EVERYMAN, I will go with thee,
and be thy guide,
In thy most need to go by thy side.

JEAN-JACQUES ROUSSEAU

Born at Geneva 28 June 1712, the son of a watch-maker. Ran away aged fifteen and became a convert to Catholicism. After a year wandering in Italy, he returned to France and lived with Mme de Warens at Chambéry for ten years. Settled in Paris in 1742, where he formed a liaison with Thérèse Levasseur, whom he married many years later, and by whom he had five children, all put into a found-lings' home. Left France for Switzerland in 1762 on the condemnation of *Émile* and the *Contrat social*, and in 1766 visited England at the invitation of David Hume. Returned to France the following year and to Paris in 1770. Died 2 July 1778, at Ermenonville, near Paris.

JEAN-JACQUES ROUSSEAU

Émile

Translated by Barbara Foxley

Introduction by P. D. Jimack
Professor of French, University of Stirling

Dent: London and Melbourne

EVERYMAN'S LIBRARY

Made in Great Britain by
Guernsey Press Co. Ltd, Guernsey, C. I. for
J. M. Dent & Sons Ltd
Aldine House, 33 Welbeck Street, London W1M 8LX

This edition was first published in
Everyman's Library in 1911
Last reprinted 1986

No 518   Hardback ISBN 0 460 00518 9
No 1518   Paperback ISBN 0 460 11518 9

INTRODUCTION

'Émile' in Rousseau's life

Like his great contemporaries, Voltaire and Diderot, Rousseau was a many-faceted writer, who achieved eminence in various fields—*littérateur*, moralist, political theorist, as well as a composer of some distinction. Yet it is doubtful if any of his works holds as much current interest for the modern reader as *Émile*. Rousseau's educational ideas, revolutionary in their day, continue to be discussed, and not just as historical curiosities; they are still controversial, they continue even today to surprise, to annoy and to excite.

With any work of educational reform, it is tempting to speculate about the author's own life, to wonder, for example, how far his mature thought is fundamentally a reaction against his own childhood experiences. There is, however, little evidence that this was true in Rousseau's case. His own 'education' was certainly unusual; indeed, in the sense of 'formal education', it was non-existent. He was born in Geneva in 1712, and as his mother died within a few days of his birth, he was brought up by a charming aunt, with whom he seems to have been half in love, and a grieving but indulgent father. According to his *Confessions*, Rousseau's childhood was idyllically happy, spent in an atmosphere of harmony and protective gentleness —he relates with pride that he was never allowed to play out in the street with other children. By the age of six or seven, he was reading avidly and precociously, first the sentimental novels which had belonged to his mother (he and his father sometimes stayed up all night reading them), and then the uplifting *Lives* of Plutarch, an author whose exaltation of civic virtue made him much in favour in Geneva. When he was nearly thirteen, Rousseau was apprenticed to an engraver, whose brutality, he claimed, began to induce in him the vices from which his earlier upbringing had preserved him, and he was not yet sixteen when he ran away from Geneva. In little more than a month he had renounced Calvinism and been baptized a Catholic in Turin. He spent a further year in Italy, part of the time as a servant, and then returned to France. After another two years of wanderings and adventures, he finally settled down, at the age of nineteen, to live at Chambéry with Mme de Warens, who was soon to become his mistress.

It was only in his mid twenties that Rousseau began systematically to educate himself in the intellectual sense. His inauspicious career as a teacher, however, could be said to have begun a few years earlier when, aged eighteen, we find him in Neuchâtel giving music lessons— and learning music himself in the process. But the real test came in

1740 when he accepted the post of tutor to the children of a M. de
Mably, in Lyon: it was soon clear to all concerned that, whatever
Rousseau's talents may have been, they did not lie in teaching two
small boys, and he left Lyon after about a year. The experience was
not, however, intellectually unproductive, for it at least prompted
Rousseau to think about education and to present to his employer a
memoir on the subject. The work itself was a conventional enough
project of educational reform, drawing extensively on Montaigne
and even more on Locke, and had it not been written by the future
author of *Émile*, it would surely have been long since forgotten.

It was more than fifteen years later that Rousseau began thinking
seriously about a major work on education, and in those fifteen years
much had happened on the French intellectual scene. It was during
this period that there appeared some of the most influential works of
the century, works which were to change the course of men's thinking: Montesquieu's *De l'Esprit des Lois*, for example, was published
in 1748, and the following year saw the first three volumes of Buffon's
monumental *Histoire naturelle*; the two most significant works of
sensationalist philosophy in French, Condillac's *Essai sur l'origine
des connaissances humaines* and *Traité des sensations*, were published
in 1746 and 1754 respectively; and most important of all, perhaps,
the famous *Encyclopédie* of Diderot and d'Alembert, to which
Rousseau was himself a contributor, began appearing in 1751. It was
during the same period too that Rousseau's own career as a writer
and moralist took shape. His 'illumination' while he was on the
way to visit Diderot, imprisoned in the Château de Vincennes,
marked a dramatic development in his thinking, and the resultant
Discours sur les Sciences et les Arts (1750), and even more the *Discours
sur l'inégalité* (1755), were already the works of a profound and
original mind.

So it was that the Rousseau who wrote *Émile* was a very different
person, living in a very different intellectual climate, from the
tentative young author of the *Mémoire* presented to M. de Mably.
On a personal level too, much had happened. In particular, Rousseau's liaison with Thérèse Levasseur began in 1745, and in the
next few years she bore him five children, all of them placed more or
less immediately (and against their mother's wishes) in a foundlings'
home—a course of action he was to come to regret bitterly, and
to which he clearly refers in a passage of Book I of *Émile* (page 17
of the present edition).

In the spring of 1756, to avoid the obligations and 'corruption' of
Parisian society, Rousseau, now a celebrity, took up residence in the
Hermitage, a small house on the edge of the forest of Montmorency
belonging to Mme d'Epinay. It was in this peaceful seclusion that
he was soon to compose his great novel, *La Nouvelle Héloise*, and
shortly afterwards to begin work on a treatise on education. At
least in their origin, two works could hardly be more different. The
Nouvelle Héloise was begun as a conscious attempt by Rousseau to

attain in the world of the imagination the emotional fulfilment which he felt had been denied him in reality: he deliberately identified himself with the characters he had created, Julie d'Etanges and her tutor (and lover) Saint-Preux, as they exchanged the passionate letters which were to become the first part of his novel. But once Julie had rejected Saint-Preux and married the sedate rationalist Wolmar, the emphasis of the work changed, and the later parts were concerned to paint a picture of the domestic bliss of the ideal family. Inevitably the question of education arose, and there are two long letters towards the end of the novel in which Saint-Preux describes eulogistically how the Wolmars are bringing up their children; the two letters cannot have been written more than, at most, a few months before the beginning of *Émile*, and to a very great extent they coincide, often textually, with parts of Books I and II.

It was probably at the end of 1758 that Rousseau began work in earnest on his treatise on education. Now quite apart from its subject matter, one of the most striking things about *Émile* is its form, half treatise half novel; indeed, when one reads the love story of Émile and Sophie in Book V, it may well seem more novel than treatise. Yet it was as a treatise that it was begun, and in his correspondence at the time of its publication, Rousseau referred to the work most often as 'mon Traité d'éducation'. The curious hybrid form of *Émile* seems to have come into existence during the actual writing of the work, more by accident than by design. The first manuscript draft reveals that all the references in Book I of the published text to the method Rousseau was to employ, namely the creation of an individual pupil, with Jean-Jacques as his tutor, are subsequent additions, as are all specific mentions of Émile before the beginning of what is now Book III, which is where the character of the pupil first appears on the scene. It seems too that it was by a process not unlike the one which lay at the origin of the *Nouvelle Héloïse* that the characters of Émile and his tutor came into being: each time Rousseau illustrated his treatise with an example, he identified himself, not unexpectedly, with the tutor, referring increasingly to 'my' pupil; but rather more significant, the pupil himself acquired more substance with each appearance . . . until, by the end of the book, Émile is as much a wishful-thinking Jean-Jacques as Saint-Preux had been.

Émile was completed in the autumn of 1760. Having quarrelled with Mme d'Epinay (as well as Grimm and Diderot), Rousseau had left the Hermitage in December 1757 and moved to Montmorency, where he became friendly with the Maréchal de Luxembourg and his wife, who had a château in the neighbourhood. It was to Mme de Luxembourg, at her suggestion, that he entrusted arrangements for the publication of his new work. In fact, nearly a year passed before he signed a contract with a Parisian publisher, Duchesne, and there then began one of the most tormented periods of Rousseau's life. The printing proceeded erratically and somewhat mysteriously,

and Rousseau's anxiety verged on panic: the only explanation
he could see for the mysterious delays was in some double-dealing,
perhaps the secret seizure of his manuscript by the Jesuits. The
story is a complex one. Although the contract with Duchesne had
been ostensibly for the work to be printed by Néaulme in Holland,
in reality Duchesne was printing it himself in Paris, though at
first without Rousseau's knowledge, for the latter had insisted
from the beginning that there was very little chance of the French
authorities permitting publication of such a book. The reasons for
the printing in Paris were presumably commercial (Dutch editions
were very costly), and the intention was to present the book as if
it had in fact been published in Holland, a conventional enough
deception in the eighteenth century. It was thus that the work
finally appeared in May 1762, bearing the imprint 'A La Haye,
chez Jean Néaulme'.

Less than three weeks later, on 8th June, Rousseau was awakened
in the middle of the night by an emissary of Mme de Luxembourg
and warned that on the following day the Paris *Parlement* was certain
to condemn *Émile* and to order the arrest of its author. The prediction proved true, but by the time the officers came for him,
Rousseau had left, *en route* for Switzerland, and the *Parlement*
had to be content with burning *Émile*. The condemnations had
begun. When Rousseau arrived a few days later at Yverdon, in
Bernese territory, he may well have looked towards Geneva; but
the Genevan authorities forestalled him: on 19th June they condemned *Émile* and the *Contrat social*, published a few months
earlier, to be burned, as 'rash, scandalous, impious, tending to destroy the Christian religion and all governments . . .', and added a
warning that Rousseau would be arrested if he set foot on Genevan
soil. Other condemnations followed, in Berne and Amsterdam, in
Paris by the Sorbonne and by the Archbishop of Paris, and of course
in Rome.

The publication of *Émile* was indeed a turning point in Rousseau's
life. He had already broken with the anti-Christian *philosophes*,
incurring the dangerous enmity of Voltaire, Diderot and Grimm,
and now he was rejected by the opposite camp. After wandering from
haven to haven, including spending more than a year in England,
he finally returned to France only in 1767, and then under the
assumed name of M. Renou, and still officially liable to arrest.
With minor exceptions, the only works he wrote after 1762 were
those defending and justifying what he had already written, mainly
in *Émile* and the *Contrat social* (*Lettre à Christophe de Beaumont*,
1763, *Lettres écrites de la Montagne*, 1764), and finally the self-
justifying autobiographical works, the *Confessions*, the *Dialogues*
and the *Rêveries du Promeneur solitaire*.

'Émile' in *Rousseau's thought*

Although Rousseau usually referred to *Émile* as his 'Traité d'éducation', he tended always to play down the educational aspect of the book, which he saw primarily as a work of moral philosophy, based on his belief that man was naturally good. 'You are quite right to say that it is impossible to form an Émile,' he wrote to a correspondent in 1764, 'but I cannot believe that you take the book which bears this name for a true treatise on education. It is a rather philosophical work on the principle. . . that *man is naturally good.*' And some years later, when he discussed his earlier works in the *Dialogues*, he described *Émile* as 'merely a treatise on the original goodness of man, intended to show how vice and error, alien to his constitution, are introduced into it from outside and imperceptibly distort it'. But Rousseau also maintained that *Émile* formed part of a philosophical system, which, even if false, was a coherent one, stemming from his sudden and remarkable inspiration on the way to Vincennes: 'All that I was able to remember of the vast number of great truths which, in a quarter of an hour, illuminated me beneath that tree, has been but thinly diffused throughout my three principal works, namely the first *Discours*, the one on inequality, and the treatise on education, which three works are inseparable and form together a single whole' (Letter to Malesherbes, January 1762).

Rousseau's famous principle of the goodness of natural man was not in fact enunciated in the first *Discours*, in which he set out to show that modern man, for all his knowledge and culture, was inferior to the unsophisticated citizens of ancient Rome or Sparta. It was only in the second *Discours* that natural man came on the scene for the first time as Rousseau's ideal. In a quasi-historical reconstruction, he drew a nostalgic picture of the contented self-sufficiency and implicit goodness of natural, pre-social man, and attempted to demonstrate that the very creation of society, based on the notion of property, was the root cause of the corruption and unhappiness of modern man. If the ideal had apparently changed from the citizen to natural man, the common factor in the two *Discours* is clearly Rousseau's awareness of the inadequacy of contemporary social man, and it is this, rather than the goodness of man, which is the true starting point of his thought. It is obvious from the first *Discours* that Rousseau was not rejecting social man as such, but only the unsuccessful social man he saw around him, and the ideal social man of Greece and Rome was as desirable an alternative as natural man, a point he makes perfectly clear at the beginning of *Émile*. The two *Discours*, however, had been merely analytical and expository: any solution to the problem they analysed must lie either in the reform of society, which was the subject of the *Contrat social*, or in the reform of man himself, in other words in education.

But if man was to be reformed, a choice of model had surely to be made between natural man and social man, and it is thus appropriate that the discussion of this choice should form the matter of the opening pages of *Émile*. The choice was made all the more crucial by the fact that for Rousseau the two ideals were totally opposed: 'The natural man lives for himself; he is the unit, the whole, dependent only on himself and on his like. The citizen is but the numerator of a fraction, whose value depends on its denominator; his value depends upon the whole, that is, on the community.' Now it is precisely because he is torn between these conflicting demands that modern man is unhappy; Rousseau's aim is thus to pave the way for his happiness by uniting the two ideals: 'If the twofold aims could be resolved into one by removing the man's self-contradictions, one great obstacle to his happiness would be gone.' Émile will be a natural man, not in the historical sense of the second *Discours*, but a man whose natural goodness has been protected and allowed to develop uncontaminated by the corrupting influence of society. Yet at the same time he will be a member of a society, able to play in it whatever role his duty as a citizen should require.

It is undoubtedly helpful to consider *Émile* in this way as a part of Rousseau's system. Yet if ever an author's life and personality threw important light upon his work, it is surely Rousseau's, and quite apart from the fact that some of his most important works (the *Nouvelle Héloïse* and the autobiographical works) were not included by him in the system, the significance of the system itself cannot be fully appreciated without some reference to the man. The fundamental opposition which Rousseau saw between natural man, existing only for himself, and the ideal social man who existed only for others, corresponds strikingly to the two opposing elements which seem to underlie his whole life as well as his writings. On the one hand, he was born and brought up in Calvinist Geneva and remained all his life imbued with the austere ideal of self-renunciation. The hero of his first important literary work was, as we have seen, the dedicated patriot of Greece or Rome, and when at the beginning of *Émile* he described examples of the ideal citizen, there is no doubting his admiration for this particular brand of civic virtue, which placed the good of the state above all personal considerations. On the other hand, he was endowed with a particularly sensitive and emotional temperament, which was reinforced no doubt by his childhood knowledge that his birth had caused his mother's death. Thus, while his Genevan side was reflected and strengthened by his early addiction to Plutarch, he had already indulged tastes of an opposite kind in devouring his mother's novels, gaining thereby, according to the *Confessions*, a dangerously premature experience of the passions which was subsequently to cause him much unhappiness. (It is surely no coincidence that the education of Émile's emotions will be delayed until he has reached adoleseence, by which time he will have acquired a sound foundation of reason and judgment.)

The same dichotomy will still be apparent some forty years later, for if Rousseau claimed that it was for the guidance of his fellow men that he composed the works which formed his system, he confessed freely that he had begun writing the *Nouvelle Héloïse* as a conscious act of self-indulgence. The author of the passionate love story of Julie and Saint-Preux seems to be hardly the same man as the fervent admirer of Sparta, who interrupted the composition of his novel to write the *Lettre à d'Alembert*, in which he warned his compatriots not to establish a theatre in Geneva for fear of corrupting the purity of their morals by the mere spectacle of love. But the *Nouvelle Héloïse* itself reflects the two contrasting sides of Rousseau's personality. If the first half of the work, characterized by the emotional and headstrong young Saint-Preux, narrates a destructive and abortive love affair, the second half, after Julie's marriage to a self-disciplined Wolmar, is very different: whereas Saint-Preux has been a kind of natural man, living only for his own happiness, Wolmar and Julie together found a model society and are conscious above all of their duties to others.

Émile offers similar contrasts. Though its composition was not undertaken in the same self-indulgent way, we have noted that Rousseau soon began to involve himself emotionally with his characters. As a parallel to Saint-Preux the ideal lover and Julie the ideal mistress become the ideal wife and mother, we may choose to see in Émile both a substitute son and the child Rousseau would himself have liked to have been, and in his tutor Jean-Jacques yet another idealized version of the author, as well perhaps as the father he would have liked to have had. This might appear to be merely of psychological interest, with no implications for the subject matter of the work, and it is true that the internal contrasts in *Émile* are less striking than in the *Nouvelle Héloïse*. Yet as Rousseau dwells lovingly on the story of Émile and Sophie in Book V, it is difficult to believe that this section of the work at least is not dependent on the author's emotional involvement, and equally difficult to reconcile it with what is to come, the stern message of the tutor's long speech to Émile, which is intended specifically as a warning against self-indulgence and surely comes as a shock to the reader, nearly as much as to Émile: 'Nature and fortune had left you free. You could face poverty, you could bear bodily pain; the sufferings of the heart were unknown to you; you were then dependent on nothing but your position as a human being; now you depend on all the ties you have formed for yourself; you have learnt to desire, and you are now the slave of your desires. . . . Now is the time for real freedom; learn to be your own master; control your heart, my Émile, and you will be virtuous. . . .'

Now at the beginning of the first manuscript draft of *Émile*,

Rousseau noted a brief plan of his proposed treatise: the plan listed
the different ages of man, and the one corresponding to Book V,
from twenty to twenty-five, is described as 'the Age of Wisdom', to
be followed by 'the Age of Happiness—all the rest of life'. The
implication would seem to be that the acquisition of wisdom is a
necessary condition for achieving happiness, a principle which is
implied still more clearly near the beginning of Book II: 'What
then is human wisdom or the path of true happiness?' The same
passage goes on to clarify exactly what Rousseau understood by
'wisdom', which lay for him in 'decreasing the difference between
our desires and our powers, in establishing a perfect equilibrium
between the power and the will'. It was essentially a form of self-
restriction based on enlightened self-interest: if man desires only
what he can obtain and wills only what he can achieve, he cannot be
unhappy. As the tutor later explained to Émile, 'Nature forbids us
to extend our relations beyond the limits of our strength; reason
forbids us to want what we cannot get. ...'

It was this same self-restriction, the rational limitation of the
desires to the attainable, that Julie and Saint-Preux had to accept
in the second half of the *Nouvelle Héloïse*. In *Émile* the lesson
became explicit. In Book II Rousseau foreshadows the Age of Wisdom
when he points to the folly of the happy man made suddenly unhappy
by a letter, a mere piece of paper. By his failure to live only within
himself, man has made himself more vulnerable to unhappiness:
'We spread ourselves, so to speak, over the whole world, and all
this vast expanse becomes sensitive. No wonder our woes increase
when we may be wounded on every side.' It is above all of course
the tutor's long speech in Book V already referred to that expounds
Rousseau's doctrine on this subject. Yet some two-thirds of Book V
has already gone by with almost no mention of 'wisdom', and this
one speech can hardly be said to dominate the whole book, which
might be more aptly characterized as 'the age of love' or 'the age of
marriage'. There is certainly no indication at the end of the work
that Émile has learnt his tutor's lesson and kept his love for Sophie
under firm control.

It appears then that the transformation of the Treatise on Education into *Émile* probably involved at least one important change
in subject matter, and that Émile himself had not at the end learnt
what had been intended as perhaps his most important lesson.
This interpretation is supported by an unfinished continuation of
Émile, entitled *Émile et Sophie, ou les Solitaires*, which reveals a
future very different from the lasting happiness predicted in the
plan. Sophie has been unfaithful to Émile, who has reacted at first
with predictably extravagant distress. But then, gradually, he
remembers his tutor's lessons, and he asks himself: 'What harm
has been done to my person? What crime have I committed? What
have I lost of myself? . . .' And so he regains his self-control
and his happiness, reflecting admiringly how wise he is: '. . . the

first wisdom is to will what is and to order one's heart according to one's destiny. . . .' In spite of all you have lost, Émile tells himself, 'what is real, what exists for you, is your life, your health, your youth, your reason, your talents, your knowledge, and, if you choose, your virtues, and consequently your happiness'.

This stoic view of the happiness of the wise man may well reveal the influence of Seneca, Plutarch and Montaigne, all of whom Rousseau knew well and admired greatly. But whatever its literary sources, the principle had become fully Rousseau's own, and one moreover which he tried to apply as much in his life as in his writings. In particular, the last of his autobiographical works, the *Rêveries du Promeneur solitaire*, offers a curious parallel with *Émile et Sophie*: we behold Rousseau in the last years of his life, believing himself (not entirely without justification) rejected and persecuted by his fellow men, seeking and sometimes finding a kind of solace in the self-sufficiency of emotional detachment from the rest of mankind which had been preached by the tutor at the end of *Émile*.

'*Émile*' as a work on education

Although, as we have seen, Rousseau himself subordinated the educational aspect of *Émile* to the philosophical, there is no doubt that it is primarily as a work of educational reform that it became and has remained famous—using 'educational' as applying to every aspect of the raising of children. Certainly reform was needed. The usual treatment of babies (at least in 'society') seems to have been a calamitous mixture of mollycoddling and neglect. The fashionable practice was for them to be looked after by wet-nurses, usually peasants, who frequently neglected them horribly. Hygiene was virtually non-existent. The babies were tightly bound in swaddling clothes, partly as a convenience, and partly for fear of their coming to harm if left free to move. As they grew older they continued to be protected from such evils as fresh air and exercise, while being beaten for disobedience. At a very early age, sometimes five or six, formal instruction began. Whether they were taught at home by private tutors, or later went to a college, children were usually subject to the harshest discipline, and practically as soon as they could read they were forced to devote long hours to the study of subjects quite remote from them—scripture, ancient history, geography, heraldry, for instance, and above all, Latin. The idea of childhood being not only an apprenticeship, but in its own right a valid stage of human existence was scarcely entertained: whether or not children were happy was irrelevant; they were seen merely as miniature, imperfect adults.

There was no lack of works in the eighteenth century, even before *Émile*, containing proposals for educational reform: in particular, the failure of mothers to feed their own babies and the use of swaddling clothes were frequent targets for criticism, and several authors followed Locke in advocating that more attention should be given to physical education generally. But there was no serious challenge to the tradition of intellectual education; and most works dealing with the subject, even after *Émile*, confined themselves to discussing minor details of the curriculum, and perhaps some changes in the methods of learning the traditional subjects. The most striking work of reform in this respect remained in fact Locke's *Thoughts on Education*, first translated into French in 1695; for Locke at least wanted learning to be an enjoyable process, based as far as possible on interest, and warned against trying to teach children too much before their reason was sufficiently developed.

Locke's *Thoughts* were widely read, running through several editions in the first half of the eighteenth century, and Rousseau was by no means the first to borrow extensively from him. Many of the details of *Émile*, especially on physical education, apparently taken from Locke, had by that time become commonplaces. Yet if numerous other writers had anticipated Rousseau in details, *Émile* was none the less original: for in its predecessors there was nothing but the details, the details were the whole. It was unusual enough to deal, as did Rousseau, with every aspect of the child's life from birth—indeed from before birth—to full adulthood, even to parenthood, the restarting of the cycle; but Rousseau stood out from his precursors above all in subordinating the details of education to an overall conception of man and of the development proper to him.

The education he proposes is rigorously structured according to clear principles; the life of man is divided into a succession of ages corresponding to the different stages of his development, and the characteristics of each stage determine what education is appropriate. Broadly speaking, the first two books of *Émile*, up to the age of twelve approximately (called in the manuscript plan 'the Age of Nature'), are concerned with the physical being. Book III, from twelve to fifteen, begins the constructive learning process, with the child gradually becoming skilled in the exercise of his reason, which is still not fully developed. Book IV deals with adolescence: the now mature reason is complicated and complemented by the passions awaking, so that this is the period both of true intellectual education and of moral education.

Rousseau starts from the premise, axiomatic for him, that natural man, man as he is born, is good; he is also free, both a cause and a result of being good. If then man as we know him appears bad, this demonstrates not that Rousseau's premise is wrong, but that man's education has been faulty, or in other words that he has been corrupted by men, in the form of society. Good education will consist merely in the protection of natural good from this corrupting influence (a principle which will have various consequences, including the removal of Émile from the town to the country), and thus protected, the child's natural self will be free to develop of its own accord. To support and elucidate his argument, Rousseau appeals to the example of those who have remained close to nature—peasants, primitive peoples, even animals, all of whom treat their young with a kind of judicious, health-giving neglect. On their model, he urges mothers to feed their children themselves, to abandon their swaddling clothes, to bath them regularly in cold water; then as they grow older, to make them robust in body and temperament by letting them become hardened, for instance, to pain and to extremes of temperature. The young Émile will spend most of his time out of doors, running about thinly clad and barefoot, leading the vigorous, natural and free life of a young animal.

Rousseau actually maintains that the guiding principle during the Age of Nature should be 'to let well alone', describing the ideal education of this period as 'merely negative'. The striking formula is obviously intended to contrast with the excessive academic instruction young children were usually subjected to: Émile will have no lessons, he will never learn anything by heart, he will not even read books, 'the curse of childhood'. But his education will in reality be far from negative, and it is only the education of the mind that Rousseau wishes to delay: 'Exercise his body, his limbs, his senses, his strength, but keep his mind idle as long as you can.'

In placing so much emphasis on physical education, however, Rousseau was not seeking merely to redress the balance, in the spirit of *mens sana in corpore sano*, desirable though such a reform may have been. By the middle of the eighteenth century, most thinkers, Rousseau among them, had rejected Descartes' doctrine of innate ideas in favour of the sensationalist description of man given by Locke: all knowledge, all ideas are acquired through the experience of the physical senses. The development of the senses is thus of primary importance for the whole of education, and Rousseau stresses the fact repeatedly: 'His sense experiences are the raw material of thought; they should, therefore, be presented to him in fitting order. . .', he wrote in Book I; and in Book II: 'The senses are the first of our faculties to mature, and they are therefore the first that should be cultivated. . .' In consequence, the latter part of Book II is devoted in detail to the cultivation of each of the five senses in turn. The full and positive significance of Rousseau's 'negative education' now becomes clear: unhampered as a baby by swaddling clothes and later unrestricted by lessons, the child is free virtually from birth to explore the world about him and to gain a continually widening physical experience; he will acquire a mass of sense experience to be used as the 'raw material' for future development, while at the same time his senses themselves, 'the first instruments of our knowledge', will be systematically perfected.

Moreover, just as the Age of Nature lays the foundations for the child's intellectual education, so too it marks an invaluable first stage in his moral development, though the process is always by experience, never by instruction: 'Give your child no verbal lessons; he should be taught by experience alone. . . .' Perhaps the most important of the lessons he learns is submission to the inevitable and the immovable—what Rousseau calls 'la dépendance des choses'. In accepting the irrevocable finality of 'there is none left', the child is learning not to want what he cannot have, learning, in other words, to bow to 'the stern law of necessity'. Not only is he thus protected from one of the principal causes of unhappiness ('Do you know the surest way to make your child miserable? Let him have everything he wants. . .'), but he has already done much towards guaranteeing his future happiness by taking the first important steps along the path of human wisdom.

If Rousseau was so reluctant to embark on any direct moral or intellectual instruction, it was because he believed the child was not yet ready for it. Premature attempts to give such lessons, inevitably using words the child was too young to understand properly, could only lead him into error, and such error would have disastrous consequences: 'The first mistaken idea he gets into his head is the germ of error and vice. . .' Indeed ignorance is infinitely preferable to this false knowledge: 'I care not if he knows nothing provided he is not mistaken,' says Rousseau, referring to the pre-adolescent Émile of Book III. By this time the child is ready to begin learning more positively, since his reason is already well developed and not yet disturbed by the awaking passions. But Rousseau is still most circumspect: the child must learn only what he wants to learn; his curiosity for the subject must be aroused and he must always be able to see its utility for him. In short, though he will learn, he must still not be taught. Émile's progress in Book III will be by ingeniously guided discovery: he must seem to achieve everything by himself, he will have no lessons, he will read no books—except *Robinson Crusoe*, which will provide the ideal model—he will even have no ready made instruments, for he and his tutor will make all their own. It is true that he will learn far less by this method than ordinary children in their colleges; but he will learn what is useful and above all he will understand what he learns: 'Do not teach the child many things, but let him perceive only accurate and clear ideas . . . it matters little what he learns provided he understands it and knows how to use it. . . .' At the end of Book III, 'Émile knows little, but what he knows is really his own . . .' And what is more, in full possession of his natural freedom, he will still be happy, which alone would justify Rousseau's method.

An important part of the education of Book III is to be devoted to the learning of a manual trade, carpentry in Émile's case. Useful and constructive in itself, this also has other advantages. Émile will be functioning as a social as well as a natural man, for the first time fulfilling some of his civic responsibility—and Rousseau takes the opportunity to make some forthright social criticisms: 'Man in society is bound to work; rich or poor, weak or strong, every idler is a thief.' At the same time, Émile is helping to secure his own future well-being, for who can be sure that the existing order will continue? Rousseau prophetically foresees a future in which 'the great become small, the rich poor, the king a commoner'. But this is not only a political point: in learning to be a carpenter, Émile is preparing the true freedom that comes only from self-sufficiency, and if the work ends without his having needed his trade, he will one day discover its full value in *Les Solitaires*.

At the end of Book III, a kind of transitional stage between childhood proper and adolescence, Rousseau assesses how far he has come and what still remains to be done: 'We have made him a worker and a thinker; we have now to make him loving and tender-hearted, to perfect reason through feeling.' It is only with puberty that the child's emotional, moral and aesthetic faculties are awakened and his reason thereby completed and perfected. Thus it is Book IV which marks the full development of these aspects of his education. Now is the time for all that has hitherto been deferred because Émile was not yet ready for it, and he will learn all the more quickly and all the more effectively because the soundest of foundations have been laid. But he will still retain the freedom of the earlier books: he will have no formal lessons, he will learn nothing on the authority of others, he will study only what he wants to, either because it is useful, or because it is pleasing. It is thus that Rousseau imagines Émile studying poetry and languages: 'If he has the least glimmering of taste for poetry, how eagerly will he study the languages of the poets, Greek, Latin and Italian! These studies will afford him unlimited amusement and will be none the less valuable; they will be a delight to him at an age and in circumstances when the heart finds so great a charm in every kind of beauty which affects it.' Yet even such diversions have their place in the overall educational scheme. In cultivating Émile's aesthetic taste, Rousseau is cultivating his reliance on his own inner resources and once again preparing his future self-sufficiency: 'My main object in teaching him to feel and love beauty of every kind is to fix his affections and his taste on these, to prevent the corruption of his natural appetites, lest he should have to seek some day in the midst of his wealth for the means of happiness which should be found close at hand.'

It is now that Émile is at last ready to return to society and to take his place among his fellow men. Having learnt to think for himself, and having been thus far preserved from error and prejudice, he is now in little danger of being corrupted by society. But the final touch to his preparation will be the study of history, which will enable him to observe the true nature of man and of society, to see how the natural goodness of the one is corrupted by the other, while himself remaining a mere spectator, personally uninvolved.

Émile is now ready too for religion. At a time when religious
instruction usually began by the age of seven at the latest, the delay
in any form of religious education until after the age of fifteen was
not surprisingly one of the most controversial points in the work.
But far from being anti-religious in so delaying, Rousseau was in
fact stressing the importance of religion. Like all the other aspects of
education which depended on more than the mechanical reason of
the child, the discussion of religion had to wait until Émile was
mature enough to understand it, so that in religion too he would
avoid false knowledge and prejudice. And needless to say, on the
subject of God as on every other subject, he would proceed not by
instruction, but by weighing the evidence and by thinking for
himself.

As far as Émile's education is concerned, it only remains for him in
Book V to learn the final lesson of true wisdom, the complete self-
sufficiency which has already been systematically prepared in earlier
books—though, as we have seen, it is open to question whether or
not he actually succeeds. The greater part of Book V is, however,
concerned with feminine education, and here Rousseau is as retro-
grade as he was enlightened on the subject of masculine education.
All the principles, all the carefully structured progression of the
previous books, are abandoned, and the education of women is
entirely subordinated to the needs of man: Sophie will be little more
than a charming plaything for Émile.

Enlightened though it is, the education of Émile himself contains
of course obvious weaknesses. Yet some of them are more apparent
than real. Rousseau is prone to categorical and extreme statements,
as for instance: 'The only habit the child should be allowed to
contract is that of having no habits. . .', 'Reverse the usual practice
and you will almost always do right. . .', 'I hate books. . .'. Yet all
these statements are clearly exaggerations used for rhetorical effect
and obviously not intended to be taken literally. Far from being
dogmatic and inflexible, Rousseau is frequently at pains to stress
the importance of careful observation to enable one to base education on the particular character of the individual: 'Every mind has
its own form, in accordance with which it must be controlled. . . . Oh,
wise man, take time to observe nature; watch your scholar well
before you say a word to him; first leave the germ of his character
free to show itself. . .' His advice is usually much more moderate than
at first appears, as for instance when he is most careful to recommend
that babies should be bathed in ice-cold water only after a very
gradual process of acclimatization.

A more serious defect might seem to be Rousseau's claim that 'the
first impulses of nature are always right', which can scarcely be
dismissed as a mere rhetorical exaggeration since he repeatedly
claimed it to be the fundamental principle on which *Émile* was built.
Such apparently uncritical trust in nature seems perhaps unduly
optimistic until one realizes it is all a question of definition; for what

Rousseau does not consider to be good he does not call natural. Though he suggests ways of correcting a lazy child, for example, the child is not Émile, for such a failing can only be the result of a faulty upbringing; because laziness is not good, it cannot be natural, any more than imperiousness, cruelty or any other vice, all of which must be prevented or corrected. Rousseau's belief, therefore, in natural goodness, though important, seems to have fewer pedagogical implications than one might think, since it does not blind him to the existence of what other people might term natural faults.

The other principle associated with man's goodness, and which Rousseau stresses throughout *Émile*, namely his freedom, is similarly ambiguous. It is true that Émile is subject to hardly any obvious restrictions; but particularly as he grows older, he is increasingly controlled, if only indirectly, by his tutor: even his chance meeting with Sophie and their consequent falling in love have been carefully planned in advance. Such subtle manipulation might well seem to encroach far more seriously on the child's natural freedom than the traditional restraints. Yet Émile is not conscious of any infringement of his liberty, and it is surely with *feeling* free that Rousseau is concerned. Man feels free when he wants only what is within his reach: 'That man is truly free who desires only what he is able to perform, and does what he desires.' The happiness Rousseau is finally aiming at will derive from the only true freedom, that of voluntary self-restriction.

The most frequent contemporary criticism to be made of the educational system of *Émile* was probably that it was impracticable, and in many ways the criticism seems justified. Not only does the tutor have only one pupil (a not unusual arrangement in aristocratic eighteenth-century society), but he must devote himself totally—and without payment!—to his pupil's education. The child must be kept in near isolation from society, and the tutor has to have absolute control over his whole environment. Though it is no doubt desirable for the child to learn only what he wants to, and then only when his interest has been aroused, is it really possible to arouse the ordinary child's interest as easily as Rousseau imagines? And however desirable it may be to acquire knowledge only by first-hand discovery, is it really feasible that an ordinary child would acquire enough in this way for his future needs, especially in the modern world?

But Rousseau's answer to such objections would be that Émile, certainly by Book III, was indeed no ordinary child, for he was the product of his upbringing in Books I and II. Thus one can make no assumptions about Émile based on experience of other children, any more than one can use his behaviour as a guide for them: 'The real Émile, a child so different from the rest, would not serve as an illustration for anything.' Rousseau was in fact little concerned with piecemeal remedies and reforms; the education of *Émile* is essentially a whole, and as such impracticable in any immediate sense. There was no lack in the eighteenth century of works containing useful and enlightened practical precepts; what made *Émile* so different, so original, was its very impracticability, Rousseau's refusal to limit his vision to details. He examines critically the very foundations on which all educational practice must be based and proposes a new way of looking at children and at their education; the pedagogical doctrine of *Émile* is a structured whole, in which each age is important both in its own right—children are at last seen as children—and as a preparation for future development. It is this overall conception rather than any of the component parts which has had such a profound influence on subsequent thinkers and made *Émile* one of the most stimulating and fruitful works on education ever written.

The 'Profession de foi du Vicaire savoyard'

In spite of the sustained influence of the educational thought of *Émile*, it is probable that the aspect of the work which made the most immediate impact on Rousseau's contemporaries was rather the discussion of religion contained in the *Profession de foi du Vicaire savoyard* ('The Creed of a Savoyard Priest'). Now although Émile's religious initiation is an important element in his education, it is clear from the text alone that the *Profession de foi* is far more than just that, and far more too than what the autobiographical introduction claims it to be, the advice given to Rousseau himself some thirty years previously. In a letter to his Genevan friend, Moultou, written shortly before the publication of *Émile*, Rousseau admitted openly that the 'profession of faith' was his own, and many years later, in the *Rêveries du Promeneur solitaire*, he explained that it had been the result of an attempt to establish once and for all the beliefs and principles on which he would base the rest of his life. So that although the *Profession de foi du Vicaire savoyard* is an integral part of *Émile*, it is at the same time a separate work which has to be considered in its own right.

To appreciate fully Rousseau's aims and achievement in the *Profession de foi*, one needs to remember something of the historical background against which he wrote it. Far more than political controversy, the *cause célèbre* of mid eighteenth-century France was the religious battle between two bitterly opposed camps, an authoritarian and intolerant Catholic Church and the irreligious *philosophes*. Most of Rousseau's friends were anti-Christian deists or even atheists, and it was to a large extent the disquieting ethical implications of the more extreme materialist views which prompted him to seek to clarify and formulate his own religious position. Although he started from a sensationalist standpoint ('I exist, and I have senses through which I receive impressions. . .'), the first half of the *Profession de foi* is clearly intended as a rejection of the materialist description of man, and especially that given by Helvétius in his notorious book *De l'Esprit*, published (and condemned) in 1758. In specific refutation of Helvétius, who had claimed that '*to judge* is *to feel*', Rousseau declares that 'to judge and to feel are not the same'; he demonstrates that man is a thinking, willing, moral being and proceeds to establish the existence of a personal God, concerned for the well-being of man. The first part of the *Profession de foi* concludes with an impassioned assertion that man has intuitive knowledge of moral truth by means of that 'sure guide', his conscience, 'divine instinct', 'infallible judge of good and evil'. Thus 'we may be men without being scholars'; all, however ignorant or unintelligent, are capable by themselves of sound moral judgment.

In the second half of the *Profession*, Rousseau embarks on the discussion of revealed religion. The discussion has been to some extent prejudged, however; for the only important truths he recognizes are the moral ones, which, in his view, man can attain unaided. In spite of the value attached to conscience, reason is by no means abandoned: Rousseau retains it as a kind of critical filter by which all allegedly revealed religions must be assessed. He emphasizes the enormous problems involved in examining the claims of rival revelations and points to the folly and injustice of religious intolerance. Turning to Christianity itself, he considers it virtually impossible to judge the authenticity of its so-called miracles and mysteries, which remain unacceptable to his reason. In spite of his eloquent eulogy of Christ (which nevertheless contrives to avoid unambiguous acceptance of his divinity), Rousseau's position is one of unwilling scepticism.

In the moving conclusion of the *Profession de foi*, the *Vicaire savoyard* describes his humble acceptance of his office and its duties. But such conformity was scarcely likely to mollify those who had been incensed by his earlier rejection of the authority of the Church: his 'acceptance' still involved rejection of much that the Church considered essential, including the belief that there was only one true religion, only one way of worshipping God, for 'true worship is of the heart'. For all their humility, Rousseau and his priest retained the right to decide for themselves exactly what they would and would not believe.

It is this refusal to accept authority which is one of the most striking characteristics not only of the *Profession de foi*, but of much of Émile's education in the rest of the work. Just as he must learn not from other people or from books, but from his own experience and reflexion, so, in the matter of religion, man's conscience and reason alone will enable him to discover whatever truths he may need. No doubt this repeated stressing of total self-reliance owes much to Rousseau's own personality, and his cry of 'How many men between God and me!' may well throw important light on his reluctance to accept the authority of the Church. But whatever the psychological origins of this attitude, it results in *Émile*, and in the *Profession de foi* in particular, in an emphatic assertion of confidence in man, in the status and capacity of the human individual. And such a view was in complete opposition both to the Church's insistence on the humility and subordination of man, and to the materialists' picture of an amoral automaton, suffering from delusions of freedom in a determined world of necessary causes and effects.

The Condemnation of 'Émile'

The condemnation of *Émile* in Geneva, which coupled it with the *Contrat social*, was, it is true, concerned more with the latter work and the politically subversive nature of Rousseau's writings. But the other condemnations were based almost entirely on the *Profession de foi*, and it was in fact Rousseau's rejection of the authority of the Church, his replacement of Christian revelation by the judgment of man, which was the principal charge levelled at him. And yet, ironically, Rousseau saw himself as the champion of the religious cause, one of the few defenders of Christianity in a hostile, irreligious age. In his reply to the condemnation by the Archbishop of Paris, Christophe de Beaumont, he protested indignantly that he was most certainly a Christian, convinced of 'the truths essential to Christianity': he had in the *Profession* established the existence of a providential God and affirmed his view of man as a moral being; he had even written with admiration and reverence of Christ, in a passage about which the archbishop himself admitted: 'It would be difficult to pay a more glowing tribute to the authenticity of the Scriptures.' Indeed until *Émile* was actually condemned, Rousseau continued to assert his confidence in his own safety, refusing to believe that the authorities who took no action against the authors of so many openly materialist and atheistic works could possibly seek to prosecute the author of the *Profession de foi du Vicaire savoyard*.

Nevertheless, not only was the *Profession de foi* the object of numerous condemnations and refutations, but Rousseau himself would, it seems, have been arrested had he not fled from Paris, and one must ask why he should have been singled out for such exceptional treatment. Now it is true that many other works had challenged the authority of the Church; but they rarely did so as directly as Rousseau's, and in any case they did not seriously purport to be anything other than anti-religious and so presented few dangers for the faithful. What made Rousseau different was precisely his attack on the materialists and his professed sympathy for Christianity. The *Profession* was calculated to appeal not to the irreligious but to those believers for whom Christianity as preached by the established Church presented difficulties. When Rousseau proudly claimed he was a Christian in the *Lettre à Christophe de Beaumont*, he merely reasserted the heresy he had already made clear in the *Profession*: 'My lord, I am a Christian, and a sincere Christian, according to the doctrine of the Scriptures. I am a Christian, not as a disciple of the priests, but as a disciple of Jesus Christ.' In other words, it was he rather than the Church who was to decide what truths *were* essential to Christianity—and Rousseau did not disguise his view that the interpretation of 'the priests' (including, presumably, the archbishop) was false.

As much as anything, it was this unconscious arrogance of Rousseau's that provoked such extreme measures against him, for he constituted a far more serious danger to the Church than those authors (like Voltaire and Diderot) who implicitly admitted their wickedness by denying authorship of the works they had published anonymously. When, on the contrary, the name of Jean-Jacques Rousseau appeared shamelessly on the title-page of *Émile*, it presented a direct challenge which the authorities could not afford to let pass, as the *Avocat général* pointed out in his denunciation of the book to the Paris *Parlement*: 'Since the author of this book has not been afraid to declare his own name, he cannot be too speedily prosecuted.'

The fears of those who condemned *Émile* proved, at least in one respect, to be well founded. There is little doubt that the *Profession de foi* was a major factor in the rapid and widespread popularity achieved by *Émile*, and in the next few years Rousseau received many grateful and enthusiastic letters from disciples of the *Vicaire savoyard*. Whether or not one considers Rousseau as a Christian must depend on one's definition of Christianity. But his influence certainly seems to have been for rather than against religion, even the Christian religion: although refutations continued to couple him with the rationalist opponents of religion, the main appeal of the *Profession de foi* was a spiritual if not religious one, contrasting with the increasing popularity of materialism, and it has even been seen as an important preparatory cause of the Catholic revival of the early nineteenth century.

The success of 'Émile'

The violence of the initial reaction provoked by Rousseau's religious views tended both to distract attention from the educational aspect of *Émile* and also to make people wary of expressing any public approval of the work. The immediate response, at least in print, was on the whole unfavourable. Almost everyone, it is true, expressed admiration for Rousseau's eloquence, which continued to be admired throughout the century, even by some of his bitterest enemies. But admiration for his eloquence was usually allied to a condemnation of his brilliant paradoxes, the result of a wilful 'singularity', a love of originality for its own sake. As for the educational content of *Émile*, much of the physical education of Books I and II was approved, while the deferring of intellectual (and of course religious) education was generally deplored: in other words, praise was reserved for the conventional reforms, while all that was original was rejected.

Yet undoubtedly, *Émile* was an immediate success. In spite of the
ban, it was widely read almost as soon as it appeared, and from the
first it seems to have aroused great enthusiasm among the general
educated public—a fact which is confirmed by the many critics who
complained about its popularity. The abbé Yvon, for instance,
referred sadly to the 'prodigious esteem' which Paris bestowed
on Rousseau's book. Nor did this popularity diminish as the years
went by. Quite quickly, considering it was banned, *Émile* became
more or less respectable, and an increasing number of writers on
education openly took much of it for granted. Some were still rather
timorous: the abbé Le More, for example, in a treatise published in
1774, referred frequently and with approval both to Rousseau and
Émile, without once mentioning either by name. But by that date,
such caution was rather exceptional. More typical perhaps was the
abbé Auger, who, as *Professeur d'éloquence* at the Royal College of
Rouen, could be seen as a pillar of the establishment Rousseau
had attacked. It is true that in the speeches he delivered in 1772 and
1774 on the occasion of the beginning of the school year, which were
based extensively on the ideas of *Émile*, Auger referred specifically
to Rousseau only once (a disagreement), and then not by name but as
'a famous Philosopher, renowned for the beauty of his style'. But
when he published the speeches in 1775, he appended numerous
supporting quotations, mostly from Rousseau (named this time),
and inserted an introductory discussion of *Émile*, which he described
as 'a rich treasure, containing, on the subject of education, a host
of luminous new truths, the wisest and most judicious reflexions,
and the most severe morality'.

The aspect of *Émile* most usually admired, however, continued to
be the education of the 'age of nature', and more especially some of
the details of Book I, notably Rousseau's exhortations on the
subject of maternal breast-feeding and swaddling clothes. This
seems too to have been the only area in which there was any considerable influence of *Émile* in practice. More and more mothers
took to feeding their own babies, a reform which was popularly
attributed to Rousseau's influence, and it became fashionable
among 'enlightened' parents to bring children up 'in the Rousseau
manner' ('à la Jean-Jacques'). A good idea of what this entailed
can be gained from the complaints of Fourcroy de Guillerville, who
wrote in 1770 that everyone said that his children were being brought
up 'à la Jean-Jacques', whereas he had merely 'followed nature' in
bathing them virtually from birth in ice-cold water and letting
them run about lightly clothed in the bitterest winter weather.

The popularity of *Émile* both contributed to and profited from the
remarkable wave of enthusiasm, even veneration, which was
produced by Rousseau's death in 1778 and found expression, for
instance, in the vast number of admirers who, during the next
few years, made the pilgrimage to his tomb at Ermenonville. There
seems to have been widespread agreement at this time, particularly

among those who disapproved, that a great many of Rousseau's educational principles had been generally adopted; even some of his admirers conceded that the devotees of *Émile* sometimes went too far in attempting to adopt its every detail. More frequently, however, Rousseau was credited with having been responsible for a wholly desirable reform which had transformed the lives of young children. 'Everyone has adopted Rousseau's physical system of education ,' wrote Mme de Staël in 1788, and she went on: 'A sure success has permitted no disagreement. . . . He has succeeded in restoring happiness to childhood. . . .'

The confidence with which people attributed the changes to the influence of Rousseau might appear surprising, since, as it was frequently pointed out, the physical details of *Émile* were far from original, and maternal breast-feeding and the abandonment of swaddling clothes in particular, the two reforms principally associated with Rousseau, had been frequently advocated since long before 1762. But the general opinion was that it was Rousseau whose genius and passionate eloquence had convinced where others had merely attempted unsuccessfully to persuade. When someone reminded the great naturalist, Buffon, that he had demonstrated before Rousseau that mothers should breast-feed their babies themselves, he is reputed to have answered: 'Yes, we all said it . . . but M. Rousseau alone commanded it and made people obey him.'

But the changes in educational practice were not confined to such details: all contemporary accounts seem to confirm that since the publication of *Émile* there had indeed been a fundamental transformation in the attitude of parents to children, and the consensus of opinion was certainly that this transformation was due to the influence of Rousseau. Approval of the result was not of course shared by everyone. Restif de la Bretonne, for instance, in 1788, paints a curiously modern picture of this Rousseau-infected younger generation: 'Their hair straggles in a hideous and disgusting way. . . . They are no longer checked, but clamber on to you with their muddy feet. When you visit their parents, they deafen you with their noise, and just when their father or mother is about to reply to you on some important matter, you see them choose instead to answer some childish question of their darling son or daughter. . . . It is *Émile* which is responsible for this provoking, obstinate, insolent, impudent, arrogant generation. . . .' But the freedom that irritated Restif was precisely what, on the eve of the French Revolution, a great many people saw as Rousseau's most important legacy. Writer after writer spoke of *Émile* firstly as having liberated mothers from the prejudices which had prevented them savouring the joys of feeding their own babies, but most of all as having liberated children from the barbarous clutches of mercenary wet-nurses and the cruel bonds of swaddling clothes, as he was later to free them from the traditional academic shackles which had oppressed them.

The impact of *Émile* on pre-revolutionary France is nevertheless a very small fragment of the history of Rousseau's book, a history which it would be quite impossible even to attempt to summarize. *Émile* rapidly became famous throughout Europe, and from the moment it appeared it began to exercise a profound influence on both the theory and the practice of education in many different countries: it is doubtful whether any major educational reformer since Rousseau has not in some measure drawn inspiration from him. Perhaps it is some indication of *Émile*'s greatness that it has meant different things to different ages and different societies. Today, more than two hundred years since it was published, it has still not been left behind. Recent critics have, for instance, demonstrated that many of Rousseau's principles, particularly on the psychology of learning, anticipate uncannily the findings of modern scientific investigators. At the same time, though wet-nurses and swaddling clothes no longer trouble us, the two fundamental concepts of *Émile*, natural goodness and controlled freedom, continue to be at the root of much modern educational debate. Posterity has surely avenged Rousseau on those of his contemporaries who condemned the specious, wilful originality of *Émile*, while taking comfort from the fact that the enthusiasm aroused by the book, irksome though it was, could not possibly last.

1974.   P. D. JIMACK.

SELECT BIBLIOGRAPHY

PRINCIPAL WORKS (with date of first publication)

Discours sur les Sciences et les Arts (1750); *Le Devin du Village* (opera) (1753); *Narcisse ou l'amant de lui-même* (play) (1753); *Lettre sur la musique française* (1753); *Discours sur l'origine et les fondements de l'inégalité* (1755); *Économie politique* (article in Vol. V of the *Encyclopédie* of Diderot and d'Alembert, 1755); *Lettre à d'Alembert sur les Spectacles* (1758); *Julie ou la Nouvelle Héloïse* (1761); *Du Contrat Social* (1762); *Émile ou de l'Éducation* (1762); *Lettre à Christophe de Beaumont, Archévêque de Paris* (1763); *Lettres écrites de la Montagne* (1764); *Dictionnaire de Musique* (1767); *Émile et Sophie ou les Solitaires* (1780, written 1762-5); *Considérations sur le gouvernement de la Pologne* (1782, written 1771); *Les Confessions* (Part I 1782, Part II 1789; written 1766-70); *Rousseau juge de Jean-Jacques, Dialogues* (1st Dialogue 1780, complete 1782; written 1772-6); *Les Rêveries du Promeneur Solitaire* (1782, written 1776-8).

EDITIONS

(N.B. Details of editions of Rousseau's works up to 1949 are to be found in J. Sénelier, *Bibliographie générale des Œuvres de J.-J. Rousseau*, Paris, 1750.)

Complete works

The first reasonably complete edition of Rousseau's works was published by his friends Du Peyrou and Moultou from 1780 to 1789, and there have been many others since. All previous editions have, however, been superseded by what must now be regarded as the standard edition of Rousseau's works, in the Bibliothèque de la Pléiade, published by Gallimard. This edition comprises scholarly introductions and very full notes and is arranged as follows: Vol. I (1959), autobiographical writings; Vol. II (1964), *Nouvelle Héloïse*, theatre, poetry, etc.: Vol. III (1964), political writings; Vol. IV (1969), *Émile* and associated works; Vol. V (1985).

Émile

First edition 1762, in two forms: 'A La Haye, Chez Jean Néaulme' and 'A Amsterdam, Chez Jean Néaulme'; in reality published by Duchesne in Paris. There have been many different editions since then. The best is Vol. IV of the Pléiade *Œuvres Complètes*, but two useful small critical editions are those in Classiques Garnier (ed. F. and P. Richard) and Garnier-Flammarion (ed. M. Launay). The edition of *Émile* in the series 'Les Classiques du Peuple' (Éditions Sociales, Paris, 1978) is a volume of extracts which contains valuable introductory studies by Henri Wallon and J. L. Lecercle. There have been several separate editions of the *Profession du foi du Vicaire savoyard*. The best remains the remarkable critical edition of P.-M. Masson (1914), but a useful recent edition can be found in Rousseau, *Religious Writings*, ed. R. Grimsley (Clarendon Press, 1970).

Correspondence

A scholarly edition of Rousseau's correspondence is in course of publication (*Correspondance Complète*, ed. R. A. Leigh, published by The Voltaire Foundation). Letters that have not yet appeared in this edition may be found in the earlier and less accurate *Correspondance Générale*, ed. T. Dufour and P.-P. Plan (Paris, 1924-34).

Translations

Many of Rousseau's works were translated into English within a year or two of publication, but by no means all of them are available in modern translations. The *Contrat Social*, together with the two *Discours*, is in Everyman's Library. There is also a recent translation of the *Lettre à d'Alembert* (by Bloom, Glencoe, Ill., 1960).

BIOGRAPHY AND CRITICISM

A very great number of critical studies have been published on Rousseau and his works, and the following is a short selection of some of the most important: J. H. Broome, *Rousseau – a Study of his Thought* (London, 1963), P. Burgelin, *La Philosophie de l'Existence de Rousseau* (Paris, 1952), L. G. Crocker, *Jean-Jacques Rousseau*, especially Vol. II, 'The Prophetic Years' (New York and London, 1973), R. Derathé, *Le Rationalisme de J.-J. Rousseau* (Paris, 1948), F. C. Green, *J.-J. Rousseau – a Critical Study of his Life and Writings* (Cambridge, 1955), R. Grimsley, *The Philosophy of Rousseau* (Oxford, 1973), J. Guéhenno, *Jean-Jacques, Histoire d'une Conscience* (Paris, 1948-52) (English translation by J. and D. Weightman, London, 1966), John Hope Mason, *The Indispensable Rousseau* (London, 1979), M. L. and W. S. Sahakian, *Rousseau as Educator* (New York, 1974), J. Starobinski, *J.-J. Rousseau: la Transparence el l'Obstacle* (Paris, 1958). Most of these books contain sections on *Émile*, but see also Peter Jimack, *Rousseau: Emile* (Critical Guides to French texts, London, 1983). For other critical reading on the subject see the very full list of works relating to the educational aspect of *Émile* published by P. Chanover in his article 'Rousseau: A pedagogical bibliography' (in *The French Review*, Vol. XLVI, No. 6, May 1973). A useful addition to Chanover's bibliography is C. H. Dobinson, *Jean-Jacques Rousseau* (The Library of Educational Thought, London, 1969), and an excellent book on the pedagogical background to *Émile* is G. Snyders, *La Pédagogie en France au XVIIe and XVIIIe Siècles* (Paris, 1965). Mention must also be made of the *Index – Correspondance d'Émile*, published by E. Brunet (Geneva and Paris, 1980), a most valuable work of reference. On Rousseau's religious thought, see particularly P.-M. Masson, *La Religion de Rousseau* (Paris, 1916), and R. Grimsley, *Rousseau and the Religious Quest* (Oxford, 1968), as well as parts of Derathé's book, already referred to. On the education of women in the 18th century, see P. Hoffmann's detailed study *La Femme dans la pensée des Lumières* (Paris, 1977), and for the general reader, Vera Lee, *The Reign of Women in 18th-Century France* (Cambridge, Mass., 1975). A periodical devoted to Rousseau studies in general is the *Annales J.-J. Rousseau*, and many relevant articles may also be found in *Studies on Voltaire and the 18th Century* (both published in Geneva).

AUTHOR'S PREFACE

This collection of scattered thoughts and observations has little order or continuity; it was begun to give pleasure to a good mother who thinks for herself. My first idea was to write a tract a few pages long, but I was carried away by my subject, and before I knew what I was doing my tract had become a kind of book, too large indeed for the matter contained in it, but too small for the subject of which it treats. For a long time I hesitated whether to publish it or not, and I have often felt, when at work upon it, that it is one thing to publish a few pamphlets and another to write a book. After vain attempts to improve it, I have decided that it is my duty to publish it as it stands. I consider that public attention requires to be directed to this subject, and even if my own ideas are mistaken, my time will not have been wasted if I stir up others to form right ideas. A solitary who casts his writings before the public without any one to advertise them, without any party ready to defend them, one who does not even know what is thought and said about those writings, is at least free from one anxiety—if he is mistaken, no one will take his errors for gospel.

I shall say very little about the value of a good education, nor shall I stop to prove that the customary method of education is bad; this has been done again and again, and I do not wish to fill my book with things which everyone knows. I will merely state that, go as far back as you will, you will find a continual outcry against the established method, but no attempt to suggest a better. The literature and science of our day tend rather to destroy than to build up. We find fault after the manner of a master; to suggest, we must adopt another style, a style less in accordance with the pride of the philosopher. In spite of all those books, whose only aim, so they say, is public utility, the most useful of all arts, the art of training men, is still neglected. Even after Locke's book was written the subject remained almost untouched, and I fear that my book will leave it pretty much as it found it.

We know nothing of childhood; and with our mistaken notions the further we advance the further we go astray. The wisest writers devote themselves to what a man ought to know, without asking what a child is capable of learning. They are always looking for the man in the child, without considering what he is before he becomes a man. It is to this study that I have chiefly devoted myself, so that if my method is fanciful and unsound, my observations may still be of service. I may be greatly mistaken as to what ought to be done, but I think I have clearly perceived the material which is to be worked upon. Begin thus by making a more careful study of your scholars, for it is clear that you know nothing about them; yet if you read this book with that end in view, I think you will find that it is not entirely useless.

With regard to what will be called the systematic portion of the book, which is nothing more than the course of nature, it is here that the reader will probably go wrong, and no doubt I shall be attacked on this side, and perhaps my critics may be right. You will tell me, "This is not so much a treatise on education as the visions of a dreamer with regard to education." What can I do? I have not written about other people's ideas of education, but about my own. My thoughts are not those of others; this reproach has been brought against me again and again. But is it within my power to furnish myself with other eyes, or to adopt other ideas? It is within my power to refuse to be wedded to my own opinions and to refuse to think myself wiser than others. I cannot change my mind; I can distrust myself. This is all I can do, and this I have done. If I sometimes adopt a confident tone, it is not to impress the reader, it is to make my meaning plain to him. Why should I profess to suggest as doubtful that which is not a matter of doubt to myself? I say just what I think.

When I freely express my opinion, I have so little idea of claiming authority that I always give my reasons, so that you may weigh and judge them for yourselves; but though I would not obstinately defend my ideas, I think it my duty to put them forward; for the principles with regard to which I differ from other writers are not matters of indifference; we must know whether they are true or false, for on them depends the happiness or the misery of mankind.

People are always telling me to make *practicable* suggestions. You might as well tell me to suggest what people are doing already, or at least to suggest improvements which may be incorporated with the wrong methods at present in use. There are matters with regard to which such a suggestion is far more chimerical than my own, for in such a connection the good is corrupted and the bad is none the better for it. I would rather follow exactly the established method than adopt a better method by halves. There would be fewer contradictions in the man; he cannot aim at one and the same time at two different objects. Fathers and mothers, what you desire that you can do. May I count on your goodwill?

There are two things to be considered with regard to any scheme. In the first place, "Is it good in itself?" In the second, "Can it be easily put into practice?"

With regard to the first of these it is enough that the scheme should be intelligible and feasible in itself, that what is good in it should be adapted to the nature of things, in this case, for example, that the proposed method of education should be suitable to man and adapted to the human heart.

The second consideration depends upon certain given conditions in particular cases; these conditions are accidental and therefore variable; they may vary indefinitely. Thus one kind of education would be possible in Switzerland and not in France; another would be adapted to the middle classes but not to the nobility. The scheme can be carried out, with more or less success, according to a multitude of circumstances, and its results can only be determined by its special application to one country or another, to this class or that. Now all these particular applications are not essential to my subject, and they form no part of my scheme. It is enough for me that, wherever men are born into the world, my suggestions with regard to them may be carried out, and when you have made them what I would have them be, you have done what is best for them and best for other people. If I fail to fulfil this promise, no doubt I am to blame; but if I fulfil my promise, it is your own fault if you ask anything more of me, for I have promised you nothing more.

BOOK I

GOD makes all things good; man meddles with them and they become evil. He forces one soil to yield the products of another, one tree to bear another's fruit. He confuses and confounds time, place, and natural conditions. He mutilates his dog, his horse, and his slave. He destroys and defaces all things; he loves all that is deformed and monstrous; he will have nothing as nature made it, not even man himself, who must learn his paces like a saddle-horse, and be shaped to his master's taste like the trees in his garden.

Yet things would be worse without this education, and mankind cannot be made by halves. Under existing conditions a man left to himself from birth would be more of a monster than the rest. Prejudice, authority, necessity, example, all the social conditions into which we are plunged, would stifle nature in him and put nothing in her place. She would be like a sapling chance sown in the midst of the highway, bent hither and thither and soon crushed by the passers-by.

Tender, anxious mother,[1] I appeal to you. You can remove this young tree from the highway and shield it from the crushing force

[1] The earliest education is most important and it undoubtedly is woman's work. If the author of nature had meant to assign it to men he would have given them milk to feed the child. Address your treatises on education to the women, for not only are they able to watch over it more closely than men, not only is their influence always predominant in education, its success concerns them more nearly, for most widows are at the mercy of their children, who show them very plainly whether their education was good or bad. The laws, always more concerned about property than about people, since their object is not virtue but peace, the laws give too little authority to the mother. Yet her position is more certain than that of the father, her duties are more trying; the right ordering of the family depends more upon her, and she is usually fonder of her children. There are occasions when a son may be excused for lack of respect for his father, but if a child could be so unnatural as to fail in respect for the mother who bore him and nursed him at her breast, who for so many years devoted herself to his care, such a monstrous wretch should be smothered at once as unworthy to live. You say mothers spoil their children, and no doubt that is wrong, but it is worse to deprave them as you do. The mother wants her child to be happy now. She is right, and if her method is wrong, she must be taught a better. Ambition, avarice, tyranny, the mistaken foresight of fathers, their neglect, their harshness, are a hundredfold more harmful to the child than the blind affection of the mother. Moreover, I must explain what I mean by a mother and that explanation follows.

5

of social conventions. Tend and water it ere it dies. One day its fruit will reward your care. From the outset raise a wall round your child's soul; another may sketch the plan, you alone should carry it into execution.

Plants are fashioned by cultivation, man by education. If a man were born tall and strong, his size and strength would be of no good to him till he had learnt to use them; they would even harm him by preventing others from coming to his aid; [1] left to himself he would die of want before he knew his needs. We lament the helplessness of infancy; we fail to perceive that the race would have perished had not man begun by being a child.

We are born weak, we need strength; helpless, we need aid; foolish, we need reason. All that we lack at birth, all that we need when we come to man's estate, is the gift of education.

This education comes to us from nature, from men, or from things. The inner growth of our organs and faculties is the education of nature, the use we learn to make of this growth is the education of men, what we gain by our experience of our surroundings is the education of things.

Thus we are each taught by three masters. If their teaching conflicts, the scholar is ill-educated and will never be at peace with himself; if their teaching agrees, he goes straight to his goal, he lives at peace with himself, he is well-educated.

Now of these three factors in education nature is wholly beyond our control, things are only partly in our power; the education of men is the only one controlled by us; and even here our power is largely illusory, for who can hope to direct every word and deed of all with whom the child has to do.

Viewed as an art, the success of education is almost impossible, since the essential conditions of success are beyond our control. Our efforts may bring us within sight of the goal, but fortune must favour us if we are to reach it.

What is this goal? As we have just shown, it is the goal of nature. Since all three modes of education must work together, the two that we can control must follow the lead of that which is beyond our control. Perhaps this word Nature has too vague a meaning. Let us try to define it.

Nature, we are told, is merely habit. What does that mean? Are there not habits formed under compulsion, habits which never stifle nature? Such, for example, are the habits of plants trained horizontally. The plant keeps its artificial shape, but the sap has not changed its course, and any new growth the plant may make will be vertical. It is the same with a man's disposition; while the conditions remain the same, habits, even the least natural of them, hold good; but change the conditions, habits vanish, nature re-

---

[1] Like them in externals, but without speech and without the ideas which are expressed by speech, he would be unable to make his wants known, while there would be nothing in his appearance to suggest that he needed their help.

asserts herself. Education itself is but habit, for are there not people who forget or lose their education and others who keep it? Whence comes this difference? If the term nature is to be restricted to habits conformable to nature we need say no more.

We are born sensitive and from our birth onwards we are affected in various ways by our environment. As soon as we become conscious of our sensations we tend to seek or shun the things that cause them, at first because they are pleasant or unpleasant, then because they suit us or not, and at last because of judgments formed by means of the ideas of happiness and goodness which reason gives us. These tendencies gain strength and permanence with the growth of reason, but hindered by our habits they are more or less warped by our prejudices. Before this change they are what I call Nature within us.

Everything should therefore be brought into harmony with these natural tendencies, and that might well be if our three modes of education merely differed from one another; but what can be done when they conflict, when instead of training man for himself you try to train him for others? Harmony becomes impossible. Forced to combat either nature or society, you must make your choice between the man and the citizen, you cannot train both.

The smaller social group, firmly united in itself and dwelling apart from others, tends to withdraw itself from the larger society. Every patriot hates foreigners; they are only men, and nothing to him.[1] This defect is inevitable, but of little importance. The great thing is to be kind to our neighbours. Among strangers the Spartan was selfish, grasping, and unjust, but unselfishness, justice, and harmony ruled his home life. Distrust those cosmopolitans who search out remote duties in their books and neglect those that lie nearest. Such philosophers will love the Tartars to avoid loving their neighbour.

The natural man lives for himself; he is the unit, the whole, dependent only on himself and on his like. The citizen is but the numerator of a fraction, whose value depends on its denominator; his value depends upon the whole, that is, on the community. Good social institutions are those best fitted to make a man unnatural, to exchange his independence for dependence, to merge the unit in the group, so that he no longer regards himself as one, but as a part of the whole, and is only conscious of the common life. A citizen of Rome was neither Caius nor Lucius, he was a Roman; he ever loved his country better than his life. The captive Regulus professed himself a Carthaginian; as a foreigner he refused to take his seat in the Senate except at his master's bidding. He scorned the attempt to save his life. He had his will, and returned in triumph to a cruel death. There is no great likeness between Regulus and the men of our own day.

---

[1] Thus the wars of republics are more cruel than those of monarchies. But if the wars of kings are less cruel, their peace is terrible; better be their foe than their subject.

The Spartan Pedaretes presented himself for admission to the council of the Three Hundred and was rejected; he went away rejoicing that there were three hundred Spartans better than himself. I suppose he was in earnest; there is no reason to doubt it. That was a citizen.

A Spartan mother had five sons with the army. A Helot arrived; trembling she asked his news. "Your five sons are slain." "Vile slave, was that what I asked thee?" "We have won the victory." She hastened to the temple to render thanks to the gods. That was a citizen.

He who would preserve the supremacy of natural feelings in social life knows not what he asks. Ever at war with himself, hesitating between his wishes and his duties, he will be neither a man nor a citizen. He will be of no use to himself nor to others. He will be a man of our day, a Frenchman, an Englishman, one of the great middle class.

To be something, to be himself, and always at one with himself, a man must act as he speaks, must know what course he ought to take, and must follow that course with vigour and persistence. When I meet this miracle it will be time enough to decide whether he is a man or a citizen, or how he contrives to be both.

Two conflicting types of educational systems spring from these conflicting aims. One is public and common to many, the other private and domestic.

If you wish to know what is meant by public education, read Plato's *Republic*. Those who merely judge books by their titles take this for a treatise on politics, but it is the finest treatise on education ever written.

In popular estimation the Platonic Institute stands for all that is fanciful and unreal. For my own part I should have thought the system of Lycurgus far more impracticable had he merely committed it to writing. Plato only sought to purge man's heart; Lycurgus turned it from its natural course.

The public institute does not and cannot exist, for there is neither country nor patriot. The very words should be struck out of our language. The reason does not concern us at present, so that though I know it I refrain from stating it.

I do not consider our ridiculous colleges [1] as public institutes, nor do I include under this head a fashionable education, for this education facing two ways at once achieves nothing. It is only fit to turn out hypocrites, always professing to live for others, while thinking of themselves alone. These professions, however, deceive

[1] There are teachers dear to me in many schools and especially in the University of Paris, men for whom I have a great respect, men whom I believe to be quite capable of instructing young people, if they were not compelled to follow the established custom. I exhort one of them to publish the scheme of reform which he has thought out. Perhaps people would at length seek to cure the evil if they realised that there was a remedy.

no one, for every one has his share in them; they are so much labour wasted.

Our inner conflicts are caused by these contradictions. Drawn this way by nature and that way by man, compelled to yield to both forces, we make a compromise and reach neither goal. We go through life, struggling and hesitating, and die before we have found peace, useless alike to ourselves and to others.

There remains the education of the home or of nature; but how will a man live with others if he is educated for himself alone? If the twofold aims could be resolved into one by removing the man's self-contradictions, one great obstacle to his happiness would be gone. To judge of this you must see the man full-grown; you must have noted his inclinations, watched his progress, followed his steps; in a word you must really know a natural man. When you have read this work, I think you will have made some progress in this inquiry.

What must be done to train this exceptional man! We can do much, but the chief thing is to prevent anything being done. To sail against the wind we merely follow one tack and another; to keep our position in a stormy sea we must cast anchor. Beware, young pilot, lest your boat slip its cable or drag its anchor before you know it.

In the social order where each has his own place a man must be educated for it. If such a one leave his own station he is fit for nothing else. His education is only useful when fate agrees with his parents' choice; if not, education harms the scholar, if only by the prejudices it has created. In Egypt, where the son was compelled to adopt his father's calling, education had at least a settled aim; where social grades remain fixed, but the men who form them are constantly changing, no one knows whether he is not harming his son by educating him for his own class.

In the natural order men are all equal and their common calling is that of manhood, so that a well-educated man cannot fail to do well in that calling and those related to it. It matters little to me whether my pupil is intended for the army, the church, or the law. Before his parents chose a calling for him nature called him to be a man. Life is the trade I would teach him. When he leaves me, I grant you, he will be neither a magistrate, a soldier, nor a priest; he will be a man. All that becomes a man he will learn as quickly as another. In vain will fate change his station, he will always be in his right place. "Occupavi te, fortuna, atque cepi; omnes-que aditus tuos interclusi, ut ad me aspirare non posses." The real object of our study is man and his environment. To my mind those of us who can best endure the good and evil of life are the best educated; hence it follows that true education consists less in precept than in practice. We begin to learn when we begin to live; our education begins with ourselves, our first teacher is our nurse. The ancients used the word "Education" in a different sense, it meant "Nurture." "Educit obstetrix," says Varro, "Educat nutrix, instituit pædagogus, docet magister." Thus, education, discipline, and instruction are three things as different in their purpose as the dame, the usher, and the teacher. But these distinctions are undesirable and the child should only follow one guide.

We must therefore look at the general rather than the particular, and consider our scholar as man in the abstract, man exposed to all the changes and chances of mortal life. If men were born attached to the soil of our country, if one season lasted all the year round, if every man's fortune were so firmly grasped that he could never lose it, then the established method of education would have certain advantages; the child brought up to his own calling would never leave it, he could never have to face the difficulties of any other condition. But when we consider the fleeting nature of human affairs, the restless and uneasy spirit of our times, when every generation overturns the work of its predecessor, can we conceive a more senseless plan than to educate a child as if he would never leave his room, as if he would always have his servants about him? If the wretched creature takes a single step up or down he is lost. This is not teaching him to bear pain; it is training him to feel it.

People think only of preserving their child's life; this is not enough, he must be taught to preserve his own life when he is a man, to bear the buffets of fortune, to brave wealth and poverty, to live at need among the snows of Iceland or on the scorching rocks of Malta. In vain you guard against death; he must needs die; and even if you do not kill him with your precautions, they are mistaken. Teach him to live rather than to avoid death: life is not breath, but action, the use of our senses, our mind, our faculties, every part of ourselves which makes us conscious of our being. Life consists less in length of days than in the keen sense of living. A man may be buried at a hundred and may never have lived at all. He would have fared better had he died young.

Our wisdom is slavish prejudice, our customs consist in control, constraint, compulsion. Civilised man is born and dies a slave. The infant is bound up in swaddling clothes, the corpse is nailed down in his coffin. All his life long man is imprisoned by our institutions.

I am told that many midwives profess to improve the shape of the infant's head by rubbing, and they are allowed to do it. Our heads are not good enough as God made them, they must be moulded outside by the nurse and inside by the philosopher. The Caribs are better off than we are. "The child has hardly left the mother's womb, it has hardly begun to move and stretch its limbs, when it is deprived of its freedom. It is wrapped in swaddling bands, laid down with its head fixed, its legs stretched out, and its arms by its sides; it is wound round with linen and bandages of all sorts so that it cannot move. It is fortunate if it has room to breathe, and it is laid on its side so that water which should flow from its mouth can escape, for it is not free to turn its head on one side for this purpose."

The new-born child requires to stir and stretch his limbs to free them from the stiffness resulting from being curled up so long. His limbs are stretched indeed, but he is not allowed to move them. Even the head is confined by a cap. One would think they were afraid the child should look as if it were alive.

Thus the internal impulses which should lead to growth find an insurmountable obstacle in the way of the necessary movements. The child exhausts his strength in vain struggles, or he gains strength very slowly. He was freer and less constrained in the womb; he has gained nothing by birth.

The inaction, the constraint to which the child's limbs are subjected can only check the circulation of the blood and humours; it can only hinder the child's growth in size and strength, and injure its constitution. Where these absurd precautions are absent, all the men are tall, strong, and well-made. Where children are swaddled, the country swarms with the hump-backed, the lame, the bow-legged, the rickety, and every kind of deformity. In our fear lest the body should become deformed by free movement, we hasten to deform it by putting it in a press. We make our children helpless lest they should hurt themselves.

Is not such a cruel bondage certain to affect both health and temper? Their first feeling is one of pain and suffering; they find every necessary movement hampered; more miserable than a galley slave, in vain they struggle, they become angry, they cry. Their first words you say are tears. That is so. From birth you are always checking them, your first gifts are fetters, your first treatment, torture. Their voice alone is free; why should they not raise it in complaint? They cry because you are hurting them; if you were swaddled you would cry louder still.

What is the origin of this senseless and unnatural custom? Since mothers have despised their first duty and refused to nurse their own children, they have had to be entrusted to hired nurses. Finding themselves the mothers of a stranger's children, without the ties of nature, they have merely tried to save themselves trouble. A child unswaddled would need constant watching; well swaddled it is cast into a corner and its cries are unheeded. So long as the nurse's negligence escapes notice, so long as the nursling does not break its arms or legs, what matter if it dies or becomes a weakling for life. Its limbs are kept safe at the expense of its body, and if anything goes wrong it is not the nurse's fault.

These gentle mothers, having got rid of their babies, devote themselves gaily to the pleasures of the town. Do they know how their children are being treated in the villages? If the nurse is at all busy, the child is hung up on a nail like a bundle of clothes and is left crucified while the nurse goes leisurely about her business. Children have been found in this position purple in the face, their tightly bandaged chest forbade the circulation of the blood, and it went to the head; so the sufferer was considered very quiet because he had not strength to cry. How long a child might survive under such conditions I do not know, but it could not be long. That, I fancy, is one of the chief advantages of swaddling clothes.

It is maintained that unswaddled infants would assume faulty positions and make movements which might injure the proper development of their limbs. That is one of the empty arguments of our false wisdom which has never been confirmed by experience. Out of all the crowds of children who grow up with the full use of their limbs among nations wiser than ourselves, you never find one who hurts himself or maims himself; their movements are too feeble to be dangerous, and when they assume an injurious position, pain warns them to change it.

We have not yet decided to swaddle our kittens and puppies; are they any the worse for this neglect? Children are heavier, I admit, but they are also weaker. They can scarcely move, how could they hurt themselves? If you lay them on their backs, they will lie there till they die, like the turtle, unable to turn itself over.

Not content with having ceased to suckle their children, women no longer wish to do it; with the natural result—motherhood becomes a burden; means are found to avoid it. They will destroy their work to begin it over again, and they thus turn to the injury of the race the charm which was given them for its increase. This practice, with other causes of depopulation, forbodes the coming fate of Europe. Her arts and sciences, her philosophy and morals, will shortly reduce her to a desert. She will be the home of wild beasts, and her inhabitants will hardly have changed for the worse.

I have sometimes watched the tricks of young wives who pretend that they wish to nurse their own children. They take care to be dissuaded from this whim. They contrive that husbands, doctors, and especially mothers should intervene. If a husband should let his wife nurse her own baby it would be the ruin of him; they would make him out a murderer who wanted to be rid of her. A prudent husband must sacrifice paternal affection to domestic peace. Fortunately for you there are women in the country districts more continent than your wives. You are still more fortunate if the time thus gained is not intended for another than yourself.

There can be no doubt about a wife's duty, but, considering the contempt in which it is held, it is doubtful whether it is not just as good for the child to be suckled by a stranger. This is a question for the doctors to settle, and in my opinion they have settled it according to the women's wishes,[1] and for my own part I think it is better that the child should suck the breast of a healthy nurse rather than of a petted mother, if he has any further evil to fear from her who has given him birth.

Ought the question, however, to be considered only from the

[1] The league between the women and the doctors has always struck me as one of the oddest things in Paris. The doctors' reputation depends on the women, and by means of the doctors the women get their own way. It is easy to see what qualifications a doctor requires in Paris if he is to become celebrated.

physiological point of view? Does not the child need a mother's care as much as her milk? Other women, or even other animals, may give him the milk she denies him, but there is no substitute for a mother's love.

The woman who nurses another's child in place of her own is a bad mother; how can she be a good nurse? She may become one in time; use will overcome nature, but the child may perish a hundred times before his nurse has developed a mother's affection for him.

And this affection when developed has its drawbacks, which should make any feeling woman afraid to put her child out to nurse. Is she prepared to divide her mother's rights, or rather to abdicate them in favour of a stranger; to see her child loving another more than herself; to feel that the affection he retains for his own mother is a favour, while his love for his foster-mother is a duty; for is not some affection due where there has been a mother's care?

To remove this difficulty, children are taught to look down on their nurses, to treat them as mere servants. When their task is completed the child is withdrawn or the nurse is dismissed. Her visits to her foster-child are discouraged by a cold reception. After a few years the child never sees her again. The mother expects to take her place, and to repair by her cruelty the results of her own neglect. But she is greatly mistaken; she is making an ungrateful foster-child, not an affectionate son; she is teaching him ingratitude, and she is preparing him to despise at a later day the mother who bore him, as he now despises his nurse.

How emphatically would I speak if it were not so hopeless to keep struggling in vain on behalf of a real reform. More depends on this than you realise. Would you restore all men to their primal duties, begin with the mothers; the results will surprise you. Every evil follows in the train of this first sin; the whole moral order is disturbed, nature is quenched in every breast, the home becomes gloomy, the spectacle of a young family no longer stirs the husband's love and the stranger's reverence. The mother whose children are out of sight wins scanty esteem; there is no home life, the ties of nature are not strengthened by those of habit; fathers, mothers, children, brothers, and sisters cease to exist. They are almost strangers; how should they love one another? Each thinks of himself first. When the home is a gloomy solitude pleasure will be sought elsewhere.

But when mothers deign to nurse their own children, then will be a reform in morals; natural feeling will revive in every heart; there will be no lack of citizens for the state; this first step by itself will restore mutual affection. The charms of home are the best antidote to vice. The noisy play of children, which we thought so trying, becomes a delight; mother and father rely more on each other and grow dearer to one another; the marriage tie is strengthened. In the cheerful home life the mother finds her sweetest duties and the father his pleasantest recreation. Thus the cure of this one evil would work a wide-spread reformation; nature would regain her rights. When women become good mothers, men will be good husbands and fathers.

My words are vain! When we are sick of worldly pleasures we do not return to the pleasures of the home. Women have ceased to be mothers, they do not and will not return to their duty. Could they do it if they would? The contrary custom is firmly established; each would have to overcome the opposition of her neighbours, leagued together against the example which some have never given and others do not desire to follow.

Yet there are still a few young women of good natural disposition who refuse to be the slaves of fashion and rebel against the clamour of other women, who fulfil the sweet task imposed on them by nature. Would that the reward in store for them might draw others to follow their example. My conclusion is based upon plain reason, and upon facts I have never seen disputed; and I venture to promise these worthy mothers the firm and steadfast affection of their husbands and the truly filial love of their children and the respect of all the world. Child-birth will be easy and will leave no ill-results, their health will be strong and vigorous, and they will see their daughters follow their example, and find that example quoted as a pattern to others.

No mother, no child; their duties are reciprocal, and when ill done by the one they will be neglected by the other. The child should love his mother before he knows what he owes her. If the voice of instinct is not strengthened by habit it soon dies, the heart is still-born. From the outset we have strayed from the path of nature.

There is another by-way which may tempt our feet from the path of nature. The mother may lavish excessive care on her child instead of neglecting him; she may make an idol of him; she may develop and increase his weakness to prevent him feeling it; she wards off every painful experience in the hope of withdrawing him from the power of nature, and fails to realise that for every trifling ill from which she preserves him the future holds in store many accidents and dangers, and that it is a cruel kindness to prolong the child's weakness when the grown man must bear fatigue.

Thetis, so the story goes, plunged her son in the waters of Styx to make him invulnerable. The truth of this allegory is apparent. The cruel mothers I speak of do otherwise; they plunge their children into softness, and they are preparing suffering for them, they open the way to every kind of ill, which their children will not fail to experience after they grow up.

Fix your eyes on nature, follow the path traced by her. She keeps children at work, she hardens them by all kinds of difficulties, she soon teaches them the meaning of pain and grief. They cut their teeth and are feverish, sharp colics bring on convulsions, they are choked by fits of coughing and tormented by worms, evil humours corrupt the blood, germs of various kinds ferment in it, causing dangerous eruptions. Sickness and danger play the chief part in infancy. One half of the children who are born die before their eighth year. The child who has overcome hardships has gained strength, and as soon as he can use his life he holds it more securely.

This is nature's law; why contradict it? Do you not see that in your efforts to improve upon her handiwork you are destroying it; her cares are wasted? To do from without what she does within is according to you to increase the danger twofold. On the contrary, it is the way to avert it; experience shows that children delicately nurtured are more likely to die. Provided we do not overdo it, there is less risk in using their strength than in sparing it. Accustom them therefore to the hardships they will have to face; train them to endure extremes of temperature, climate, and condition, hunger, thirst, and weariness. Dip them in the waters of Styx. Before bodily habits become fixed you may teach what habits you will without any risk, but once habits are established any change is fraught with peril. A child will bear changes which a man cannot bear, the muscles of the one are soft and flexible, they take whatever direction you give them without any effort; the muscles of the grown man are harder and they only change their accustomed mode of action when subjected to violence. So we can make a child strong without risking his life or health, and even if there were some risk, it should not be taken into consideration. Since human life is full of dangers, can we do better than face them at a time when they can do the least harm?

A child's worth increases with his years. To his personal value must be added the cost of the care bestowed upon him. For himself there is not only loss of life, but the consciousness of death. We must therefore think most of his future in our efforts for his preservation. He must be protected against the ills of youth before he reaches them: for if the value of life increases until the child reaches an age when he can be useful, what madness to spare some suffering in infancy only to multiply his pain when he reaches the age of reason. Is that what our master teaches us?

Man is born to suffer; pain is the means of his preservation. His childhood is happy, knowing only pain of body. These bodily sufferings are much less cruel, much less painful, than other forms of suffering, and they rarely lead to self-destruction. It is not the twinges of gout which make a man kill himself, it is mental suffering that leads to despair. We pity the sufferings of childhood; we should pity ourselves; our worst sorrows are of our own making.

The new-born infant cries, his early days are spent in crying. He is alternately petted and shaken by way of soothing him; sometimes he is threatened, sometimes beaten, to keep him quiet. We do what he wants or we make him do what we want, we submit to his whims or subject him to our own. There is no middle course; he must rule or obey. Thus his earliest ideas are those of the tyrant or the slave. He commands before he can speak, he obeys before he can act, and sometimes he is punished for faults before he is aware of them, or rather before they are committed. Thus early are the seeds of evil passions sown in his young heart. At a later day these are attributed to nature, and when we have taken pains to make him bad we lament his badness.

In this way the child passes six or seven years in the hands of women, the victim of his own caprices or theirs, and after they have taught him all sorts of things, when they have burdened his memory with words he cannot understand, or things which are of no use to him, when nature has been stifled by the passions they have implanted in him, this sham article is sent to a tutor. The tutor completes the development of the germs of artificiality which he finds already well grown, he teaches him everything except self-knowledge and self-control, the arts of life and happiness. When at length this infant slave and tyrant, crammed with knowledge but empty of sense, feeble alike in mind and body, is flung upon the world, and his helplessness, his pride, and his other vices are displayed, we begin to lament the wretchedness and perversity of mankind. We are wrong; this is the creature of our fantasy; the natural man is cast in another mould.

Would you keep him as nature made him? Watch over him from his birth. Take possession of him as soon as he comes into the world and keep him till he is a man; you will never succeed otherwise. The real nurse is the mother and the real teacher is the father. Let them agree in the ordering of their duties as well as in their method, let the child pass from one to the other. He will be better educated by a sensible though ignorant father than by the cleverest master in the world. For zeal will atone for lack of knowledge, rather than knowledge for lack of zeal. But the duties of public and private business! Duty indeed! Does a father's duty come last.[1] It is not surprising that the man whose wife despises the duty of suckling her child should despise its education. There is no more charming picture than that of family life; but when one feature is wanting the whole is marred. If the mother is too delicate to nurse her child, the father will be too busy to teach him. Their children, scattered about in schools, convents, and colleges, will find the home of their affections elsewhere, or rather they will form the habit of caring for nothing. Brothers and sisters will scarcely know each other; when they are together in company they will behave as strangers. When there is no confidence between

[1] When we read in Plutarch that Cato the Censor, who ruled Rome with such glory, brought up his own sons from the cradle, and so carefully that he left everything to be present when their nurse, that is to say their mother, bathed them; when we read in Suetonius that Augustus, the master of the world which he had conquered and which he himself governed, himself taught his grandsons to write, to swim, to understand the beginnings of science, and that he always had them with him, we cannot help smiling at the little people of those days who amused themselves with such follies, and who were too ignorant, no doubt, to attend to the great affairs of the great people of our own time.

relations, when the family society ceases to give savour to life, its place is soon usurped by vice. Is there any man so stupid that he cannot see how all this hangs together?

A father has done but a third of his task when he begets children and provides a living for them. He owes men to humanity, citizens to the state. A man who can pay this threefold debt and neglects to do so is guilty, more guilty, perhaps, if he pays it in part than when he neglects it entirely. He has no right to be a father if he cannot fulfil a father's duties. Poverty, pressure of business, mistaken social prejudices, none of these can excuse a man from his duty, which is to support and educate his own children. If a man of any natural feeling neglects these sacred duties he will repent it with bitter tears and will never be comforted.

But what does this rich man do, this father of a family, compelled, so he says, to neglect his children? He pays another man to perform those duties which are his alone. Mercenary man! do you expect to purchase a second father for your child? Do not deceive yourself; it is not even a master you have hired for him, it is a flunkey, who will soon train such another as himself.

There is much discussion as to the characteristics of a good tutor. My first requirement, and it implies a good many more, is that he should not take up his task for reward. There are callings so great that they cannot be undertaken for money without showing our unfitness for them; such callings are those of the soldier and the teacher.

"But who must train my child?" "I have just told you, you should do it yourself." "I cannot." "You cannot! Then find a friend. I see no other course."

A tutor! What a noble soul! Indeed for the training of a man one must either be a father or more than man. It is this duty you would calmly hand over to a hireling!

The more you think of it the harder you will find it. The tutor must have been trained for his pupil, his servants must have been trained for their master, so that all who come near him may have received the impression which is to be transmitted to him. We must pass from education to education, I know not how far. How can a child be well educated by one who has not been well educated himself?

Can such a one be found? I know not. In this age of degradation who knows the height of virtue to which man's soul may attain? But let us assume that this prodigy has been discovered. We shall learn what he should be from the consideration of his duties. I fancy the father who realises the value of a good tutor will contrive to do without one, for it will be harder to find one than to become such a tutor himself; he need search no further, nature herself having done half the work.

Some one whose rank alone is known to me suggested that I should educate his son. He did me a great honour, no doubt, but far from regretting my refusal, he ought to congratulate himself on my prudence. Had the offer been accepted, and had I been mistaken in my method, there would have been an education ruined; had I succeeded, things would have been worse—his son would have renounced his title and refused to be a prince.

I feel too deeply the importance of a tutor's duties and my own unfitness, ever to accept such a post, whoever offered it, and even the claims of friendship would be only an additional motive for my refusal. Few, I think, will be tempted to make me such an offer when they have read this book, and I beg any one who would do so to spare his pains. I have had enough experience of the task to convince myself of my own unfitness, and my circumstances would make it impossible, even if my talents were such as to fit me for it. I have thought it my duty to make this public declaration to those who apparently refuse to do me the honour of believing in the sincerity of my determination. If I am unable to undertake the more useful task, I will at least venture to attempt the easier one; I will follow the example of my predecessors and take up, not the task, but my pen; and instead of doing the right thing I will try to say it.

I know that in such an undertaking the author, who ranges at will among theoretical systems, utters many fine precepts impossible to practise, and even when he says what is practicable it remains undone for want of details and examples as to its application.

I have therefore decided to take an imaginary pupil, to assume on my own part the age, health, knowledge, and talents required for the work of his education, to guide him from birth to manhood, when he needs no guide but himself. This method seems to me useful for an author who fears lest he may stray from the practical to the visionary; for as soon as he departs from common practice he has only to try his method on his pupil; he will soon know, or the reader will know for him, whether he is following the development of the child and the natural growth of the human heart.

This is what I have tried to do. Lest my book should be unduly bulky, I have been content to state those principles the truth of which is self-evident. But as to the rules which call for proof, I have applied them to Emile or to others, and I have shown, in very great detail, how my theories may be put into practice. Such at least is my plan; the reader must decide whether I have succeeded. At first I have said little about Emile, for my earliest maxims of education, though very different from those generally accepted, are so plain that it is hard for a man of sense to refuse to accept them, but as I advance, my scholar, educated after another fashion than yours, is no longer an ordinary child, he needs a special system. Then he appears upon the scene more frequently, and towards the end I never lose sight of him for a moment, until, whatever he may say, he needs me no longer.

I pass over the qualities required in a good tutor; I take them for granted, and assume that I am endowed with them. As you read this book you will see how generous I have been to myself.

I will only remark that, contrary to the received opinion, a child's tutor should be young, as young indeed as a man may well be who is also wise. Were it possible, he should become a child himself, that he may be the companion of his pupil and win his confidence by sharing his games. Childhood and age have too little in common for the formation of a really firm affection. Children sometimes flatter old men; they never love them.

People seek a tutor who has already educated one pupil. This is too much; one man can only educate one pupil; if two were essential to success, what right would he have to undertake the first? With more experience you may know better what to do, but you are less capable of doing it; once this task has been well done, you will know too much of its difficulties to attempt it a second time—if ill done, the first attempt augurs badly for the second.

It is one thing to follow a young man about for four years, another to be his guide for five-and-twenty. You find a tutor for your son when he is already formed; I want one for him before he is born. Your man may change his pupil every five years; mine will never have but one pupil. You distinguish between the teacher and the tutor. Another piece of folly! Do you make any distinction between the pupil and the scholar? There is only one science for children to learn—the duties of man. This science is one, and, whatever Xenophon may say of the education of the Persians, it is indivisible. Besides, I prefer to call the man who has this knowledge master rather than teacher, since it is a question of guidance rather than instruction. He must not give precepts, he must let the scholar find them out for himself.

If the master is to be so carefully chosen, he may well choose his pupil, above all when he proposes to set a pattern for others. This choice cannot depend on the child's genius or character, as I adopt him before he is born, and they are only known when my task is finished. If I had my choice I would take a child of ordinary mind, such as I assume in my pupil. It is ordinary people who have to be educated, and their education alone can serve as a pattern for the education of their fellows. The others find their way alone.

The birthplace is not a matter of indifference in the education of man; it is only in temperate climes that he comes to his full growth. The disadvantages of extremes are easily seen. A man is not planted in one place like a tree, to stay there the rest of his life, and to pass from one extreme to another you must travel twice as far as he who starts half-way.

If the inhabitant of a temperate climate passes in turn through both extremes his advantage is plain, for although he may be changed as much as he who goes from one extreme to the other, he only removes half-way from his natural condition. A Frenchman can live in New Guinea or in Lapland, but a negro cannot live in Tornea nor a Samoyed in Benin. It seems also as if the brain were less perfectly organised in the two extremes. Neither the negroes nor the Laps are as wise as Europeans. So if I want my pupil to be a citizen of the world I will choose him in the temperate zone, in France for example, rather than elsewhere.

In the north with its barren soil men devour much food, in the fertile south they eat little. This produces another difference: the one is industrious, the other contemplative. Society shows us, in one and the same spot, a similar difference between rich and poor. The one dwells in a fertile land, the other in a barren land.

The poor man has no need of education. The education of his own station in life is forced upon him, he can have no other; the education received by the rich man from his own station is least fitted for himself and for society. Moreover, a natural education should fit a man for any position. Now it is more unreasonable to train a poor man for wealth than a rich man for poverty, for in proportion to their numbers more rich men are ruined and fewer poor men become rich. Let us choose our scholar among the rich; we shall at least have made another man; the poor may come to manhood without our help.

For the same reason I should not be sorry if Emile came of a good family. He will be another victim snatched from prejudice.

Emile is an orphan. No matter whether he has father or mother, having undertaken their duties I am invested with their rights. He must honour his parents, but he must obey me. That is my first and only condition.

I must add that there is just one other point arising out of this; we must never be separated except by mutual consent. This clause is essential, and I would have tutor and scholar so inseparable that they should regard their fate as one. If once they perceive the time of their separation drawing near, the time which must make them strangers to one another, they become strangers then and there; each makes his own little world, and both of them being busy in thought with the time when they will no longer be together, they remain together against their will. The disciple regards his master as the badge and scourge of childhood, the master regards his scholar as a heavy burden which he longs to be rid of. Both are looking forward to the time when they will part, and as there is never any real affection between them, there will be scant vigilance on the one hand, and on the other scant obedience.

But when they consider they must always live together, they must needs love one another, and in this way they really learn to love one another. The pupil is not ashamed to follow as a child the friend who will be with him in manhood; the tutor takes an interest in the efforts whose fruits he will enjoy, and the virtues he is cultivating in his pupil form a store laid up for his old age.

This agreement made beforehand assumes a normal birth, a strong, well-made, healthy child. A father has no choice, and should have no preference within the limits of the family God has given him; all his children are his alike, the same care and affection is due to all. Crippled or well-made, weak or strong, each of them is a trust for which he is responsible to the Giver, and nature is a party to the marriage contract along with husband and wife.

But if you undertake a duty not imposed upon you by nature, you must secure beforehand the means for its fulfilment, unless you would undertake duties you cannot fulfil. If you take the care of a sickly, unhealthy child, you are a sick nurse, not a tutor. To preserve a useless life you are wasting the time which should be spent in increasing its value, you risk the sight of a despairing mother reproaching you for the death of her child, who ought to have died long ago.

I would not undertake the care of a feeble, sickly child, should he live to four score years. I want no pupil who is useless alike to himself and others, one whose sole business is to keep himself alive, one whose body is always a hindrance to the training of his mind. If I vainly lavish my care upon him, what can I do but double the loss to society by robbing it of two men, instead of one? Let another tend this weakling for me; I am quite willing, I approve his charity, but I myself have no gift for such a task; I could never teach the art of living to one who needs all his strength to keep himself alive.

The body must be strong enough to obey the mind; a good servant must be strong. I know that intemperance stimulates the passions; in course of time it also destroys the body; fasting and penance often produce the same results in an opposite way. The weaker the body, the more imperious its demands; the stronger it is, the better it obeys. All sensual passions find their home in effeminate bodies; the less satisfaction they can get the keener their sting.

A feeble body makes a feeble mind. Hence the influence of physic, an art which does more harm to man than all the evils it professes to cure. I do not know what the doctors cure us of, but I know this: they infect us with very deadly diseases, cowardice, timidity, credulity, the fear of death. What matter if they make the dead walk, we have no need of corpses; they fail to give us men, and it is men we need.

Medicine is all the fashion in these days, and very naturally. It is the amusement of the idle and unemployed, who do not know what to do with their time, and so spend it in taking care of themselves. If by ill-luck they had happened to be born immortal, they would have been the most miserable of men; a life they could not lose would be of no value to them. Such men must have doctors to threaten and flatter them, to give them the only pleasure they can enjoy, the pleasure of not being dead.

I will say no more at present as to the uselessness of medicine. My aim is to consider its bearings on morals. Still I cannot refrain from saying that men employ the same sophism about medicine as they do about the search for truth. They assume that the patient is cured and that the seeker after truth finds it. They fail to see that against one life saved by the doctors you must set a hundred slain, and against the value of one truth discovered the errors which creep in with it. The science which instructs and the medicine which heals are no doubt excellent, but the science which misleads us and the medicine which kills us are evil. Teach us to know them apart. That is the real difficulty. If we were content to be ignorant of truth we should not be the dupes of falsehood; if we did not want to be cured in spite of nature, we should not be killed by the doctors. We should do well to steer clear of both, and we should evidently be the gainers. I do not deny that medicine is useful to some men; I assert that it is fatal to mankind.

You will tell me, as usual, that the doctors are to blame, that medicine herself is infallible. Well and good, then give us the medicine without the doctor, for when we have both, the blunders of the artist are a hundredfold greater than our hopes from the art.

This lying art, invented rather for the ills of the mind than of the body, is useless to both alike; it does less to cure us of our diseases than to fill us with alarm. It does less to ward off death than to make us dread its approach. It exhausts life rather than prolongs it; should it even prolong life it would only be to the prejudice of the race, since it makes us set its precautions before society and our fears before our duties. It is the knowledge of danger that makes us afraid. If we thought ourselves invulnerable we should know no fear. The poet armed Achilles against danger and so robbed him of the merit of courage; on such terms any man would be an Achilles.

Would you find a really brave man? Seek him where there are no doctors, where the results of disease are unknown, and where death is little thought of. By nature a man bears pain bravely and dies in peace. It is the doctors with their rules, the philosophers with their precepts, the priests with their exhortations, who debase the heart and make us afraid to die.

Give me a pupil who has no need of these, or I will have nothing to do with him. No one else shall spoil my work, I will educate him myself or not at all. That wise man, Locke, who had devoted part of his life to the study of medicine, advises us to give no drugs to the child, whether as a precaution, or on account of slight ailments. I will go farther, and will declare that, as I never call in a doctor for myself, I will never send for one for Emile, unless his life is clearly in danger, when the doctor can but kill him.

I know the doctor will make capital out of my delay If the child dies, he was called in too late; if he recovers, it is his doing. So be it; let the doctor boast, but do not call him in except in extremity.

As the child does not know how to be cured, he knows how to be ill. The one art takes the place of the other and is often more successful; it is the art of nature. When a beast is ill, it keeps quiet and suffers in silence; but we see fewer sickly animals than sick men. How many men have been slain by impatience, fear, anxiety, and above all by medicine, men whom disease would have spared, and time alone have cured. I shall be told that animals, who live according to nature, are less liable to disease than ourselves. Well, that way of living is just what I mean to teach my pupil; he should profit by it in the same way.

Hygiene is the only useful part of medicine, and hygiene is rather a virtue than a science. Temperance and industry are man's true remedies; work sharpens his appetite and temperance teaches him to control it.

To learn what system is most beneficial you have only to study those races remarkable for health, strength, and length of days. If common observation shows us that medicine neither increases health nor prolongs life, it follows that this useless art is worse than useless, since it wastes time, men, and things on what is pure loss. Not only must we deduct the time spent, not in using life, but preserving it, but if this time is spent in tormenting ourselves it is worse than wasted, it is so much to the bad, and to reckon fairly a corresponding share must be deducted from what remains to us. A man who lives ten years for himself and others without the help of doctors lives more for himself and others than one who spends thirty years as their victim. I have tried both, so I think I have a better right than most to draw my own conclusions.

For these reasons I decline to take any but a strong and healthy pupil, and these are my principles for keeping him in health. I will not stop to prove at length the value of manual labour and bodily exercise for strengthening the health and constitution; no one denies it. Nearly all the instances of long life are to be found among the men who have taken most exercise, who have endured fatigue and labour.[1] Neither will I enter into details as to the care I shall take for this alone. It will be clear that it forms such an essential part of my practice that it is enough to get hold of the idea without further explanation.

When our life begins our needs begin too. The new-born infant must have a nurse. If his mother will do her duty, so much the better; her instructions will be given her in writing, but this advantage has its drawbacks, it removes the tutor from his charge. But it is to be hoped that the child's own interests, and her respect for the person to whom she is about to confide so precious a treasure,

[1] I cannot help quoting the following passage from an English newspaper, as it throws much light on my opinions: " A certain Patrick O'Neil, born in 1647, has just married his seventh wife in 1760. In the seventeenth year of Charles II. he served in the dragoons and in other regiments up to 1740, when he took his discharge. He served in all the campaigns of William III. and Marlborough. This man has never drunk anything but small beer; he has always lived on vegetables, and has never eaten meat except on few occasions when he made a feast for his relations. He has always been accustomed to rise with the sun and go to bed at sunset unless prevented by his military duties. He is now in his 130th year; he is healthy, his hearing is good, and he walks with the help of a stick. In spite of his great age he is never idle, and every Sunday he goes to his parish church accompanied by his children, grandchildren, and great grandchildren."

will induce the mother to follow the master's wishes, and whatever she does you may be sure she will do better than another. If we must have a strange nurse, make a good choice to begin with.

It is one of the misfortunes of the rich to be cheated on all sides; what wonder they think ill of mankind! It is riches that corrupt men, and the rich are rightly the first to feel the defects of the only tool they know. Everything is ill-done for them, except what they do themselves, and they do next to nothing. When a nurse must be selected the choice is left to the doctor. What happens? The best nurse is the one who offers the highest bribe. I shall not consult the doctor about Emile's nurse, I shall take care to choose her myself. I may not argue about it so elegantly as the surgeon, but I shall be more reliable, I shall be less deceived by my zeal than the doctor by his greed.

There is no mystery about this choice; its rules are well known, but I think we ought probably to pay more attention to the age of the milk as well as its quality. The first milk is watery, it must be almost an aperient, to purge the remains of the meconium curdled in the bowels of the new-born child. Little by little the milk thickens and supplies more solid food as the child is able to digest it. It is surely not without cause that nature changes the milk in the female of every species according to the age of the offspring.

Thus a new-born child requires a nurse who has recently become a mother. There is, I know, a difficulty here, but as soon as we leave the path of nature there are difficulties in the way of all well-doing. The wrong course is the only right one under the circumstances, so we take it.

The nurse must be healthy alike in disposition and in body. The violence of the passions as well as the humours may spoil her milk. Moreover, to consider the body only is to keep only half our aim in view. The milk may be good and the nurse bad; a good character is as necessary as a good constitution. If you choose a vicious person, I do not say her foster-child will acquire her vices, but he will suffer for them. Ought she not to bestow on him day by day, along with her milk, a care which calls for zeal, patience, gentleness, and cleanliness. If she is intemperate and greedy her milk will soon be spoilt; if she is careless and hasty what will become of a poor little wretch left to her mercy, and unable either to protect himself or to complain. The wicked are never good for anything.

The choice is all the more important because her foster-child should have no other guardian, just as he should have no teacher but his tutor. This was the custom of the ancients, who talked less but acted more wisely than we. The nurse never left her foster-daughter; this is why the nurse is the confidante in most of their plays. A child who passes through many hands in turn, can never be well brought up.

At every change he makes a secret comparison, which continually tends to lessen his respect for those who control him, and with it their

authority over him. If once he thinks there are grown-up people
with no more sense than children the authority of age is destroyed
and his education is ruined. A child should know no betters but
its father and mother, or failing them its foster-mother and its
tutor, and even this is one too many, but this division is inevitable,
and the best that can be done in the way of remedy is that the man
and woman who control him shall be so well agreed with regard to
him that they seem like one.

The nurse must live rather more comfortably, she must have
rather more substantial food, but her whole way of living must not
be altered, for a sudden change, even a change for the better, is
dangerous to health, and since her usual way of life has made her
healthy and strong, why change it?

Country women eat less meat and more vegetables than towns-
women, and this vegetarian diet seems favourable rather than
otherwise to themselves and their children. When they take
nurslings from the upper classes they eat meat and broth with the
idea that they will form better chyle and supply more milk. I do
not hold with this at all, and experience is on my side, for we do not
find children fed in this way less liable to colic and worms.

That need not surprise us, for decaying animal matter swarms
with worms, but this is not the case with vegetable matter.[1] Milk,
although manufactured in the body of an animal, is a vegetable
substance; this is shown by analysis; it readily turns acid, and far
from showing traces of any volatile alkali like animal matter, it
gives a neutral salt like plants.

The milk of herbivorous creatures is sweeter and more wholesome
than the milk of the carnivorous; formed of a substance similar to
its own, it keeps its goodness and becomes less liable to putrifaction.
If quantity is considered, it is well known that farinaceous foods
produce more blood than meat, so they ought to yield more milk.
If a child were not weaned too soon, and if it were fed on vegetarian
food, and its foster-mother were a vegetarian, I do not think it
would be troubled with worms.

Milk derived from vegetable foods may perhaps be more liable to
go sour, but I am far from considering sour milk an unwholesome
food; whole nations have no other food and are none the worse,
and all the array of absorbents seems to me mere humbug. There
are constitutions which do not thrive on milk, others can take it
without absorbents. People are afraid of the milk separating or
curdling; that is absurd, for we know that milk always curdles in
the stomach. This is how it becomes sufficiently solid to nourish
children and young animals; if it did not curdle it would merely
pass away without feeding them.[2] In vain you dilute milk and use

[1] Women eat bread, vegetables, and dairy produce; female dogs and
cats do the same; the she-wolves eat grass. This supplies vegetable
juices to their milk. There are still those species which are unable to eat
anything but flesh, if such there are, which I very much doubt.
[2] Although the juices which nourish us are liquid, they must be extracted

absorbents; whoever swallows milk digests cheese, this rule is without exception; rennet is made from a calf's stomach.

Instead of changing the nurse's usual diet, I think it would be enough to give food in larger quantities and better of its kind. It is not the nature of the food that makes a vegetable diet indigestible, but the flavouring that makes it unwholesome. Reform your cookery, use neither butter nor oil for frying. Butter, salt, and milk should never be cooked. Let your vegetables be cooked in water and only seasoned when they come to table. The vegetable diet, far from disturbing the nurse, will give her a plentiful supply of milk.[1] If a vegetable diet is best for the child, how can meat food be best for his nurse? The things are contradictory.

Fresh air affects children's constitutions, particularly in early years. It enters every pore of a soft and tender skin, it has a powerful effect on their young bodies. Its effects can never be destroyed. So I should not agree with those who take a country woman from her village and shut her up in one room in a town and her nursling with her. I would rather send him to breathe the fresh air of the country than the foul air of the town. He will take his new mother's position, will live in her cottage, where his tutor will follow him. The reader will bear in mind that this tutor is not a paid servant, but the father's friend. But if this friend cannot be found, if this transfer is not easy, if none of my advice can be followed, you will say to me, " What shall I do instead? " I have told you already—" Do what you are doing; " no advice is needed there.

Men are not made to be crowded together in ant-hills, but scattered over the earth to till it. The more they are massed together, the more corrupt they become. Disease and vice are the sure results of over-crowded cities. Of all creatures man is least fitted to live in herds. Huddled together like sheep, men would very soon die. Man's breath is fatal to his fellows. This is literally as well as figuratively true.

Men are devoured by our towns. In a few generations the race dies out or becomes degenerate; it needs renewal, and it is always renewed from the country. Send your children to renew themselves, so to speak, send them to regain in the open fields the strength lost in the foul air of our crowded cities. Women hurry home that their children may be born in the town; they ought to do just the opposite, especially those who mean to nurse their own children. They would lose less than they think, and in more natural surroundings the pleasures associated by nature with maternal duties would soon destroy the taste for other delights.

The new-born infant is first bathed in warm water to which a

from solids. A hard-working man who ate nothing but soup would soon waste away. He would be far better fed on milk, just because it curdles.

[1] Those who wish to study a full account of the advantages and disadvantages of the Pythagorean régime, may consult the works of Dr. Cocchi and his opponent Dr. Bianchi on this important subject.

little wine is usually added. I think the wine might be dispensed with. As nature does not produce fermented liquors, it is not likely that they are of much value to her creatures.

In the same way it is unnecessary to take the precaution of heating the water; in fact among many races the new-born infants are bathed with no more ado in rivers or in the sea. Our children, made tender before birth by the softness of their parents, come into the world with a constitution already enfeebled, which cannot be at once exposed to all the trials required to restore it to health. Little by little they must be restored to their natural vigour. Begin then by following this custom, and leave it off gradually. Wash your children often, their dirty ways show the need of this. If they are only wiped their skin is injured; but as they grow stronger gradually reduce the heat of the water, till at last you bathe them winter and summer in cold, even in ice-cold water. To avoid risk this change must be slow, gradual, and imperceptible, so you may use the thermometer for exact measurements.

This habit of the bath, once established, should never be broken off, it must be kept up all through life. I value it not only on grounds of cleanliness and present health, but also as a wholesome means of making the muscles supple, and accustoming them to bear without risk or effort extremes of heat and cold. As he gets older I would have the child trained to bathe occasionally in hot water of every bearable degree, and often in every degree of cold water. Now water being a denser fluid touches us at more points than air, so that, having learnt to bear all the variations of temperature in water, we shall scarcely feel this of the air.[1]

When the child draws its first breath do not confine it in tight wrappings. No cap, no bandages, nor swaddling clothes. Loose and flowing flannel wrappers, which leave its limbs free and are not too heavy to check his movements, not too warm to prevent his feeling the air.[2] Put him in a big cradle, well padded, where he can move easily and safely. As he begins to grow stronger, let him crawl about the room; let him develop and stretch his tiny limbs; you will see him gain strength from day to day. Compare him with a well swaddled child of the same age and you will be surprised at their different rates of progress.[3]

[1] Children in towns are stifled by being kept indoors and too much wrapped up. Those who control them have still to learn that fresh air, far from doing them harm, will make them strong, while hot air will make them weak, will give rise to fevers, and will eventually kill them.

[2] I say " cradle " using the common word for want of a better, though I am convinced that it is never necessary and often harmful to rock children in the cradle.

[3] The ancient Peruvians wrapped their children in loose swaddling bands, leaving the arms quite free. Later they placed them unswaddled in a hole in the ground, lined with cloths, so that the lower part of the body was in the hole, and their arms were free and they could move the head and bend the body at will without falling or hurting themselves. When they began to walk they were enticed to come to the breast. The little negroes are often in a position much more difficult for sucking. They cling to the

You must expect great opposition from the nurses, who find a half strangled baby needs much less watching. Besides his dirtiness is more perceptible in an open garment; he must be attended to more frequently. Indeed, custom is an unanswerable argument in some lands and among all classes of people.

Do not argue with the nurses; give your orders, see them carried out, and spare no pains to make the attention you prescribe easy in practice. Why not take your share in it? With ordinary nurslings, where the body alone is thought of, nothing matters so long as the child lives and does not actually die, but with us, when education begins with life, the new-born child is already a disciple, not of his tutor, but of nature. The tutor merely studies under this master, and sees that his orders are not evaded. He watches over the infant, he observes it, he looks for the first feeble glimmering of intelligence, as the Moslem looks for the moment of the moon's rising in her first quarter.

We are born capable of learning, but knowing nothing, perceiving nothing. The mind, bound up within imperfect and half grown organs, is not even aware of its own existence. The movements and cries of the new-born child are purely reflex, without knowledge or will.

Suppose a child born with the size and strength of manhood, entering upon life full grown like Pallas from the brain of Jupiter; such a child-man would be a perfect idiot, an automaton, a statue without motion and almost without feeling; he would see and hear nothing, he would recognise no one, he could not turn his eyes towards what he wanted to see; not only would he perceive no external object, he would not even be aware of sensation through the several sense-organs. His eye would not perceive colour, his ear sounds, his body would be unaware of contact with neighbouring bodies, he would not even know he had a body, what his hands handled would be in his brain alone; all his sensations would be united in one place, they would exist only in the common "sensorium," he would have only one idea, that of self, to which he would refer all his sensations; and this idea, or rather this feeling, would be the only thing in which he excelled an ordinary child.

This man, full grown at birth, would also be unable to stand on his feet, he would need a long time to learn how to keep his balance; perhaps he would not even be able to try to do it, and you would see the big strong body left in one place like a stone, or creeping and crawling like a young puppy.

He would feel the discomfort of bodily needs without knowing

mother's hip, and cling so tightly that the mother's arm is often not needed to support them. They clasp the breast with their hand and continue sucking while their mother goes on with her ordinary work. These children begin to walk at two months, or rather to crawl. Later on they can run on all fours almost as well as on their feet.—*Buffon.* M. Buffon might also have quoted the example of England, where the senseless and barbarous swaddling clothes have become almost obsolete. Cf. *Le Longue Voyage de Siam, Le Beau Voyage de Canada*, etc.

what was the matter and without knowing how to provide for these needs. There is no immediate connection between the muscles of the stomach and those of the arms and legs to make him take a step towards food, or stretch a hand to seize it, even were he surrounded with it; and as his body would be full grown and his limbs well developed he would be without the perpetual restlessness and movement of childhood, so that he might die of hunger without stirring to seek food. However little you may have thought about the order and development of our knowledge, you cannot deny that such a one would be in the state of almost primitive ignorance and stupidity natural to man before he has learnt anything from experience or from his fellows.

We know then, or we may know, the point of departure from which we each start towards the usual level of understanding; but who knows the other extreme? Each progresses more or less according to his genius, his taste, his needs, his talents, his zeal, and his opportunities for using them. No philosopher, so far as I know, has dared to say to man, "Thus far shalt thou go and no further." We know not what nature allows us to be, none of us has measured the possible difference between man and man. Is there a mind so dead that this thought has never kindled it, that has never said in his pride, "How much have I already done, how much more may I achieve? Why should I lag behind my fellows?"

As I said before, man's education begins at birth; before he can speak or understand he is learning. Experience precedes instruction; when he recognises his nurse he has learnt much. The knowledge of the most ignorant man would surprise us if we had followed his course from birth to the present time. If all human knowledge were divided into two parts, one common to all, the other peculiar to the learned, the latter would seem very small compared with the former. But we scarcely heed this general experience, because it is acquired before the age of reason. Moreover, knowledge only attracts attention by its rarity, as in algebraic equations common factors count for nothing. Even animals learn much. They have senses and must learn to use them; they have needs, they must learn to satisfy them; they must learn to eat, walk, or fly. Quadrupeds which can stand on their feet from the first cannot walk for all that; from their first attempts it is clear that they lack confidence. Canaries who escape from their cage are unable to fly, having never used their wings. Living and feeling creatures are always learning. If plants could walk they would need senses and knowledge, else their species would die out. The child's first mental experiences are purely affective, he is only aware of pleasure and pain; it takes him a long time to acquire the definite sensations which show him things outside himself, but before these things present and withdraw themselves, so to speak, from his sight, taking size and shape for him, the recurrence of emotional experiences is beginning to subject the child to the rule of habit. You see his eyes constantly follow the light, and if the light comes from the

*ᴅ 51b

side the eyes turn towards it, so that one must be careful to turn his head towards the light lest he should squint. He must also be accustomed from the first to the dark, or he will cry if he misses the light. Food and sleep, too, exactly measured, become necessary at regular intervals, and soon desire is no longer the effect of need, but of habit, or rather habit adds a fresh need to those of nature. You must be on your guard against this.

The only habit the child should be allowed to contract is that of having no habits; let him be carried on either arm, let him be accustomed to offer either hand, to use one or other indifferently; let him not want to eat, sleep, or do anything at fixed hours, nor be unable to be left alone by day or night. Prepare the way for his control of his liberty and the use of his strength by leaving his body its natural habit, by making him capable of lasting self-control, of doing all that he wills when his will is formed.

As soon as the child begins to take notice, what is shown him must be carefully chosen. The natural man is interested in all new things. He feels so feeble that he fears the unknown: the habit of seeing fresh things without ill effects destroys this fear. Children brought up in clean houses where there are no spiders are afraid of spiders, and this fear often lasts through life. I never saw peasants, man, woman, or child, afraid of spiders.

Since the mere choice of things shown him may make the child timid or brave, why should not his education begin before he can speak or understand? I would have him accustomed to see fresh things, ugly, repulsive, and strange beasts, but little by little, and far off till he is used to them, and till having seen others handle them he handles them himself. If in childhood he sees toads, snakes, and crayfish, he will not be afraid of any animal when he is grown up. Those who are continually seeing terrible things think nothing of them.

All children are afraid of masks. I begin by showing Emile a mask with a pleasant face, then some one puts this mask before his face; I begin to laugh, they all laugh too, and the child with them. By degrees I accustom him to less pleasing masks, and at last hideous ones. If I have arranged my stages skilfully, far from being afraid of the last mask, he will laugh at it as he did at the first. After that I am not afraid of people frightening him with masks.

When Hector bids farewell to Andromache, the young Astyanax, startled by the nodding plumes on the helmet, does not know his father; he flings himself weeping upon his nurse's bosom and wins from his mother a smile mingled with tears. What must be done to stay this terror? Just what Hector did; put the helmet on the ground and caress the child. In a calmer moment one would do more; one would go up to the helmet, play with the plumes, let the child feel them; at last the nurse would take the helmet and place it laughingly on her own head, if indeed a woman's hand dare touch the armour of Hector.

If Emile must get used to the sound of a gun, I first fire a pistol with a small charge. He is delighted with this sudden flash, this sort of lightning; I repeat the process with more powder; gradually I add a small charge without a wad, then a larger; in the end I accustom him to the sound of a gun, to fireworks, cannon, and the most terrible explosions.

I have observed that children are rarely afraid of thunder unless the peals are really terrible and actually hurt the ear, otherwise this fear only comes to them when they know that thunder sometimes hurts or kills. When reason begins to cause fear, let use reassure them. By slow and careful stages man and child learn to fear nothing.

In the dawn of life, when memory and imagination have not begun to function, the child only attends to what affects its senses. His sense experiences are the raw material of thought; they should, therefore, be presented to him in fitting order, so that memory may at a future time present them in the same order to his understanding; but as he only attends to his sensations it is enough, at first, to show him clearly the connection between these sensations and the things which cause them. He wants to touch and handle everything; do not check these movements which teach him invaluable lessons. Thus he learns to perceive the heat, cold, hardness, softness, weight, or lightness of bodies, to judge their size and shape and all their physical properties, by looking, feeling,[1] listening, and, above all, by comparing sight and touch, by judging with the eye what sensation they would cause to his hand.

It is only by movement that we learn the difference between self and not self; it is only by our own movements that we gain the idea of space. The child has not this idea, so he stretches out his hand to seize the object within his reach or that which is a hundred paces from him. You take this as a sign of tyranny, an attempt to bid the thing draw near, or to bid you bring it. Nothing of the kind, it is merely that the object first seen in his brain, then before his eyes, now seems close to his arms, and he has no idea of space beyond his reach. Be careful, therefore, to take him about, to move him from place to place, and to let him perceive the change in his surroundings, so as to teach him to judge of distances.

When he begins to perceive distances then you must change your plan, and only carry him when you please, not when he pleases; for as soon as he is no longer deceived by his senses, there is another motive for his effort. This change is remarkable and calls for explanation.

The discomfort caused by real needs is shown by signs, when the help of others is required. Hence the cries of children; they often cry; it must be so. Since they are only conscious of feelings, when those feelings are pleasant they enjoy them in silence; when they

---

[1] Of all the senses that of smell is the latest to develop in children; up to two or three years of age they appear to be insensible of pleasant or unpleasant odours; in this respect they are as indifferent or rather as insensible as many animals.

are painful they say so in their own way and demand relief. Now when they are awake they can scarcely be in a state of indifference; either they are asleep or else they are feeling something.

All our languages are the result of art. It has long been a subject of inquiry whether there ever was a natural language common to all; no doubt there is, and it is the language of children before they begin to speak. This language is inarticulate, but it has tone, stress, and meaning. The use of our own language has led us to neglect it so far as to forget it altogether. Let us study children and we shall soon learn it afresh from them. Nurses can teach us this language; they understand all their nurslings say to them, they answer them, and keep up long conversations with them; and though they use words, these words are quite useless. It is not the hearing of the word, but its accompanying intonation that is understood.

To the language of intonation is added the no less forcible language of gesture. The child uses, not its weak hands, but its face. The amount of expression in these undeveloped faces is extraordinary; their features change from one moment to another with incredible speed. You see smiles, desires, terror, come and go like lightning; every time the face seems different. The muscles of the face are undoubtedly more mobile than our own. On the other hand the eyes are almost expressionless. Such must be the sort of signs they use at an age when their only needs are those of the body. Grimaces are the sign of sensation, the glance expresses sentiment.

As man's first state is one of want and weakness, his first sounds are cries and tears. The child feels his needs and cannot satisfy them, he begs for help by his cries. Is he hungry or thirsty? there are tears; is he too cold or too hot? more tears; he needs movement and is kept quiet, more tears; he wants to sleep and is disturbed, he weeps. The less comfortable he is, the more he demands change. He has only one language because he has, so to say, only one kind of discomfort. In the imperfect state of his sense organs he does not distinguish their several impressions; all ills produce one feeling of sorrow.

These tears, which you think so little worthy of your attention, give rise to the first relation between man and his environment; here is forged the first link in the long chain of social order.

When the child cries he is uneasy, he feels some need which he cannot satisfy; you watch him, seek this need, find it, and satisfy it. If you can neither find it nor satisfy it, the tears continue and become tiresome. The child is petted to quiet him, he is rocked or sung to sleep; if he is obstinate, the nurse becomes impatient and threatens him; cruel nurses sometimes strike him. What strange lessons for him at his first entrance into life!

I shall never forget seeing one of these troublesome crying children thus beaten by his nurse. He was silent at once. I thought he was frightened, and said to myself, " This will be a servile being from whom nothing can be got but by harshness." I was wrong, the poor wretch was choking with rage, he could not breathe, he was black in the face. A moment later there were bitter cries, every sign of the anger, rage, and despair of this age was in his tones. I thought he would die. Had I doubted the innate sense of justice and injustice in man's heart, this one instance would have convinced me. I am sure that a drop of boiling liquid falling by chance on that child's hand would have hurt him less than that blow, slight in itself, but clearly given with the intention of hurting him.

This tendency to anger, vexation, and rage needs great care. Boerhaave thinks that most of the diseases of children are of the nature of convulsions, because the head being larger in proportion and the nervous system more extensive than in adults, they are more liable to nervous irritation. Take the greatest care to remove from them any servants who tease, annoy, or vex them. They are a hundredfold more dangerous and more fatal than fresh air and changing seasons. When children only experience resistance in things and never in the will of man, they do not become rebellious or passionate, and their health is better. This is one reason why the children of the poor, who are freer and more independent, are generally less frail and weakly, more vigorous than those who are supposed to be better brought up by being constantly thwarted; but you must always remember that it is one thing to refrain from thwarting them, but quite another to obey them. The child's first tears are prayers, beware lest they become commands; he begins by asking for aid, he ends by demanding service. Thus from his own weakness, the source of his first consciousness of dependence, springs the later idea of rule and tyranny; but as this idea is aroused rather by his needs than by our services, we begin to see moral results whose causes are not in nature; thus we see how important it is, even at the earliest age, to discern the secret meaning of the gesture or cry.

When the child tries to seize something without speaking, he thinks he can reach the object, for he does not rightly judge its distance; when he cries and stretches out his hands he no longer misjudges the distance, he bids the object approach, or orders you to bring it to him. In the first case bring it to him slowly; in the second do not even seem to hear his cries. The more he cries the less you should heed him. He must learn in good time not to give commands to men, for he is not their master, nor to things, for they cannot hear him. Thus when the child wants something you mean to give him, it is better to carry him to it rather than to bring the thing to him. From this he will draw a conclusion suited to his age, and there is no other way of suggesting it to him.

The Abbé Saint-Pierre calls men big children; one might also call children little men. These statements are true, but they require explanation. But when Hobbes calls the wicked a strong child, his statement is contradicted by facts. All wickedness comes from weakness. The child is only naughty because he is weak; make him strong and he will be good; if we could do everything we should never do wrong. Of all the attributes of the Almighty, goodness is that which it would be hardest to dissociate from our conception of Him. All nations who have acknowledged a good and an evil power, have always regarded the evil as inferior to the good; otherwise their opinion would have been absurd. Compare this with the creed of the Savoyard clergyman later on in this book.

Reason alone teaches us to know good and evil. Therefore conscience, which makes us love the one and hate the other, though it is independent of reason, cannot develop without it. Before the age of reason we do good or ill without knowing it, and there is no morality in our actions, although there is sometimes in our feeling with regard to other people's actions in relation to ourselves. A child wants to overturn everything he sees. He breaks and smashes everything he can reach; he seizes a bird as he seizes a stone, and strangles it without knowing what he is about.

Why so? In the first place philosophy will account for this by inbred sin, man's pride, love of power, selfishness, spite; perhaps it will say in addition to this that the child's consciousness of his own weakness makes him eager to use his strength, to convince himself of it. But watch that broken down old man reduced in the downward course of life to the weakness of a child; not only is he quiet and peaceful, he would have all about him quiet and peaceful too; the least change disturbs and troubles him, he would like to see universal calm. How is it possible that similar feebleness and similar passions should produce such different effects in age and in infancy, if the original cause were not different? And where can we find this difference in cause except in the bodily condition of the two. The active principle, common to both, is growing in one case and declining in the other; it is being formed in the one and destroyed in the other; one is moving towards life, the other towards death. The failing activity of the old man is centred in his heart, the child's overflowing activity spreads abroad. He feels, if we may say so, strong enough to give life to all about him. To make or to destroy, it is all one to him; change is what he seeks, and all change involves action. If he seems to enjoy destructive activity it is only that it takes time to make things and very little time to break them, so that the work of destruction accords better with his eagerness.

While the Author of nature has given children this activity, He takes care that it shall do little harm by giving them small power to use it. But as soon as they can think of people as tools to be used, they use them to carry out their wishes and to supplement their own weakness. This is how they become tiresome, masterful, imperious, naughty, and unmanageable; a development which does not spring from a natural love of power, but one which has been taught them, for it does not need much experience to realise how pleasant it is to set others to work and to move the world by a word.

As the child grows it gains strength and becomes less restless and unquiet and more independent. Soul and body become better balanced and nature no longer asks for more movement than is required for self-preservation. But the love of power does not die with the need that aroused it; power arouses and flatters self-love, and habit strengthens it; thus caprice follows upon need, and the first seeds of prejudice and obstinacy are sown.

First Maxim.—Far from being too strong, children are not strong enough for all the claims of nature. Give them full use of such strength as they have; they will not abuse it.

Second Maxim.—Help them and supply the experience and strength they lack whenever the need is of the body.

Third Maxim.—In the help you give them confine yourself to what is really needful, without granting anything to caprice or unreason; for they will not be tormented by caprice if you do not call it into existence, seeing it is no part of nature.

Fourth Maxim.—Study carefully their speech and gestures, so that at an age when they are incapable of deceit you may discriminate between those desires which come from nature and those which spring from perversity.

The spirit of these rules is to give children more real liberty and less power, to let them do more for themselves and demand less of others; so that by teaching them from the first to confine their wishes within the limits of their powers they will scarcely feel the want of whatever is not in their power.

This is another very important reason for leaving children's limbs and bodies perfectly free, only taking care that they do not fall, and keeping anything that might hurt them out of their way.

The child whose body and arms are free will certainly cry much less than a child tied up in swaddling clothes. He who knows only bodily needs, only cries when in pain; and this is a great advantage, for then we know exactly when he needs help, and if possible we should not delay our help for an instant. But if you cannot relieve his pain, stay where you are and do not flatter him by way of soothing him; your caresses will not cure his colic, but he will remember what he must do to win them; and if he once finds out how to gain your attention at will, he is your master; the whole education is spoilt.

Their movements being less constrained, children will cry less; less wearied with their tears, people will not take so much trouble to check them. With fewer threats and promises, they will be less timid and less obstinate, and will remain more nearly in their natural state. Ruptures are produced less by letting children cry than by the means taken to stop them, and my evidence for this is the fact that the most neglected children are less liable to them than others. I am very far from wishing that they should be neglected; on the contrary, it is of the utmost importance that their wants should be anticipated, so that they need not proclaim their wants by crying. But neither would I have unwise care bestowed on them. Why should they think it wrong to cry when they find they can get so much by it? When they have learned the value of their silence they take good care not to waste it. In the end they will so exaggerate its importance that no one will be able to pay its price; then worn out with crying they become exhausted, and are at length silent.

Prolonged crying on the part of a child neither swaddled nor out of health, a child who lacks nothing, is merely the result of habit or obstinacy. Such tears are no longer the work of nature, but the work of the child's nurse, who could not resist its importunity and so has increased it, without considering that while she quiets the child to-day she is teaching him to cry louder to-morrow.

Moreover, when caprice or obstinacy is the cause of their tears, there is a sure way of stopping them by distracting their attention by some pleasant or conspicuous object which makes them forget that they want to cry. Most nurses excel in this art, and rightly used it is very useful; but it is of the utmost importance that the child should not perceive that you mean to distract his attention, and that he should be amused without suspecting you are thinking about him; now this is what most nurses cannot do.

Most children are weaned too soon. The time to wean them is when they cut their teeth. This generally causes pain and suffering. At this time the child instinctively carries everything he gets hold of to his mouth to chew it. To help forward this process he is given as a plaything some hard object such as ivory or a wolf's tooth. I think this is a mistake. Hard bodies applied to the gums do not soften them; far from it, they make the process of cutting the teeth more difficult and painful. Let us always take instinct as our guide; we never see puppies practising their budding teeth on pebbles, iron, or bones, but on wood, leather, rags, soft materials which yield to their jaws, and on which the tooth leaves its mark.

We can do nothing simply, not even for our children. Toys of silver, gold, coral, cut crystal, rattles of every price and kind; what vain and useless appliances. Away with them all! Let us have no corals or rattles; a small branch of a tree with its leaves and fruit, a stick of liquorice which he may suck and chew, will amuse him as well as these splendid trifles, and they will have this advantage at least, he will not be brought up to luxury from his birth.

It is admitted that pap is not a very wholesome food. Boiled milk and uncooked flour cause gravel and do not suit the stomach. In pap the flour is less thoroughly cooked than in bread and it has not fermented. I think bread and milk or rice-cream are better. If you will have pap, the flour should be lightly cooked beforehand. In my own country they make a very pleasant and wholesome soup from flour thus heated. Meat-broth or soup is not a very suitable food and should be used as little as possible. The child must first get used to chewing his food; this is the right way to bring the teeth through, and when the child begins to swallow, the saliva mixed with the food helps digestion.

I would have them first chew dried fruit or crusts. I should give them as playthings little bits of dry bread or biscuits, like the Piedmont bread, known in the country as " grisses." By dint of softening this bread in the mouth some of it is eventually swallowed, the teeth come through of themselves, and the child is weaned almost imperceptibly. Peasants have usually very good digestions, and they are weaned with no more ado.

From the very first children hear spoken language; we speak to them before they can understand or even imitate spoken sounds. The vocal organs are still stiff, and only gradually lend themselves to the reproduction of the sounds heard; it is even doubtful whether these sounds are heard distinctly as we hear them. The nurse may amuse the child with songs and with very merry and varied intonation, but I object to her bewildering the child with a multitude of vain words of which it understands nothing but her tone of voice. I would have the first words he hears few in number, distinctly and often repeated, while the words themselves should be related to things which can first be shown to the child. That fatal facility in the use of words we do not understand begins earlier than we think. In the schoolroom the scholar listens to the verbiage of his master as he listened in the cradle to the babble of his nurse. I think it would be a very useful education to leave him in ignorance of both.

All sorts of ideas crowd in upon us when we try to consider the development of speech and the child's first words. Whatever we do they all learn to talk in the same way, and all philosophical speculations are utterly useless.

To begin with, they have, so to say, a grammar of their own, whose rules and syntax are more general than our own; if you attend carefully you will be surprised to find how exactly they follow certain analogies, very much mistaken if you like, but very regular; these forms are only objectionable because of their harshness or because they are not recognised by custom. I have just heard a child severely scolded by his father for saying, "Mon père, irai-je-t-y?" Now we see that this child was following the analogy more closely than our grammarians, for as they say to him, "Vas-y," why should he not say, "Irai-je-t-y?" Notice too the skilful way in which he avoids the hiatus in irai-je-y or y-irai-je? Is it the poor child's fault that we have so unskilfully deprived the phrase of this determinative adverb "y," because we did not know what to do with it? It is an intolerable piece of pedantry and most superfluous attention to detail to make a point of correcting all children's little sins against the customary expression, for they always cure themselves with time. Always speak correctly before them, let them never be so happy with any one as with you, and be sure that their speech will be imperceptibly modelled upon yours without any correction on your part.

But a much greater evil, and one far less easy to guard against, is that they are urged to speak too much, as if people were afraid they would not learn to talk of themselves. This indiscreet zeal produces an effect directly opposite to what is meant. They speak later and more confusedly; the extreme attention paid to everything they say makes it unnecessary for them to speak distinctly, and as they will scarcely open their mouths, many of them contract a vicious pronunciation and a confused speech, which last all their life and make them almost unintelligible.

I have lived much among peasants, and I never knew one of them lisp, man or woman, boy or girl. Why is this? Are their speech organs differently made from our own? No, but they are differently used. There is a hillock facing my window on which the children of the place assemble for their games. Although they are far enough away, I can distinguish perfectly what they say, and often get good notes for this book. Every day my ear deceives me as to their age. I hear the voices of children of ten; I look and see the height and features of children of three or four. This experience is not confined to me; the townspeople who come to see me, and whom I consult on this point, all fall into the same mistake.

This results from the fact that, up to five or six, children in town, brought up in a room and under the care of a nursery governess, do not need to speak above a whisper to make themselves heard. As soon as their lips move people take pains to make out what they mean; they are taught words which they repeat inaccurately, and by paying great attention to them the people who are always with them rather guess what they meant to say than what they said.

It is quite a different matter in the country. A peasant woman is not always with her child; he is obliged to learn to say very clearly and loudly what he wants, if he is to make himself understood. Children scattered about the fields at a distance from their fathers, mothers and other children, gain practice in making themselves heard at a distance, and in adapting the loudness of the voice to the distance which separates them from those to whom they want to speak. This is the real way to learn pronunciation, not by stammering out a few vowels into the ear of an attentive governess. So when you question a peasant child, he may be too shy to answer, but what he says he says distinctly, while the nurse must serve as interpreter for the town child; without her one can understand nothing of what he is muttering between his teeth.[1]

As they grow older, the boys are supposed to be cured of this fault at college, the girls in the convent schools; and indeed both usually speak more clearly than children brought up entirely at home. But they are prevented from acquiring as clear a pronunciation as the peasants in this way—they are required to learn all sorts of things by heart, and to repeat aloud what they have learnt; for when they are studying they get into the way of gabbling and pronouncing carelessly and ill; it is still worse when they repeat their lessons; they cannot find the right words, they drag out their syllables. This is only possible when the memory hesitates, the

[1] There are exceptions to this; and often those children who at first are most difficult to hear, become the noisiest when they begin to raise their voices. But if I were to enter into all these details I should never make an end; every sensible reader ought to see that defect and excess, caused by the same abuse, are both corrected by my method. I regard the two maxims as inseperable — always enough — never too much. When the first is well established, the latter necessarily follows on it.

tongue does not stammer of itself. Thus they acquire or continue habits of bad pronunciation. Later on you will see that Emile does not acquire such habits or at least not from this cause.

I grant you uneducated people and villagers often fall into the opposite extreme. They almost always speak too loud; their pronunciation is too exact, and leads to rough and coarse articulation; their accent is too pronounced, they choose their expressions badly, etc.

But, to begin with, this extreme strikes me as much less dangerous than the other, for the first law of speech is to make oneself understood, and the chief fault is to fail to be understood. To pride ourselves on having no accent is to pride ourselves on ridding our phrases of strength and elegance. Emphasis is the soul of speech, it gives it its feeling and truth. Emphasis deceives less than words; perhaps that is why well-educated people are so afraid of it. From the custom of saying everything in the same tone has arisen that of poking fun at people without their knowing it. When emphasis is proscribed, its place is taken by all sorts of ridiculous, affected, and ephemeral pronunciations, such as one observes especially among the young people about court. It is this affectation of speech and manner which makes Frenchmen disagreeable and repulsive to other nations on first acquaintance. Emphasis is found, not in their speech, but in their bearing. That is not the way to make themselves attractive.

All these little faults of speech, which you are so afraid the children will acquire, are mere trifles; they may be prevented or corrected with the greatest ease, but the faults which are taught them when you make them speak in a low, indistinct, and timid voice, when you are always criticising their tone and finding fault with their words, are never cured. A man who has only learnt to speak in society of fine ladies could not make himself heard at the head of his troops, and would make little impression on the rabble in a riot. First teach the child to speak to men; he will be able to speak to the women when required.

Brought up in all the rustic simplicity of the country, your children will gain a more sonorous voice; they will not acquire the hesitating stammer of town children, neither will they acquire the expressions nor the tone of the villagers, or if they do they will easily lose them; their master being with them from their earliest years, and more and more in their society the older they grow, will be able to prevent or efface by speaking correctly himself the impression of the peasants' talk. Emile will speak the purest French I know, but he will speak it more distinctly and with a better articulation than myself.

The child who is trying to speak should hear nothing but words he can understand, nor should he say words he cannot articulate; his efforts lead him to repeat the same syllable as if he were practising its clear pronunciation. When he begins to stammer, do not try to understand him. To expect to be always listened to is a form of tyranny which is not good for the child. See carefully to his real needs, and let him try to make you understand the rest. Still less should you hurry him into speech; he will learn to talk when he feels the want of it.

It has indeed been remarked that those who begin to speak very late never speak so distinctly as others; but it is not because they talked late that they are hesitating; on the contrary, they began to talk late because they hesitate; if not, why did they begin to talk so late? Have they less need of speech, have they been less urged to it? On the contrary, the anxiety aroused with the first suspicion of this backwardness leads people to tease them much more to begin to talk than those who articulated earlier; and this mistaken zeal may do much to make their speech confused, when with less haste they might have had time to bring it to greater perfection.

Children who are forced to speak too soon have no time to learn either to pronounce correctly or to understand what they are made to say; while left to themselves they first practise the easiest syllables, and then, adding to them little by little some meaning which their gestures explain, they teach you their own words before they learn yours. By this means they do not acquire your words till they have understood them. Being in no hurry to use them, they begin by carefully observing the sense in which you use them, and when they are sure of them they adopt them.

The worst evil resulting from the precocious use of speech by young children is that we not only fail to understand the first words they use, we misunderstand them without knowing it; so that while they seem to answer us correctly, they fail to understand us and we them. This is the most frequent cause of our surprise at children's sayings; we attribute to them ideas which they did not attach to their words. This lack of attention on our part to the real meaning which words have for children seems to me the cause of their earliest misconceptions; and these misconceptions, even when corrected, colour their whole course of thought for the rest of their life. I shall have several opportunities of illustrating these by examples later on.

Let the child's vocabulary, therefore, be limited; it is very undesirable that he should have more words than ideas, that he should be able to say more than he thinks. One of the reasons why peasants are generally shrewder than townsfolk is, I think, that their vocabulary is smaller. They have few ideas, but those few are thoroughly grasped.

The infant is progressing in several ways at once; he is learning to talk, eat, and walk about the same time. This is really the first phase of his life. Up till now, he was little more than he was before birth; he had neither feeling nor thought, he was barely capable of sensation; he was unconscious of his own existence.

" Vivit, et est vitæ nescius ipse suæ."—OVID.

BOOK II

WE have now reached the second phase of life; infancy, strictly so-called, is over; for the words *infans* and *puer* are not synonymous. The latter includes the former, which means literally " one who cannot speak; " thus Valerius speaks of *puerum infantem*. But I shall continue to use the word child (French *enfant*) according to the custom of our language till an age for which there is another term.

When children begin to talk they cry less. This progress is quite natural; one language supplants another. As soon as they can say " It hurts me," why should they cry, unless the pain is too sharp for words? If they still cry, those about them are to blame. When once Emile has said, " It hurts me," it will take a very sharp pain to make him cry.

If the child is delicate and sensitive, if by nature he begins to cry for nothing, I let him cry in vain and soon check his tears at their source. So long as he cries I will not go near him; I come at once when he leaves off crying. He will soon be quiet when he wants to call me, or rather he will utter a single cry. Children learn the meaning of signs by their effects; they have no other meaning for them. However much a child hurts himself when he is alone, he rarely cries, unless he expects to be heard.

Should he fall or bump his head, or make his nose bleed, or cut his fingers, I shall show no alarm, nor shall I make any fuss over him; I shall take no notice, at any rate at first. The harm is done; he must bear it; all my zeal could only frighten him more and make him more nervous. Indeed it is not the blow but the fear of it which distresses us when we are hurt. I shall spare him this suffering at least, for he will certainly regard the injury as he sees me regard it; if he finds that I hasten anxiously to him, if I pity him or comfort him, he will think he is badly hurt. If he finds I take no notice, he will soon recover himself, and will think the wound is healed when it ceases to hurt. This is the time for his first lesson in courage, and by bearing slight ills without fear we gradually learn to bear greater.

I shall not take pains to prevent Emile hurting himself; far from it, I should be vexed if he never hurt himself, if he grew up unacquainted with pain. To bear pain is his first and most useful lesson. It seems as if children were small and weak on purpose to teach them these valuable lessons without danger. The child has such a little way to fall he will not break his leg; if he knocks himself with a stick he will not break his arm; if he seizes a sharp knife he will not grasp it tight enough to make a deep wound. So far as I know, no child, left to himself, has ever been known to kill or maim itself, or even to do itself any serious harm, unless it has been foolishly left on a high place, or alone near the fire, or within reach of dangerous weapons. What is there to be said for all the paraphernalia with which the child is surrounded to shield him on every side so that he grows up at the mercy of pain, with neither courage nor experience, so that he thinks he is killed by a pin-prick and faints at the sight of blood?

With our foolish and pedantic methods we are always preventing children from learning what they could learn much better by themselves, while we neglect what we alone can teach them. Can anything be sillier than the pains taken to teach them to walk, as if there were any one who was unable to walk when he grows up through his nurse's neglect? How many we see walking badly all their life because they were ill taught?

Emile shall have no head-pads, no go-carts, no leading-strings; or at least as soon as he can put one foot before another he shall only be supported along pavements, and he shall be taken quickly across them.[1] Instead of keeping him mewed up in a stuffy room, take him out into a meadow every day; let him run about, let him struggle and fall again and again, the oftener the better; he will learn all the sooner to pick himself up. The delights of liberty will make up for many bruises. My pupil will hurt himself oftener than yours, but he will always be merry; your pupils may receive fewer injuries, but they are always thwarted, constrained, and sad. I doubt whether they are any better off.

As their strength increases, children have also less need for tears. They can do more for themselves, they need the help of others less frequently. With strength comes the sense to use it. It is with this second phase that the real personal life has its beginning; it is then that the child becomes conscious of himself. During every moment of his life memory calls up the feeling of self; he becomes really one person, always the same, and therefore capable of joy or sorrow. Hence we must begin to consider him as a moral being.

Although we know approximately the limits of human life and our chances of attaining those limits, nothing is more uncertain than the length of the life of any one of us. Very few reach old age. The chief risks occur at the beginning of life; the shorter our past life, the less we must hope to live. Of all the children who are born scarcely one half reach adolescence, and it is very likely your pupil will not live to be a man.

What is to be thought, therefore, of that cruel education which sacrifices the present to an uncertain future, that burdens a child with all sorts of restrictions and begins by making him miserable, in order to prepare him for some far-off happiness which he may

---

[1] There is nothing so absurd and hesitating as the gait of those who have been kept too long in leading-strings when they were little. This is one of the observations which are considered trivial because they are true.

never enjoy? Even if I considered that education wise in its aims, how could I view without indignation those poor wretches subjected to an intolerable slavery and condemned like galley-slaves to endless toil, with no certainty that they will gain anything by it? The age of harmless mirth is spent in tears, punishments, threats, and slavery. You torment the poor thing for his good; you fail to see that you are calling Death to snatch him from these gloomy surroundings. Who can say how many children fall victims to the excessive care of their fathers and mothers? They are happy to escape from this cruelty; this is all that they gain from the ills they are forced to endure: they die without regretting, having known nothing of life but its sorrows.

Men, be kind to your fellow-men; this is your first duty, kind to every age and station, kind to all that is not foreign to humanity. What wisdom can you find that is greater than kindness? Love childhood, indulge its sports, its pleasures, its delightful instincts. Who has not sometimes regretted that age when laughter was ever on the lips, and when the heart was ever at peace? Why rob these innocents of the joys which pass so quickly, of that precious gift which they cannot abuse? Why fill with bitterness the fleeting days of early childhood, days which will no more return for them than for you? Fathers, can you tell when death will call your children to him? Do not lay up sorrow for yourselves by robbing them of the short span which nature has allotted to them. As soon as they are aware of the joy of life, let them rejoice in it, so that whenever God calls them they may not die without having tasted the joy of life.

How people will cry out against me! I hear from afar the shouts of that false wisdom which is ever dragging us onwards, counting the present as nothing, and pursuing without a pause a future which flies as we pursue, that false wisdom which removes us from our place and never brings us to any other.

Now is the time, you say, to correct his evil tendencies; we must increase suffering in childhood, when it is less keenly felt, to lessen it in manhood. But how do you know that you can carry out all these fine schemes; how do you know that all this fine teaching with which you overwhelm the feeble mind of the child will not do him more harm than good in the future? How do you know that you can spare him anything by the vexations you heap upon him now? Why inflict on him more ills than befit his present condition unless you are quite sure that these present ills will save him future ill? And what proof can you give me that those evil tendencies you profess to cure are not the result of your foolish precautions rather than of nature? What a poor sort of foresight, to make a child wretched in the present with the more or less doubtful hope of making him happy at some future day. If such blundering thinkers fail to distinguish between liberty and licence, between a merry child and a spoilt darling, let them learn to discriminate.

Let us not forget what befits our present state in the pursuit of vain fancies. Mankind has its place in the sequence of things; childhood has its place in the sequence of human life; the man must be treated as a man and the child as a child. Give each his place, and keep him there. Control human passions according to man's nature; that is all we can do for his welfare. The rest depends on external forces, which are beyond our control.

Absolute good and evil are unknown to us. In this life they are blended together; we never enjoy any perfectly pure feeling, nor do we remain for more than a moment in the same state. The feelings of our minds, like the changes in our bodies, are in a continual flux. Good and ill are common to all, but in varying proportions. The happiest is he who suffers least; the most miserable is he who enjoys least. Ever more sorrow than joy—this is the lot of all of us. Man's happiness in this world is but a negative state; it must be reckoned by the fewness of his ills.

Every feeling of hardship is inseparable from the desire to escape from it; every idea of pleasure from the desire to enjoy it. All desire implies a want, and all wants are painful; hence our wretchedness consists in the disproportion between our desires and our powers. A conscious being whose powers were equal to his desires would be perfectly happy.

What then is human wisdom? Where is the path of true happiness? The mere limitation of our desires is not enough, for if they were less than our powers, part of our faculties would be idle, and we should not enjoy our whole being; neither is the mere extension of our powers enough, for if our desires were also increased we should only be the more miserable. True happiness consists in decreasing the difference between our desires and our powers, in establishing a perfect equilibrium between the power and the will. Then only, when all its forces are employed, will the soul be at rest and man will find himself in his true position.

In this condition, nature, who does everything for the best, has placed him from the first. To begin with, she gives him only such desires as are necessary for self-preservation and such powers as are sufficient for their satisfaction. All the rest she has stored in his mind as a sort of reserve, to be drawn upon at need. It is only in this primitive condition that we find the equilibrium between desire and power, and then alone man is not unhappy. As soon as his potential powers of mind begin to function, imagination, more powerful than all the rest, awakes, and precedes all the rest. It is imagination which enlarges the bounds of possibility for us, whether for good or ill, and therefore stimulates and feeds desires by the hope of satisfying them. But the object which seemed within our grasp flies quicker than we can follow; when we think we have grasped it, it transforms itself and is again far ahead of us. We no longer perceive the country we have traversed, and we think nothing of it; that which lies before us becomes vaster and stretches still before us. Thus we exhaust our strength, yet never reach our goal, and the nearer we are to pleasure, the further we are from happiness.

On the other hand, the more nearly a man's condition approximates to this state of nature the less difference is there between his desires and his powers, and happiness is therefore less remote. Lacking everything, he is never less miserable; for misery consists, not in the lack of things, but in the needs which they inspire.

The world of reality has its bounds, the world of imagination is boundless; as we cannot enlarge the one, let us restrict the other; for all the sufferings which really make us miserable arise from the difference between the real and the imaginary. Health, strength, and a good conscience excepted, all the good things of life are a matter of opinion; except bodily suffering and remorse, all our woes are imaginary. You will tell me this is a commonplace; I admit it, but its practical application is no commonplace, and it is with practice only that we are now concerned.

What do you mean when you say, "Man is weak"? The term weak implies a relation, a relation of the creature to whom it is applied. An insect or a worm whose strength exceeds its needs is strong; an elephant, a lion, a conqueror, a hero, a god himself, whose needs exceed his strength is weak. The rebellious angel who fought against his own nature was weaker than the happy mortal who is living at peace according to nature. When man is content to be himself he is strong indeed; when he strives to be more than man he is weak indeed. But do not imagine that you can increase your strength by increasing your powers. Not so; if your pride increases more rapidly than your strength is diminished. Let us measure the extent of our sphere and remain in its centre like the spider in its web; we shall have strength sufficient for our needs, we shall have no cause to lament our weakness, for we shall never be aware of it.

The other animals possess only such powers as are required for self-preservation; man alone has more. Is it not very strange that this superfluity should make him miserable? In every land a man's labour yields more than a bare living. If he were wise enough to disregard this surplus he would always have enough, for he would never have too much. "Great needs," said Favorin, "spring from great wealth; and often the best way of getting what we want is to get rid of what we have." By striving to increase our happiness we change it into wretchedness. If a man were content to live, he would live happy; and he would therefore be good, for what would he have to gain by vice?

If we were immortal we should all be miserable; no doubt it is hard to die, but it is sweet to think that we shall not live for ever, and that a better life will put an end to the sorrows of this world. If we had the offer of immortality here below, who would accept the sorrowful gift?[1] What resources, what hopes, what consolation would be left against the cruelties of fate and man's injustice? The ignorant man never looks before; he knows little of the value of

[1] You understand I am speaking of those who think, and not of the crowd.

life and does not fear to lose it; the wise man sees things of greater worth and prefers them to it. Half knowledge and sham wisdom set us thinking about death and what lies beyond it; and they thus create the worst of our ills. The wise man bears life's ills all the better because he knows he must die. Life would be too dearly bought did we not know that sooner or later death will end it.

Our moral ills are the result of prejudice, crime alone excepted, and that depends on ourselves; our bodily ills either put an end to themselves or to us. Time or death will cure them, but the less we know how to bear it, the greater is our pain, and we suffer more in our efforts to cure our diseases than if we endured them. Live according to nature; be patient, get rid of the doctors; you will not escape death, but you will only die once, while the doctors make you die daily through your diseased imagination; their lying art, instead of prolonging your days, robs you of all delight in them. I am always asking what real good this art has done to mankind. True, the doctors cure some who would have died, but they kill millions who would have lived. If you are wise you will decline to take part in this lottery when the odds are so great against you. Suffer, die, or get better; but whatever you do, live while you are alive.

Human institutions are one mass of folly and contradiction. As our life loses its value we set a higher price upon it. The old regret life more than the young; they do not want to lose all they have spent in preparing for its enjoyment. At sixty it is cruel to die when one has not begun to live. Man is credited with a strong desire for self-preservation, and this desire exists; but we fail to perceive that this desire, as felt by us, is largely the work of man. In a natural state man is only eager to preserve his life while he has the means for its preservation; when self-preservation is no longer possible, he resigns himself to his fate and dies without vain torments. Nature teaches us the first law of resignation. Savages, like wild beasts, make very little struggle against death, and meet it almost without a murmur. When this natural law is overthrown reason establishes another, but few discern it, and man's resignation is never so complete as nature's.

Prudence! Prudence which is ever bidding us look forward into the future, a future which in many cases we shall never reach; here is the real source of all our troubles! How mad it is for so short-lived a creature as man to look forward into a future to which he rarely attains, while he neglects the present which is his? this madness is all the more fatal since it increases with years, and the old, always timid, prudent, and miserly, prefer to do without necessaries to-day that they may have luxuries at a hundred. Thus we grasp everything, we cling to everything; we are anxious about time, place, people, things, all that is and will be; we ourselves are but the least part of ourselves. We spread ourselves, so to speak, over the whole world, and all this vast expanse becomes sensitive. No wonder our woes increase when we may be wounded on every side. How many princes make themselves miserable for the loss of lands they never saw, and how many merchants lament in Paris over some misfortune in the Indies!

Is it nature that carries men so far from their real selves? Is it her will that each should learn his fate from others and even be the last to learn it; so that a man dies happy or miserable before he knows what he is about. There is a healthy, cheerful, strong. and vigorous man; it does me good to see him; his eyes tell of content and well-being; he is the picture of happiness. A letter comes by post; the happy man glances at it, it is addressed to him, he opens it and reads it. In a moment he is changed, he turns pale and falls into a swoon. When he comes to himself he weeps, laments, and groans, he tears his hair, and his shrieks re-echo through the air. You would say he was in convulsions. Fool, what harm has this bit of paper done you? What limb has it torn away? What crime has it made you commit? What change has it wrought in you to reduce you to this state of misery?

Had the letter miscarried, had some kindly hand thrown it into the fire, it strikes me that the fate of this mortal, at once happy and unhappy, would have offered us a strange problem. His misfortunes, you say, were real enough. Granted; but he did not feel them. What of that? His happiness was imaginary. I admit it; health, wealth, a contented spirit, are mere dreams. We no longer live in our own place, we live outside it. What does it profit us to live in such fear of death, when all that makes life worth living is our own?

Oh, man! live your own life and you will no longer be wretched. Keep to your appointed place in the order of nature and nothing can tear you from it. Do not kick against the stern law of necessity, nor waste in vain resistance the strength bestowed on you by heaven, not to prolong or extend your existence, but to preserve it so far and so long as heaven pleases. Your freedom and your power extend as far and no further than your natural strength; anything more is but slavery, deceit, and trickery. Power itself is servile when it depends upon public opinion; for you are dependent on the prejudices of others when you rule them by means of those prejudices. To lead them as you will, they must be led as they will. They have only to change their way of thinking and you are forced to change your course of action. Those who approach you need only contrive to sway the opinions of those you rule, or of the favourite by whom you are ruled, or those of your own family or theirs. Had you the genius of Themistocles,[1] viziers, courtiers, priests, soldiers, servants, babblers, the very children themselves, would lead you like a child in the midst of your legions. Whatever

---

[1] " You see that little boy," said Themistocles to his friends, " the fate of Greece is in his hands, for he rules his mother and his mother rules me, I rule the Athenians and the Athenians rule the Greeks." What petty creatures we should often find controlling great empires if we traced the course of power from the prince to those who secretly put that power in motion.

you do, your actual authority can never extend beyond your own powers. As soon as you are obliged to see with another's eyes you must will what he wills. You say with pride, " My people are my subjects." Granted, but what are you? The subject of your ministers. And your ministers, what are they? The subjects of their clerks, their mistresses, the servants of their servants. Grasp all, usurp all, and then pour out your silver with both hands; set up your batteries, raise the gallows and the wheel; make laws, issue proclamations, multiply your spies, your soldiers, your hangmen, your prisons, and your chains. Poor little men, what good does it do you? You will be no better served, you will be none the less robbed and deceived, you will be no nearer absolute power. You will say continually, " It is our will," and you will continually do the will of others.

There is only one man who gets his own way—he who can get it single-handed; therefore freedom, not power, is the greatest good. That man is truly free who desires what he is able to perform, and does what he desires. This is my fundamental maxim. Apply it to childhood, and all the rules of education spring from it.

Society has enfeebled man, not merely by robbing him of the right to his own strength, but still more by making his strength insufficient for his needs. This is why his desires increase in proportion to his weakness; and this is why the child is weaker than the man. If a man is strong and a child is weak it is not because the strength of the one is absolutely greater than the strength of the other, but because the one can naturally provide for himself and the other cannot. Thus the man will have more desires and the child more caprices, a word which means, I take it, desires which are not true needs, desires which can only be satisfied with the help of others.

I have already given the reason for this state of weakness. Parental affection is nature's provision against it; but parental affection may be carried to excess, it may be wanting, or it may be ill applied. Parents who live under our ordinary social conditions bring their child into these conditions too soon. By increasing his needs they do not relieve his weakness; they rather increase it. They further increase it by demanding of him what nature does not demand, by subjecting to their will what little strength he has to further his own wishes, by making slaves of themselves or of him instead of recognising that mutual dependence which should result from his weakness or their affection.

The wise man can keep his own place; but the child who does not know what his place is, is unable to keep it. There are a thousand ways out of it, and it is the business of those who have charge of the child to keep him in his place, and this is no easy task. He should be neither beast nor man, but a child. He must feel his weakness, but not suffer through it; he must be dependent, but he must not obey; he must ask, not command. He is only subject to others because of his needs, and because they see better than he what he really needs, what may help or hinder his existence. No one, not even his father, has the right to bid the child do what is of no use to him.

When our natural tendencies have not been interfered with by human prejudice and human institutions, the happiness alike of children and of men consists in the enjoyment of their liberty. But the child's liberty is restricted by his lack of strength. He who does as he likes is happy provided he is self-sufficing; it is so with the man who is living in a state of nature. He who does what he likes is not happy if his desires exceed his strength; it is so with a child in like conditions. Even in a state of nature children only enjoy an imperfect liberty, like that enjoyed by men in social life. Each of us, unable to dispense with the help of others, becomes so far weak and wretched. We were meant to be men, laws and customs thrust us back into infancy. The rich and great, the very kings themselves are but children; they see that we are ready to relieve their misery; this makes them childishly vain, and they are quite proud of the care bestowed on them, a care which they would never get if they were grown men.

These are weighty considerations, and they provide a solution for all the conflicting problems of our social system. There are two kinds of dependence: dependence on things, which is the work of nature; and dependence on men, which is the work of society. Dependence on things, being non-moral, does no injury to liberty and begets no vices; dependence on men, being out of order,[1] gives rise to every kind of vice, and through this master and slave become mutually depraved. If there is any cure for this social evil, it is to be found in the substitution of law for the individual; in arming the general will with a real strength beyond the power of any individual will. If the laws of nations, like the laws of nature, could never be broken by any human power, dependence on men would become dependence on things; all the advantages of a state of nature would be combined with all the advantages of social life in the commonwealth. The liberty which preserves a man from vice would be united with the morality which raises him to virtue.

Keep the child dependent on things only. By this course of education you will have followed the order of nature. Let his unreasonable wishes meet with physical obstacles only, or the punishment which results from his own actions, lessons which will be recalled when the same circumstances occur again. It is enough to prevent him from wrong doing without forbidding him to do wrong. Experience or lack of power should take the place of law. Give him, not what he wants, but what he needs. Let there be no question of obedience for him or tyranny for you. Supply the strength he lacks just so far as is required for freedom, not for power, so that he may receive your services with a sort of shame, and look forward to the time when he may dispense with them and may achieve the honour of self-help.

[1] In my *Principles of Political Law* it is proved that no private will can be ordered in the social system.

Nature provides for the child's growth in her own fashion, and this should never be thwarted. Do not make him sit still when he wants to run about, nor run when he wants to be quiet. If we did not spoil our children's wills by our blunders their desires would be free from caprice. Let them run, jump, and shout to their heart's content. All their own activities are instincts of the body for its growth in strength; but you should regard with suspicion those wishes which they cannot carry out for themselves, those which others must carry out for them. Then you must distinguish carefully between natural and artificial needs, between the needs of budding caprice and the needs which spring from the overflowing life just described.

I have already told you what you ought to do when a child cries for this thing or that. I will only add that as soon as he has words to ask for what he wants and accompanies his demands with tears, either to get his own way quicker or to over-ride a refusal, he should never have his way. If his words were prompted by a real need you should recognise it and satisfy it at once; but to yield to his tears is to encourage him to cry, to teach him to doubt your kindness, and to think that you are influenced more by his importunity than your own good-will. If he does not think you kind he will soon think you unkind; if he thinks you weak he will soon become obstinate; what you mean to give must be given at once. Be chary of refusing, but, having refused, do not change your mind.

Above all, beware of teaching the child empty phrases of politeness, which serve as spells to subdue those around him to his will, and to get him what he wants at once. The artificial education of the rich never fails to make them politely imperious, by teaching them the words to use so that no one will dare to resist them. Their children have neither the tone nor the manner of suppliants; they are as haughty or even more haughty in their entreaties than in their commands, as though they were more certain to be obeyed. You see at once that " If you please " means " It pleases me," and " I beg " means " I command." What a fine sort of politeness which only succeeds in changing the meaning of words so that every word is a command! For my own part, I would rather Emile were rude than haughty, that he should say " Do this " as a request, rather than " Please " as a command. What concerns me is his meaning, not his words.

There is such a thing as excessive severity as well as excessive indulgence, and both alike should be avoided. If you let children suffer you risk their health and life; you make them miserable now; if you take too much pains to spare them every kind of uneasiness you are laying up much misery for them in the future; you are making them delicate and over-sensitive; you are taking them out of their place among men, a place to which they must sooner or later return, in spite of all your pains. You will say I am falling into the same mistake as those bad fathers whom I blamed for sacrificing the present happiness of their children to a future which may never be theirs.

Not so; for the liberty I give my pupil makes up for the slight hardships to which he is exposed. I see little fellows playing in the snow, stiff and blue with cold, scarcely able to stir a finger. They could go and warm themselves if they chose, but they do not choose; if you forced them to come in they would feel the harshness of constraint a hundredfold more than the sharpness of the cold. Then what becomes of your grievance? Shall I make your child miserable by exposing him to hardships which he is perfectly ready to endure? I secure his present good by leaving him his freedom, and his future good by arming him against the evils he will have to bear. If he had his choice, would he hesitate for a moment between you and me?

Do you think any man can find true happiness elsewhere than in his natural state; and when you try to spare him all suffering, are you not taking him out of his natural state? Indeed I maintain that to enjoy great happiness he must experience slight ills; such is his nature. Too much bodily prosperity corrupts the morals. A man who knew nothing of suffering would be incapable of tenderness towards his fellow-creatures and ignorant of the joys of pity; he would be hard-hearted, unsocial, a very monster among men.

Do you know the surest way to make your child miserable? Let him have everything he wants; for as his wants increase in proportion to the ease with which they are satisfied, you will be compelled, sooner or later, to refuse his demands, and this unlooked-for refusal will hurt him more than the lack of what he wants. He will want your stick first, then your watch, the bird that flies, or the star that shines above him. He will want all he sets eyes on, and unless you were God himself, how could you satisfy him?

Man naturally considers all that he can get as his own. In this sense Hobbes' theory is true to a certain extent: Multiply both our wishes and the means of satisfying them, and each will be master of all. Thus the child, who has only to ask and have, thinks himself the master of the universe; he considers all men as his slaves; and when you are at last compelled to refuse, he takes your refusal as an act of rebellion, for he thinks he has only to command. All the reasons you give him, while he is still too young to reason, are so many pretences in his eyes; they seem to him only unkindness the sense of injustice embitters his disposition; he hates every one. Though he has never felt grateful for kindness, he resents all opposition.

How should I suppose that such a child can ever be happy? He is the slave of anger, a prey to the fiercest passions. Happy! He is a tyrant, at once the basest of slaves and the most wretched of creatures. I have known children brought up like this who expected you to knock the house down, to give them the weather-cock on the steeple, to stop a regiment on the march so that they might listen to the band; when they could not get their way they screamed and cried and would pay no attention to any one. In vain everybody strove to please them; as their desires were stimulated by the ease with which they got their own way, they set their hearts on impossibilities, and found themselves face to face with opposition and difficulty, pain and grief. Scolding, sulking, or in a rage, they wept and cried all day. Were they really so greatly favoured? Weakness, combined with love of power, produces nothing but folly and suffering. One spoilt child beats the table; another whips the sea. They may beat and whip long enough before they find contentment.

If their childhood is made wretched by these notions of power and tyranny, what of their manhood, when their relations with their fellow-men begin to grow and multiply? They are used to find everything give way to them; what a painful surprise to enter society and meet with opposition on every side, to be crushed beneath the weight of a universe which they expected to move at will. Their insolent manners, their childish vanity, only draw down upon them mortification, scorn, and mockery; they swallow insults like water; sharp experience soon teaches them that they have realised neither their position nor their strength. As they cannot do everything, they think they can do nothing. They are daunted by unexpected obstacles, degraded by the scorn of men; they become base, cowardly, and deceitful, and fall as far below their true level as they formerly soared above it.

Let us come back to the primitive law. Nature has made children helpless and in need of affection; did she make them to be obeyed and feared? Has she given them an imposing manner, a stern eye, a loud and threatening voice with which to make themselves feared? I understand how the roaring of the lion strikes terror into the other beasts, so that they tremble when they behold his terrible mane, but of all unseemly, hateful, and ridiculous sights, was there ever anything like a body of statesmen in their robes of office with their chief at their head bowing down before a swaddled babe, addressing him in pompous phrases, while he cries and slavers in reply?

If we consider childhood itself, is there anything so weak and wretched as a child, anything so utterly at the mercy of those about it, so dependent on their pity, their care, and their affection? Does it not seem as if his gentle face and touching appearance were intended to interest every one on behalf of his weakness and to make them eager to help him? And what is there more offensive, more unsuitable, than the sight of a sulky or imperious child, who commands those about him, and impudently assumes the tones of a master towards those without whom he would perish?

On the other hand, do you not see how children are fettered by the weakness of infancy? Do you not see how cruel it is to increase this servitude by obedience to our caprices, by depriving them of such liberty as they have? a liberty which they can scarcely abuse, a liberty the loss of which will do so little good to them or us. If there is nothing more ridiculous than a haughty child, there is nothing that claims our pity like a timid child. With the age of reason the child becomes the slave of the community; then why forestall this by slavery in the home? Let this brief hour of life be free from a yoke which nature has not laid upon it; leave the child the use of his natural liberty, which, for a time at least, secures him from the vices of the slave. Bring me those harsh masters, and those fathers who are the slaves of their children, bring them both with their frivolous objections, and before they boast of their own methods let them for once learn the method of nature.

I return to practical matters. I have already said your child must not get what he asks, but what he needs;[1] he must never act from obedience, but from necessity.

The very words *obey* and *command* will be excluded from his vocabulary, still more those of *duty* and *obligation*; but the words strength, necessity, weakness, and constraint must have a large place in it. Before the age of reason it is impossible to form any idea of moral beings or social relations; so avoid, as far as may be, the use of words which express these ideas, lest the child at an early age should attach wrong ideas to them, ideas which you cannot or will not destroy when he is older. The first mistaken idea he gets into his head is the germ of error and vice; it is the first step that needs watching. Act in such a way that while he only notices external objects his ideas are confined to sensations; let him only see the physical world around him. If not, you may be sure that either he will pay no heed to you at all, or he will form fantastic ideas of the moral world of which you prate, ideas which you will never efface as long as he lives.

"Reason with children" was Locke's chief maxim; it is in the height of fashion at present, and I hardly think it is justified by its results; those children who have been constantly reasoned with strike me as exceedingly silly. Of all man's faculties, reason, which is, so to speak, compounded of all the rest, is the last and choicest growth, and it is this you would use for the child's early training. To make a man reasonable is the coping stone of a good education, and yet you profess to train a child through his reason! You begin at the wrong end, you make the end the means. If children understood reason they would not need education, but by talking to them from their earliest age in a language they do not understand you accustom them to be satisfied with words, to question all that is said to them, to think themselves as wise as their teachers; you train them to be argumentative and rebellious; and whatever you

---

[1] We must recognise that pain is often necessary, pleasure is sometimes needed. So there is only one of the child's desires which should never be complied with, the desire for power. Hence, whenever they ask for anything we must pay special attention to their motive in asking. As far as possible give them everything they ask for, provided it can really give them pleasure; refuse everything they demand from mere caprice or love of power.

think you gain from motives of reason, you really gain from greediness, fear, or vanity with which you are obliged to reinforce your reasoning.

Most of the moral lessons which are and can be given to children may be reduced to this formula:

Master. You must not do that.

Child. Why not?

Master. Because it is wrong.

Child. Wrong! What is wrong?

Master. What is forbidden.

Child. Why is it wrong to do what is forbidden?

Master. You will be punished for disobedience.

Child. I will do it when no one is looking.

Master. We shall watch you.

Child. I will hide.

Master. We shall ask you what you were doing.

Child. I shall tell a lie.

Master. You must not tell lies.

Child. Why must not I tell lies?

Master. Because it is wrong, etc.

That is the inevitable circle. Go beyond it, and the child will not understand you. What sort of use is there in such teaching? I should greatly like to know what you would substitute for this dialogue. It would have puzzled Locke himself. It is no part of a child's business to know right and wrong, to perceive the reason for a man's duties.

Nature would have them children before they are men. If we try to invert this order we shall produce a forced fruit immature and flavourless, fruit which will be rotten before it is ripe; we shall have young doctors and old children. Childhood has its own ways of seeing, thinking, and feeling; nothing is more foolish than to try and substitute our ways; and I should no more expect judgment in a ten-year-old child than I should expect him to be five feet high. Indeed, what use would reason be to him at that age? It is the curb of strength, and the child does not need the curb.

When you try to persuade your scholars of the duty of obedience, you add to this so-called persuasion compulsion and threats, or still worse, flattery and bribes. Attracted by selfishness or constrained by force, they pretend to be convinced by reason. They see as soon as you do that obedience is to their advantage and disobedience to their disadvantage. But as you only demand disagreeable things of them, and as it is always disagreeable to do another's will, they hide themselves so that they may do as they please, persuaded that they are doing no wrong so long as they are not found out, but ready, if found out, to own themselves in the wrong for fear of worse evils. The reason for duty is beyond their age, and there is not a man in the world who could make them really aware of it; but the fear of punishment, the hope of forgiveness, importunity, the difficulty of answering, wrings from them as many confessions as you want; and you think you have convinced them when you have only wearied or frightened them.

What does it all come to? In the first place, by imposing on them a duty which they fail to recognise, you make them disinclined to submit to your tyranny, and you turn away their love; you teach them deceit, falsehood, and lying as a way to gain rewards or escape punishment; then by accustoming them to conceal a secret motive under the cloak of an apparent one, you yourself put into their hands the means of deceiving you, of depriving you of a knowledge of their real character, of answering you and others with empty words whenever they have the chance. Laws, you say, though binding on conscience, exercise the same constraint over grown-up men. That is so, but what are these men but children spoilt by education? This is just what you should avoid. Use force with children and reasoning with men; this is the natural order; the wise man needs no laws.

Treat your scholar according to his age. Put him in his place from the first, and keep him in it, so that he no longer tries to leave it. Then before he knows what goodness is, he will be practising its chief lesson. Give him no orders at all, absolutely none. Do not even let him think that you claim any authority over him. Let him only know that he is weak and you are strong, that his condition and yours puts him at your mercy; let this be perceived, learned, and felt. Let him early find upon his proud neck, the heavy yoke which nature has imposed upon us, the heavy yoke of necessity, under which every finite being must bow. Let him find this necessity in things, not in the caprices[1] of man; let the curb be force, not authority. If there is something he should not do, do not forbid him, but prevent him without explanation or reasoning; what you give him, give it at his first word without prayers or entreaties, above all without conditions. Give willingly, refuse unwillingly, but let your refusal be irrevocable; let no entreaties move you; let your "No," once uttered, be a wall of brass, against which the child may exhaust his strength some five or six times, but in the end he will try no more to overthrow it.

Thus you will make him patient, equable, calm, and resigned, even when he does not get all he wants; for it is in man's nature to bear patiently with the nature of things, but not with the ill-will of another. A child never rebels against, "There is none left," unless he thinks the reply is false. Moreover, there is no middle course; you must either make no demands on him at all, or else you must fashion him to perfect obedience. The worst education of all is to leave him hesitating between his own will and yours, constantly disputing whether you or he is master; I would rather a hundred times that he were master.

It is very strange that ever since people began to think about

[1] You may be sure the child will regard as caprice any will which opposes his own or any will which he does not understand. Now the child does not understand anything which interferes with his own fancies.

education they should have hit upon no other way of guiding children than emulation, jealousy, envy, vanity, greediness, base cowardice, all the most dangerous passions, passions ever ready to ferment, ever prepared to corrupt the soul even before the body is full-grown. With every piece of precocious instruction which you try to force into their minds you plant a vice in the depths of their hearts; foolish teachers think they are doing wonders when they are making their scholars wicked in order to teach them what goodness is, and then they tell us seriously, "Such is man." Yes, such is man, as you have made him. Every means has been tried except one, the very one which might succeed — well-regulated liberty. Do not undertake to bring up a child if you cannot guide him merely by the laws of what can or cannot be. The limits of the possible and the impossible are alike unknown to him, so they can be extended or contracted around him at your will. Without a murmur he is restrained, urged on, held back, by the hands of necessity alone; he is made adaptable and teachable by the mere force of things, without any chance for vice to spring up in him; for passions do not arise so long as they have accomplished nothing.

Give your scholar no verbal lessons; he should be taught by experience alone; never punish him, for he does not know what it is to do wrong; never make him say, "Forgive me," for he does not know how to do you wrong. Wholly unmoral in his actions, he can do nothing morally wrong, and he deserves neither punishment nor reproof.

Already I see the frightened reader comparing this child with those of our time; he is mistaken. The perpetual restraint imposed upon your scholars stimulates their activity; the more subdued they are in your presence, the more boisterous they are as soon as they are out of your sight. They must make amends to themselves in some way or other for the harsh constraint to which you subject them. Two schoolboys from the town will do more damage in the country than all the children of the village. Shut up a young gentleman and a young peasant in a room; the former will have upset and smashed everything before the latter has stirred from his place. Why is that, unless that the one hastens to misuse a moment's licence, while the other, always sure of freedom, does not use it rashly. And yet the village children, often flattered or constrained, are still very far from the state in which I would have them kept.

Let us lay it down as an incontrovertible rule that the first impulses of nature are always right; there is no original sin in the human heart, the how and why of the entrance of every vice can be traced. The only natural passion is self-love or selfishness taken in a wider sense. This selfishness is good in itself and in relation to ourselves; and as the child has no necessary relations to other people he is naturally indifferent to them; his self-love only becomes good or bad by the use made of it and the relations established by its means. Until the time is ripe for the appearance of reason, that guide of selfishness, the main thing is that the child shall do nothing because you are watching him or listening to him; in a word, nothing because of other people, but only what nature asks of him; then he will never do wrong.

I do not mean to say that he will never do any mischief, never hurt himself, never break a costly ornament if you leave it within his reach. He might do much damage without doing wrong, since wrong-doing depends on the harmful intention which will never be his. If once he meant to do harm, his whole education would be ruined; he would be almost hopelessly bad.

Greed considers some things wrong which are not wrong in the eyes of reason. When you leave free scope to a child's heedlessness, you must put anything he could spoil out of his way, and leave nothing fragile or costly within his reach. Let the room be furnished with plain and solid furniture; no mirrors, china, or useless ornaments. My pupil Emile, who is brought up in the country, shall have a room just like a peasant's. Why take such pains to adorn it when he will be so little in it? I am mistaken, however; he will ornament it for himself, and we shall soon see how.

But if, in spite of your precautions, the child contrives to do some damage, if he breaks some useful article, do not punish him for your carelessness, do not even scold him; let him hear no word of reproval, do not even let him see that he has vexed you; behave just as if the thing had come to pieces of itself; you may consider you have done great things if you have managed to hold your tongue.

May I venture at this point to state the greatest, the most important, the most useful rule of education? It is: Do not save time, but lose it. I hope that every-day readers will excuse my paradoxes; you cannot avoid paradox if you think for yourself, and whatever you may say I would rather fall into paradox than into prejudice. The most dangerous period in human life lies between birth and the age of twelve. It is the time when errors and vices spring up, while as yet there is no means to destroy them; when the means of destruction are ready, the roots have gone too deep to be pulled up. If the infant sprang at one bound from its mother's breast to the age of reason, the present type of education would be quite suitable, but its natural growth calls for quite a different training. The mind should be left undisturbed till its faculties have developed; for while it is blind it cannot see the torch you offer it, nor can it follow through the vast expanse of ideas a path so faintly traced by reason that the best eyes can scarcely follow it.

Therefore the education of the earliest years should be merely negative. It consists, not in teaching virtue or truth, but in preserving the heart from vice and from the spirit of error. If only you could let well alone, and get others to follow your example; if you could bring your scholar to the age of twelve strong and healthy, but unable to tell his right hand from his left, the eyes of his understanding would be open to reason as soon as you began to teach him. Free from prejudices and free from habits, there would be nothing in him to counteract the effects of your labours. In your hands he would soon become the wisest of men; by doing nothing to begin with, you would end with a prodigy of education.

Reverse the usual practice and you will almost always do right. Fathers and teachers who want to make the child, not a child but a man of learning, think it never too soon to scold, correct, reprove, threaten, bribe, teach, and reason. Do better than they; be reasonable, and do not reason with your pupil, more especially do not try to make him approve what he dislikes; for if reason is always connected with disagreeable matters, you make it distasteful to him, you discredit it at an early age in a mind not yet ready to understand it. Exercise his body, his limbs, his senses, his strength, but keep his mind idle as long as you can. Distrust all opinions which appear before the judgment to discriminate between them. Restrain and ward off strange impressions; and to prevent the birth of evil do not hasten to do well, for goodness is only possible when enlightened by reason. Regard all delays as so much time gained; you have achieved much, you approach the boundary without loss. Leave childhood to ripen in your children. In a word, beware of giving anything they need to-day if it can be deferred without danger to to-morrow.

There is another point to be considered which confirms the suitability of this method: it is the child's individual bent, which must be thoroughly known before we can choose the fittest moral training. Every mind has its own form, in accordance with which it must be controlled; and the success of the pains taken depends largely on the fact that he is controlled in this way and no other. Oh, wise man, take time to observe nature; watch your scholar well before you say a word to him; first leave the germ of his character free to show itself, do not constrain him in anything, the better to see him as he really is. Do you think this time of liberty is wasted? On the contrary, your scholar will be the better employed, for this is the way you yourself will learn not to lose a single moment when time is of more value. If, however, you begin to act before you know what to do, you act at random; you may make mistakes, and must retrace your steps; your haste to reach your goal will only take you further from it. Do not imitate the miser who loses much lest he should lose a little. Sacrifice a little time in early childhood, and it will be repaid you with usury when your scholar is older. The wise physician does not hastily give prescriptions at first sight, but he studies the constitution of the sick man before he prescribes anything; the treatment is begun later, but the patient is cured, while the hasty doctor kills him.

But where shall we find a place for our child so as to bring him up as a senseless being, an automaton? Shall we keep him in the moon, or on a desert island? Shall we remove him from human society? Will he not always have around him the sight and the pattern of the passions of other people? Will he never see children of his own age? Will he not see his parents, his neighbours, his nurse, his governess, his man-servant, his tutor himself, who after all will not be an angel? Here we have a real and serious objection. But did I tell you that an education according to nature would be an easy task? Oh, men! is it my fault that you have made all good things difficult? I admit that I am aware of these difficulties; perhaps they are insuperable; but nevertheless it is certain that we do to some extent avoid them by trying to do so. I am showing what we should try to attain, I do not say we can attain it, but I do say that whoever comes nearest to it is nearest to success.

Remember you must be a man yourself before you try to train a man; you yourself must set the pattern he shall copy. While the child is still unconscious there is time to prepare his surroundings, so that nothing shall strike his eye but what is fit for his sight. Gain the respect of every one, begin to win their hearts, so that they may try to please you. You will not be master of the child if you cannot control every one about him; and this authority will never suffice unless it rests upon respect for your goodness. There is no question of squandering one's means and giving money right and left; I never knew money win love. You must neither be harsh nor niggardly, nor must you merely pity misery when you can relieve it; but in vain will you open your purse if you do not open your heart along with it, the hearts of others will always be closed to you. You must give your own time, attention, affection, your very self; for whatever you do, people always perceive that your money is not you. There are proofs of kindly interest which produce more results and are really more useful than any gift; how many of the sick and wretched have more need of comfort than of charity; how many of the oppressed need protection rather than money? Reconcile those who are at strife, prevent lawsuits; incline children to duty, fathers to kindness; promote happy marriages; prevent annoyances; freely use the credit of your pupil's parents on behalf of the weak who cannot obtain justice, the weak who are oppressed by the strong. Be just, human, kindly. Do not give alms alone, give charity; works of mercy do more than money for the relief of suffering; love others and they will love you; serve them and they will serve you; be their brother and they will be your children.

This is one reason why I want to bring up Emile in the country, far from those miserable lacqueys, the most degraded of men except their masters; far from the vile morals of the town, whose gilded surface makes them seductive and contagious to children; while the vices of peasants, unadorned and in their naked grossness, are more fitted to repel than to seduce, when there is no motive for imitating them.

In the village a tutor will have much more control over the things he wishes to show the child; his reputation, his words, his example, will have a weight they would never have in the town; he is of use to every one, so every one is eager to oblige him, to win his esteem, to appear before the disciple what the master would have him be;

if vice is not corrected, public scandal is at least avoided, which is all that our present purpose requires.

Cease to blame others for your own faults; children are corrupted less by what they see than by your own teaching. With your endless preaching, moralising, and pedantry, for one idea you give your scholars, believing it to be good, you give them twenty more which are good for nothing; you are full of what is going on in your own minds, and you fail to see the effect you produce on theirs. In the continual flow of words with which you overwhelm them, do you think there is none which they get hold of in a wrong sense? Do you suppose they do not make their own comments on your long-winded explanations, that they do not find material for the construction of a system they can understand—one which they will use against you when they get the chance?

Listen to a little fellow who has just been under instruction; let him chatter freely, ask questions, and talk at his ease, and you will be surprised to find the strange forms your arguments have assumed in his mind; he confuses everything, and turns everything topsy-turvy; you are vexed and grieved by his unforeseen objections; he reduces you to be silent yourself or to silence him: and what can he think of silence in one who is so fond of talking? If ever he gains this advantage and is aware of it, farewell education; from that moment all is lost; he is no longer trying to learn, he is trying to refute you.

Zealous teachers, be simple, sensible, and reticent; be in no hurry to act unless to prevent the actions of others. Again and again I say, reject, if it may be, a good lesson for fear of giving a bad one. Beware of playing the tempter in this world, which nature intended as an earthly paradise for men, and do not attempt to give the innocent child the knowledge of good and evil; since you cannot prevent the child learning by what he sees outside himself, restrict your own efforts to impressing those examples on his mind in the form best suited for him.

The explosive passions produce a great effect upon the child when he sees them; their outward expression is very marked; he is struck by this and his attention is arrested. Anger especially is so noisy in its rage that it is impossible not to perceive it if you are within reach. You need not ask yourself whether this is an opportunity for a pedagogue to frame a fine disquisition. What! no fine disquisition, nothing, not a word! Let the child come to you; impressed by what he has seen, he will not fail to ask you questions. The answer is easy; it is drawn from the very things which have appealed to his senses. He sees a flushed face, flashing eyes, a threatening gesture, he hears cries; everything shows that the body is ill at ease. Tell him plainly, without affectation or mystery, "This poor man is ill, he is in a fever." You may take the opportunity of giving him in a few words some idea of disease and its effects; for that too belongs to nature, and is one of the bonds of necessity which he must recognise. By means of this idea, which is not false in itself, may he not early acquire a certain aversion to giving way to excessive passions, which he regards as diseases; and do you not think that such a notion, given at the right moment, will produce a more wholesome effect than the most tedious sermon? But consider the after effects of this idea; you have authority, if ever you find it necessary, to treat the rebellious child as a sick child; to keep him in his room, in bed if need be, to diet him, to make him afraid of his growing vices, to make him hate and dread them without ever regarding as a punishment the strict measures you will perhaps have to use for his recovery. If it happens that you yourself in a moment's heat depart from the calm and self-control which you should aim at, do not try to conceal your fault, but tell him frankly, with a gentle reproach, " My dear, you have hurt me."

Moreover, it is a matter of great importance that no notice should be taken in his presence of the quaint sayings which result from the simplicity of the ideas in which he is brought up, nor should they be quoted in a way he can understand. A foolish laugh may destroy six months' work and do irreparable damage for life. I cannot repeat too often that to control the child one must often control oneself.

I picture my little Emile at the height of a dispute between two neighbours going up to the fiercest of them and saying in a tone of pity, " You are ill, I am very sorry for you." This speech will no doubt have its effect on the spectators and perhaps on the disputants. Without laughter, scolding, or praise I should take him away, willing or no, before he could see this result, or at least before he could think about it; and I should make haste to turn his thoughts to other things, so that he would soon forget all about it.

I do not propose to enter into every detail, but only to explain general rules and to give illustrations in cases of difficulty. I think it is impossible to train a child up to the age of twelve in the midst of society, without giving him some idea of the relations between one man and another, and of the morality of human actions. It is enough to delay the development of these ideas as long as possible, and when they can no longer be avoided to limit them to present needs, so that he may neither think himself master of everything nor do harm to others without knowing or caring. There are calm and gentle characters which can be led a long way in their first innocence without any danger; but there are also stormy dispositions whose passions develop early; you must hasten to make men of them lest you should have to keep them in chains.

Our first duties are to ourselves; our first feelings are centred on self; all our instincts are at first directed to our own preservation and our own welfare. Thus the first notion of justice springs not from what we owe to others, but from what is due to us. Here is another error in popular methods of education. If you talk to children of their duties, and not of their rights, you are beginning at the wrong end, and telling them what they cannot understand, what cannot be of any interest to them.

If I had to train a child such as I have just described, I should say to myself, " A child never attacks people,[1] only things; and he soon learns by experience to respect those older and stronger than himself. Things, however, do not defend themselves. Therefore the first idea he needs is not that of liberty but of property, and that he may get this idea he must have something of his own." It is useless to enumerate his clothes, furniture, and playthings; although he uses these he knows not how or why he has come by them. To tell him they were given him is little better, for giving implies having; so here is property before his own, and it is the principle of property that you want to teach him; moreover, giving is a convention, and the child as yet has no idea of conventions. I hope my reader will note, in this and many other cases, how people think they have taught children thoroughly, when they have only thrust on them words which have no intelligible meaning to them.[2]

We must therefore go back to the origin of property, for that is where the first idea of it must begin. The child, living in the country, will have got some idea of field work; eyes and leisure suffice for that, and he will have both. In every age, and especially in childhood, we want to create, to copy, to produce, to give all the signs of power and activity. He will hardly have seen the gardener at work twice, sowing, planting, and growing vegetables, before he will want to garden himself.

According to the principles I have already laid down, I shall not thwart him; on the contrary, I shall approve of his plan, share his hobby, and work with him, not for his pleasure but my own; at least, so he thinks; I shall be his under-gardener, and dig the ground for him till his arms are strong enough to do it; he will take possession of it by planting a bean, and this is surely a more sacred possession, and one more worthy of respect, than that of Nuñes Balboa, who took possession of South America in the name of the King of Spain, by planting his banner on the coast of the Southern Sea.

We water the beans every day, we watch them coming up with the greatest delight. Day by day I increase this delight by saying, " Those belong to you." To explain what that word " belong " means, I show him how he has given his time, his labour, and his trouble, his very self to it; that in this ground there is a part of himself which he can claim against all the world, as he could with-

[1] A child should never be allowed to play with grown-up people as if they were his inferiors, nor even as if they were only his equals. If he ventured to strike any one in earnest, were it only the footman, were it the hangman himself, let the sufferer return his blows with interest, so that he will not want to do it again. I have seen silly women inciting children to rebellion, encouraging them to hit people, allowing themselves to be beaten, and laughing at the harmless blows, never thinking that those blows were in intention the blows of a murderer, and that the child who desires to beat people now will desire to kill them when he is grown up.
[2] This is why most children want to take back what they have given, and cry if they cannot get it. They do not do this when once they know what a gift is; only they are more careful about giving things away.

draw his arm from the hand of another man who wanted to keep it against his will.

One fine day he hurries up with his watering-can in his hand. What a scene of woe! Alas! all the beans are pulled up, the soil is dug over, you can scarcely find the place. Oh! what has become of my labour, my work, the beloved fruits of my care and effort? Who has stolen my property? Who has taken my beans? The young heart revolts; the first feeling of injustice brings its sorrow and bitterness; tears come in torrents, the unhappy child fills the air with cries and groans. I share his sorrow and anger; we look around us, we make inquiries. At last we discover that the gardener did it. We send for him.

But we are greatly mistaken. The gardener, hearing our complaint, begins to complain louder than we:—

What, gentlemen, was it you who spoilt my work! I had sown some Maltese melons; the seed was given me as something quite out of the common, and I meant to give you a treat when they were ripe; but you have planted your miserable beans and destroyed my melons, which were coming up so nicely, and I can never get any more. You have behaved very badly to me and you have deprived yourselves of the pleasure of eating most delicious melons.

Jean Jacques. My poor Robert, you must forgive us. You had given your labour and your pains to it. I see we were wrong to spoil your work, but we will send to Malta for some more seed for you, and we will never dig the ground again without finding out if some one else has been beforehand with us.

Robert. Well, gentlemen, you need not trouble yourselves, for there is no more waste ground. I dig what my father tilled; every one does the same, and all the land you see has been occupied time out of mind.

Emile. Mr. Robert, do people often lose the seed of Maltese melons?

Robert. No indeed, sir; we do not often find such silly little gentlemen as you. No one meddles with his neighbour's garden; every one respects other people's work so that his own may be safe.

Emile. But I have not got a garden.

Robert. I don't care; if you spoil mine I won't let you walk in it, for you see I do not mean to lose my labour.

Jean Jacques. Could not we suggest an arrangement with this kind Robert? Let him give my young friend and myself a corner of his garden to cultivate, on condition that he has half the crop.

Robert. You may have it free. But remember I shall dig up your beans if you touch my melons.

In this attempt to show how a child may be taught certain primitive ideas we see how the notion of property goes back naturally to the right of the first occupier to the results of his work. That is plain and simple, and quite within the child's grasp. From that to the rights of property and exchange there is but a step, after which you must stop short.

You also see that an explanation which I can give in writing in a couple of pages may take a year in practice, for in the course of moral ideas we cannot advance too slowly, nor plant each step too firmly. Young teacher, pray consider this example, and remember that your lessons should always be in deeds rather than words, for children soon forget what they say or what is said to them, but not what they have done nor what has been done to them.

Such teaching should be given, as I have said, sooner or later, as the scholar's disposition, gentle or turbulent, requires it. The way of using it is unmistakable; but to omit no matter of importance in a difficult business let us take another example.

Your ill-tempered child destroys everything he touches. Do not vex yourself; put anything he can spoil out of his reach. He breaks the things he is using; do not be in a hurry to give him more; let him feel the want of them. He breaks the windows of his room; let the wind blow upon him night and day, and do not be afraid of his catching cold; it is better to catch cold than to be reckless. Never complain of the inconvenience he causes you, but let him feel it first. At last you will have the windows mended without saying anything. He breaks them again; then change your plan; tell him dryly and without anger, "The windows are mine, I took pains to have them put in, and I mean to keep them safe." Then you will shut him up in a dark place without a window. At this unexpected proceeding he cries and howls; no one heeds. Soon he gets tired and changes his tone; he laments and sighs; a servant appears, the rebel begs to be let out. Without seeking any excuse for refusing, the servant merely says, "I, too, have windows to keep," and goes away. At last, when the child has been there several hours, long enough to get very tired of it, long enough to make an impression on his memory, some one suggests to him that he should offer to make terms with you, so that you may set him free and he will never break windows again. That is just what he wants. He will send and ask you to come and see him; you will come, he will suggest his plan, and you will agree to it at once, saying, "That is a very good idea; it will suit us both; why didn't you think of it sooner?" Then without asking for any affirmation or confirmation of his promise, you will embrace him joyfully and take him back at once to his own room, considering this agreement as sacred as if he had confirmed it by a formal oath. What idea do you think he will form from these proceedings, as to the fulfilment of a promise and its usefulness? If I am not greatly mistaken, there is not a child upon earth, unless he is utterly spoilt already, who could resist this treatment, or one who would ever dream of breaking windows again on purpose. Follow out the whole train of thought. The naughty little fellow hardly thought when he was making a hole for his beans that he was hewing out a cell in which his own knowledge would soon imprison him.[1]

[1] Moreover if the duty of keeping his word were not established in the child's mind by its own utility, the child's growing consciousness would

We are now in the world of morals, the door to vice is open. Deceit and falsehood are born along with conventions and duties. As soon as we can do what we ought not to do, we try to hide what we ought not to have done. As soon as self-interest makes us give a promise, a greater interest may make us break it; it is merely a question of doing it with impunity; we naturally take refuge in concealment and falsehood. As we have not been able to prevent vice, we must punish it. The sorrows of life begin with its mistakes.

I have already said enough to show that children should never receive punishment merely as such; it should always come as the natural consequence of their fault. Thus you will not exclaim against their falsehood, you will not exactly punish them for lying, but you will arrange that all the ill effects of lying, such as not being believed when we speak the truth, or being accused of what we have not done in spite of our protests, shall fall on their heads when they have told a lie. But let us explain what lying means to the child.

There are two kinds of lies; one concerns an accomplished fact, the other concerns a future duty. The first occurs when we falsely deny or assert that we did or did not do something, or, to put it in general terms, when we knowingly say what is contrary to facts. The other occurs when we promise what we do not mean to perform, or, in general terms, when we profess an intention which we do not really mean to carry out. These two kinds of lie are sometimes found in combination,[1] but their differences are my present business.

He who feels the need of help from others, he who is constantly experiencing their kindness, has nothing to gain by deceiving them; it is plainly to his advantage that they should see things as they are, lest they should mistake his interests. It is therefore plain that lying with regard to actual facts is not natural to children, but lying is made necessary by the law of obedience; since obedience is disagreeable, children disobey as far as they can in secret, and the present good of avoiding punishment or reproof outweighs the remoter good of speaking the truth. Under a free and natural education why should your child lie? What has he to conceal from you? You do not thwart him, you do not punish him, you demand nothing from him. Why should he not tell everything to you as simply as to his little playmate? He cannot see anything more risky in the one course than in the other.

The lie concerning duty is even less natural, since promises to do

soon impress it on him as a law of conscience, as an innate principle, only requiring suitable experiences for its development. This first outline is not sketched by man, it is engraved on the heart by the author of al justice. Take away the primitive law of contract and the obligation imposed by contract and there is nothing left of human society but vanity and empty show. He who only keeps his word because it is to his own profit is hardly more pledged than if he had given no promise at all. This principle is of the utmost importance, and deserves to be thoroughly studied, for man is now beginning to be at war with himself.

[1] Thus the guilty person, accused of some evil deed, defends himself by asserting that he is a good man. His statement is false in itself and false in its application to the matter in hand.

or refrain from doing are conventional agreements which are outside the state of nature and detract from our liberty. Moreover, all promises made by children are in themselves void; when they pledge themselves they do not know what they are doing, for their narrow vision cannot look beyond the present. A child can hardly lie when he makes a promise; for he is only thinking how he can get out of the present difficulty, any means which has not an immediate result is the same to him; when he promises for the future he promises nothing, and his imagination is as yet incapable of projecting him into the future while he lives in the present. If he could escape a whipping or get a packet of sweets by promising to throw himself out of the window to-morrow, he would promise on the spot. This is why the law disregards all promises made by minors, and when fathers and teachers are stricter and demand that promises shall be kept, it is only when the promise refers to something the child ought to do even if he had made no promise.

The child cannot lie when he makes a promise, for he does not know what he is doing when he makes his promise. The case is different when he breaks his promise, which is a sort of retrospective falsehood; for he clearly remembers making the promise, but he fails to see the importance of keeping it. Unable to look into the future, he cannot foresee the results of things, and when he breaks his promises he does nothing contrary to his stage of reasoning.

Children's lies are therefore entirely the work of their teachers, and to teach them to speak the truth is nothing less than to teach them the art of lying. In your zeal to rule, control, and teach them, you never find sufficient means at your disposal. You wish to gain fresh influence over their minds by baseless maxims, by unreasonable precepts; and you would rather they knew their lessons and told lies, than leave them ignorant and truthful.

We, who only give our scholars lessons in practice, who prefer to have them good rather than clever, never demand the truth lest they should conceal it, and never claim any promise lest they should be tempted to break it. If some mischief has been done in my absence and I do not know who did it, I shall take care not to accuse Emile, nor to say, " Did you do it ? " [1] For in so doing what should I do but teach him to deny it ? If his difficult temperament compels me to make some agreement with him, I will take good care that the suggestion always comes from him, never from me; that when he undertakes anything he has always a present and effective interest in fulfilling his promise, and if he ever fails this lie will bring down on him all the unpleasant consequences which he sees arising from the natural order of things, and not from his tutor's vengeance.

---

[1] Nothing could be more indiscreet than such a question, especially if the child is guilty. Then if he thinks you know what he has done, he will think you are setting a trap for him, and this idea can only set him against you. If he thinks you do not know, he will say to himself, " Why should I make my fault known ? " And here we have the first temptation to falsehood as the direct result of your foolish question.

But far from having recourse to such cruel measures, I feel almost certain that Emile will not know for many years what it is to lie, and that when he does find out, he will be astonished and unable to understand what can be the use of it. It is quite clear that the less I make his welfare dependent on the will or the opinions of others, the less is it to his interest to lie.

When we are in no hurry to teach there is no hurry to demand, and we can take our time, so as to demand nothing except under fitting conditions. Then the child is training himself, in so far as he is not being spoilt. But when a fool of a tutor, who does not know how to set about his business, is always making his pupil promise first this and then that, without discrimination, choice, or proportion, the child is puzzled and overburdened with all these promises, and neglects, forgets or even scorns them, and considering them as so many empty phrases he makes a game of making and breaking promises. Would you have him keep his promise faithfully, be moderate in your claims upon him.

The detailed treatment I have just given to lying may be applied in many respects to all the other duties imposed upon children, whereby these duties are made not only hateful but impracticable. For the sake of a show of preaching virtue you make them love every vice; you instil these vices by forbidding them. Would you have them pious, you take them to church till they are sick of it; you teach them to gabble prayers until they long for the happy time when they will not have to pray to God. To teach them charity you make them give alms as if you scorned to give yourself. It is not the child, but the master, who should give; however much he loves his pupil he should vie with him for this honour; he should make him think that he is too young to deserve it. Alms-giving is the deed of a man who can measure the worth of his gift and the needs of his fellow-men. The child, who knows nothing of these, can have no merit in giving; he gives without charity, without kindness; he is almost ashamed to give, for, to judge by your practice and his own, he thinks it is only children who give, and that there is no need for charity when we are grown up.

Observe that the only things children are set to give are things of which they do not know the value, bits of metal carried in their pockets for which they have no further use. A child would rather give a hundred coins than one cake. But get this prodigal giver to distribute what is dear to him, his toys, his sweets, his own lunch, and we shall soon see if you have made him really generous.

People try yet another way; they soon restore what he gave to the child, so that he gets used to giving everything which he knows will come back to him. I have scarcely seen generosity in children except of these two types, giving what is of no use to them, or what they expect to get back again. "Arrange things," says Locke, "so that experience may convince them that the most generous giver gets the biggest share." That is to make the child superficially generous but really greedy. He adds that "children will thus form the habit of liberality." Yes, a usurer's liberality, which expects cent. per cent. But when it is a question of real giving, good-bye to the habit; when they do not get things back, they will not give. It is the habit of the mind, not of the hands, that needs watching. All the other virtues taught to children are like this, and to preach these baseless virtues you waste their youth in sorrow. What a sensible sort of education!

Teachers, have done with these shams; be good and kind; let your example sink into your scholars' memories till they are old enough to take it to heart. Rather than hasten to demand deeds of charity from my pupil I prefer to perform such deeds in his presence, even depriving him of the means of imitating me, as an honour beyond his years; for it is of the utmost importance that he should not regard a man's duties as merely those of a child. If when he sees me help the poor he asks me about it, and it is time to reply to his questions,[1] I shall say, " My dear boy, the rich only exist through the good-will of the poor, so they have promised to feed those who have not enough to live on, either in goods or labour." " Then you promised to do this ? " " Certainly; I am only master of the wealth that passes through my hands on the condition attached to its ownership."

After this talk (and we have seen how a child may be brought to understand it) another than Emile would be tempted to imitate me and behave like a rich man; in such a case I should at least take care that it was done without ostentation; I would rather he robbed me of my privilege and hid himself to give. It is a fraud suitable to his age, and the only one I could forgive in him.

I know that all these imitative virtues are only the virtues of a monkey, and that a good action is only morally good when it is done as such and not because of others. But at an age when the heart does not yet feel anything, you must make children copy the deeds you wish to grow into habits, until they can do them with understanding and for the love of what is good. Man imitates, as do the beasts. The love of imitating is well regulated by nature; in society it becomes a vice. The monkey imitates man, whom he fears, and not the other beasts, which he scorns; he thinks what is done by his betters must be good. Among ourselves, our harlequins imitate all that is good to degrade it and bring it into ridicule; knowing their owners' baseness they try to equal what is better than they are, or they strive to imitate what they admire, and their bad taste appears in their choice of models, they would rather deceive others or win applause for their own talents than become wiser or better. Imitation has its roots in our desire to escape from ourselves. If I succeed in my undertaking, Emile will certainly have no such wish. So we must dispense with any seeming good that might arise from it.

Examine your rules of education; you will find them all topsy-

---

[1] It must be understood that I do not answer his questions when he wants; that would be to subject myself to his will and to place myself in the most dangerous state of dependence that ever a tutor was in.

turvy, especially in all that concerns virtue and morals. The only moral lesson which is suited for a child—the most important lesson for every time of life—is this: "Never hurt anybody." The very rule of well-doing, if not subordinated to this rule, is dangerous, false, and contradictory. Who is there who does no good? Every one does some good, the wicked as well as the righteous; he makes one happy at the cost of the misery of a hundred, and hence spring all our misfortunes. The noblest virtues are negative, they are also the most difficult, for they make little show, and do not even make room for that pleasure so dear to the heart of man, the thought that some one is pleased with us. If there be a man who does no harm to his neighbours, what good must he have accomplished! What a bold heart, what a strong character it needs! It is not in talking about this maxim, but in trying to practise it, that we discover both its greatness and its difficulty.[1]

This will give you some slight idea of the precautions I would have you take in giving children instruction which cannot always be refused without risk to themselves or others, or the far greater risk of the formation of bad habits, which would be difficult to correct later on; but be sure this necessity will not often arise with children who are properly brought up, for they cannot possibly become rebellious, spiteful, untruthful, or greedy, unless the seeds of these vices are sown in their hearts. What I have just said applies therefore rather to the exception than the rule. But the oftener children have the opportunity of quitting their proper condition, and contracting the vices of men, the oftener will these exceptions arise. Those who are brought up in the world must receive more precocious instruction than those who are brought up in retirement. So this solitary education would be preferable, even if it did nothing more than leave childhood time to ripen.

There is quite another class of exceptions: those so gifted by nature that they rise above the level of their age. As there are men who never get beyond infancy, so there are others who are never, so to speak, children, they are men almost from birth. The difficulty is that these cases are very rare, very difficult to distinguish; while every mother, who knows that a child may be a prodigy, is convinced that her child is that one. They go further; they mistake the common signs of growth for marks of exceptional talent. Liveliness, sharp sayings, romping, amusing simplicity, these are the characteristic marks of this age, and show that the child is a child

---

[1] The precept "Never hurt anybody," implies the greatest possible independence of human society; for in the social state one man's good is another man's evil. This relation is part of the nature of things; it is inevitable. You may apply this test to man in society and to the hermit to discover which is best. A distinguished author says, "None but the wicked can live alone." I say, "None but the good can live alone." This proposition, if less sententious, is truer and more logical than the other. If the wicked were alone, what evil would he do? It is among his fellows that he lays his snares for others. If they wish to apply this argument to the man of property, my answer is to be found in the passage to which this note is appended.

indeed. Is it strange that a child who is encouraged to chatter and allowed to say anything, who is restrained neither by consideration nor convention, should chance to say something clever? Were he never to hit the mark, his case would be stranger than that of the astrologer who, among a thousand errors, occasionally predicts the truth. "They lie so often," said Henry IV., "that at last they say what is true." If you want to say something clever, you have only to talk long enough. May Providence watch over those fine folk who have no other claim to social distinction.

The finest thoughts may spring from a child's brain, or rather the best words may drop from his lips, just as diamonds of great worth may fall into his hands, while neither the thoughts nor the diamonds are his own; at that age neither can be really his. The child's sayings do not mean to him what they mean to us, the ideas he attaches to them are different. His ideas, if indeed he has any ideas at all, have neither order nor connection; there is nothing sure, nothing certain, in his thoughts. Examine your so-called prodigy. Now and again you will discover in him extreme activity of mind and extraordinary clearness of thought. More often this same mind will seem slack and spiritless, as if wrapped in mist. Sometimes he goes before you, sometimes he will not stir. One moment you would call him a genius, another a fool. You would be mistaken in both; he is a child, an eaglet who soars aloft for a moment, only to drop back into the nest.

Treat him, therefore, according to his age, in spite of appearances, and beware of exhausting his strength by over-much exercise. If the young brain grows warm and begins to bubble, let it work freely, but do not heat it any further, lest it lose its goodness, and when the first gases have been given off, collect and compress the rest so that in after years they may turn to life-giving heat and real energy. If not, your time and your pains will be wasted, you will destroy your own work, and after foolishly intoxicating yourself with these heady fumes, you will have nothing left but an insipid and worthless wine.

Silly children grow into ordinary men. I know no generalisation more certain than this. It is the most difficult thing in the world to distinguish between genuine stupidity, and that apparent and deceitful stupidity which is the sign of a strong character. At first sight it seems strange that the two extremes should have the same outward signs; and yet it may well be so, for at an age when man has as yet no true ideas, the whole difference between the genius and the rest consists in this: the latter only take in false ideas, while the former, finding nothing but false ideas, receives no ideas at all. In this he resembles the fool; the one is fit for nothing, the other finds nothing fit for him. The only way of distinguishing between them depends upon chance, which may offer the genius some idea which he can understand, while the fool is always the same. As a child, the young Cato was taken for an idiot by his parents; he was obstinate and silent, and that was all they perceived in him; it was only in Sulla's ante-chamber that his uncle discovered what was in him. Had he never found his way there, he might have passed for a fool till he reached the age of reason. Had Cæsar never lived, perhaps this same Cato, who discerned his fatal genius, and foretold his great schemes, would have passed for a dreamer all his days. Those who judge children hastily are apt to be mistaken; they are often more childish than the child himself. I knew a middle-aged man,[1] whose friendship I esteemed an honour, who was reckoned a fool by his family. All at once he made his name as a philosopher, and I have no doubt posterity will give him a high place among the greatest thinkers and the profoundest metaphysicians of his day.

Hold childhood in reverence, and do not be in any hurry to judge it for good or ill. Leave exceptional cases to show themselves, let their qualities be tested and confirmed, before special methods are adopted. Give nature time to work before you take over her business, lest you interfere with her dealings. You assert that you know the value of time and are afraid to waste it. You fail to perceive that it is a greater waste of time to use it ill than to do nothing, and that a child ill taught is further from virtue than a child who has learnt nothing at all. You are afraid to see him spending his early years doing nothing. What! is it nothing to be happy, nothing to run and jump all day? He will never be so busy again all his life long. Plato, in his *Republic*, which is considered so stern, teaches the children only through festivals, games, songs, and amusements. It seems as if he had accomplished his purpose when he had taught them to be happy; and Seneca, speaking of the Roman lads in olden days, says, " They were always on their feet, they were never taught anything which kept them sitting." Were they any the worse for it in manhood? Do not be afraid, therefore, of this so-called idleness. What would you think of a man who refused to sleep lest he should waste part of his life? You would say, " He is mad; he is not enjoying his life, he is robbing himself of part of it; to avoid sleep he is hastening his death." Remember that these two cases are alike, and that childhood is the sleep of reason.

The apparent ease with which children learn is their ruin. You fail to see that this very facility proves that they are not learning. Their shining, polished brain reflects, as in a mirror, the things you show them, but nothing sinks in. The child remembers the words and the ideas are reflected back; his hearers understand them, but to him they are meaningless.

Although memory and reason are wholly different faculties, the one does not really develop apart from the other. Before the age of reason the child receives images, not ideas; and there is this difference between them: images are merely the pictures of external objects, while ideas are notions about those objects determined by their relations. An image when it is recalled may exist by itself in

[1] The Abbé de Condillac

the mind, but every idea implies other ideas. When we image we merely perceive, when we reason we compare. Our sensations are merely passive, our notions or ideas spring from an active principle which judges. The proof of this will be given later.

I maintain, therefore, that as children are incapable of judging, they have no true memory. They retain sounds, form, sensation, but rarely ideas, and still more rarely relations. You tell me they acquire some rudiments of geometry, and you think you prove your case; not so, it is mine you prove; you show that far from being able to reason themselves, children are unable to retain the reasoning of others; for if you follow the method of these little geometricians you will see they only retain the exact impression of the figure and the terms of the demonstration. They cannot meet the slightest new objection; if the figure is reversed they can do nothing. All their knowledge is on the sensation-level, nothing has penetrated to their understanding. Their memory is little better than their other powers, for they always have to learn over again, when they are grown up, what they learnt as children.

I am far from thinking, however, that children have no sort of reason.[1] On the contrary, I think they reason very well with regard to things that affect their actual and sensible well-being. But people are mistaken as to the extent of their information, and they attribute to them knowledge they do not possess, and make them reason about things they cannot understand. Another mistake is to try to turn their attention to matters which do not concern them in the least, such as their future interest, their happiness when they are grown up, the opinion people will have of them when they are men—terms which are absolutely meaningless when addressed to creatures who are entirely without foresight. But all the forced studies of these poor little wretches are directed towards matters utterly remote from their minds. You may judge how much attention they can give to them.

The pedagogues, who make a great display of the teaching they give their pupils, are paid to say just the opposite; yet their actions show that they think just as I do. For what do they teach? Words! words! words! Among the various sciences they boast

[1] I have noticed again and again that it is impossible in writing a lengthy work to use the same words always in the same sense. There is no language rich enough to supply terms and expressions sufficient for the modifications of our ideas. The method of defining every term and constantly substituting the definition for the term defined looks well, but it is impracticable. For how can we escape from our vicious circle? Definitions would be all very well if we did not use words in the making of them. In spite of this I am convinced that even in our poor language we can make our meaning clear, not by always using words in the same sense, but by taking care that every time we use a word the sense in which we use it is sufficiently indicated by the sense of the context, so that each sentence in which the word occurs acts as a sort of definition. Sometimes I say children are incapable of reasoning. Sometimes I say they reason cleverly. I must admit that my words are often contradictory, but I do not think there is any contradiction in my ideas.

of teaching their scholars, they take good care never to choose those which might be really useful to them, for then they would be compelled to deal with things and would fail utterly; the sciences they choose are those we seem to know when we know their technical terms—heraldry, geography, chronology, languages, etc., studies so remote from man, and even more remote from the child, that it is a wonder if he can ever make any use of any part of them.

You will be surprised to find that I reckon the study of languages among the useless lumber of education; but you must remember that I am speaking of the studies of the earliest years, and whatever you may say, I do not believe any child under twelve or fifteen ever really acquired two languages.

If the study of languages were merely the study of words, that is, of the symbols by which language expresses itself, then this might be a suitable study for children; but languages, as they change the symbols, also modify the ideas which the symbols express. Minds are formed by language, thoughts take their colour from its ideas. Reason alone is common to all. Every language has its own form, a difference which may be partly cause and partly effect of differences in national character; this conjecture appears to be confirmed by the fact that in every nation under the sun speech follows the changes of manners, and is preserved or altered along with them.

By use the child acquires one of these different forms, and it is the only language he retains till the age of reason. To acquire two languages he must be able to compare their ideas, and how can he compare ideas he can barely understand? Everything may have a thousand meanings to him, but each idea can only have one form, so he can only learn one language. You assure me he learns several languages; I deny it. I have seen those little prodigies who are supposed to speak half a dozen languages. I have heard them speak first in German, then in Latin, French, or Italian; true, they used half a dozen different vocabularies, but they always spoke German. In a word, you may give children as many synonyms as you like; it is not their language but their words that you change; they will never have but one language.

To conceal their deficiencies teachers choose the dead languages, in which we have no longer any judges whose authority is beyond dispute. The familiar use of these tongues disappeared long ago, so they are content to imitate what they find in books, and they call that talking. If the master's Greek and Latin is such poor stuff, what about the children? They have scarcely learnt their primer by heart, without understanding a word of it, when they are set to translate a French speech into Latin words; then when they are more advanced they piece together a few phrases of Cicero for prose or a few lines of Vergil for verse. Then they think they can speak Latin, and who will contradict them?

In any study whatsoever the symbols are of no value without the idea of the things symbolised. Yet the education of the child is confined to those symbols, while no one ever succeeds in making him understand the thing signified. You think you are teaching him what the world is like; he is only learning the map; he is taught the names of towns, countries, rivers, which have no existence for him except on the paper before him. I remember seeing a geography somewhere which began with: " What is the world? "— " A sphere of cardboard." That is the child's geography. I maintain that after two years' work with the globe and cosmography, there is not a single ten-year-old child who could find his way from Paris to Saint Denis by the help of the rules he has learnt. I maintain that not one of these children could find his way by the map about the paths on his father's estate without getting lost. These are the young doctors who can tell us the position of Pekin, Ispahan, Mexico, and every country in the world.

You tell me the child must be employed on studies which only need eyes. That may be; but if there are any such studies, they are unknown to me.

It is a still more ridiculous error to set them to study history, which is considered within their grasp because it is merely a collection of facts. But what is meant by this word " fact "? Do you think the relations which determine the facts of history are so easy to grasp that the corresponding ideas are easily-developed in the child's mind? Do you think that a real knowledge of events can exist apart from the knowledge of their causes and effects, and that history has so little relation to words that the one can be learnt without the other? If you perceive nothing in a man's actions beyond merely physical and external movements, what do you learn from history? Absolutely nothing; while this study, robbed of all that makes it interesting, gives you neither pleasure nor information. If you want to judge actions by their moral bearings, try to make these moral bearings intelligible to your scholars. You will soon find out if they are old enough to learn history.

Remember, reader, that he who speaks to you is neither a scholar nor a philosopher, but a plain man and a lover of truth; a man who is pledged to no one party or system, a hermit, who mixes little with other men, and has less opportunity of imbibing their prejudices, and more time to reflect on the things that strike him in his intercourse with them. My arguments are based less on theories than on facts, and I think I can find no better way to bring the facts home to you than by quoting continually some example from the observations which suggested my arguments.

I had gone to spend a few days in the country with a worthy mother of a family who took great pains with her children and their education. One morning I was present while the eldest boy had his lessons. His tutor, who had taken great pains to teach him ancient history, began upon the story of Alexander and lighted on the well-known anecdote of Philip the Doctor. There is a picture of it, and the story is well worth study. The tutor, worthy man, made several reflections which I did not like with regard to Alexander's courage, but I did not argue with him lest I should lower him in the eyes of his pupil. At dinner they did not fail to set the little fellow talking, French fashion. The eager spirit of a child of his age, and the confident expectation of applause, made him say a number of silly things, and among them from time to time there were things to the point, and these made people forget the rest. At last came the story of Philip the Doctor. He told it very distinctly and prettily. After the usual meed of praise, demanded by his mother and expected by the child himself, they discussed what he had said. Most of them blamed Alexander's rashness, some of them, following the tutor's example, praised his resolution, which showed me that none of those present really saw the beauty of the story. "For my own part," I said, "if there was any courage or any steadfastness at all in Alexander's conduct I think it was only a piece of bravado." Then every one agreed that it was a piece of bravado. I was getting angry, and would have replied, when a lady sitting beside me, who had not hitherto spoken, bent towards me and whispered in my ear. "Jean Jacques," said she, "say no more, they will never understand you." I looked at her, I recognised the wisdom of her advice, and I held my tongue.

Several things made me suspect that our young professor had not in the least understood the story he told so prettily. After dinner I took his hand in mine and we went for a walk in the park. When I had questioned him quietly, I discovered that he admired the vaunted courage of Alexander more than any one. But in what do you suppose he thought this courage consisted? Merely in swallowing a disagreeable drink at a single draught without hesitation and without any signs of dislike. Not a fortnight before the poor child had been made to take some medicine which he could hardly swallow, and the taste of it was still in his mouth. Death, and death by poisoning, were for him only disagreeable sensations, and senna was his only idea of poison. I must admit, however, that Alexander's resolution had made a great impression on his young mind, and he was determined that next time he had to take medicine he would be an Alexander. Without entering upon explanations which were clearly beyond his grasp, I confirmed him in his praiseworthy intention, and returned home smiling to myself over the great wisdom of parents and teachers who expect to teach history to children.

Such words as king, emperor, war, conquest, law, and revolution are easily put into their mouths; but when it is a question of attaching clear ideas to these words the explanations are very different from our talk with Robert the gardener.

I feel sure some readers dissatisfied with that "Say no more, Jean Jacques," will ask what I really saw to admire in the conduct of Alexander. Poor things! if you need telling, how can you comprehend it? Alexander believed in virtue, he staked his head, he staked his own life on that faith, his great soul was fitted to hold such a faith. To swallow that draught was to make a noble profession of the faith that was in him. Never did mortal man recite a finer creed. If there is an Alexander in our own days, show me such deeds.

If children have no knowledge of words, there is no study that is suitable for them. If they have no real ideas they have no real memory, for I do not call that a memory which only recalls sensations. What is the use of inscribing on their brains a list of symbols which mean nothing to them? They will learn the symbols when they learn the things signified; why give them the useless trouble of learning them twice over? And yet what dangerous prejudices are you implanting when you teach them to accept as knowledge words which have no meaning for them. The first meaningless phrase, the first thing taken for granted on the word of another person without seeing its use for himself, this is the beginning of the ruin of the child's judgment. He may dazzle the eyes of fools long enough before he recovers from such a loss.[1]

No, if nature has given the child this plasticity of brain which fits him to receive every kind of impression, it was not that you should imprint on it the names and dates of kings, the jargon of heraldry, the globe and geography, all those words without present meaning or future use for the child, which flood of words overwhelms his sad and barren childhood. But by means of this plasticity all the ideas he can understand and use, all that concern his happiness and will some day throw light upon his duties, should be traced at an early age in indelible characters upon his brain, to guide him to live in such a way as befits his nature and his powers.

Without the study of books, such a memory as the child may possess is not left idle; everything he sees and hears makes an impression on him, he keeps a record of men's sayings and doings, and his whole environment is the book from which he unconsciously enriches his memory, till his judgment is able to profit by it.

To select these objects, to take care to present him constantly with those he may know, to conceal from him those he ought not to know, this is the real way of training his early memory; and in this way you must try to provide him with a storehouse of knowledge which will serve for his education in youth and his conduct throughout life. True, this method does not produce infant prodigies, nor will it reflect glory upon their tutors and governesses, but it produces men, strong, right-thinking men, vigorous both in mind

[1] The learning of most philosophers is like the learning of children. Vast erudition results less in the multitude of ideas than in a multitude of images. Dates, names, places, all objects isolated or unconnected with ideas are merely retained in the memory for symbols, and we rarely recall any of these without seeing the right or left page of the book in which we read it, or the form in which we first saw it. Most science was of this kind till recently. The science of our times is another matter; study and observation are things of the past; we dream and the dreams of a bad night are given to us as philosophy. You will say I too am a dreamer; I admit it, but I do what the others fail to do, I give my dreams as dreams, and leave the reader to discover whether there is anything in them which may prove useful to those who are awake.

and body, men who do not win admiration as children, but honour as men.

Emile will not learn anything by heart, not even fables, not even the fables of La Fontaine, simple and delightful as they are, for the words are no more the fable than the words of history are history. How can people be so blind as to call fables the child's system of morals, without considering that the child is not only amused by the apologue but misled by it? He is attracted by what is false and he misses the truth, and the means adopted to make the teaching pleasant prevent him profiting by it. Men may be taught by fables; children require the naked truth.

All children learn La Fontaine's fables, but not one of them understands them. It is just as well that they do not understand, for the morality of the fables is so mixed and so unsuitable for their age that it would be more likely to incline them to vice than to virtue. "More paradoxes!" you exclaim. Paradoxes they may be; but let us see if there is not some truth in them.

I maintain that the child does not understand the fables he is taught, for however you try to explain them, the teaching you wish to extract from them demands ideas which he cannot grasp, while the poetical form which makes it easier to remember makes it harder to understand, so that clearness is sacrificed to facility. Without quoting the host of wholly unintelligible and useless fables which are taught to children because they happen to be in the same book as the others, let us keep to those which the author seems to have written specially for children.

In the whole of La Fontaine's works I only know five or six fables conspicuous for child-like simplicity; I will take the first of these as an example, for it is one whose moral is most suitable for all ages, one which children get hold of with the least difficulty, which they have most pleasure in learning, one which for this very reason the author has placed at the beginning of his book. If his object were really to delight and instruct children, this fable is his masterpiece. Let us go through it and examine it briefly.

THE FOX AND THE CROW

A FABLE

"Maître corbeau, sur un arbre perché" (Mr. Crow perched on a tree).—"Mr.!" what does that word really mean? What does it mean before a proper noun? What is its meaning here? What is a crow? What is "un arbre perché"? We do not say "on a tree perched," but perched on a tree. So we must speak of poetical inversions, we must distinguish between prose and verse.

"Tenait dans son bec un fromage" (Held a cheese in his beak)—What sort of a cheese? Swiss, Brie, or Dutch? If the child has never seen crows, what is the good of talking about them? If he has seen crows will he believe that they can hold a cheese in their beak? Your illustrations should always be taken from nature.

"Maître renard, par l'odeur alléché" (Mr. Fox, attracted by the smell).—Another Master! But the title suits the fox, who is master of all the tricks of his trade. You must explain what a fox is, and distinguish between the real fox and the conventional fox of the fables.

"Alléché." The word is obsolete; you will have to explain it. You will say it is only used in verse. Perhaps the child will ask why people talk differently in verse. How will you answer that question?

"Alléché, par l'odeur d'un fromage." The cheese was held in his beak by a crow perched on a tree; it must indeed have smelt strong if the fox, in his thicket or his earth, could smell it. This is the way you train your pupil in that spirit of right judgment, which rejects all but reasonable arguments, and is able to distinguish between truth and falsehood in other tales.

"Lui tient à peu près ce langage" (Spoke to him after this fashion).—"Ce langage." So foxes talk, do they! They talk like crows! Mind what you are about, oh, wise tutor; weigh your answer before you give it, it is more important than you suspect.

"Eh! Bonjour, Monsieur le Corbeau!" ("Good-day, Mr. Crow!")—Mr.! The child sees this title laughed to scorn before he knows it is a title of honour. Those who say "Monsieur du Corbeau" will find their work cut out for them to explain that "du."

"Que vous êtes joli! Que vous me semblez beau!" ("How handsome you are, how beautiful in my eyes!")—Mere padding. The child, finding the same thing repeated twice over in different words, is learning to speak carelessly. If you say this redundance is a device of the author, a part of the fox's scheme to make his praise seem all the greater by his flow of words, that is a valid excuse for me, but not for my pupil.

"Sans mentir, si votre ramage" ("Without lying, if your song").—"Without lying." So people do tell lies sometimes. What will the child think of you if you tell him the fox only says "Sans mentir" because he is lying?

"Repondait à votre plumage" ("Answered to your fine feathers").—"Answered!" What does that mean? Try to make the child compare qualities so different as those of song and plumage; you will see how much he understands.

"Vous seriez le phénix des hôtes de ces bois!" ("You would be the phœnix of all the inhabitants of this wood!")—The phœnix! What is a phœnix? All of a sudden we are floundering in the lies of antiquity—we are on the edge of mythology.

"The inhabitants of this wood." What figurative language! The flatterer adopts the grand style to add dignity to his speech, to make it more attractive. Will the child understand this cunning? Does he know, how could he possibly know, what is meant by grand style and simple style?

"A ces mots le corbeau ne se sent pas de joie" (At these words, the crow is beside himself with delight).—To realise the full force of this proverbial expression we must have experienced very strong feeling.

"Et, pour montrer sa belle voix" (And, to show his fine voice).— Remember that the child, to understand this line and the whole fable, must know what is meant by the crow's fine voice.

"Il ouvre un large bec, laisse tomber sa proie" (He opens his wide beak and drops his prey).—This is a splendid line; its very sound suggests a picture. I see the great big ugly gaping beak, I hear the cheese crashing through the branches; but this kind of beauty is thrown away upon children.

"Le renard s'en saisit, et dit, 'Mon bon monsieur'" (The fox catches it, and says, "My dear sir").—So kindness is already folly. You certainly waste no time in teaching your children.

"Apprenez que tout flatteur" ("You must learn that every flatterer").—A general maxim. The child can make neither head nor tail of it.

"Vit au depens de celui qui l'écoute" ("Lives at the expense of the person who listens to his flattery").—No child of ten ever understood that.

"Ce leçon vaut bien un fromage, sans doute" ("No doubt this lesson is well worth a cheese").—This is intelligible and its meaning is very good. Yet there are few children who could compare a cheese and a lesson, few who would not prefer the cheese. You will therefore have to make them understand that this is said in mockery. What subtlety for a child!

"Le corbeau, honteux et confus" (The crow, ashamed and confused).—Anothing pleonasm, and there is no excuse for it this time.

"Jura, mais un peu tard, qu'on ne l'y prendrait plus" (Swore, but rather too late, that he would not be caught in that way again). —"Swore." What master will be such a fool as to try to explain to a child the meaning of an oath?

What a host of details! but much more would be needed for the analysis of all the ideas in this fable and their reduction to the simple and elementary ideas of which each is composed. But who thinks this analysis necessary to make himself intelligible to children? Who of us is philosopher enough to be able to put himself in the child's place? Let us now proceed to the moral.

Should we teach a six-year-old child that there are people who flatter and lie for the sake of gain? One might perhaps teach them that there are people who make fools of little boys and laugh at their foolish vanity behind their backs. But the whole thing is spoilt by the cheese. You are teaching them how to make another drop his cheese rather than how to keep their own. This is my second paradox, and it is not less weighty than the former one.

Watch children learning their fables and you will see that when they have a chance of applying them they almost always use them exactly contrary to the author's meaning; instead of being on their guard against the fault which you would prevent or cure, they are disposed to like the vice by which one takes advantage of another's defects. In the above fable children laugh at the crow, but they all love the fox. In the next fable you expect them to follow the example of the grasshopper. Not so, they will choose the ant. They do not care to abase themselves, they will always choose the principal part—this is the choice of self-love, a very natural choice. But what a dreadful lesson for children! There could be no monster more detestable than a harsh and avaricious child, who realised what he was asked to give and what he refused. The ant does more; she teaches him not merely to refuse but to revile.

In all the fables where the lion plays a part, usually the chief part, the child pretends to be the lion, and when he has to preside over some distribution of good things, he takes care to keep everything for himself; but when the lion is overthrown by the gnat, the child is the gnat. He learns how to sting to death those whom he dare not attack openly.

From the fable of the sleek dog and the starving wolf he learns a lesson of licence rather than the lesson of moderation which you profess to teach him. I shall never forget seeing a little girl weeping bitterly over this tale, which had been told her as a lesson in obedience. The poor child hated to be chained up; she felt the chain chafing her neck; she was crying because she was not a wolf.

So from the first of these fables the child learns the basest flattery; from the second, cruelty; from the third, injustice; from the fourth, satire; from the fifth, insubordination. The last of these lessons is no more suitable for your pupils than for mine, though he has no use for it. What results do you expect to get from your teaching when it contradicts itself? But perhaps the same system of morals which furnishes me with objections against the fables supplies you with as many reasons for keeping to them. Society requires a rule of morality in our words; it also requires a rule of morality in our deeds; and these two rules are quite different. The former is contained in the Catechism and it is left there; the other is contained in La Fontaine's fables for children and his tales for mothers. The same author does for both.

Let us make a bargain, M. de la Fontaine. For my own part, I undertake to make your books my favourite study; I undertake to love you, and to learn from your fables, for I hope I shall not mistake their meaning. As to my pupil, permit me to prevent him studying any one of them till you have convinced me that it is good for him to learn things three-fourths of which are unintelligible to him, and until you can convince me that in those fables he can understand he will never reverse the order and imitate the villain instead of taking warning from his dupe.

When I thus get rid of children's lessons, I get rid of the chief cause of their sorrows, namely their books. Reading is the curse of childhood, yet it is almost the only occupation you can find for children. Emile, at twelve years old, will hardly know what a book is. "But," you say, "he must, at least, know how to read."

When reading is of use to him, I admit he must learn to read, but till then he will only find it a nuisance.

If children are not to be required to do anything as a matter of obedience, it follows that they will only learn what they perceive to be of real and present value, either for use or enjoyment; what other motive could they have for learning? The art of speaking to our absent friends, of hearing their words; the art of letting them know at first hand our feelings, our desires, and our longings, is an art whose usefulness can be made plain at any age. How is it that this art, so useful and pleasant in itself, has become a terror to children? Because the child is compelled to acquire it against his will, and to use it for purposes beyond his comprehension. A child has no great wish to perfect himself in the use of an instrument of torture, but make it a means to his pleasure, and soon you will not be able to keep him from it.

People make a great fuss about discovering the best way to teach children to read. They invent " bureaux " [1] and cards, they turn the nursery into a printer's shop. Locke would have them taught to read by means of dice. What a fine idea! And the pity of it! There is a better way than any of those, and one which is generally overlooked—it consists in the desire to learn. Arouse this desire in your scholar and have done with your " bureaux " and your dice —any method will serve.

Present interest, that is the motive power, the only motive power that takes us far and safely. Sometimes Emile receives notes of invitation from his father or mother, his relations or friends; he is invited to a dinner, a walk, a boating expedition, to see some public entertainment. These notes are short, clear, plain, and well written. Some one must read them to him, and he cannot always find anybody when wanted; no more consideration is shown to him than he himself showed to you yesterday. Time passes, the chance is lost. The note is read to him at last, but it is too late. Oh! if only he had known how to read! He receives other notes, so short, so interesting, he would like to try to read them. Sometimes he gets help, sometimes none. He does his best, and at last he makes out half the note; it is something about going to-morrow to drink cream— Where? With whom? He cannot tell—how hard he tries to make out the rest! I do not think Emile will need a " bureau." Shall I proceed to the teaching of writing? No, I am ashamed to toy with these trifles in a treatise on education.

I will just add a few words which contain a principle of great importance. It is this—What we are in no hurry to get is usually obtained with speed and certainty. I am pretty sure Emile will learn to read and write before he is ten, just because I care very little whether he can do so before he is fifteen; but I would rather

[1] *Translator's note.*—The " bureau " was a sort of case containing letters to be put together to form words. It was a favourite device for the teaching of reading and gave its name to a special method, called the bureau-method, of learning to read.

he never learnt to read at all, than that this art should be acquired at the price of all that makes reading useful. What is the use of reading to him if he always hates it? " Id imprimis cavere oportebit, ne studia, qui amare nondum potest, oderit, et amaritudinem semel perceptam etiam ultra rudes annos reformidet."—Qvintil.

The more I urge my method of letting well alone, the more objections I perceive against it. If your pupil learns nothing from you, he will learn from others. If you do not instil truth he will learn falsehoods; the prejudices you fear to teach him he will acquire from those about him, they will find their way through every one of his senses; they will either corrupt his reason before it is fully developed or his mind will become torpid through inaction, and will become engrossed in material things. If we do not form the habit of thinking as children, we shall lose the power of thinking for the rest of our life.

I fancy I could easily answer that objection, but why should I answer every objection? If my method itself answers your objections, it is good; if not, it is good for nothing. I continue my explanation.

If, in accordance with the plan I have sketched, you follow rules which are just the opposite of the established practice, if instead of taking your scholar far afield, instead of wandering with him in distant places, in far-off lands, in remote centuries, in the ends of the earth, and in the very heavens themselves, you try to keep him to himself, to his own concerns, you will then find him able to perceive, to remember, and even to reason; this is nature's order. As the sentient being becomes active his discernment develops along with his strength. Not till his strength is in excess of what is needed for self-preservation, is the speculative faculty developed, the faculty adapted for using this superfluous strength for other purposes. Would you cultivate your pupil's intelligence, cultivate the strength it is meant to control. Give his body constant exercise, make it strong and healthy, in order to make him good and wise; let him work, let him do things, let him run and shout, let him be always on the go; make a man of him in strength, and he will soon be a man in reason.

Of course by this method you will make him stupid if you are always giving him directions, always saying come here, go there, stop, do this, don't do that. If your head always guides his hands, his own mind will become useless. But remember the conditions we laid down; if you are a mere pedant it is not worth your while to read my book.

It is a lamentable mistake to imagine that bodily activity hinders the working of the mind, as if these two kinds of activity ought not to advance hand in hand, and as if the one were not intended to act as guide to the other.

There are two classes of men who are constantly engaged in bodily activity, peasants and savages, and certainly neither of these pays the least attention to the cultivation of the mind. Peasants are rough, coarse, and clumsy; savages are noted, not only for their keen senses, but for great subtility of mind. Speaking generally, there is nothing duller than a peasant or sharper than a savage. What is the cause of this difference? The peasant has always done as he was told, what his father did before him, what he himself has always done; he is the creature of habit, he spends his life almost like an automaton on the same tasks; habit and obedience have taken the place of reason.

The case of the savage is very different; he is tied to no one place, he has no prescribed task, no superior to obey, he knows no law but his own will; he is therefore forced to reason at every step he takes. He can neither move nor walk without considering the consequences. Thus the more his body is exercised, the more alert is his mind; his strength and his reason increase together, and each helps to develop the other.

Oh, learned tutor, let us see which of our two scholars is most like the savage and which is most like the peasant. Your scholar is subject to a power which is continually giving him instruction; he acts only at the word of command; he dare not eat when he is hungry, nor laugh when he is merry, nor weep when he is sad, nor offer one hand rather than the other, nor stir a foot unless he is told to do it; before long he will not venture to breathe without orders. What would you have him think about, when you do all the thinking for him? He rests securely on your foresight, why should he think for himself? He knows you have undertaken to take care of him, to secure his welfare, and he feels himself freed from this responsibility. His judgment relies on yours; what you have not forbidden that he does, knowing that he runs no risk. Why should he learn the signs of rain? He knows you watch the clouds for him. Why should he time his walk? He knows there is no fear of your letting him miss his dinner hour. He eats till you tell him to stop, he stops when you tell him to do so; he does not attend to the teaching of his own stomach, but yours. In vain do you make his body soft by inaction; his understanding does not become subtle. Far from it, you complete your task of discrediting reason in his eyes, by making him use such reasoning power as he has on the things which seem of least importance to him. As he never finds his reason any use to him, he decides at last that it is useless. If he reasons badly he will be found fault with; nothing worse will happen to him; and he has been found fault with so often that he pays no attention to it, such a common danger no longer alarms him.

Yet you will find he has a mind. He is quick enough to chatter with the women in the way I spoke of further back; but if he is in danger, if he must come to a decision in difficult circumstances, you will find him a hundredfold more stupid and silly than the son of the roughest labourer.

As for my pupil, or rather Nature's pupil, he has been trained from the outset to be as self-reliant as possible, he has not formed the habit of constantly seeking help from others, still less of displaying his stores of learning. On the other hand, he exercises discrimination and forethought, he reasons about everything that concerns himself. He does not chatter, he acts. Not a word does he know of what is going on in the world at large, but he knows very thoroughly what affects himself. As he is always stirring he is compelled to notice many things, to recognise many effects; he soon acquires a good deal of experience. Nature, not man, is his schoolmaster, and he learns all the quicker because he is not aware that he has any lesson to learn. So mind and body work together. He is always carrying out his own ideas, not those of other people, and thus he unites thought and action; as he grows in health and strength he grows in wisdom and discernment. This is the way to attain later on to what is generally considered incompatible, though most great men have achieved it, strength of body and strength of mind, the reason of the philosopher and the vigour of the athlete.

Young teacher, I am setting before you a difficult task, the art of controlling without precepts, and doing everything without doing anything at all. This art is, I confess, beyond your years, it is not calculated to display your talents nor to make your value known to your scholar's parents; but it is the only road to success. You will never succeed in making wise men if you do not first make little imps of mischief. This was the education of the Spartans; they were not taught to stick to their books, they were set to steal their dinners. Were they any the worse for it in after life? Ever ready for victory, they crushed their foes in every kind of warfare, and the prating Athenians were as much afraid of their words as of their blows.

When education is most carefully attended to, the teacher issues his orders and thinks himself master, but it is the child who is really master. He uses the tasks you set him to obtain what he wants from you, and he can always make you pay for an hour's industry by a week's complaisance. You must always be making bargains with him. These bargains, suggested in your fashion, but carried out in his, always follow the direction of his own fancies, especially when you are foolish enough to make the condition some advantage he is almost sure to obtain, whether he fulfils his part of the bargain or not. The child is usually much quicker to read the master's thoughts than the master to read the child's feelings. And that is as it should be, for all the sagacity which the child would have devoted to self-preservation, had he been left to himself, is now devoted to the rescue of his native freedom from the chains of his tyrant; while the latter, who has no such pressing need to understand the child, sometimes finds that it pays him better to leave him in idleness or vanity.

Take the opposite course with your pupil; let him always think he is master while you are really master. There is no subjection so complete as that which preserves the forms of freedom; it is thus that the will itself is taken captive. Is not this poor child, without knowledge, strength, or wisdom, entirely at your mercy? Are you not master of his whole environment so far as it affects him? Cannot you make of him what you please ? His work and play, his pleasure and pain, are they not, unknown to him, under your control ? No doubt he ought only to do what he wants, but he ought to want to do nothing but what you want him to do. He should never take a step you have not foreseen, nor utter a word you could not foretell.

Then he can devote himself to the bodily exercises adapted to his age without brutalising his mind; instead of developing his cunning to evade an unwelcome control, you will then find him entirely occupied in getting the best he can out of his environment with a view to his present welfare, and you will be surprised by the subtlety of the means he devises to get for himself such things as he can obtain, and to really enjoy things without the aid of other people's ideas. You leave him master of his own wishes, but you do not multiply his caprices. When he only does what he wants, he will soon only do what he ought, and although his body is constantly in motion, so far as his sensible and present interests are concerned, you will find him developing all the reason of which he is capable, far better and in a manner much better fitted for him than in purely theoretical studies.

Thus when he does not find you continually thwarting him, when he no longer distrusts you, no longer has anything to conceal from you, he will neither tell you lies nor deceive you; he will show himself fearlessly as he really is, and you can study him at your ease, and surround him with all the lessons you would have him learn, without awaking his suspicions.

Neither will he keep a curious and jealous eye on your own conduct, nor take a secret delight in catching you at fault. It is a great thing to avoid this. One of the child's first objects is, as I have said, to find the weak spots in its rulers. Though this leads to spitefulness, it does not arise from it, but from the desire to evade a disagreeable control. Overburdened by the yoke laid upon him, he tries to shake it off, and the faults he finds in his master give him a good opportunity for this. Still the habit of spying out faults and delighting in them grows upon people. Clearly we have stopped another of the springs of vice in Emile's heart. Having nothing to gain from my faults, he will not be on the watch for them, nor will he be tempted to look out for the faults of others.

All these methods seem difficult because they are new to us, but they ought not to be really difficult. I have a right to assume that you have the knowledge required for the business you have chosen; that you know the usual course of development of the human thought, that you can study mankind and man, that you know beforehand the effect on your pupil's will of the various objects suited to his age which you put before him. You have the tools and the art to use them; are you not master of your trade ?

You speak of childish caprice; you are mistaken. Children's caprices are never the work of nature, but of bad discipline; they have either obeyed or given orders, and I have said again and again, they must do neither. Your pupil will have the caprices you have taught him; it is fair you should bear the punishment of your own faults. "But how can I cure them?" do you say? That may still be done by better conduct on your own part and great patience. I once undertook the charge of a child for a few weeks; he was accustomed not only to have his own way, but to make every one else do as he pleased; he was therefore capricious. The very first day he wanted to get up at midnight, to try how far he could go with me. When I was sound asleep he jumped out of bed, got his dressing-gown, and waked me up. I got up and lighted the candle, which was all he wanted. After a quarter of an hour he became sleepy and went back to bed quite satisfied with his experiment. Two days later he repeated it, with the same success and with no sign of impatience on my part. When he kissed me as he lay down, I said to him very quietly, "My little dear, this is all very well, but do not try it again." His curiosity was aroused by this, and the very next day he did not fail to get up at the same time and woke me to see whether I should dare to disobey him. I asked what he wanted, and he told me he could not sleep. "So much the worse for you," I replied, and I lay quiet. He seemed perplexed by this way of speaking. He felt his way to the flint and steel and tried to strike a light. I could not help laughing when I heard him strike his fingers. Convinced at last that he could not manage it, he brought the steel to my bed; I told him I did not want it, and I turned my back to him. Then he began to rush wildly about the room, shouting, singing, making a great noise, knocking against chairs and tables, but taking, however, good care not to hurt himself seriously, but screaming loudly in the hope of alarming me. All this had no effect, but I perceived that though he was prepared for scolding or anger, he was quite unprepared for indifference.

However, he was determined to overcome my patience with his own obstinacy, and he continued his racket so successfully that at last I lost my temper. I foresaw that I should spoil the whole business by an unseemly outburst of passion. I determined on another course. I got up quietly, went to the tinder box, but could not find it; I asked him for it, and he gave it me, delighted to have won the victory over me. I struck a light, lighted the candle, took my young gentleman by the hand and led him quietly into an adjoining dressing-room with the shutters firmly fastened, and nothing he could break.

I left him there without a light; then locking him in I went back to my bed without a word. What a noise there was! That was what I expected, and took no notice. At last the noise ceased; I listened, heard him settling down, and I was quite easy about him. Next morning I entered the room at daybreak, and my little rebel was lying on a sofa enjoying a sound and much needed sleep after his exertions.

The matter did not end there. His mother heard that the child had spent a great part of the night out of bed. That spoilt the whole thing; her child was as good as dead. Finding a good chance for revenge, he pretended to be ill, not seeing that he would gain nothing by it. They sent for the doctor. Unluckily for the mother, the doctor was a practical joker, and to amuse himself with her terrors he did his best to increase them. However, he whispered to me, " Leave it to me, I promise to cure the child of wanting to be ill for some time to come." As a matter of fact he prescribed bed and dieting, and the child was handed over to the apothecary. I sighed to see the mother. cheated on every hand except by me, whom she hated because I did not deceive her.

After pretty severe reproaches, she told me her son was delicate, that he was the sole heir of the family, his life must be preserved at all costs, and she would not have him contradicted. In that I thoroughly agreed with her, but what she meant by contradicting was not obeying him in everything. I saw I should have to treat the mother as I had treated the son. " Madam," I said coldly, " I do not know how to educate the heir to a fortune, and what is more, I do not mean to study that art. You can take that as settled." I was wanted for some days longer, and the father smoothed things over. The mother wrote to the tutor to hasten his return, and the child, finding he got nothing by disturbing my rest, nor yet by being ill, decided at last to get better and to go to sleep.

You can form no idea of the number of similar caprices to which the little tyrant had subjected his unlucky tutor; for his education was carried on under his mother's eye, and she would not allow her son and heir to be disobeyed in anything. Whenever he wanted to go out, you must be ready to take him, or rather to follow him, and he always took good care to choose the time when he knew his tutor was very busy. He wished to exercise the same power over me and to avenge himself by day for having to leave me in peace at night. I gladly agreed and began by showing plainly how pleased I was to give him pleasure; after that when it was a matter of curing him of his fancies I set about it differently.

In the first place, he must be shown that he was in the wrong. This was not difficult; knowing that children think only of the present, I took the easy advantage which foresight gives; I took care to provide him with some indoor amusement of which he was very fond. Just when he was most occupied with it, I went and suggested a short walk, and he sent me away. I insisted, but he paid no attention. I had to give in, and he took note of this sign of submission.

The next day it was my turn. As I expected, he got tired of his occupation; I, however, pretended to be very busy. That was enough to decide him. He came to drag me from my work, to take him at once for a walk. I refused; he persisted. " No," I said, " when I did what you wanted, you taught me how to get my own way; I shall not go out." " Very well," he replied eagerly, " I shall go out by myself." " As you please," and I returned to my work.

He put on his things rather uneasily when he saw I did not follow his example. When he was ready he came and made his bow; I bowed too; he tried to frighten me with stories of the expeditions he was going to make; to hear him talk you would think he was going to the world's end. Quite unmoved, I wished him a pleasant journey. He became more and more perplexed. However, he put a good face on it, and when he was ready to go out he told his footman to follow him. The footman, who had his instructions, replied that he had no time, and that he was busy carrying out my orders, and he must obey me first. For the moment the child was taken aback. How could he think they would really let him go out alone, him, who, in his own eyes, was the most important person in the world, who thought that everything in heaven and earth was wrapped up in his welfare? However, he was beginning to feel his weakness, he perceived that he should find himself alone among people who knew nothing of him. He saw beforehand the risks he would run; obstinacy alone sustained him; very slowly and unwillingly he went downstairs. At last he went out into the street, consoling himself a little for the harm that might happen to himself, in the hope that I should be held responsible for it.

This was just what I expected. All was arranged beforehand, and as it meant some sort of public scene I had got his father's consent. He had scarcely gone a few steps, when he heard, first on this side then on that, all sorts of remarks about himself. "What a pretty little gentleman, neighbour? Where is he going all alone? He will get lost! I will ask him into our house." "Take care you don't. Don't you see he is a naughty little boy, who has been turned out of his own house because he is good for nothing? You must not stop naughty boys; let him go where he likes." "Well, well; the good God take care of him. I should be sorry if anything happened to him." A little further on he met some young urchins of about his own age who teased him and made fun of him. The further he got the more difficulties he found. Alone and unprotected he was at the mercy of everybody, and he found to his great surprise that his shoulder knot and his gold lace commanded no respect.

However, I had got a friend of mine, who was a stranger to him, to keep an eye on him. Unnoticed by him, this friend followed him step by step, and in due time he spoke to him. The rôle, like that of Sbrigani in *Pourceaugnac*, required an intelligent actor, and it was played to perfection. Without making the child fearful and timid by inspiring excessive terror, he made him realise so thoroughly the folly of his exploit that in half an hour's time he brought him home to me, ashamed and humble, and afraid to look me in the face.

To put the finishing touch to his discomfiture, just as he was coming in his father came down on his way out and met him on the stairs. He had to explain where he had been, and why I was not with him.[1] The poor child would gladly have sunk into the earth

---

[1] In a case like this there is no danger in asking a child to tell the truth, for he knows very well that it cannot be hid, and that if he ventured to tell a lie he would be found out at once.

His father did not take the trouble to scold him at length, but said with more severity than I should have expected, " When you want to go out by yourself, you can do so, but I will not have a rebel in my house, so when you go, take good care that you never come back."

As for me, I received him somewhat gravely, but without blame and without mockery, and for fear he should find out we had been playing with him, I declined to take him out walking that day. Next day I was well pleased to find that he passed in triumph with me through the very same people who had mocked him the previous day, when they met him out by himself. You may be sure he never threatened to go out without me again.

By these means and other like them I succeeded during the short time I was with him in getting him to do everything I wanted without bidding him or forbidding him to do anything, without preaching or exhortation, without wearying him with unnecessary lessons. So he was pleased when I spoke to him, but when I was silent he was frightened, for he knew there was something amiss, and he always got his lesson from the thing itself. But let us return to our subject.

The body is strengthened by this constant exercise under the guidance of nature herself, and far from brutalising the mind, this exercise develops in it the only kind of reason of which young children are capable, the kind of reason most necessary at every age. It teaches us how to use our strength, to perceive the relations between our own and neighbouring bodies, to use the natural tools, which are within our reach and adapted to our senses. Is there anything sillier than a child brought up indoors under his mother's eye, who, in his ignorance of weight and resistance, tries to uproot a tall tree or pick up a rock. The first time I found myself outside Geneva I tried to catch a galloping horse, and I threw stones at Mont Salève, two leagues away; I was the laughing stock of the whole village, and was supposed to be a regular idiot. At eighteen we are taught in our natural philosophy the use of the lever; every village boy of twelve knows how to use a lever better than the cleverest mechanician in the academy. The lessons the scholars learn from one another in the playground are worth a hundredfold more than what they learn in the class-room.

Watch a cat when she comes into a room for the first time; she goes from place to place, she sniffs about and examines everything, she is never still for a moment; she is suspicious of everything till she has examined it and found out what it is. It is the same with the child when he begins to walk, and enters, so to speak, the room of the world around him. The only difference is that, while both use sight, the child uses his hands and the cat that subtle sense of smell which nature has bestowed upon it. It is this instinct, rightly or wrongly educated, which makes children skilful or clumsy, quick or slow, wise or foolish.

As a man's first natural impulse is to measure himself with his environment, to discover in every object he sees those sensible qualities which may concern himself, so his first study is a kind of experimental physics for his own preservation. He is turned away from this and sent to speculative studies before he has found his proper place in the world. While his delicate and flexible limbs can adjust themselves to the bodies upon which they are intended to act, while his senses are keen and as yet free from illusions, then is the time to exercise both limbs and senses in their proper business. It is the time to learn to perceive the physical relations between ourselves and things. Since everything that comes into the human mind enters through the gates of sense, man's first reason is a reason of sense-experience. It is this that serves as a foundation for the reason of the intelligence; our first teachers in natural philosophy are our feet, hands, and eyes. To substitute books for them does not teach us to reason, it teaches us to use the reason of others rather than our own; it teaches us to believe much and know little.

Before you can practise an art you must first get your tools; and if you are to make good use of those tools, they must be fashioned sufficiently strong to stand use. To learn to think we must therefore exercise our limbs, our senses, and our bodily organs, which are the tools of the intellect; and to get the best use out of these tools, the body which supplies us with them must be strong and healthy. Not only is it quite a mistake that true reason is developed apart from the body, but it is a good bodily constitution which makes the workings of the mind easy and correct.

While I am showing how the child's long period of leisure should be spent, I am entering into details which may seem absurd. You will say, " This is a strange sort of education, and it is subject to your own criticism, for it only teaches what no one needs to learn. Why spend your time in teaching what will come of itself without care or trouble? Is there any child of twelve who is ignorant of all you wish to teach your pupil, while he also knows what his master has taught him."

Gentlemen, you are mistaken. I am teaching my pupil an art the acquirement of which demands much time and trouble, an art which your scholars certainly do not possess; it is the art of being ignorant; for the knowledge of any one who only thinks he knows, what he really does know is a very small matter. You teach science; well and good; I am busy fashioning the necessary tools for its acquisition. Once upon a time, they say the Venetians were displaying the treasures of the Cathedral of Saint Mark to the Spanish ambassador; the only comment he made was, " Qui non c'e la radice." When I see a tutor showing off his pupil's learning, I am always tempted to say the same to him.

Every one who has considered the manner of life among the ancients, attributes the strength of body and mind by which they are distinguished from the men of our own day to their gymnastic exercises. The stress laid by Montaigne upon this opinion, shows that it had made a great impression on him; he returns to it again and again. Speaking of a child's education he says, "To strengthen the mind you must harden the muscles; by training the child to labour you train him to suffering; he must be broken in to the hardships of gymnastic exercises to prepare him for the hardships of dislocations, colics, and other bodily ills." The philosopher Locke, the worthy Rollin, the learned Fleury, the pedant De Crouzas, differing as they do so widely from one another, are agreed in this one matter of sufficient bodily exercise for children. This is the wisest of their precepts, and the one which is certain to be neglected. I have already dwelt sufficiently on its importance, and as better reasons and more sensible rules cannot be found than those in Locke's book, I will content myself with referring to it, after taking the liberty of adding a few remarks of my own.

The limbs of a growing child should be free to move easily in his clothing; nothing should cramp their growth or movement; there should be nothing tight, nothing fitting closely to the body, no belts of any kind. The French style of dress, uncomfortable and un-healthy for a man, is especially bad for children. The stagnant humours, whose circulation is interrupted, putrify in a state of inaction, and this process proceeds more rapidly in an inactive and sedentary life; they become corrupt and give rise to scurvy; this disease, which is continually on the increase among us, was almost unknown to the ancients, whose way of dressing and living pro-tected them from it. The hussar's dress, far from correcting this fault, increases it, and compresses the whole of the child's body, by way of dispensing with a few bands. The best plan is to keep children in frocks as long as possible and then to provide them with loose clothing, without trying to define the shape which is only another way of deforming it. Their defects of body and mind may all be traced to the same source, the desire to make men of them before their time.

There are bright colours and dull; children like the bright colours best, and they suit them better too. I see no reason why such natural suitability should not be taken into consideration; but as soon as they prefer a material because it is rich, their hearts are already given over to luxury, to every caprice of fashion, and this taste is certainly not their own. It is impossible to say how much education is influenced by this choice of clothes, and the motives for this choice. Not only do short-sighted mothers offer ornaments as rewards to their children, but there are foolish tutors who threaten to make their pupils wear the plainest and coarsest clothes as a punishment. "If you do not do your lessons better, if you do not take more care of your clothes, you shall be dressed like that little peasant boy." This is like saying to them, "Understand that clothes make the man." Is it to be wondered at that our young people profit by such wise teaching, that they care for nothing but dress, and that they only judge of merit by its outside.

If I had to bring such a spoilt child to his senses, I would take care that his smartest clothes were the most uncomfortable, that he was always cramped, constrained, and embarrassed in every way; freedom and mirth should flee before his splendour. If he wanted to take part in the games of children more simply dressed, they should cease their play and run away. Before long I should make him so tired and sick of his magnificence, such a slave to his gold-laced coat, that it would become the plague of his life, and he would be less afraid to behold the darkest dungeon than to see the preparations for his adornment. Before the child is enslaved by our prejudices his first wish is always to be free and comfortable. The plainest and most comfortable clothes, those which leave him most liberty, are what he always likes best.

There are habits of body suited for an active life and others for a sedentary life. The latter leaves the humours an equable and uniform course, and the body should be protected from changes in temperature; the former is constantly passing from action to rest, from heat to cold, and the body should be inured to these changes. Hence people, engaged in sedentary pursuits indoors, should always be warmly dressed, to keep their bodies as nearly as possible at the same temperature at all times and seasons. Those, however, who come and go in sun, wind, and rain, who take much exercise, and spend most of their time out of doors, should always be lightly clad, so as to get used to the changes in the air and to every degree of temperature without suffering inconvenience. I would advise both never to change their clothes with the changing seasons, and that would be the invariable habit of my pupil Emile. By this I do not mean that he should wear his winter clothes in summer like many people of sedentary habits, but that he should wear his summer clothes in winter like hard-working folk. Sir Isaac Newton always did this, and he lived to be eighty.

Emile should wear little or nothing on his head all the year round. The ancient Egyptians always went bareheaded; the Persians used to wear heavy tiaras and still wear large turbans, which according to Chardin are required by their climate. I have remarked elsewhere on the difference observed by Herodotus on a battle-field between the skulls of the Persians and those of the Egyptians. Since it is desirable that the bones of the skull should grow harder and more substantial, less fragile and porous, not only to protect the brain against injuries but against colds, fever, and every influence of the air, you should therefore accustom your children to go bareheaded winter and summer, day and night. If you make them wear a night-cap to keep their hair clean and tidy, let it be thin and transparent like the nets with which the Basques cover their hair. I am aware that most mothers will be more impressed by Chardin's observations than my arguments, and will think that all climates are the climate of Persia, but I did not choose a European pupil to turn him into an Asiatic.

Children are generally too much wrapped up, particularly in infancy. They should be accustomed to cold rather than heat;

great cold never does them any harm, if they are exposed to it soon enough; but their skin is still too soft and tender and leaves too free a course for perspiration, so that they are inevitably exhausted by excessive heat. It has been observed that infant mortality is greatest in August. Moreover, it seems certain from a comparison of northern and southern races that we become stronger by bearing extreme cold rather than excessive heat. But as the child's body grows bigger and his muscles get stronger, train him gradually to bear the rays of the sun. Little by little you will harden him till he can face the burning heat of the tropics without danger.

Locke, in the midst of the manly and sensible advice he gives us, falls into inconsistencies one would hardly expect in such a careful thinker. The same man who would have children take an ice-cold bath summer and winter, will not let them drink cold water when they are hot, or lie on damp grass. But he would never have their shoes water-tight; and why should they let in more water when the child is hot than when he is cold, and may we not draw the same inference with regard to the feet and body that he draws with regard to the hands and feet and the body and face? If he would have a man all face, why blame me if I would have him all feet?

To prevent children drinking when they are hot, he says they should be trained to eat a piece of bread first. It is a strange thing to make a child eat because he is thirsty; I would as soon give him a drink when he is hungry. You will never convince me that our first instincts are so ill-regulated that we cannot satisfy them without endangering our lives. Were that so, the man would have perished over and over again before he had learned how to keep himself alive.

Whenever Emile is thirsty let him have a drink, and let him drink fresh water just as it is, not even taking the chill off it in the depths of winter and when he is bathed in perspiration. The only precaution I advise is to take care what sort of water you give him. If the water comes from a river, give it him just as it is; if it is spring-water let it stand a little exposed to the air before he drinks it. In warm weather rivers are warm; it is not so with springs, whose water has not been in contact with the air. You must wait till the temperature of the water is the same as that of the air. In winter, on the other hand, spring water is safer than river water. It is, however, unusual and unnatural to perspire greatly in winter, especially in the open air, for the cold air constantly strikes the skin and drives the perspiration inwards, and prevents the pores opening enough to give it passage. Now I do not intend Emile to take his exercise by the fireside in winter, but in the open air and among the ice. If he only gets warm with making and throwing snowballs, let him drink when he is thirsty, and go on with his game after drinking, and you need not be afraid of any ill effects. And if any other exercise makes him perspire let him drink cold water even in winter provided he is thirsty. Only take care to take him to get the water some little distance away. In such cold as I am supposing, he would have cooled down sufficiently when he got there to be able to drink without danger. Above all, take care to conceal these precautions from him. I would rather he were ill now and then, than always thinking about his health.

Since children take such violent exercise they need a great deal of sleep. The one makes up for the other, and this shows that both are necessary. Night is the time set apart by nature for rest. It is an established fact that sleep is quieter and calmer when the sun is below the horizon, and that our senses are less calm when the air is warmed by the rays of the sun. So it is certainly the healthiest plan to rise with the sun and go to bed with the sun. Hence in our country man and all the other animals with him want more sleep in winter than in summer. But town life is so complex, so unnatural, so subject to chances and changes, that it is not wise to accustom a man to such uniformity that he cannot do without it. No doubt he must submit to rules; but the chief rule is this—be able to break the rule if necessary. So do not be so foolish as to soften your pupil by letting him always sleep his sleep out. Leave him at first to the law of nature without any hindrance, but never forget that under our conditions he must rise above this law; he must be able to go to bed late and rise early, be awakened suddenly, or sit up all night without ill effects. Begin early and proceed gently, a step at a time, and the constitution adapts itself to the very conditions which would destroy it if they were imposed for the first time on the grown man.

In the next place he must be accustomed to sleep in an uncomfortable bed, which is the best way to find no bed uncomfortable. Speaking generally, a hard life, when once we have become used to it, increases our pleasant experiences; an easy life prepares the way for innumerable unpleasant experiences. Those who are too tenderly nurtured can only sleep on down; those who are used to sleep on bare boards can find them anywhere. There is no such thing as a hard bed for the man who falls asleep at once.

The body is, so to speak, melted and dissolved in a soft bed where one sinks into feathers and eider-down. The reins when too warmly covered become inflamed. Stone and other diseases are often due to this, and it invariably produces a delicate constitution, which is the seed-ground of every ailment.

The best bed is that in which we get the best sleep. Emile and I will prepare such a bed for ourselves during the daytime. We do not need Persian slaves to make our beds; when we are digging the soil we are turning our mattresses. I know that a healthy child may be made to sleep or wake almost at will. When the child is put to bed and his nurse grows weary of his chatter, she says to him, " Go to sleep." That is much like saying, " Get well," when he is ill. The right way is to let him get tired of himself. Talk so much that he is compelled to hold his tongue, and he will soon be asleep. Here is at least one use for sermons, and you may as well preach to him as rock his cradle; but if you use this narcotic at night, do not use it by day.

I shall sometimes rouse Emile, not so much to prevent his sleeping too much, as to accustom him to anything—even to waking with a start. Moreover, I should be unfit for my business if I could not make him wake himself, and get up, so to speak, at my will, without being called.

If he wakes too soon, I shall let him look forward to a tedious morning, so that he will count as gain any time he can give to sleep. If he sleeps too late I shall show him some favourite toy when he wakes. If I want him to wake at a given hour I shall say, "Tomorrow at six I am going fishing," or "I shall take a walk to such and such a place. Would you like to come too?" He assents, and begs me to wake him. I promise, or do not promise, as the case requires. If he wakes too late, he finds me gone. There is something amiss if he does not soon learn to wake himself.

Moreover, should it happen, though it rarely does, that a sluggish child desires to stagnate in idleness, you must not give way to this tendency, which might stupefy him entirely, but you must apply some stimulus to wake him. You must understand that is no question of applying force, but of arousing some appetite which leads to action, and such an appetite, carefully selected on the lines laid down by nature, kills two birds with one stone.

If one has any sort of skill, I can think of nothing for which a taste, a very passion, cannot be aroused in children, and that without vanity, emulation, or jealousy. Their keenness, their spirit of imitation, is enough of itself; above all, there is their natural liveliness, of which no teacher so far has contrived to take advantage. In every game, when they are quite sure it is only play, they endure without complaint, or even with laughter, hardships which they would not submit to otherwise without floods of tears. The sports of the young savage involve long fasting, blows, burns, and fatigue of every kind, a proof that even pain has a charm of its own, which may remove its bitterness. It is not every master, however, who knows how to season this dish, nor can every scholar eat it without making faces. However, I must take care or I shall be wandering off again after exceptions.

It is not to be endured that man should become the slave of pain, disease, accident, the perils of life, or even death itself; the more familiar he becomes with these ideas the sooner he will be cured of that over-sensitiveness which adds to the pain by impatience in bearing it; the sooner he becomes used to the sufferings which may overtake him, the sooner he shall, as Montaigne has put it, rob those pains of the sting of unfamiliarity, and so make his soul strong and invulnerable; his body will be the coat of mail which stops all the darts which might otherwise find a vital part. Even the approach of death, which is not death itself, will scarcely be felt as such; he will not die, he will be, so to speak, alive or dead and nothing more. Montaigne might say of him as he did of a certain king of Morocco, " No man ever prolonged his life so far into death." A child serves his apprenticeship in courage and endurance as well as in other virtues; but you cannot teach children these virtues by name alone; they must learn them unconsciously through experience.

But speaking of death, what steps shall I take with regard to my pupil and the smallpox? Shall he be inoculated in infancy, or shall I wait till he takes it in the natural course of things? The former plan is more in accordance with our practice, for it preserves his life at a time when it is of greater value, at the cost of some danger when his life is of less worth; if indeed we can use the word danger with regard to inoculation when properly performed.

But the other plan is more in accordance with our general principles—to leave nature to take the precautions she delights in, precautions she abandons whenever man interferes. The natural man is always ready; let nature inoculate him herself, she will choose the fitting occasion better than we.

Do not think I am finding fault with inoculation, for my reasons for exempting my pupil from it do not in the least apply to yours. Your training does not prepare them to escape catching smallpox as soon as they are exposed to infection. If you let them take it any-how, they will probably die. I perceive that in different lands the resistance to inoculation is in proportion to the need for it; and the reason is plain. So I scarcely condescend to discuss this question with regard to Emile. He will be inoculated or not according to time, place, and circumstances; it is almost a matter of indifference, as far as he is concerned. If it gives him smallpox, there will be the advantage of knowing what to expect, knowing what the disease is; that is a good thing, but if he catches it naturally it will have kept him out of the doctor's hands, which is better.

An exclusive education, which merely tends to keep those who have received it apart from the mass of mankind, always selects such teaching as is costly rather than cheap, even when the latter is of more use. Thus all carefully educated young men learn to ride, because it is costly, but scarcely any of them learn to swim, as it costs nothing, and an artisan can swim as well as any one. Yet without passing through the riding school, the traveller learns to mount his horse, to stick on it, and to ride well enough for practical purposes; but in the water if you cannot swim you will drown, and we cannot swim unless we are taught. Again, you are not forced to ride on pain of death, while no one is sure of escaping such a common danger as drowning. Emile shall be as much at home in the water as on land. Why should he not be able to live in every element? If he could learn to fly, he should be an eagle; I would make him a salamander, if he could bear the heat.

People are afraid lest the child should be drowned while he is learning to swim; if he dies while he is learning, or if he dies because he has not learnt, it will be your own fault. Foolhardiness is the result of vanity; we are not rash when no one is looking. Emile will not be foolhardy, though all the world were watching him. As the exercise does not depend on its danger, he will learn to swim the Hellespont by swimming, without any danger, a stream in his father's park; but he must get used to danger too, so as not to be flustered by it. This is an essential part of the apprenticeship I spoke of just now. Moreover, I shall take care to proportion the danger to his strength, and I shall always share it myself, so that I need scarcely fear any imprudence if I take as much care for his life as for my own.

A child is smaller than a man; he has not the man's strength or reason, but he sees and hears as well or nearly as well; his sense of taste is very good, though he is less fastidious, and he distinguishes scents as clearly though less sensuously. The senses are the first of our faculties to mature; they are those most frequently overlooked or neglected.

To train the senses it is not enough merely to use them; we must learn to judge by their means, to learn to feel, so to speak; for we cannot touch, see, or hear, except as we have been taught.

There is a mere natural and mechanical use of the senses which strengthens the body without improving the judgment. It is all very well to swim, run, jump, whip a top, throw stones; but have we nothing but arms and legs? Have we not eyes and ears as well; and are not these organs necessary for the use of the rest? Do not merely exercise the strength, exercise all the senses by which it is guided; make the best use of every one of them, and check the results of one by the other. Measure, count, weigh, compare. Do not use force till you have estimated the resistance; let the estimation of the effect always precede the application of the means. Get the child interested in avoiding insufficient or superfluous efforts. If in this way you train him to calculate the effects of all his movements, and to correct his mistakes by experience, is it not clear that the more he does the wiser he will become?

Take the case of moving a heavy mass; if he takes too long a lever, he will waste his strength; if it is too short, he will not have strength enough; experience will teach him to use the very stick he needs. This knowledge is not beyond his years. Take, for example, a load to be carried; if he wants to carry as much as he can, and not to take up more than he can carry, must he not calculate the weight by the appearance? Does he know how to compare masses of like substance and different size, or to choose between masses of the same size and different substances? he must set to work to compare their specific weights. I have seen a young man, very highly educated, who could not be convinced, till he had tried it, that a bucket full of blocks of oak weighed less than the same bucket full of water.

All our senses are not equally under our control. One of them, touch, is always busy during our waking hours; it is spread over the whole surface of the body, like a sentinel ever on the watch to warn us of anything which may do us harm. Whether we will or not, we learn to use it first of all by experience, by constant practice, and therefore we have less need for special training for it. Yet we know that the blind have a surer and more delicate sense of touch than we, for not being guided by the one sense, they are forced to get from the touch what we get from sight. Why, then, are not we trained to walk as they do in the dark, to recognise what we touch, to distinguish things about us; in a word, to do at night and in the dark what they do in the daytime without sight? We are better off than they while the sun shines; in the dark it is their turn to be our guide. We are blind half our time, with this difference: the really blind always know what to do, while we are afraid to stir in the dark. We have lights, you say. What! always artificial aids. Who can insure that they will always be at hand when required. I had rather Emil's eyes were in his finger tips, than in the chandler's shop.

If you are shut up in a building at night, clap your hands, you will know from the sound whether the space is large or small, if you are in the middle or in one corner. Half a foot from a wall the air, which is refracted and does not circulate freely, produces a different effect on your face. Stand still in one place and turn this way and that; a slight draught will tell you if there is a door open. If you are on a boat you will perceive from the way the air strikes your face not merely the direction in which you are going, but whether the current is bearing you slow or fast. These observations and many others like them can only be properly made at night; however much attention we give to them by daylight, we are always helped or hindered by sight, so that the results escape us. Yet here we use neither hand nor stick. How much may be learnt by touch, without ever touching anything!

I would have plenty of games in the dark! This suggestion is more valuable than it seems at first sight. Men are naturally afraid of the dark; so are some animals.[1] Only a few men are freed from this burden by knowledge, determination, and courage. I have seen thinkers, unbelievers, philosophers, exceedingly brave by daylight, tremble like women at the rustling of a leaf in the dark. This terror is put down to nurses' tales; this is a mistake; it has a natural cause. What is this cause? What makes the deaf suspicious and the lower classes superstitious? Ignorance of the things about us, and of what is taking place around us.[2] Accustomed

[1] This terror is very noticeable during great eclipses of the sun.

[2] Another cause has been well explained by a philosopher, often quoted in this work, a philosopher to whose wide views I am very greatly indebted.

" When under special conditions we cannot form a fair idea of distance, when we can only judge things by the size of the angle or rather of the image formed in our eyes, we cannot avoid being deceived as to the size of these objects. Every one knows by experience how when we are travelling at night we take a bush near at hand for a great tree at a distance, and *vice versa*. In the same way, if the objects were of a shape unknown to us, so that we could not tell their size in that way, we should be equally mistaken with regard to it. If a fly flew quickly past a few inches from our

to perceive things from a distance and to calculate their effects, how can I help supposing, when I cannot see, that there are hosts of creatures and all sorts of movements all about me which may do me harm, and against which I cannot protect myself? In vain do I know I am safe where I am; I am never so sure of it as when I can actually see it, so that I have always a cause for fear which did not exist in broad daylight. I know, indeed, that a foreign body can scarcely act upon me without some slight sound, and how intently I listen! At the least sound which I cannot explain, the desire of self-preservation makes me picture everything that would put me on my guard, and therefore everything most calculated to alarm me.

I am just as uneasy if I hear no sound, for I might be taken unawares without a sound. I must picture things as they were before, as they ought to be; I must see what I do not see. Thus driven to exercise my imagination, it soon becomes my master, and

eyes, we should think it was a distant bird; a horse standing still at a distance from us in the midst of open country, in a position somewhat like that of a sheep, would be taken for a large sheep, so long as we did not perceive that it was a horse; but as soon as we recognise what it is, it seems as large as a horse, and we at once correct our former judgment.

"Whenever one finds oneself in unknown places at night where we cannot judge of distance, and where we cannot recognise objects by their shape on account of the darkness, we are in constant danger of forming mistaken judgments as to the objects which present themselves to our notice. Hence that terror, that kind of inward fear experienced by most people on dark nights. This is foundation for the supposed appearances of spectres, or gigantic and terrible forms which so many people profess to have seen. They are generally told that they imagined these things, yet they may really have seen them, and it is quite possible they really saw what they say they did see; for it will always be the case that when we can only estimate the size of an object by the angle it forms in the eye, that object will swell and grow as we approach it; and if the spectator thought it several feet high when it was thirty or forty feet away, it will seem very large indeed when it is a few feet off; this must indeed astonish and alarm the spectator until he touches it and perceives what it is, for as soon as he perceives what it is, the object which seemed so gigantic will suddenly shrink and assume its real size, but if we run away or are afraid to approach, we shall certainly form no other idea of the thing than the image formed in the eye, and we shall have really seen a gigantic figure of alarming size and shape. There is, therefore, a natural ground for the tendency to see ghosts, and these appearances are not merely the creation of the imagination, as the men of science would have us think."— Buffon, *Nat. Hist.*

In the text I have tried to show that they are always partly the creation of the imagination, and with regard to the cause explained in this quotation, it is clear that the habit of walking by night should teach us to distinguish those appearances which similarity of form and diversity of distance lend to the objects seen in the dark. For if the air is light enough for us to see the outlines there must be more air between us and them when they are further off, so that we ought to see them less distinctly when further off, which should be enough, when we are used to it, to prevent the error described by M. Buffon. Whichever explanation you prefer, my mode of procedure is still efficacious, and experience entirely confirms it.

what I did to reassure myself only alarms me more. I hear a noise, it is a robber; I hear nothing, it is a ghost. The watchfulness inspired by the instinct of self-preservation only makes me more afraid. Everything that ought to reassure me exists only for my reason, and the voice of instinct is louder than that of reason. What is the good of thinking there is nothing to be afraid of, since in that case there is nothing we can do?

The cause indicates the cure. In everything habit overpowers imagination; it is only aroused by what is new. It is no longer imagination, but memory which is concerned with what we see every day, and that is the reason of the maxim, " Ab assuetis non fit passio," for it is only at the flame of imagination that the passions are kindled. Therefore do not argue with any one whom you want to cure of the fear of darkness; take him often into dark places and be assured this practice will be of more avail than all the arguments of philosophy. The tiler on the roof does not know what it is to be dizzy, and those who are used to the dark will not be afraid.

There is another advantage to be gained from our games in the dark. But if these games are to be a success I cannot speak too strongly of the need for gaiety. Nothing is so gloomy as the dark; do not shut your child up in a dungeon, let him laugh when he goes into a dark place, let him laugh when he comes out, so that the thought of the game he is leaving and the games he will play next may protect him from the fantastic imagination which might lay hold on him.

There comes a stage in life beyond which we progress backwards. I feel I have reached this stage. I am, so to speak, returning to a past career. The approach of age makes us recall the happy days of our childhood. As I grow old I become a child again, and I recall more readily what I did at ten than at thirty. Reader, forgive me if I sometimes draw my examples from my own experience. If this book is to be well written, I must enjoy writing it.

I was living in the country with a pastor called M. Lambercier. My companion was a cousin richer than myself, who was regarded as the heir to some property, while I, far from my father, was but a poor orphan. My big cousin Bernard was unusually timid, especially at night. I laughed at his fears, till M. Lambercier was tired of my boasting, and determined to put my courage to the proof. One autumn evening, when it was very dark, he gave me the church key, and told me to go and fetch a Bible he had left in the pulpit. To put me on my mettle he said something which made it impossible for me to refuse.

I set out without a light; if I had had one, it would perhaps have been even worse. I had to pass through the graveyard; I crossed it bravely, for as long as I was in the open air I was never afraid of the dark.

As I opened the door I heard a sort of echo in the roof; it sounded like voices and it began to shake my Roman courage. Having opened the door I tried to enter, but when I had gone a few steps I

stopped. At the sight of the profound darkness in which the vast
building lay I was seized with terror and my hair stood on end. I
turned, I went out through the door, and took to my heels. In the
yard I found a little dog, called Sultan, whose caresses reassured me.
Ashamed of my fears, I retraced my steps, trying to take Sultan
with me, but he refused to follow. Hurriedly I opened the door
and entered the church. I was hardly inside when terror again got
hold of me and so firmly that I lost my head, and though the pulpit
was on the right, as I very well knew, I sought it on the left, and
entangling myself among the benches I was completely lost.
Unable to find either pulpit or door, I fell into an indescribable
state of mind. At last I found the door and managed to get out of the
church and run away as I had done before, quite determined never
to enter the church again except in broad daylight.

I returned to the house; on the doorstep I heard M. Lambercier
laughing, laughing, as I supposed, at me. Ashamed to face his
laughter, I was hesitating to open the door, when I heard Miss
Lambercier, who was anxious about me, tell the maid to get the
lantern, and M. Lambercier got ready to come and look for me,
escorted by my gallant cousin, who would have got all the credit
for the expedition. All at once my fears departed, and left me
merely surprised at my terror. I ran, I fairly flew, to the church;
without losing my way, without groping about, I reached the
pulpit, took the Bible, and ran down the steps. In three strides I
was out of the church, leaving the door open. Breathless, I entered
the room and threw the Bible on the table, frightened indeed, but
throbbing with pride that I had done it without the proposed
assistance.

You will ask if I am giving this anecdote as an example, and as an
illustration, of the mirth which I say should accompany these games.
Not so, but I give it as a proof that there is nothing so well calculated
to reassure any one who is afraid in the dark as to hear sounds of
laughter and talking in an adjoining room. Instead of playing alone
with your pupil in the evening, I would have you get together a
number of merry children; do not send them alone to begin with,
but several together, and do not venture to send any one quite alone,
until you are quite certain beforehand that he will not be too
frightened.

I can picture nothing more amusing and more profitable than such
games, considering how little skill is required to organise them. In
a large room I should arrange a sort of labyrinth of tables, arm-
chairs, chairs, and screens. In the inextricable windings of this
labyrinth I should place some eight or ten sham boxes, and one real
box almost exactly like them, but well filled with sweets. I should
describe clearly and briefly the place where the right box would be
found. I should give instructions sufficient to enable people more
attentive and less excitable than children to find it.[1] Then having

[1] To practise them in attention, only tell them things which it is clearly
to their present interest that they should understand thoroughly; above

made the little competitors draw lots, I should send first one and then another till the right box was found. I should increase the difficulty of the task in proportion to their skill.

Picture to yourself a youthful Hercules returning, box in hand, quite proud of his expedition. The box is placed on the table and opened with great ceremony. I can hear the bursts of laughter and the shouts of the merry party when, instead of the looked-for sweets, he finds, neatly arranged on moss or cotton-wool, a beetle, a snail, a bit of coal, a few acorns, a turnip, or some such thing. Another time in a newly whitewashed room, a toy or some small article of furniture would be hung on the wall and the children would have to fetch it without touching the wall. When the child who fetches it comes back, if he has failed ever so little to fulfil the conditions, a dab of white on the brim of his cap, the tip of his shoe, the flap of his coat or his sleeve, will betray his lack of skill.

This is enough, or more than enough, to show the spirit of these games. Do not read my book if you expect me to tell you everything.

What great advantages would be possessed by a man so educated, when compared with others. His feet ar accustomed to tread firmly in the dark, and his hands to touch lightly; they will guide him safely in the thickest darkness. His imagination is busy with the evening games of his childhood, and will find it difficult to turn towards objects of alarm. If he thinks he hears laughter, it will be the laughter of his former playfellows, not of frenzied spirits; if he thinks there is a host of people, it will not be the witches' sabbath, but the party in his tutor's study. Night only recalls these cheerful memories, and it will never alarm him; it will inspire delight rather than fear. He will be ready for a military expedition at any hour, with or without his troop. He will enter the camp of Saul, he will find his way, he will reach the king's tent without waking any one, and he will return unobserved. Are the steeds of Rhesus to be stolen, you may trust him. You will scarcely find a Ulysses among men educated in any other fashion.

I have known people who tried to train the children not to fear the dark by startling them. This is a very bad plan; its effects are just the opposite of those desired, and it only makes children more timid. Neither reason nor habit can secure us from the fear of a present danger whose degree and kind are unknown, nor from the fear of surprises which we have often experienced. Yet how will you make sure that you can preserve your pupil from such accidents ? I consider this the best advice to give him beforehand. I should say to Emile, " This is a matter of self-defence, for the aggressor does not let you know whether he means to hurt or frighten you, and as the advantage is on his side you cannot even take refuge in flight. Therefore seize boldly anything, whether man or beast, which takes you unawares in the dark. Grasp it, squeeze it

all be brief, never say a word more than is necessary. But neither let your speech be obscure nor of doubtful meaning.

with all your might; if it struggles, strike, and do not spare your blows; and whatever he may say or do, do not let him go till you know just who he is. The event will probably prove that you had little to be afraid of, but this way of treating practical jokers would naturally prevent their trying it again.

Although touch is the sense oftenest used, its discrimination remains, as I have already pointed out, coarser and more imperfect than that of any other sense, because we always use sight along with it; the eye perceives the thing first, and the mind almost always judges without the hand. On the other hand, discrimination by touch is the surest just because of its limitations; for extending only as far as our hands can reach, it corrects the hasty judgments of the other senses, which pounce upon objects scarcely perceived, while what we learn by touch is learnt thoroughly. Moreover, touch, when required, unites the force of our muscles to the action of the nerves; we associate by simultaneous sensations our ideas of temperature, size, and shape, to those of weight and density. Thus touch is the sense which best teaches us the action of foreign bodies upon ourselves, the sense which most directly supplies us with the knowledge required for self-preservation.

As the trained touch takes the place of sight, why should it not, to some extent, take the place of hearing, since sounds set up, in sonorous bodies, vibrations perceptible by touch? By placing the hand on the body of a 'cello one can distinguish without the use of eye or ear, merely by the way in which the wood vibrates and trembles, whether the sound given out is sharp or flat, whether it is drawn from the treble string or the base. If our touch were trained to note these differences, no doubt we might in time become so sensitive as to hear a whole tune by means of our fingers. But if we admit this, it is clear that one could easily speak to the deaf by means of music; for tone and measure are no less capable of regular combination than voice and articulation, so that they might be used as the elements of speech.

There are exercises by which the sense of touch is blunted and deadened, and others which sharpen it and make it delicate and discriminating. The former, which employ much movement and force for the continued impression of hard bodies, make the skin hard and thick, and deprive it of its natural sensitiveness. The latter are those which give variety to this feeling, by slight and repeated contact, so that the mind is attentive to constantly recurring impressions, and readily learns to discern their variations. This difference is clear in the use of musical instruments. The harsh and painful touch of the 'cello, bass-viol, and even of the violin, hardens the finger-tips, although it gives flexibility to the fingers. The soft and smooth touch of the harpsichord makes the fingers both flexible and sensitive. In this respect the harpsichord is to be preferred.

The skin protects the rest of the body, so it is very important to harden it to the effects of the air that it may be able to bear its changes. With regard to this I may say I would not have the hand roughened by too servile application to the same kind of work, nor should the skin of the hand become hardened so as to lose its delicate sense of touch which keeps the body informed of what is going on, and by the kind of contact sometimes makes us shudder in different ways even in the dark.

Why should my pupil be always compelled to wear the skin of an ox under his foot? What harm would come of it if his own skin could serve him at need as a sole. It is clear that a delicate skin could never be of any use in this way, and may often do harm. The Genevese, aroused at midnight by their enemies in the depth of winter, seized their guns rather than their shoes. Who can tell whether the town would have escaped capture if its citizens had not been able to go barefoot?

Let a man be always fore-armed against the unforeseen. Let Emile run about barefoot all the year round, upstairs, downstairs, and in the garden. Far from scolding him, I shall follow his example; only I shall be careful to remove any broken glass. I shall soon proceed to speak of work and manual occupations. Meanwhile, let him learn to perform every exercise which encourages agility of body; let him learn to hold himself easily and steadily in any position, let him practise jumping and leaping, climbing trees and walls. Let him always find his balance, and let his every movement and gesture be regulated by the laws of weight, long before he learns to explain them by the science of statics. By the way his foot is planted on the ground, and his body supported on his leg, he ought to know if he is holding himself well or ill. An easy carriage is always graceful, and the steadiest positions are the most elegant. If I were a dancing master I would refuse to play the monkey tricks of Marcel, which are only fit for the stage where they are performed; but instead of keeping my pupil busy with fancy steps, I would take him to the foot of a cliff. There I would show him how to hold himself, how to carry his body and head, how to place first a foot then a hand, to follow lightly the steep, toilsome, and rugged paths, to leap from point to point, either up or down. He should emulate the mountain-goat, not the ballet dancer.

As touch confines its operations to the man's immediate surroundings, so sight extends its range beyond them; it is this which makes it misleading; man sees half his horizon at a glance. In the midst of this host of simultaneous impressions and the thoughts excited by them, how can he fail now and then to make mistakes? Thus sight is the least reliable of our senses, just because it has the widest range; it functions long before our other senses, and its work is too hasty and on too large a scale to be corrected by the rest Moreover, the very illusions of perspective are necessary if we are to arrive at a knowledge of space and compare one part of space with another. Without false appearances we should never see anything at a distance; without the gradations of size and tone we could not judge of distance, or rather distance would have no existence for us. If two trees, one of which was a hundred paces from us and the other ten, looked equally large and distinct, we should think they were side by side. If we perceived the real dimensions of things, we should know nothing of space; everything would seem close to our eyes.

The angle formed between any objects and our eye is the only means by which our sight estimates their size and distance, and as this angle is the simple effect of complex causes, the judgment we form does not distinguish between the several causes; we are compelled to be inaccurate. For how can I tell, by sight alone, whether the angle at which an object appears to me smaller than another, indicates that it is really smaller or that it is further off.

Here we must just reverse our former plan. Instead of simplifying the sensation, always reinforce it and verify it by means of another sense. Subject the eye to the hand, and, so to speak, restrain the precipitation of the former sense by the slower and more reasoned pace of the latter. For want of this sort of practice our sight measurements are very imperfect. We cannot correctly, and at a glance, estimate height, length, breadth, and distance; and the fact that engineers, surveyors, architects, masons, and painters are generally quicker to see and better able to estimate distances correctly, proves that the fault is not in our eyes, but in our use of them. Their occupations give them the training we lack, and they check the equivocal results of the angle of vision by its accompanying experiences, which determine the relations of the two causes of this angle for their eyes.

Children will always do anything that keeps them moving freely. There are countless ways of rousing their interest in measuring, perceiving, and estimating distance. There is a very tall cherry tree; how shall we gather the cherries? Will the ladder in the barn be big enough? There is a wide stream; how shall we get to the other side? Would one of the wooden planks in the yard reach from bank to bank? From our windows we want to fish in the moat; how many yards of line are required? I want to make a swing between two trees; will two fathoms of cord be enough? They tell me our room in the new house will be twenty-five feet square; do you think it will be big enough for us? Will it be larger than this? We are very hungry; here are two villages, which can we get to first for our dinner?

An idle, lazy child was to be taught to run. He had no liking for this or any other exercise, though he was intended for the army. Somehow or other he had got it into his head that a man of his rank need know nothing and do nothing—that his birth would serve as a substitute for arms and legs, as well as for every kind of virtue. The skill of Chiron himself would have failed to make a fleet-footed Achilles of this young gentleman. The difficulty was increased by my determination to give him no kind of orders. I had renounced all right to direct him by preaching, promises, threats, emulation, or the desire to show off. How should I make him want to run without saying anything? I might run myself, but he might not follow my example, and this plan had other drawbacks. Moreover, I must find some means of teaching him through this exercise, so as to train mind and body to work together. This is how I, or rather how the teacher who supplied me with this illustration, set about it.

When I took him a walk of an afternoon I sometimes put in my pocket a couple of cakes, of a kind he was very fond of; we each ate one while we were out, and we came back well pleased with our outing. One day he noticed I had three cakes; he could have easily eaten six, so he ate his cake quickly and asked for the other. " No," said I, " I could eat it myself, or we might divide it, but I would rather see those two little boys run a race for it." I called them to us, showed them the cake, and suggested that they should race for it. They were delighted. The cake was placed on a large stone which was to be the goal; the course was marked out, we sat down, and at a given signal off flew the children! The victor seized the cake and ate it without pity in the sight of the spectators and of his defeated rival.

The sport was better than the cake; but the lesson did not take effect all at once, and produced no result. I was not discouraged, nor did I hurry; teaching is a trade at which one must be able to lose time and save it. Our walks were continued, sometimes we took three cakes, sometimes four, and from time to time there were one or two cakes for the racers. If the prize was not great, neither was the ambition of the competitors. The winner was praised and petted, and everything was done with much ceremony. To give room to run and to add interest to the race I marked out a longer course and admitted several fresh competitors. Scarcely had they entered the lists than all the passers-by stopped to watch. They were encouraged by shouting, cheering, and clapping. I sometimes saw my little man trembling with excitement, jumping up and shouting when one was about to reach or overtake another—to him these were the Olympian games.

However, the competitors did not always play fair, they got in each other's way, or knocked one another down, or put stones on the track. That led us to separate them and make them start from different places at equal distances from the goal. You will soon see the reason for this, for I must describe this important affair at length.

Tired of seeing his favourite cakes devoured before his eyes, the young lord began to suspect that there was some use in being a quick runner, and seeing that he had two legs of his own, he began to practise running on the quiet. I took care to see nothing, but I knew my stratagem had taken effect. When he thought he was good enough (and I thought so too), he pretended to tease me to give him the other cake. I refused; he persisted, and at last he said angrily, " Well, put it on the stone and mark out the course, and we shall see." " Very good," said I, laughing, " You will get a good appetite, but you will not get the cake." Stung by my mockery, he took heart, won the prize, all the more easily because I had marked out a very short course and taken care that the best runner was out of the way. It will be evident that, after the first step, I had no difficulty in keeping him in training. Soon he took such a fancy for this form of exercise that without any favour he was almost certain to beat the little peasant boys at running, however long the course.

The advantage thus obtained led unexpectedly to another. So long as he seldom won the prize, he ate it himself like his rivals, but as he got used to victory he grew generous, and often shared it with the defeated. That taught me a lesson in morals and I saw what was the real root of generosity.

While I continued to mark out a different starting place for each competitor, he did not notice that I had made the distances unequal, so that one of them, having farther to run to reach the goal, was clearly at a disadvantage. But though I left the choice to my pupil he did not know how to take advantage of it. Without thinking of the distance, he always chose the smoothest path, so that I could easily predict his choice, and could almost make him win or lose the cake at my pleasure. I had more than one end in view in this stratagem; but as my plan was to get him to notice the difference himself, I tried to make him aware of it. Though he was generally lazy and easy going, he was so eager in his sports and trusted me so completely that I had great difficulty in making him see that I was cheating him. When at last I managed to make him see it in spite of his excitement, he was angry with me. "What have you to complain of?" said I. "In a gift which I propose to give of my own free will am not I master of the conditions? Who makes you run? Did I promise to make the courses equal? Is not the choice yours? Do not you see that I am favouring you, and that the inequality you complain of is all to your advantage, if you knew how to use it?" That was plain to him; and to choose he must observe more carefully. At first he wanted to count the paces, but a child measures paces slowly and inaccurately; moreover, I decided to have several races on one day; and the game having become a sort of passion with the child, he was sorry to waste in measuring the portion of time intended for running. Such delays are not in accordance with a child's impatience; he tried therefore to see better and to reckon the distance more accurately at sight. It was now quite easy to extend and develop this power. At length, after some months' practice, and the correction of his errors, I so trained his power of judging at sight that I had only to place an imaginary cake on any distant object and his glance was nearly as accurate as the surveyor's chain.

Of all the senses, sight is that which we can least distinguish from the judgments of the mind; so it takes a long time to learn to see. It takes a long time to compare sight and touch, and to train the former sense to give a true report of shape and distance. Without touch, without progressive motion, the sharpest eyes in the world could give us no idea of space. To the oyster the whole world must seem a point, and it would seem nothing more to it even if it had a human mind. It is only by walking, feeling, counting, measuring the dimensions of things, that we learn to judge them rightly; but, on the other hand, if we were always measuring, our senses would trust to the instrument and would never gain confidence. Nor must the child pass abruptly from measurement to judgment; he must continue to compare the parts when he could not compare the whole; he must substitute his estimated aliquot parts for exact aliquot parts, and instead of always applying the measure by hand he must get used to applying it by eye alone. I would, however, have his first estimates tested by measurement, so that he may correct his errors, and if there is a false impression left upon the senses he may correct it by a better judgment. The same natural standards of measurement are in use almost everywhere, the man's foot, the extent of his outstretched arms, his height. When the child wants to measure the height of a room, his tutor may serve as a measuring rod; if he is estimating the height of a steeple let him measure it by the house; if he wants to know how many leagues of road there are, let him count the hours spent in walking along it. Above all, do not do this for him; let him do it himself.

One cannot learn to estimate the extent and size of bodies without at the same time learning to know and even to copy their shape; for at bottom this copying depends entirely on the laws of perspective, and one cannot estimate distance without some feeling for these laws. All children in the course of their endless imitation try to draw; and I would have Emile cultivate this art; not so much for art's sake, as to give him exactness of eye and flexibility of hand. Generally speaking, it matters little whether he is acquainted with this or that occupation, provided he gains clearness of sense-perception and the good bodily habits which belong to the exercise in question. So I shall take good care not to provide him with a drawing master, who would only set him to copy copies and draw from drawings. Nature should be his only teacher, and things his only models. He should have the real thing before his eyes, not its copy on paper. Let him draw a house from a house, a tree from a tree, a man from a man; so that he may train himself to observe objects and their appearance accurately and not to take false and conventional copies for truth. I would even train him to draw only from objects actually before him and not from memory, so that, by repeated observation, their exact form may be impressed on his imagination, for fear lest he should substitute absurd and fantastic forms for the real truth of things, and lose his sense of proportion and his taste for the beauties of nature.

Of course I know that in this way he will make any number of daubs before he produces anything recognisable, that it will be long before he attains to the graceful outline and light touch of the draughtsman; perhaps he will never have an eye for picturesque effect or a good taste in drawing. On the other hand, he will certainly get a truer eye, a surer hand, a knowledge of the real relations of form and size between animals, plants, and natural objects, together with a quicker sense of the effects of perspective. That is just what I wanted, and my purpose is rather that he should know things than copy them. I would rather he showed me a plant of acanthus even if he drew a capital with less accuracy.

Moreover, in this occupation as in others, I do not intend my pupil to play by himself; I mean to make it pleasanter for him by always sharing it with him. He shall have no other rival; but mine will be a continual rivalry, and there will be no risk attaching to it; it will give interest to his pursuits without awaking jealousy between us. I shall follow his example and take up a pencil; at first I shall use it as unskilfully as he. I should be an Apelles if I did not set myself daubing. To begin with, I shall draw a man such as lads draw on walls, a line for each arm, another for each leg, with the fingers longer than the arm. Long after, one or other of us will notice this lack of proportion; we shall observe that the leg is thick, that this thickness varies, that the length of the arm is proportionate to the body. In this improvement I shall either go side by side with my pupil, or so little in advance that he will always overtake me easily and sometimes get ahead of me. We shall get brushes and paints, we shall try to copy the colours of things and their whole appearance, not merely their shape. We shall colour prints, we shall paint, we shall daub; but in all our daubing we shall be searching out the secrets of nature, and whatever we do shall be done under the eye of that master.

We badly needed ornaments for our room, and now we have them ready to our hand. I will have our drawings framed and covered with good glass, so that no one will touch them, and thus seeing them where we put them, each of us has a motive for taking care of his own. I arrange them in order round the room, each drawing repeated some twenty or thirty times, thus showing the author's progress in each specimen, from the time when the house is merely a rude square, till its front view, its side view, its proportions, its light and shade are all exactly portrayed. These gradations will certainly furnish us with pictures, a source of interest to ourselves and of curiosity to others, which will spur us on to further emulation. The first and roughest drawings I put in very smart gilt frames to show them off; but as the copy becomes more accurate and the drawing really good, I only give it a very plain dark frame; it needs no other ornament than itself, and it would be a pity if the frame distracted the attention which the picture itself deserves. Thus we each aspire to a plain frame, and when we desire to pour scorn on each other's drawings, we condemn them to a gilded frame. Some day perhaps "the gilt frame" will become a proverb among us, and we shall be surprised to find how many people show what they are really made of by demanding a gilt frame.

I have said already that geometry is beyond the child's reach; but that is our own fault. We fail to perceive that their method is not ours, that what is for us the art of reasoning, should be for them the art of seeing. Instead of teaching them our way, we should do better to adopt theirs, for our way of learning geometry is quite as much a matter of imagination as of reasoning. When a proposition is enunciated you must imagine the proof; that is, you must discover on what proposition already learnt it depends, and of all the possible deductions from that proposition you must choose just the one required.

In this way the closest reasoner, if he is not inventive, may find himself at a loss. What is the result? Instead of making us discover proofs, they are dictated to us; instead of teaching us to reason, our memory only is employed.

Draw accurate figures, combine them together, put them one upon another, examine their relations, and you will discover the whole of elementary geometry in passing from one observation to another, without a word of definitions, problems, or any other form of demonstration but super-position. I do not profess to teach Emile geometry; he will teach me; I shall seek for relations, he will find them, for I shall seek in such a fashion as to make him find. For instance, instead of using a pair of compasses to draw a circle, I shall draw it with a pencil at the end of bit of string attached to a pivot. After that, when I want to compare the radii one with another, Emile will laugh at me and show me that the same thread at full stretch cannot have given distances of unequal length. If I wish to measure an angle of 60° I describe from the apex of the angle, not an arc, but a complete circle, for with children nothing must be taken for granted. I find that the part of the circle contained between the two lines of the angle is the sixth part of a circle. Then I describe another and larger circle from the same centre, and I find the second arc is again the sixth part of its circle. I describe a third concentric circle with a similar result, and I continue with more and more circles till Emile, shocked at my stupidity, shows me that every arc, large or small, contained by the same angle will always be the sixth part of its circle. Now we are ready to use the protractor.

To prove that two adjacent angles are equal to two right angles people describe a circle. On the contrary I would have Emile observe the fact in a circle, and then I should say, " If we took away the circle and left the straight lines, would the angles have changed their size, etc. ? "

Exactness in the construction of figures is neglected; it is taken for granted and stress is laid on the proof. With us, on the other hand, there will be no question of proof. Our chief business will be to draw very straight, accurate, and even lines, a perfect square, a really round circle. To verify the exactness of a figure we will test it by each of its sensible properties, and that will give us a chance to discover fresh properties day by day. We will fold the two semi-circles along the diameter, the two halves of the square by the diagonal; he will compare our two figures to see who has got the edges to fit most exactly, *i.e.*, who has done it best; we should argue whether this equal division would always be possible in parallelograms, trapezes, etc. We shall sometimes try to forecast the result of an experiment, to find reasons, etc.

Geometry means to my scholar the successful use of the rule and compass; he must not confuse it with drawing, in which these instruments are not used. The rule and compass will be locked up, so that he will not get into the way of messing about with them, but we may sometimes take our figures with us when we go for a walk, and talk over what we have done, or what we mean to do.

I shall never forget seeing a young man at Turin, who had learnt as a child the relations of contours and surfaces by having to choose every day isoperimetric cakes among cakes of every geometrical figure. The greedy little fellow had exhausted the art of Archimedes to find which were the biggest.

When the child flies a kite he is training eye and hand to accuracy; when he whips a top, he is increasing his strength by using it, but without learning anything. I have sometimes asked why children are not given the same games of skill as men; tennis, mall, billiards, archery, football, and musical instruments. I was told that some of these are beyond their strength, that the child's senses are not sufficiently developed for others. These do not strike me as valid reasons; a child is not as tall as a man, but he wears the same sort of coat; I do not want him to play with our cues at a billiard-table three feet high; I do not want him knocking about among our games, nor carrying one of our racquets in his little hand; but let him play in a room whose windows have been protected; at first let him only use soft balls, let his first racquets be of wood, then of parchment, and lastly of gut, according to his progress. You prefer the kite because it is less tiring and there is no danger. You are doubly wrong. Kite-flying is a sport for women, but every woman will run away from a swift ball. Their white skins were not meant to be hardened by blows and their faces were not made for bruises. But we men are made for strength; do you think we can attain it without hardship, and what defence shall we be able to make if we are attacked? People always play carelessly in games where there is no danger. A falling kite hurts nobody, but nothing makes the arm so supple as protecting the head, nothing makes the sight so accurate as having to guard the eye. To dash from one end of the room to another, to judge the rebound of a ball before it touches the ground, to return it with strength and accuracy, such games are not so much sports fit for a man, as sports fit to make a man of him.

The child's limbs, you say, are too tender. They are not so strong as those of a man, but they are more supple. His arm is weak, still it is an arm, and it should be used with due consideration as we use other tools. Children have no skill in the use of their hands. That is just why I want them to acquire skill; a man with as little practice would be just as clumsy. We can only learn the use of our limbs by using them. It is only by long experience that we learn to make the best of ourselves, and this experience is the real object of study to which we cannot apply ourselves too early.

What is done can be done. Now there is nothing commoner than to find nimble and skilful children whose limbs are as active as those of a man. They may be seen at any fair, swinging, walking on their hands, jumping, dancing on the tight rope. For many years past, troops of children have attracted spectators to the ballets at the Italian Comedy House. Who is there in Germany and Italy who has not heard of the famous pantomime company of Nicolini? Has it ever occurred to any one that the movements of these children were less finished, their postures less graceful, their ears less true, their dancing more clumsy than those of grown-up dancers? If at first the fingers are thick, short, and awkward, the dimpled hands unable to grasp anything, does this prevent many children from learning to read and write at an age when others cannot even hold a pen or pencil? All Paris still recalls the little English girl of ten who did wonders on the harpsichord. I once saw a little fellow of eight, the son of a magistrate, who was set like a statuette on the table among the dishes, to play on a fiddle almost a big as himself, and even artists were surprised at his execution.

To my mind, these and many more examples prove that the supposed incapacity of children for our games is imaginary, and that if they are unsuccessful in some of them, it is for want of practice.

You will tell me that with regard to the body I am falling into the same mistake of precocious development which I found fault with for the mind. The cases are very different: in the one, progress is apparent only; in the other it is real. I have shown that children have not the mental development they appear to have, while they really do what they seem to do. Besides, we must never forget that all this should be play, the easy and voluntary control of the movements which nature demands of them, the art of varying their games to make them pleasanter, without the least bit of constraint to transform them into work; for what games do they play in which I cannot find material for instruction for them? And even if I could not do so, so long as they are amusing themselves harmlessly and passing the time pleasantly, their progress in learning is not yet of such great importance. But if one must be teaching them this or that at every opportunity, it cannot be done without constraint, vexation, or tedium.

What I have said about the use of the two senses whose use is most constant and most important, may serve as an example of how to train the rest. Sight and touch are applied to bodies at rest and bodies in motion, but as hearing is only affected by vibrations of the air, only a body in motion can make a noise or sound; if everything were at rest we should never hear. At night, when we ourselves only move as we choose, we have nothing to fear but moving bodies; hence we need a quick ear, and power to judge from the sensations experienced whether the body which causes them is large or small, far off or near, whether its movements are gentle or violent When once the air is set in motion, it is subject to repercussions which produce echoes, these renew the sensations and make us hear a loud or penetrating sound in another quarter. If you put your ear to the ground you may hear the sound of men's voices or horses' feet in a plain or valley much further off than when you stand upright.

As we have made a comparison between sight and touch, it will be as well to do the same for hearing, and to find out which of the two impressions starting simultaneously from a given body first reaches the sense-organ. When you see the flash of a cannon, you have still time to take cover; but when you hear the sound it is too late, the ball is close to you. One can reckon the distance of a thunderstorm by the interval between the lightning and the thunder. Let the child learn all these facts, let him learn those that are within his reach by experiment, and discover the rest by induction; but I would far rather he knew nothing at all about them, than that you should tell him.

In the voice we have an organ answering to hearing; we have no such organ answering to sight, and we do not repeat colours as we repeat sounds. This supplies an additional means of cultivating the ear by practising the active and passive organs one with the other.

Man has three kinds of voice, the speaking or articulate voice, the singing or melodious voice, and the pathetic or expressive voice, which serves as the language of the passions, and gives life to song and speech. The child has these three voices, just as the man has them, but he does not know how to use them in combination. Like us, he laughs, cries, laments, shrieks, and groans, but he does not know how to combine these inflexions with speech or song. These three voices find their best expression in perfect music. Children are incapable of such music, and their singing lacks feeling. In the same way their spoken language lacks expression; they shout, but they do not speak with emphasis, and there is as little power in their voice as there is emphasis in their speech. Our pupil's speech will be plainer and simpler still, for his passions are still asleep, and will not blend their tones with his. Do not, therefore, set him to recite tragedy or comedy, nor try to teach declamation so-called. He will have too much sense to give voice to things he cannot understand, or expression to feelings he has never known.

Teach him to speak plainly and distinctly, to articulate clearly, to pronounce correctly and without affectation, to perceive and imitate the right accent in prose and verse, and always to speak loud enough to be heard, but without speaking too loud—a common fault with school-children. Let there be no waste in anything.

The same method applies to singing; make his voice smooth and true, flexible and full, his ear alive to time and tune, but nothing more. Descriptive and theatrical music is not suitable at his age—

I would rather he sang no words; if he must have words, I would try to compose songs on purpose for him, songs interesting to a child, and as simple as his own thoughts.

You may perhaps suppose that as I am in no hurry to teach Emile to read and write, I shall not want to teach him to read music. Let us spare his brain the strain of excessive attention, and let us be in no hurry to turn his mind towards conventional signs. I grant you there seems to be a difficulty here, for if at first sight the knowledge of notes seems no more necessary for singing than the knowledge of letters for speaking, there is really this difference between them: When we speak, we are expressing our own thoughts; when we sing we are expressing the thoughts of others. Now in order to express them we must read them.

But at first we can listen to them instead of reading them, and a song is better learnt by ear than by eye. Moreover, to learn music thoroughly we must make songs as well as sing them, and the two processes must be studied together, or we shall never have any real knowledge of music. First give your young musician practice in very regular, well-cadenced phrases; then let him connect these phrases with the very simplest modulations; then show him their relation one to another by correct accent, which can be done by a fit choice of cadences and rests. On no account give him anything unusual, or anything that requires pathos or expression. A simple, tuneful air, always based on the common chords of the key, with its bass so clearly indicated that it is easily felt and accompanied, for to train his voice and ear he should always sing with the harpsi-chord.

We articulate the notes we sing the better to distinguish them; hence the custom of sol-faing with certain syllables. To tell the keys one from another they must have names and fixed intervals; hence the names of the intervals, and also the letters of the alphabet attached to the keys of the clavier and the notes of the scale. *C* and *A* indicate fixed sounds, invariable and always rendered by the same keys; *Ut* and *La* are different. *Ut* is always the dominant of a major scale, or the leading-note of a minor scale. *La* is always the dominant of a minor scale or the sixth of a major scale. Thus the letters indicate fixed terms in our system of music, and the syllables indicate terms homologous to the similar relations in different keys. The letters show the keys on the piano, and the syllables the degrees in the scale. French musicians have made a strange muddle of this. They have confused the meaning of the syllables with that of the letters, and while they have unnecessarily given us two sets of symbols for the keys of the piano, they have left none for the chords of the scales; so that *Ut* and *C* are always the same for them; this is not and ought not to be; if so, what is the use of *C?* Their method of sol-faing is, therefore, extremely and needlessly difficult, neither does it give any clear idea to the mind; since, by this method, *Ut* and *Me*, for example, may mean either a major third, a minor third, an augmented third, or a diminished third. What a strange thing that the country which produces the finest books about music should be the very country where it is hardest to learn music!

Let us adopt a simpler and clearer plan with our pupil; let him have only two scales whose relations remain unchanged, and indicated by the same symbols. Whether he sings or plays, let him learn to fix his scale on one of the twelve tones which may serve as a base, and whether he modulates in *D*, *C*, or *G*, let the close be always *Ut* or *La*, according to the scale. In this way he will understand what you mean, and the essential relations for correct singing and playing will always be present in his mind; his execution will be better and his progress quicker. There is nothing funnier than what the French call " natural sol-faing; " it consists in removing the real meaning of things and putting in their place other meanings which only distract us. There is nothing more natural than sol-faing by transposition, when the scale is transposed. But I have said enough, and more than enough, about music; teach it as you please, so long as it is nothing but play.

We are now thoroughly acquainted with the condition of foreign bodies in relation to our own, their weight, form, colour, density, size, distance, temperature, stability, or motion. We have learnt which of them to approach or avoid, how to set about overcoming their resistance or to resist them so as to prevent ourselves from injury; but this is not enough. Our own body is constantly wasting and as constantly requires to be renewed. Although we have the power of changing other substances into our own, our choice is not a matter of indifference. Everything is not food for man, and what may be food for him is not all equally suitable; it depends on his racial constitution, the country he lives in, his individual temperament, and the way of living which his condition demands.

If we had to wait till experience taught us to know and choose fit food for ourselves, we should die of hunger or poison; but a kindly providence which has made pleasure the means of self-preservation to sentient beings teaches us through our palate what is suitable for our stomach. In a state of nature there is no better doctor than a man's own appetite, and no doubt in a state of nature man could find the most palateable food the most wholesome.

Nor is this all. Our Maker provides, not only for those needs he has created, but for those we create for ourselves; and it is to keep the balance between our wants and our needs that he has caused our tastes to change and vary with our way of living. The further we are from a state of nature, the more we lose our natural tastes; or rather, habit becomes a second nature, and so completely replaces our real nature, that we have lost all knowledge of it.

From this it follows that the most natural tastes should be the simplest, for those are more easily changed; but when they are sharpened and stimulated by our fancies they assume a form which is incapable of modification. The man who so far has not adapted himself to one country can learn the ways of any country whatsoever; but the man who has adopted the habits of one particular country can never shake them off.

This seems to be true of all our senses, especially of taste. Our first food is milk; we only become accustomed by degrees to strong flavours; at first we dislike them. Fruit, vegetables, herbs, and then fried meat without salt or seasoning. formed the feasts of primitive man. When the savage tastes wine for the first time, he makes a grimace and spits it out; and even among ourselves a man who has not tasted fermented liquors before twenty cannot get used to them; we should all be sober if we did not have wine when we were children. Indeed, the simpler our tastes are, the more general they are; made dishes are those most frequently disliked. Did you ever meet with any one who disliked bread or water? Here is the finger of nature, this then is our rule. Preserve the child's primitive tastes as long as possible; let his food be plain and simple, let strong flavours be unknown to his palate, and do not let his diet be too uniform.

I am not asking, for the present, whether this way of living is healthier or no; that is not what I have in view. It is enough for me to know that my choice is more in accordance with nature, and that it can be more readily adapted to other conditions. In my opinion, those who say children should be accustomed to the food they will have when they are grown up are mistaken. Why should their food be the same when their way of living is so different? A man worn out by labour, anxiety, and pain needs tasty foods to give fresh vigour to his brain; a child fresh from his games, a child whose body is growing, needs plentiful food which will supply more chyle. Moreover the grown man has already a settled profession, occupation, and home, but who can tell what Fate holds in store for the child? Let us not give him so fixed a bent in any direction that he cannot change it if required without hardship. Do not bring him up so that he would die of hunger in a foreign land if he does not take a French cook about with him; do not let him say at some future time that France is the only country where the food is fit to eat. By the way, that is a strange way of praising one's country. On the other hand, I myself should say that the French are the only people who do not know what good food is, since they require such a special art to make their dishes eatable.

Of all our different senses, we are usually most affected by taste. Thus it concerns us more nearly to judge aright of what will actually become part of ourselves, than of that which will merely form part of our environment. Many things are matters of indifference to touch, hearing, and sight; but taste is affected by almost everything. Moreover the activity of this sense is wholly physical and material; of all the senses, it alone makes no appeal to the imagination, or at least, imagination plays a smaller part in its sensations; while imitation and imagination often bring morality into the impressions of the other senses. Thus, speaking generally, soft and pleasure - loving minds, passionate and truly sensitive dispositions, which are easily stirred by the other senses, are usually indifferent to this. From this very fact, which apparently places taste below our other senses and makes our inclination towards it the more despicable, I draw just the opposite conclusion—that the best way to lead children is by the mouth. Greediness is a better motive than vanity; for the former is a natural appetite directly dependent on the senses, while the latter is the outcome of convention, it is the slave of human caprice and liable to every kind of abuse. Believe me the child will cease to care about his food only too soon, and when his heart is too busy, his palate will be idle. When he is grown up greediness will be expelled by a host of stronger passions, while vanity will only be stimulated by them; for this latter passion feeds upon the rest till at length they are all swallowed up in it. I have sometimes studied those men who pay great attention to good eating, men whose first waking thought is—What shall we have to eat to-day? men who describe their dinner with as much detail as Polybius describes a combat. I have found these so-called men were only children of forty, without strength or vigour—*fruges consumere nati*. Gluttony is the vice of feeble minds. The gourmand has his brains in his palate, he can do nothing but eat; he is so stupid and incapable that the table is the only place for him, and dishes are the only things he knows anything about. Let us leave him to this business without regret; it is better for him and for us.

It is a small mind that fears lest greediness should take root in the child who is fit for something better. The child thinks of nothing but his food, the youth pays no heed to it at all; every kind of food is good, and we have other things to attend to. Yet I would not have you use the low motive unwisely. I would not have you trust to dainties rather than to the honour which is the reward of a good deed. But childhood is, or ought to be, a time of play and merry sports, and I do not see why the rewards of purely bodily exercises should not be material and sensible rewards. If a little lad in Majorca sees a basket on the tree-top and brings it down with his sling, is it not fair that he should get something by this, and a good breakfast should repair the strength spent in getting it. If a young Spartan, facing the risk of a hundred stripes, slips skilfully into the kitchen, and steals a live fox-cub, carries it off in his garment, and is scratched, bitten till the blood comes, and for shame lest he should be caught the child allows his bowels to be torn out without a movement or a cry, is it not fair that he should keep his spoils, that he should eat his prey after it has eaten him? A good meal should never be a reward; but why should it not be sometimes the result of efforts made to get it. Emile does not consider the cake I put on the stone as a reward for good running; he knows that the only way to get the cake is to get there first.

This does not contradict my previous rules about simple food; for to tempt a child's appetite you need not stimulate it, you need only satisfy it; and the commonest things will do this if you do not attempt to refine children's taste. Their perpetual hunger, the result of their need for growth, will be the best sauce. Fruit, milk, a piece of cake just a little better than ordinary bread, and above all the art of dispensing these things prudently, by these means you may lead a host of children to the world's end, without on the one hand giving them a taste for strong flavours, nor on the other hand letting them get tired of their food.

The indifference of children towards meat is one proof that the taste for meat is unnatural; their preference is for vegetable foods, such as milk, pastry, fruit, etc. Beware of changing this natural taste and making children flesh-eaters, if not for their health's sake, for the sake of their character; for how can one explain away the fact that great meat-eaters are usually fiercer and more cruel than other men; this has been recognised at all times and in all places. The English are noted for their cruelty[1] while the Gaures[2] are the gentlest of men. All savages are cruel, and it is not their customs that tend in this direction; their cruelty is the result of their food. They go to war as to the chase, and treat men as they would treat bears. Indeed in England butchers are not allowed to give evidence in a court of law,[3] no more can surgeons. Great criminals prepare themselves for murder by drinking blood. Homer makes his flesh-eating Cyclops a terrible man, while his Lotus-eaters are so delightful that those who went to trade with them forgot even their own country to dwell among them.

" You ask me," said Plutarch, " why Pythagoras abstained from eating the flesh of beasts, but I ask you, what courage must have been needed by the first man who raised to his lips the flesh of the slain, who broke with his teeth the bones of a dying beast, who had dead bodies, corpses, placed before him and swallowed down limbs which a few moments ago were bleating, bellowing, walking, and seeing? How could his hand plunge the knife into the heart of a sentient creature, how could his eyes look on murder, how could he behold a poor helpless animal bled to death, scorched, and dismembered? how can he bear the sight of this quivering flesh? does not the very smell of it turn his stomach? is he not repelled, disgusted, horror-struck, when he has to handle the blood from these wounds, and to cleanse his fingers from the dark and viscous bloodstains?

[1] I am aware that the English make a boast of their humanity and of the kindly disposition of their race, which they call " good-natured people;" but in vain do they proclaim this fact; no one else says it of them.
[2] The Banians, who abstain from flesh even more completely than the Gaures, are almost as gentle as the Gaures themselves, but as their morality is less pure and their form of worship less reasonable they are not such good men.
[3] One of the English translators of my book has pointed out my mistake, and both of them have corrected it. Butchers and surgeons are allowed to give evidence in the law courts, but butchers may not serve on juries in criminal cases, though surgeons are allowed to do so.

"The scorched skins wriggled upon the ground,
The shrinking flesh bellowed upon the spit.
Man cannot eat them without a shudder;
He seems to hear their cries within his breast.

"Thus must he have felt the first time he did despite to nature and made this horrible meal; the first time he hungered for the living creature, and desired to feed upon the beast which was still grazing; when he bade them slay, dismember, and cut up the sheep which licked his hands. It is those who began these cruel feasts, not those who abandon them, who should cause surprise, and there were excuses for those primitive men, excuses which we have not, and the absence of such excuses multiplies our barbarity a hundredfold.

"'Mortals, beloved of the gods,' says this primitive man, 'compare our times with yours; see how happy you are, and how wretched were we. The earth, newly formed, the air heavy with moisture, were not yet subjected to the rule of the seasons. Three-fourths of the surface of the globe was flooded by the ever-shifting channels of rivers uncertain of their course, and covered with pools, lakes, and bottomless morasses. The remaining quarter was covered with woods and barren forests. The earth yielded no good fruit, we had no instruments of tillage, we did not even know the use of them, and the time of harvest never came for those who had sown nothing. Thus hunger was always in our midst. In winter, mosses and the bark of trees were our common food. A few green roots of dogs-bit or heather were a feast, and when men found beech-mast, nuts, or acorns, they danced for joy round the beech or oak, to the sound of some rude song, while they called the earth their mother and their nurse. This was their only festival, their only sport; all the rest of man's life was spent in sorrow, pain, and hunger.

"'At length, when the bare and naked earth no longer offered us any food, we were compelled in self-defence to outrage nature, and to feed upon our companions in distress, rather than perish with them. But you, oh, cruel men! who forces you to shed blood? Behold the wealth of good things about you, the fruits yielded by the earth, the wealth of field and vineyard; the animals give their milk for your drink and their fleece for your clothing. What more do you ask? What madness compels you to commit such murders, when you have already more than you can eat or drink? Why do you slander our mother earth, and accuse her of denying you food? Why do you sin against Ceres, the inventor of the sacred laws, and against the gracious Bacchus, the comforter of man, as if their lavish gifts were not enough to preserve mankind? Have you the heart to mingle their sweet fruits with the bones upon your table, to eat with the milk the blood of the beasts which gave it? The lions and panthers, wild beasts as you call them, are driven to follow their natural instinct, and they kill other beasts that they may live. But, a hundredfold fiercer than they, you fight against your instincts without cause, and abandon yourselves to the most cruel pleasures. The animals you eat are not those who devour others; you do not eat the carnivorous beasts, you take them as your pattern. You only hunger for the sweet and gentle creatures which harm no one, which follow you, serve you, and are devoured by you as the reward of their service.

"'O unnatural murderer! if you persist in the assertion that nature has made you to devour your fellow-creatures, beings of flesh and blood, living and feeling like yourself, stifle if you can that horror with which nature makes you regard these horrible feasts; slay the animals yourself, slay them, I say, with your own hands, without knife or mallet; tear them with your nails like the lion and the bear, take this ox and rend him in pieces, plunge your claws into his hide; eat this lamb while it is yet alive, devour its warm flesh, drink its soul with its blood. You shudder! you dare not feel the living throbbing flesh between your teeth? Ruthless man; you begin by slaying the animal and then you devour it, as if to slay it twice. It is not enough. You turn against the dead flesh, it revolts you, it must be transformed by fire, boiled and roasted, seasoned and disguised with drugs; you must have butchers, cooks, turnspits, men who will rid the murder of its horrors, who will dress the dead bodies so that the taste deceived by these disguises will not reject what is strange to it, and will feast on corpses, the very sight of which would sicken you.'"

Although this quotation is irrelevant, I cannot resist the temptation to transcribe it, and I think few of my readers will resent it.

In conclusion, whatever food you give your children, provided you accustom them to nothing but plain and simple dishes, let them eat and run and play as much as they want; you may be sure they will never eat too much and will never have indigestion; but if you keep them hungry half their time, when they do contrive to evade your vigilance, they will take advantage of it as far as they can; they will eat till they are sick, they will gorge themselves till they can eat no more. Our appetite is only excessive because we try to impose on it rules other than those of nature, opposing, controlling, prescribing, adding, or substracting; the scales are always in our hands, but the scales are the measure of our caprices not of our stomachs. I return to my usual illustration; among peasants the cupboard and the apple-loft are always left open, and indigestion is unknown alike to children and grown-up people.

If, however, it happened that a child were too great an eater, though, under my system, I think it is impossible, he is so easily distracted by his favourite games that one might easily starve him without his knowing it. How is it that teachers have failed to use such a safe and easy weapon. Herodotus records that the Lydians,[1]

[1] The ancient historians are full of opinions which may be useful, even if the facts which they present are false. But we do not know how to make any real use of history. Criticism and erudition are our only care; as if it mattered more that a statement were true or false than that

under the pressure of great scarcity, decided to invent sports and other amusements with which to cheat their hunger, and they passed whole-days without thought of food. Your learned teachers may have read this passage time after time without seeing how it might be applied to children. One of these teachers will probably tell me that a child does not like to leave his dinner for his lessons. You are right, sir—I was not thinking of that sort of sport.

The sense of smell is to taste what sight is to touch; it goes before it and gives it warning that it will be affected by this or that substance; and it inclines it to seek or shun this experience according to the impressions received beforehand. I have been told that savages receive impressions quite different from ours, and that they have quite different ideas with regard to pleasant or unpleasant odours. I can well believe it. Odours alone are slight sensations; they affect the imagination rather than the senses, and they work mainly through the anticipations they arouse. This being so, and the tastes of savages being so unlike the taste of civilised men, they should lead them to form very different ideas with regard to flavours and therefore with regard to the odours which announce them. A Tartar must enjoy the smell of a haunch of putrid horseflesh, much as a sportsman enjoys a very high partridge.

Our idle sensations, such as the scents wafted from the flower beds, must pass unnoticed among men who walk too much to care for strolling in a garden, and do not work enough to find pleasure in repose. Hungry men would find little pleasure in scents which did not proclaim the approach of food.

Smell is the sense of the imagination; as it gives tone to the nerves it must have a great effect on the brain; that is why it revives us for the time, but eventually causes exhaustion. Its effects on love are pretty generally recognised. The sweet perfumes of a dressing-room are not so slight a snare as you may fancy them, and I hardly know whether to congratulate or condole with that wise and somewhat insensible person whose senses are never stirred by the scent of the flowers his mistress wears in her bosom.

Hence the sense of smell should not be over-active in early childhood; the imagination, as yet unstirred by changing passions, is scarcely susceptible of emotion, and we have not enough experience to discern beforehand from one sense the promise of another. This view is confirmed by observation, and it is certain that the sense of smell is dull and almost blunted in most children. Not that their sensations are less acute than those of grown-up people, but that there is no idea associated with them; they do not easily experience pleasure or pain, and are not flattered or hurt as we are. Without going beyond my system, and without recourse to comparative anatomy, I think we can easily see why women are generally fonder of perfumes than men.

we should be able to get a useful lesson from it. A wise man should consider history a tissue of fables whose morals are well adapted to the human heart.

It is said that from early childhood the Redskins of Canada train their sense of smell to such a degree of subtlety that, although they have dogs, they do not condescend to use them in hunting— they are their own dogs Indeed I believe that if children were trained to scent their dinner as a dog scents game, their sense of smell might be nearly as perfect; but I see no very real advantage to be derived from this sense, except by teaching the child to observe the relation between smell and taste. Nature has taken care to compel us to learn these relations. She has made the exercise of the latter sense practically inseparable from that of the former, by placing their organs close together, and by providing, in the mouth, a direct pathway between them, so that we taste nothing without smelling it too. Only I would not have these natural relations disturbed in order to deceive the child, *e.g.*, to conceal the taste of medicine with an aromatic odour, for the discord between the senses is too great for deception, the more active sense overpowers the other, the medicine is just as distasteful, and this disagreeable association extends to every sensation experienced at the time; so the slightest of these sensations recalls the rest to his imagination and a very pleasant perfume is for him only a nasty smell; thus our foolish precautions increase the sum total of his unpleasant sensations at the cost of his pleasant sensations.

In the following books I have still to speak of the training of a sort of sixth sense, called common-sense, not so much because it is common to all men, but because it results from the well-regulated use of the other five, and teaches the nature of things by the sumtotal of their external aspects. So this sixth sense has no special organ, it has its seat in the brain, and its sensations which are purely internal are called percepts or ideas. The number of these ideas is the measure of our knowledge; exactness of thought depends on their clearness and precision; the art of comparing them one with another is called human reason. Thus what I call the reasoning of the senses, or the reasoning of the child, consists in the formation of simple ideas through the associated experience of several sensations; what I call the reasoning of the intellect, consists in the formation of complex ideas through the association of several simple ideas.

If my method is indeed that of nature, and if I am not mistaken in the application of that method, we have led our pupil through the region of sensation to the bounds of the child's reasoning; the first step we take beyond these bounds must be the step of a man. But before we make this fresh advance, let us glance back for a moment at the path we have hitherto followed. Every age, every station in life, has a perfection, a ripeness, of its own. We have often heard the phrase " a grown man; " but we will consider " a grown child." This will be a new experience and none the less pleasing.

The life of finite creatures is so poor and narrow that the mere sight of what is arouses no emotion. It is fancy which decks reality, and if imagination does not lend its charm to that which touches our senses, our barren pleasure is confined to the senses alone, while the heart remains cold. The earth adorned with the treasures of autumn displays a wealth of colour which the eye admires; but this admiration fails to move us, it springs rather from thought than from feeling. In spring the country is almost bare and leafless, the trees give no shade, the grass has hardly begun to grow, yet the heart is touched by the sight. In this new birth of nature, we feel the revival of our own life; the memories of past pleasures surround us; tears of delight, those companions of pleasure ever ready to accompany a pleasing sentiment, tremble on our eyelids. Animated. lively, and delightful though the vintage may be, we behold it without a tear.

And why is this? Because imagination adds to the sight of spring the image of the seasons which are yet to come; the eye sees the tender shoot, the mind's eye beholds its flowers, fruit, and foliage. and even the mysteries they may conceal. It blends successive stages into one moment's experience; we see things, not so much as they will be, but as we would have them be, for imagination has only to take her choice. In autumn, on the other hand, we only behold the present; if we wish to look forward to spring, winter bars the way, and our shivering imagination dies away among its frost and snow.

This is the source of the charm we find in beholding the beauties of childhood, rather than the perfection of manhood. When do we really delight in beholding a man? When the memory of his deeds leads us to look back over his life and his youth is renewed in our eyes. If we are reduced to viewing him as he is, or to picturing him as he will be in old age, the thought of declining years destroys all our pleasure. There is no pleasure in seeing a man hastening to his grave; the image of death makes all hideous.

But when I think of a child of ten or twelve, strong, healthy, well-grown for his age, only pleasant thoughts are called up, whether of the present or the future. I see him keen, eager, and full of life, free from gnawing cares and painful forebodings, absorbed in this present state, and delighting in a fullness of life which seems to extend beyond himself. I look forward to a time when he will use his daily increasing sense, intelligence and vigour, those growing powers of which he continually gives fresh proof. I watch the child with delight, I picture to myself the man with even greater pleasure. His eager life seems to stir my own pulses, I seem to live his life and in his vigour I renew my own.

The hour strikes, the scene is changed. All of a sudden his eye grows dim, his mirth has fled. Farewell mirth, farewell untrammelled sports in which he delighted. A stern, angry man takes him by the hand, saying gravely, "Come with me, sir," and he is led away. As they are entering the room, I catch a glimpse of books. Books, what dull food for a child of his age! The poor child allows himself to be dragged away; he casts a sorrowful look on all about him, and departs in silence, his eyes swollen with the tears he dare not shed, and his heart bursting with the sighs he dare not utter.

You who have no such cause for fear, you for whom no period of life is a time of weariness and tedium, you who welcome days without care and nights without impatience, you who only reckon time by your pleasures, come, my happy kindly pupil, and console us for the departure of that miserable creature. Come! Here he is and at his approach I feel a thrill of delight which I see he shares. It is his friend, his comrade, who meets him; when he sees me he knows very well that he will not be long without amusement; we are never dependent on each other, but we are always on good terms, and we are never so happy as when together.

His face, his bearing, his expression, speak of confidence and contentment; health shines in his countenance, his firm step speaks of strength; his colour, delicate but not sickly, has nothing of softness or effeminacy. Sun and wind have already set the honourable stamp of manhood on his countenance; his rounded muscles already begin to show some signs of growing individuality; his eyes, as yet unlighted by the flame of feeling, have at least all their native calm. They have not been darkened by prolonged sorrow, nor are his cheeks furrowed by ceaseless tears. Behold in his quick and certain movements the natural vigour of his age and the confidence of independence. His manner is free and open, but without a trace of insolence or vanity; his head which has not been bent over books does not fall upon his breast; there is no need to say, " Hold your head up," he will neither hang his head for shame or fear.

Make room for him, gentlemen, in your midst; question him boldly; have no fear of importunity, chatter, or impertinent questions. You need not be afraid that he will take possession of you and expect you to devote yourself entirely to him, so that you cannot get rid of him.

Neither need you look for compliments from him; nor will he tell you what I have taught him to say; expect nothing from him but the plain, simple truth, without addition or ornament and without vanity. He will tell you the wrong things he has done and thought as readily as the right, without troubling himself in the least as to the effect of his words upon you; he will use speech with all the simplicity of its first beginnings.

We love to augur well of our children, and we are continually regretting the flood of folly which overwhelms the hopes we would fain have rested on some chance phrase. If my scholar rarely gives me cause for such prophecies, neither will he give me cause for such regrets, for he never says a useless word, and does not exhaust himself by chattering when he knows there is no one to listen to him. His ideas are few but precise, he knows nothing by rote but much by experience. If he reads our books worse than other children, he reads far better in the book of nature; his thoughts are not in his tongue but in his brain; he has less memory and more judgment; he can only speak one language, but he understands what he is saying, and if his speech is not so good as that of other children his deeds are better.

He does not know the meaning of habit, routine, and custom; what he did yesterday has no control over what he is doing [1] to-day; he follows no rule, submits to no authority, copies no pattern, and only acts or speaks as he pleases. So do not expect set speeches or studied manners from him, but just the faithful expression of his thoughts and the conduct that springs from his inclinations.

You will find he has a few moral ideas concerning his present state and none concerning manhood; what use could he make of them, for the child is not, as yet, an active member of society. Speak to him of freedom, of property, or even of what is usually done; he may understand you so far; he knows why his things are his own, and why other things are not his, and nothing more. Speak to him of duty or obedience; he will not know what you are talking about; bid him do something and he will pay no attention; but say to him, " If you will give me this pleasure, I will repay it when required," and he will hasten to give you satisfaction, for he asks nothing better than to extend his domain, to acquire rights over you, which will, he knows, be respected. Maybe he is not sorry to have a place of his own, to be reckoned of some account; but if he has formed this latter idea, he has already left the realms of nature, and you have failed to bar the gates of vanity.

For his own part, should he need help, he will ask it readily of the first person he meets. He will ask it of a king as readily as of his servant; all men are equals in his eyes. From his way of asking you will see he knows you owe him nothing, that he is asking a favour. He knows too that humanity moves you to grant this favour; his words are few and simple. His voice, his look, his gesture are those of a being equally familiar with compliance and refusal. It is neither the crawling, servile submission of the slave, nor the imperious tone of the master, it is a modest confidence in mankind; it is the noble and touching gentleness of a creature, free, yet sensitive and feeble, who asks aid of a being, free, but strong and kindly. If you grant his request he will not thank you, but he will feel he has incurred a debt. If you refuse he will neither complain nor insist; he knows it is useless; he will not say, " They refused to help me," but " It was impossible," and as I have already said, we do not rebel against necessity when once we have perceived it.

Leave him to himself and watch his actions without speaking; consider what he is doing and how he sets about it. He does not require to convince himself that he is free, so he never acts thought-

---

[1] Habit owes its charm to man's natural idleness, and this idleness grows upon us if indulged; it is easier to do what we have already done, there is a beaten path which is easily followed. Thus we may observe that habit is very strong in the aged and in the indolent, and very weak in the young and active. The rule of habit is only good for feeble hearts, and it makes them more and more feeble day by day. The only useful habit for children is to be accustomed to submit without difficulty to necessity, and the only useful habit for man is to submit without difficulty to the rule of reason. Every other habit is a vice.

lessly and merely to show that he can do what he likes; does he not know that he is always his own master? He is quick, alert, and ready; his movements are eager as befits his age, but you will not find one which has no end in view. Whatever he wants, he will never attempt what is beyond his powers, for he has learnt by experience what those powers are; his means will always be adapted to the end in view, and he will rarely attempt anything without the certainty of success; his eye is keen and true; he will not be so stupid as to go and ask other people about what he sees; he will examine it on his own account, and before he asks he will try every means at his disposal to discover what he wants to know for himself. If he lights upon some unexpected difficulty, he will be less upset than others; if there is danger he will be less afraid. His imagination is still asleep and nothing has been done to arouse it; he only sees what is really there, and rates the danger at its true worth; so he never loses his head. He does not rebel against necessity, her hand is too heavy upon him; he has borne her yoke all his life long, he is well used to it; he is always ready for anything.

Work or play are all one to him, his games are his work; he knows no difference. He brings to everything the cheerfulness of interest, the charm of freedom, and he snows the bent of his own mind and the extent of his knowledge. Is there anything better worth seeing, anything more touching or more delightful, than a pretty child, with merry, cheerful glance, easy contented manner, open smiling countenance, playing at the most important things, or working at the lightest amusements?

Would you now judge him by comparison? Set him among other children and leave him to himself. You will soon see which has made most progress, which comes nearer to the perfection of childhood. Among all the children in the town there is none more skilful and none so strong. Among young peasants he is their equal in strength and their superior in skill. In everything within a child's grasp he judges, reasons, and shows a forethought beyond the rest. Is it a matter of action, running, jumping, or shifting things, raising weights or estimating distance, inventing games, carrying off prizes; you might say, " Nature obeys his word," so easily does he bend all things to his will. He is made to lead, to rule his fellows; talent and experience take the place of right and authority. In any garb, under any name, he will still be first; everywhere he will rule the rest, they will always feel his superiority, he will be master without knowing it, and they will serve him unawares.

He has reached the perfection of childhood; he has lived the life of a child; his progress has not been bought at the price of his happiness, he has gained both. While he has acquired all the wisdom of a child, he has been as free and happy as his health permits. If the Reaper Death should cut him off and rob us of our hopes, we need not bewail alike his life and death, we shall not have the added grief of knowing that we caused him pain; we will say,

"His childhood, at least, was happy; we have robbed him of nothing that nature gave him."

The chief drawback to this early education is that it is only appreciated by the wise; to vulgar eyes the child so carefully educated is nothing but a rough little boy. A tutor thinks rather of the advantage to himself than to his pupil; he makes a point of showing that there has been no time wasted; he provides his pupil with goods which can be readily displayed in the shop window, accomplishments which can be shown off at will; no matter whether they are useful, provided they are easily seen. Without choice or discrimination he loads his memory with a pack of rubbish. If the child is to be examined he is set to display his wares; he spreads them out, satisfies those who behold them, packs up his bundle and goes his way. My pupil is poorer, he has no bundle to display, he has only himself to show. Now neither child nor man can be read at a glance. Where are the observers who can at once discern the characteristics of this child? There are such people, but they are few and far between; among a thousand fathers you will scarcely find one.

Too many questions are tedious and revolting to most of us and especially to children. After a few minutes their attention flags, they cease to listen to your everlasting questions and reply at random. This way of testing them is pedantic and useless; a chance word will often show their sense and intelligence better than much talking, but take care that the answer is neither a matter of chance nor yet learnt by heart. A man must needs have a good judgment if he is to estimate the judgment of a child.

I heard the late Lord Hyde tell the following story about one of his friends. He had returned from Italy after a three years' absence, and was anxious to test the progress of his son, a child of nine or ten. One evening he took a walk with the child and his tutor across a level space where the schoolboys were flying their kites. As they went, the father said to his son, "Where is the kite that casts this shadow?" Without hesitating and without glancing upwards the child replied, "Over the high road." "And indeed," said Lord Hyde, "the high road was between us and the sun." At these words, the father kissed his child, and having finished his examination he departed. The next day he sent the tutor the papers settling an annuity on him in addition to his salary.

What a father! and what a promising child! The question is exactly adapted to the child's age, the answer is perfectly simple; but see what precision it implies in the child's judgment. Thus did the pupil of Aristotle master the famous steed which no squire had ever been able to tame.

BOOK III

THE whole course of man's life up to adolescence is a period of weakness; yet there comes a time during these early years when the child's strength overtakes the demands upon it, when the growing creature, though absolutely weak, is relatively strong. His needs are not fully developed and his present strength is more than enough for them. He would be a very feeble man, but he is a strong child.

What is the cause of man's weakness? It is to be found in the disproportion between his strength and his desires. It is our passions that make us weak, for our natural strength is not enough for their satisfaction. To limit our desires comes to the same thing, therefore, as to increase our strength. When we can do more than we want, we have strength enough and to spare, we are really strong. This is the third stage of childhood, the stage with which I am about to deal. I still speak of childhood for want of a better word; for our scholar is approaching adolescence, though he has not yet reached the age of puberty.

About twelve or thirteen the child's strength increases far more rapidly than his needs. The strongest and fiercest of the passions is still unknown, his physical development is still imperfect and seems to await the call of the will. He is scarcely aware of extremes of heat and cold and braves them with impunity. He needs no coat, his blood is warm; no spices, hunger is his sauce, no food comes amiss at this age; if he is sleepy he stretches himself on the ground and goes to sleep; he finds all he needs within his reach; he is not tormented by any imaginary wants; he cares nothing what others think; his desires are not beyond his grasp; not only is he self-sufficing, but for the first and last time in his life he has more strength than he needs.

I know beforehand what you will say. You will not assert that the child has more needs than I attribute to him, but you will deny his strength. You forget that I am speaking of my own pupil, not of those puppets who walk with difficulty from one room to another, who toil indoors and carry bundles of paper. Manly strength, you say, appears only with manhood; the vital spirits, distilled in their proper vessels and spreading through the whole body, can alone make the muscles firm, sensitive, tense, and springy, can alone cause real strength. This is the philosophy of the study; I appeal to that of experience. In the country districts, I see big lads hoeing, digging, guiding the plough, filling the wine-cask, driving the cart, like their fathers; you would take them for grown men if their voices did not betray them. Even in our towns, iron-workers', tool makers', and blacksmiths' lads are almost as strong as their masters and would be scarcely less skilful had their training begun earlier. If there is a difference, and I do not deny that there is, it is, I repeat, much less than the difference between the stormy passions of the man and the few wants of the child. Moreover, it is not merely a question of bodily strength, but more especially of strength of mind, which reinforces and directs the bodily strength.

This interval in which the strength of the individual is in excess of his wants is, as I have said, relatively though not absolutely the time of greatest strength. It is the most precious time in his life; it comes but once; it is very short, all too short, as you will see when you consider the importance of using it aright.

He has, therefore, a surplus of strength and capacity which he will never have again. What use shall he make of it? He will strive to use it in tasks which will help at need. He will, so to speak, cast his present surplus into the storehouse of the future; the vigorous child will make provision for the feeble man; but he will not store his goods where thieves may break in, nor in barns which are not his own. To store them aright, they must be in the hands and the head, they must be stored within himself. This is the time for work, instruction, and inquiry. And note that this is no arbitrary choice of mine, it is the way of nature herself.

Human intelligence is finite, and not only can no man know everything, he cannot even acquire all the scanty knowledge of others. Since the contrary of every false proposition is a truth, there are as many truths as falsehoods. We must, therefore, choose what to teach as well as when to teach it. Some of the information within our reach is false, some is useless, some merely serves to puff up its possessor. The small store which really contributes to our welfare alone deserves the study of a wise man, and therefore of a child whom one would have wise. He must know not merely what is, but what is useful.

From this small stock we must also deduct those truths which require a full grown mind for their understanding, those which suppose a knowledge of man's relations to his fellow-men—a knowledge which no child can acquire; these things, although in themselves true, lead an inexperienced mind into mistakes with regard to other matters.

We are now confined to a circle, small indeed compared with the whole of human thought, but this circle is still a vast sphere when measured by the child's mind. Dark places of the human understanding, what rash hand shall dare to raise your veil? What pitfalls does our so-called science prepare for the miserable child. Would you guide him along this dangerous path and draw the veil from the face of nature? Stay your hand. First make sure that neither he nor you will become dizzy. Beware of the specious charms of error and the intoxicating fumes of pride. Keep this truth ever before you—Ignorance never did any one any harm, error alone is fatal, and we do not lose our way through ignorance but through self-confidence.

His progress in geometry may serve as a test and a true measure of the growth of his intelligence, but as soon as he can distinguish between what is useful and what is useless, much skill and discretion are required to lead him towards theoretical studies. For example, would you have him find a mean proportional between two lines, contrive that he should require to find a square equal to a given rectangle; if two mean proportionals are required, you must first contrive to interest him in the doubling of the cube. See how we are gradually approaching the moral ideas which distinguish between good and evil. Hitherto we have known no law but necessity, now we are considering what is useful; we shall soon come to what is fitting and right.

Man's diverse powers are stirred by the same instinct. The bodily activity, which seeks an outlet for its energies, is succeeded by the mental activity which seeks for knowledge. Children are first restless, then curious; and this curiosity, rightly directed, is the means of development for the age with which we are dealing. Always distinguish between natural and acquired tendencies. There is a zeal for learning which has no other foundation than a wish to appear learned, and there is another which springs from man's natural curiosity about all things far or near which may affect himself. The innate desire for comfort and the impossibility of its complete satisfaction impel him to the endless search for fresh means of contributing to its satisfaction. This is the first principle of curiosity; a principle natural to the human heart, though its growth is proportional to the development of our feeling and knowledge. If a man of science were left on a desert island with his books and instruments and knowing that he must spend the rest of his life there, he would scarcely trouble himself about the solar system, the laws of attraction, or the differential calculus. He might never even open a book again; but he would never rest till he had explored the furthest corner of his island, however large it might be. Let us therefore omit from our early studies such knowledge as has no natural attraction for us, and confine ourselves to such things as instinct impels us to study.

Our island is this earth; and the most striking object we behold is the sun. As soon as we pass beyond our immediate surroundings, one or both of these must meet our eye. Thus the philosophy of most savage races is mainly directed to imaginary divisions of the earth or to the divinity of the sun.

What a sudden change you will say. Just now we were concerned with what touches ourselves, with our immediate environment, and all at once we are exploring the round world and leaping to the bounds of the universe. This change is the result of our growing strength and of the natural bent of the mind. While we were weak and feeble, self-preservation concentrated our attention on ourselves; now that we are strong and powerful, the desire for a wider sphere carries us beyond ourselves as far as our eyes can reach. But as the intellectual world is still unknown to us, our thoughts are bounded by the visible horizon, and our understanding only develops within the limits of our vision.

Let us transform our sensations into ideas, but do not let us jump all at once from the objects of sense to objects of thought. The latter are attained by means of the former. Let the senses be the only guide for the first workings of reason. No book but the world, no teaching but that of fact. The child who reads ceases to think, he only reads. He is acquiring words not knowledge.

Teach your scholar to observe the phenomena of nature; you will soon rouse his curiosity, but if you would have it grow, do not be in too great a hurry to satisfy this curiosity. Put the problems before him and let him solve them himself. Let him know nothing because you have told him, but because he has learnt it for himself. Let him not be taught science, let him discover it. If ever you substitute authority for reason he will cease to reason; he will be a mere plaything of other people's thoughts.

You wish to teach this child geography and you provide him with globes, spheres, and maps. What elaborate preparations! What is the use of all these symbols; why not begin by showing him the real thing so that he may at least know what you are talking about?

One fine evening we are walking in a suitable place where the wide horizon gives us a full view of the setting sun, and we note the objects which mark the place where it sets. Next morning we return to the same place for a breath of fresh air before sun-rise. We see the rays of light which announce the sun's approach; the glow increases, the east seems afire, and long before the sun appears the light leads us to expect its return. Every moment you expect to see it. There it is at last! A shining point appears like a flash of lightning and soon fills the whole space; the veil of darkness rolls away, man perceives his dwelling place in fresh beauty. During the night the grass has assumed a fresher green; in the light of early dawn, and gilded by the first rays of the sun, it seems covered with a shining network of dew reflecting the light and colour. The birds raise their chorus of praise to greet the Father of life, not one of them is mute; their gentle warbling is softer than by day, it expresses the langour of a peaceful waking. All these produce an impression of freshness which seems to reach the very soul. It is a brief hour of enchantment which no man can resist; a sight so grand, so fair, so delicious, that none can behold it unmoved.

Fired with this enthusiasm, the master wishes to impart it to the child. He expects to rouse his emotion by drawing attention to his own. Mere folly! The splendour of nature lives in man's heart; to be seen, it must be felt. The child sees the objects themselves, but does not perceive their relations, and cannot hear their harmony. It needs knowledge he has not yet acquired, feelings he has not yet experienced, to receive the complex impression which results from all these separate sensations. If he has not wandered over arid plains, if his feet have not been scorched by the burning sands of the desert, if he has not breathed the hot and oppressive air reflected from the glowing rocks, how shall he delight in the fresh air of a fine morning. The scent of flowers, the beauty of foliage, the moistness of the dew, the soft turf beneath his feet, how shall all these delight his senses. How shall the song of the birds arouse voluptuous emotion if love and pleasure are still unknown to him? How shall he behold with rapture the birth of this fair day, if his imagination cannot paint the joys it may bring in its track? How can he feel the beauty of nature, while the hand that formed it is unknown?

Never tell the child what he cannot understand: no descriptions, no eloquence, no figures of speech, no poetry. The time has not come for feeling or taste. Continue to be clear and cold; the time will come only too soon when you must adopt another tone.

Brought up in the spirit of our maxims, accustomed to make his own tools and not to appeal to others until he has tried and failed, he will examine everything he sees carefully and in silence. He thinks rather than questions. Be content, therefore, to show him things at a fit season; then, when you see that his curiosity is thoroughly aroused, put some brief question which will set him trying to discover the answer.

On the present occasion when you and he have carefully observed the rising sun, when you have called his attention to the mountains and other objects visible from the same spot, after he has chattered freely about them, keep quiet for a few minutes as if lost in thought and then say, "I think the sun set over there last night; it rose here this morning. How can that be?" Say no more; if he asks questions, do not answer them; talk of something else. Let him alone, and be sure he will think about it.

To train a child to be really attentive so that he may be really impressed by any truth of experience, he must spend anxious days before he discovers that truth. If he does not learn enough in this way, there is another way of drawing his attention to the matter. Turn the question about. If he does not know how the sun gets from the place where it sets to where it rises, he knows at least how it travels from sunrise to sunset, his eyes teach him that. Use the second question to throw light on the first; either your pupil is a regular dunce or the analogy is too clear to be missed. This is his first lesson in cosmography.

As we always advance slowly from one sensible idea to another, and as we give time enough to each for him to become really familiar with it before we go on to another, and lastly as we never force our scholar's attention, we are still a long way from a knowledge of the course of the sun or the shape of the earth; but as all the apparent movements of the celestial bodies depend on the same principle, and the first observation leads on to all the rest, less effort is needed, though more time, to proceed from the diurnal revolution to the calculation of eclipses, than to get a thorough understanding of day and night.

Since the sun revolves round the earth it describes a circle, and every circle must have a centre; that we know already. This centre is invisible, it is in the middle of the earth, but we can mark out two opposite points on the earth's surface which correspond to it. A skewer passed through the three points and prolonged to the sky at either end would represent the earth's axis and the sun's daily course. A round teetotum revolving on its point represents the sky turning on its axis, the two points of the teetotum are the two poles; the child will be delighted to find one of them, and I show him the tail of the Little bear. Here is a another game for the dark. Little by little we get to know the stars, and from this comes a wish to know the planets and observe the constellations.

We saw the sun rise at midsummer, we shall see it rise at Christmas or some other fine winter's day; for you know we are no lie-a-beds and we enjoy the cold. I take care to make this second observation in the same place as the first, and if skilfully lead up to, one or other will certainly exclaim, "What a funny thing! The sun is not rising in the same place; here are our land-marks, but it is rising over there. So there is the summer east and the winter east, etc." Young teacher, you are on the right track. These examples should show you how to teach the sphere without any difficulty, taking the earth for the earth and the sun for the sun.

As a general rule—never substitute the symbol for the thing signified, unless it is impossible to show the thing itself; for the child's attention is so taken up with the symbol that he will forget what it signifies.

I consider the armillary sphere a clumsy disproportioned bit of apparatus. The confused circles and the strange figures described on it suggest witchcraft and frighten the child. The earth is too small, the circles too large and too numerous, some of them, the colures, for instance, are quite useless, and the thickness of the pasteboard gives them an appearance of solidity so that they are taken for circular masses having a real existence, and when you tell the child that these are imaginary circles, he does not know what he is looking at and is none the wiser.

We are unable to put ourselves in the child's place, we fail to enter into his thoughts, we invest him with our own ideas, and while we are following our own chain of reasoning, we merely fill his head with errors and absurdities.

Should the method of studying science be analytic or synthetic? People dispute over this question, but it is not always necessary to choose between them. Sometimes the same experiments allow one to use both analysis and synthesis, and thus to guide the child by the method of instruction when he fancies he is only analysing. Then, by using both at once, each method confirms the results of the other. Starting from opposite ends, without thinking of follow-ing the same road, he will unexpectedly reach their meeting place and this will be a delightful surprise. For example, I would begin geography at both ends and add to the study of the earth's revolution the measurement of its divisions, beginning at home. While the child is studying the sphere and is thus transported to the heavens, bring him back to the divisions of the globe and show him his own home.

His geography will begin with the town he lives in and his father's country house, then the places between them, the rivers near them, and then the sun's aspect and how to find one's way by its aid. This is the meeting place. Let him make his own map, a very simple map, at first containing only two places; others may be added from time to time, as he is able to estimate their distance and position. You see at once what a good start we have given him by making his eye his compass.

No doubt he will require some guidance in spite of this, but very little, and that little without his knowing it. If he goes wrong let him alone, do not correct his mistakes; hold your tongue till he finds them out for himself and corrects them, or at most arrange something, as opportunity offers, which may show him his mistakes. If he never makes mistakes he will never learn anything thoroughly. Moreover, what he needs is not an exact knowledge of local topography, but how to find out for himself. No matter whether he carries maps in his head provided he understands what they mean, and has a clear idea of the art of making them. See what a difference there is already between the knowledge of your scholars and the ignorance of mine. They learn maps, he makes them. Here are fresh ornaments for his room.

Remember that this is the essential point in my method—Do not teach the child many things, but never to let him form inaccurate or confused ideas. I care not if he knows nothing provided he is not mistaken, and I only acquaint him with truths to guard him against the errors he might put in their place. Reason and judgment come slowly, prejudices flock to us in crowds, and from these he must be protected. But if you make science itself your object, you embark on an unfathomable and shoreless ocean, an ocean strewn with reefs from which you will never return. When I see a man in love with knowledge, yielding to its charms and flitting from one branch to another unable to stay his steps, he seems to me like a child gathering shells on the sea-shore, now picking them up, then throwing them aside for others which he sees beyond them, then taking them again, till overwhelmed by their number and unable to choose between them, he flings them all away and returns empty handed.

Time was long during early childhood; we only tried to pass our time for fear of using it ill; now it is the other way; we have not time enough for all that would be of use. The passions, remember, are drawing near, and when they knock at the door your scholar will have no ear for anything else. The peaceful age of intelligence is so short, it flies so swiftly, there is so much to be done, that it is madness to try to make your child learned. It is not your business to teach him the various sciences, but to give him a taste for them and methods of learning them when this taste is more mature. That is assuredly a fundamental principle of all good education.

This is also the time to train him gradually to prolonged attention to a given object; but this attention should never be the result of constraint, but of interest or desire; you must be very careful that it is not too much for his strength, and that it is not carried to the point of tedium. Watch him, therefore, and whatever happens, stop before he is tired, for it matters little what he learns; it does matter that he should do nothing against his will.

If he asks questions let your answers be enough to whet his curiosity but not enough to satisfy it; above all, when you find him talking at random and overwhelming you with silly questions instead of asking for information, at once refuse to answer; for it is clear that he no longer cares about the matter in hand, but wants to make you a slave to his questions. Consider his motives rather than his words. This warning, which was scarcely needed before, becomes of supreme importance when the child begins to reason.

There is a series of abstract truths by means of which all the sciences are related to common principles and are developed each in its turn. This relationship is the method of the philosophers. We are not concerned with it at present. There is quite another method by which every concrete example suggests another and always points to the next in the series. This succession, which stimulates the curiosity and so arouses the attention required by every object in turn, is the order followed by most men, and it is the right order for all children. To take our bearings so as to make our maps we must find meridians. Two points of intersection between the equal shadows morning and evening supply an excellent meridian for a thirteen-year-old astronomer. But these meridians disappear, it takes time to trace them, and you are obliged to work in one place. So much trouble and attention will at last become irksome. We foresaw this and are ready for it.

Again I must enter into minute and detailed explanations. I hear my readers murmur, but I am prepared to meet their disapproval; I will not sacrifice the most important part of this book to your impatience. You may think me as long-winded as you please; I have my own opinion as to your complaints.

Long ago my pupil and I remarked that some substances such as amber, glass, and wax, when well rubbed, attracted straws, while others did not. We accidentally discover a substance which has a more unusual property, that of attracting filings or other small particles of iron from a distance and without rubbing. How much time do we devote to this game to the exclusion of everything else! At last we discover that this property is communicated to the iron itself, which is, so to speak, endowed with life. We go to the fair one day [1] and a conjuror has a wax duck floating in a basin of water,

[1] I could not help laughing when I read an elaborate criticism of this little tale by M. de Formy. "This conjuror," says he, "who is afraid of

and he makes it follow a bit of bread. We are greatly surprised, but we do not call him a wizard, never having heard of such persons. As we are continually observing effects whose causes are unknown to us, we are in no hurry to make up our minds, and we remain in ignorance till we find an opportunity of learning.

When we get home we discuss the duck till we try to imitate it. We take a needle thoroughly magnetised, we imbed it in white wax, shaped as far as possible like a duck, with the needle running through the body, so that its eye forms the beak. We put the duck in water and put the end of a key near its beak, and you will readily understand our delight when we find that our duck follows the key just as the duck at the fair followed the bit of bread. Another time we may note the direction assumed by the duck when left in the basin; for the present we are wholly occupied with our work and we want nothing more.

The same evening we return to the fair with some bread specially prepared in our pockets, and as soon as the conjuror has performed his trick, my little doctor, who can scarcely sit still, exclaims, " The trick is quite easy; I can do it myself." " Do it then." He at once takes the bread with a bit of iron hidden in it from his pocket; his heart throbs as he approaches the table and holds out the bread, his hand trembles with excitement. The duck approaches and follows his hand. The child cries out and jumps for joy. The applause, the shouts of the crowd, are too much for him, he is beside himself. The conjuror, though disappointed, embraces him, congratulates him, begs the honour of his company on the following day, and promises to collect a still greater crowd to applaud his skill. My young scientist is very proud of himself and is beginning to chatter, but I check him at once and take him home overwhelmed with praise.

The child counts the minutes till to-morrow with absurd anxiety. He invites every one he meets, he wants all mankind to behold his glory; he can scarcely wait till the appointed hour. He hurries to the place; the hall is full already; as he enters his young heart swells with pride. Other tricks are to come first. The conjuror surpasses himself and does the most surprising things. The child sees none of these; he wriggles, perspires, and hardly breathes; the time is spent in fingering with a trembling hand the bit of bread in his pocket. His turn comes at last; the master announces it to the audience with all ceremony; he goes up looking somewhat shamefaced and takes out his bit of bread. Oh fleeting joys of human life! the duck, so tame yesterday, is quite wild to-day; instead of offering its beak it turns tail and swims away; it avoids the bread and the hand that holds it as carefully as it followed them

a child's competition and preaches to his tutor is the sort of person we meet with in the world in which Emile and such as he are living " This witty M. de Formy could not guess that this little scene was arranged beforehand, and that the juggler was taught his part in it; indeed I did not state this fact. But I have said again and again that I was not writing for people who expected to be told everything.

yesterday. After many vain attempts accompanied by derisive shouts from the audience the child complains that he is being cheated, that is not the same duck, and he defies the conjuror to attract it.

The conjuror, without further words, takes a bit of bread and offers it to the duck, which at once follows it and comes to the hand which holds it. The child takes the same bit of bread with no better success; the duck mocks his efforts and swims round the basin. Overwhelmed with confusion he abandons the attempt, ashamed to face the crowd any longer. Then the conjuror takes the bit of bread the child brought with him and uses it as successfully as his own. He takes out the bit of iron before the audience—another laugh at our expense—then with this same bread he attracts the duck as before. He repeats the experiment with a piece of bread cut by a third person in full view of the audience. He does it with his glove, with his finger-tip. Finally he goes into the middle of the room and in the emphatic tones used by such persons he declares that his duck will obey his voice as readily as his hand; he speaks and the duck obeys; he bids him go to the right and he goes, to come back again and he comes. The movement is as ready as the command. The growing applause completes our discomfiture. We slip away unnoticed and shut ourselves up in our room, without relating our successes to everybody as we had expected.

Next day there is a knock at the door. When I open it there is the conjuror, who makes a modest complaint with regard to our conduct. What had he done that we should try to discredit his tricks and deprive him of his livelihood? What is there so wonderful in attracting a duck that we should purchase this honour at the price of an honest man's living? "My word, gentlemen! had I any other trade by which I could earn a living I would not pride myself on this. You may well believe that a man who has spent his life at this miserable trade knows more about it than you who only give your spare time to it. If I did not show you my best tricks at first, it was because one must not be so foolish as to display all one knows at once. I always take care to keep my best tricks for emergencies; and I have plenty more to prevent young folks from meddling. However, I have come, gentlemen, in all kindness, to show you the trick that gave you so much trouble; I only beg you not to use it to my hurt, and to be more discreet in future."

He then shows us his apparatus, and to our great surprise we find it is merely a strong magnet in the hand of a boy concealed under the table. The man puts up his things, and after we have offered our thanks and apologies, we try to give him something. He refuses it. "No, gentlemen," says he, "I owe you no gratitude and I will not accept your gift. I leave you in my debt in spite of all, and that is my only revenge. Generosity may be found among all sorts of people, and I earn my pay by doing my tricks not by teaching them."

As he is going he blames me out-right. "I can make excuses for

the child," he says, " he sinned in ignorance. But you, sir, should
know better. Why did you let him do it? As you are living
together and you are older than he, you should look after him and
give him good advice. Your experience should be his guide. When
he is grown up he will reproach, not only himself, but you, for the
faults of his youth."

When he is gone we are greatly downcast. I blame myself for
my easy-going ways. I promise the child that another time I will
put his interests first and warn him against faults before he falls
into them, for the time is coming when our relations will be changed,
when the severity of the master must give way to the friendliness
of the comrade; this change must come gradually, you must look
ahead, and very far ahead.

We go to the fair again the next day to see the trick whose secret
we know. We approach our Socrates, the conjuror, with profound
respect, we scarcely dare to look him in the face. He overwhelms
us with politeness, gives us the best places, and heaps coals of fire
on our heads. He goes through his performance as usual, but he
lingers affectionately over the duck, and often glances proudly in
our direction. We are in the secret, but we do not tell. If my
pupil did but open his mouth he would be worthy of death.

There is more meaning than you suspect in this detailed illustration. How many lessons in one! How mortifying are the results
of a first impulse towards vanity! Young tutor, watch this first
impulse carefully. If you can use it to bring about shame and
disgrace, you may be sure it will not recur for many a day. What
a fuss you will say. Just so; and all to provide a compass which
will enable us to dispense with a meridian!

Having learnt that a magnet acts through other bodies, our next
business is to construct a bit of apparatus similar to that shown us.
A bare table, a shallow bowl placed on it and filled with water, a
duck rather better finished than the first, and so on. We often
watch the thing and at last we notice that the duck, when at rest,
always turns the same way. We follow up this observation; we
examine the direction, we find that it is from south to north.
Enough! we have found our compass or its equivalent; the study
of physics is begun.

There are various regions of the earth, and these regions differ
in temperature. The variation is more evident as we approach the
poles; all bodies expand with heat and contract with cold; this is
best measured in liquids and best of all in spirits; hence the
thermometer. The wind strikes the face, then the air is a body, a
fluid; we feel it though we cannot see it. I invert a glass in water;
the water will not fill it unless you leave a passage for the escape of
the air; so air is capable of resistance. Plunge the glass further in
the water; the water will encroach on the air-space without filling
it entirely; so air yields somewhat to pressure. A ball filled with
compressed air bounces better than one filled with anything else;
so air is elastic. Raise your arm horizontally from the water when

you are lying in your bath; you will feel a terrible weight on it; so air is a heavy body. By establishing an equilib:ium between air and other fluids its weight can be measured, hence the barometer, the siphon, the air-gun, and the air-pump. All the laws of statics and hydrostatics are discovered by such rough experiments. For none of these would I take the child into a physical cabinet; I dislike that array of instruments and apparatus. The scientific atmosphere destroys science. Either the child is frightened by these instruments or his attention, which should be fixed on their effects, is distracted by their appearance.

We shall make all our apparatus ourselves, and I would not make it beforehand, but having caught a glimpse of the experiment by chance we mean to invent step by step an instrument for its verification. I would rather our apparatus was somewhat clumsy and imperfect, but our ideas clear as to what the apparatus ought to be, and the results to be obtained by means of it. For my first lesson in statics, instead of fetching a balance, I lay a stick across the back of a chair, I measure the two parts when it is balanced; add equal or unequal weights to either end; by pulling or pushing it as required, I find at last that equilibrium is the result of a reciprocal proportion between the amount of the weights and the length of the levers. Thus my little physicist is ready to rectify a balance before ever he sees one.

Undoubtedly the notions of things thus acquired for oneself are clearer and much more convincing than those acquired from the teaching of others; and not only is our reason not accustomed to a slavish submission to authority, but we develop greater ingenuity in discovering relations, connecting ideas and inventing apparatus, than when we merely accept what is given us and allow our minds to be enfeebled by indifference, like the body of a man whose servants always wait on him, dress him and put on his shoes, whose horse carries him, till he loses the use of his limbs. Boileau used to boast that he had taught Racine the art of rhyming with difficulty. Among the many short cuts to science, we badly need some one to teach us the art of learning with difficulty.

The most obvious advantage of these slow and laborious inquiries is this: the scholar, while engaged in speculative studies, is actively using his body, gaining suppleness of limb, and training his hands to labour so that he will be able to make them useful when he is a man. Too much apparatus, designed to guide us in our experiments and to supplement the exactness of our senses, makes us neglect to use those senses. The theodolite makes it unnecessary to estimate the size of angles; the eye which used to judge distances with much precision, trusts to the chain for its measurements; the steel yard dispenses with the need of judging weight by the hand as I used to do. The more ingenious our apparatus, the coarser and more unskilful are our senses. We surround ourselves with tools and fail to use those with which nature has provided every one of us.

But when we devote to the making of these instruments the

skill which did instead of them, when for their construction we use the intelligence which enabled us to dispense with them, this is gain not loss, we add art to nature, we gain ingenuity without loss of skill. If instead of making a child stick to his books I employ him in a workshop, his hands work for the development of his mind. While he fancies himself a workman he is becoming a philosopher. Moreover, this exercise has other advantages of which I shall speak later; and you will see how, through philosophy in sport, one may rise to the real duties of man.

I have said already that purely theoretical science is hardly suitable for children, even for children approaching adolescence; but without going far into theoretical physics, take care that all their experiments are connected together by some chain of reasoning, so that they may follow an orderly sequence in the mind, and may be recalled at need; for it is very difficult to remember isolated facts or arguments, when there is no cue for their recall.

In your inquiry into the laws of nature always begin with the commonest and most conspicuous phenomena, and train your scholar not to accept these phenomena as causes but as facts. I take a stone and pretend to place it in the air; I open my hand, the stone falls. I see Emile watching my action and I say, "Why does this stone fall?"

What child will hesitate over this question? None, not even Emile, unless I have taken great pains to teach him not to answer. Every one will say, "The stone falls because it is heavy." "And what do you mean by heavy?" "That which falls." "So the stone falls because it falls?" Here is a poser for my little philosopher. This is his first lesson in systematic physics, and whether he learns physics or no it is a good lesson in common-sense.

As the child develops in intelligence other important considerations require us to be still more careful in our choice of his occupations. As soon as he has sufficient self-knowledge to understand what constitutes his well-being, as soon as he can grasp such far-reaching relations as to judge what is good for him and what is not, then he is able to discern the difference between work and play, and to consider the latter merely as relaxation. The objects of real utility may be introduced into his studies and may lead him to more prolonged attention than he gave to his games. The ever-recurring law of necessity soon teaches a man to do what he does not like, so as to avert evils which he would dislike still more. Such is the use of foresight, and this foresight, well or ill used, is the source of all the wisdom or the wretchedness of mankind.

Every one desires happiness, but to secure it he must know what happiness is. For the natural man happiness is as simple as his life; it consists in the absence of pain; health, freedom, the necessaries of life are its elements. The happiness of the moral man is another matter, but it does not concern us at present. I cannot repeat too often that it is only objects which can be perceived by the senses which can have any interest for children, especially children whose vanity has not been stimulated nor their minds corrupted by social conventions.

As soon as they foresee their needs before they feel them, their intelligence has made a great step forward, they are beginning to know the value of time. They must then be trained to devote this time to useful purposes, but this usefulness should be such as they can readily perceive and should be within the reach of their age and experience. What concerns the moral order and the customs of society should not yet be given them, for they are not in a condition to understand it. It is folly to expect them to attend to things vaguely described as good for them, when they do not know what this good is, things which they are assured will be to their advantage when they are grown up, though for the present they take no interest in this so-called advantage, which they are unable to understand.

Let the child do nothing because he is told; nothing is good for him but what he recognises as good. When you are always urging him beyond his present understanding, you think you are exercising a foresight which you really lack. To provide him with useless tools which he may never require, you deprive him of man's most useful tool—common-sense. You would have him docile as a child; he will be a credulous dupe when he grows up. You are always saying, "What I ask is for your good, though you cannot understand it. What does it matter to me whether you do it or not; my efforts are entirely on your account." All these fine speeches with which you hope to make him good, are preparing the way, so that the visionary, the tempter, the charlatan, the rascal, and every kind of fool may catch him in his snare or draw him into his folly.

A man must know many things which seem useless to a child, but need the child learn, or can he indeed learn, all that the man must know? Try to teach the child what is of use to a child and you will find that it takes all his time. Why urge him to the studies of an age he may never reach, to the neglect of those studies which meet his present needs? "But," you ask, "will it not be too late to learn what he ought to know when the time comes to use it?" I cannot tell; but this I do know, it is impossible to teach it sooner, for our real teachers are experience and emotion, and man will never learn what befits a man except under its own conditions. A child knows he must become a man; all the ideas he may have as to man's estate are so many opportunities for his instruction, but he should remain in complete ignorance of those ideas which are beyond his grasp. My whole book is one continued argument in support of this fundamental principle of education.

As soon as we have contrived to give our pupil an idea of the word "Useful," we have got an additional means of controlling him, for this word makes a great impression on him, provided that its meaning for him is a meaning relative to his own age, and provided he clearly sees its relation to his own well-being. This word makes no impression on your scholars because you have taken no pains to give it a meaning they can understand, and because other people always undertake to supply their needs so that they never require to think for themselves, and do not know what utility is.

"What is the use of that?" In future this is the sacred formula, the formula by which he and I test every action of our lives. This is the question with which I invariably answer all his questions; it serves to check the stream of foolish and tiresome questions with which children weary those about them. These incessant questions produce no result, and their object is rather to get a hold over you than to gain any real advantage. A pupil, who has been really taught only to want to know what is useful, questions like Socrates; he never asks a question without a reason for it, for he knows he will be required to give his reason before he gets an answer.

See what a powerful instrument I have put into your hands for use with your pupil. As he does not know the reason for anything you can reduce him to silence almost at will; and what advantages do your knowledge and experience give you to show him the usefulness of what you suggest. For, make no mistake about it, when you put this question to him, you are teaching him to put it to you, and you must expect that whatever you suggest to him in the future he will follow your own example and ask, "What is the use of this?"

Perhaps this is the greatest of the tutor's difficulties. If you merely try to put the child off when he asks a question, and if you give him a single reason he is not able to understand, if he finds that you reason according to your own ideas, not his, he will think what you tell him is good for you but not for him; you will lose his confidence and all your labour is thrown away. But what master will stop short and confess his faults to his pupil? We all make it a rule never to own to the faults we really have. Now I would make it a rule to admit even the faults I have not, if I could not make my reasons clear to him; as my conduct will always be intelligible to him, he will never doubt me and I shall gain more credit by confessing my imaginary faults than those who conceal their real defects.

In the first place do not forget that it is rarely your business to suggest what he ought to learn; it is for him to want to learn, to seek and to find it. You should put it within his reach, you should skilfully awaken the desire and supply him with means for its satisfaction. So your questions should be few and well-chosen, and as he will always have more questions to put to you than you to him, you will always have the advantage and will be able to ask all the oftener, "What is the use of that question?" Moreover, as it matters little what he learns provided he understands it and knows how to use it, as soon as you cannot give him a suitable explanation give him none at all. Do not hesitate to say, "I have no good answer to give you; I was wrong, let us drop the subject." If your teaching was really ill-chosen there is no harm in dropping it altogether; if it was not, with a little care you will soon find an opportunity of making its use apparent to him.

I do not like verbal explanations. Young people pay little heed to them, nor do they remember them. Things! Things! I cannot repeat it too often. We lay too much stress upon words; we teachers babble, and our scholars follow our example.

Suppose we are studying the course of the sun and the way to find our bearings, when all at once Emile interrupts me with the question, " What is the use of that ? " what a fine lecture I might give, how many things I might take occasion to teach him in reply to his question, especially if there is any one there. I might speak of the advantages of travel, the value of commerce, the special products of different lands and the peculiar customs of different nations, the use of the calendar, the way to reckon the seasons for agriculture, the art of navigation, how to steer our course at sea, how to find our way without knowing exactly where we are. Politics, natural history, astronomy, even morals and international law are involved in my explanation, so as to give my pupil some idea of all these sciences and a great wish to learn them. When I have finished I shall have shown myself a regular pedant, I shall have made a great display of learning, and not one single idea has he understood. He is longing to ask me again, " What is the use of taking one's bearings ? " but he dare not for fear of vexing me. He finds it pays best to pretend to listen to what he is forced to hear. This is the practical result of our fine systems of education.

But Emile is educated in a simpler fashion. We take so much pains to teach him a difficult idea that he will have heard nothing of all this. At the first word he does not understand, he will run away, he will prance about the room, and leave me to speechify by myself. Let us seek a more commonplace explanation; my scientific learning is of no use to him.

We were observing the position of the forest to the north of Montmorency when he interrupted me with the usual question, " What is the use of that ? " " You are right," I said. " Let us take time to think it over, and if we find it is no use we will drop it, for we only want useful games." We find something else to do and geography is put aside for the day.

Next morning I suggest a walk before breakfast; there is nothing he would like better; children are always ready to run about, and he is a good walker. We climb up to the forest, we wander through its clearings and lose ourselves; we have no idea where we are, and when we want to retrace our steps we cannot find the way. Time passes, we are hot and hungry; hurrying vainly this way and that we find nothing but woods, quarries, plains, not a landmark to guide us. Very hot, very tired, very hungry, we only get further astray. At last we sit down to rest and to consider our position. I assume that Emile has been educated like an ordinary child. He does not think, he begins to cry; he has no idea we are close to Montmorency, which is hidden from our view by a mere thicket; but this thicket is a forest to him, a man of his size is buried among bushes. After a few minutes' silence I begin anxiously—

Jean Jacques. My dear Emile, what shall we do to get out?

Emile. I am sure I do not know. I am tired, I am hungry, I am thirsty. I cannot go any further.

Jean Jacques. Do you suppose I am any better off? I would cry too if I could make my breakfast off tears. Crying is no use, we must look about us. Let us see your watch; what time is it?

Emile. It is noon and I am so hungry!

Jean Jacques. Just so; it is noon and I am so hungry too.

Emile. You must be very hungry indeed.

Jean Jacques. Unluckily my dinner won't come to find me. It is twelve o'clock. This time yesterday we were observing the position of the forest from Montmorency. If only we could see the position of Montmorency from the forest——

Emile. But yesterday we could see the forest, and here we cannot see the town.

Jean Jacques. That is just it. If we could only find it without seeing it.

Emile. Oh! my dear friend!

Jean Jacques. Did not we say the forest was——

Emile. North of Montmorency.

Jean Jacques. Then Montmorency must lie——

Emile. South of the forest.

Jean Jacques. We know how to find the north at midday.

Emile. Yes, by the direction of the shadows.

Jean Jacques. But the south?

Emile. What shall we do?

Jean Jacques. The south is opposite the north.

Emile. That is true; we need only find the opposite of the shadows. That is the south! That is the south! Montmorency must be over there! Let us look for it there!

Jean Jacques. Perhaps you are right; let us follow this path through the wood.

Emile. (*Clapping his hands.*) Oh, I can see Montmorency! there it is, quite plain, just in front of us! Come to luncheon, come to dinner, make haste! Astronomy is some use after all.

Be sure that he thinks this if he does not say it; no matter which, provided I do not say it myself. He will certainly never forget this day's lesson as long as he lives, while if I had only led him to think of all this at home, my lecture would have been forgotten the next day. Teach by doing whenever you can, and only fall back upon words when doing is out of the question.

The reader will not expect me to have such a poor opinion of him as to supply him with an example of every kind of study; but, whatever is taught, I cannot too strongly urge the tutor to adapt his instances to the capacity of his scholar; for once more I repeat the risk is not in what he does not know, but in what he thinks he knows.

I remember how I once tried to give a child a taste for chemistry. After showing him several metallic precipitates, I explained how ink was made. I told him how its blackness was merely the result of fine particles of iron separated from the vitriol and precipitated by an alkaline solution. In the midst of my learned explanation the little rascal pulled me up short with the question I myself had taught him. I was greatly puzzled. After a few moments' thought I decided what to do. I sent for some wine from the cellar of our landlord, and some very cheap wine from a wine-merchant. I took a small [1] flask of an alkaline solution, and placing two glasses before me filled with the two sorts of wine, I said—

Food and drink are adulterated to make them seem better than they really are. These adulterations deceive both the eye and the palate, but they are unwholesome and make the adulterated article even worse than before in spite of its fine appearance.

All sorts of drinks are adulterated, and wine more than others; for the fraud is more difficult to detect, and more profitable to the fraudulent person.

Sour wine is adulterated with litharge; litharge is a preparation of lead. Lead in combination with acids forms a sweet salt which corrects the harsh taste of the sour wine, but it is poisonous. So before we drink wine of doubtful quality we should be able to tell if there is lead in it. This is how I should do it.

Wine contains not merely an inflammable spirit as you have seen from the brandy made from it; it also contains an acid as you know from the vinegar made from it.

This acid has an affinity for metals, it combines with them and forms salts, such as iron-rust, which is only iron dissolved by the acid in air or water, or such as verdegris, which is only copper dissolved in vinegar.

But this acid has a still greater affinity for alkalis than for metals, so that when we add alkalis to the above-mentioned salts, the acid sets free the metal with which it had combined, and combines with the alkali.

Then the metal, set free by the acid which held it in solution, is precipitated and the liquid becomes opaque.

If then there is litharge in either of these glasses of wine, the acid holds the litharge in solution. When I pour into it an alkaline solution, the acid will be forced to set the lead free in order to combine with the alkali. The lead, no longer held in solution, will reappear, the liquor will become thick, and after a time the lead will be deposited at the bottom of the glass.

If there is no lead [2] nor other metal in the wine the alkali will

[1] Before giving any explanation to a child a little bit of apparatus serves to fix his attention.

[2] The wine sold by retail dealers in Paris is rarely free from lead, though some of it does not contain litharge, for the counters are covered with lead and when the wine is poured into the measures and some of it spilt upon the counter and the measures left standing on the counter, some of the lead is always dissolved. It is strange that so obvious and dangerous an abuse should be tolerated by the police. But indeed well-to-do people, who rarely drink these wines, are not likely to be poisoned by them.

slowly [1] combine with the acid, all will remain clear and there will be no precipitate.

Then I poured my alkaline solution first into one glass and then into the other. The wine from our own house remained clear and unclouded, the other at once became turbid, and an hour later the lead might be plainly seen, precipitated at the bottom of the glass.

"This," said I, "is a pure natural wine and fit to drink; the other is adulterated and poisonous. You wanted to know the use of knowing how to make ink. If you can make ink you can find out what wines are adulterated."

I was very well pleased with my illustration, but I found it made little impression on my pupil. When I had time to think about it I saw I had been a fool, for not only was it impossible for a child of twelve to follow my explanations, but the usefulness of the experiment did not appeal to him; he had tasted both glasses of wine and found them both good, so he attached no meaning to the word "adulterated" which I thought I had explained so nicely. Indeed, the other words, "unwholesome" and "poison," had no meaning whatever for him; he was in the same condition as the boy who told the story of Philip and his doctor. It is the condition of all children.

The relation of causes and effects whose connection is unknown to us, good and ill of which we have no idea, the needs we have never felt, have no existence for us. It is impossible to interest ourselves in them sufficiently to make us do anything connected with them. At fifteen we become aware of the happiness of a good man, as at thirty we become aware of the glory of Paradise. If we had no clear idea of either we should make no effort for their attainment; and even if we had a clear idea of them, we should make little or no effort unless we desired them and unless we felt we were made for them. It is easy to convince a child that what you wish to teach him is useful, but it is useless to convince if you cannot also persuade. Pure reason may lead us to approve or censure, but it is feeling which leads to action, and how shall we care about that which does not concern us?

Never show a child what he cannot see. Since mankind is almost unknown to him, and since you cannot make a man of him, bring the man down to the level of the child. While you are thinking what will be useful to him when he is older, talk to him of what he knows he can use now. Moreover, as soon as he begins to reason let there be no comparison with other children, no rivalry, no competition, not even in running races. I would far rather he did not learn anything than have him learn it through jealousy or self-conceit. Year by year I shall just note the progress he had made, I shall compare the results with those of the following year, I shall say, "You have grown so much; that is the ditch you jumped,

[1] The vegetable acid is very gentle in its action. If it were a mineral acid and less diluted, the combination would not take place without effervescence.

the weight you carried, the distance you flung a pebble, the race you ran without stopping to take breath, etc.; let us see what you can do now."

In this way he is stimulated to further effort without jealousy. He wants to excel himself as he ought to do; I see no reason why he should not emulate his own performances.

I hate books; they only teach us to talk about things we know nothing about. Hermes, they say, engraved the elements of science on pillars lest a deluge should destroy them. Had he imprinted them on men's hearts they would have been preserved by tradition. Well-trained minds are the pillars on which human knowledge is most deeply engraved.

Is there no way of correlating so many lessons scattered through so many books, no way of focussing them on some common object, easy to see, interesting to follow, and stimulating even to a child? Could we but discover a state in which all man's needs appear in such a way as to appeal to the child's mind, a state in which the ways of providing for these needs are as easily developed, the simple and stirring portrayal of this state should form the earliest training of the child's imagination.

Eager philosopher, I see your own imagination at work. Spare yourself the trouble; this state is already known, it is described, with due respect to you, far better than you could describe it, at least with greater truth and simplicity. Since we must have books, there is one book which, to my thinking, supplies the best treatise on an education according to nature. This is the first book Emile will read; for a long time it will form his whole library, and it will always retain an honoured place. It will be the text to which all our talks about natural science are but the commentary. It will serve to test our progress towards a right judgment, and it will always be read with delight, so long as our taste is unspoilt. What is this wonderful book? Is it Aristotle? Pliny? Buffon? No; it is *Robinson Crusoe*.

Robinson Crusoe on his island, deprived of the help of his fellow-men, without the means of carrying on the various arts, yet finding food, preserving his life, and procuring a certain amount of comfort; this is the thing to interest people of all ages, and it can be made attractive to children in all sorts of ways. We shall thus make a reality of that desert island which formerly served as an illustration. The condition, I confess, is not that of a social being, nor is it in all probability Emile's own condition, but he should use it as a standard of comparison for all other conditions. The surest way to raise him above prejudice and to base his judgments on the true relations of things, is to put him in the place of a solitary man, and to judge all things as they would be judged by such a man in relation to their own utility.

This novel, stripped of irrelevant matter, begins with Robinson's shipwreck on his island, and ends with the coming of the ship which bears him from it, and it will furnish Emile with material, both for work and play, during the whole period we are considering. His head should be full of it, he should always be busy with his castle, his goats, his plantations. Let him learn in detail, not from books but from things, all that is necessary in such a case. Let him think he is Robinson himself; let him see himself clad in skins, wearing a tall cap, a great cutlass, all the grotesque get-up of Robinson Crusoe, even to the umbrella which he will scarcely need. He should anxiously consider what steps to take; will this or that be wanting. He should examine his hero's conduct; has he omitted nothing; is there nothing he could have done better? He should carefully note his mistakes, so as not to fall into them himself in similar circumstances, for you may be sure he will plan out just such a settlement for himself. This is the genuine castle in the air of this happy age, when the child knows no other happiness but food and freedom.

What a motive will this infatuation supply in the hands of a skilful teacher who has aroused it for the purpose of using it. The child who wants to build a storehouse on his desert island will be more eager to learn than the master to teach. He will want to know all sorts of useful things and nothing else; you will need the curb as well as the spur. Make haste, therefore, to establish him on his island while this is all he needs to make him happy; for the day is at hand, when, if he must still live on his island, he will not be content to live alone, when even the companionship of Man Friday, who is almost disregarded now, will not long suffice.

The exercise of the natural arts, which may be carried on by one man alone, leads on to the industrial arts which call for the co-operation of many hands. The former may be carried on by hermits, by savages, but the others can only arise in a society, and they make society necessary. So long as only bodily needs are recognised man is self-sufficing; with superfluity comes the need for division and distribution of labour, for though one man working alone can earn a man's living, one hundred men working together can earn the living of two hundred. As soon as some men are idle, others must work to make up for their idleness.

Your main object should be to keep out of your scholar's way all idea of such social relations as he cannot understand, but when the development of knowledge compels you to show him the mutual dependence of mankind, instead of showing him its moral side, turn all his attention at first towards industry and the mechanical arts which make men useful to one another. While you take him from one workshop to another, let him try his hand at every trade you show him, and do not let him leave it till he has thoroughly learnt why everything is done, or at least everything that has attracted his attention. With this aim you should take a share in his work and set him an example. Be yourself the apprentice that he may become a master; you may expect him to learn more in one hour's work than he would retain after a whole day's explanation.

The value set by the general public on the various arts is in inverse ratio to their real utility. They are even valued directly according to their uselessness. This might be expected. The most useful arts are the worst paid, for the number of workmen is regulated by the demand, and the work which everybody requires must necessarily be paid at a rate which puts it within the reach of the poor. On the other hand, those great people who are called artists, not artisans, who labour only for the rich and idle, put a fancy price on their trifles; and as the real value of this vain labour is purely imaginary, the price itself adds to their market value, and they are valued according to their costliness. The rich think so much of these things, not because they are useful, but because they are beyond the reach of the poor. *Nolo habere bona, nisi quibus populus inviderit.*

What will become of your pupils if you let them acquire this foolish prejudice, if you share it yourself? If, for instance, they see you show more politeness in a jeweller's shop than in a locksmith's. What idea will they form of the true worth of the arts and the real value of things when they see, on the one hand, a fancy price and, on the other, the price of real utility, and that the more a thing costs the less it is worth? As soon as you let them get hold of these ideas, you may give up all attempt at further education; in spite of you they will be like all the other scholars—you have wasted fourteen years.

Emile, bent on furnishing his island, will look at things from another point of view. Robinson would have thought more of a toolmaker's shop than all Saide's trifles put together. He would have reckoned the toolmaker a very worthy man, and Saide little more than a charlatan.

" My son will have to take the world as he finds it, he will not live among the wise but among fools; he must therefore be acquainted with their follies, since they must be led by this means. A real knowledge of things may be a good thing in itself, but the knowledge of men and their opinions is better, for in human society man is the chief tool of man, and the wisest man is he who best knows the use of this tool. What is the good of teaching children an imaginary system, just the opposite of the established order of things, among which they will have to live? First teach them wisdom, then show them the follies of mankind."

These are the specious maxims by which fathers, who mistake them for prudence, strive to make their children the slaves of the prejudices in which they are educated, and the puppets of the senseless crowd, which they hope to make subservient to their passions. How much must be known before we attain to a knowledge of man. This is the final study of the philosopher, and you expect to make it the first lesson of the child! Before teaching him our sentiments, first teach him to judge of their worth. Do you perceive folly when you mistake it for wisdom? To be wise we must discern between good and evil. How can your child know men, when he can neither judge of their judgments nor unravel their mistakes? It is a misfortune to know what they think, with out knowing whether their thoughts are true or false. First teach him things as they really are, afterwards you will teach him how they appear to us. He will then be able to make a comparison between popular ideas and truth, and be able to rise above the vulgar crowd; for you are unaware of the prejudices you adopt, and you do not lead a nation when you are like it. But if you begin to teach the opinions of other people before you teach how to judge of their worth, of one thing you may be sure, your pupil will adopt those opinions whatever you may do, and you will not succeed in uprooting them. I am therefore convinced that to make a young man judge rightly, you must form his judgment rather than teach him your own.

So far you see I have not spoken to my pupil about men; he would have too much sense to listen to me. His relations to other people are as yet not sufficiently apparent to him to enable him to judge others by himself. The only person he knows is himself, and his knowledge of himself is very imperfect. But if he forms few opinions about others, those opinions are correct. He knows nothing of another's place, but he knows his own and keeps to it. I have bound him with the strong cord of necessity, instead of social laws, which are beyond his knowledge. He is still little more than a body; let us treat him as such.

Every substance in nature and every work of man must be judged in relation to his own use, his own safety, his own preservation, his own comfort. Thus he should value iron far more than gold, and glass than diamonds; in the same way he has far more respect for a shoemaker or a mason than for a Lempereur, a Le Blanc, or all the jewellers in Europe. In his eyes a confectioner is a really great man, and he would give the whole academy of sciences for the smallest pastrycook in Lombard Street. Goldsmiths, engravers, gilders, and embroiderers, he considers lazy people, who play at quite useless games. He does not even think much of a clockmaker. The happy child enjoys Time without being a slave to it; he uses it, but he does not know its value. The freedom from passion which makes every day alike to him, makes any means of measuring time unnecessary. When I assumed that Emile had a watch,[1] just as I assumed that he cried, it was a commonplace Emile that I chose to serve my purpose and make myself understood. The real Emile, a child so different from the rest, would not serve as an illustration for anything.

There is an order no less natural and even more accurate, by which the arts are valued according to bonds of necessity which connect them; the highest class consists of the most independent, the lowest of those most dependent on others. This classification,

[1] When our hearts are abandoned to the sway of passion, then it is that we need a measure of time. The wise man's watch is his equable temper and his peaceful heart. He is always punctual, and he always knows the time.

Emile

which suggests important considerations on the order of society in general, is like the preceding one in that it is subject to the same inversion in popular estimation, so that the use of raw material is the work of the lowest and worst paid trades, while the oftener the material changes hands, the more the work rises in price and in honour. I do not ask whether industry is really greater and more deserving of reward when engaged in the delicate arts which give the final shape to these materials, than in the labour which first gave them to man's use; but this I say, that in everything the art which is most generally useful and necessary, is undoubtedly that which most deserves esteem, and that art which requires the least help from others, is more worthy of honour than those which are dependent on other arts, since it is freer and more nearly independent. These are the true laws of value in the arts; all others are arbitrary and dependent on popular prejudice.

Agriculture is the earliest and most honourable of arts; metal work I put next, then carpentry, and so on. This is the order in which the child will put them, if he has not been spoilt by vulgar prejudices. What valuable considerations Emile will derive from his Robinson in such matters. What will he think when he sees the arts only brought to perfection by sub-division, by the infinite multiplication of tools. He will say, " All those people are as silly as they are ingenious; one would think they were afraid to use their eyes and their hands, they invent so many tools instead. To carry on one trade they become the slaves of many others; every single workman needs a whole town. My friend and I try to gain skill; we only make tools we can take about with us; these people, who are so proud of their talents in Paris, would be no use at all on our island; they would have to become apprentices."

Reader, do not stay to watch the bodily exercises and manual skill of our pupil, but consider the bent we are giving to his childish curiosity; consider his common-sense, his inventive spirit, his foresight; consider what a head he will have on his shoulders. He will want to know all about everything he sees or does, to learn the why and the wherefore of it; from tool to tool he will go back to the first beginning, taking nothing for granted; he will decline to learn anything that requires previous knowledge which he has not acquired. If he sees a spring made he will want to know how they got the steel from the mine; if he sees the pieces of a chest put together, he will want to know how the tree was cut down; when at work he will say of each tool, " If I had not got this, how could I make one like it, or how could I get along without it ? "

It is, however, difficult to avoid another error. When the master is very fond of certain occupations, he is apt to assume that the child shares his tastes; beware lest you are carried away by the interest of your work, while the child is bored by it, but is afraid to show it. The child must come first, and you must devote yourself entirely to him. Watch him, study him constantly, without his knowing it; consider his feelings beforehand, and provide against those which are undesirable, keep him occupied in such a way that he not only feels the usefulness of the thing, but takes a pleasure in understanding the purpose which his work will serve.

The solidarity of the arts consists in the exchange of industry, that of commerce in the exchange of commodities, that of banks in the exchange of money or securities. All these ideas hang together, and their foundation has already been laid in early childhood with the help of Robert the gardener. All we have now to do is to substitute general ideas for particular, and to enlarge these ideas by means of numerous examples, so as to make the child understand the game of business itself, brought home to him by means of particular instances of natural history with regard to the special products of each country, by particular instances of the arts and sciences which concern navigation and the difficulties of transport, greater or less in proportion to the distance between places, the position of land, seas, rivers, etc.

There can be no society without exchange, no exchange without a common standard of measurement, no common standard of measurement without equality. Hence the first law of every society is some conventional equality either in men or things.

Conventional equality between men, a very different thing from natural equality, leads to the necessity for positive law, i.e., government and kings. A child's political knowledge should be clear and restricted; he should know nothing of government in general, beyond what concerns the rights of property, of which he has already some idea.

Conventional equality between things has led to the invention of money, for money is only one term in a comparison between the values of different sorts of things; and in this sense money is the real bond of society; but anything may be money; in former days it was cattle; shells are used among many tribes at the present day; Sparta used iron; Sweden, leather; while we use gold and silver.

Metals, being easier to carry, have generally been chosen as the middle term of every exchange, and these metals have been made into coin to save the trouble of continual weighing and measuring, for the stamp on the coin is merely evidence that the coin is of given weight; and the sole right of coining money is vested in the ruler because he alone has the right to demand the recognition of his authority by the whole nation.

The stupidest person can perceive the use of money when it is explained in this way. It is difficult to make a direct comparison between various things, for instance, between cloth and corn; but when we find a common measure, in money, it is easy for the manufacturer and the farmer to estimate the value of the goods they wish to exchange in terms of this common measure. If a given quantity of cloth is worth a given some of money, and a given quantity of corn is worth the same sum of money, then the seller, receiving the corn in exchange for his cloth, makes a fair bargain.

Thus by means of money it becomes possible to compare the values of goods of various kinds.

Be content with this, and do not touch upon the moral effects of this institution. In everything you must show clearly the use before the abuse. If you attempt to teach children how the sign has led to the neglect of the thing signified, how money is the source of all the false ideas of society, how countries rich in silver must be poor in everything else, you will be treating these children as philosophers, and not only as philosophers but as wise men, for you are professing to teach them what very few philosophers have grasped.

What a wealth of interesting objects, towards which the curiosity of our pupil may be directed without ever quitting the real and material relations he can understand, and without permitting the formation of a single idea beyond his grasp! The teacher's art consists in this: To turn the child's attention from trivial details and to guide his thoughts continually towards relations of importance which he will one day need to know, that he may judge rightly of good and evil in human society. The teacher must be able to adapt the conversation with which he amuses his pupil to the turn already given to his mind. A problem which another child would never heed will torment Emile half a year.

We are going to dine with wealthy people; when we get there everything is ready for a feast, many guests, many servants, many dishes, dainty and elegant china. There is something intoxicating in all these preparations for pleasure and festivity when you are not used to them. I see how they will affect my young pupil. While dinner is going on, while course follows course, and conversation is loud around us, I whisper in his ear, " How many hands do you suppose the things on this table passed through before they got here? " What a crowd of ideas is called up by these few words. In a moment the mists of excitement have rolled away. He is thinking, considering, calculating, and anxious. The child is philosophising, while philosophers, excited by wine or perhaps by female society, are babbling like children. If he asks questions I decline to answer and put him off to another day. He becomes impatient, he forgets to eat and drink, he longs to get away from table and talk as he pleases. What an object of curiosity, what a text for instruction. Nothing has so far succeeded in corrupting his healthy reason; what will he think of luxury when he finds that every quarter of the globe has been ransacked, that some 2,000,000 men have laboured for years, that many lives have perhaps been sacrificed, and all to furnish him with fine clothes to be worn at midday and laid by in the wardrobe at night.

Be sure you observe what private conclusions he draws from all his observations. If you have watched him less carefully than I suppose, his thoughts may be tempted in another direction; he may consider himself a person of great importance in the world, when he sees so much labour concentrated on the preparation of his dinner. If you suspect his thoughts will take this direction you can easily prevent it, or at any rate promptly efface the false impression. As yet he can only appropriate things by personal enjoyment, he can only judge of their fitness or unfitness by their outward effects. Compare a plain rustic meal, preceded by exercise, seasoned by hunger, freedom, and delight, with this magnificent but tedious repast. This will suffice to make him realise that he has got no real advantage from the splendour of the feast, that his stomach was as well satisfied when he left the table of the peasant, as when he left the table of the banker; from neither had he gained anything he could really call his own.

Just fancy what a tutor might say to him on such an occasion. Consider the two dinners and decide for yourself which gave you most pleasure, which seemed the merriest, at which did you eat and drink most heartily, which was the least tedious and required least change of courses? Yet note the difference—this black bread you so enjoy is made from the peasant's own harvest; his wine is dark in colour and of a common kind, but wholesome and refreshing; it was made in his own vineyard; the cloth is made of his own hemp, spun and woven in the winter by his wife and daughters and the maid; no hands but theirs have touched the food. His world is bounded by the nearest mill and the next market. How far did you enjoy all that the produce of distant lands and the service of many people had prepared for you at the other dinner? If you did not get a better meal, what good did this wealth do you? how much of it was made for you? Had you been the master of the house, the tutor might say, it would have been of still less use to you; for the anxiety of displaying your enjoyment before the eyes of others would have robbed you of it; the pains would be yours, the pleasure theirs.

This may be a very fine speech, but it would be thrown away upon Emile, as he cannot understand it, and he does not accept second-hand opinions. Speak more simply to him. After these two experiences, say to him some day, " Where shall we have our dinner to-day? Where that mountain of silver covered three quarters of the table and those beds of artificial flowers on looking glass were served with the dessert, where those smart ladies treated you as a toy and pretended you said what you did not mean; or in that village two leagues away, with those good people who were so pleased to see us and gave us such delicious cream ? " Emile will not hesitate; he is not vain and he is no chatterbox; he cannot endure constraint, and he does not care for fine dishes; but he is always ready for a run in the country and is very fond of good fruit and vegetables, sweet cream and kindly people.[1] On our way, the

---

[1] This taste, which I assume my pupil to have acquired, is a natural result of his education. Moreover, he has nothing foppish or affected about him, so that the ladies take little notice of him and he is less petted than other children; therefore he does not care for them, and is less spoilt by their company; he is not yet of an age to feel its charm. I have taken

thought will occur to him, "All those people who laboured to prepare that grand feast were either wasting their time or they have no idea how to enjoy themselves."

My example may be right for one child and wrong for the rest. If you enter into their way of looking at things you will know how to vary your instances as required; the choice depends on the study of the individual temperament, and this study in turn depends on the opportunities which occur to show this temperament. You will not suppose that, in the three or four years at our disposal, even the most gifted child can get an idea of all the arts and sciences, sufficient to enable him to study them for himself when he is older; but by bringing before him what he needs to know, we enable him to develop his own tastes, his own talents, to take the first step towards the object which appeals to his individuality and to show us the road we must open up to aid the work of nature.

There is another advantage of these trains of limited but exact bits of knowledge; he learns by their connection and interdependence how to rank them in his own estimation and to be on his guard against those prejudices, common to most men, which draw them towards the gifts they themselves cultivate and away from those they have neglected. The man who clearly sees the whole, sees where each part should be; the man who sees one part clearly and knows it thoroughly may be a learned man, but the former is a wise man, and you remember it is wisdom rather than knowledge that we hope to acquire.

However that may be, my method does not depend on my examples; it depends on the amount of a man's powers at different ages, and the choice of occupations adapted to those powers. I think it would be easy to find a method which appeared to give better results, but if it were less suited to the type, sex, and age of the scholar, I doubt whether the results would really be as good.

At the beginning of this second period we took advantage of the fact that our strength was more than enough for our needs, to enable us to get outside ourselves. We have ranged the heavens and measured the earth; we have sought out the laws of nature; we have explored the whole of our island. Now let us return to ourselves, let us unconsciously approach our own dwelling. We are happy indeed if we do not find it already occupied by the dreaded foe, who is preparing to seize it.

What remains to be done when we have observed all that lies around us? We must turn to our own use all that we can get, we must increase our comfort by means of our curiosity. Hitherto we have provided ourselves with tools of all kinds, not knowing which we require. Perhaps those we do not want will be useful to others, and perhaps we may need theirs. Thus we discover the use

care not to teach him to kiss their hands, to pay them compliments, or even to be more polite to them than to men. It is my constant rule to ask nothing from him but what he can understand, and there is no good reason why a child should treat one sex differently from the other.

of exchange; but for this we must know each other's needs, what tools other people use, what they can offer in exchange. Given ten men, each of them has ten different requirements. To get what he needs for himself each must work at ten different trades; but considering our different talents, one will do better at this trade, another at that. Each of them, fitted for one thing, will work at all, and will be badly served. Let us form these ten men into a society, and let each devote himself to the trade for which he is best adapted, and let him work at it for himself and for the rest. Each will reap the advantage of the others' talents, just as if they were his own; by practice each will perfect his own talent, and thus all the ten, well provided for, will still have something to spare for others. This is the plain foundation of all our institutions. It is not my aim to examine its results here; I have done so in another book (*Discours sur l'inégalité*).

According to this principle, any one who wanted to consider himself as an isolated individual, self-sufficing and independent of others, could only be utterly wretched. He could not even continue to exist, for finding the whole earth appropriated by others while he had only himself, how could he get the means of subsistence? When we leave the state of nature we compel others to do the same; no one can remain in a state of nature in spite of his fellow-creatures, and to try to remain in it when it is no longer practicable, would really be to leave it, for self-preservation is nature's first law.

Thus the idea of social relations is gradually developed in the child's mind, before he can really be an active member of human society. Emile sees that to get tools for his own use, other people must have theirs, and that he can get in exchange what he needs and they possess. I easily bring him to feel the need of such exchange and to take advantage of it.

"Sir, I must live," said a miserable writer of lampoons to the minister who reproved him for his infamous trade. "I do not see the necessity," replied the great man coldly. This answer, excellent from the minister, would have been barbarous and untrue in any other mouth. Every man must live; this argument, which appeals to every one with more or less force in proportion to his humanity, strikes me as unanswerable when applied to oneself. Since our dislike of death is the strongest of those aversions nature has implanted in us, it follows that everything is permissible to the man who has no other means of living. The principles, which teach the good man to count his life a little thing and to sacrifice it at duty's call, are far removed from this primitive simplicity. Happy are those nations where one can be good without effort, and just without conscious virtue. If in this world there is any condition so miserable that one cannot live without wrong-doing, where the citizen is driven into evil, you should hang, not the criminal, but those who drove him into crime.

As soon as Emile knows what life is, my first care will be to teach him to preserve his life. Hitherto I have made no distinction of condition, rank, station, or fortune; nor shall I distinguish between them in the future, since man is the same in every station; the rich man's stomach is no bigger than the poor man's, nor is his digestion any better; the master's arm is neither longer nor stronger than the slave's; a great man. is no taller than one of the people, and indeed the natural needs are the same to all, and the means of satisfying them should be equally within the reach of all. Fit a man's education to his real self, not to what is no part of him. Do you not see that in striving to fit him merely for one station, you are unfitting him for anything else, so that some caprice of Fortune may make your work really harmful to him ? What could be more absurd than a nobleman in rags, who carries' with him into his poverty the prejudices of his birth ? What is more despicable than a rich man fallen into poverty, who recalls the scorn with which he himself regarded the poor, and feels that he has sunk to the lowest depth of degradation ? The one may become a professional thief, the other a cringing servant, with this fine saying, " I must live."

You reckon on the present order of society, without considering that this order is itself subject to inscrutable changes, and that you can neither foresee nor provide against the revolution which may affect your children. The great become small, the rich poor, the king a commoner. Does fate strike so seldom that you can count on immunity from her blows ? The crisis is approaching, and we are on the edge of a revolution.[1] Who can answer for your fate ? What man has made, man may destroy. Nature's characters alone are ineffaceable, and nature makes neither the prince, the rich man, nor the nobleman. This satrap whom you have educated for greatness, what will become of him in his degradation ? This farmer of the taxes who can only live on gold, what will he do in poverty ? This haughty fool who cannot use his own hands, who prides himself on what is not really his, what will he do when he is stripped of all ? In that day, happy will he be who can give up the rank which is no longer his, and be still a man in Fate's despite. Let men praise as they will that conquered monarch who like a madman would be buried beneath the fragments of his throne; I behold him with scorn; to me he is merely a crown, and when that is gone he is nothing. But he who loses his crown and lives without it, is more than a king; from the rank of a king, which may be held by a coward, a villain, or madman, he rises to the rank of a man, a position few can fill. Thus he triumphs over Fortune, he dares to look her in the face; he depends on himself alone, and when he has nothing left to show but himself he is not a nonentity, he is somebody. Better a thousandfold the king of Corinth a schoolmaster at Syracuse, than a wretched Tarquin, unable to be anything but a

[1] In my opinion it is impossible that the great kingdoms of Europe should last much longer. Each of them has had its period of splendour, after which it must inevitably decline. I have my own opinions as to the special applications of this general statement, but this is not the place to enter into details, and they are only too evident to everybody.

king, or the heir of the ruler of three kingdoms, the sport of all who would scorn his poverty, wandering from court to court in search of help, and finding nothing but insults, for want of knowing any trade but one which he can no longer practise.

The man and the citizen, whoever he may be, has no property to invest in society but himself, all his other goods belong to society in spite of himself, and when a man is rich, either he does not enjoy his wealth, or the public enjoys it too; in the first case he robs others as well as himself; in the second he gives them nothing. Thus his debt to society is still unpaid, while he only pays with his property. "But my father was serving society while he was acquiring his wealth." Just so; he paid his own debt, not yours. You owe more to others than if you had been born with nothing, since you were born under favourable conditions. It is not fair that what one man has done for society should pay another's debt, for since every man owes all that he is, he can only pay his own debt, and no father can transmit to his son any right to be of no use to mankind. "But," you say, "this is just what he does when he leaves me his wealth, the reward of his labour." The man who eats in idleness what he has not himself earned, is a thief, and in my eyes, the man who lives on an income paid him by the state for doing nothing, differs little from a highwayman who lives on those who travel his way. Outside the pale of society, the solitary, owing nothing to any man, may live as he pleases, but in society either he lives at the cost of others, or he owes them in labour the cost of his keep; there is no exception to this rule. Man in society is bound to work; rich or poor, weak or strong, every idler is a thief.

Now of all the pursuits by which a man may earn his living, the nearest to a state of nature is manual labour; of all stations that of the artisan is least dependent on Fortune. The artisan depends on his labour alone, he is a free man while the ploughman is a slave; for the latter depends on his field where the crops may be destroyed by others. An enemy, a prince, a powerful neighbour, or a law-suit may deprive him of his field; through this field he may be harassed in all sorts of ways. But if the artisan is ill-treated his goods are soon packed and he takes himself off. Yet agriculture is the earliest, the most honest of trades, and more useful than all the rest, and therefore more honourable for those who practise it. I do not say to Emile, "Study agriculture," he is already familiar with it. He is acquainted with every kind of rural labour, it was his first occupation, and he returns to it continually. So I say to him, "Cultivate your father's lands, but if you lose this inheritance, or if you have none to lose, what will you do? Learn a trade."

"A trade for my son! My son a working man! What are you thinking of, sir?" Madam, my thoughts are wiser than yours; you want to make him fit for nothing but a lord, a marquis, or a prince; and some day he may be less than nothing. I want to give him a rank which he cannot lose, a rank which will always do him honour; I want to raise him to the status of a man, and, whatever you may say, he will have fewer equals in that rank than in your own.

The letter killeth, the spirit giveth life. Learning a trade matters less than overcoming the prejudices he despises. You will never be reduced to earning your livelihood; so much the worse for you. No matter; work for honour, not for need; stoop to the position of a working man, to rise above your own. To conquer Fortune and everything else, begin by independence. To rule through public opinion, begin by ruling over it.

Remember I demand no talent, only a trade, a genuine trade, a mere mechanical art, in which the hands work harder than the head, a trade which does not lead to fortune but makes you independent of her. In households far removed from all danger of want I have known fathers carry prudence to such a point as to provide their children not only with ordinary teaching but with knowledge by means of which they could get a living if anything happened. These far-sighted parents thought they were doing a great thing. It is nothing, for the resources they fancy they have secured depend on that very fortune of which they would make their children independent; so that unless they found themselves in circumstances fitted for the display of their talents, they would die of hunger as if they had none.

As soon as it is a question of influence and intrigue you may as well use these means to keep yourself in plenty, as to acquire, in the depths of poverty, the means of returning to your former position. If you cultivate the arts which depend on the artist's reputation, if you fit yourself for posts which are only obtained by favour, how will that help you when, rightly disgusted with the world, you scorn the steps by which you must climb. You have studied politics and state-craft, so far so good; but how will you use this knowledge, if you cannot gain the ear of the ministers, the favourites, or the officials? if you have not the secret of winning their favour, if they fail to find you a rogue to their taste? You are an architect or a painter; well and good; but your talents must be displayed. Do you suppose you can exhibit in the salon without further ado? That is not the way to set about it. Lay aside the rule and the pencil, take a cab and drive from door to door; there is the road to fame. Now you must know that the doors of the great are guarded by porters and flunkeys, who only understand one language, and their ears are in their palms. If you wish to teach what you have learned, geography, mathematics, languages, music, drawing, even to find pupils, you must have friends who will sing your praises. Learning, remember, gains more credit than skill, and with no trade but your own none will believe in your skill. See how little you can depend on these fine " Resources," and how many other resources are required before you can use what you have got. And what will become of you in your degradation? Misfortune will make you worse rather than better. More than ever the sport of public opinion, how will you rise above the pre-

judices on which your fate depends? How will you despise the
vices and the baseness from which you get your living? You were
dependent on wealth, now you are dependent on the wealthy; you
are still a slave and a poor man into the bargain. Poverty without
freedom, can a man sink lower than this!

But if instead of this recondite learning adapted to feed the mind,
not the body, you have recourse, at need, to your hands and your
handiwork, there is no call for deceit, your trade is ready when
required. Honour and honesty will not stand in the way of your
living. You need no longer cringe and lie to the great, nor creep
and crawl before rogues, a despicable flatterer of both, a borrower
or a thief, for there is little to choose between them when you are
penniless. Other people's opinions are no concern of yours, you
need not pay court to any one, there is no fool to flatter, no flunkey
to bribe, no woman to win over. Let rogues conduct the affairs
of state; in your lowly rank you can still be an honest man and yet
get a living. You walk into the first workshop of your trade.
" Master, I want work." " Comrade, take your place and work."
Before dinner-time you have earned your dinner. If you are sober
and industrious, before the week is out you will have earned your
keep for another week; you will have lived in freedom, health,
truth, industry, and righteousness. Time is not wasted when it
brings these returns.

Emile shall learn a trade. " An honest trade, at least," you say.
What do you mean by honest? Is not every useful trade honest?
I would not make an embroiderer, a gilder, a polisher of him, like
Locke's young gentleman. Neither would I make him a musician,
an actor, or an author.[1] With the exception of these and others like
them, let him choose his own trade, I do not mean to interfere with
his choice. I would rather have him a shoemaker than a poet, I
would rather he paved streets than painted flowers on china. " But,"
you will say, " policemen, spies, and hangmen are useful people."
There would be no use for them if it were not for the government.
But let that pass. I was wrong. It is not enough to choose an
honest trade, it must be a trade which does not develop detestable
qualities in the mind, qualities incompatible with humanity. To
return to our original expression, " Let us choose an honest trade,"
but let us remember there can be no honesty without usefulness.

A famous writer of this century, whose books are full of great
schemes and narrow views, was under a vow, like the other priests
of his communion, not to take a wife. Finding himself more
scrupulous than others with regard to his neighbour's wife, he
decided, so they say, to employ pretty servants, and so did his best
to repair the wrong done to the race by his rash promise. He
thought it the duty of a citizen to breed children for the state, and

---

[1] You are an author yourself, you will reply. Yes, for my sins; and
my ill deeds, which I think I have fully expiated, are no reason why others
should be like me. I do not write to excuse my faults, but to prevent
my readers from copying them.

he made his children artisans. As soon as they were old enough they were taught whatever trade they chose; only idle or useless trades were excluded, such as that of the wigmaker who is never necessary, and may any day cease to be required, so long as nature does not get tired of providing us with hair.

This spirit shall guide our choice of trade for Emile, or rather, not our choice but his; for the maxims he has imbibed make him despise useless things, and he will never be content to waste his time on vain labours; his trade must be of use to Robinson on his island.

When we review with the child the productions of art and nature, when we stimulate his curiosity and follow its lead, we have great opportunities of studying his tastes and inclinations, and perceiving the first spark of genius, if he has any decided talent in any direction. You must, however, be on your guard against the common error which mistakes the effects of environment for the ardour of genius, or imagines there is a decided bent towards any one of the arts, when there is nothing more than that spirit of emulation, common to men and monkeys, which impels them instinctively to do what they see others doing, without knowing why. The world is full of artisans, and still fuller of artists, who have no native gift for their calling, into which they were driven in early childhood, either through the conventional ideas of other people, or because those about them were deceived by an appearance of zeal, which would have led them to take to any other art they saw practised. One hears a drum and fancies he is a general; another sees a building and wants to be an architect. Every one is drawn towards the trade he sees before him if he thinks it is held in honour.

I once knew a footman who watched his master drawing and painting and took it into his head to become a designer and artist. He seized a pencil which he only abandoned for a paint-brush, to which he stuck for the rest of his days. Without teaching or rules of art he began to draw everything he saw. Three whole years were devoted to these daubs, from which nothing but his duties could stir him, nor was he discouraged by the small progress resulting from his very mediocre talents. I have seen him spend the whole of a broiling summer in a little ante-room towards the south, a room where one was suffocated merely passing through it; there he was, seated or rather nailed all day to his chair, before a globe, drawing it again and again and yet again, with invincible obstinacy till he had reproduced the rounded surface to his own satisfaction. At last with his master's help and under the guidance of an artist he got so far as to abandon his livery and live by his brush. Perseverance does instead of talent up to a certain point; he got so far, but no further. This honest lad's perseverance and ambition are praiseworthy; he will always be respected for his industry and steadfastness of purpose, but his paintings will always be third-rate. Who would not have been deceived by his zeal and taken it for real talent? There is all the difference in the world between a liking and an aptitude. To make sure of real genius or real taste in a child calls for more accurate observations than is generally suspected, for the child displays his wishes not his capacity, and we judge by the former instead of considering the latter. I wish some trustworthy person would give us a treatise on the art of child-study. This art is well worth studying, but neither parents nor teachers have mastered its elements.

Perhaps we are laying too much stress on the choice of a trade; as it is a manual occupation, Emile's choice is no great matter, and his apprenticeship is more than half accomplished already, through the exercises which have hitherto occupied him. What would you have him do? He is ready for anything. He can handle the spade and hoe, he can use the lathe, hammer, plane, or file; he is already familiar with these tools which are common to many trades. He only needs to acquire sufficient skill in the use of any one of them to rival the speed, the familiarity, and the diligence of good workmen, and he will have a great advantage over them in suppleness of body and limb, so that he can easily take any position and can continue any kind of movements without effort. Moreover his senses are acute and well-practised, he knows the principles of the various trades; to work like a master of his craft he only needs experience, and experience comes with practice. To which of these trades which are open to us will he give sufficient time to make himself master of it? That is the whole question.

Give a man a trade befitting his sex, to a young man a trade befitting his age. Sedentary indoor employments, which make the body tender and effeminate, are neither pleasing nor suitable. No lad ever wanted to be a tailor. It takes some art to attract a man to this woman's work.[1] The same hand cannot hold the needle and the sword. If I were king I would only allow needlework and dressmaking to be done by women and cripples who are obliged to work at such trades. If eunuchs were required I think the Easterns were very foolish to make them on purpose. Why not take those provided by nature, that crowd of base persons without natural feeling? There would be enough and to spare. The weak, feeble, timid man is condemned by nature to a sedentary life, he is fit to live among women or in their fashion. Let him adopt one of their trades if he likes; and if there must be eunuchs let them take those men who dishonour their sex by adopting trades unworthy of it. Their choice proclaims a blunder on the part of nature; correct it one way or other, you will do no harm.

An unhealthy trade I forbid to my pupil, but not a difficult or dangerous one. He will exercise himself in strength and courage; such trades are for men not women, who claim no share in them. Are not men ashamed to poach upon the women's trades?

" Luctantur paucæ, comedunt coliphia paucæ.
Vos lanam trahitis, calathisque peracta refertis
Vellera."—Juven. *Sat.* ii. v. 55.

[1] There were no tailors among the ancients; men's clothes were made at home by the women.

Women are not seen in shops in Italy, and to persons accustomed to the streets of England and France nothing could look gloomier. When I saw drapers selling ladies ribbons, pompons, net, and chenille, I thought these delicate ornaments very absurd in the coarse hands fit to blow the bellows and strike the anvil. I said to myself, " In this country women should set up as steel-polishers and armourers." Let each make and sell the weapons of his or her own sex; knowledge is acquired through use.

I know I have said too much for my agreeable contemporaries, but I sometimes let myself be carried away by my argument. If any one is ashamed to be seen wearing a leathern apron or handling a plane, I think him a mere slave of public opinion, ready to blush for what is right when people poke fun at it. But let us yield to parents' prejudices so long as they do not hurt the children. To honour trades we are not obliged to practise every one of them, so long as we do not think them beneath us. When the choice is ours and we are under no compulsion, why not choose the pleasanter, more attractive and more suitable trade. Metal work is useful, more useful, perhaps, than the rest, but unless for some special reason Emile shall not be a blacksmith, a locksmith nor an iron-worker. I do not want to see him a Cyclops at the forge. Neither would I have him a mason, still less a shoemaker. All trades must be carried on, but when the choice is ours, cleanliness should be taken into account; this is not a matter of class prejudice, our senses are our guides. In conclusion, I do not like those stupid trades in which the workmen mechanically perform the same action without pause and almost without mental effort. Weaving, stocking-knitting, stone-cutting; why employ intelligent men on such work? it is merely one machine employed on another.

All things considered, the trade I should choose for my pupil, among the trades he likes, is that of a carpenter. It is clean and useful; it may be carried on at home; it gives enough exercise; it calls for skill and industry, and while fashioning articles for everyday use, there is scope for elegance and taste. If your pupil's talents happened to take a scientific turn, I should not blame you if you gave him a trade in accordance with his tastes, for instance, he might learn to make mathematical instruments, glasses, telescopes, etc.

When Emile learns his trade I shall learn it too. I am convinced he will never learn anything thoroughly unless we learn it together. So we shall both serve our apprenticeship, and we do not mean to be treated as gentlemen, but as real apprentices who are not there for fun; why should not we actually be apprenticed? Peter the Great was a ship's carpenter and drummer to his own troops; was not that prince at least your equal in birth and merit? You understand this is addressed not to Emile but to you—to you, whoever you may be.

Unluckily we cannot spend the whole of our time at the workshop. We are not only 'prentice-carpenters but 'prentice-men—a trade whose apprenticeship is longer and more exacting than the rest.

What shall we do? Shall we take a master to teach us the use of the plane and engage him by the hour like the dancing-master? In that case we should be not apprentices but students, and our ambition is not merely to learn carpentry but to be carpenters. Once or twice a week I think we should spend the whole day at our master's; we should get up when he does, we should be at our work before him, we should take our meals with him, work under his orders, and after having had the honour of supping at his table we may if we please return to sleep upon our own hard beds. This is the way to learn several trades at once, to learn to do manual work without neglecting our apprenticeship to life.

Let us do what is right without ostentation; let us not fall into vanity through our efforts to resist it. To pride ourselves on our victory over prejudice is to succumb to prejudice. It is said that in accordance with an old custom of the Ottomans, the sultan is obliged to work with his hands, and, as every one knows, the handiwork of a king is a masterpiece. So he royally distributes his masterpieces among the great lords of the Porte and the price paid is in accordance with the rank of the workman. It is not this so-called abuse to which I object; on the contrary, it is an advantage, and by compelling the lords to share with him the spoils of the people it is so much the less necessary for the prince to plunder the people himself. Despotism needs some such relaxation, and without it that hateful rule could not last.

The real evil in such a custom is the idea it gives that poor man of his own worth. Like King Midas he sees all things turn to gold at his touch, but he does not see the ass' ears growing. Let us keep Emile's hands from money lest he should become an ass, let him take the work but not the wages. Never let his work be judged by any standard but that of the work of a master. Let it be judged as work, not because it is his. If anything is well done, I say, " That is a good piece of work," but do not ask who did it. If he is pleased and proud and says, " I did it," answer indifferently, " No matter who did it, it is well done."

Good mother, be on your guard against the deceptions prepared for you. If your son knows many things, distrust his knowledge; if he is unlucky enough to be rich and educated in Paris he is ruined. As long as there are clever artists he will have every talent, but apart from his masters he will have none. In Paris a rich man knows everything, it is the poor who are ignorant. Our capital is full of amateurs, especially women, who do their work as M. Gillaume invents his colours. Among the men I know three striking exceptions, among the women I know no exceptions, and I doubt if there are any. In a general way a man becomes an artist and a judge of art as he becomes a Doctor of Laws and a magistrate.

If then it is once admitted that it is a fine thing to have a trade, your children would soon have one without learning it. They would become postmasters like the councillors of Zurich. Let us have no such ceremonies for Emile; let it be the real thing not the sham.

Do not say what he knows, let him learn in silence. Let him make his masterpiece, but not be hailed as master; let him be a workman not in name but in deed.

If I have made my meaning clear you ought to realise how bodily exercise and manual work unconsciously arouse thought and reflexion in my pupil, and counteract the idleness which might result from his indifference to men's judgments, and his freedom from passion. He must work like a peasant and think like a philosopher, if he is not to be as idle as a savage. The great secret of education is to use exercise of mind and body as relaxation one to the other.

But beware of anticipating teaching which demands more maturity of mind. Emile will not long be a workman before he discovers those social inequalities he had not previously observed. He will want to question me in turn on the maxims I have given him, maxims he is able to understand. When he derives everything from me, when he is so nearly in the position of the poor, he will want to know why I am so far removed from it. All of a sudden he may put scathing questions to me. " You are rich, you tell me, and I see you are. A rich man owes his work to the community like the rest because he is a man. What are you doing for the community ? " What would a fine tutor say to that ? I do not know. He would perhaps be foolish enough to talk to the child of the care he bestows upon him. The workshop will get me out of the difficulty. " My dear Emile that is a very good question; I will undertake to answer for myself, when you can answer for yourself to your own satisfaction. Meanwhile I will take care to give what I can spare to you and to the poor, and to make a table or a bench every week, so as not to be quite useless."

We have come back to ourselves. Having entered into possession of himself, our child is now ready to cease to be a child. He is more than ever conscious of the necessity which makes him dependent on things. After exercising his body and his senses you have exercised his mind and his judgment. Finally we have joined together the use of his limbs and his faculties. We have made him a worker and a thinker; we have now to make him loving and tender-hearted, to perfect reason through feeling. But before we enter on this new order of things, let us cast an eye over the stage we are leaving behind us, and perceive as clearly as we can how far we have got.

At first our pupil had merely sensations, now he has ideas; he could only feel, now he reasons. For from the comparison of many successive or simultaneous sensations and the judgment arrived at with regard to them, there springs a sort of mixed or complex sensation which I call an idea.

The way in which ideas are formed gives a character to the human mind. The mind which derives its ideas from real relations is thorough; the mind which relies on apparent relations is superficial. He who sees relations as they are has an exact mind; he who fails to estimate them aright has an inaccurate mind; he who concocts imaginary relations, which have no real existence, is a madman; he who does not perceive any relation at all is an imbecile. Clever men are distinguished from others by their greater or less aptitude for the comparison of ideas and the discovery of relations between them.

Simple ideas consist merely of sensations compared one with another. Simple sensations involve judgments, as do the complex sensations which I call simple ideas. In the sensation the judgment is purely passive; it affirms that I feel what I feel. In the percept or idea the judgment is active; it connects, compares, it discriminates between relations not perceived by the senses. That is the whole difference; but it is a great difference. Nature never deceives us; we deceive ourselves.

I see some one giving an ice-cream to an eight-year-old child; he does not know what it is and puts the spoon in his mouth. Struck by the cold he cries out, "Oh, it burns!" He feels a very keen sensation, and the heat of the fire is the keenest sensation he knows, so he thinks that is what he feels. Yet he is mistaken; cold hurts, but it does not burn; and these two sensations are different, for persons with more experience do not confuse them. So it is not the sensation that is wrong, but the judgment formed with regard to it.

It is just the same with those who see a mirror or some optical instrument for the first time, or enter a deep cellar in the depths of winter or at midsummer, or dip a very hot or cold hand into tepid water, or roll a little ball between two crossed fingers. If they are content to say what they really feel, their judgment, being purely passive, cannot go wrong; but when they judge according to appearances, their judgment is active; it compares and establishes by induction relations which are not really perceived. Then these inductions may or may not be mistaken. Experience is required to correct or prevent error.

Show your pupil the clouds at night passing between himself and the moon; he will think the moon is moving in the opposite direction and that the clouds are stationary. He will think this through a hasty induction, because he generally sees small objects moving and larger ones at rest, and the clouds seems larger than the moon, whose distance is beyond his reckoning. When he watches the shore from a moving boat he falls into the opposite mistake and thinks the earth is moving because he does not feel the motion of the boat and considers it along with the sea or river as one motionless whole, of which the shore, which appears to move, forms no part.

The first time a child sees a stick half immersed in water he thinks he sees a broken stick; the sensation is true and would not cease to be true even if he knew the reason of this appearance. So if you ask him what he sees, he replies, "A broken stick," for he is quite sure he is experiencing this sensation. But when deceived by his judgment he goes further and, after saying he sees a broken stick, he affirms that it really is broken he says what is not true. Why? Because he becomes active and judges no longer by observation but by induction, he affirms what he does not perceive, *i.e.*, that the judgment he receives through one of his senses would be confirmed by another.

Since all our errors arise in our judgment, it is clear, that had we no need for judgment, we should not need to learn; we should never be liable to mistakes, we should be happier in our ignorance than we can be in our knowledge. Who can deny that a vast number of things are known to the learned, which the unlearned will never know? Are the learned any nearer truth? Not so, the further they go the further they get from truth, for their pride in their judgment increases faster than their progress in knowledge, so that for every truth they acquire they draw a hundred mistaken conclusions. Every one knows that the learned societies of Europe are mere schools of falsehood, and there are assuredly more mistaken notions in the Academy of Sciences than in a whole tribe of American Indians.

The more we know, the more mistakes we make; therefore ignorance is the only way to escape error. Form no judgments and you will never be mistaken. This is the teaching both of nature and reason. We come into direct contact with very few things, and these are very readily perceived; the rest we regard with profound indifference. A savage will not turn his head to watch the working of the finest machinery or all the wonders of electricity. "What does that matter to me?" is the common saying of the ignorant; it is the fittest phrase for the wise.

Unluckily this phrase will no longer serve our turn. Everything matters to us, as we are dependent on everything, and our curiosity naturally increases with our needs. This is why I attribute much curiosity to the man of science and none to the savage. The latter needs no help from anybody; the former requires every one, and admirers most of all.

You will tell me I am going beyond nature. I think not. She chooses her instruments and orders them, not according to fancy, but necessity. Now a man's needs vary with his circumstances. There is all the difference in the world between a natural man living in a state of nature, and a natural man living in society. Emile is no savage to be banished to the desert, he is a savage who has to live in the town. He must know how to get his living in a town, how to use its inhabitants, and how to live among them, if not of them.

In the midst of so many new relations and dependent on them, he must reason whether he wants to or no. Let us therefore teach him to reason correctly.

The best way of learning to reason aright is that which tends to simplify our experiences, or to enable us to dispense with them altogether without falling into error. Hence it follows that we must learn to confirm the experiences of each sense by itself, without recourse to any other, though we have been in the habit of verifying the experience of one sense by that of another. Then each of our sensations will become an idea, and this idea will always correspond to the truth. This is the sort of knowledge I have tried to accumulate during this third phase of man's life.

This method of procedure demands a patience and circumspection which few teachers possess; without them the scholar will never learn to reason. For example, if you hasten to take the stick out of the water when the child is deceived by its appearance, you may perhaps undeceive him, but what have you taught him? Nothing more than he would soon have learnt for himself. That is not the right thing to do. You have not got to teach him truths so much as to show him how to set about discovering them for himself. To teach him better you must not be in such a hurry to correct his mistakes. Let us take Emile and myself as an illustration.

To begin with, any child educated in the usual way could not fail to answer the second of my imaginary questions in the affirmative. He will say, " That is certainly a broken stick." I very much doubt whether Emile will give the same reply. He sees no reason for knowing everything or pretending to know it; he is never in a hurry to draw conclusions. He only reasons from evidence and on this occasion he has not got the evidence. He knows how appearances deceive us, if only through perspective.

Moreover, he knows by experience that there is always a reason for my slightest questions, though he may not see it at once; so he has not got into the habit of giving silly answers; on the contrary, he is on his guard, he considers things carefully and attentively before answering. He never gives me an answer unless he is satisfied with it himself, and he is hard to please. Lastly we neither of us take any pride in merely knowing a thing, but only in avoiding mistakes. We should be more ashamed to deceive ourselves with bad reasoning, than to find no explanation at all. There is no phrase so appropriate to us, or so often on our lips, as, " I do not know; " neither of us are ashamed to use it. But whether he gives the silly answer or whether he avoids it by our convenient phrase " I do not know," my answer is the same. " Let us examine it."

This stick immersed half way in the water is fixed in an upright position. To know if it is broken, how many things must be done before we take it out of the water or even touch it.

1. First we walk round it, and we see that the broken part follows us. So it is only our eye that changes it; looks do not make things move.

2. We look straight down on that end of the stick which is above the water, the stick is no longer bent,[1] the end near our eye exactly hides the other end. Has our eye set the stick straight?

3. We stir the surface of the water; we see the stick break into several pieces, it moves in zigzags and follows the ripples of the

---

[1] I have since found by more exact experiment that this is not the case. Refraction acts in a circle, and the stick appears larger at the end which is in the water, but this makes no difference to the strength of the argument, and the conclusion is correct.

water. Can the motion we gave the water suffice to break, soften, or melt the stick like this?

4. We draw the water off, and little by little we see the stick straightening itself as the water sinks. Is not this more than enough to clear up the business and to discover refraction? So it is not true that our eyes deceive us, for nothing more has been required to correct the mistakes attributed to it.

Suppose the child were stupid enough not to perceive the result of these experiments, then you must call touch to the help of sight. Instead of taking the stick out of the water, leave it where it is and let the child pass his hand along it from end to end; he will feel no angle, therefore the stick is not broken.

You will tell me this is not mere judgment but formal reasoning. Just so; but do not you see that as soon as the mind has got any ideas at all, every judgment is a process of reasoning? So that as soon as we compare one sensation with another, we are beginning to reason. The art of judging and the art of reasoning are one and the same.

Emile will never learn dioptrics unless he learns with this stick. He will not have dissected insects nor counted the spots on the sun; he will not know what you mean by a microscope or a telescope. Your learned pupils will laugh at his ignorance and rightly. I intend him to invent these instruments before he uses them, and you will expect that to take some time.

This is the spirit of my whole method at this stage. If the child rolls a little ball between two crossed fingers and thinks he feels two balls, I shall not let him look until he is convinced there is only one.

This explanation will suffice, I hope, to show plainly the progress made by my pupil hitherto and the route followed by him. But perhaps the number of things I have brought to his notice alarms you. I shall crush his mind beneath this weight of knowledge. Not so, I am rather teaching him to be ignorant of things than to know them. I am showing him the path of science, easy indeed, but long, far-reaching and slow to follow. I am taking him a few steps along this path, but I do not allow him to go far.

Compelled to learn for himself, he uses his own reason not that of others, for there must be no submission to authority if you would have no submission to convention. Most of our errors are due to others more than ourselves. This continual exercise should develop a vigour of mind like that acquired by the body through labour and weariness. Another advantage is that his progress is in proportion to his strength, neither mind nor body carries more than it can bear. When the understanding lays hold of things before they are stored in the memory, what is drawn from that store is his own; while we are in danger of never finding anything of our own in a memory over-burdened with undigested knowledge.

Emile knows little, but what he knows is really his own; he has no half-knowledge. Among the few things he knows and knows thoroughly this is the most valuable, that there are many things he does not know now but may know some day, many more that other men know but he will never know, and an infinite number which nobody will ever know. He is large-minded, not through knowledge, but through the power of acquiring it; he is open-minded, intelligent, ready for anything, and, as Montaigne says, capable of learning if not learned. I am content if he knows the "Wherefore" of his actions and the "Why" of his beliefs. For once more my object is not to supply him with exact knowledge, but the means of getting it when required, to teach him to value it at its true worth, and to love truth above all things. By this method progress is slow but sure, and we never need to retrace our steps.

Emile's knowledge is confined to nature and things. The very name of history is unknown to him, along with metaphysics and morals. He knows the essential relations between men and things, but nothing of the moral relations between man and man. He has little power of generalisation, he has no skill in abstraction. He perceives that certain qualities are common to certain things, without reasoning about these qualities themselves. He is acquainted with the abstract idea of space by the help of his geometrical figures; he is acquainted with the abstract idea of quantity by the help of his algebraical symbols. These figures and signs are the supports on which these ideas may be said to rest, the supports on which his senses repose. He does not attempt to know the nature of things, but only to know things in so far as they affect himself. He only judges what is outside himself in relation to himself, and his judgment is exact and certain. Caprice and prejudice have no part in it. He values most the things which are of use to himself, and as he never departs from this standard of values, he owes nothing to prejudice.

Emile is industrious, temperate, patient, stedfast, and full of courage. His imagination is still asleep, so he has no exaggerated ideas of danger; the few ills he feels he knows how to endure in patience, because he has not learnt to rebel against fate. As to death, he knows not what it means; but accustomed as he is to submit without resistance to the law of necessity, he will die, if die he must, without a groan and without a struggle; that is as much as we can demand of human nature, in that hour which we all abhor. To live in freedom, and to be independent of human affairs, is the best way to learn how to die.

In a word Emile is possessed of all that portion of virtue which concerns himself. To acquire the social virtues he only needs a knowledge of the relations which make those virtues necessary; he only lacks knowledge which he is quite ready to receive.

He thinks not of others but of himself, and prefers that others should do the same. He makes no claim upon them, and acknowledges no debt to them. He is alone in the midst of human society, he depends on himself alone, for he is all that a boy can be at his age. He has no errors, or at least only such as are inevitable; he has no vices, or only those from which no man can escape. His body is healthy, his limbs are supple, his mind is accurate and unprejudiced, his heart is free and untroubled by passion. Pride, the earliest and the most natural of passions, has scarcely shown itself. Without disturbing the peace of others, he has passed his life contented, happy, and free, so far as nature allows. Do you think that the earlier years of a child, who has reached his fifteenth year in this condition, have been wasted?

BOOK IV

How swiftly life passes here below! The first quarter of it is gone before we know how to use it; the last quarter finds us incapable of enjoying life. At first we do not know how to live; and when we know how to live it is too late. In the interval between these two useless extremes we waste three-fourths of our time sleeping, working, sorrowing, enduring restraint and every kind of suffering. Life is short, not so much because of the short time it lasts, but because we are allowed scarcely any time to enjoy it. In vain is there a long interval between the hour of death and that of birth; life is still too short, if this interval is not well spent.

We are born, so to speak, twice over; born into existence, and born into life; born a human being, and born a man. Those who regard woman as an imperfect man are no doubt mistaken, but they have external resemblance on their side. Up to the age of puberty children of both sexes have little to distinguish them to the eye, the same face and form, the same complexion and voice, everything is the same; girls are children and boys are children; one name is enough for creatures so closely resembling one another. Males whose development is arrested preserve this resemblance all their lives; they are always big children; and women who never lose this resemblance seem in many respects never to be more than children.

But, speaking generally, man is not meant to remain a child. He leaves childhood behind him at the time ordained by nature; and this critical moment, short enough in itself, has far-reaching consequences.

As the roaring of the waves precedes the tempest, so the murmur of rising passions announces this tumultuous change; a suppressed excitement warns us of the approaching danger. A change of temper, frequent outbreaks of anger, a perpetual stirring of the mind, make the child almost ungovernable. He becomes deaf to the voice he used to obey; he is a lion in a fever; he distrusts his keeper and refuses to be controlled.

With the moral symptoms of a changing temper there are perceptible changes in appearance. His countenance develops and takes the stamp of his character; the soft and sparse down upon his cheeks becomes darker and stiffer. His voice grows hoarse or rather he loses it altogether. He is neither a child nor a man and cannot speak like either of them. His eyes, those organs of the soul which till now were dumb, find speech and meaning; a kindling fire illumines them, there is still a sacred innocence in their ever brightening glance, but they have lost their first meaningless expression; he is already aware that they can say too much; he is beginning to learn to lower his eyes and blush, he is becoming sensitive, though he does not know what it is that he feels; he is uneasy without knowing why. All this may happen gradually and give you time enough; but if his keenness becomes impatience, his eagerness madness, if he is angry and sorry all in a moment, if he weeps without cause, if in the presence of objects which are beginning to be a source of danger his pulse quickens and his eyes sparkle, if he trembles when a woman's hand touches his, if he is troubled or timid in her presence, O Ulysses, wise Ulysses! have a care! The passages you closed with so much pains are open; the winds are unloosed; keep your hand upon the helm or all is lost.

This is the second birth I spoke of; then it is that man really enters upon life; henceforth no human passion is a stranger to him. Our efforts so far have been child's play, now they are of the greatest importance. This period when education is usually finished is just the time to begin; but to explain this new plan properly, let us take up our story where we left it.

Our passions are the chief means of self-preservation; to try to destroy them is therefore as absurd as it is useless; this would be to overcome nature, to reshape God's handiwork. If God bade man annihilate the passions he has given him, God would bid him be and not be; He would contradict himself. He has never given such a foolish commandment, there is nothing like it written on the heart of man, and what God will have a man do, He does not leave to the words of another man, He speaks Himself; His words are written in the secret heart.

Now I consider those who would prevent the birth of the passions almost as foolish as those who would destroy them, and those who think this has been my object hitherto are greatly mistaken.

But should we reason rightly, if from the fact that passions are natural to man, we inferred that all the passions we feel in ourselves and behold in others are natural? Their source, indeed, is natural; but they have been swollen by a thousand other streams; they are a great river which is constantly growing, one in which we can scarcely find a single drop of the original stream. Our natural passions are few in number; they are the means to freedom, they tend to self-preservation. All those which enslave and destroy us have another source; nature does not bestow them on us; we seize on them in her despite.

The origin of our passions, the root and spring of all the rest, the only one which is born with man, which never leaves him as long as he lives, is self-love; this passion is primitive, instinctive, it precedes all the rest, which are in a sense only modifications of it. In this sense, if you like, they are all natural. But most of these modifications are the result of external influences, without which they would never occur, and such modifications, far from being advantageous to us, are harmful. They change the original purpose and work against its end; then it is that man finds himself outside nature and at strife with himself.

Self-love is always good, always in accordance with the order of nature. The preservation of our own life is specially entrusted to each one of us, and our first care is, and must be, to watch over our own life; and how can we continually watch over it, if we do not take the greatest interest in it?

Self-preservation requires, therefore, that we shall love ourselves; we must love ourselves above everything, and it follows directly from this that we love what contributes to our preservation. Every child becomes fond of its nurse; Romulus must have loved the she-wolf who suckled him. At first this attachment is quite unconscious; the individual is attracted to that which contributes to his welfare and repelled by that which is harmful; this is merely blind instinct. What transforms this instinct into feeling, the liking into love, the aversion into hatred, is the evident intention of helping or hurting us. We do not become passionately attached to objects without feeling, which only follow the direction given them; but those from which we expect benefit or injury from their internal disposition, from their will, those we see acting freely for or against us, inspire us with like feelings to those they exhibit towards us. Something does us good, we seek after it; but we love the person who does us good; something harms us and we shrink from it, but we hate the person who tries to hurt us.

The child's first sentiment is self-love, his second, which is derived from it, is love of those about him; for in his present state of weakness he is only aware of people through the help and attention received from them. At first his affection for his nurse and his governess is mere habit. He seeks them because he needs them and because he is happy when they are there; it is rather perception than kindly feeling. It takes a long time to discover not merely that they are useful to him, but that they desire to be useful to him, and then it is that he begins to love them.

So a child is naturally disposed to kindly feeling because he sees that every one about him is inclined to help him, and from this experience he gets the habit of a kindly feeling towards his species; but with the expansion of his relations, his needs, his dependence, active or passive, the consciousness of his relations to others is awakened, and leads to the sense of duties and preferences. Then the child becomes masterful, jealous, deceitful, and vindictive. If he is not compelled to obedience, when he does not see the usefulness of what he is told to do, he attributes it to caprice, to an intention of tormenting him, and he rebels. If people give in to him, as soon as anything opposes him he regards it as rebellion, as a determination to resist him; he beats the chair or table for disobeying him. Self-love, which concerns itself only with ourselves, is content to satisfy our own needs; but selfishness, which is always comparing self with others, is never satisfied and never can be; for this feeling, which prefers ourselves to others, requires that they should prefer us to themselves, which is impossible. Thus the tender and gentle passions spring from self-love, while the hateful and angry passions spring from selfishness. So it is the fewness of his needs, the narrow limits within which he can compare himself with others, that makes a man really good; what makes him really bad is a multiplicity of needs and dependence on the opinions of others. It is easy to see how we can apply this principle and guide every passion of children and men towards good or evil. True, man cannot always live alone, and it will be hard therefore to remain good; and this difficulty will increase of necessity as his relations with others are extended. For this reason, above all, the dangers of social life demand that the necessary skill and care shall be devoted to guarding the human heart against the depravity which springs from fresh needs.

Man's proper study is that of his relation to his environment. So long as he only knows that environment through his physical nature, he should study himself in relation to things; this is the business of his childhood; when he begins to be aware of his moral nature, he should study himself in relation to his fellow-men; this is the business of his whole life, and we have now reached the time when that study should be begun.

As soon as a man needs a companion he is no longer an isolated creature, his heart is no longer alone. All his relations with his species, all the affections of his heart, come into being along with this. His first passion soon arouses the rest.

The direction of the instinct is uncertain. One sex is attracted by the other; that is the impulse of nature. Choice, preferences, individual likings, are the work of reason, prejudice, and habit; time and knowledge are required to make us capable of love; we do not love without reasoning or prefer without comparison. These judgments are none the less real, although they are formed unconsciously. True love, whatever you may say, will always be held in honour by mankind; for although its impulses lead us astray, although it does not bar the door of the heart to certain detestable qualities, although it even gives rise to these, yet it always presupposes certain worthy characteristics, without which we should be incapable of love. This choice, which is supposed to be contrary to reason, really springs from reason. We say Love is blind because his eyes are better than ours, and he perceives relations which we cannot discern. All women would be alike to a man who had no idea of virtue or beauty, and the first comer would always be the most charming. Love does not spring from nature, far from it; it is the curb and law of her desires; it is love that makes one sex indifferent to the other, the loved one alone excepted.

We wish to inspire the preference we feel; love must be mutual. To be loved we must be worthy of love; to be preferred we must be more worthy than the rest, at least in the eyes of our beloved. Hence we begin to look around among our fellows; we begin to compare ourselves with them, there is emulation, rivalry, and jealousy. A heart full to overflowing loves to make itself known; from the need of a mistress there soon springs the need of a friend He who feels how sweet it is to be loved, desires to be loved by everybody; and there could be no preferences if there were not many that fail to find satisfaction. With love and friendship there begin dissensions, enmity, and hatred. I behold deference to other people's opinions enthroned among all these divers passions, and foolish mortals, enslaved by her power, base their very existence merely on what other people think.

Expand these ideas and you will see where we get that form of selfishness which we call natural selfishness, and how selfishness ceases to be a simple feeling and becomes pride in great minds, vanity in little ones, and in both feeds continually at our neighbour's cost. Passions of this kind, not having any germ in the child's heart, cannot spring up in it of themselves; it is we who sow the seeds, and they never take root unless by our fault. Not so with the young man; they will find an entrance in spite of us. It is therefore time to change our methods.

Let us begin with some considerations of importance with regard to the critical stage under discussion. The change from childhood to puberty is not so clearly determined by nature but that it varies according to individual temperament and racial conditions. Everybody knows the differences which have been observed with regard to this between hot and cold countries, and every one sees that ardent temperaments mature earlier than others; but we may be mistaken as to the causes, and we may often attribute to physical causes what is really due to moral: this is one of the commonest errors in the philosophy of our times. The teaching of nature comes slowly; man's lessons are mostly premature. In the former case, the senses kindle the imagination, in the latter the imagination kindles the senses; it gives them a precocious activity which cannot fail to enervate the individual and, in the long run, the race. It is a more general and more trustworthy fact than that of climatic influences, that puberty and sexual power is always more precocious among educated and civilised races, than among the ignorant and barbarous.[1] Children are preternaturally quick to discern immoral habits under the cloak of decency with which they are concealed.

[1] "In towns," says M. Buffon, "and among the well-to-do classes, children accustomed to plentiful and nourishing food sooner reach this state; in the country and among the poor, children are more backward, because of their poor and scanty food." I admit the fact but not the explanation, for in the districts where the food of the villagers is plentiful and good, as in the Valais and even in some of the mountain districts of Italy, such as Friuli, the age of puberty for both sexes is quite as much later than in the heart of the towns, where, in order to gratify their vanity, people are often extremely parsimonious in the matter of food, and where most people, in the words of the proverb, have a velvet coat and an empty belly. It is astonishing to find in these mountainous regions big lads as strong as a man with shrill voices and smooth chins, and tall girls, well developed in other respects, without any trace of the periodic functions of their sex. This difference is, in my opinion, solely due to the fact that in the simplicity of their manners the imagination remains calm and peaceful, and does not stir the blood till much later, and thus their temperament is much less precocious.

The prim speech imposed upon them, the lessons in good behaviour, the veil of mystery you profess to hang before their eyes, serve but to stimulate their curiosity. It is plain, from the way you set about it, that they are meant to learn what you profess to conceal; and of all you teach them this is most quickly assimilated.

Consult experience and you will find how far this foolish method hastens the work of nature and ruins the character. This is one of the chief causes of physical degeneration in our towns. The young people, prematurely exhausted, remain small, puny, and misshapen, they grow old instead of growing up, like a vine forced to bear fruit in spring, which fades and dies before autumn.

To know how far a happy ignorance may prolong the innocence of children, you must live among rude and simple people. It is a sight both touching and amusing to see both sexes, left to the protection of their own hearts, continuing the sports of childhood in the flower of youth and beauty, showing by their very familiarity the purity of their pleasures. When at length those delightful young people marry, they bestow on each other the first fruits of their person, and are all the dearer therefore. Swarms of strong and healthy children are the pledges of a union which nothing can change, and the fruit of the virtue of their early years.

If the age at which a man becomes conscious of his sex is deferred as much by the effects of education as by the action of nature, it follows that this age may be hastened or retarded according to the way in which the child is brought up; and if the body gains or loses strength in proportion as its development is accelerated or retarded, it also follows that the more we try to retard it the stronger and more vigorous will the young man be. I am still speaking of purely physical consequences; you will soon see that this is not all.

From these considerations I arrive at the solution of the question so often discussed—Should we enlighten children at an early period as to the objects of their curiosity, or is it better to put them off with decent shams? I think we need do neither. In the first place, this curiosity will not arise unless we give it a chance. We must therefore take care not to give it an opportunity. In the next place, questions one is not obliged to answer do not compel us to deceive those who ask them; it is better to bid the child hold his tongue than to tell him a lie. He will not be greatly surprised at this treatment if you have already accustomed him to it in matters of no importance. Lastly, if you decide to answer his questions, let it be with the greatest plainness, without mystery or confusion, without a smile. It is much less dangerous to satisfy a child's curiosity than to stimulate it.

Let your answers be always grave, brief, decided, and without trace of hesitation. I need not add that they should be true. We cannot teach children the danger of telling lies to men without realising, on the man's part, the danger of telling lies to children. A single untruth on the part of the master will destroy the results of his education.

Complete ignorance with regard to certain matters is perhaps the best thing for children; but let them learn very early what it is impossible to conceal from them permanently. Either their curiosity must never be aroused, or it must be satisfied before the age when it becomes a source of danger. Your conduct towards your pupil in this respect depends greatly on his individual circumstances, the society in which he moves, the position in which he may find himself, etc. Nothing must be left to chance; and if you are not sure of keeping him in ignorance of the difference between the sexes till he is sixteen, take care you teach him before he is ten.

I do not like people to be too fastidious in speaking with children, nor should they go out of their way to avoid calling a spade a spade; they are always found out if they do. Good manners in this respect are always perfectly simple; but an imagination soiled by vice makes the ear over-sensitive and compels us to be constantly refining our expressions. Plain words do not matter; it is lascivious ideas which must be avoided.

Although modesty is natural to man, it is not natural to children. Modesty only begins with the knowledge of evil; and how should children without this knowledge of evil have the feeling which results from it? To give them lessons in modesty and good conduct is to teach them that there are things shameful and wicked, and to give them a secret wish to know what these things are. Sooner or later they will find out, and the first spark which touches the imagination will certainly hasten the awakening of the senses. Blushes are the sign of guilt; true innocence is ashamed of nothing.

Children have not the same desires as men; but they are subject like them to the same disagreeable needs which offend the senses, and by this means they may receive the same lessons in propriety. Follow the mind of nature which has located in the same place the organs of secret pleasures and those of disgusting needs; she teaches us the same precautions at different ages, sometimes by means of one idea and sometimes by another; to the man through modesty, to the child through cleanliness.

I can only find one satisfactory way of preserving the child's innocence, to surround him by those who respect and love him. Without this all our efforts to keep him in ignorance fail sooner or later; a smile, a wink, a careless gesture tells him all we sought to hide; it is enough to teach him to perceive that there is something we want to hide from him. The delicate phrases and expressions employed by persons of politeness assume a knowledge which children ought not to possess, and they are quite out of place with them, but when we truly respect the child's innocence we easily find in talking to him the simple phrases which befit him. There is a certain directness of speech which is suitable and pleasing to innocence; this is the right tone to adopt in order to turn the child from dangerous curiosity. By speaking simply to him about everything you do not let him suspect there is anything left unsaid. By connecting coarse words with the unpleasant ideas which belong to them, you quench the first spark of imagination; you do not forbid the child to say these words or to form these ideas; but without his knowing it you make him unwilling to recall them. And how much confusion is spared to those who speaking from the heart always say the right thing, and say it as they themselves have felt it!

"Where do little children come from?" This is an embarrassing question, which occurs very naturally to children, one which foolishly or wisely answered may decide their health and their morals for life. The quickest way for a mother to escape from it without deceiving her son is to tell him to hold his tongue. That will serve its turn if he has always been accustomed to it in matters of no importance, and if he does not suspect some mystery from this new way of speaking. But the mother rarely stops there. "It is the married people's secret," she will say, "little boys should not be so curious." That is all very well so far as the mother is concerned, but she may be sure that the little boy, piqued by her scornful manner, will not rest till he has found out the married people's secret, which will very soon be the case.

Let me tell you a very different answer which I heard given to the same question, one which made all the more impression on me, coming, as it did, from a woman, modest in speech and behaviour, but one who was able on occasion, for the welfare of her child and for the cause of virtue, to cast aside the false fear of blame and the silly jests of the foolish. Not long before the child had passed a small stone which had torn the passage, but the trouble was over and forgotten. "Mamma," said the eager child, "where do little children come from?" "My child," replied his mother without hesitation, "women pass them with pains that sometimes cost their life." Let fools laugh and silly people be shocked; but let the wise inquire if it is possible to find a wiser answer and one which would better serve its purpose.

In the first place the thought of a need of nature with which the child is well acquainted turns his thoughts from the idea of a mysterious process. The accompanying ideas of pain and death cover it with a veil of sadness which deadens the imagination and suppresses curiosity; everything leads the mind to the results, not the causes, of child-birth. This is the information to which this answer leads. If the repugnance inspired by this answer should permit the child to inquire further, his thoughts are turned to the infirmities of human nature, disgusting things, images of pain. What chance is there for any stimulation of desire in such a conversation? And yet you see there is no departure from truth, no need to deceive the scholar in order to teach him.

Your children read; in the course of their reading they meet with things they would never have known without reading. Are they students, their imagination is stimulated and quickened in the silence of the study. Do they move in the world of society, they hear a strange jargon, they see conduct which makes a great impression on them; they have been told so continually that they are men that in everything men do in their presence they at once try to find how that will suit themselves; the conduct of others must indeed serve as their pattern when the opinions of others are their law. Servants, dependent on them, and therefore anxious to please them, flatter them at the expense of their morals; giggling governesses say things to the four-year-old child which the most shameless woman would not dare to say to them at fifteen. They soon forget what they said, but the child has not forgotten what he heard. Loose conversation prepares the way for licentious conduct; the child is debauched by the cunning lacquey, and the secret of the one guarantees the secret of the other.

The child brought up in accordance with his age is alone. He knows no attachment but that of habit, he loves his sister like his watch, and his friend like his dog. He is unconscious of his sex and his species; men and women are alike unknown; he does not connect their sayings and doings with himself, he neither sees nor hears, or he pays no heed to them; he is no more concerned with their talk than their actions; he has nothing to do with it. This is no artificial error induced by our method, it is the ignorance of nature. The time is at hand when that same nature will take care to enlighten her pupil, and then only does she make him capable of profiting by the lessons without danger. This is our principle; the details of its rules are outside my subject; and the means I suggest with regard to other matters will still serve to illustrate this.

Do you wish to establish law and order among the rising passions, prolong the period of their development, so that they may have time to find their proper place as they arise. Then they are controlled by nature herself, not by man; your task is merely to leave it in her hands. If your pupil were alone, you would have nothing to do; but everything about him enflames his imagination. He is swept along on the torrent of conventional ideas; to rescue him you must urge him in the opposite direction. Imagination must be curbed by feeling and reason must silence the voice of conventionality. Sensibility is the source of all the passions, imagination determines their course. Every creature who is aware of his relations must be disturbed by changes in these relations and when he imagines or fancies he imagines others better adapted to his nature. It is the errors of the imagination which transmute into vices the passions of finite beings, of angels even, if indeed they have passions; for they must needs know the nature of every creature to realise what relations are best adapted to themselves.

This is the sum of human wisdom with regard to the use of the passions. First, to be conscious of the true relations of man both in the species and the individual; second, to control all the affections in accordance with these relations.

But is man in a position to control his affections according to such and such relations? No doubt he is, if he is able to fix his imagination on this or that object, or to form this or that habit. Moreover, we are not so much concerned with what a man can do

for himself, as with what we can do for our pupil through our choice
of the circumstances in which he shall be placed. To show the
means by which he may be kept in the path of nature is to show
plainly enough how he might stray from that path.

So long as his consciousness is confined to himself there is no
morality in his actions; it is only when it begins to extend beyond
himself that he forms first the sentiments and then the ideas of
good and ill, which make him indeed a man, and an integral part
of his species. To begin with we must therefore confine our
observations to this point.

These observations are difficult to make, for we must reject the
examples before our eyes, and seek out those in which the
successive developments follow the order of nature.

A child sophisticated, polished, and civilised, who is only awaiting
the power to put into practice the precocious instruction he has
received, is never mistaken with regard to the time when this power
is acquired. Far from awaiting it, he accelerates it; he stirs his
blood to a premature ferment; he knows what should be the object
of his desires long before those desires are experienced. It is not
nature which stimulates him; it is he who forces the hand of nature;
she has nothing to teach him when he becomes a man; he was a
man in thought long before he was a man in reality.

The true course of nature is slower and more gradual. Little by
little the blood grows warmer, the faculties expand, the character
is formed. The wise workman who directs the process is careful to
perfect every tool before he puts it to use; the first desires are
preceded by a long period of unrest, they are deceived by a prolonged ignorance, they know not what they want. The blood
ferments and bubbles; overflowing vitality seeks to extend its
sphere. The eye grows brighter and surveys others, we begin to be
interested in those about us, we begin to feel that we are not meant
to live alone; thus the heart is thrown open to human affection,
and becomes capable of attachment.

The first sentiment of which the well-trained youth is capable is
not love but friendship. The first work of his rising imagination is
to make known to him his fellows; the species affects him before the
sex. Here is another advantage to be gained from prolonged
innocence; you may take advantage of his dawning sensibility to
sow the first seeds of humanity in the heart of the young adolescent.
This advantage is all the greater because this is the only time in
his life when such efforts may be really successful.

I have always observed that young men, corrupted in early youth
and addicted to women and debauchery, are inhuman and cruel;
their passionate temperament makes them impatient, vindictive, and
angry; their imagination fixed on one object only, refuses all others;
mercy and pity are alike unknown to them; they would have
sacrificed father, mother, the whole world, to the least of their
pleasures. A young man, on the other hand, brought up in happy
innocence, is drawn by the first stirrings of nature to the tender and

affectionate passions; his warm heart is touched by the sufferings of his fellow-creatures; he trembles with delight when he meets his comrade, his arms can embrace tenderly, his eyes can shed tears of pity; he learns to be sorry for offending others through his shame at causing annoyance. If the eager warmth of his blood makes him quick, hasty, and passionate, a moment later you see all his natural kindness of heart in the eagerness of his repentance; he weeps, he groans over the wound he has given; he would atone for the blood he has shed with his own; his anger dies away, his pride abases itself before the consciousness of his wrong-doing. Is he the injured party, in the height of his fury an excuse, a word, disarms him; he forgives the wrongs of others as whole-heartedly as he repairs his own. Adolescence is not the age of hatred or vengeance; it is the age of pity, mercy, and generosity. Yes, I maintain, and I am not afraid of the testimony of experience, a youth of good birth, one who has preserved his innocence up to the age of twenty, is at that age the best, the most generous, the most loving, and the most lovable of men. You never heard such a thing; I can well believe that philosophers such as you, brought up among the corruption of the public schools, are unaware of it.

Man's weakness makes him sociable. Our common sufferings draw our hearts to our fellow-creatures; we should have no duties to mankind if we were not men. Every affection is a sign of insufficiency; if each of us had no need of others, we should hardly think of associating with them. So our frail happiness has its roots in our weakness. A really happy man is a hermit; God only enjoys absolute happiness; but which of us has any idea what that means? If any imperfect creature were self-sufficing, what would he have to enjoy? To our thinking he would be wretched and alone. I do not understand how one who has need of nothing could love anything, nor do I understand how he who loves nothing can be happy.

Hence it follows that we are drawn towards our fellow-creatures less by our feeling for their joys than for their sorrows; for in them we discern more plainly a nature like our own, and a pledge of their affection for us. If our common needs create a bond of interest our common sufferings create a bond of affection. The sight of a happy man arouses in others envy rather than love, we are ready to accuse him of usurping a right which is not his, of seeking happiness for himself alone, and our selfishness suffers an additional pang in the thought that this man has no need of us. But who does not pity the wretch when he beholds his sufferings? who would not deliver him from his woes if a wish could do it? Imagination puts us more readily in the place of the miserable man than of the happy man; we feel that the one condition touches us more nearly than the other. Pity is sweet, because, when we put ourselves in the place of one who suffers, we are aware, nevertheless, of the pleasure of not suffering like him. Envy is bitter, because the sight of a happy man, far from putting the envious in his place, inspires him with regret that he is not there. The one seems to exempt us from the

pains he suffers, the other seems to deprive us of the good things he
enjoys.

Do you desire to stimulate and nourish the first stirrings of
awakening sensibility in the heart of a young man, do you desire to
incline his disposition towards kindly deed and thought, do not
cause the seeds of pride, vanity, and envy to spring up in him
through the misleading picture of the happiness of mankind; do
not show him to begin with the pomp of courts, the pride of palaces,
the delights of pageants; do not take him into society and into
brilliant assemblies; do not show him the outside of society till you
have made him capable of estimating it at its true worth. To show
him the world before he is acquainted with men, is not to train him,
but to corrupt him; not to teach, but to mislead.

By nature men are neither kings, nobles, courtiers, nor millionaires.
All men are born poor and naked, all are liable to the sorrows of life,
its disappointments, its ills, its needs, its suffering of every kind;
and all are condemned at length to die. This is what it really means
to be a man, this is what no mortal can escape. Begin then with
the study of the essentials of humanity, that which really constitutes
mankind.

At sixteen the adolescent knows what it is to suffer, for he himself has suffered; but he scarcely realises that others suffer too; to
see without feeling is not knowledge, and as I have said again and
again the child who does not picture the feelings of others knows no
ills but his own; but when his imagination is kindled by the first
beginnings of growing sensibility, he begins to perceive himself in
his fellow-creatures, to be touched by their cries, to suffer in their
sufferings. It is at this time that the sorrowful picture of suffering
humanity should stir his heart with the first touch of pity he has
ever known.

If it is not easy to discover this opportunity in your scholars,
whose fault is it? You taught them so soon to play at feeling, you
taught them so early its language, that speaking continually in the
same strain they turn your lessons against yourself, and give you
no chance of discovering when they cease to lie, and begin to feel
what they say. But look at Emile; I have led him up to this age,
and he has neither felt nor pretended to feel. He has never said,
" I love you dearly," till he knew what it was to love; he has never
been taught what expression to assume when he enters the room of
his father, his mother, or his sick tutor; he has not learnt the art of
affecting a sorrow he does not feel. He has never pretended to
weep for the death of any one, for he does not know what it is to die.
There is the same insensibility in his heart as in his manners. Indifferent, like every child, to every one but himself, he takes no
interest in any one; his only peculiarity is that he will not pretend
to take such an interest; he is less deceitful than others.

Emile having thought little about creatures of feeling will be a
long time before he knows what is meant by pain and death. Groans
and cries will begin to stir his compassion, he will turn away his

eyes at the sight of blood; the convulsions of a dying animal will cause him I know not what anguish before he knows the source of these impulses. If he were still stupid and barbarous he would not feel them; if he were more learned he would recognise their source; he has compared ideas too frequently already to be insensible, but not enough to know what he feels.

So pity is born, the first relative sentiment which touches the human heart according to the order of nature. To become sensitive and pitiful the child must know that he has fellow-creatures who suffer as he has suffered, who feel the pains he has felt, and others which he can form some idea of, being capable of feeling them himself. Indeed, how can we let ourselves be stirred by pity unless we go beyond ourselves, and identify ourselves with the suffering animal, by leaving, so to speak, our own nature and taking his. We only suffer so far as we suppose he suffers; the suffering is not ours but his. So no one becomes sensitive till his imagination is aroused and begins to carry him outside himself.

What should we do to stimulate and nourish this growing sensibility, to direct it, and to follow its natural bent? Should we not present to the young man objects on which the expansive force of his heart may take effect, objects which dilate it, which extend it to other creatures, which take him outside himself? should we not carefully remove everything that narrows, concentrates, and strengthens the power of the human self? that is to say, in other words, we should arouse in him kindness, goodness, pity, and beneficence, all the gentle and attractive passions which are naturally pleasing to man; those passions prevent the growth of envy, covetousness, hatred, all the repulsive and cruel passions which make our sensibility not merely a cipher but a minus quantity, passions which are the curse of those who feel them.

I think I can sum up the whole of the preceding reflections in two or three maxims, definite, straightforward, and easy to understand.

First Maxim.—It is not in human nature to put ourselves in the place of those who are happier than ourselves, but only in the place of those who can claim our pity.

If you find exceptions to this rule, they are more apparent than real. Thus we do not put ourselves in the place of the rich or great when we become fond of them; even when our affection is real, we only appropriate to ourselves a part of their welfare. Sometimes we love the rich man in the midst of misfortunes; but so long as he prospers he has no real friend, except the man who is not deceived by appearances, who pities rather than envies him in spite of his prosperity.

The happiness belonging to certain states of life appeals to us; take, for instance, the life of a shepherd in the country. The charm of seeing these good people so happy is not poisoned by envy; we are genuinely interested in them. Why is this? Because we feel we can descend into this state of peace and innocence and enjoy the same happiness; it is an alternative which only calls up pleasant thoughts, so long as the wish is as good as the deed. It is always pleasant to examine our stores, to contemplate our own wealth, even when we do not mean to spend it.

From this we see that to incline a young man to humanity you must not make him admire the brilliant lot of others; you must show him life in its sorrowful aspects and arouse his fears. Thus it becomes clear that he must force his own way to happiness, without interfering with the happiness of others.

Second Maxim.—We never pity another's woes unless we know we may suffer in like manner ourselves.

"Non ignara mali, miseris succurrere disco."—VIRGIL.

I know nothing so fine, so full of meaning, so touching, so true as these words.

Why have kings no pity on their people? Because they never expect to be ordinary men. Why are the rich so hard on the poor? Because they have no fear of becoming poor. Why do the nobles look down upon the people? Because a nobleman will never be one of the lower classes. Why are the Turks generally kinder and more hospitable than ourselves? Because, under their wholly arbitrary system of government, the rank and wealth of individuals are always uncertain and precarious, so that they do not regard poverty and degradation as conditions with which they have no concern; to-morrow, any one may himself be in the same position as those on whom he bestows alms to-day. This thought, which occurs again and again in eastern romances, lends them a certain tenderness which is not to be found in our pretentious and harsh morality.

So do not train your pupil to look down from the height of his glory upon the sufferings of the unfortunate, the labours of the wretched, and do not hope to teach him to pity them while he considers them as far removed from himself. Make him thoroughly aware of the fact that the fate of these unhappy persons may one day be his own, that his feet are standing on the edge of the abyss, into which he may be plunged at any moment by a thousand unexpected irresistible misfortunes. Teach him to put no trust in birth, health, or riches; show him all the changes of fortune; find him examples—there are only too many of them—in which men of higher rank than himself have sunk below the condition of these wretched ones. Whether by their own fault or another's is for the present no concern of ours; does he indeed know the meaning of the word fault? Never interfere with the order in which he acquires knowledge, and teach him only through the means within his reach; it needs no great learning to perceive that all the prudence of mankind cannot make certain whether he will be alive or dead in an hour's time, whether before nightfall he will not be grinding his teeth in the pangs of nephritis, whether a month hence he will be rich or poor, whether in a year's time he may not be rowing an Algerian galley under the lash of the slave-driver. Above all do not teach him this, like his catechism, in cold blood; let him see and feel the calamities which overtake men; surprise and startle his imagination with the perils which lurk continually about a man's path; let him see the pitfalls all about him, and when he hears you speak of them, let him cling more closely to you for fear lest he should fall. "You will make him timid and cowardly," do you say? We shall see; let us make him kindly to begin with, that is what matters most.

Third Maxim.—The pity we feel for others is proportionate, not to the amount of the evil, but to the feelings we attribute to the sufferers.

We only pity the wretched so far as we think they feel the need of pity. The bodily effect of our sufferings is less than one would suppose; it is memory that prolongs the pain, imagination which projects it into the future, and makes us really to be pitied. This is, I think, one of the reasons why we are more callous to the sufferings of animals than of men, although a fellow-feeling ought to make us identify ourselves equally with either. We scarcely pity the cart-horse in his shed, for we do not suppose that while he is eating his hay he is thinking of the blows he has received and the labours in store for him. Neither do we pity the sheep grazing in the field, though we know it is about to be slaughtered, for we believe it knows nothing of the fate in store for it. In this way we also become callous to the fate of our fellow-men, and the rich console themselves for the harm done by them to the poor, by the assumption that the poor are too stupid to feel. I usually judge of the value any one puts on the welfare of his fellow-creatures by what he seems to think of them. We naturally think lightly of the happiness of those we despise. It need not surprise you that politicians speak so scornfully of the people, and philosophers profess to think mankind so wicked.

The people are mankind; those who do not belong to the people are so few in number that they are not worth counting. Man is the same in every station of life; if that be so, those ranks to which most men belong deserve most honour. All distinctions of rank fade away before the eyes of a thoughtful person; he sees the same passions, the same feelings in the noble and the guttersnipe; there is merely a slight difference in speech, and more or less artificiality of tone; and if there is indeed any essential difference between them, the disadvantage is all on the side of those who are more sophisticated. The people show themselves as they are, and they are not attractive; but the fashionable world is compelled to adopt a disguise; we should be horrified if we saw it as it really is.

There is, so our wiseacres tell us, the same amount of happiness and sorrow in every station. This saying is as deadly in its effects as it is incapable of proof; if all are equally happy why should I trouble myself about any one? Let every one stay where he is; leave the slave to be ill-treated, the sick man to suffer, and the wretched to perish; they have nothing to gain by any change in their condition. You enumerate the sorrows of the rich, and show the vanity of his empty pleasures; what barefaced sophistry! The rich man's sufferings do not come from his position, but from himself alone when he abuses it. He is not to be pitied were he indeed more miserable than the poor, for his ills are of his own making, and he could be happy if he chose. But the sufferings of the poor man come from external things, from the hardships fate has imposed upon him. No amount of habit can accustom him to the bodily ills of fatigue, exhaustion, and hunger. Neither head nor heart can serve to free him from the sufferings of his condition. How is Epictetus the better for knowing beforehand that his master will break his leg for him; does he do it any the less? He has to endure not only the pain itself but the pains of anticipation. If the people were as wise as we assume them to be stupid, how could they be other than they are? Observe persons of this class; you will see that, with a different way of speaking, they have as much intelligence and more common-sense than yourself. Have respect then for your species; remember that it consists essentially of the people, that if all the kings and all the philosophers were removed they would scarcely be missed, and things would go on none the worse. In a word, teach your pupil to love all men, even those who fail to appreciate him; act in such way that he is not a member of any class, but takes his place in all alike: speak in his hearing of the human race with tenderness, and even with pity, but never with scorn. You are a man; do not dishonour mankind.

It is by these ways and others like them—how different from the beaten paths—that we must reach the heart of the young adolescent and stimulate in him the first impulses of nature; we must develop that heart and open its doors to his fellow-creatures, and there must be as little self-interest as possible mixed up with these impulses; above all, no vanity, no emulation, no boasting, none of those sentiments which force us to compare ourselves with others; for such comparisons are never made without arousing some measure of hatred against those who dispute our claim to the first place, were it only in our own estimation. Then we must be either blind or angry, a bad man or a fool; let us try to avoid this dilemma. Sooner or later these dangerous passions will appear, so you tell me, in spite of us. I do not deny it. There is a time and place for everything; I am only saying that we should not help to arouse these passions.

This is the spirit of the method to be laid down. In this case examples and illustrations are useless, for here we find the beginning of the countless differences of character, and every example I gave would possibly apply to only one case in a hundred thousand. It is at this age that the clever teacher begins his real business, as a student and a philosopher who knows how to probe the heart and strives to guide it aright. While the young man has not learnt to pretend, while he does not even know the meaning of pretence, you see by his look, his manner, his gestures, the impression he has received from any object presented to him; you read in his countenance every impulse of his heart; by watching his expression you learn to protect his impulses and actually to control them.

It has been commonly observed that blood, wounds, cries and groans, the preparations for painful operations, and everything which directs the senses towards things connected with suffering, are usually the first to make an impression on all men. The idea of destruction, a more complex matter, does not have so great an effect; the thought of death affects us later and less forcibly, for no one knows from his own experience what it is to die; you must have seen corpses to feel the agonies of the dying. But when once this idea is established in the mind, there is no spectacle more dreadful in our eyes, whether because of the idea of complete destruction which it arouses through our senses, or because we know that this moment must come for each one of us and we feel ourselves all the more keenly affected by a situation from which we know there is no escape.

These various impressions differ in manner and in degree, according to the individual character of each one of us and his former habits, but they are universal and no one is altogether free from them. There are other impressions less universal and of a later growth, impressions most suited to sensitive souls, such impressions as we receive from moral suffering, inward grief, the sufferings of the mind, depression, and sadness. There are men who can be touched by nothing but groans and tears; the suppressed sobs of a heart labouring under sorrow would never win a sigh; the sight of a downcast visage, a pale and gloomy countenance, eyes which can weep no longer, would never draw a tear from them. The sufferings of the mind are as nothing to them; they weigh them, their own mind feels nothing; expect nothing from such persons but inflexible severity, harshness, cruelty. They may be just and upright, but not merciful, generous, or pitiful. They may, I say, be just, if a man can indeed be just without being merciful.

But do not be in a hurry to judge young people by this standard, more especially those who have been educated rightly, who have no idea of the moral sufferings they have never had to endure; for once again they can only pity the ills they know, and this apparent insensibility is soon transformed into pity when they begin to feel that there are in human life a thousand ills of which they know nothing As for Emile, if in childhood he was distinguished by simplicity and good sense, in his youth he will show a warm and tender heart; for the reality of the feelings depends to a great extent on the accuracy of the ideas.

But why call him hither? More than one reader will reproach me no doubt for departing from my first intention and forgetting the lasting happiness I promised my pupil. The sorrowful, the dying, such sights of pain and woe, what happiness, what delight is this for a young heart on the threshold of life? His gloomy tutor, who proposed to give him such a pleasant education, only introduces him to life that he may suffer. This is what they will say, but what care I? I promised to make him happy, not to make him seem happy. Am I to blame if, deceived as usual by the outward appearances, you take them for the reality?

Let us take two young men at the close of their early education, and let them enter the world by opposite doors. The one mounts at once to Olympus, and moves in the smartest society; he is taken to court, he is presented in the houses of the great, of the rich, of the pretty women. I assume that he is everywhere made much of, and I do not regard too closely the effect of this reception on his reason; I assume it can stand it. Pleasures fly before him, every day provides him with fresh amusements; he flings himself into everything with an eagerness which carries you away. You find him busy, eager, and curious; his first wonder makes a great impression on you; you think him happy; but behold the state of his heart; you think he is rejoicing, I think he suffers.

What does he see when first he opens his eyes? all sorts of so-called pleasures, hitherto unknown. Most of these pleasures are only for a moment within his reach, and seem to show themselves only to inspire regret for their loss. Does he wander through a palace; you see by his uneasy curiosity that he is asking why his father's house is not like it. Every question shows you that he is comparing himself all the time with the owner of this grand place. And all the mortification arising from this comparison at once revolts and stimulates his vanity. If he meets a young man better dressed than himself, I find him secretly complaining of his parents' meanness. If he is better dressed than another, he suffers because the latter is his superior in birth or in intellect, and all his gold lace is put to shame by a plain cloth coat. Does he shine unrivalled in some assembly, does he stand on tiptoe that they may see him better, who is there who does not secretly desire to humble the pride and vanity of the young fop? Everybody is in league against him; the disquieting glances of a solemn man, the biting phrases of some satirical person, do not fail to reach him, and if it were only one man who despised him, the scorn of that one would poison in a moment the applause of the rest.

Let us grant him everything, let us not grudge him charm and worth; let him be well-made, witty, and attractive; the women will run after him; but by pursuing him before he is in love with them, they will inspire rage rather than love; he will have successes, but neither rapture nor passion to enjoy them. As his desires are always anticipated; they never have time to spring up among his pleasures, so he only feels the tedium of restraint. Even before he knows it he is disgusted and satiated with the sex formed to be the delight of his own; if he continues its pursuit it is only through vanity, and even should he really be devoted to women, he will not be the only brilliant, the only attractive young man, nor will he always find his mistresses prodigies of fidelity.

I say nothing of the vexation, the deceit, the crimes, and the remorse of all kinds, inseparable from such a life. We know that

experience of the world disgusts us with it; I am speaking only
of the drawbacks belonging to youthful illusions.

Hitherto the young man has lived in the bosom of his family and
his friends, and has been the sole object of their care; what a change
to enter all at once into a region where he counts for so little; to
find himself plunged into another sphere, he who has been so long
the centre of his own. What insults, what humiliation, must he
endure, before he loses among strangers the ideas of his own importance which have been formed and nourished among his own
people! As a child everything gave way to him, everybody flocked
to him; as a young man he must give place to every one, or if he
preserves ever so little of his former airs, what harsh lessons will
bring him to himself! Accustomed to get everything he wants
without any difficulty, his wants are many, and he feels continual
privations. He is tempted by everything that flatters him; what
others have, he must have too; he covets everything, he envies
every one, he would always be master. He is devoured by vanity,
his young heart is enflamed by unbridled passions, jealousy and
hatred among the rest; all these violent passions burst out at once;
their sting rankles in him in the busy world, they return with him
at night, he comes back dissatisfied with himself, with others; he
falls asleep among a thousand foolish schemes disturbed by a
thousand fancies, and his pride shows him even in his dreams those
fancied pleasures; he is tormented by a desire which will never be
satisfied. So much for your pupil; let us turn to mine.

If the first thing to make an impression on him is something
sorrowful his first return to himself is a feeling of pleasure. When
he sees how many ills he has escaped he thinks he is happier than
he fancied. He shares the suffering of his fellow-creatures, but
he shares it of his own free will and finds pleasure in it. He enjoys
at once the pity he feels for their woes and the joy of being exempt
from them; he feels in himself that state of vigour which projects
us beyond ourselves, and bids us carry elsewhere the superfluous
activity of our well-being. To pity another's woes we must indeed
know them, but we need not feel them. When we have suffered,
when we are in fear of suffering, we pity those who suffer; but when
we suffer ourselves, we pity none but ourselves. But if all of us,
being subject ourselves to the ills of life, only bestow upon others
the sensibility we do not actually require for ourselves, it follows
that pity must be a very pleasant feeling, since it speaks on our
behalf; and, on the other hand, a hard-hearted man is always
unhappy, since the state of his heart leaves him no superfluous
sensibility to bestow on the sufferings of others.

We are too apt to judge of happiness by appearances; we suppose
it is to be found in the most unlikely places, we seek for it where it
cannot possibly be; mirth is a very doubtful indication of its
presence. A merry man is often a wretch who is trying to deceive
others and distract himself. The men who are jovial, friendly, and
contented at their club are almost always gloomy grumblers at

home, and their servants have to pay for the amusement they give among their friends. True contentment is neither merry nor noisy; we are jealous of so sweet a sentiment, when we enjoy it we think about it, we delight in it for fear it should escape us. A really happy man says little and laughs little; he hugs his happiness, so to speak, to his heart. Noisy games, violent delight, conceal the disappointment of satiety. But melancholy is the friend of pleasure; tears and pity attend our sweetest enjoyment, and great joys call for tears rather than laughter.

If at first the number and variety of our amusements seem to contribute to our happiness, if at first the even tenor of a quiet life seems tedious, when we look at it more closely we discover that the pleasantest habit of mind consists in a moderate enjoyment which leaves little scope for desire and aversion. The unrest of passion causes curiosity and fickleness; the emptiness of noisy pleasures causes weariness. We never weary of our state when we know none more delightful. Savages suffer less than other men from curiosity and from tedium; everything is the same to them —themselves, not their possessions—and they are never weary.

The man of the world almost always wears a mask. He is scarcely ever himself and is almost a stranger to himself; he is ill at ease when he is forced into his own company. Not what he is, but what he seems, is all he cares for.

I cannot help picturing in the countenance of the young man I have just spoken of an indefinable but unpleasant impertinence, smoothness, and affectation, which is repulsive to a plain man, and in the countenance of my own pupil a simple and interesting expression which indicates the real contentment and the calm of his mind; an expression which inspires respect and confidence, and seems only to await the establishment of friendly relations to bestow his own confidence in return. It is thought that the expression is merely the development of certain features designed by nature. For my own part I think that over and above this development a man's face is shaped, all unconsciously, by the frequent and habitual influence of certain affections of the heart. These affections are shown on the face, there is nothing more certain; and when they become habitual, they must surely leave lasting traces. This is why I think the expression shows the character, and that we can sometimes read one another without seeking mysterious explanations in powers we do not possess.

A child has only two distinct feelings, joy and sorrow; he laughs or he cries; he knows no middle course, and he is constantly passing from one extreme to the other. On account of these perpetual changes there is no lasting impression on the face, and no expression; but when the child is older and more sensitive, his feelings are keener or more permanent, and these deeper impressions leave traces more difficult to erase; and the habitual state of the feelings has an effect on the features which in course of time becomes ineffaceable. Still it is not uncommon to meet with men whose expression varies with their age. I have met with several, and I have always found that those whom I could observe and follow had also changed their habitual temper. This one observation thoroughly confirmed would seem to me decisive, and it is not out of place in a treatise on education, where it is a matter of importance, that we should learn to judge the feelings of the heart by external signs.

I do not know whether my young man will be any the less amiable for not having learnt to copy conventional manners and to feign sentiments which are not his own; that does not concern me at present, I only know he will be more affectionate; and I find it difficult to believe that he, who cares for nobody but himself, can so far disguise his true feelings as to please as readily as he who finds fresh happiness for himself in his affection for others. But with regard to this feeling of happiness, I think I have said enough already for the guidance of any sensible reader, and to show that I have not contradicted myself.

I return to my system, and I say, when the critical age approaches, present to young people spectacles which restrain rather than excite them; put off their dawning imagination with objects which, far from inflaming their senses, put a check to their activity. Remove them from great cities, where the flaunting attire and the boldness of the women hasten and anticipate the teaching of nature, where everything presents to their view pleasures of which they should know nothing till they are of an age to choose for themselves. Bring them back to their early home, where rural simplicity allows the passions of their age to develop more slowly; or if their taste for the arts keeps them in town, guard them by means of this very taste from a dangerous idleness. Choose carefully their company, their occupations, and their pleasures; show them nothing but modest and pathetic pictures which are touching but not seductive, and nourish their sensibility without stimulating their senses. Remember also, that the danger of excess is not confined to any one place, and that immoderate passions always do irreparable damage. You need not make your pupil a sick-nurse or a Brother of Pity; you need not distress him by the perpetual sight of pain and suffering; you need not take him from one hospital to another, from the gallows to the prison. He must be softened, not hardened, by the sight of human misery. When we have seen a sight it ceases to impress us, use is second nature, what is always before our eyes no longer appeals to the imagination, and it is only through the imagination that we can feel the sorrows of others; this is why priests and doctors who are always beholding death and suffering become so hardened. Let your pupil therefore know something of the lot of man and the woes of his fellow-creatures, but let him not see them too often. A single thing, carefully selected and shown at the right time, will fill him with pity and set him thinking for a month. His opinion about anything depends not so much on what he sees, but on how it reacts on himself; and his lasting impression of any object depends less on the object itself than on the point of view from which he regards it. Thus by a sparing use of examples, lessons, and pictures, you may blunt the sting of sense and delay nature while following her own lead.

As he acquires knowledge, choose what ideas he shall attach to it; as his passions awake, select scenes calculated to repress them. A veteran, as distinguished for his character as for his courage, once told me that in early youth his father, a sensible man but extremely pious, observed that through his growing sensibility he was attracted by women, and spared no pains to restrain him; but at last when, in spite of all his care, his son was about to escape from his control, he decided to take him to a hospital, and, without telling him what to expect, he introduced him into a room where a number of wretched creatures were expiating, under a terrible treatment, the vices which had brought them into this plight. This hideous and revolting spectacle sickened the young man. " Miserable libertine," said his father vehemently, " begone; follow your vile tastes; you will soon be only too glad to be admitted to this ward, and a victim to the most shameful sufferings, you will compel your father to thank God when you are dead."

These few words, together with the striking spectacle he beheld, made an impression on the young man which could never be effaced. Compelled by his profession to pass his youth in garrison, he preferred to face all the jests of his comrades rather than to share their evil ways. " I have been a man," he said to me, " I have had my weaknesses, but even to the present day the sight of a harlot inspires me with horror." Say little to your pupil, but choose time, place, and people; then rely on concrete examples for your teaching, and be sure it will take effect.

The way childhood is spent is no great matter; the evil which may find its way is not irremediable, and the good which may spring up might come later. But it is not so in those early years when a youth really begins to live. This time is never long enough for what there is to be done, and its importance demands unceasing attention; this is why I lay so much stress on the art of prolonging it. One of the best rules of good farming is to keep things back as much as possible. Let your progress also be slow and sure; prevent the youth from becoming a man all at once. While the body is growing the spirits destined to give vigour to the blood and strength to the muscles are in process of formation and elaboration. If you turn them into another channel, and permit that strength which should have gone to the perfecting of one person to go to the making of another, both remain in a state of weakness and the work of nature is unfinished. The workings of the mind, in their turn, are affected by this change, and the mind, as sickly as the body, functions languidly and feebly. Length and strength of limb are not the same thing as courage or genius, and I grant that strength of mind does not always accompany strength of body, when the means of connection between the two are otherwise faulty. But however well planned they may be, they will always work feebly if for motive power they depend upon an exhausted, impoverished supply of blood, deprived of the substance which gives strength and elasticity to all the springs of the machinery. There is generally more vigour of mind to be found among men whose early years have been preserved from precocious vice, than among those whose evil living has begun at the earliest opportunity; and this is no doubt the reason why nations whose morals are pure are generally superior in sense and courage to those whose morals are bad. The latter shine only through I know not what small and trifling qualities, which they call wit, sagacity, cunning; but those great and noble features of goodness and reason, by which a man is distinguished and honoured through good deeds, virtues, really useful efforts, are scarcely to be found except among the nations whose morals are pure.

Teachers complain that the energy of this age makes their pupils unruly; I see that it is so, but are not they themselves to blame? When once they have let this energy flow through the channel of the senses, do they not know that they cannot change its course? Will the long and dreary sermons of the pedant efface from the mind of his scholar the thoughts of pleasure when once they have found an entrance; will they banish from his heart the desires by which it is tormented; will they chill the heat of a passion whose meaning the scholar realises? Will not the pupil be roused to anger by the obstacles opposed to the only kind of happiness of which he has any notion? And in the harsh law imposed upon him before he can understand it, what will he see but the caprice and hatred of a man who is trying to torment him? Is it strange that he rebels and hates you too?

I know very well that if one is easy-going one may be tolerated, and one may keep up a show of authority. But I fail to see the use of an authority over the pupil which is only maintained by fomenting the vices it ought to repress; it is like attempting to soothe a fiery steed by making it leap over a precipice.

Far from being a hindrance to education, this enthusiasm of adolescence is its crown and coping-stone; this it is that gives you a hold on the youth's heart when he is no longer weaker than you. His first affections are the reins by which you control his movements; he was free, and now I behold him in your power. So long as he loved nothing, he was independent of everything but himself and his own necessities; as soon as he loves, he is dependent on his affections. Thus the first ties which unite him to his species are already formed. When you direct his increasing sensibility in this direction, do not expect that it will at once include all men, and that the word " mankind " will have any meaning for him. Not so; this sensibility will at first confine itself to those like himself, and these will not be strangers to him, but those he knows, those whom habit has made dear to him or necessary to him, those who are evidently thinking and feeling as he does, those whom he perceives to be exposed to the pains he has endured, those who enjoy the pleasures he has enjoyed; in a word, those who are so like himself that he is the more disposed to self-love. It is only after long training, after much consideration as to his own feelings and the feelings he observes in others, that he will be able to generalise his individual notions under the abstract idea of humanity, and add to his individual affections those which may identify him with the race.

When he becomes capable of affection, he becomes aware of the affection of others,[1] and he is on the lookout for the signs of that affection. Do you not see how you will acquire a fresh hold on him? What bands have you bound about his heart while he was yet unaware of them! What will he feel, when he beholds himself and sees what you have done for him; when he can compare himself with other youths, and other tutors with you! I say, "When he sees it," but beware lest you tell him of it; if you tell him he will not perceive it. If you claim his obedience in return for the care bestowed upon him, he will think you have over-reached him; he will see that while you profess to have cared for him without reward, you meant to saddle him with a debt and to bind him to a bargain which he never made. In vain you will add that what you demand is for his own good; you demand it, and you demand it in virtue of what you have done without his consent. When a man down on his luck accepts the shilling which the sergeant professes to give him, and finds he has enlisted without knowing what he was about, you protest against the injustice; is it not still more unjust to demand from your pupil the price of care which he has not even accepted?

Ingratitude would be rarer if kindness were less often the investment of a usurer. We love those who have done us a kindness; what a natural feeling! Ingratitude is not to be found in the heart of man, but self-interest is there; those who are ungrateful for benefits received are fewer than those who do a kindness for their own ends. If you sell me your gifts, I will haggle over the price; but if you pretend to give, in order to sell later on at your own price, you are guilty of fraud; it is the free gift which is beyond price. The heart is a law to itself; if you try to bind it, you lose it; give it its liberty, and you make it your own.

When the fisherman baits his line, the fish come round him without suspicion; but when they are caught on the hook concealed in the bait, they feel the line tighten and they try to escape. Is the fisherman a benefactor? Is the fish ungrateful? Do we find a man forgotten by his benefactor, unmindful of that benefactor? On the contrary, he delights to speak of him, he cannot think of him

[1] Affection may be unrequited; not so friendship. Friendship is a bargain, a contract like any other; though a bargain more sacred than the rest. The word " friend " has no other correlation. Any man who is not the friend of his friend is undoubtedly a rascal; for one can only obtain friendship by giving it, or pretending to give it.

without emotion; if he gets a chance of showing him, by some unexpected service, that he remembers what he did for him, how delighted he is to satisfy his gratitude; what a pleasure it is to earn the gratitude of his benefactor. How delightful to say, " It is my turn now." This is indeed the teaching of nature; a good deed never caused ingratitude.

If therefore gratitude is a natural feeling, and you do not destroy its effects by your blunders, be sure your pupil, as he begins to understand the value of your care for him, will be grateful for it, provided you have not put a price upon it; and this will give you an authority over his heart which nothing can overthrow. But beware of losing this advantage before it is really yours, beware of insisting on your own importance. Boast of your services and they become intolerable; forget them and they will not be forgotten. Until the time comes to treat him as a man let there be no question of his duty to you, but his duty to himself. Let him have his freedom if you would make him docile; hide yourself so that he may seek you; raise his heart to the noble sentiment of gratitude by only speaking of his own interest. Until he was able to understand I would not have him told that what was done was for his good; he would only have understood such words to mean that you were dependent on him and he would merely have made you his servant. But now that he is beginning to feel what love is, he also knows what a tender affection may bind a man to what he loves; and in the zeal which keeps you busy on his account, he now sees not the bonds of a slave, but the affection of a friend. Now there is nothing which carries so much weight with the human heart as the voice of friendship recognised as such, for we know that it never speaks but for our good. We may think our friend is mistaken, but we never believe he is deceiving us. We may reject his advice now and then, but we never scorn it.

We have reached the moral order at last; we have just taken the second step towards manhood. If this were the place for it, I would try to show how the first impulses of the heart give rise to the first stirrings of conscience, and how from the feelings of love and hatred spring the first notions of good and evil. I would show that justice and kindness are no mere abstract terms, no mere moral conceptions framed by the understanding, but true affections of the heart enlightened by reason, the natural outcome of our primitive affections; that by reason alone, unaided by conscience, we cannot establish any natural law, and that all natural right is a vain dream if it does not rest upon some instinctive need of the human heart.[1]

[1] The precept " Do unto others as you would have them do unto you " has no true foundation but that of conscience and feeling; for what valid reason is there why I, being myself, should do what I would do if I were some one else, especially when I am morally certain I never shall find myself in exactly the same case; and who will answer for it that if I faithfully follow out this maxim I shall get others to follow it with regard to me? The wicked takes advantage both of the uprightness of the just and of his own injustice; he will gladly have everybody just but himself.

But I do not think it is my business at present to prepare treatises on metaphysics and morals, nor courses of study of any kind whatsoever; it is enough if I indicate the order and development of our feelings and our knowledge in relation to our growth. Others will perhaps work out what I have here merely indicated.

Hitherto my Emile has thought only of himself, so his first glance at his equals leads him to compare himself with them; and the first feeling excited by this comparison is the desire to be first. It is here that self-love is transformed into selfishness, and this is the starting point of all the passions which spring from selfishness. But to determine whether the passions by which his life will be governed shall be humane and gentle or harsh and cruel, whether they shall be the passions of benevolence and pity or those of envy and covetousness, we must know what he believes his place among men to be, and what sort of obstacles he expects to have to overcome in order to attain to the position he seeks.

To guide him in this inquiry, after we have shown him men by means of the accidents common to the species, we must now show him them by means of their differences. This is the time for estimating inequality natural and civil, and for the scheme of the whole social order.

Society must be studied in the individual and the individual in society; those who desire to treat politics and morals apart from one another will never understand either. By confining ourselves at first to the primitive relations, we see how men should be influenced by them and what passions should spring from them; we see that it is in proportion to the development of these passions that a man's relations with others expand or contract. It is not so much strength of arm as moderation of spirit which makes men free and independent. The man whose wants are few is dependent on but few people, but those who constantly confound our vain desires with our bodily needs, those who have made these needs the basis of human society, are continually mistaking effects for causes, and they have only confused themselves by their own reasoning.

Since it is impossible in the state of nature that the difference between man and man should be great enough to make one dependent on another, there is in fact in this state of nature an actual and indestructible equality. In the civil state there is a vain and chimerical equality of right; the means intended for its maintenance, themselves serve to destroy it; and the power of the

This bargain, whatever you may say, is not greatly to the advantage of the just. But if the enthusiasm of an overflowing heart identifies me with my fellow-creature, if I feel, so to speak, that I will not let him suffer lest I should suffer too, I care for him because I care for myself, and the reason of the precept is found in nature herself, which inspires me with the desire for my own welfare wherever I may be. From this I conclude that it is false to say that the precepts of natural law are based on reason only; they have a firmer and more solid foundation. The love of others, springing from self-love, is the source of human justice. The whole of morality is summed up in the gospel in this summary of the law.

community, added to the power of the strongest for the oppression
of the weak, disturbs the sort of equilibrium which nature has established between them.[1]   From this first contradiction spring all the
other contradictions between the real and the apparent, which are
to be found in the civil order.   The many will always be sacrificed to
the few, the common weal to private interest; those specious words—
justice and subordination—will always serve as the tools of violence
and the weapons of injustice; hence it follows that the higher classes
which claim to be useful to the rest are really only seeking their own
welfare at the expense of others; from this we may judge how much
consideration is due to them according to right and justice.   It
remains to be seen if the rank to which they have attained is more
favourable to their own happiness to know what opinion each one
of us should form with regard to his own lot.   This is the study
with which we are now concerned; but to do it thoroughly we must
begin with a knowledge of the human heart.

If it were only a question of showing young people man in his
mask, there would be no need to point him out, and he would always
be before their eyes; but since the mask is not the man, and since
they must not be led away by its specious appearance, when you
paint men for your scholar, paint them as they are, not that he may
hate them, but that he may pity them and have no wish to be like
them.   In my opinion that is the most reasonable view a man can
hold with regard to his fellow-men.

With this object in view we must take the opposite way from
that hitherto followed, and instruct the youth rather through the
experience of others than through his own.   If men deceive him he
will hate them; but, if, while they treat him with respect, he sees
them deceiving each other, he will pity them.   " The spectacle of
the world," said Pythagoras, " is like the Olympic games; some are
buying and selling and think only of their gains; others take an
active part and strive for glory; others, and these not the worst,
are content to be lookers-on."

I would have you so choose the company of a youth that he
should think well of those among whom he lives, and I would have
you so teach him to know the world that he should think ill of all
that takes place in it.   Let him know that man is by nature good,
let him feel it, let him judge his neighbour by himself; but let him
see how men are depraved and perverted by society; let him find
the source of all their vices in their preconceived opinions; let him
be disposed to respect the individual, but to despise the multitude;
let him see that all men wear almost the same mask, but let him also
know that some faces are fairer than the mask that conceals them.

It must be admitted that this method has its drawbacks, and it
is not easy to carry it out; for if he becomes too soon engrossed
in watching other people, if you train him to mark too closely the

[1] The universal spirit of the laws of every country is always to take the
part of the strong against the weak, and the part of him who has against
him who has not; this defect is inevitable, and there is no exception to it.

actions of others, you will make him spiteful and satirical, quick and decided in his judgments of others; he will find a hateful pleasure in seeking bad motives, and will fail to see the good even in that which is really good. He will, at least, get used to the sight of vice, he will behold the wicked without horror, just as we get used to seeing the wretched without pity. Soon the perversity of mankind will be not so much a warning as an excuse; he will say, "Man is made so," and he will have no wish to be different from the rest.

But if you wish to teach him theoretically to make him acquainted, not only with the heart of man, but also with the application of the external causes which turn our inclinations into vices; when you thus transport him all at once from the objects of sense to the objects of reason, you employ a system of metaphysics which he is not in a position to understand; you fall back into the error, so carefully avoided hitherto, of giving him lessons which are like lessons, of substituting in his mind the experience and the authority of the master for his own experience and the development of his own reason.

To remove these two obstacles at once, and to bring the human heart within his reach without risk of spoiling his own, I would show him men from afar, in other times or in other places, so that he may behold the scene but cannot take part in it. This is the time for history; with its help he will read the hearts of men without any lessons in philosophy; with its help he will view them as a mere spectator, dispassionate and without prejudice; he will view them as their judge, not as their accomplice or their accuser.

To know men you must behold their actions. In society we hear them talk; they show their words and hide their deeds; but in history the veil is drawn aside, and they are judged by their deeds. Their sayings even help us to understand them; for comparing what they say and what they do, we see not only what they are but what they would appear; the more they disguise themselves the more thoroughly they stand revealed.

Unluckily this study has its dangers, its drawbacks of several kinds. It is difficult to adopt a point of view which will enable one to judge one's fellow-creatures fairly. It is one of the chief defects of history to paint men's evil deeds rather than their good ones; it is revolutions and catastrophes that make history interesting; so long as a nation grows and prospers quietly in the tranquillity of a peaceful government, history says nothing; she only begins to speak of nations when, no longer able to be self-sufficing, they interfere with their neighbours' business, or allow their neighbours to interfere with their own; history only makes them famous when they are on the downward path; all our histories begin where they ought to end. We have very accurate accounts of declining nations; what we lack is the history of those nations which are multiplying; they are so happy and so good that history has nothing to tell us of them; and we see indeed in our own times that the most successful governments are least talked of. We only hear what is bad; the good is scarcely mentioned. Only the wicked become famous, the good are forgotten or laughed to scorn, and thus history, like philosophy, is for ever slandering mankind.

Moreover, it is inevitable that the facts described in history should not give an exact picture of what really happened; they are transformed in the brain of the historian, they are moulded by his interests and coloured by his prejudices. Who can place the reader precisely in a position to see the event as it really happened? Ignorance or partiality disguises everything. What a different impression may be given merely by expanding or contracting the circumstances of the case without altering a single historical incident. The same object may be seen from several points of view, and it will hardly seem the same thing, yet there has been no change except in the eye that beholds it. Do you indeed do honour to truth when what you tell me is a genuine fact, but you make it appear something quite different? A tree more or less, a rock to the right or to the left, a cloud of dust raised by the wind, how often have these decided the result of a battle without any one knowing it? Does that prevent history from telling you the cause of defeat or victory with as much assurance as if she had been on the spot? But what are the facts to me, while I am ignorant of their causes, and what lessons can I draw from an event, whose true cause is unknown to me? The historian indeed gives me a reason, but he invents it; and criticism itself, of which we hear so much, is only the art of guessing, the art of choosing from among several lies, the lie that is most like truth.

Have you ever read Cleopatra or Cassandra or any books of the kind? The author selects some well-known event, he then adapts it to his purpose, adorns it with details of his own invention, with people who never existed, with imaginary portraits; thus he piles fiction on fiction to lend a charm to his story. I see little difference between such romances and your histories, unless it is that the novelist draws more on his own imagination, while the historian slavishly copies what another has imagined; I will also admit, if you please, that the novelist has some moral purpose good or bad, about which the historian scarcely concerns himself.

You will tell me that accuracy in history is of less interest than a true picture of men and manners; provided the human heart is truly portrayed, it matters little that events should be accurately recorded; for after all you say, what does it matter to us what happened two thousand years ago? You are right if the portraits are indeed truly given according to nature; but if the model is to be found for the most part in the historian's imagination, are you not falling into the very error you intended to avoid, and surrendering to the authority of the historian what you would not yield to the authority of the teacher? If my pupil is merely to see fancy pictures, I would rather draw them myself; they will, at least, be better suited to him.

The worst historians for a youth are those who give their opinions.

Facts! Facts! and let him decide for himself; this is how he will learn to know mankind. If he is always directed by the opinion of the author, he is only seeing through the eyes of another person, and when those eyes are no longer at his disposal he can see nothing.

I leave modern history on one side, not only because it has no character and all our people are alike, but because our historians, wholly taken up with effect, think of nothing but highly coloured portraits, which often represent nothing.[1] The old historians generally give fewer portraits and bring more intelligence and common-sense to their judgments; but even among them there is plenty of scope for choice, and you must not begin with the wisest but with the simplest. I would not put Polybius or Sallust into the hands of a youth; Tacitus is the author of the old, young men cannot understand him; you must learn to see in human actions the simplest features of the heart of man before you try to sound its depths. You must be able to read facts clearly before you begin to study maxims. Philosophy in the form of maxims is only fit for the experienced. Youth should never deal with the general, all its teaching should deal with individual instances.

To my mind Thucydides is the true model of historians. He relates facts without giving his opinion; but he omits no circumstance adapted to make us judge for ourselves. He puts everything that he relates before his reader; far from interposing between the facts and the readers, he conceals himself; we seem not to read but to see. Unfortunately he speaks of nothing but war, and in his stories we only see the least instructive part of the world, that is to say the battles. The virtues and defects of the Retreat of the Ten Thousand and the Commentaries of Cæsar are almost the same. The kindly Herodotus, without portraits, without maxims, yet flowing, simple, full of details calculated to delight and interest in the highest degree, would be perhaps the best historian if these very details did not often degenerate into childish folly, better adapted to spoil the taste of youth than to form it; we need discretion before we can read him. I say nothing of Livy, his turn will come; but he is a statesman, a rhetorician, he is everything which is unsuitable for a youth.

History in general is lacking because it only takes note of striking and clearly marked facts which may be fixed by names, places, and dates; but the slow evolution of these facts, which cannot be definitely noted in this way, still remains unknown. We often find in some battle, lost or won, the ostensible cause of a revolution which was inevitable before this battle took place. War only makes manifest events already determined by moral causes, which few historians can perceive.

The philosophic spirit has turned the thoughts of many of the historians of our times in this direction; but I doubt whether truth

---

[1] Take, for instance, Guicciardini, Streda, Solis, Machiavelli, and sometimes even De Thou himself. Vertot is almost the only one who knows how to describe without giving fancy portraits.

has profited by their labours. The rage for systems has got possession of all alike, no one seeks to see things as they are, but only as
they agree with his system.

Add to all these considerations the fact that history shows us
actions rather than men, because she only seizes men at certain
chosen times in full dress; she only portrays the statesman when
he is prepared to be seen; she does not follow him to his home, to
his study, among his family and his friends; she only shows him
in state; it is his clothes rather than himself that she describes.

I would prefer to begin the study of the human heart with reading
the lives of individuals; for then the man hides himself in vain,
the historian follows him everywhere; he never gives him a
moment's grace nor any corner where he can escape the piercing
eye of the spectator; and when he thinks he is concealing himself,
then it is that the writer shows him up most plainly.

"Those who write lives," says Montaigne, "in so far as they
delight more in ideas than in events, more in that which comes
from within than in that which comes without, these are the
writers I prefer; for this reason Plutarch is in every way the man
for me."

It is true that the genius of men in groups or nations is very
different from the character of the individual man, and that we
have a very imperfect knowledge of the human heart if we do not
also examine it in crowds; but it is none the less true that to judge
of men we must study the individual man, and that he who had
a perfect knowledge of the inclinations of each individual might
foresee all their combined effects in the body of the nation.

We must go back again to the ancients, for the reasons already
stated, and also because all the details common and familiar, but
true and characteristic, are banished by modern stylists, so that
men are as much tricked out by our modern authors in their private
life as in public. Propriety, no less strict in literature than in life,
no longer permits us to say anything in public which we might not
do in public; and as we may only show the man dressed up for his
part, we never see a man in our books any more than we do on the
stage. The lives of kings may be written a hundred times, but to
no purpose; we shall never have another Suetonius.

The excellence of Plutarch consists in these very details which we
are no longer permitted to describe. With inimitable grace he
paints the great man in little things; and he is so happy in the choice
of his instances that a word, a smile, a gesture, will often suffice to
indicate the nature of his hero. With a jest Hannibal cheers his
frightened soldiers, and leads them laughing to the battle which will
lay Italy at his feet; Agesilaus riding on a stick makes me love the
conqueror of the great king; Cæsar passing through a poor village
and chatting with his friends unconsciously betrays the traitor who
professed that he only wished to be Pompey's equal. Alexander
swallows a draught without a word—it is the finest moment in his
life; Aristides writes his own name on the shell and so justifies his

title; Philopœmen, his mantle laid aside, chops firewood in the kitchen of his host. This is the true art of portraiture. Our disposition does not show itself in our features, nor our character in our great deeds; it is trifles that show what we really are. What is done in public is either too commonplace or too artificial, and our modern authors are almost too grand to tell us anything else.

M. de Turenne was undoubtedly one of the greatest men of the last century. They have had the courage to make his life interesting by the little details which make us know and love him; but how many details have they felt obliged to omit which might have made us know and love him better still? I will only quote one which I have on good authority, one which Plutarch would never have omitted, and one which Ramsai would never have inserted had he been acquainted with it.

On a hot summer's day Viscount Turenne in a little white vest and nightcap was standing at the window of his antechamber; one of his men came up and, misled by the dress, took him for one of the kitchen lads whom he knew. He crept up behind him and smacked him with no light hand. The man he struck turned round hastily. The valet saw it was his master and trembled at the sight of his face. He fell on his knees in desperation. "Sir, I thought it was George." "Well, even if it was George," exclaimed Turenne rubbing the injured part, "you need not have struck so hard." You do not dare to say this, you miserable writers! Remain for ever without humanity and without feeling; steel your hard hearts in your vile propriety, make yourselves contemptible through your high-mightiness. But as for you, dear youth, when you read this anecdote, when you are touched by all the kindliness displayed even on the impulse of the moment, read also the littleness of this great man when it was a question of his name and birth. Remember it was this very Turenne who always professed to yield precedence to his nephew, so that all men might see that this child was the head of a royal house. Look on this picture and on that, love nature, despise popular prejudice, and know the man as he was.

There are few people able to realise what an effect such reading, carefully directed, will have upon the unspoilt mind of a youth. Weighed down by books from our earliest childhood, accustomed to read without thinking, what we read strikes us even less, because we already bear in ourselves the passions and prejudices with which history and the lives of men are filled; all that they do strikes us as only natural, for we ourselves are unnatural and we judge others by ourselves. But imagine my Emile, who has been carefully guarded for eighteen years with the sole object of preserving a right judgment and a healthy heart, imagine him when the curtain goes up casting his eyes for the first time upon the world's stage; or rather picture him behind the scenes watching the actors don their costumes, and counting the cords and pulleys which deceive with their feigned shows the eyes of the spectators. His first surprise will soon give place to feelings of shame and scorn of his fellow-man; he will be indignant at the sight of the whole human race deceiving itself and stooping to this childish folly; he will grieve to see his brothers tearing each other limb from limb for a mere dream, and transforming themselves into wild beasts because they could not be content to be men.

Given the natural disposition of the pupil, there is no doubt that if the master exercises any sort of prudence or discretion in his choice of reading, however little he may put him in the way of reflecting on the subject-matter, this exercise will serve as a course in practical philosophy, a philosophy better understood and more thoroughly mastered than all the empty speculations with which the brains of lads are muddled in our schools. After following the romantic schemes of Pyrrhus, Cineas asks him what real good he would gain by the conquest of the world, which he can never enjoy without such great sufferings; this only arouses in us a passing interest as a smart saying; but Emile will think it a very wise thought, one which had already occurred to himself, and one which he will never forget, because there is no hostile prejudice in his mind to prevent it sinking in. When he reads more of the life of this madman, he will find that all his great plans resulted in his death at the hands of a woman, and instead of admiring this pinchbeck heroism, what will he see in the exploits of this great captain and the schemes of this great statesman but so many steps towards that unlucky tile which was to bring life and schemes alike to a shameful death?

All conquerors have not been killed; all usurpers have not failed in their plans; to minds imbued with vulgar prejudices many of them will seem happy, but he who looks below the surface and reckons men's happiness by the condition of their hearts will perceive their wretchedness even in the midst of their successes; he will see them panting after advancement and never attaining their prize, he will find them like those inexperienced travellers among the Alps, who think that every height they see is the last, who reach its summit only to find to their disappointment there are loftier peaks beyond.

Augustus, when he had subdued his fellow-citizens and destroyed his rivals, reigned for forty years over the greatest empire that ever existed; but all this vast power could not hinder him from beating his head against the walls, and filling his palace with his groans as he cried to Varus to restore his slaughtered legions. If he had conquered all his foes what good would his empty triumphs have done him, when troubles of every kind beset his path, when his life was threatened by his dearest friends, and when he had to mourn the disgrace or death of all near and dear to him? The wretched man desired to rule the world and failed to rule his own household. What was the result of this neglect? He beheld his nephew, his adopted child, his son-in-law, perish in the flower of youth, his grandson reduced to eat the stuffing of his mattress to prolong his wretched existence for a few hours; his daughter and his granddaughter, after they had covered him with infamy, died, the one of hunger and want on a desert island, the other in prison by the hand of a common archer. He himself, the last survivor of his unhappy house, found himself compelled by his own wife to acknowledge a monster as his heir. Such was the fate of the master of the world, so famous for his glory and his good fortune. I cannot believe that any one of those who admire his glory and fortune would accept them at the same price.

I have taken ambition as my example, but the play of every human passion offers similar lessons to any one who will study history to make himself wise and good at the expense of those who went before. The time is drawing near when the teaching of the life of Anthony will appeal more forcibly to the youth than the life of Augustus. Emile will scarcely know where he is among the many strange sights in his new studies; but he will know beforehand how to avoid the illusion of passions before they arise, and seeing how in all ages they have blinded men's eyes, he will be forewarned of the way in which they may one day blind his own should he abandon himself to them.[1] These lessons, I know, are unsuited to him, perhaps at need they may prove scanty and ill-timed; but remember they are not the lessons I wished to draw from this study. To begin with, I had quite another end in view; and indeed, if this purpose is unfulfilled, the teacher will be to blame.

Remember that, as soon as selfishness has developed, the self in its relations to others is always with us, and the youth never observes others without coming back to himself and comparing himself with them. From the way young men are taught to study history I see that they are transformed, so to speak, into the people they behold, that you strive to make a Cicero, a Trajan, or an Alexander of them, to discourage them when they are themselves again, to make every one regret that he is merely himself. There are certain advantages in this plan which I do not deny; but, so far as Emile is concerned, should it happen at any time when he is making these comparisons that he wishes to be any one but himself—were it Socrates or Cato—I have failed entirely; he who begins to regard himself as a stranger will soon forget himself altogether.

It is not philosophers who know most about men; they only view them through the preconceived ideas of philosophy, and I know no one so prejudiced as philosophers. A savage would judge us more sanely. The philosopher is aware of his own vices, he is indignant at ours, and he says to himself, " We are all bad alike; " the savage beholds us unmoved and says, " You are mad." He is right, for no one does evil for evil's sake. My pupil is that savage, with this difference: Emile has thought more, he has compared

<hr/>

[1] It is always prejudice which stirs up passion in our heart. He who only sees what really exists and only values what he knows, rarely becomes angry. The errors of our judgment produce the warmth of our desires.

ideas, seen our errors at close quarters, he is more on his guard against himself, and only judges of what he knows.

It is our own passions that excite us against the passions of others; it is our self-interest which makes us hate the wicked; if they did us no harm we should pity rather than hate them. We should readily forgive their vices if we could perceive how their own heart punishes those vices. We are aware of the offence, but we do not see the punishment; the advantages are plain, the penalty is hidden. The man who thinks he is enjoying the fruits of his vices is no less tormented by them than if they had not been successful; the object is different, the anxiety is the same; in vain he displays his good fortune and hides his heart; in spite of himself his conduct betrays him; but to discern this, our own heart must be utterly unlike his.

We are led astray by those passions which we share; we are disgusted by those that militate against our own interests; and with a want of logic due to these very passions, we blame in others what we fain would imitate. Aversion and self-deception are inevitable when we are forced to endure at another's hands what we ourselves would do in his place.

What then is required for the proper study of men? A great wish to know men, great impartiality of judgment, a heart sufficiently sensitive to understand every human passion, and calm enough to be free from passion. If there is any time in our life when this study is likely to be appreciated, it is this that I have chosen for Emile; before this time men would have been strangers to him; later on he would have been like them. Convention, the effects of which he already perceives, has not yet made him its slave, the passions, whose consequences he realises, have not yet stirred his heart. He is a man; he takes an interest in his brethren; he is a just man and he judges his peers. Now it is certain that if he judges them rightly he will not want to change places with any one of them, for the goal of all their anxious efforts is the result of prejudices which he does not share, and that goal seems to him a mere dream. For his own part, he has all he wants within his reach. How should he be dependent on any one when he is self-sufficing and free from prejudice? Strong arms, good health,[1] moderation, few needs, together with the means to satisfy those needs, are his. He has been brought up in complete liberty and servitude is the greatest ill he understands. He pities these miserable kings, the slaves of all who obey them; he pities these false prophets fettered by their empty fame; he pities these rich fools, martyrs to their own pomp; he pities these ostentatious voluptuaries, who spend their life in deadly dullness that they may seem to enjoy its pleasures. He would pity the very foe who harmed him, for he would discern his wretchedness beneath his cloak of spite. He

[1] I think I may fairly reckon health and strength among the advantages he has obtained by his education, or rather among the gifts of nature which his education has preserved for him.

would say to himself, "This man has yielded to his desire to hurt me, and this need of his places him at my mercy."

One step more and our goal is attained. Selfishness is a dangerous tool though a useful one; it often wounds the hand that uses it, and it rarely does good unmixed with evil. When Emile considers his place among men, when he finds himself so fortunately situated, he will be tempted to give credit to his own reason for the work of yours, and to attribute to his own deserts what is really the result of his good fortune. He will say to himself, "I am wise and other men are fools." He will pity and despise them and will congratulate himself all the more heartily; and as he knows he is happier than they, he will think his deserts are greater. This is the fault we have most to fear, for it is the most difficult to eradicate. If he remained in this state of mind, he would have profited little by all our care; and if I had to choose, I hardly know whether I would not rather choose the illusions of prejudice than those of pride.

Great men are under no illusion with respect to their superiority; they see it and know it, but they are none the less modest. The more they have, the better they know what they lack. They are less vain of their superiority over us than ashamed by the consciousness of their weakness, and among the good things they really possess, they are too wise to pride themselves on a gift which is none of their getting. The good man may be proud of his virtue for it is his own, but what cause for pride has the man of intellect? What has Racine done that he is not Pradon, and Boileau that he is not Cotin?

The circumstances with which we are concerned are quite different. Let us keep to the common level. I assumed that my pupil had neither surpassing genius nor a defective understanding. I chose him of an ordinary mind to show what education could do for man. Exceptions defy all rules. If, therefore, as a result of my care, Emile prefers his way of living, seeing, and feeling to that of others, he is right; but if he thinks because of this that he is nobler and better born than they, he is wrong; he is deceiving himself; he must be undeceived, or rather let us prevent the mistake, lest it be too late to correct it.

Provided a man is not mad, he can be cured of any folly but vanity; there is no cure for this but experience, if indeed there is any cure for it at all; when it first appears we can at least prevent its further growth. But do not on this account waste your breath on empty arguments to prove to the youth that he is like other men and subject to the same weaknesses. Make him feel it or he will never know it. This is another instance of an exception to my own rules; I must voluntarily expose my pupil to every accident which may convince him that he is no wiser than we. The adventure with the conjurer will be repeated again and again in different ways; I shall let flatterers take advantage of him; if rash comrades draw him into some perilous adventure, I will let him run the risk; if he falls into the hands of sharpers at the card-table, I will abandon him to them as their dupe.[1] I will let them flatter him, pluck him, and rob him; and when having sucked him dry they turn and mock him, I will even thank them to his face for the lessons they have been good enough to give him. The only snares from which I will guard him with my utmost care are the wiles of wanton women. The only precaution I shall take will be to share all the dangers I let him run, and all the insults I let him receive. I will bear everything in silence, without a murmur or reproach, without a word to him, and be sure that if this wise conduct is faithfully adhered to, what he sees me endure on his account will make more impression on his heart than what he himself suffers.

I cannot refrain at this point from drawing attention to the sham dignity of tutors, who foolishly pretend to be wise, who discourage their pupils by always professing to treat them as children, and by emphasising the difference between themselves and their scholars in everything they do. Far from damping their youthful spirits in this fashion, spare no effort to stimulate their courage; that they may become your equals, treat them as such already, and if they cannot rise to your level, do not scruple to come down to theirs without being ashamed of it. Remember that your honour is no longer in your own keeping but in your pupil's. Share his faults that you may correct them, bear his disgrace that you may wipe it out; follow the example of that brave Roman who, unable to rally his fleeing soldiers, placed himself at their head, exclaiming, " They do not flee, they follow their captain ! " Did this dishonour him ? Not so; by sacrificing his glory he increased it. The power of duty, the beauty of virtue, compel our respect in spite of all our foolish prejudices. If I received a blow in the course of my duties to Emile, far from avenging it I would boast of it; and I doubt whether there is in the whole world a man so vile as to respect me any the less on this account.

I do not intend the pupil to suppose his master to be as ignorant, or as liable to be led astray, as he is himself. This idea is all very well for a child who can neither see nor compare things, who thinks everything is within his reach, and only bestows his confidence on those who know how to come down to his level. But a youth of Emile's age and sense is no longer so foolish as to make this

---

[1] Moreover our pupil will be little tempted by this snare; he has so many amusements about him, he has never been bored in his life, and he scarcely knows the use of money. As children have been led by these two motives, self-interest and vanity, rogues and courtesans use the same means to get hold of them later. When you see their greediness encouraged by prizes and rewards, when you find their public performances at ten years old applauded at school or college, you see too how at twenty they will be induced to leave their purse in a gambling hell and their health in a worse place. You may safely wager that the sharpest boy in the class will become the greatest gambler and debauchee. Now the means which have not been employed in childhood have not the same effect in youth. But we must bear in mind my constant plan and take the thing at its worst. First I try to prevent the vice; then I assume its existence in order to correct it.

mistake, and it would not be desirable that he should. The confidence he ought to have in his tutor is of another kind; it should rest on the authority of reason, and on superior knowledge, advantages which the young man is capable of appreciating while he perceives how useful they are to himself. Long experience has convinced him that his tutor loves him, that he is a wise and good man who desires his happiness and knows how to procure it. He ought to know that it is to his own advantage to listen to his advice. But if the master lets himself be taken in like the disciple, he will lose his right to expect deference from him, and to give him instruction. Still less should the pupil suppose that his master is purposely letting him fall into snares or preparing pitfalls for his inexperience. How can we avoid these two difficulties? Choose the best and most natural means; be frank and straightforward like himself; warn him of the dangers to which he is exposed, point them out plainly and sensibly, without exaggeration, without temper, without pedantic display, and above all without giving your opinions in the form of orders, until they have become such, and until this imperious tone is absolutely necessary. Should he still be obstinate as he often will be, leave him free to follow his own choice, follow him, copy his example, and that cheerfully and frankly; if possible fling yourself into things, amuse yourself as much as he does. If the consequences become too serious, you are at hand to prevent them; and yet when this young man has beheld your foresight and your kindliness, will he not be at once struck by the one and touched by the other? All his faults are but so many bands with which he himself provides you to restrain him at need. Now under these circumstances the great art of the master consists in controlling events and directing his exhortations so that he may know beforehand when the youth will give in, and when he will refuse to do so, so that all around him he may encompass him with the lessons of experience, and yet never let him run too great a risk.

Warn him of his faults before he commits them; do not blame him when once they are committed; you would only stir his self-love to mutiny. We learn nothing from a lesson we detest. I know nothing more foolish than the phrase, "I told you so." The best way to make him remember what you told him is to seem to have forgotten it. Go further than this, and when you find him ashamed of having refused to believe you, gently smooth away the shame with kindly words. He will indeed hold you dear when he sees how you forget yourself on his account, and how you console him instead of reproaching him. But if you increase his annoyance by your reproaches he will hate you, and will make it a rule never to heed you, as if to show you that he does not agree with you as to the value of your opinion.

The turn you give to your consolation may itself be a lesson to him, and all the more because he does not suspect it. When you tell him, for example, that many other people have made the same mistakes, this is not what he was expecting; you are administering correction under the guise of pity; for when one thinks oneself better than other people it is a very mortifying excuse to console oneself by their example; it means that we must realise that the most we can say is that they are no better than we.

The time of faults is the time for fables. When we blame the guilty under the cover of a story we instruct without offending him; and he then understands that the story is not untrue by means of the truth he finds in its application to himself. The child who has never been deceived by flattery understands nothing of the fable I recently examined; but the rash youth who has just become the dupe of a flatterer perceives only too readily that the crow was a fool. Thus he acquires a maxim from the fact, and the experience he would soon have forgotten is engraved on his mind by means of the fable. There is no knowledge of morals which cannot be acquired through our own experience or that of others. When there is danger, instead of letting him try the experiment himself, we have recourse to history. When the risk is comparatively slight, it is just as well that the youth should be exposed to it; then by means of the apologue the special cases with which the young man is now acquainted are transformed into maxims.

It is not, however, my intention that these maxims should be explained, nor even formulated. Nothing is so foolish and unwise as the moral at the end of most of the fables; as if the moral was not, or ought not to be so clear in the fable itself that the reader cannot fail to perceive it. Why then add the moral at the end, and so deprive him of the pleasure of discovering it for himself. The art of teaching consists in making the pupil wish to learn. But if the pupil is to wish to learn, his mind must not remain in such a passive state with regard to what you tell him that there is really nothing for him to do but listen to you. The master's vanity must always give way to the scholars; he must be able to say, I understand, I see it, I am getting at it, I am learning something. One of the things which makes the Pantaloon in the Italian comedies so wearisome is the pains taken by him to explain to the audience the platitudes they understand only too well already. We must always be intelligible, but we need not say all there is to be said. If you talk much you will say little, for at last no one will listen to you. What is the sense of the four lines at the end of La Fontaine's fable of the frog who puffed herself up. Is he afraid we should not understand it? Does this great painter need to write the names beneath the things he has painted? His morals, far from generalising, restrict the lesson to some extent to the examples given, and prevent our applying them to others. Before I put the fables of this inimitable author into the hands of a youth, I should like to cut out all the conclusions with which he strives to explain what he has just said so clearly and pleasantly. If your pupil does not understand the fable without the explanation, he will not understand it with it.

Moreover, the fables would require to be arranged in a more

didactic order, one more in agreement with the feelings and knowledge of the young adolescent. Can you imagine anything so foolish
as to follow the mere numerical order of the book without regard to
our requirements or our opportunities. First the grasshopper, then
the crow, then the frog, then the two mules, etc. I am sick of these
two mules; I remember seeing a child who was being educated for
finance; they never let him alone, but were always insisting on the
profession he was to follow; they made him read this fable, learn it,
say it, repeat it again and again without finding in it the slightest
argument against his future calling. Not only have I never found
children make any real use of the fables they learn, but I have never
found anybody who took the trouble to see that they made such a
use of them. The study claims to be instruction in morals; but
the real aim of mother and child is nothing but to set a whole party
watching the child while he recites his fables; when he is too old to
recite them and old enough to make use of them, they are altogether
forgotten. Only men, I repeat, can learn from fables, and Emile
is now old enough to begin.

I do not mean to tell you everything, so I only indicate the paths
which diverge from the right way, so that you may know how to
avoid them. If you follow the road I have marked out for you,
I think your pupil will buy his knowledge of mankind and his
knowledge of himself in the cheapest market; you will enable him
to behold the tricks of fortune without envying the lot of her
favourites, and to be content with himself without thinking himself
better than others. You have begun by making him an actor that
he may learn to be one of the audience; you must continue your
task, for from the theatre things are what they seem, from the stage
they seem what they are. For the general effect we must get a
distant view, for the details we must observe more closely. But
how can a young man take part in the business of life? What
right has he to be initiated into its dark secrets? His interests are
confined within the limits of his own pleasures, he has no power over
others, it is much the same as if he had no power at all. Man is
the cheapest commodity on the market, and among all our important
rights of property, the rights of the individual are always considered
last of all.

When I see the studies of young men at the period of their greatest
activity confined to purely speculative matters, while later on they
are suddenly plunged, without any sort of experience, into the world
of men and affairs, it strikes me as contrary alike to reason and to
nature, and I cease to be surprised that so few men know what to
do. How strange a choice to teach us so many useless things, while
the art of doing is never touched upon! They profess to fit us for
society, and we are taught as if each of us were to live a life of contemplation in a solitary cell, or to discuss theories with persons
whom they did not concern. You think you are teaching your
scholars how to live, and you teach them certain bodily contortions
and certain forms of words without meaning. I, too, have taught

Emile how to live; for I have taught him to enjoy his own society and, more than that, to earn his own bread. But this is not enough. To live in the world he must know how to get on with other people, he must know what forces move them, he must calculate the action and re-action of self-interest in civil society, he must estimate the results so accurately that he will rarely fail in his undertakings, or he will at least have tried in the best possible way. The law does not allow young people to manage their own affairs nor to dispose of their own property; but what would be the use of these precautions if they never gained any experience until they were of age. They would have gained nothing by the delay, and would have no more experience at five-and-twenty than at fifteen. No doubt we must take precautions, so that a youth, blinded by ignorance or misled by passion, may not hurt himself; but at any age there are opportunities when deeds of kindness and of care for the weak may be performed under the direction of a wise man, on behalf of the unfortunate who need help.

Mothers and nurses grow fond of children because of the care they lavish on them; the practice of social virtues touches the very heart with the love of humanity; by doing good we become good; and I know no surer way to this end. Keep your pupil busy with the good deeds that are within his power, let the cause of the poor be his own, let him help them not merely with his money, but with his service; let him work for them, protect them, let his person and his time be at their disposal; let him be their agent; he will never all his life long have a more honourable office. How many of the oppressed, who have never got a hearing, will obtain justice when he demands it for them with that courage and firmness which the practice of virtue inspires; when he makes his way into the presence of the rich and great, when he goes, if need be, to the footstool of the king himself, to plead the cause of the wretched, the cause of those who find all doors closed to them by their poverty, those who are so afraid of being punished for their misfortunes that they do not dare to complain?

But shall we make of Emile a knight-errant, a redresser of wrongs, a paladin? Shall he thrust himself into public life, play the sage and the defender of the laws before the great, before the magistrates, before the king? Shall he lay petitions before the judges and plead in the law courts? That I cannot say. The nature of things is not changed by terms of mockery and scorn. He will do all that he knows to be useful and good. He will do nothing more, and he knows that nothing is useful and good for him which is unbefitting his age. He knows that his first duty is to himself; that young men should distrust themselves; that they should act circumspectly; that they should show respect to those older than themselves, reticence and discretion in talking without cause, modesty in things indifferent, but courage in well doing, and boldness to speak the truth. Such were those illustrious Romans who, having been admitted into public life, spent their days in bringing criminals to justice and in protecting the innocent, without any motives beyond those of learning, and of the furtherance of justice and of the protection of right conduct.

Emile is not fond of noise or quarrelling, not only among men, but among animals.[1] He will never set two dogs to fight, he will never set a dog to chase a cat. This peaceful spirit is one of the results of his education, which has never stimulated self-love or a high opinion of himself, and so has not encouraged him to seek his pleasure in domination and in the sufferings of others. The sight of suffering makes him suffer too; this is a natural feeling. It is one of the after effects of vanity that hardens a young man and makes him take a delight in seeing the torments of a living and feeling creature; it makes him consider himself beyond the reach of similar sufferings through his superior wisdom or virtue. He who is beyond the reach of vanity cannot fall into the vice which results from vanity. So Emile loves peace. He is delighted at the sight of happiness, and if he can help to bring it about, this is an additional reason for sharing it. I do not assume that when he sees the unhappy he will merely feel for them that barren and cruel pity which is content to pity the ills it can heal. His kindness is active and teaches him much he would have learnt far more slowly, or he would never have learnt at all, if his heart had been harder. If he finds his comrades at strife, he tries to reconcile them; if he sees the afflicted, he inquires as to the cause of their sufferings; if he meets two men who hate each other, he wants to know the reason of their enmity; if he finds one who is down-trodden groaning under the oppression of the rich and powerful, he tries to discover by what means he can counteract this oppression, and in the interest he takes with regard to all these unhappy persons, the means of removing their sufferings

---

[1] " But what will he do if any one seeks a quarrel with him? " My answer is that no one will ever quarrel with him, he will never lend himself to such a thing. But, indeed, you continue, who can be safe from a blow, or an insult from a bully, a drunkard, a bravo, who for the joy of killing his man begins by dishonouring him? That is another matter. The life and honour of the citizens should not be at the mercy of a bully, a drunkard, or a bravo, and one can no more insure oneself against such an accident than against a falling tile. A blow given, or a lie in the teeth, if he submit to them, have social consequences which no wisdom can prevent and no tribunal can avenge. The weakness of the laws, therefore, so far restores a man's independence; he is the sole magistrate and judge between the offender and himself, the sole interpreter and administrator of natural law. Justice is his due, and he alone can obtain it, and in such a case there is no government on earth so foolish as to punish him for so doing. I do not say he must fight; that is absurd; I say justice is his due, and he alone can dispense it. If I were king, I promise you that in my kingdom no one would ever strike a man or call him a liar, and yet I would do without all those useless laws against duels; the means are simple and require no law courts. However that may be, Emile knows what is due to himself in such a case, and the example due from him to the safety of men of honour. The strongest of men cannot prevent insult, but he can take good care that his adversary has no opportunity to boast of that insult.

are never out of his sight.   What use shall we make of this disposition so that it may re-act in a way suited to his age?   Let us direct
his efforts and his knowledge, and use his zeal to increase them.

I am never weary of repeating: let all the lessons of young people
take the form of doing rather than talking; let them learn nothing
from books which they can learn from experience.   How absurd
to attempt to give them practice in speaking when they have nothing
to say, to expect to make them feel, at their school desks, the vigour
of the language of passion and all the force of the arts of persuasion
when they have nothing and nobody to persuade!   All the rules of
rhetoric are mere waste of words to those who do not know how to
use them for their own purposes.   How does it concern a schoolboy
to know how Hannibal encouraged his soldiers to cross the Alps?
If instead of these grand speeches you showed him how to induce his
prefect to give him a holiday, you may be sure he would pay more
attention to your rules.

If I wanted to teach rhetoric to a youth whose passions were as
yet undeveloped, I would draw his attention continually to things
that would stir his passions, and I would discuss with him how he
should talk to people so as to get them to regard his wishes favour
ably.   But Emile is not in a condition so favourable to the art of
oratory.   Concerned mainly with his physical well-being, he has
less need of others than they of him; and having nothing to ask of
others on his own account, what he wants to persuade them to do
does not affect him sufficiently to awake any very strong feeling.
From this it follows that his language will be on the whole simple
and literal.   He usually speaks to the point and only to make himself understood.   He is not sententious, for he has not learnt to
generalise; he does not speak in figures, for he is rarely impassioned.

Yet this is not because he is altogether cold and phlegmatic,
neither his age, his character, nor his tastes permit of this.   In the
fire of adolescence the life-giving spirits, retained in the blood and
distilled again and again, inspire his young heart with a warmth
which glows in his eye, a warmth which is felt in his words and
perceived in his actions.   The lofty feeling with which he is inspired
gives him strength and nobility; imbued with tender love for
mankind his words betray the thoughts of his heart; I know not
how it is, but there is more charm in his open-hearted generosity
than in the artificial eloquence of others; or rather this eloquence
of his is the only true eloquence, for he has only to show what he
feels to make others share his feelings.

The more I think of it the more convinced I am that by thus
translating our kindly impulses into action, by drawing from our
good or ill success conclusions as to their cause, we shall find that
there is little useful knowledge that cannot be imparted to a youth;
and that together with such true learning as may be got at college
he will learn a science of more importance than all the rest together,
the application of what he has learned to the purposes of life.
Taking such an interest in his fellow-creatures, it is impossible that

he should fail to learn very quickly how to note and weigh their actions, their tastes, their pleasures, and to estimate generally at their true value what may increase or diminish the happiness of men; he should do this better than those who care for nobody and never do anything for any one. The feelings of those who are always occupied with their own concerns are too keenly affected for them to judge wisely of things. They consider everything as it affects themselves, they form their ideas of good and ill solely on their own experience, their minds are filled with all sorts of absurd prejudices, and anything which affects their own advantage ever so little, seems an upheaval of the universe.

Extend self-love to others and it is transformed into virtue, a virtue which has its root in the heart of every one of us. The less the object of our care is directly dependent on ourselves, the less we have to fear from the illusion of self-interest; the more general this interest becomes, the juster it is; and the love of the human race is nothing but the love of justice within us. If therefore we desire Emile to be a lover of truth, if we desire that he should indeed perceive it, let us keep him far from self-interest in all his business. The more care he bestows upon the happiness of others the wiser and better he is, and the fewer mistakes he will make between good and evil; but never allow him any blind preference founded merely on personal predilection or unfair prejudice. Why should he harm one person to serve another? What does it matter to him who has the greater share of happiness, providing he promotes the happiness of all? Apart from self-interest this care for the general well-being is the first concern of the wise man, for each of us forms part of the human race and not part of any individual member of that race.

To prevent pity degenerating into weakness we must generalise it and extend it to mankind. Then we only yield to it when it is in accordance with justice, since justice is of all the virtues that which contributes most to the common good. Reason and self-love compel us to love mankind even more than our neighbour, and to pity the wicked is to be very cruel to other men.

Moreover, you must bear in mind that all these means employed to project my pupil beyond himself have also a distinct relation to himself; since they not only cause him inward delight, but I am also endeavouring to instruct him, while I am making him kindly disposed towards others.

First I showed the means employed, now I will show the result. What wide prospects do I perceive unfolding themselves before his mind! What noble feelings stifle the lesser passions in his heart! What clearness of judgment, what accuracy in reasoning, do I see developing from the inclinations we have cultivated, from the experience which concentrates the desires of a great heart within the narrow bounds of possibility, so that a man superior to others can come down to their level if he cannot raise them to his own! True principles of justice, true types of beauty, all moral relations between man and man, all ideas of order, these are engraved on his understanding; he sees the right place for everything and the causes which drive it from that place; he sees what may do good, and what hinders it. Without having felt the passions of mankind, he knows the illusions they produce and their mode of action.

I proceed along the path which the force of circumstances compels me to tread, but I do not insist that my readers shall follow me. Long ago they have made up their minds that I am wandering in the land of chimeras, while for my part I think they are dwelling in the country of prejudice. When I wander so far from popular beliefs I do not cease to bear them in mind; I examine them, I consider them, not that I may follow them or shun them, but that I may weigh them in the balance of reason. Whenever reason compels me to abandon these popular beliefs, I know by experience that my readers will not follow my example; I know that they will persist in refusing to go beyond what they can see, and that they will take the youth I am describing for the creation of my fanciful imagination, merely because he is unlike the youths with whom they compare him; they forget that he must needs be different, because he has been brought up in a totally different fashion; he has been influenced by wholly different feelings, instructed in a wholly different manner, so that it would be far stranger if he were like your pupils than if he were what I have supposed. He is a man of nature's making, not man's. No wonder men find him strange.

When I began this work I took for granted nothing but what could be observed as readily by others as by myself; for our starting-point, the birth of man, is the same for all; but the further we go, while I am seeking to cultivate nature and you are seeking to deprave it, the further apart we find ourselves. At six years old my pupil was not so very unlike yours, whom you had not yet had time to disfigure; now there is nothing in common between them; and when they reach the age of manhood, which is now approaching, they will show themselves utterly different from each other, unless all my pains have been thrown away. There may not be so very great a difference in the amount of knowledge they possess, but there is all the difference in the world in the kind of knowledge. You are amazed to find that the one has noble sentiments of which the others have not the smallest germ, but remember that the latter are already philosophers and theologians while Emile does not even know what is meant by a philosopher and has scarcely heard the name of God.

But if you come and tell me, "There are no such young men, young people are not made that way; they have this passion or that, they do this or that," it is as if you denied that a pear tree could ever be a tall tree because the pear trees in our gardens are all dwarfs.

I beg these critics who are so ready with their blame to consider that I am as well acquainted as they are with everything they say, that I have probably given more thought to it, and that, as I have no private end to serve in getting them to agree with me, I have a right to demand that they should at least take time to find out where I am mistaken. Let them thoroughly examine the nature of man, let them follow the earliest growth of the heart in any given circumstances, so as to see what a difference education may make in the individual; then let them compare my method of education with the results I ascribe to it; and let them tell me where my reasoning is unsound, and I shall have no answer to give them.

It is this that makes me speak so strongly, and as I think with good excuse: I have not pledged myself to any system, I depend as little as possible on arguments, and I trust to what I myself have observed. I do not base my ideas on what I have imagined, but on what I have seen. It is true that I have not confined my observations within the walls of any one town, nor to a single class of people; but having compared men of every class and every nation which I have been able to observe in the course of a life spent in this pursuit, I have discarded as artificial what belonged to one nation and not to another, to one rank and not to another; and I have regarded as proper to mankind what was common to all, at any age, in any station, and in any nation whatsoever.

Now if in accordance with this method you follow from infancy the course of a youth who has not been shaped to any special mould, one who depends as little as possible on authority and the opinions of others, which will he most resemble, my pupil or yours? It seems to me that this is the question you must answer if you would know if I am mistaken.

It is not easy for a man to begin to think; but when once he has begun he will never leave off. Once a thinker, always a thinker, and the understanding once practised in reflection will never rest. You may therefore think that I do too much or too little; that the human mind is not by nature so quick to unfold; and that after having given it opportunities it has not got, I keep it too long confined within a circle of ideas which it ought to have outgrown.

But remember, in the first place, that when I want to train a natural man, I do not want to make him a savage and to send him back to the woods, but that living in the whirl of social life it is enough that he should not let himself be carried away by the passions and prejudices of men; let him see with his eyes and feel with his heart, let him own no sway but that of reason. Under these conditions it is plain that many things will strike him; the oft-recurring feelings which affect him, the different ways of satisfying his real needs, must give him many ideas he would not otherwise have acquired or would only have acquired much later. The natural progress of the mind is quickened but not reversed. The same man who would remain stupid in the forests should become wise and reasonable in towns, if he were merely a spectator in them. Nothing is better fitted to make one wise than the sight of follies we do not share, and even if we share them, we still learn, provided

(we are not the dupe of our follies and provided we do not bring to)
them the same mistakes as the others.

Consider also that while our faculties are confined to the things
of sense, we offer scarcely any hold to the abstractions of philosophy
or to purely intellectual ideas.   To attain to these we require either
to free ourselves from the body to which we are so strongly bound,
or to proceed step by step in a slow and gradual course, or else to
leap across the intervening space with a gigantic bound of which
no child is capable, one for which grown men even require many
steps hewn on purpose for them; but I find it very difficult to see
how you propose to construct such steps.

The Incomprehensible embraces all, he gives its motion to the
earth, and shapes the system of all creatures, but our eyes cannot
see him nor can our hands search him out, he evades the efforts of
our senses; we behold the work, but the workman is hidden from
our eyes.   It is no small matter to know that he exists, and when
we have got so far, and when we ask. What is he? Where is he? our
mind is overwhelmed, we lose ourselves, we know not what to think.

Locke would have us begin with the study of spirits and go on
to that of bodies.   This is the method of superstition, prejudice,
and error; it is not the method of nature, nor even that of well-
ordered reason; it is to learn to see by shutting our eyes.   We
must have studied bodies long enough before we can form any true
idea of spirits, or even suspect that there are such beings.   The
contrary practice merely puts materialism on a firmer footing.

Since our senses are the first instruments to our learning, corporeal
and sensible bodies are the only bodies we directly apprehend.   The
word "spirit" has no meaning for any one who has not philosophised.
To the unlearned and to the child a spirit is merely a body.   Do
they not fancy that spirits groan, speak, fight, and make noises?
Now you must own that spirits with arms and voices are very like
bodies.   This is why every nation on the face of the earth, not even
excepting the Jews, have made to themselves idols.   We, ourselves,
with our words, Spirit, Trinity, Persons, are for the most part quite
anthropomorphic.   I admit that we are taught that God is everywhere; but we also believe that there is air everywhere, at least
in our atmosphere; and the word Spirit meant originally nothing
more than breath and wind.   Once you teach people to say what
they do not understand, it is easy enough to get them to say
anything you like.

The perception of our action upon other bodies must have first
induced us to suppose that their action upon us was effected in like
manner.   Thus man began by thinking that all things whose action
affected him were alive.   He did not recognise the limits of their
powers, and he therefore supposed that they were boundless; as
soon as he had supplied them with bodies they became his gods.
In the earliest times men went in terror of everything and everything in nature seemed alive.   The idea of matter was developed
as slowly as that of spirit, for the former is itself an abstraction.

Thus the universe was peopled with gods like themselves. The stars, the winds and the mountains, rivers, trees, and towns, their very dwellings, each had its soul, its god, its life. The teraphim of Laban, the manitos of savages, the fetishes of the negroes, every work of nature and of man, were the first gods of mortals; polytheism was their first religion and idolatry their earliest form of worship. The idea of one God was beyond their grasp, till little by little they formed general ideas, and they rose to the idea of a first cause and gave meaning to the word "substance," which is at bottom the greatest of abstractions. So every child who believes in God is of necessity an idolater or at least he regards the Deity as a man, and when once the imagination has perceived God, it is very seldom that the understanding conceives him. Locke's order leads us into this same mistake.

Having arrived, I know not how, at the idea of substance, it is clear that to allow of a single substance it must be assumed that this substance is endowed with incompatible and mutually exclusive properties, such as thought and size, one of which is by its nature divisible and the other wholly incapable of division. Moreover it is assumed that thought or, if you prefer it, feeling is a primitive quality inseparable from the substance to which it belongs, that its relation to the substance is like the relation between substance and size. Hence it is inferred that beings who lose one of these attributes lose the substance to which it belongs, and that death is, therefore, but a separation of substances, and that those beings in whom the two attributes are found are composed of the two substances to which those two qualities belong.

But consider what a gulf there still is between the idea of two substances and that of the divine nature, between the incomprehensible idea of the influence of our soul upon our body and the idea of the influence of God upon every living creature. The ideas of creation, destruction, ubiquity, eternity, almighty power, those of the divine attributes—these are all ideas so confused and obscure that few men succeed in grasping them; yet there is nothing obscure about them to the common people, because they do not understand them in the least; how then should they present themselves in full force, that is to say in all their obscurity, to the young mind which is still occupied with the first working of the senses, and fails to realise anything but what it handles? In vain do the abysses of the Infinite open around us, a child does not know the meaning of fear; his weak eyes cannot gauge their depths. To children everything is infinite, they cannot assign limits to anything; not that their measure is so large, but because their understanding is so small. I have even noticed that they place the infinite rather below than above the dimensions known to them. They judge a distance to be immense rather by their feet than by their eyes; infinity is bounded for them, not so much by what they can see, but how far they can go. If you talk to them of the power of God, they will think he is nearly as strong as their father. As their own knowledge is in everything the standard by which they judge of what is possible, they always picture what is described to them as rather smaller than what they know. Such are the natural reasonings of an ignorant and feeble mind. Ajax was afraid to measure his strength against Achilles, yet he challenged Jupiter to combat, for he knew Achilles and did not know Jupiter. A Swiss peasant thought himself the richest man alive; when they tried to explain to him what a king was, he asked with pride, "Has the king got a hundred cows on the high pastures?"

I am aware that many of my readers will be surprised to find me tracing the course of my scholar through his early years without speaking to him of religion. At fifteen he will not even know that he has a soul, at eighteen even he may not be ready to learn about it. For if he learns about it too soon, there is the risk of his never really knowing anything about it.

If I had to depict the most heart-breaking stupidity, I would paint a pedant teaching children the catechism; if I wanted to drive a child crazy I would set him to explain what he learned in his catechism. You will reply that as most of the Christian doctrines are mysteries, you must wait, not merely till the child is a man, but till the man is dead, before the human mind will understand those doctrines. To that I reply, that there are mysteries which the heart of man can neither conceive nor believe, and I see no use in teaching them to children, unless you want to make liars of them. Moreover, I assert that to admit that there are mysteries, you must at least realise that they are incomprehensible, and children are not even capable of this conception! At an age when everything is mysterious, there are no mysteries properly so-called.

"We must believe in God if we would be saved." This doctrine wrongly understood is the root of bloodthirsty intolerance and the cause of all the futile teaching which strikes a deadly blow at human reason by training it to cheat itself with mere words. No doubt there is not a moment to be lost if we would deserve eternal salvation; but if the repetition of certain words suffices to obtain it, I do not see why we should not people heaven with starlings and magpies as well as with children.

The obligation of faith assumes the possibility of belief. The philosopher who does not believe is wrong, for he misuses the reason he has cultivated, and he is able to understand the truths he rejects. But the child who professes the Christian faith—what does he believe? Just what he understands; and he understands so little of what he is made to repeat that if you tell him to say just the opposite he will be quite ready to do it. The faith of children and the faith of many men is a matter of geography. Will they be rewarded for having been born in Rome rather than in Mecca? One is told that Mahomet is the prophet of God and he says, "Mahomet is the prophet of God." The other is told that Mahomet is a rogue and he says, "Mahomet is a rogue." Either of them would have said just the opposite had he stood in the other's shoes.

When they are so much alike to begin with, can the one be con-
signed to Paradise and the other to Hell? When a child says he
believes in God, it is not God he believes in, but Peter or James
who told him that there is something called God, and he believes it
after the fashion of Euripides—

"O Jupiter, of whom I know nothing but thy name."[1]

We hold that no child who dies before the age of reason will be
deprived of everlasting happiness; the Catholics believe the same
of all children who have been baptised, even though they have never
heard of God. There are, therefore, circumstances in which one
can be saved without belief in God, and these circumstances occur
in the case of children or madmen when the human mind is incapable
of the operations necessary to perceive the Godhead. The only
difference I see between you and me is that you profess that children
of seven years old are able to do this and I do not think them ready
for it at fifteen. Whether I am right or wrong depends, not on an
article of the creed, but on a simple observation in natural history.

From the same principle it is plain that any man having reached
old age without faith in God will not, therefore, be deprived of God's
presence in another life if his blindness was not wilful; and I maintain that it is not always wilful. You admit that it is so in the
case of lunatics deprived by disease of their spiritual faculties, but
not of their manhood, and therefore still entitled to the goodness of
their Creator. Why then should we not admit it in the case of
those brought up from infancy in seclusion, those who have led the
life of a savage and are without the knowledge that comes from
intercourse with other men.[2] For it is clearly impossible that such
a savage could ever raise his thoughts to the knowledge of the true
God. Reason tells that man should only be punished for his wilful
faults, and that invincible ignorance can never be imputed to
him as a crime. Hence it follows that in the sight of the Eternal
Justice every man who would believe if he had the necessary knowledge is counted a believer, and that there will be no unbelievers
to be punished except those who have closed their hearts against
the truth.

Let us beware of proclaiming the truth to those who cannot as
yet comprehend it, for to do so is to try to inculcate error. It
would be better to have no idea at all of the Divinity than to have
mean, grotesque, harmful, and unworthy ideas; to fail to perceive
the Divine is a lesser evil than to insult it. The worthy Plutarch
says, "I would rather men said, 'There is no such person as
Plutarch,' than that they should say, 'Plutarch is unjust, envious,
jealous, and such a tyrant that he demands more than can be
performed.'"

[1] Plutarch. It is thus that the tragedy of Menalippus originally began,
but the clamour of the Athenians compelled Euripides to change these
opening lines.
[2] For the natural condition of the human mind and its slow development,
cf. the first part of the *Discours sur Inégalité.*

*H 518

The chief harm which results from the monstrous ideas of God which are instilled into the minds of children is that they last all their life long, and as men they understand no more of God than they did as children. In Switzerland I once saw a good and pious mother who was so convinced of the truth of this maxim that she refused to teach her son religion when he was a little child for fear lest he should be satisfied with this crude teaching and neglect a better teaching when he reached the age of reason. This child never heard the name of God pronounced except with reverence and devotion, and as soon as he attempted to say the word he was told to hold his tongue, as if the subject were too sublime and great for him. This reticence aroused his curiosity and his self-love; he looked forward to the time when he would know this mystery so carefully hidden from him. The less they spoke of God to him, the less he was himself permitted to speak of God, the more he thought about Him; this child beheld God everywhere. What I should most dread as the result of this unwise affectation of mystery is this: by over-stimulating the youth's imagination you may turn his head, and make him at the best a fanatic rather than a believer.

But we need fear nothing of the sort for Emile, who always declines to pay attention to what is beyond his reach, and listens with profound indifference to things he does not understand. There are so many things of which he is accustomed to say, "That is no concern of mine," that one more or less makes little difference to him; and when he does begin to perplex himself with these great matters, it is because the natural growth of his knowledge is turning his thoughts that way.

We have seen the road by which the cultivated human mind approaches these mysteries, and I am ready to admit that it would not attain to them naturally, even in the bosom of society, till a much later age. But as there are in this same society inevitable causes which hasten the development of the passions, if we did not also hasten the development of the knowledge which controls these passions we should indeed depart from the path of nature and disturb her equilibrium. When we can no longer restrain a precocious development in one direction we must promote a corresponding development in another direction, so that the order of nature may not be inverted, and so that things should progress together, not separately, so that the man, complete at every moment of his life, may never find himself at one stage in one of his faculties and at another stage in another faculty.

What a difficulty do I see before me! A difficulty all the greater because it depends less on actual facts than on the cowardice of those who dare not look the difficulty in the face. Let us at least venture to state our problem. A child should always be brought up in his father's religion; he is always given plain proofs that this religion, whatever it may be, is the only true religion, that all others are ridiculous and absurd. The force of the argument depends entirely on the country in which it is put forward. Let a Turk,

who thinks Christianity so absurd at Constantinople, come to Paris
and see what they think of Mahomet. It is in matters of religion
more than in anything else that prejudice is triumphant. But
when we who profess to shake off its yoke entirely, we who refuse to
yield any homage to authority, decline to teach Emile anything
which he could not learn for himself in any country, what religion
shall we give him, to what sect shall this child of nature belong?
The answer strikes me as quite easy. We will not attach him to
any sect, but we will give him the means to choose for himself
according to the right use of his own reason.

> Incedo per ignes
> Suppositos cineri doloso.—HORACE, lib. ii. ode I.

No matter! Thus far zeal and prudence have taken the place of
caution. I hope that these guardians will not fail me now. Reader,
do not fear lest I should take precautions unworthy of a lover of
truth; I shall never forget my motto, but I distrust my own judgment all too easily. Instead of telling you what I think myself,
I will tell you the thoughts of one whose opinions carry more weight
than mine. I guarantee the truth of the facts I am about to relate;
they actually happened to the author whose writings I am about to
transcribe; it is for you to judge whether we can draw from them
any considerations bearing on the matter in hand. I do not offer
you my own idea or another's as your rule; I merely present them
for your examination.

Thirty years ago there was a young man in an Italian town; he
was an exile from his native land and found himself reduced to the
depths of poverty. He had been born a Calvinist, but the consequences of his own folly had made him a fugitive in a strange land;
he had no money and he changed his religion for a morsel of bread.
There was a hostel for proselytes in that town to which he gained
admission. The study of controversy inspired doubts he had never
felt before, and he made acquaintance with evil hitherto unsuspected
by him; he heard strange doctrines and he met with morals still
stranger to him; he beheld this evil conduct and nearly fell a victim
to it. He longed to escape, but he was locked up; he complained,
but his complaints were unheeded; at the mercy of his tyrants, he
found himself treated as a criminal because he would not share
their crimes. The anger kindled in a young and untried heart by
the first experience of violence and injustice may be realised by
those who have themselves experienced it. Tears of anger flowed
from his eyes, he was wild with rage; he prayed to heaven and to
man, and his prayers were unheard; he spoke to every one and no one
listened to him. He saw no one but the vilest servants under the
control of the wretch who insulted him, or accomplices in the same
crime who laughed at his resistance and encouraged him to follow
their example. He would have been ruined had not a worthy priest
visited the hostel on some matter of business. He found an opportunity of consulting him secretly. The priest was poor and in need

of help himself, but the victim had more need of his assistance, and he did not hesitate to help him to escape at the risk of making a dangerous enemy.

Having escaped from vice to return to poverty, the young man struggled vainly against fate: for a moment he thought he had gained the victory. At the first gleam of good fortune his woes and his protector were alike forgotten. He was soon punished for this ingratitude; all his hopes vanished; youth indeed was on his side, but his romantic ideas spoiled everything. He had neither talent nor skill to make his way easily, he could neither be commonplace nor wicked, he expected so much that he got nothing. When he had sunk to his former poverty, when he was without food or shelter and ready to die of hunger, he remembered his benefactor.

He went back to him, found him, and was kindly welcomed; the sight of him reminded the priest of a good deed he had done; such a memory always rejoices the heart. This man was by nature humane and pitiful; he felt the sufferings of others through his own, and his heart had not been hardened by prosperity; in a word, the lessons of wisdom and an enlightened virtue had reinforced his natural kindness of heart. He welcomed the young man, found him a lodging, and recommended him; he shared with him his living which was barely enough for two. He did more, he instructed him, consoled him, and taught him the difficult art of bearing adversity in patience. You prejudiced people, would you have expected to find all this in a priest and in Italy?

This worthy priest was a poor Savoyard clergyman who had offended his bishop by some youthful fault; he had crossed the Alps to find a position which he could not obtain in his own country. He lacked neither wit nor learning, and with his interesting countenance he had met with patrons who found him a place in the household of one of the ministers, as tutor to his son. He preferred poverty to dependence, and he did not know how to get on with the great. He did not stay long with this minister, and when he departed he took with him his good opinion; and as he lived a good life and gained the hearts of everybody, he was glad to be forgiven by his bishop and to obtain from him a small parish among the mountains, where he might pass the rest of his life. This was the limit of his ambition.

He was attracted by the young fugitive and he questioned him closely. He saw that ill-fortune had already seared his heart, that scorn and disgrace had overthrown his courage, and that his pride, transformed into bitterness and spite, led him to see nothing in the harshness and injustice of men but their evil disposition and the vanity of all virtue. He had seen that religion was but a mask for selfishness, and its holy services but a screen for hypocrisy; he had found in the subtleties of empty disputations heaven and hell awarded as prizes for mere words; he had seen the sublime and primitive idea of Divinity disfigured by the vain fancies of men; and when, as he thought, faith in God required him to renounce the reason God himself had given him, he held in equal scorn our foolish imaginings and the object with which they are concerned. With no knowledge of things as they are, without any idea of their origins, he was immersed in his stubborn ignorance and utterly despised those who thought they knew more than himself.

The neglect of all religion soon leads to the neglect of a man's duties. The heart of this young libertine was already far on this road. Yet his was not a bad nature, though incredulity and misery were gradually stifling his natural disposition and dragging him down to ruin; they were leading him into the conduct of a rascal and the morals of an atheist.

The almost inevitable evil was not actually consummated. The young man was not ignorant, his education had not been neglected. He was at that happy age when the pulse beats strongly and the heart is warm, but is not yet enslaved by the madness of the senses. His heart had not lost its elasticity. A native modesty, a timid disposition restrained him, and prolonged for him that period during which you watch your pupil so carefully. The hateful example of brutal depravity, of vice without any charm, had not merely failed to quicken his imagination, it had deadened it. For a long time disgust rather than virtue preserved his innocence, which would only succumb to more seductive charms.

The priest saw the danger and the way of escape. He was not discouraged by difficulties, he took a pleasure in his task; he determined to complete it and to restore to virtue the victim he had snatched from vice. He set about it cautiously; the beauty of the motive gave him courage and inspired him with means worthy of his zeal. Whatever might be the result, his pains would not be wasted. We are always successful when our sole aim is to do good.

He began to win the confidence of the proselyte by not asking any price for his kindness, by not intruding himself upon him, by not preaching at him, by always coming down to his level, and treating him as an equal. It was, so I think, a touching sight to see a serious person becoming the comrade of a young scamp, and virtue putting up with the speech of licence in order to triumph over it more completely. When the young fool came to him with his silly confidences and opened his heart to him, the priest listened and set him at his ease; without giving his approval to what was bad, he took an interest in everything; no tactless reproof checked his chatter or closed his heart; the pleasure which he thought was given by his conversation increased his pleasure in telling everything; thus he made his general confession without knowing he was confessing anything.

After he had made a thorough study of his feelings and disposition, the priest saw plainly that, although he was not ignorant for his age, he had forgotten everything that he most needed to know, and that the disgrace which fortune had brought upon him had stifled in him all real sense of good and evil. There is a stage of degradation which robs the soul of its life; and the inner voice cannot be heard by one whose whole mind is bent on getting food. To protect the unlucky youth from the moral death which threatened him, he began to revive his self-love and his good opinion of himself. He showed him a happier future in the right use of his talents; he revived the generous warmth of his heart by stories of the noble deeds of others; by rousing his admiration for the doers of these deeds he revived his desire to do like deeds himself. To draw him gradually from his idle and wandering life, he made him copy out extracts from well-chosen books; he pretended to want these extracts, and so nourished in him the noble feeling of gratitude. He taught him indirectly through these books, and thus he made him sufficiently regain his good opinion of himself so that he would no longer think himself good for nothing, and would not make himself despicable in his own eyes.

A trifling incident will show how this kindly man tried, unknown to him, to raise the heart of his disciple out of its degradation, without seeming to think of teaching. The priest was so well known for his uprightness and his discretion, that many people preferred to entrust their alms to him, rather than to the wealthy clergy of the town. One day some one had given him some money to distribute among the poor, and the young man was mean enough to ask for some of it on the score of poverty. "No," said he, "we are brothers, you belong to me and I must not touch the money entrusted to me." Then he gave him the sum he had asked for out of his own pocket. Lessons of this sort seldom fail to make an impression on the heart of young people who are not wholly corrupt.

I am weary of speaking in the third person, and the precaution is unnecessary; for you are well aware, my dear friend, that I myself was this unhappy fugitive; I think I am so far removed from the disorders of my youth that I may venture to confess them, and the hand which rescued me well deserves that I should at least do honour to its goodness at the cost of some slight shame.

What struck me most was to see in the private life of my worthy master, virtue without hypocrisy, humanity without weakness, speech always plain and straightforward, and conduct in accordance with this speech. I never saw him trouble himself whether those whom he assisted went to vespers or confession, whether they fasted at the appointed seasons and went without meat; nor did he impose upon them any other like conditions, without which you might die of hunger before you could hope for any help from the devout.

Far from displaying before him the zeal of a new convert, I was encouraged by these observations and I made no secret of my way of thinking, nor did he seem to be shocked by it. Sometimes I would say to myself, he overlooks my indifference to the religion I have adopted because he sees I am equally indifferent to the religion in which I was brought up; he knows that my scorn for religion is not confined to one sect. But what could I think when I sometimes heard him give his approval to doctrines contrary to those of the Roman Catholic Church, and apparently having but a poor opinion of its ceremonies. I should have thought him a Protestant in disguise if I had not beheld him so faithful to those very customs which he seemed to value so lightly; but I knew he fulfilled his priestly duties as carefully in private as in public, and I knew not what to think of these apparent contradictions. Except for the fault which had formerly brought about his disgrace, a fault which he had only partially overcome, his life was exemplary, his conduct beyond reproach, his conversation honest and discreet. While I lived on very friendly terms with him, I learnt day by day to respect him more; and when he had completely won my heart by such great kindness, I awaited with eager curiosity the time when I should learn what was the principle on which the uniformity of this strange life was based.

This opportunity was a long time coming. Before taking his disciple into his confidence, he tried to get the seeds of reason and kindness which he had sown in my heart to germinate. The most difficult fault to overcome in me was a certain haughty misanthropy, a certain bitterness against the rich and successful, as if their wealth and happiness had been gained at my own expense, and as if their supposed happiness had been unjustly taken from my own. The foolish vanity of youth, which kicks against the pricks of humiliation, made me only too much inclined to this angry temper; and the self-respect, which my mentor strove to revive, led to pride, which made men still more vile in my eyes, and only added scorn to my hatred.

Without directly attacking this pride, he prevented it from developing into hardness of heart; and without depriving me of my self-esteem, he made me less scornful of my neighbours. By continually drawing my attention from the empty show, and directing it to the genuine sufferings concealed by it, he taught me to deplore the faults of my fellows and feel for their sufferings, to pity rather than envy them. Touched with compassion towards human weaknesses through the profound conviction of his own failings, he viewed all men as the victims of their own vices and those of others; he beheld the poor groaning under the tyranny of the rich, and the rich under the tyranny of their own prejudices. "Believe me," said he, "our illusions, far from concealing our woes, only increase them by giving value to what is in itself valueless, in making us aware of all sorts of fancied privations which we should not otherwise feel. Peace of heart consists in despising everything that might disturb that peace; the man who clings most closely to life is the man who can least enjoy it; and the man who most eagerly desires happiness is always most miserable."

"What gloomy ideas!" I exclaimed bitterly. "If we must deny ourselves everything, we might as well never have been born; and if we must despise even happiness itself who can be happy?" "I am," replied the priest one day, in a tone which made a great impression on me. "You happy! So little favoured by fortune, so poor, an exile and persecuted, you are happy! How have you contrived to be happy?" "My child," he answered, "I will gladly tell you."

Thereupon he explained that, having heard my confessions, he would confess to me. "I will open my whole heart to yours," he said, embracing me. "You will see me, if not as I am, at least as I seem to myself. When you have heard my whole confession of faith, when you really know the condition of my heart, you will know why I think myself happy, and if you think as I do, you will know how to be happy too. But these explanations are not the affair of a moment, it will take time to show you all my ideas about the lot of man and the true value of life; let us choose a fitting time and a place where we may continue this conversation without interruption."

I showed him how eager I was to hear him. The meeting was fixed for the very next morning. It was summer time; we rose at daybreak. He took me out of the town on to a high hill above the river Po, whose course we beheld as it flowed between its fertile banks; in the distance the landscape was crowned by the vast chain of the Alps; the beams of the rising sun already touched the plains and cast across the fields long shadows of trees, hillocks, and houses, and enriched with a thousand gleams of light the fairest picture which the human eye can see. You would have thought that nature was displaying all her splendour before our eyes to furnish a text for our conversation. After contemplating this scene for a space in silence, the man of peace spoke to me.

THE CREED OF A SAVOYARD PRIEST

My child, do not look to me for learned speeches or profound arguments. I am no great philosopher, nor do I desire to be one. I have, however, a certain amount of common-sense and a constant devotion to truth. I have no wish to argue with you nor even to convince you; it is enough for me to show you, in all simplicity of heart, what I really think. Consult your own heart while I speak; that is all I ask. If I am mistaken, I am honestly mistaken, and therefore my error will not be counted to me as a crime; if you, too, are honestly mistaken, there is no great harm done. If I am right, we are both endowed with reason, we have both the same motive for listening to the voice of reason. Why should not you think as I do?

By birth I was a peasant and poor; to till the ground was my portion; but my parents thought it a finer thing that I should learn to get my living as a priest and they found means to send me to college. I am quite sure that neither my parents nor I had any idea of seeking after what was good, useful, or true; we only sought what was wanted to get me ordained. I learned what was taught me, I said what I was told to say, I promised all that was required, and I became a priest. But I soon discovered that when I promised not to be a man, I had promised more than I could perform.

Conscience, they tell us, is the creature of prejudice, but I know from experience that conscience persists in following the order of nature in spite of all the laws of man. In vain is this or that forbidden; remorse makes her voice heard but feebly when what we do is permitted by well-ordered nature, and still more when we are doing her bidding. My good youth, nature has not yet appealed to your senses; may you long remain in this happy state when her voice is the voice of innocence. Remember that to anticipate her teaching is to offend more deeply against her than to resist her teaching; you must first learn to resist, that you may know when to yield without wrong-doing.

From my youth up I had reverenced the married state as the first and most sacred institution of nature. Having renounced the right to marry, I was resolved not to profane the sanctity of marriage; for in spite of my education and reading I had always led a simple and regular life, and my mind had preserved the innocence of its natural instincts; these instincts had not been obscured by worldly wisdom, while my poverty kept me remote from the temptations dictated by the sophistry of vice.

This very resolution proved my ruin. My respect for marriage led to the discovery of my misconduct. The scandal must be expiated; I was arrested, suspended, and dismissed; I was the victim of my scruples rather than of my incontinence, and I had reason to believe, from the reproaches which accompanied my disgrace, that one can often escape punishment by being guilty of a worse fault.

A thoughtful mind soon learns from such experiences. I found my former ideas of justice, honesty, and every duty of man overturned by these painful events, and day by day I was losing my hold on one or another of the opinions I had accepted. What was left was not enough to form a body of ideas which could stand alone, and I felt that the evidence on which my principles rested was being weakened; at last I knew not what to think, and I came to the same conclusion as yourself, but with this difference: My lack of faith was the slow growth of manhood, attained with great difficulty, and all the harder to uproot.

I was in that state of doubt and uncertainty which Descartes considers essential to the search for truth. It is a state which cannot continue, it is disquieting and painful; only vicious tendencies and an idle heart can keep us in that state. My heart was not so corrupt as to delight in it, and there is nothing which so maintains the habit of thinking as being better pleased with oneself than with one's lot.

I pondered, therefore, on the sad fate of mortals, adrift upon this sea of human opinions, without compass or rudder, and abandoned to their stormy passions with no guide but an inexperienced pilot who does not know whence he comes or whither he is going. I said to myself, "I love truth, I seek her, and cannot find her. Show me truth and I will hold her fast; why does she hide her face from the eager heart that would fain worship her?"

Although I have often experienced worse sufferings, I have never led a life so uniformly distressing as this period of unrest and anxiety, when I wandered incessantly from one doubt to another, gaining nothing from my prolonged meditations but uncertainty, darkness, and contradiction with regard to the source of my being and the rule of my duties.

I cannot understand how any one can be a sceptic sincerely and on principle. Either such philosophers do not exist or they are the most miserable of men. Doubt with regard to what we ought to know is a condition too violent for the human mind; it cannot long be endured; in spite of itself the mind decides one way or another, and it prefers to be deceived rather than to believe nothing.

My perplexity was increased by the fact that I had been brought up in a church which decides everything and permits no doubts, so that having rejected one article of faith I was forced to reject the rest; as I could not accept absurd decisions, I was deprived of those which were not absurd. When I was told to believe everything, I could believe nothing, and I knew not where to stop.

I consulted the philosophers, I searched their books and examined their various theories; I found them all alike proud, assertive, dogmatic, professing, even in their so-called scepticism, to know everything, proving nothing, scoffing at each other. This last trait, which was common to all of them, struck me as the only point in which they were right. Braggarts in attack, they are weaklings in defence. Weigh their arguments, they are all destructive; count their voices, every one speaks for himself; they are only agreed in arguing with each other. I could find no way out of my uncertainty by listening to them.

I suppose this prodigious diversity of opinion is caused, in the first place, by the weakness of the human intellect; and, in the second, by pride. We have no means of measuring this vast machine, we are unable to calculate its workings; we know neither its guiding principles nor its final purpose; we do not know ourselves, we know neither our nature nor the spirit that moves us; we scarcely know whether man is one or many; we are surrounded by impenetrable mysteries. These mysteries are beyond the region of sense, we think we can penetrate them by the light of reason, but we fall back on our imagination. Through this imagined world each forces a way for himself which he holds to be right; none can tell whether his path will lead him to the goal. Yet we long to know and understand it all. The one thing we do not know is the limit of the knowable. We prefer to trust to chance and to believe what is not true, rather than to own that not one of us can see what really is. A fragment of some vast whole whose bounds are beyond our gaze, a fragment abandoned by its Creator to our foolish quarrels, we are vain enough to want to determine the nature of that whole and our own relations with regard to it.

If the philosophers were in a position to declare the truth, which of them would care to do so? Every one of them knows that his own system rests on no surer foundations than the rest, but he maintains it because it is his own. There is not one of them who, if he chanced to discover the difference between truth and falsehood, would not prefer his own lie to the truth which another had discovered. Where is the philosopher who would not deceive the whole world for his own glory? If he can rise above the crowd, if he can excel his rivals, what more does he want? Among believers he is an atheist; among atheists he would be a believer.

The first thing I learned from these considerations was to restrict my inquiries to what directly concerned myself, to rest in profound ignorance of everything else, and not even to trouble myself to doubt anything beyond what I required to know.

I also realised that the philosophers, far from ridding me of my vain doubts, only multiplied the doubts that tormented me and failed to remove any one of them. So I chose another guide and said, " Let me follow the Inner Light; it will not lead me so far astray as others have done, or if it does it will be my own fault, and I shall not go so far wrong if I follow my own illusions as if I trusted to their deceits."

I then went over in my mind the various opinions which I had held in the course of my life, and I saw that although no one of them was plain enough to gain immediate belief, some were more probable than others, and my inward consent was given or withheld in proportion to this improbability. Having discovered this, I made an unprejudiced comparison of all these different ideas, and I perceived that the first and most general of them was also the simplest and the most reasonable, and that it would have been accepted by every one if only it had been last instead of first. Imagine all your philosophers, ancient and modern, having exhausted their strange systems of force, chance, fate, necessity, atoms, a living world, animated matter, and every variety of materialism. Then comes the illustrious Clarke who gives light to the world and proclaims the Being of beings and the Giver of things. What universal admiration, what unanimous applause would have greeted this new system —a system so great, so illuminating, and so simple. Other systems are full of absurdities; this system seems to me to contain fewer things which are beyond the understanding of the human mind. I said to myself, " Every system has its insoluble problems, for the finite mind of man is too small to deal with them; these difficulties are therefore no final arguments, against any system. But what a difference there is between the direct evidence on which these systems are based! Should we not prefer that theory which alone explains all the facts, when it is no more difficult than the rest?

Bearing thus within my heart the love of truth as my only philosophy, and as my only method a clear and simple rule which dispensed with the need for vain and subtle arguments, I returned with the help of this rule to the examination of such knowledge as concerned myself; I was resolved to admit as self-evident all that I could not honestly refuse to believe, and to admit as true all that seemed to follow directly from this; all the rest I determined to leave undecided, neither accepting nor rejecting it, nor yet troubling myself to clear up difficulties which did not lead to any practical ends.

But who am I? What right have I to decide? What is it that determines my judgments? If they are inevitable, if they are the results of the impressions I receive, I am wasting my strength in such inquiries; they would be made or not without any interference of mine. I must therefore first turn my eyes upon myself to acquaint myself with the instrument I desire to use, and to discover how far it is realiable.

I exist, and I have senses through which I receive impressions. This is the first truth that strikes me and I am forced to accept it. Have I any independent knowledge of my existence, or am I only aware of it through my sensations? This is my first difficulty, and so far I cannot solve it. For I continually experience sensations, either directly or indirectly through memory, so how can I know if the feeling of *self* is something beyond these sensations or if it can exist independently of them?

My sensations take place in myself, for they make me aware of my own existence; but their cause is outside me, for they affect me whether I have any reason for them or not, and they are produced or destroyed independently of me. So I clearly perceive that my sensation, which is within me, and its cause or its object, which is outside me, are different things.

Thus, not only do I exist, but other entities exist also, that is to say, the objects of my sensations; and even if these objects are merely ideas, still these ideas are not me.

But everything outside myself, everything which acts upon my senses, I call matter, and all the particles of matter which I suppose to be united into separate entities I call bodies. Thus all the disputes of the idealists and the realists have no meaning for me; their distinctions between the appearance and the reality of bodies are wholly fanciful.

I am now as convinced of the existence of the universe as of my own. I next consider the objects of my sensations, and I find that I have the power of comparing them, so I perceive that I am endowed with an active force of which I was not previously aware.

To perceive is to feel; to compare is to judge; to judge and to feel are not the same. Through sensation objects present themselves to me separately and singly as they are in nature; by comparing them I rearrange them, I shift them so to speak, I place one upon another to decide whether they are alike or different, or more generally to find out their relations. To my mind, the distinctive faculty of an active or intelligent being is the power of understand-

ing this word " is." I seek in vain in the merely sensitive entity
that intelligent force which compares and judges; I can find no
trace of it in its nature. This passive entity will be aware of each
object separately, it will even be aware of the whole formed by the
two together, but having no power to place them side by side it
can never compare them, it can never form a judgment with regard
to them.

To see two things at once is not to see their relations nor to judge
of their differences; to perceive several objects, one beyond the
other, is not to relate them. I may have at the same moment an
idea of a big stick and a little stick without comparing them, without
judging that one is less than the other, just as I can see my whole
hand without counting my fingers.[1] These comparative ideas,
greater, *smaller*, together with number ideas of *one*, *two*, etc., are
certainly not sensations, although my mind only produces them
when my sensations occur.

We are told that a sensitive being distinguishes sensations from
each other by the inherent differences in the sensations; this
requires explanation. When the sensations are different, the
sensitive being distinguishes them by their differences; when they
are alike, he distinguishes them because he is aware of them one
beyond the other. Otherwise, how could he distinguish between two
equal objects simultaneously experienced? He would necessarily
confound the two objects and take them for one object, especially
under a system which professed that the representative sensations
of space have no extension.

When we become aware of the two sensations to be compared,
their impression is made, each object is perceived, both are perceived,
but for all that their relation is not perceived. If the judgment of
this relation were merely a sensation, and came to me solely from
the object itself, my judgments would never be mistaken, for it is
never untrue that I feel what I feel.

Why then am I mistaken as to the relation between these two
sticks, especially when they are not parallel? Why, for example,
do I say the small stick is a third of the large, when it is only a
quarter? Why is the picture, which is the sensation, unlike its
model which is the object? It is because I am active when I judge,
because the operation of comparison is at fault; because my understanding, which judges of relations, mingles its errors with the truth
of sensations, which only reveal to me things.

Add to this a consideration which will, I feel sure, appeal to you
when you have thought about it: it is this—If we were purely
passive in the use of our senses, there would be no communication
between them; it would be impossible to know that the body we are
touching and the thing we are looking at is the same. Either we
should never perceive anything outside ourselves, or there would

[1] M. de le Cordamines' narratives tell of a people who only know how
to count up to three. Yet the men of this nation, having hands, have
often seen their fingers without learning to count up to five.

be for us five substances perceptible by the senses, whose identity we should have no means of perceiving.

This power of my mind which brings my sensations together and compares them may be called by any name; let it be called attention, meditation, reflection, or what you will; it is still true that it is in me and not in things, that it is I alone who produce it, though I only produce it when I receive an impression from things. Though I am compelled to feel or not to feel, I am free to examine more or less what I feel.

Being now, so to speak, sure of myself, I begin to look at things outside myself, and I behold myself with a sort of shudder flung at random into this vast universe, plunged as it were into the vast number of entities, knowing nothing of what they are in themselves or in relation to me. I study them, I observe them; and the first object which suggests itself for comparison with them is myself.

All that I perceive through the senses is matter, and I deduce all the essential properties of matter from the sensible qualities which make me perceive it, qualities which are inseparable from it. I see it sometimes in motion, sometimes at rest,[1] hence I infer that neither motion nor rest is essential to it, but motion, being an action, is the result of a cause of which rest is only the absence. When, therefore, there is nothing acting upon matter it does not move, and for the very reason that rest and motion are indifferent to it, its natural state is a state of rest.

I perceive two sorts of motions of bodies, acquired motion and spontaneous or voluntary motion. In the first the cause is external to the body moved, in the second it is within. I shall not conclude from that that the motion, say of a watch, is spontaneous, for if no external cause operated upon the spring it would run down and the watch would cease to go. For the same reason I should not admit that the movements of fluids are spontaneous, neither should I attribute spontaneous motion to fire which causes their fluidity.[2]

You ask me if the movements of animals are spontaneous; my answer is, "I cannot tell," but analogy points that way. You ask me again, how do I know that there are spontaneous movements? I tell you, "I know it because I feel them." I want to move my arm and I move it without any other immediate cause of the movement but my own will. In vain would any one try to argue me out of this feeling, it is stronger than any proofs; you might as well try to convince me that I do not exist.

If there were no spontaneity in men's actions, nor in anything that happens on this earth, it would be all the more difficult to imagine

[1] This repose is, if you prefer it, merely relative; but as we perceive more or less of motion, we may plainly conceive one of two extremes, which is rest; and we conceive it so clearly that we are even disposed to take for absolute rest what is only relative. But it is not true that motion is of the essence of matter, if matter may be conceived of as at rest.

[2] Chemists regard phlogiston or the element of fire as diffused, motionless, and stagnant in the compounds of which it forms part, until external forces set it free, collect it and set in in motion, and change it into fire.

a first cause for all motion. For my own part, I feel myself so thoroughly convinced that the natural state of matter is a state of rest, and that it has no power of action in itself, that when I see a body in motion I at once assume that it is either a living body or that this motion has been imparted to it. My mind declines to accept in any way the idea of inorganic matter moving of its own accord, or giving rise to any action.

Yet this visible universe consists of matter, matter diffused and dead,[1] matter which has none of the cohesion, the organisation, the common feeling of the parts of a living body, for it is certain that we who are parts of the whole have no consciousness of the whole. This same universe is in motion, and in its movements, ordered, uniform, and subject to fixed laws, it has none of that freedom which appears in the spontaneous movements of men and animals. So the world is not some huge animal which moves of its own accord; its movements are therefore due to some external cause, a cause which I cannot perceive, but the inner voice makes this cause so apparent to me that I cannot watch the course of the sun without imagining a force which drives it, and when the earth revolves I think I see the hand that sets it in motion.

If I must accept general laws whose essential relation to matter is unperceived by me, how much further have I got? These laws, not being real things, not being substances, have therefore some other basis unknown to me. Experiment and observation have acquainted us with the laws of motion; these laws determine the results without showing their causes; they are quite inadequate to explain the system of the world and the course of the universe. With the help of dice Descartes made heaven and earth; but he could not set his dice in motion, nor start the action of his centrifugal force without the help of rotation. Newton discovered the law of gravitation; but gravitation alone would soon reduce the universe to a motionless mass; he was compelled to add a projectile force to account for the elliptical course of the celestial bodies; let Newton show us the hand that launched the planets in the tangent of their orbits.

The first causes of motion are not to be found in matter; matter receives and transmits motion, but does not produce it. The more I observe the action and reaction of the forces of nature playing on one another, the more I see that we must always go back from one effect to another, till we arrive at a first cause in some will; for to assume an infinite succession of causes is to assume that there is no first cause. In a word, no motion which is not caused by another motion can take place, except by a spontaneous, voluntary action; inanimate bodies have no action but motion, and there is no real action without will. This is my first principle. I believe, therefore,

---

[1] I have tried hard to grasp the idea of a living molecule, but in vain. The idea of matter feeling without any senses seems to me unintelligible and self-contradictory. To accept or reject this idea one must first understand it, and I confess that so far I have not succeeded.

that there is a will which sets the universe in motion and gives life to nature. This is my first dogma, or the first article of my creed.

How does a will produce a physical and corporeal action? I cannot tell, but I perceive that it does so in myself; I will to do something and I do it; I will to move my body and it moves, but if an inanimate body, when at rest, should begin to move itself, the thing is incomprehensible and without precedent. The will is known to me in its action, not in its nature. I know this will as a cause of motion, but to conceive of matter as producing motion is clearly to conceive of an effect without a cause, which is not to conceive at all.

It is no more possible for me to conceive how my will moves my body than to conceive how my sensations affect my mind. I do not even know why one of these mysteries has seemed less inexplicable than the other. For my own part, whether I am active or passive, the means of union of the two substances seem to me absolutely incomprehensible. It is very strange that people make this very incomprehensibility a step towards the compounding of the two substances, as if operations so different in kind were more easily explained in one case than in two.

The doctrine I have just laid down is indeed obscure; but at least it suggests a meaning and there is nothing in it repugnant to reason or experience; can we say as much of materialism? Is it not plain that if motion is essential to matter it would be inseparable from it, it would always be present in it in the same degree, always present in every particle of matter, always the same in each particle of matter, it would not be capable of transmission, it could neither increase nor diminish, nor could we ever conceive of matter at rest. When you tell me that motion is not essential to matter but necessary to it, you try to cheat me with words which would be easier to refute if there was a little more sense in them. For either the motion of matter arises from the matter itself and is therefore essential to it; or it arises from an external cause and is not necessary to the matter, because the motive cause acts upon it; we have got back to our original difficulty.

The chief source of human error is to be found in general and abstract ideas; the jargon of metaphysics has never led to the discovery of any single truth, and it has filled philosophy with absurdities of which we are ashamed as soon as we strip them of their long words. Tell me, my friend, when they talk to you of a blind force diffused throughout nature, do they present any real idea to your mind? They think they are saying something by these vague expressions—universal force, essential motion—but they are saying nothing at all. The idea of motion is nothing more than the idea of transference from place to place; there is no motion without direction; for no individual can move all ways at once. In what direction then does matter move of necessity? Has the whole body of matter a uniform motion, or has each atom its own motion? According to the first idea the whole universe must form a solid and indivisible mass; according to the second it can only form a diffused and incoherent fluid, which would make the union of any two atoms impossible. What direction shall be taken by this motion common to all matter? Shall it be in a straight line, in a circle, or from above downwards, to the right or to the left? If each molecule has its own direction, what are the causes of all these directions and all these differences? If every molecule or atom only revolved on its own axis, nothing would ever leave its place and there would be no transmitted motion, and even then this circular movement would require to follow some direction. To set matter in motion by an abstraction is to utter words without meaning, and to attribute to matter a given direction is to assume a determining cause. The more examples I take, the more causes I have to explain, without ever finding a common agent which controls them. Far from being able to picture to myself an entire absence of order in the fortuitous concurrence of elements, I cannot even imagine such a strife, and the chaos of the universe is less conceivable to me than its harmony. I can understand that the mechanism of the universe may not be intelligible to the human mind, but when a man sets to work to explain it, he must say what men can understand.

If matter in motion points me to a will, matter in motion according to fixed laws points me to an intelligence; that is the second article of my creed. To act, to compare, to choose, are the operations of an active, thinking being; so this being exists. Where do you find him existing, you will say? Not merely in the revolving heavens, nor in the sun which gives us light, not in myself alone, but in the sheep that grazes, the bird that flies, the stone that falls, and the leaf blown by the wind.

I judge of the order of the world, although I know nothing of its purpose, for to judge of this order it is enough for me to compare the parts one with another, to study their co-operation, their relations, and to observe their united action. I know not why the universe exists, but I see continually how it is changed; I never fail to perceive the close connection by which the entities of which it consists lend their aid one to another. I am like a man who sees the works of a watch for the first time; he is never weary of admiring the mechanism, though he does not know the use of the instrument and has never seen its face. I do not know what this is for, says he, but I see that each part of it is fitted to the rest, I admire the workman in the details of his work, and I am quite certain that all these wheels only work together in this fashion for some common end which I cannot perceive.

Let us compare the special ends, the means, the ordered relations of every kind, then let us listen to the inner voice of feeling; what healthy mind can reject its evidence? Unless the eyes are blinded by prejudices, can they fail to see that the visible order of the universe proclaims a supreme intelligence? What sophisms must be brought together before we fail to understand the harmony of existence and the wonderful co-operation of every part for the maintenance of the rest? Say what you will of combinations and probabilities; what do you gain by reducing me to silence if you cannot gain my consent? And how can you rob me of the spontaneous feeling which, in spite of myself, continually gives you the lie? If organised bodies had come together fortuitously in all sorts of ways before assuming settled forms, if stomachs are made without mouths, feet without heads, hands without arms, imperfect organs of every kind which died because they could not preserve their life, why do none of these imperfect attempts now meet our eyes; why has nature at length prescribed laws to herself which she did not at first recognise? I must not be surprised if that which is possible should happen, and if the improbability of the event is compensated for by the number of the attempts. I grant this; yet if any one told me that printed characters scattered broadcast had produced the Æneid all complete, I would not condescend to take a single step to verify this falsehood. You will tell me I am forgetting the multitude of attempts. But how many such attempts must I assume to bring the combination within the bounds of probability? For my own part the only possible assumption is that the chances are infinity to one that the product is not the work of chance. In addition to this, chance combinations yield nothing but products of the same nature as the elements combined, so that life and organisation will not be produced by a flow of atoms, and a chemist when making his compounds will never give them thought and feeling in his crucible.[1]

I was surprised and almost shocked when I read Neuwentit. How could this man desire to make a book out of the wonders of nature, wonders which show the wisdom of the author of nature? His book would have been as large as the world itself before he had exhausted his subject, and as soon as we attempt to give details, that greatest wonder of all, the concord and harmony of the whole, escapes us. The mere generation of living organic bodies is the despair of the human mind; the insurmountable barrier raised by nature between the various species, so that they should not mix with one another, is the clearest proof of her intention. She is not content to have established order, she has taken adequate measures to prevent the disturbance of that order.

There is not a being in the universe which may not be regarded as in some respects the common centre of all, around which they are grouped, so that they are all reciprocally end and means in relation to each other. The mind is confused and lost amid these in-

[1] Could one believe, if one had not seen it, that human absurdity could go so far? Amatus Lusitanus asserts that he saw a little man an inch long enclosed in a glass, which Julius Camillus, like a second Prometheus, had made by alchemy. Paracelsus (De natura rerum) teaches the method of making these tiny men, and he maintains that the pygmies, fauns, satyrs, and nymphs have been made by chemistry. Indeed I cannot see that there is anything more to be done, to establish the possibility of these facts, unless it is to assert that organic matter resists the heat of fire and that its molecules can preserve their life in the hottest furnace.

numerable relations, not one of which is itself confused or lost in the crowd. What absurd assumptions are required to deduce all this harmony from the blind mechanism of matter set in motion by chance! In vain do those who deny the unity of intention manifested in the relations of all the parts of this great whole, in vain do they conceal their nonsense under abstractions, co-ordinations, general principles, symbolic expressions; whatever they do I find it impossible to conceive of a system of ent.ties so firmly ordered unless I believe in an intelligence that orders them. It is not in my power to believe that passive and dead matter can have brought forth living and feeling beings, that blind chance has brought forth intelligent beings, that that which does not think has brought forth thinking beings.

I believe, therefore, that the world is governed by a wise and powerful will; I see it or rather I feel it, and it is a great thing to know this. But has this same world always existed, or has it been created? Is there one source of all things? Are there two or many? What is their nature? I know not; and what concern is it of mine? When these things become of importance to me I will try to learn them; till then I abjure these idle speculations, which may trouble my peace, but cannot affect my conduct nor be comprehended by my reason.

Recollect that I am not preaching my own opinion but explaining it. Whether matter is eternal or created, whether its origin is passive or not, it is still certain that the whole is one, and that it proclaims a single intelligence; for I see nothing that is not part of the same ordered system, nothing which does not co-operate to the same end, namely, the conservation of all within the established order. This being who wills and can perform his will, this being active through his own power, this being, whoever he may be, who moves the universe and orders all things, is what I call God. To this name I add the ideas of intelligence, power, will, which I have brought together, and that of kindness which is their necessary consequence; but for all this I know no more of the being to which I ascribe them. He hides himself alike from my senses and my understanding; the more I think of him, the more perplexed I am; I know full well that he exists, and that he exists of himself alone; I know that my existence depends on his, and that everything I know depends upon him also. I see God everywhere in his works; I feel him within myself; I behold him all around me; but if I try to ponder him himself, if I try to find out where he is, what he is, what is his substance, he escapes me and my troubled spirit finds nothing.

Convinced of my unfitness, I shall never argue about the nature of God unless I am driven to it by the feeling of his relations with myself. Such reasonings are always rash; a wise man should venture on them with trembling, he should be certain that he can never sound their abysses; for the most insolent attitude towards God is not to abstain from thinking of him, but to think evil of him.

After the discovery of such of his attributes as enable me to conceive of his existence, I return to myself, and I try to discover what is my place in the order of things which he governs, and I can myself examine. At once, and beyond possibility of doubt, I discover my species; for by my own will and the instruments I can control to carry out my will, I have more power to act upon all bodies about me, either to make use of or to avoid their action at my pleasure, than any of them has power to act upon me against my will by mere physical impulsion; and through my intelligence I am the only one who can examine all the rest. What being here below, except man, can observe others, measure, calculate, forecast their motions, their effects, and unite, so to speak, the feeling of a common existence with that of his individual existence? What is there so absurd in the thought that all things are made for me, when I alone can relate all things to myself?

It is true, therefore, that man is lord of the earth on which he dwells; for not only does he tame all the beasts, not only does he control its elements through his industry; but he alone knows how to control it; by contemplation he takes possession of the stars which he cannot approach. Show me any other creature on earth who can make a fire and who can behold with admiration the sun. What! can I observe and know all creatures and their relations; can I feel what is meant by order, beauty, and virtue; can I consider the universe and raise myself towards the hand that guides it; can I love good and perform it; and should I then liken myself to the beasts? Wretched soul, it is your gloomy philosophy which makes you like the beasts; or rather in vain do you seek to degrade yourself; your genius belies your principles, your kindly heart belies your doctrines, and even the abuse of your powers proves their excellence in your own despite.

For myself, I am not pledged to the support of any system. I am a plain and honest man, one who is not carried away by party spirit, one who has no ambition to be head of a sect; I am content with the place where God has set me; I see nothing, next to God himself, which is better than my species; and if I had to choose my place in the order of creation, what more could I choose than to be a man!

I am not puffed up by this thought, I am deeply moved by it; for this state was no choice of mine, it was not due to the deserts of a creature who as yet did not exist. Can I behold myself thus distinguished without congratulating myself on this post of honour, without blessing the hand which bestowed it? The first return to self has given birth to a feeling of gratitude and thankfulness to the author of my species, and this feeling calls forth my first homage to the beneficent Godhead. I worship his Almighty power and my heart acknowledges his mercies. Is it not a natural consequence of our self-love to honour our protector and to love our benefactor?

But when, in my desire to discover my own place within my

species, I consider its different ranks and the men who fill them, where am I now? What a sight meets my eyes! Where is now the order I perceived? Nature showed me a scene of harmony and proportion; the human race shows me nothing but confusion and disorder. The elements agree together; men are in a state of chaos. The beasts are happy; their king alone is wretched. O Wisdom, where are thy laws? O Providence, is this thy rule over the world? Merciful God, where is thy Power? I behold the earth, and there is evil upon it.

Would you believe it, dear friend, from these gloomy thoughts and apparent contradictions, there was shaped in my mind the sublime idea of the soul, which all my seeking had hitherto failed to discover? While I meditated upon man's nature, I seemed to discover two distinct principles in it; one of them raised him to the study of the eternal truths, to the love of justice, and of true morality, to the regions of the world of thought, which the wise delight to contemplate; the other led him downwards to himself, made him the slave of his senses, of the passions which are their instruments, and thus opposed everything suggested to him by the former principle. When I felt myself carried away, distracted by these conflicting motives, I said, No; man is not one; I will and I will not; I feel myself at once a slave and a free man; I perceive what is right, I love it, and I do what is wrong; I am active when I listen to the voice of reason; I am passive when I am carried away by my passions; and when I yield, my worst suffering is the knowledge that I might have resisted.

Young man, hear me with confidence. I will always be honest with you. If conscience is the creature of prejudice, I am certainly wrong, and there is no such thing as a proof of morality; but if to put oneself first is an inclination natural to man, and if the first sentiment of justice is moreover inborn in the human heart, let those who say man is a simple creature remove these contradictions and I will grant that there is but one substance.

You will note that by this term *substance* I understand generally the being endowed with some primitive quality, apart from all special and secondary modifications. If then all the primitive qualities which are known to us can be united in one and the same being, we should only acknowledge one substance; but if there are qualities which are mutually exclusive, there are as many different substances as there are such exclusions. You will think this over; for my own part, whatever Locke may say, it is enough for me to recognise matter as having merely extension and divisibility to convince myself that it cannot think, and if a philosopher tells me that trees feel and rocks think [1] in vain will he perplex me with his

---

[1] It seems to me that modern philosophy, far from saying that rocks think, has discovered that men do not think. It perceives nothing more in nature than sensitive beings; and the only difference it finds between a man and a stone is that a man is a sensitive being which experiences sensations, and a stone is a sensitive being which does not experience

cunning arguments; I merely regard him as a dishonest sophist, who prefers to say that stones have feeling rather than that men have souls.

Suppose a deaf man denies the existence of sounds because he has never heard them. I put before his eyes a stringed instrument and cause it to sound in unison by means of another instrument concealed from him; the deaf man sees the chord vibrate. I tell him, " The sound makes it do that." " Not at all," says he, " the string itself is the cause of the vibration; to vibrate in that way is a quality common to all bodies." " Then show me this vibration in other bodies," I answer, " or at least show me its cause in this string." " I cannot," replies the deaf man; " but because I do not understand how that string vibrates why should I try to explain it by means of your sounds, of which I have not the least idea? It is explaining one obscure fact by means of a cause still more obscure. Make me perceive your sounds; or I say there are no such things."

The more I consider thought and the nature of the human mind, the more likeness I find between the arguments of the materialists and those of the deaf man. Indeed, they are deaf to the inner voice which cries aloud to them, in a tone which can hardly be mistaken. A machine does not think, there is neither movement nor form which can produce reflection; something within thee tries to break the bands which confine it; space is not thy measure, the whole universe does not suffice to contain thee; thy sentiments, thy desires, thy anxiety, thy pride itself, have another origin than this small body in which thou art imprisoned.

No material creature is in itself active, and I am active. In vain do you argue this point with me; I feel it, and it is this feeling which speaks to me more forcibly than the reason which disputes it. I have a body which is acted upon by other bodies, and it acts in

sensations. But if it is true that all matter feels, where shall I find the sensitive unit, the individual ego? Shall it be in each molecule of matter or in bodies as aggregates of molecules? Shall I place this unity in fluids and solids alike, in compounds and in elements? You tell me nature consists of individuals. But what are these individuals? Is that stone an individual or an aggregate of individuals? Is it a single sensitive being, or are there as many beings in it as there are grains of sand? If every elementary atom is a sensitive being, how shall I conceive of that intimate communication by which one feels within the other, so that their two egos are blended in one? Attraction may be a law of nature whose mystery is unknown to us; but at least we conceive that there is nothing in attraction acting in proportion to mass which is contrary to extension and divisibility. Can you conceive of sensation in the same way? The sensitive parts have extension, but the sensitive being is one and indivisible; he cannot be cut in two, he is a whole or he is nothing; therefore the sensitive being is not a material body. I know not how our materialists understand it, but it seems to me that the same difficulties which have led them to reject thought, should have made them also reject feeling; and I see no reason why, when the first step has been taken, they should not take the second too; what more would it cost them? Since they are certain they do not think, why do they dare to affirm that they feel?

turn upon them; there is no doubt about this reciprocal action; but my will is independent of my senses; I consent or I resist; I yield or I win the victory, and I know very well in myself when I have done what I wanted and when I have merely given way to my passions. I have always the power to will, but not always the strength to do what I will. When I yield to temptation I surrender myself to the action of external objects. When I blame myself for this weakness, I listen to my own will alone; I am a slave in my vices, a free man in my remorse; the feeling of freedom is never effaced in me but when I myself do wrong, and when I at length prevent the voice of the soul from protesting against the authority of the body.

I am only aware of will through the consciousness of my own will, and intelligence is no better known to me. When you ask me what is the cause which determines my will, it is my turn to ask what cause determines my judgment; for it is plain that these two causes are but one; and if you understand clearly that man is active in his judgments, that his intelligence is only the power to compare and judge, you will see that his freedom is only a similar power or one derived from this; he chooses between good and evil as he judges between truth and falsehood; if his judgment is at fault, he chooses amiss. What then is the cause that determines his will? It is his judgment. And what is the cause that determines his judgment? It is his intelligence, his power of judging; the determining cause is in himself. Beyond that, I understand nothing.

No doubt I am not free not to desire my own welfare, I am not free to desire my own hurt; but my freedom consists in this very thing, that I can will what is for my own good, or what I esteem as such, without any external compulsion. Does it follow that I am not my own master because I cannot be other than myself?

The motive power of all action is in the will of a free creature; we can go no farther. It is not the word freedom that is meaningless, but the word necessity. To suppose some action which is not the effect of an active motive power is indeed to suppose effects without cause, to reason in a vicious circle. Either there is no original impulse, or every original impulse has no antecedent cause, and there is no will properly so-called without freedom. Man is therefore free to act, and as such he is animated by an immaterial substance; that is the third article of my creed. From these three you will easily deduce the rest, so that I need not enumerate them.

If man is at once active and free, he acts of his own accord; what he does freely is no part of the system marked out by Providence and it cannot be imputed to Providence. Providence does not will the evil that man does when he misuses the freedom given to him; neither does Providence prevent him doing it, either because the wrong done by so feeble a creature is as nothing in ts eyes, or because it could not prevent it without doing a greater wrong and degrading his nature. Providence has made him free that he may chouse the good and refuse the evil. It has made him capable of this choice if he uses rightly the faculties bestowed upon him, but it has so strictly limited his powers that the misuse of his freedom cannot disturb the general order. The evil that man does reacts upon himself without affecting the system of the world, without preventing the preservation of the human species in spite of itself. To complain that God does not prevent us from doing wrong is to complain because he has made man of so excellent a nature, that he has endowed his actions with that morality by which they are ennobled, that he has made virtue man's birthright. Supreme happiness consists in self-content; that we may gain this self-content we are placed upon this earth and endowed with freedom, we are tempted by our passions and restrained by conscience. What more could divine power itself have done on our behalf? Could it have made our nature a contradiction, and have given the prize of well-doing to one who was incapable of evil? To prevent a man from wickedness, should Providence have restricted him to instinct and made him a fool? Not so, O God of my soul, I will never reproach thee that thou hast created me in thine own image, that I may be free and good and happy like my Maker!

It is the abuse of our powers that makes us unhappy and wicked. Our cares, our sorrows, our sufferings are of our own making. Moral ills are undoubtedly the work of man, and physical ills would be nothing but for our vices which have made us liable to them. Has not nature made us feel our needs as a means to our preservation? Is not bodily suffering a sign that the machine is out of order and needs attention? Death. . . . Do not the wicked poison their own life and ours? Who would wish to live for ever? Death is the cure for the evils you bring upon yourself; nature would not have you suffer perpetually. How few sufferings are felt by man living in a state of primitive simplicity! His life is almost entirely free from suffering and from passion; he neither fears nor feels death; if he feels it, his sufferings make him desire it; henceforth it is no evil in his eyes. If we were but content to be ourselves we should have no cause to complain of our lot; but in the search for an imaginary good we find a thousand real ills. He who cannot bear a little pain must expect to suffer greatly. If a man injures his constitution by dissipation, you try to cure him with medicine; the ill he fears is added to the ill he feels; the thought of death makes it horrible and hastens its approach; the more we seek to escape from it, the more we are aware of it; and we go through life in the fear of death, blaming nature for the evils we have inflicted on ourselves by our neglect of her laws.

O Man! seek no further for the author of evil; thou art he. There is no evil but the evil you do or the evil you suffer, and both come from yourself. Evil in general can only spring from disorder, and in the order of the world I find a never-failing system. Evil in particular cases exists only in the mind of those who experience it; and this feeling is not the gift of nature, but the work of man himself.

Pain has little power over those who, having thought little, look neither before nor after. Take away our fatal progress, take away our faults and our vices, take away man's handiwork, and all is well.

Where all is well, there is no such thing as injustice. Justice and goodness are inseparable; now goodness is the necessary result of boundless power and of that self-love which is innate in all sentient beings. The omnipotent projects himself, so to speak, into the being of his creatures. Creation and preservation are the everlasting work of power; it does not act on that which has no existence; God is not the God of the dead; he could not harm and destroy without injury to himself. The omnipotent can only will what is good.[1] Therefore he who is supremely good, because he is supremely powerful, must also be supremely just, otherwise he would contradict himself; for that love of order which creates order we call goodness and that love of order which preserves order we call justice.

Men say God owes nothing to his creatures. I think he owes them all he promised when he gave them their being. Now to give them the idea of something good and to make them feel the need of it, is to promise it to them. The more closely I study myself, the more carefully I consider, the more plainly do I read these words, " Be just and you will be happy." It is not so, however, in the present condition of things, the wicked prospers and the oppression of the righteous continues. Observe how angry we are when this expectation is disappointed. Conscience revolts and murmurs against her Creator; she exclaims with cries and groans, " Thou hast deceived me."

" I have deceived thee, rash soul! Who told thee this? Is thy soul destroyed? Hast thou ceased to exist? O Brutus! O my son! let there be no stain upon the close of thy noble life; do not abandon thy hope and thy glory with thy corpse upon the plains of Philippi. Why dost thou say, ' Virtue is naught,' when thou art about to enjoy the reward of virtue? Thou art about to die! Nay, thou shalt live, and thus my promise is fulfilled."

One might judge from the complaints of impatient men that God owes them the reward before they have deserved it, that he is bound to pay for virtue in advance. Oh! let us first be good and then we shall be happy. Let us not claim the prize before we have won it, nor demand our wages before we have finished our work. " It is not in the lists that we crown the victors in the sacred games," says Plutarch, " it is when they have finished their course."

If the soul is immaterial, it may survive the body; and if it so survives, Providence is justified. Had I no other proof of the immaterial nature of the soul, the triumph of the wicked and the oppression of the righteous in this world would be enough to convince me. I should seek to resolve so appalling a discord in

[1] The ancients were right when they called the supreme God *Optimus Maximus*, but it would have been better to say *Maximus Optimus*, for his goodness springs from his power, he is good because he is great.

the universal harmony. I should say to myself, "All is not over with life, everything finds its place at death." I should still have to answer the question, "What becomes of man when all we know of him through our senses has vanished?" This question no longer presents any difficulty to me when I admit the two substances. It is easy to understand that what is imperceptible to those senses escapes me, during my bodily life, when I perceive through my senses only. When the union of soul and body is destroyed, I think one may be dissolved and the other may be preserved. Why should the destruction of the one imply the destruction of the other? On the contrary, so unlike in their nature, they were during their union in a highly unstable condition, and when this union comes to an end they both return to their natural state; the active vital substance regains all the force which it expended to set in motion the passive dead substance. Alas! my vices make me only too well aware that man is but half alive during this life; the life of the soul only begins with the death of the body.

But what is that life? Is the soul of man in its nature immortal? I know not. My finite understanding cannot hold the infinite; what is called eternity eludes my grasp. What can I assert or deny, how can I reason with regard to what I cannot conceive? I believe that the soul survives the body for the maintenance of order; who knows if this is enough to make it eternal? However, I know that the body is worn out and destroyed by the division of its parts, but I cannot conceive a similar destruction of the conscious nature, and as I cannot imagine how it can die, I presume that it does not die. As this assumption is consoling and in itself not unreasonable, why should I fear to accept it?

I am aware of my soul; it is known to me in feeling and in thought; I know what it is without knowing its essence; I cannot reason about ideas which are unknown to me. What I do know is this, that my personal identity depends upon memory, and that to be indeed the same self I must remember that I have existed. Now after death I could not recall what I was when alive unless I also remembered what I felt and therefore what I did; and I have no doubt that this remembrance will one day form the happiness of the good and the torment of the bad. In this world our inner consciousness is absorbed by the crowd of eager passions which cheat remorse. The humiliation and disgrace involved in the practice of virtue do not permit us to realise its charm. But when, freed from the illusions of the bodily senses, we behold with joy the supreme Being and the eternal truths which flow from him; when all the powers of our soul are alive to the beauty of order and we are wholly occupied in comparing what we have done with what we ought to have done, then it is that the voice of conscience will regain its strength and sway; then it is that the pure delight which springs from self-content, and the sharp regret for our own degradation of that self, will decide by means of overpowering feeling what shall be the fate which each has prepared for himself. My good friend, do not ask me whether there are other sources of happiness or suffering; I cannot tell; that which my fancy pictures is enough to console me in this life and to bid me look for a life to come. I do not say the good will be rewarded, for what greater good can a truly good being expect than to exist in accordance with his nature? But I do assert that the good will be happy, because their maker, the author of all justice, who has made them capable of feeling, has not made them that they may suffer; moreover, they have not abused their freedom upon earth and they have not changed their fate through any fault of their own; yet they have suffered in this life and it will be made up to them in the life to come. This feeling relies not so much on man's deserts as on the idea of good which seems to me inseparable from the divine essence. I only assume that the laws of order are constant and that God is true to himself.

Do not ask me whether the torments of the wicked will endure for ever, whether the goodness of their creator can condemn them to the eternal suffering; again, I cannot tell, and I have no empty curiosity for the investigation of useless problems. How does the fate of the wicked concern me? I take little interest in it. All the same I find it hard to believe that they will be condemned to everlasting torments. If the supreme justice calls for vengeance, it claims it in this life. The nations of the world with their errors are its ministers. Justice uses self-inflicted ills to punish the crimes which have deserved them. It is in your own insatiable souls, devoured by envy, greed, and ambition, it is in the midst of your false prosperity, that the avenging passions find the due reward of your crimes. What need to seek a hell in the future life? It is here in the breast of the wicked.

When our fleeting needs are over, and our mad desires are at rest, there should also be an end of our passions and our crimes. Can pure spirits be capable of any perversity? Having need of nothing, why should they be wicked? If they are free from our gross senses, if their happiness consists in the contemplation of other beings, they can only desire what is good; and he who ceases to be bad can never be miserable. This is what I am inclined to think though I have not been at the pains to come to any decision. O God, merciful and good, whatever thy decrees may be I adore them; if thou should t commit the wicked to everlasting punishment, I abandon my feeble reason to thy justice; but if the remorse of these wretched beings should in the course of time be extinguished, if their sufferings should come to an end, and if the same peace shall one day be the lot of all mankind, I give thanks to thee for this. Is not the wicked my brother? How often have I been tempted to be like him? Let him be delivered from his misery and freed from the spirit of hatred that accompanied it; let him be as happy as I myself; his happiness, far from arousing my jealousy, will only increase my own.

Thus it is that, in the contemplation of God in his works, and in the study of such of his attributes as it concerned me to know, I have slowly grasped and developed the idea, at first partial and imperfect, which I have formed of this Infinite Being. But if this idea has become nobler and greater it is also more suited to the human reason. As I approach in spirit the eternal light, I am confused and dazzled by its glory, and compelled to abandon all the earthly notions which helped me to picture it to myself. God is no longer corporeal and sensible; the supreme mind which rules the world is no longer the world itself; in vain do I strive to grasp his inconceivable essence. When I think that it is he that gives life and movement to the living and moving substance which controls all living bodies; when I hear it said that my soul is spiritual and that God is a spirit, I revolt against this abasement of the divine essence; as if God and my soul were of one and the same nature! As if God were not the one and only absolute being, the only really active, feeling, thinking, willing being, from whom we derive our thought, feeling, motion, will, our freedom and our very existence! We are free because he wills our freedom, and his inexplicable substance is to our souls what our souls are to our bodies. I know not whether he has created matter, body, soul, the world itself. The idea of creation confounds me and eludes my grasp; so far as I can conceive of it I believe it; but I know that he has formed the universe and all that is, that he has made and ordered all things. No doubt God is eternal; but can my mind grasp the idea of eternity? Why should I cheat myself with meaningless words? This is what I do understand; before things were—God was; he will be when they are no more, and if all things come to an end he will still endure. That a being beyond my comprehension should give life to other beings, this is merely difficult and beyond my understanding; but that Being and Nothing should be convertible terms, this is indeed a palpable contradiction, an evident absurdity.

God is intelligent, but how? Man is intelligent when he reasons, but the Supreme Intelligence does not need to reason; there is neither premise nor conclusion for him, there is not even a proposition. The Supreme Intelligence is wholly intuitive, it sees what is and what shall be; all truths are one for it, as all places are but one point and all time but one moment. Man's power makes use of means, the divine power is self-active. God can because he wills; his will is his power. God is good; this is certain; but man finds his happiness in the welfare of his kind, God's happiness consists in the love of order; for it is through order that he maintains what is, and unites each part in the whole. God is just; of this I am sure, it is a consequence of his goodness; man's injustice is not God's work, but his own; that moral justice which seems to the philosophers a presumption against Providence, is to me a proof of its existence. But man's justice consists in giving to each his due; God's justice consists in demanding from each of us an account of that which he has given us.

If I have succeeded in discerning these attributes of which I have no absolute idea, it is in the form of unavoidable deductions, and by the right use of my reason; but I affirm them without understanding them, and at bottom that is no affirmation at all. In vain do I say, God is thus, I feel it, I experience it, none the more do I understand how God can be thus.

In a word: the more I strive to envisage his infinite essence the less do I comprehend it; but it is, and that is enough for me; the less I understand, the more I adore. I abase myself, saying, " Being of beings, I am because thou art; to fix my thoughts on thee is to ascend to the source of my being. The best use I can make of my reason is to resign it before thee; my mind delights, my weakness rejoices, to feel myself overwhelmed by thy greatness."

Having thus deduced from the perception of objects of sense and from my inner consciousness, which leads me to judge of causes by my native reason, the principal truths which I require to know, I must now seek such principles of conduct as I can draw from them, and such rules as I must lay down for my guidance in the fulfilment of my destiny in this world, according to the purpose of my Maker. Still following the same method, I do not derive these rules from the principles of the higher philosophy, I find them in the depths of my heart, traced by nature in characters which nothing can efface. I need only consult myself with regard to what I wish to do; what I feel to be right is right, what I feel to be wrong is wrong; conscience is the best casuist; and it is only when we haggle with conscience that we have recourse to the subtleties of argument. Our first duty is towards ourself; yet how often does the voice of others tell us that in seeking our good at the expense of others we are doing ill? We think we are following the guidance of nature, and we are resisting it; we listen to what she says to our senses, and we neglect what she says to our heart; the active being obeys, the passive commands. Conscience is the voice of the soul, the passions are the voice of the body. It is strange that these voices often contradict each other? And then to which should we give heed? Too often does reason deceive us; we have only too good a right to doubt her; but conscience never deceives us; she is the true guide of man; it is to the soul what instinct is to the body; [1] he who obeys his conscience

---

[1] Modern philosophy, which only admits what it can understand, is careful not to admit this obscure power called instinct which seems to guide the animals to some end without any acquired experience. Instinct, according to some of our wise philosophers, is only a secret habit of reflection, acquired by reflection; and from the way in which they explain this development one ought to suppose that children reflect more than grown-up people: a paradox strange enough to be worth examining. Without entering upon this discussion I must ask what name I shall give to the eagerness with which my dog makes war on the moles he does not eat, or to the patience with which he sometimes watches them for hours and the skill with which he seizes them, throws them to a distance from their earth as soon as they emerge, and then kills them and leaves them. Yet no one has trained him to this sport, nor even told him there were such things as moles. Again, I ask, and this is a more important question, why, when I threatened this same dog for the first time, why did he throw himself on the ground with his paws folded, in such a suppliant attitude

is following nature and he need not fear that he will go astray. This is a matter of great importance, continued my benefactor, seeing that I was about to interrupt him; let me stop awhile to explain it more fully.

The morality of our actions consists entirely in the judgments we ourselves form with regard to them. If good is good, it must be good in the depth of our heart as well as in our actions; and the first reward of justice is the consciousness that we are acting justly. If moral goodness is in accordance with our nature, man can only be healthy in mind and body when he is good. If it is not so, and if man is by nature evil, he cannot cease to be evil without corrupting his nature, and goodness in him is a crime against nature. If he is made to do harm to his fellow-creatures, as the wolf is made to devour his prey, a humane man would be as depraved a creature as a pitiful wolf; and virtue alone would cause remorse.

My young friend, let us look within, let us set aside all personal prejudices and see wh the our inclinations lead us. Do we take more pleasure in the sight of the sufferings of others or their joys? Is it pleasanter to do a kind action or an unkind action, and which leaves the more delightful memory behind it? Why do you enjoy the theatre? Do you delight in the crimes you behold? Do you weep over the punishment which overtakes the criminal? They say we are indifferent to everything but self-interest; yet we find our consolation in our sufferings in the charms of friendship and humanity, and even in our pleasures we should be too lonely and miserable if we had no one to share them with us. If there is no such thing as morality in man's heart, what is the source of his rapturous admiration of noble deeds, his passionate devotion to great men? What connection is there between self-interest and this enthusiasm for virtue? Why should I choose to be Cato dying by his own hand, rather than Cæsar in his triumphs? Take from our hearts this love of what is noble and you rob us of the joy of life. The mean-spirited man in whom these delicious feelings have been stifled among vile passions, who by thinking of no one but himself comes at last to love no one but himself, this man feels no raptures, his cold heart no longer throbs with joy, and his eyes no longer fill with the sweet tears of sympathy, he delights in nothing; the wretch has neither life nor feeling, he is already dead.

There are many bad men in this world, but there are few of these

calculated to touch me, a position which he would have maintained if, without being touched by it, I had continued to beat him in that position? What! Had my dog, little more than a puppy, acquired moral ideas? Did he know the meaning of mercy and generosity? By what acquired knowledge did he seek to appease my wrath by yielding to my discretion? Every dog in the world does almost the same thing in similar circumstances, and I am asserting nothing but what any one can verify for himself. Will the philosophers, who so scornfully reject instinct, kindly explain this fact by the mere play of sensations and experience which they assume we have acquired? Let them give an account of it which will satisfy any sensible man; in that case I have nothing further to urge, and I will say no more of instinct.

dead souls, alive only to self-interest, and insensible to all that is right and good. We only delight in injustice so long as it is to our own advantage; in every other case we wish the innocent to be protected. If we see some act of violence or injustice in town or country, our hearts are at once stirred to their depths by an instinctive anger and wrath, which bids us go to the help of the oppressed; but we are restrained by a stronger duty, and the law deprives us of our right to protect the innocent. On the other hand, if some deed of mercy or generosity meets our eye, what reverence and love does it inspire! Do we not say to ourselves, " I should like to have done that myself " ? What does it matter to us that two thousand years ago a man was just or unjust? and yet we take the same interest in ancient history as if it happened yesterday. What are the crimes of Cataline to me? I shall not be his victim. Why then have I the same horror of his crimes as if he were living now? We do not hate the wicked merely because of the harm they do to ourselves, but because they are wicked. Not only do we wish to be happy ourselves, we wish others to be happy too, and if this happiness does not interfere with our own happiness, it increases it. In conclusion, whether we will or not, we pity the unfortunate; when we see their suffering we suffer too. Even the most depraved are not wholly without this instinct, and it often leads them to self-contradiction. The highwayman who robs the traveller, clothes the nakedness of the poor; the fiercest murderer supports a fainting man.

Men speak of the voice of remorse, the secret punishment of hidden crimes, by which such are often brought to light. Alas! who does not know its unwelcome voice? We speak from experience, and we would gladly stifle this imperious feeling which causes us such agony. Let us obey the call of nature; we shall see that her yoke is easy and that when we give heed to her voice we find a joy in the answer of a good conscience. The wicked fears and flees from her; he delights to escape from himself; his anxious eyes look around him for some object of dive sion; without bitter satire and rude mockery he would always be sorrowful; the scornful laugh is his one pleasure. Not so the just man, who finds his peace within himself; there is joy not malice in his laughter, a joy which springs from his own heart; he is as cheerful alone as in company, his satisfaction does not depend on those who approach him; it includes them.

Cast your eyes over every nation of the world; peruse every volume of its history; in the midst of all these strange and cruel forms of worship, among this amazing variety of manners and customs, you will everywhere find the same ideas of right and justice; everywhere the same principles of morality, the same ideas of good and evil. The old paganism gave birth to abominable gods who would have been punished as scoundrels here below, gods who merely offered, as a picture of supreme happiness, crimes to be committed and lust to be gratified. But in vain did vice descend from the abode of the gods armed with their sacred authority; the moral instinct refused to admit it into the heart of man. While the debaucheries of Jupiter were celebrated, the continence of Xenocrates was revered; the chaste Lucrece adored the shameless Venus; the bold Roman offered sacrifices to Fear; he invoked the god who mutilated his father, and he died without a murmur at the hand of his own father. The most unworthy gods were worshipped by the noblest men. The sacred voice of nature was stronger than the voice of the gods, and won reverence upon earth; it seemed to relegate guilt and the guilty alike to heaven.

There is therefore at the bottom of our hearts an innate principle of justice and virtue, by which, in spite of our maxims, we judge our own actions or those of others to be good or evil; and it is this principle that I call conscience.

But at this word I hear the murmurs of all the wise men so-called. Childish errors, prejudices of our upbringing, they exclaim in concert! There is nothing in the human mind but what it has gained by experience; and we judge everything solely by means of the ideas we have acquired. They go further; they even venture to reject the clear and universal agreement of all peoples, and to set against this striking unanimity in the judgment of mankind, they seek out some obscure exception known to themselves alone; as if the whole trend of nature were rendered null by the depravity of a single nation, and as if the existence of monstrosities made an end of species. But to what purpose does the sceptic Montaigne strive himself to unearth in some obscure corner of the world a custom which is contrary to the ideas of justice? To what purpose does he credit the most untrustworthy travellers, while he refuses to believe the greatest writers? A few strange and doubtful customs, based on local causes, unknown to us; shall these destroy a general inference based on the agreement of all the nations of the earth, differing from each other in all else, but agreed in this? O Montaigne, you pride yourself on your truth and honesty; be sincere and truthful, if a philosopher can be so, and tell me if there is any country upon earth where it is a crime to keep one's plighted word, to be merciful, helpful, and generous, where the good man is scorned, and the traitor is held in honour.

Self-interest, so they say, induces each of us to agree for the common good. But how is it that the good man consents to this to his own hurt? Does a man go to death from self-interest? No doubt each man acts for his own good, but if there is no such thing as moral good to be taken into consideration, self-interest will only enable you to account for the deeds of the wicked; possibly you will not attempt to do more. A philosophy which could find no place for good deeds would be too detestable; you would find yourself compelled either to find some mean purpose, some wicked motive, or to abuse Socrates and slander Regulus. If such doctrines ever took root among us, the voice of nature, together with the voice of reason, would constantly protest against them, till no adherent

of such teaching could plead an honest excuse for his parti-
sanship.

It is no part of my scheme to enter at present into metaphysical
discussions which neither you nor I can understand, discussions
which really lead nowhere. I have told you already that I do not
wish to philosophise with you, but to help you to consult your own
heart. If all the philosophers in the world should prove that I am
wrong, and you feel that I am right, that is all I ask.

For this purpose it is enough to lead you to distinguish between
our acquired ideas and our natural feelings; for feeling precedes
knowledge; and since we do not learn to seek what is good for us
and avoid what is bad for us, but get this desire from nature, in
the same way the love of good and the hatred of evil are as natural
to us as our self-love. The decrees of conscience are not judgments
but feelings. Although all our ideas come from without, the feelings
by which they are weighed are within us, and it is by these feelings
alone that we perceive fitness or unfitness of things in relation
to ourselves, which leads us to seek or shun these things.

To exist is to feel; our feeling is undoubtedly earlier than our
intelligence, and we had feelings before we had ideas.[1] Whatever
may be the cause of our being, it has provided for our preservation
by giving us feelings suited to our nature; and no one can deny
that these at least are innate. These feelings, so far as the individual
is concerned, are self-love, fear, pain, the dread of death, the desire
for comfort. Again, if, as it is impossible to doubt, man is by nature
sociable, or at least fitted to become sociable, he can only be so by
means of other innate feelings, relative to his kind; for if only
physical well-being were considered, men would certainly be scattered
rather than brought together. But the motive power of conscience
is derived from the moral system formed through this twofold
relation to himself and to his fellow-men. To know good is not to
love it; this knowledge is not innate in man; but as soon as his
reason leads him to perceive it, his conscience impels him to love it;
it is this feeling which is innate.

So I do not think, my young friend, that it is impossible to explain
the immediate force of conscience as a result of our own nature,
independent of reason itself. And even should it be impossible,
it is unnecessary; for those who deny this principle, admitted and
received by everybody else in the world, do not prove that there is
no such thing; they are content to affirm, and when we affirm its
existence we have quite as good grounds as they, while we have

---

[1] In some respects ideas are feelings and feelings are ideas. Both terms
are appropriate to any perception with which we are concerned, appropriate both to the object of that perception and to ourselves who are
affected by it; it is merely the order in which we are affected which decides
the appropriate term. When we are chiefly concerned with the object
and only think of ourselves as it were by reflection, that is an idea; when,
on the other hand, the impression received excites our chief attention
and we only think in the second place of the object which caused it, it is
a feeling.

moreover the witness within us, the voice of conscience, which speaks on its own behalf. If the first beams of judgment dazzle us and confuse the objects we behold, let us wait till our feeble sight grows clear and strong, and in the light of reason we shall soon behold these very objects as nature has already showed them to us. Or rather let us be simpler and less pretentious; let us be content with the first feelings we experience in ourselves, since science always brings us back to these, unless it has led us astray.

Conscience! Conscience! Divine instinct, immortal voice from heaven; sure guide for a creature ignorant and finite indeed, yet intelligent and free; infallible judge of good and evil, making man like to God! In thee consists the excellence of man's nature and the morality of his actions; apart from thee, I find nothing in myself to raise me above the beasts—nothing but the sad privilege of wandering from one error to another, by the help of an unbridled understanding and a reason which knows no principle.

Thank heaven we have now got rid of all that alarming show of philosophy; we may be men without being scholars; now that we need not spend our life in the study of morality, we have found a less costly and surer guide through this vast labyrinth of human thought. But it is not enough to be aware that there is such a guide; we must know her and follow her. If she speaks to all hearts, how is it that so few give heed to her voice? She speaks to us in the language of nature, and everything leads us to forget that tongue. Conscience is timid, she loves peace and retirement; she is startled by noise and numbers; the prejudices from which she is said to arise are her worst enemies. She flees before them or she is silent; their noisy voices drown her words, so that she cannot get a hearing; fanaticism dares to counterfeit her voice and to inspire crimes in her name. She is discouraged by ill-treatment; she no longer speaks to us, no longer answers to our call; when she has been scorned so long, it is as hard to recall her as it was to banish her.

How often in the course of my inquiries have I grown weary of my own coldness of heart! How often have grief and weariness poured their poison into my first meditations and made them hateful to me! My barren heart yielded nothing but a feeble zeal and a lukewarm love of truth. I said to myself: Why should I strive to find what does not exist? Moral good is a dream, the pleasures of sense are the only real good. When once we have lost the taste for the pleasures of the soul, how hard it is to recover it! How much more difficult to acquire it if we have never possessed it! If there were any man so wretched as never to have done anything all his life long which he could remember with pleasure, and which would make him glad to have lived, that man would be incapable of self-knowledge, and for want of knowledge of goodness, of which his nature is capable, he would be constrained to remain in his wickedness and would be for ever miserable. But do you think there is any one man upon earth so depraved that he has never yielded to the temptation of well-doing? This temptation is so natural, so pleasant, that it is impossible always to resist it; and the thought of the pleasure it has once afforded is enough to recall it constantly to our memory. Unluckily it is hard at first to find satisfaction for it; we have any number of reasons for refusing to follow the inclinations of our heart; prudence, so called, restricts the heart within the limits of the self; a thousand efforts are needed to break these bonds. The joy of well-doing is the prize of having done well, and we must deserve the prize before we win it. There is nothing sweeter than virtue; but we do not know this till we have tried it. Like Proteus in the fable, she first assumes a thousand terrible shapes when we would embrace her, and only shows her true self to those who refuse to let her go.

Ever at strife between my natural feelings, which spoke of the common weal, and my reason, which spoke of self, I should have drifted through life in perpetual uncertainty, hating evil, loving good, and always at war with myself, if my heart had not received further light, if that truth which determined my opinions had not also settled my conduct, and set me at peace with myself. Reason alone is not a sufficient foundation for virtue; what solid ground can be found? Virtue we are told is love of order. But can this love prevail over my love for my own well-being, and ought it so to prevail? Let them give me clear and sufficient reason for this preference. Their so-called principle is in truth a mere playing with words: for I also say that vice is love of order, differently understood. Wherever there is feeling and intelligence, there is some sort of moral order. The difference is this: the good man orders his life with regard to all men; the wicked orders it for self alone. The latter centres all things round himself; the other measures his radius and remains on the circumference. Thus his place depends on the common centre, which is God, and on all the concentric circles which are His creatures. If there is no God, the wicked is right and the good man is nothing but a fool.

My child! May you one day feel what a burden is removed when, having fathomed the vanity of human thoughts and tasted the bitterness of passion, you find at length near at hand the path of wisdom, the prize of this life's labours, the source of that happiness which you despaired of. Every duty of natural law, which man's injustice had almost effaced from my heart, is engraven there, for the second time in the name of that eternal justice which lays these duties upon me and beholds my fulfilment of them. I feel myself merely the instrument of the Omnipotent, who wills what is good, who performs it, who will bring about my own good through the co-operation of my will with his own, and by the right use of my liberty. I acquiesce in the order he establishes, certain that one day I shall enjoy that order and find my happiness in it; for what sweeter joy is there than this, to feel oneself a part of a system where all is good? A prey to pain, I bear it in patience, remembering that it will soon be over, and that it results from a body which is not mine. If I do a good deed in secret, I know that it is seen, and my conduct in this life is a pledge of the life to come. When I suffer injustice, I say to myself, the Almighty who does all things well will reward me: my bodily needs, my poverty, make the idea of death less intolerable. There will be all the fewer bonds to be broken when my hour comes.

Why is my soul subjected to my senses, and imprisoned in this body by which it is enslaved and thwarted? I know not; have I entered into the counsels of the Almighty? But I may, without rashness, venture on a modest conjecture. I say to myself: If man's soul had remained in a state of freedom and innocence, what merit would there have been in loving and obeying the order he found established, an order which it would not have been to his advantage to disturb? He would be happy, no doubt, but his happiness would not attain to the highest point, the pride of virtue, and the witness of a good conscience within him; he would be but as the angels are, and no doubt the good man will be more than they. Bound to a mortal body, by bonds as strange as they are powerful, his care for the preservation of this body tempts the soul to think only of self, and gives it an interest opposed to the general order of things, which it is still capable of knowing and loving; then it is that the right use of his freedom becomes at once the merit and the reward; then it is that it prepares for itself unending happiness, by resisting its earthly passions and following its original direction.

If even in the lowly position in which we are placed during our present life our first impulses are always good, if all our vices are of our own making, why should we complain that they are our masters? Why should we blame the Creator for the ills we have ourselves created, and the enemies we ourselves have armed against us? Oh, let us leave man unspoilt; he will always find it easy to be good and he will always be happy without remorse. The guilty, who assert that they are driven to crime, are liars as well as evil-doers; how is it that they fail to perceive that the weakness they bewail is of their own making; that their earliest depravity was the result of their own will; that by dint of wishing to yield to temptations, they at length yield to them whether they will or no and make them irresistible? No doubt they can no longer avoid being weak and wicked, but they need not have become weak and wicked. Oh, how easy would it be to preserve control of ourselves and of our passions, even in this life, if with habits still unformed, with a mind beginning to expand, we were able to keep to such things as we ought to know, in order to value rightly what is unknown; if we really wished to learn, not that we might shine before the eyes of others, but that we might be wise and good in accordance with our nature, that we might be happy in the performance of our duty. This study seems tedious and painful to us, for we do not attempt it till we are already corrupted by vice and enslaved by our passions. Our judgments and our standards of worth are determined before we have the knowledge of good and evil; and then we measure all things by this false standard, and give nothing its true worth.

There is an age when the heart is still free, but eager, unquiet, greedy of a happiness which is still unknown, a happiness which it seeks in curiosity and doubt; deceived by the senses it settles at length upon the empty show of happiness and thinks it has found it where it is not. In my own case these illusions endured for a long time. Alas! too late did I become aware of them, and I have not succeeded in overcoming them altogether; they will last as long as this mortal body from which they arise. If they lead me astray, I am at least no longer deceived by them; I know them for what they are, and even when I give way to them, I despise myself; far from regarding them as the goal of my happiness, I behold in them an obstacle to it. I long for the time when, freed from the fetters of the body, I shall be myself, at one with myself, no longer torn in two, when I myself shall suffice for my own happiness. Meanwhile I am happy even in this life, for I make small account of all its evils, in which I regard myself as having little or no part, while all the real good that I can get out of this life depends on myself alone.

To raise myself so far as may be even now to this state of happiness, strength, and freedom, I exercise myself in lofty contemplation. I consider the order of the universe, not to explain it by any futile system, but to revere it without ceasing, to adore the wise Author who reveals himself in it. I hold intercourse with him; I immerse all my powers in his divine essence; I am overwhelmed by his kindness, I bless him and his gifts, but I do not pray to him. What should I ask of him—to change the order of nature, to work miracles on my behalf? Should I, who am bound to love above all things the order which he has established in his wisdom and maintained by his providence, should I desire the disturbance of that order on my own account? No, that rash prayer would deserve to be punished rather than to be granted. Neither do I ask of him the power to do right; why should I ask what he has given me already? Has he not given me conscience that I may love the right, reason that I may perceive it, and freedom that I may choose it? If I do evil, I have no excuse; I do it of my own free will; to ask him to change my will is to ask him to do what he asks of me; it is to want him to do the work while I get the wages; to be dissatisfied with my lot is to wish to be no longer a man, to wish to be other than what I am, to wish for disorder and evil. Thou source of justice and truth, merciful and gracious God, in thee do I trust, and the desire of my heart is—Thy will be done. When I unite my will with thine, I do what thou doest; I have a share in thy goodness; I believe that I enjoy beforehand the supreme happiness which is the reward of goodness.

In my well-founded self-distrust the only thing that I ask of God, or rather expect from his justice, is to correct my error if I go astray, if that error is dangerous to me. To be honest I need not think myself infallible; my opinions, which seem to me true, may be so many lies; for what man is there who does not cling to his own beliefs; and how many men are agreed in everything? The illusion which deceives me may indeed have its source in myself, but it is God alone who can remove it. I have done all I can to attain to truth; but its source is beyond my reach; is it my fault if my strength fails me and I can go no further; it is for Truth to draw near to me.

The good priest had spoken with passion; he and I were overcome with emotion. It seemed to me as if I were listening to the divine Orpheus when he sang the earliest hymns and taught men the worship of the gods. I saw any number of objections which might be raised; yet I raised none, for I perceived that they were more perplexing than serious, and that my inclination took his part. When he spoke to me according to his conscience, my own seemed to confirm what he said.

"The novelty of the sentiments you have made known to me," said I, "strikes me all the more because of what you confess you do not know, than because of what you say you believe. They seem to be very like that theism or natural religion, which Christians profess to confound with atheism or irreligion which is their exact opposite. But in the present state of my faith I should have to ascend rather than descend to accept your views, and I find it difficult to remain just where you are unless I were as wise as you. That I may be at least as honest, I want time to take counsel with myself. By your own showing, the inner voice must be my guide, and you have yourself told me that when it has long been silenced it cannot be recalled in a moment. I take what you have said to heart, and I must consider it. If after I have thought things out, I am as convinced as you are, you will be my final teacher, and I will be your disciple till death. Continue your teaching however; you have only told me half what I must know. Speak to me of revelation, of the Scriptures, of those difficult doctrines among which I have strayed ever since I was a child, incapable either of understanding or believing them, unable to adopt or reject them."

"Yes, my child," said he, embracing me, "I will tell you all I think; I will not open my heart to you by halves; but the desire you express was necessary before I could cast aside all reserve. So far I have told you nothing but what I thought would be of service to you, nothing but what I was quite convinced of. The inquiry which remains to be made is very difficult. It seems to me full of perplexity, mystery, and darkness; I bring to it only doubt and distrust. I make up my mind with trembling, and I tell you my doubts rather than my convictions. If your own opinions were more settled I should hesitate to show you mine; but in your present condition, to think like me would be gain.[1] Moreover, give to my words only the authority of reason; I know not whether I am

[1] I think the worthy clergyman might say this at the present time to the general public.

mistaken. It is difficult in discussion to avoid assuming sometimes a dogmatic tone; but remember in this respect that all my assertions are but reasons to doubt me. Seek truth for yourself, for my own part I only promise you sincerity.

"In my exposition you find nothing but natural religion; strange that we should need more! How shall I become aware of this need? What guilt can be mine so long as I serve God according to the knowledge he has given to my mind, and the feelings he has put into my heart? What purity of morals, what dogma useful to man and worthy of its author, can I derive from a positive doctrine which cannot be derived without the aid of this doctrine by the right use of my faculties? Show me what you can add to the duties of the natural law, for the glory of God, for the good of mankind, and for my own welfare; and what virtue you will get from the new form of religion which does not result from mine. The grandest ideas of the Divine nature come to us from reason only. Behold the spectacle of nature; listen to the inner voice. Has not God spoken it all to our eyes, to our conscience, to our reason? What more can man tell us? Their revelations do but degrade God, by investing him with passions like our own. Far from throwing light upon the ideas of the Supreme Being, special doctrines seem to me to confuse these ideas; far from ennobling them, they degrade them; to the inconceivable mysteries which surround the Almighty, they add absurd contradictions, they make man proud, intolerant, and cruel; instead of bringing peace upon earth, they bring fire and sword. I ask myself what is the use of it all, and I find no answer. I see nothing but the crimes of men and the misery of mankind.

"They tell me a revelation was required to teach men how God would be served; as a proof of this they point to the many strange rites which men have instituted, and they do not perceive that this very diversity springs from the fanciful nature of the revelations. As soon as the nations took to making God speak, every one made him speak in his own fashion, and made him say what he himself wanted. Had they listened only to what God says in the heart of man, there would have been but one religion upon earth.

"One form of worship was required; just so, but was this a matter of such importance as to require all the power of the Godhead to establish it? Do not let us confuse the outward forms of religion with religion itself. The service God requires is of the heart; and when the heart is sincere that is ever the same. It is a strange sort of conceit which fancies that God takes such an interest in the shape of the priest's vestments, the form of words he utters, the gestures he makes before the altar and all his genuflections. Oh, my friend, stand upright, you will still be too near the earth. God desires to be worshipped in spirit and in truth; this duty belongs to every religion, every country, every individual. As to the form of worship, if order demands uniformity, that is only a matter of discipline and needs no revelation.

"These thoughts did not come to me to begin with. Carried

away by the prejudices of my education, and by that dangerous
vanity which always strives to lift man out of his proper sphere,
when I could not raise my feeble thoughts up to the great Being,
I tried to bring him down to my own level. I tried to reduce the
distance he has placed between his nature and mine. I desired
more immediate relations, more individual instruction; not content
to make God in the image of man that I might be favoured above
my fellows, I desired supernatural knowledge; I required a special
form of worship; I wanted God to tell me what he had not told
others, or what others had not understood like myself.

"Considering the point I had now reached as the common centre
from which all believers set out on the quest for a more enlightened
form of religion, I merely found in natural religion the elements of
all religion. I beheld the multitude of diverse sects which hold
sway upon earth, each of which accuses the other of falsehood and
error; which of these, I asked, is the right? Every one replied,
'My own;' every one said, 'I alone and those who agree with
me think rightly, all the others are mistaken.' And how do you
know that your sect is in the right? Because God said so. And
how do you know God said so?[1] And who told you that God
said it? My pastor, who knows all about it. My pastor tells me
what to believe and I believe it; he assures me that any one who
says anything else is mistaken, and I give no heed to them.

"What! thought I, is not truth one; can that which is true for
me be false for you? If those who follow the right path and those
who go astray have the same method, what merit or what blame
can be assigned to one more than to the other? Their choice is the
result of chance; it is unjust to hold them responsible for it, to
reward or punish them for being born in one country or another.
To dare to say that God judges us in this manner is an outrage on
his justice.

"Either all religions are good and pleasing to God, or if there is
one which he prescribes for men, if they will be punished for
despising it, he will have distinguished it by plain and certain signs
by which it can be known as the only true religion; these signs are
alike in every time and place, equally plain to all men, great or small,

---

[1] "All men," said a wise and good priest, "maintain that they hold
and believe their religion (and all use the same jargon), not of man, nor of
any creature, but of God. But to speak truly, without pretence or flattery,
none of them do so; whatever they may say, religions are taught by human
hands and means; take, for example, the way in which religions have been
received by the world, the way in which they are still received every day
by individuals; the nation, the country, the locality gives the religion;
we belong to the religion of the place where we are born and brought up;
we are baptised or circumcised, we are Christians, Jews, Mahometans,
before we know that we are men; we do not pick and choose our religion;
for see how ill the life and conduct agree with the religion, see for what
slight and human causes men go against the teaching of their religion."—
CHARRON, De la Sagesse.

It seems clear that the honest creed of the holy theologian of Condom
would not have differed greatly from that of the Savoyard priest.

learned or unlearned, Europeans, Indians, Africans, savages. If there were but one religion upon earth, and if all beyond its pale were condemned to eternal punishment, and if there were in any corner of the world one single honest man who was not convinced by this evidence, the God of that religion would be the most unjust and cruel of tyrants.

"Let us therefore seek honestly after truth; let us yield nothing to the claims of birth, to the authority of parents and pastors, but let us summon to the bar of conscience and of reason all that they have taught us from our childhood. In vain do they exclaim, 'Submit your reason;' a deceiver might say as much; I must have reasons for submitting my reason.

"All the theology I can get for myself by observation of the universe and by the use of my faculties is contained in what I have already told you. To know more one must have recourse to strange means. These means cannot be the authority of men, for every man is of the same species as myself, and all that a man knows by nature I am capable of knowing, and another may be deceived as much as I; when I believe what he says, it is not because he says it but because he proves its truth. The witness of man is therefore nothing more than the witness of my own reason, and it adds nothing to the natural means which God has given me for the knowledge of truth.

"Apostle of truth, what have you to tell me of which I am not the sole judge? God himself has spoken; give heed to his revelation. That is another matter. God has spoken, these are indeed words which demand attention. To whom has he spoken? He has spoken to men. Why then have I heard nothing? He has instructed others to make known his words to you. I understand; it is men who come and tell me what God has said. I would rather have heard the words of God himself; it would have been as easy for him and I should have been secure from fraud. He protects you from fraud by showing that his envoys come from him. How does he show this? By miracles. Where are these miracles? In the books. And who wrote the books? Men. And who saw the miracles? The men who bear witness to them. What! Nothing but human testimony! Nothing but men who tell me what others told them! How many men between God and me! Let us see, however, let us examine, compare, and verify. Oh! if God had but deigned to free me from all this labour, I would have served him with all my heart.

"Consider, my friend, the terrible controversy in which I am now engaged; what vast learning is required to go back to the remotest antiquity, to examine, weigh, confront prophecies, revelations, facts, all the monuments of faith set forth throughout the world, to assign their date, place, authorship, and occasion. What exactness of critical judgment is needed to distinguish genuine documents from forgeries, to compare objections with their answers, translations with their originals; to decide as to the impartiality of witnesses, their common-sense, their knowledge; to make sure that nothing has been omitted, nothing added, nothing transposed, altered, or falsified; to point out any remaining contradictions, to determine what weight should be given to the silence of our adversaries with regard to the charges brought against them; how far were they aware of those charges; did they think them sufficiently serious to require an answer; were books sufficiently well known for our books to reach them; have we been honest enough to allow their books to circulate among ourselves and to leave their strongest objections unaltered?

"When the authenticity of all these documents is accepted, we must now pass to the evidence of their authors' mission; we must know the laws of chance, and probability, to decide which prophecy cannot be fulfilled without a miracle; we must know the spirit of the original languages, to distinguish between prophecy and figures of speech; we must know what facts are in accordance with nature and what facts are not, so that we may say how far a clever man may deceive the eyes of the simple and may even astonish the learned; we must discover what are the characteristics of a prodigy and how its authenticity may be established, not only so far as to gain credence, but so that doubt may be deserving of punishment; we must compare the evidence for true and false miracles, and find sure tests to distinguish between them; lastly we must say why God chose as a witness to his words means which themselves require so much evidence on their behalf, as if he were playing with human credulity, and avoiding of set purpose the true means of persuasion.

"Assuming that the divine majesty condescends so far as to make a man the channel of his sacred will, is it reasonable, is it fair, to demand that the whole of mankind should obey the voice of this minister without making him known as such? Is it just to give him as his sole credentials certain private signs, performed in the presence of a few obscure persons, signs which everybody else can only know by hearsay? If one were to believe all the miracles that the uneducated and credulous profess to have seen in every country upon earth, every sect would be in the right; there would be more miracles than ordinary events; and it would be the greatest miracle if there were no miracles wherever there were persecuted fanatics. The unchangeable order of nature is the chief witness to the wise hand that guides it; if there were many exceptions, I should hardly know what to think; for my own part I have too great a faith in God to believe in so many miracles which are so little worthy of him.

"Let a man come and say to us: Mortals, I proclaim to you the will of the Most Highest; accept my words as those of him who has sent me; I bid the sun to change his course, the stars to range themselves in a fresh order, the high places to become smooth, the floods to rise up, the earth to change her face. By these miracles who will not recognise the master of nature? She does not obey impostors, their miracles are wrought in holes and corners, in deserts, within closed doors, where they find easy dupes among a small company of spectators already disposed to believe them. Who will venture to tell me how many eye-witnesses are required to make a miracle credible? What use are your miracles, performed if proof of your doctrine, if they themselves require so much proof? You might as well have let them alone.

"There still remains the most important inquiry of all with regard to the doctrine proclaimed; for since those who tell us God works miracles in this world, profess that the devil sometimes imitates them, when we have found the best attested miracles we have got very little further; and since the magicians of Pharaoh dared in the presence of Moses to counterfeit the very signs he wrought at God's command, why should they not, behind his back, claim a like authority? So when we have proved our doctrine by means of miracles, we must prove our miracles by means of doctrine,[1] for fear lest we should take the devil's doings for the handiwork of God. What think you of this dilemma?

"This doctrine, if it comes from God, should bear the sacred stamp of the godhead; not only should it illumine the troubled thoughts which reason imprints on our minds, but it should also offer us a form of worship, a morality, and rules of conduct in accordance with the attributes by means of which we alone conceive of God's essence. If then it teaches us what is absurd and unreasonable, if it inspires us with feelings of aversion for our fellows and terror for ourselves, if it paints us a God, angry, jealous, revengeful, partial, hating men, a God of war and battles, ever ready to strike and to destroy, ever speaking of punishment and torment, boasting even of the punishment of the innocent, my heart would not be drawn towards this terrible God, I would take good care not to quit the realm of natural religion to embrace such a religion as that; for you see plainly I must choose between them. Your God is not ours. He who begins

---

[1] This is expressly stated in many passages of Scripture, among others in Deuteronomy xiii., where it is said that when a prophet preaching strange gods confirms his words by means of miracles and what he foretells comes to pass, far from giving heed to him, this prophet must be put to death. If then the heathen put the apostles to death when they preached a strange god and confirmed their words by miracles which came to pass, I cannot see what grounds we have for complaint which they could not at once turn against us. Now, what should be done in such a case? There is only one course; to return to argument and let the miracles alone. It would have been better not to have had recourse to them at all. That is plain common-sense which can only be obscured by great subtlety of distinction. Subtleties in Christianity! So Jesus Christ was mistaken when he promised the kingdom of heaven to the simple, he was mistaken when he began his finest discourse with the praise of the poor in spirit, if so much wit is needed to understand his teaching and to get others to believe in him. When you have convinced me that submission is my duty, all will be well; but to convince me of this, come down to my level; adapt your arguments to a lowly mind, or I shall not recognise you as a true disciple of your master, and it is not his doctrine that you are teaching me.

by selecting a chosen people, and proscribing the rest of mankind, is not our common father; he who consigns to eternal punishment the greater part of his creatures, is not the merciful and gracious God revealed to me by my reason.

" Reason tells me that dogmas should be plain, clear, and striking in their simplicity.   If there is something lacking in natural religion, it is with respect to the obscurity in which it leaves the great truths it teaches; revelation should teach us these truths in a way which the mind of man can understand; it should bring them within his reach, make him comprehend them, so that he may believe them. Faith is confirmed and strengthened by understanding; the best religion is of necessity the simplest.   He who hides beneath mysteries and contradictions the religion that he preaches to me, teaches me at the same time to distrust that religion.   The God whom I adore is not the God of darkness, he has not given me understanding in order to forbid me to use it; to tell me to submit my reason is to insult the giver of reason.   The minister of truth does not tyrannise over my reason, he enlightens it.

" We have set aside all human authority, and without it I do not see how any man can convince another by preaching a doctrine contrary to reason.   Let them fight it out, and let us see what they have to say with that harshness of speech which is common to both.

" *Inspiration.* Reason tells you that the whole is greater than the part; but I tell you, in God's name, that the part is greater than the whole.

" *Reason.* And who are you to dare to tell me that God contradicts himself?   And which shall I choose to believe, God who teaches me, through my reason, the eternal truth, or you who, in his name, proclaim an absurdity?

" *Inspiration.* Believe me, for my teaching is more positive; and I will prove to you beyond all manner of doubt that he has sent me.

" *Reason.* What! you will convince me that God has sent you to bear witness against himself?   What sort of proofs will you adduce to convince me that God speaks more surely by your mouth than through the understanding he has given me?

" *Inspiration.* The understanding he has given you!   Petty, conceited creature!   As if you were the first impious person who had been led astray through his reason corrupted by sin.

" *Reason.* Man of God, you would not be the first scoundrel who asserts his arrogance as a proof of his mission.

" *Inspiration.* What! do even philosophers call names?

" *Reason.* Sometimes, when the saints set them the example.

" *Inspiration.* Oh, but I have a right to do it, for I am speaking on God's behalf.

" *Reason.* You would do well to show your credentials before you make use of your privileges.

" *Inspiration.* My credentials are authentic, earth and heaven will bear witness on my behalf.   Follow my arguments carefully, if you please.

"*Reason.* Your arguments! You forget what you are saying. When you teach me that my reason misleads me, do you not refute what it might have said on your behalf? He who denies the right of reason, must convince me without recourse to her aid. For suppose you have convinced me by reason, how am I to know that it is not my reason, corrupted by sin, which makes me accept what you say? Besides, what proof, what demonstration, can you advance, more self-evident than the axiom it is to destroy? It is more credible that a good syllogism is a lie, than that the part is greater than the whole.

"*Inspiration.* What a difference! There is no answer to my evidence; it is of a supernatural kind.

"*Reason.* Supernatural! What do you mean by the word? I do not understand it.

"*Inspiration.* I mean changes in the order of nature, prophecies, signs, and wonders of every kind.

"*Reason.* Signs and wonders! I have never seen anything of the kind.

"*Inspiration.* Others have seen them for you. Clouds of witnesses —the witness of whole nations. . . .

"*Reason.* Is the witness of nations supernatural?

"*Inspiration.* No; but when it is unanimous, it is incontestable.

"*Reason.* There is nothing so incontestable as the principles of reason, and one cannot accept an absurdity on human evidence. Once more, let us see your supernatural evidence, for the consent of mankind is not supernatural.

"*Inspiration.* Oh, hardened heart, grace does not speak to you.

"*Reason.* That is not my fault; for by your own showing, one must have already received grace before one is able to ask for it. Begin by speaking to me in its stead.

"*Inspiration.* But that is just what I am doing, and you will not listen. But what do you say to prophecy?

"*Reason.* In the first place, I say I have no more heard a prophet than I have seen a miracle. In the next, I say that no prophet could claim authority over me.

"*Inspiration.* Follower of the devil! Why should not the words of the prophets have authority over you?

"*Reason.* Because three things are required, three things which will never happen: firstly, I must have heard the prophecy; secondly, I must have seen its fulfilment; and thirdly, it must be clearly proved that the fulfilment of the prophecy could not by any possibility have been a mere coincidence; for even if it was as precise, as plain, and clear as an axiom of geometry, since the clearness of a chance prediction does not make its fulfilment impossible, this fulfilment when it does take place does not, strictly speaking, prove what was foretold.

"See what your so-called supernatural proofs, your miracles, your prophecies come to: believe all this upon the word of another, submit to the authority of men the authority of God which speaks to my reason. If the eternal truths which my mind conceives of could suffer any shock, there would be no sort of certainty for me; and far from being sure that you speak to me on God's behalf, I should not even be sure that there is a God.

"My child, here are difficulties enough, but these are not all. Among so many religions, mutually excluding and proscribing each other, one only is true, if indeed any one of them is true. To recognise the true religion we must inquire into, not one, but all; and in any question whatsoever we have no right to condemn unheard.[1] The objections must be compared with the evidence; we must know what accusation each brings against the other, and what answers they receive. The plainer any feeling appears to us, the more we must try to discover why so many other people refuse to accept it. We should be simple, indeed, if we thought it enough to hear the doctors on our own side, in order to acquaint ourselves with the arguments of the other. Where can you find theologians who pride themselves on their honesty? Where are those who, to refute the arguments of their opponents, do not begin by making out that they are of little importance? A man may make a good show among his own friends, and be very proud of his arguments, who would cut a very poor figure with those same arguments among those who are on the other side. Would you find out for yourself from books? What learning you will need! What languages you must learn; what libraries you must ransack; what an amount of reading must be got through! Who will guide me in such a choice? It will be hard to find the best books on the opposite side in any one country, and all the harder to find those on all sides; when found they would be easily answered. The absent are always in the wrong, and bad arguments boldly asserted easily efface good arguments put forward with scorn. Besides books are often very misleading, and scarcely express the opinions of their authors. If you think you can judge the Catholic faith from the writings of Bossuet, you will find yourself greatly mistaken when you have lived among us. You will see that the doctrines with which Protestants are answered are quite different from those of the pulpit. To judge a religion rightly, you must not study it in the books of its partisans, you must learn it in their lives; this is quite another matter. Each religion has its own traditions, meaning, customs, prejudices, which form the spirit of its creed, and must be taken in connection with it.

"How many great nations neither print books of their own nor read ours! How shall they judge of our opinions, or we of theirs?

[1] On the other hand, Plutarch relates that the Stoics maintained, among other strange paradoxes, that it was no use hearing both sides; for, said they, the first either proves its point or he does not prove it; if he has proved it, there is an end of it, and the other should be condemned: if he has not proved it, he himself is in the wrong and judgment should be given against him. I consider the method of those who accept an exclusive revelation very much like that of these Stoics. When each of them claims to be the sole guardian of truth, we must hear them all before we can choose between them without injustice.

We laugh at them, they despise us; and if our travellers turn them into ridicule, they need only travel among us to pay us back in our own coin. Are there not, in every country, men of common-sense, honesty, and good faith, lovers of truth, who only seek to know what truth is that they may profess it? Yet every one finds truth in his own religion, and thinks the religion of other nations absurd; so all these foreign religions are not so absurd as they seem to us, or else the reason we find for our own proves nothing.

"We have three principal forms of religion in Europe. One accepts one revelation, another two, and another three. Each hates the others, showers curses on them, accuses them of blindness, obstinacy, hardness of heart, and falsehood. What fair-minded man will dare to decide between them without first carefully weighing their evidence, without listening attentively to their arguments? That which accepts only one revelation is the oldest and seems the best established; that which accepts three is the newest and seems the most consistent; that which accepts two revelations and rejects the third may perhaps be the best, but prejudice is certainly against it: its inconsistency is glaring.

"In all three revelations the sacred books are written in languages unknown to the people who believe in them. The Jews no longer understand Hebrew, the Christians understand neither Hebrew nor Greek; the Turks and Persians do not understand Arabic, and the Arabs of our time do not speak the language of Mahomet. Is not it a very foolish way of teaching, to teach people in an unknown tongue? These books are translated, you say. What an answer! How am I to know that the translations are correct, or how am I to make sure that such a thing as a correct translation is possible? If God has gone so far as to speak to men, why should he require an interpreter?

"I can never believe that every man is obliged to know what is contained in books, and that he who is out of reach of these books, and of those who understand them, will be punished for an ignorance which is no fault of his. Books upon books! What madness! As all Europe is full of books, Europeans regard them as necessary, forgetting that they are unknown throughout three-quarters of the globe. Were not all these books written by men? Why then should a man need them to teach him his duty, and how did he learn his duty before these books were in existence? Either he must have learnt his duties for himself, or his ignorance must have been excused.

"Our Catholics talk loudly of the authority of the Church; but what is the use of it all, if they also need just as great an array of proofs to establish that authority as the other seeks to establish their doctrine? The Church decides that the Church has a right to decide. What a well-founded authority! Go beyond it, and you are back again in our discussions.

"Do you know many Christians who have taken the trouble to inquire what the Jews allege against them? If any one knows anything at all about it, it is from the writings of Christians. What a way of ascertaining the arguments of our adversaries! But what is to be done? If any one dared to publish in our day books which were openly in favour of the Jewish religion, we should punish the author, publisher, and bookseller. This regulation is a sure and certain plan for always being in the right. It is easy to refute those who dare not venture to speak.

"Those among us who have the opportunity of talking with Jews are little better off. These unhappy people feel that they are in our power; the tyranny they have suffered makes them timid; they know that Christian charity thinks nothing of injustice and cruelty; will they dare to run the risk of an outcry against blasphemy? Our greed inspires us with zeal, and they are so rich that they must be in the wrong. The more learned, the more enlightened they are, the more cautious. You may convert some poor wretch whom you have paid to slander his religion; you get some wretched old-clothes-man to speak, and he says what you want; you may triumph over their ignorance and cowardice, while all the time their men of learning are laughing at your stupidity. But do you think you would get off so easily in any place where they knew they were safe? At the Sorbonne it is plain that the Messianic prophecies refer to Jesus Christ. Among the rabbis of Amsterdam it is just as clear that they have nothing to do with him. I do not think I have ever heard the arguments of the Jews as to why they should not have a free state, schools and universities, where they can speak and argue without danger. Then alone can we know what they have to say.

"At Constantinople the Turks state their arguments, but we dare not give ours; then it is our turn to cringe. Can we blame the Turks if they require us to show the same respect for Mahomet, in whom we do not believe, as we demand from the Jews with regard to Jesus Christ in whom they do not believe? Are we right? On what grounds of justice can we answer this question?

"Two-thirds of mankind are neither Jews, Mahometans, nor Christians; and how many millions of men have never heard the name of Moses, Jesus Christ, or Mahomet? They deny it; they maintain that our missionaries go everywhere. That is easily said. But do they go into the heart of Africa, still undiscovered, where as yet no European has ever ventured? Do they go to Eastern Tartary to follow on horseback the wandering tribes, whom no stranger approaches, who not only know nothing of the pope, but have scarcely heard tell of the Grand Lama? Do they penetrate into the vast continents of America, where there are still whole nations unaware that the people of another world have set foot on their shores? Do they go to Japan, where their intrigues have led to their perpetual banishment, where their predecessors are only known to the rising generation as skilful plotters who came with feigned zeal to take possession in secret of the empire? Do they reach the harems of the Asiatic princes to preach the gospel to those thousands of poor slaves? What have the women of those countries done that no missionary may preach the faith to them? Will they all go to hell because of their seclusion?

"If it were true that the gospel is preached throughout the world, what advantage would there be? The day before the first missionary set foot in any country, no doubt somebody died who could not hear him. Now tell me what we shall do with him? If there were a single soul in the whole world, to whom Jesus Christ had never been preached, this objection would be as strong for that man as for a quarter of the human race.

"If the ministers of the gospel have made themselves heard among far-off nations, what have they told them which might reasonably be accepted on their word, without further and more exact verification? You preach to me God, born and dying, two thousand years ago, at the other end of the world, in some small town I know not where; and you tell me that all who have not believed this mystery are damned. These are strange things to be believed so quickly on the authority of an unknown person. Why did your God make these things happen so far off, if he would compel me to know about them? Is it a crime to be unaware of what is happening half a world away? Could I guess that in another hemisphere there was a Hebrew nation and a town called Jerusalem? You might as well expect me to know what was happening in the moon. You say you have come to teach me; but why did you not come and teach my father, or why do you consign that good old man to damnation because he knew nothing of all this? Must he be punished everlastingly for your laziness, he who was so kind and helpful, he who sought only for truth? Be honest; put yourself in my place; see if I ought to believe, on your word alone, all these incredible things which you have told me, and reconcile all this injustice with the just God you proclaim to me. At least allow me to go and see this distant land where such wonders, unheard of in my own country, took place; let me go and see why the inhabitants of Jerusalem put their God to death as a robber. You tell me they did not know he was God. What then shall I do, I who have only heard of him from you? You say they have been punished, dispersed, oppressed, enslaved; that none of them dare approach that town. Indeed they richly deserved it; but what do its present inhabitants say of their crime in slaying their God? They deny him; they too refuse to recognise God as God. They are no better than the children of the original inhabitants.

"What! In the very town where God was put to death, neither the former nor the latter inhabitants knew him, and you expect that I should know him, I who was born two thousand years after his time, and two thousand leagues away? Do you not see that before I can believe this book which you call sacred, but which I do not in the least understand, I must know from others than yourself when and by whom it was written, how it has been preserved, how it came into your possession, what they say about it in those lands where it is rejected, and what are their reasons for rejecting it, though

they know as well as you what you are telling me? You perceive
I must go to Europe, Asia, Palestine, to examine these things for
myself; it would be madness to listen to you before that.

" Not only does this seem reasonable to me, but I maintain that
it is what every wise man ought to say in similar circumstances;
that he ought to banish to a great distance the missionary who
wants to instruct and baptise him all of a sudden before the evidence
is verified.   Now I maintain that there is no revelation against
which these or similar objections cannot be made, and with more
force than against Christianity.   Hence it follows that if there is
but one true religion and if every man is bound to follow it under
pain of damnation, he must spend his whole life in studying, testing,
comparing all these religions, in travelling through the countries in
which they are established.   No man is free from a man's first duty;
no one has a right to depend on another's judgment.   The artisan
who earns his bread by his daily toil, the ploughboy who cannot
read, the delicate and timid maiden, the invalid who can scarcely
leave his bed, all without exception must study, consider, argue,
travel over the whole world; there will be no more fixed and settled
nations; the whole earth will swarm with pilgrims on their way, at
great cost of time and trouble, to verify, compare, and examine
for themselves the various religions to be found.   Then farewell to
the trades, the arts, the sciences of mankind, farewell to all peaceful
occupations; there can be no study but that of religion, even the
strongest, the most industrious, the most intelligent, the oldest, will
hardly be able in his last years to know where he is; and it will
be a wonder if he manages to find out what religion he ought to live
by, before the hour of his death.

" Hard pressed by these arguments, some prefer to make God
unjust and to punish the innocent for the sins of their fathers, rather
than to renounce their barbarous dogmas.   Others get out of the
difficulty by kindly sending an angel to instruct all those who in
invincible ignorance have lived a righteous life.   A good idea, that
angel!   Not content to be the slaves of their own inventions they
expect God to make use of them also!

" Behold, my son, the absurdities to which pride and intolerance
bring us, when everybody wants others to think as he does, and
everybody fancies that he has an exclusive claim upon the rest of
mankind.   I call to witness the God of Peace whom I adore, and
whom I proclaim to you, that my inquiries were honestly made;
but when I discovered that they were and always would be unsuccessful, and that I was embarked upon a boundless ocean, I
turned back, and restricted my faith within the limits of my primitive
ideas.   I could never convince myself that God would require such
learning of me under pain of hell.   So I closed all my books.   There
is one book which is open to every one—the book of nature.   In
this good and great volume I learn to serve and adore its Author.
There is no excuse for not reading this book, for it speaks to all in
a language they can understand.   Suppose I had been born in a

desert island, suppose I had never seen any man but myself, suppose
I had never heard what took place in olden days in a remote corner
of the world; yet if I use my reason, if I cultivate it, if I employ
rightly the innate faculties which God bestows upon me, I shall
learn by myself to know and love him, to love his works, to will
what he wills, and to fulfil all my duties upon earth, that I may
do his pleasure. What more can all human learning teach me?

"With regard to revelation, if I were a more accomplished dis-
putant, or a more learned person, perhaps I should feel its truth,
its usefulness for those who are happy enough to perceive it; but
if I find evidence for it which I cannot combat, I also find objections
against it which I cannot overcome. There are so many weighty
reasons for and against that I do not know what to decide, so that
I neither accept nor reject it. I only reject all obligation to be
convinced of its truth; for this so-called obligation is incompatible
with God's justice, and far from removing objections in this way
it would multiply them, and would make them insurmountable for
the greater part of mankind. In this respect I maintain an attitude
of reverent doubt. I do not presume to think myself infallible;
other men may have been able to make up their minds though the
matter seems doubtful to myself; I am speaking for myself, not for
them; I neither blame them nor follow in their steps; their judgment may be superior to mine, but it is no fault of mine that my
judgment does not agree with it.

"I own also that the holiness of the gospel speaks to my heart,
and that this is an argument which I should be sorry to refute.
Consider the books of the philosophers with all their outward show;
how petty they are in comparison! Can a book at once so grand and
so simple be the work of men? Is it possible that he whose history
is contained in this book is no more than man? Is the tone of this
book, the tone of the enthusiast or the ambitious sectary? What
gentleness and purity in his actions, what a touching grace in his
teaching, how lofty are his sayings, how profoundly wise are his
sermons, how ready, how discriminating, and how just are his answers!
What man, what sage, can live, suffer, and die without weakness or
ostentation? When Plato describes his imaginary good man,
overwhelmed with the disgrace of crime, and deserving of all the
rewards of virtue, every feature of the portrait is that of Christ;
the resemblance is so striking that it has been noticed by all the
Fathers, and there can be no doubt about it. What prejudices
and blindness must there be before we dare to compare the son
of Sophronisca with the son of Mary. How far apart they are!
Socrates dies a painless death, he is not put to open shame, and he
plays his part easily to the last; and if this easy death had not done
honour to his life, we might have doubted whether Socrates, with all
his intellect, was more than a mere sophist. He invented morality,
so they say; others before him had practised it; he only said what
they had done, and made use of their example in his teaching.
Aristides was just before Socrates defined justice; Leonidas died

for his country before Socrates declared that patriotism was a virtue; Sparta was sober before Socrates extolled sobriety; there were plenty of virtuous men in Greece before he defined virtue But among the men of his own time where did Jesus find that pure and lofty morality of which he is both the teacher and pattern ? [1] The voice of loftiest wisdom arose among the fiercest fanaticism, the simplicity of the most heroic virtues did honour to the most degraded of nations One could wish no easier death than that of Socrates, calmly discussing philosophy with his friends; one could fear nothing worse than that of Jesus, dying in torment, among the insults, the mockery, the curses of the whole nation. In the midst of these terrible sufferings, Jesus prays for his cruel murderers. Yes, if the life and death of Socrates are those of a philosopher, the life and death of Christ are those of a God. Shall we say that the gospel story is the work of the imagination ? My friend, such things are not imagined; and the doings of Socrates, which no one doubts, are less well attested than those of Jesus Christ. At best, you only put the difficulty from you; it would be still more incredible that several persons should have agreed together to invent such a book, than that there was one man who supplied its subject matter. The tone and morality of this story are not those of any Jewish authors, and the gospel indeed contains characters so great, so striking, so entirely inimitable, that their invention would be more astonishing than their hero. With all this the same gospel is full of incredible things, things repugnant to reason, things which no natural man can understand or accept. What can you do among so many contradictions ? You can be modest and wary, my child; respect in silence what you can neither reject nor understand, and humble yourself in the sight of the Divine Being who alone knows the truth.

"This is the unwilling scepticism in which I rest; but this scepticism is in no way painful to me, for it does not extend to matters of practice, and I am well assured as to the principles underlying all my duties. I serve God in the simplicity of my heart; I only seek to know what affects my conduct. As to those dogmas which have no effect upon action or morality, dogmas about which so many men torment themselves, I give no heed to them. I regard all individual religions as so many wholesome institutions which prescribe a uniform method by which each country may do honour to God in public worship; institutions which may each have its reason in the country, the government, the genius of the people, or in other local causes which make one preferable to another in a given time or place. I think them all good alike, when God is served in a fitting manner. True worship is of the heart. God rejects no homage, however offered, provided it is sincere. Called to the service of the Church in my own religion, I fulfil as scrupulously as I can all the duties prescribed to me, and my conscience would reproach me if I were knowingly wanting with regard to any

[1] Cf. in the Sermon on the Mount the parallel he himself draws between the teaching of Moses and his own.—Matt. v.

point. You are aware that after being suspended for a long time, I have, through the influence of M. Mellarede, obtained permission to resume my priestly duties, as a means of livelihood. I used to say Mass with the levity that comes from long experience even of the most serious matters when they are too familiar to us; with my new principles I now celebrate it with more reverence; I dwell upon the majesty of the Supreme Being, his presence, the insufficiency of the human mind, which so little realises what concerns its Creator. When I consider how I present before him the prayers of all the people in a form laid down for me, I carry out the whole ritual exactly; I give heed to what I say, I am careful not to omit the least word, the least ceremony; when the moment of the consecration approaches, I collect my powers, that I may do all things as required by the Church and by the greatness of this sacrament; I strive to annihilate my own reason before the Supreme Mind; I say to myself, Who art thou to measure infinite power? I reverently pronounce the sacramental words, and I give to their effect all the faith I can bestow. Whatever may be this mystery which passes understanding, I am not afraid that at the day of judgment I shall be punished for having profaned it in my heart.

Honoured with the sacred ministry, though in its lowest ranks, I will never do or say anything which may make me unworthy to fulfil these sublime duties. I will always preach virtue and exhort men to well-doing; and so far as I can I will set them a good example. It will be my business to make religion attractive; it will be my business to strengthen their faith in those doctrines which are really useful, those which every man must believe; but, please God, I shall never teach them to hate their neighbour, to say to other men, You will be damned; to say, No salvation outside the Church.[1] If I were in a more conspicuous position, this reticence might get me into trouble; but I am too obscure to have much to fear, and I could hardly sink lower than I am. Come what may, I will never blaspheme the justice of God, nor lie against the Holy Ghost.

"I have long desired to have a parish of my own; it is still my ambition, but I no longer hope to attain it. My dear friend, I think there is nothing so delightful as to be a parish priest. A good clergyman is a minister of mercy, as a good magistrate is a minister of justice. A clergyman is never called upon to do evil; if he cannot always do good himself, it is never out of place for him to beg for others, and he often gets what he asks if he knows how to gain respect. Oh! if I should ever have some poor mountain

[1] The duty of following and loving the religion of our country does not go so far as to require us to accept doctrines contrary to good morals, such as intolerance. This horrible doctrine sets men in arms against their fellow-men, and makes them all enemies of mankind. The distinction between civil toleration and theological toleration is vain and childish. These two kinds of toleration are inseparable, and we cannot accept one without the other. Even the angels could not live at peace with men whom they regarded as the enemies of God.

parish where I might minister to kindly folk, I should be happy indeed; for it seems to me that I should make my parishioners happy. I should not bring them riches, but I should share their poverty; I should remove from them the scorn and opprobrium which are harder to bear than poverty. I should make them love peace and equality, which often remove poverty, and always make it tolerable. When they saw that I was in no way better off than themselves, and that yet I was content with my lot, they would learn to put up with their fate and to be content like me. In my sermons I would lay more stress on the spirit of the gospel than on the spirit of the church; its teaching is simple, its morality sublime; there is little in it about the practices of religion, but much about works of charity. Before I teach them what they ought to do, I would try to practise it myself, that they might see that at least I think what I say. If there were Protestants in the neighbourhood or in my parish, I would make no difference between them and my own congregation so far as concerns Christian charity; I would get them to love one another, to consider themselves brethren, to respect all religions, and each to live peaceably in his own religion. To ask any one to abandon the religion in which he was born is, I consider, to ask him to do wrong, and therefore to do wrong oneself. While we await further knowledge, let us respect public order; in every country let us respect the laws, let us not disturb the form of worship prescribed by law; let us not lead its citizens into disobedience; for we have no certain knowledge that it is good for them to abandon their own opinions for others, and on the other hand we are quite certain that it is a bad thing to disobey the law.

"My young friend, I have now repeated to you my creed as God reads it in my heart; you are the first to whom I have told it; perhaps you will be the last. As long as there is any true faith left among men, we must not trouble quiet souls, nor scare the faith of the ignorant with problems they cannot solve, with difficulties which cause them uneasiness, but do not give them any guidance. But when once everything is shaken, the trunk must be preserved at the cost of the branches. Consciences, restless, uncertain, and almost quenched like yours, require to be strengthened and aroused; to set the feet again upon the foundation of eternal truth, we must remove the trembling supports on which they think they rest.

"You are at that critical age when the mind is open to conviction, when the heart receives its form and character, when we decide our own fate for life, either for good or evil. At a later date, the material has hardened and fresh impressions leave no trace. Young man, take the stamp of truth upon your heart which is not yet hardened. If I were more certain of myself, I should have adopted a more decided and dogmatic tone; but I am a man ignorant and liable to error; what could I do? I have opened my heart fully to you; and I have told what I myself hold for certain and sure; I have told you my doubts as doubts, my opinions as opinions; I have given you my reasons both for faith and doubt. It is now your turn to judge; you have asked for time; that is a wise precaution and it makes me think well of you. Begin by bringing your conscience into that state in which it desires to see clearly; be honest with yourself. Take to yourself such of my opinions as convince you, reject the rest. You are not yet so depraved by vice as to run the risk of choosing amiss. I would offer to argue with you, but as soon as men dispute they lose their temper; pride and obstinacy come in, and there is an end of honesty My friend, never argue; for by arguing we gain no light for ourselves or for others. So far as I myself am concerned, I have only made up my mind after many years of meditation; here I rest, my conscience is at peace, my heart is satisfied. If I wanted to begin afresh the examination of my feelings, I should not bring to the task a purer love of truth; and my mind, which is already less active, would be less able to perceive the truth. Here I shall rest, lest the love of contemplation, developing step by step into an idle passion, should make me lukewarm in the performance of my duties, lest I should fall into my former scepticism without strength to struggle out of it. More than half my life is spent; I have barely time to make good use of what is left, to blot out my faults by my virtues. If I am mistaken, it is against my will. He who reads my inmost heart knows that I have no love for my blindness. As my own knowledge is powerless to free me from this blindness, my only way out of it is by a good life; and if God from the very stones can raise up children to Abraham, every man has a right to hope that he may be taught the truth, if he makes himself worthy of it.

" If my reflections lead you to think as I do, if you share my feelings, if we have the same creed, I give you this advice: Do not continue to expose your life to the temptations of poverty and despair, nor waste it in degradation and at the mercy of strangers; no longer eat the shameful bread of charity. Return to your own country, go back to the religion of your fathers, and follow it in sincerity of heart, and never forsake it; it is very simple and very holy; I think there is no other religion upon earth whose morality is purer, no other more satisfying to the reason. Do not trouble about the cost of the journey, that will be provided for you. Neither do you fear the false shame of a humiliating return; we should blush to commit a fault, not to repair it. You are still at an age when all is forgiven, but when we cannot go on sinning with impunity. If you desire to listen to your conscience, a thousand empty objections will disappear at her voice. You will feel that, in our present state of uncertainty, it is an inexcusable presumption to profess any faith but that we were born into, while it is treachery not to practise honestly the faith we profess. If we go astray, we deprive ourselves of a great excuse before the tribunal of the sovereign judge. Will he not pardon the errors in which we were brought up, rather than those of our own choosing?

" My son, keep your soul in such a state that you always desire that there should be a God and you will never doubt it. Moreover, whatever decision you come to, remember that the real duties of religion are independent of human institutions; that a righteous heart is the true temple of the Godhead; that in every land, in every sect, to love God above all things and to love our neighbour as ourself is the whole law; remember there is no religion which absolves us from our moral duties; that these alone are really essential, that the service of the heart is the first of these duties, and that without faith there is no such thing as true virtue.

"Shun those who, under the pretence of explaining nature, sow destructive doctrines in the heart of men, those whose apparent scepticism is a hundredfold more self-assertive and dogmatic than the firm tone of their opponents. Under the arrogant claim, that they alone are enlightened, true, honest, they subject us imperiously to their far-reaching decisions, and profess to give us, as the true principles of all things, the unintelligible systems framed by their imagination. Moreover, they overthrow, destroy, and trample under foot all that men reverence; they rob the afflicted of their last consolation in their misery; they deprive the rich and powerful of the sole bridle of their passions; they tear from the very depths of man's heart all remorse for crime, and all hope of virtue; and they boast, moreover, that they are the benefactors of the human race. Truth, they say, can never do a man harm. I think so too, and to my mind that is strong evidence that what they teach is not true.[1]

---

[1] The rival parties attack each other with so many sophistries that it would be a rash and overwhelming enterprise to attempt to deal with all of them; it is difficult enough to note some of them as they occur. One of the commonest errors among the partisans of philosophy is to contrast a nation of good philosophers with a nation of bad Christians; as if it were easier to make a nation of good philosophers than a nation of good Christians. I know not whether in individual cases it is easier to discover one rather than the other; but I am quite certain that, as far as nations are concerned, we must assume that there will be those who misuse their philosophy without religion, just as our people misuse their religion without philosophy; and that seems to put quite a different face upon the matter.

Bayle has proved very satisfactorily that fanaticism is more harmful than atheism, and that cannot be denied; but what he has not taken the trouble to say, though it is none the less true, is this: Fanaticism, though cruel and bloodthirsty, is still a great and powerful passion, which stirs the heart of man, teaching him to despise death, and giving him an enormous motive power, which only needs to be guided rightly to produce the noblest virtues; while irreligion, and the argumentative philosophic spirit generally, on the other hand, assaults the life and enfeebles it, degrades the soul, concentrates all the passions in the basest self-interest, in the meanness of the human self; thus it saps unnoticed the very foundations of all society; for what is common to all these private interests is so small that it will never outweigh their opposing interests.

If atheism does not lead to bloodshed, it is less from love of peace than from indifference to what is good; as if it mattered little what happened to others, provided the sage remained undisturbed in his study. His principles do not kill men, but they prevent their birth, by destroying the morals by which they were multiplied, by detaching them from their fellows, by reducing all their affections to a secret selfishness, as fatal to population as to virtue. The indifference of the philosopher is like the

"My good youth, be honest and humble; learn how to be ignorant, then you will never deceive yourself or others. If ever your talents are so far cultivated as to enable you to speak to other men, always speak according to your conscience, without caring for their applause. The abuse of knowledge causes incredulity. The learned always despise the opinions of the crowd; each of them must have his own opinion. A haughty philosophy leads to atheism just as blind devotion leads to fanaticism. Avoid these extremes; keep steadfastly to the path of truth, or what seems to you truth, in simplicity of heart, and never let yourself be turned aside by pride or weakness. Dare to confess God before the philosophers; dare to preach humanity to the intolerant. It may be you will stand alone, but you will bear within you a witness which will make the witness of

peace in a despotic state; it is the repose of death; war itself is not more destructive.

Thus fanaticism, though its immediate results are more fatal than those of what is now called the philosophic mind, is much less fatal in its after effects. Moreover, it is an easy matter to exhibit fine maxims in books; but the real question is—Are they really in accordance with your teaching, are they the necessary consequences of it? and this has not been clearly proved so far. It remains to be seen whether philosophy, safely enthroned, could control successfully man's petty vanity, his self-interest, his ambition, all the lesser passions of mankind, and whether it would practise that sweet humanity which it boasts of, pen in hand.

In theory, there is no good which philosophy can bring about which is not equally secured by religion, while religion secures much that philosophy cannot secure.

In practice, it is another matter; but still we must put it to the proof. No man follows his religion in all things, even if his religion is true; most people have hardly any religion, and they do not in the least follow what they have; that is still more true; but still there are some people who have a religion and follow it, at least to some extent; and beyond doubt religious motives do prevent them from wrong-doing, and win from them virtues, praiseworthy actions, which would not have existed but for these motives.

A monk denies that money was entrusted to him; what of that? It only proves that the man who entrusted the money to him was a fool. If Pascal had done the same, that would have proved that Pascal was a hypocrite. But a monk! Are those who make a trade of religion religious people? All the crimes committed by the clergy, as by other men, do not prove that religion is useless, but that very few people are religious.

Most certainly our modern governments owe to Christianity their more stable authority, their less frequent revolutions; it has made those governments less bloodthirsty; this can be shown by comparing them with the governments of former times. Apart from fanaticism, the best known religion has given greater gentleness to Christian conduct. This change is not the result of learning; for whereverlearning has been most illustrious humanity has been no more respected on that account; the cruelties of the Athenians, the Egyptians, the Roman emperors, the Chinese bear witness to this What works of mercy spring from the gospel! How many acts of restitution, reparation, confession does the gospel lead to among Catholics! Among ourselves, as the times of communion draw near, do they not lead us to reconciliation and to alms-giving? Did not the Hebrew Jubilee make the grasping less greedy, did it not prevent much poverty? The brotherhood of the Law made the nation one; no beggar was found among them. Neither are there beggars among the Turks, men of no account with you. Let them love or hate, let them read your writings or despise them; no matter. Speak the truth and do the right; the one thing that really matters is to do one's duty in this world; and when we forget ourselves we are really working for ourselves. My child, self-interest misleads us; the hope of the just is the only sure guide."

I have transcribed this document not as a rule for the sentiments we should adopt in matters of religion, but as an example of the way in which we may reason with our pupil without forsaking the method I have tried to establish. So long as we yield nothing to human authority, nor to the prejudices of our native land, the light of reason alone, in a state of nature, can lead us no further than to natural religion; and this is as far as I should go with Emile. If he must have any other religion, I have no right to be his guide; he must choose for himself.

We are working in agreement with nature, and while she is shaping the physical man, we are striving to shape his moral being, but we do not make the same progress. The body is already strong

where there are countless pious institutions; from motives of religion they even show hospitality to the foes of their religion.

" The Mahometans say, according to Chardin, that after the interrogation which will follow the general resurrection, all bodies will traverse a bridge called Poul-Serrho, which is thrown across the eternal fires, a bridge which may be called the third and last test of the great Judgment, because it is there that the good and bad will be separated, etc.

" The Persians, continues Chardin, make a great point of this bridge; and when any one suffers a wrong which he can never hope to wipe out by any means or at any time, he finds his last consolation in these words: ' By the living God, you will pay me double at the last day; you will never get across the Poul-Serrho if you do not first do me justice; I will hold the hem of your garment, I will cling about your knees.' I have seen many eminent men, of every profession, who for fear lest this hue and cry should be raised against them as they cross that fearful bridge, beg pardon of those who complained against them; it has happened to me myself on many occasions. Men of rank, who had compelled me by their importunity to do what I did not wish to do, have come to me when they thought my anger had had time to cool, and have said to me: I pray you " Halal becon antchisra," that is, " Make this matter lawful and right." Some of them have even sent gifts and done me service, so that I might forgive them and say I did it willingly; the cause of this is nothing else but this belief that they will not be able to get across the bridge of hell until they have paid the uttermost farthing to the oppressed."

Must I think that the idea of this bridge where so many iniquities are made good is of no avail? If the Persians were deprived of this idea, if they were persuaded that there was no Poul-Serrho, nor anything of the kind, where the oppressed were avenged of their tyrants after death, is it not clear that they would be very much at their ease, and they would be freed from the care of appeasing the wretched? But it is false to say that this doctrine is hurtful, yet it would not be true.

O Philosopher, your moral laws are all very fine; but kindly show me their sanction. Cease to shirk the question, and tell me plainly what you would put in the place of Poul-Serrho.

and vigorous, the soul is still frail and delicate, and whatever can
be done by human art, the body is always ahead of the mind.
Hitherto all our care has been devoted to restrain the one and
stimulate the other, so that the man might be as far as possible at
one with himself. By developing his individuality, we have kept his
growing susceptibilities in check; we have controlled it by cultivating his reason. Objects of thought moderate the influence of
objects of sense. By going back to the causes of things, we have withdrawn him from the sway of the senses; it is an easy thing to raise
him from the study of nature to the search for the author of nature.

When we have reached this point, what a fresh hold we have
got over our pupil; what fresh ways of speaking to his heart! Then
alone does he find a real motive for being good, for doing right
when he is far from every human eye, and when he is not driven to
it by law. To be just in his own eyes and in the sight of God, to
do his duty, even at the cost of life itself, and to bear in his heart
virtue, not only for the love of order which we all subordinate to
the love of self, but for the love of the Author of his being, a love
which mingles with that self-love, so that he may at length enjoy
the lasting happiness which the peace of a good conscience and the
contemplation of that supreme being promise him in another life,
after he has used this life aright. Go beyond this, and I see nothing
but injustice, hypocrisy, and falsehood among men; private interest,
which in competition necessarily prevails over everything else,
teaches all things to adorn vice with the outward show of virtue.
Let all men do what is good for me at the cost of what is good for
themselves; let everything depend on me alone; let the whole
human race perish, if needs be, in suffering and want, to spare me
a moment's pain or hunger. Yes, I shall always maintain that
whoso says in his heart, "There is no God," while he takes the
name of God upon his lips, is either a liar or a madman.

Reader, it is all in vain; I perceive that you and I shall never
see Emile with the same eyes; you will always fancy him like
your own young people, hasty, impetuous, flighty, wandering
from fête to fête, from amusement to amusement, never able to
settle to anything. You smile when I expect to make a thinker,
a philosopher, a young theologian, of an ardent, lively, eager, and
fiery young man, at the most impulsive period of youth. This
dreamer, you say, is always in pursuit of his fancy; when he gives
us a pupil of his own making, he does not merely form him, he
creates him, he makes him up out of his own head; and while he
thinks he is treading in the steps of nature, he is getting further and
further from her. As for me, when I compare my pupil with yours,
I can scarcely find anything in common between them. So
differently brought up, it is almost a miracle if they are alike in
any respect. As his childhood was passed in the freedom they
assume in youth, in his youth he begins to bear the yoke they bore
as children; this yoke becomes hateful to them, they are sick of it,
and they see in it nothing but their masters' tyranny; when they

escape from childhood, they think they must shake off all control, they make up for the prolonged restraint imposed upon them, as a prisoner, freed from his fetters, moves and stretches and shakes his limbs.[1] Emile, however, is proud to be a man, and to submit to the yoke of his growing reason; his body, already well grown, no longer needs so much action, and begins to control itself, while his half-fledged mind tries its wings on every occasion. Thus the age of reason becomes for the one the age of licence; for the other, the age of reasoning.

Would you know which of the two is nearer to the order of nature? Consider the differences between those who are more or less removed from a state of nature. Observe young villagers and see if they are as undisciplined as your scholars. The Sieur de Beau says that savages in childhood are always active, and ever busy with sports that keep the body in motion; but scarcely do they reach adolescence than they become quiet and dreamy; they no longer devote themselves to games of skill or chance. Emile, who has been brought up in full freedom like young peasants and savages, should behave like them and change as he grows up. The whole difference is in this, that instead of merely being active in sport or for food, he has, in the course of his sports, learned to think. Having reached this stage, and by this road, he is quite ready to enter upon the next stage to which I introduce him; the subjects I suggest for his consideration rouse his curiosity, because they are fine in themselves, because they are quite new to him, and because he is able to understand them. Your young people, on the other hand, are weary and overdone with your stupid lessons, your long sermons, and your tedious catechisms; why should they not refuse to devote their minds to what has made them sad, to the burdensome precepts which have been continually piled upon them, to the thought of the Author of their being, who has been represented as the enemy of their pleasures? All this has only inspired in them aversion, disgust, and weariness; constraint has set them against it; why then should they devote themselves to it when they are beginning to choose for themselves? They require novelty, you must not repeat what they learned as children. Just so with my own pupil, when he is a man I speak to him as a man, and only tell him what is new to him; it is just because they are tedious to your pupils that he will find them to his taste.

This is how I doubly gain time for him by retarding nature to the advantage of reason. But have I indeed retarded the progress of nature? No, I have only prevented the imagination from hastening it; I have employed another sort of teaching to counter-balance the precocious instruction which the young man receives from other sources. When he is carried away by the flood of

---

[1] There is no one who looks down upon childhood with such lofty scorn as those who are barely grown-up; just as there is no country where rank is more strictly regarded than that where there is little real inequality; everybody is afraid of being confounded with his inferiors.

existing customs and I draw him in the opposite direction by means of other customs, this is not to remove him from his place, but to keep him in it.

Nature's due time comes at length, as come it must. Since man must die, he must reproduce himself, so that the species may endure and the order of the world continue. When by the signs I have spoken of you perceive that the critical moment is at hand, at once abandon for ever your former tone. He is still your disciple, but not your scholar. He is a man and your friend; henceforth you must treat him as such.

What! Must I abdicate my authority when most I need it? Must I abandon the adult to himself just when he least knows how to control himself, when he may fall into the gravest errors? Must I renounce my rights when it matters most that I should use them on his behalf? Who bids you renounce them; he is only just becoming conscious of them. Hitherto all you have gained has been won by force or guile; authority, the law of duty, were unknown to him, you had to constrain or deceive him to gain his obedience. But see what fresh chains you have bound about his heart. Reason, friendship, affection, gratitude, a thousand bonds of affection, speak to him in a voice he cannot fail to hear. His ears are not yet dulled by vice, he is still sensitive only to the passions of nature. Self-love, the first of these, delivers him into your hands; habit confirms this. If a passing transport tears him from you, regret restores him to you without delay; the sentiment which attaches him to you is the only lasting sentiment, all the rest are fleeting and self-effacing. Do not let him become corrupt, and he will always be docile; he will not begin to rebel till he is already perverted.

I grant you, indeed, that if you directly oppose his growing desires and foolishly treat as crimes the fresh needs which are beginning to make themselves felt in him, he will not listen to you for long; but as soon as you abandon my method I cannot be answerable for the consequences. Remember that you are nature's minister; you will never be her foe.

But what shall we decide to do? You see no alternative but either to favour his inclinations or to resist them; to tyrannise or to wink at his misconduct; and both of these may lead to such dangerous results that one must indeed hesitate between them.

The first way out of the difficulty is a very early marriage; this is undoubtedly the safest and most natural plan. I doubt, however, whether it is the best or the most useful. I will give my reasons later; meanwhile I admit that young men should marry when they reach a marriageable age. But this age comes too soon; we have made them precocious; marriage should be postponed to maturity.

If it were merely a case of listening to their wishes and following their lead it would be an easy matter; but there are so many contradictions between the rights of nature and the laws of society that to conciliate them we must continually contradict ourselves.

Much art is required to prevent man in society from being altogether artificial.

For the reasons just stated, I consider that by the means I have indicated and others like them the young man's desires may be kept in ignorance and his senses pure up to the age of twenty. This is so true that among the Germans a young man who lost his virginity before that age was considered dishonoured; and the writers justly attribute the vigour of constitution and the number of children among the Germans to the continence of these nations during youth.

This period may be prolonged still further, and a few centuries ago nothing was more common even in France. Among other well-known examples, Montaig e's father, a man no less scrupulously truthful than strong and healthy, swore that his was a virgin marriage at three and thirty, and he had served for a long time in the Italian wars. We may see in the writings of his son what strength and spirit were shown by the father when he was over sixty. Certainly the contrary opinion depends rather on our own morals and our own prejudices than on the experience of the race as a whole.

I may, therefore, leave on one side the experience of our young people; it proves nothing for those who have been educated in another fashion. Considering that nature has fixed no exact limits which cannot be advanced or postponed, I think I may, without going beyond the law of nature, assume that under my care Emil has so far remained in his first innocence, but I see that this happy period is drawing to a close. Surrounded by ever-increasing perils, he will escape me at the first opportunity in spite of all my efforts, and this opportunity will not long be delayed; he will follow the blind instinct of his senses; the chances are a thousand to one on his ruin. I have considered the morals of mankind too profoundly not to be aware of the irrevocable influence of this first moment on all the rest of his life. If I dissimulate and pretend to see nothing, he will take advantage of my weakness; if he thinks he can deceive me, he will despise me, and I become an accomplice in his destruction. If I try to recall him, the time is past, he no longer heeds me, he finds me tiresome, hateful, intolerable; it will not be long before he is rid of me. There is therefore only one reasonable course open to me; I must make him accountable for his own actions, I must at least preserve him from being taken unawares, and I must show him plainly the dangers which beset his path. I have restrained him so far through his ignorance; henceforward his restraint must be his own knowledge.

This new teaching is of great importance, and we will take up our story where we left it. This is the time to present my accounts, to show him how his time and mine have been spent, to make known to him what he is and what I am; what I have done, and what he has done; what we owe to each other; all his moral relations, all the undertakings to which he is pledged, all those to which others have pledged themselves in respect to him; the stage he has reached in the development of his faculties, the road that remains to be travelled, the difficulties he will meet, and the way to overcome them; how I can still help him and how he must henceforward help himself; in a word, the critical time which he has reached, the new dangers round about him, and all the valid reasons which should induce him to keep a close watch upon himself before giving heed to his growing desires.

Remember that to guide a grown man you must reverse all that you did to guide the child. Do not hesitate to speak to him of those dangerous mysteries which you have so carefully concealed from him hitherto. Since he must become aware of them, let him not learn them from another, nor from himself, but from you alone; since he must henceforth fight against them, let him know his enemy, that he may not be taken unawares.

Young people who are found to be aware of these matters, without our knowing how they obtained their knowledge, have not obtained it with impunity. This unwise teaching, which can have no honourable object, stains the imagination of those who receive it if it does nothing worse, and it inclines them to the vices of their instructors. This is not all; servants, by this means, ingratiate themselves with a child, gain his confidence, make him regard his tutor as a gloomy and tiresome person; and one of the favourite subjects of their secret colloquies is to slander him. When the pupil has got so far, the master may abandon his task; he can do no good.

But why does the child choose special confidants? Because of the tyranny of those who control him. Why should he hide himself from them if he were not driven to it? Why should he complain if he had nothing to complain of? Naturally those who control him are his first confidants; you can see from his eagerness to tell them what he thinks that he feels he has only half thought till he has told his thoughts to them. You may be sure that when the child knows you will neither preach nor scold, he will always tell you everything, and that no one will dare to tell him anything he must conceal from you, for they will know very well that he will tell you everything.

What makes me most confident in my method is this: when I follow it out as closely as possible, I find no situation in the life of my scholar which does not leave me some pleasing memory of him. Even when he is carried away by his ardent temperament or when he revolts against the hand that guides him, when he struggles and is on the point of escaping from me, I still find his first simplicity in his agitation and his anger; his heart as pure as his body, he has no more knowledge of pretence than of vice; reproach and scorn have not made a coward of him; base fears have never taught him the art of concealment. He has all the indiscretion of innocence; he is absolutely out-spoken; he does not even know the use of deceit. Every impulse of his heart is betrayed either by word or look, and I often know what he is feeling before he is aware of it himself.

So long as his heart is thus freely opened to me, so long as he delights to tell me what he feels, I have nothing to fear; the danger is not yet at hand; but if he becomes more timid, more reserved, if I perceive in his conversation the first signs of confusion and shame, his instincts are beginning to develop, he is beginning to connect the idea of evil with these instincts, there is not a moment to lose, and if I do not hasten to instruct him, he will learn in spite of me.

Some of my readers, even of those who agree with me, will think that it is only a question of a conversation with the young man at any time. Oh, this is not the way to control the human heart. What we say has no meaning unless the opportunity has been carefully chosen. Before we sow we must till the ground; the seed of virtue is hard to grow; and a long period of preparation is required before it will take root. One reason why sermons have so little effect is that they are offered to everybody alike, without discrimination or choice. How can any one imagine that the same sermon could be suitable for so many hearers, with their different dispositions, so unlike in mind, temper, age, sex, station, and opinion. Perhaps there are not two among those to whom what is addressed to all is really suitable; and all our affections are so transitory that perhaps there are not even two occasions in the life of any man when the same speech would have the same effect on him. Judge for yourself whether the time when the eager senses disturb the understanding and tyrannise over the will, is the time to listen to the solemn lessons of wisdom. Therefore never reason with young men, even when they have reached the age of reason, unless you have first prepared the way. Most lectures miss their mark more through the master's fault than the disciple's. The pedant and the teacher say much the same; but the former says it at random, and the latter only when he is sure of its effect.

As a somnambulist, wandering in his sleep, walks along the edge of a precipice, over which he would fall if he were awake, so my Emile, in the sleep of ignorance, escapes the perils which he does not see; were I to wake him with a start, he might fall. Let us first try to withdraw him from the edge of the precipice, and then we will awake him to show him it from a distance.

Reading, solitude, idleness, a soft and sedentary life, intercourse with women and young people, these are perilous paths for a young man, and these lead him constantly into danger. I divert his senses by other objects of sense; I trace another course for his spirits by which I distract them from the course they would have taken; it is by bodily exercise and hard work that I check the activity of the imagination, which was leading him astray. When the arms are hard at work, the imagination is quiet; when the body is very weary, the passions are not easily inflamed. The quickest and easiest precaution is to remove him from immediate danger. At once I take him away from towns, away from things which might lead him into temptation. But that is not enough; in what desert, in what wilds, shall he escape from the thoughts which pursue him? It is not enough to remove dangerous objects; if I fail to remove the memory of them, if I fail to find a way to detach him from everything, if I fail to distract him from himself, I might as well have left him where he was.

Emile has learned a trade, but we do not have recourse to it; he is fond of farming and understands it, but farming is not enough; the occupations he is acquainted with degenerate into routine; when he is engaged in them he is not really occupied; he is thinking of other things; head and hand are at work on different subjects. He must have some fresh occupation which has the interest of novelty—an occupation which keeps him busy, diligent, and hard at work, an occupation which he may become passionately fond of, one to which he will devote himself entirely. Now the only one which seems to possess all these characteristics is the chase. If hunting is ever an innocent pleasure, if it is ever worthy of a man, now is the time to betake ourselves to it. Emile is well-fitted to succeed in it. He is strong, skilful, patient, unwearied. He is sure to take a fancy to this sport; he will bring to it all the ardour of youth; in it he will lose, at least for a time, the dangerous inclinations which spring from softness. The chase hardens the heart as well as the body; we get used to the sight of blood and cruelty. Diana is represented as the enemy of love; and the allegory is true to life; the languors of love are born of soft repose, and tender feelings are stifled by violent exercise. In the woods and fields, the lover and the sportsman are so diversely affected that they receive very different impressions. The fresh shade, the arbours, the pleasant resting-places of the one, to the other are but feeding grounds, or places where the quarry will hide or turn to bay. Where the lover hears the flute and the nightingale, the hunter hears the horn and the hounds; one pictures to himself the nymphs and dryads, the other sees the horses, the huntsman, and the pack. Take a country walk with one or other of these men; their different conversation will soon show you that they behold the earth with other eyes, and that the direction of their thoughts is as different as their favourite pursuit.

I understand how these tastes may be combined, and that at last men find time for both. But the passions of youth cannot be divided in this way. Give the youth a single occupation which he loves, and the rest will soon be forgotten. Varied desires come with varied knowledge, and the first pleasures we know are the only ones we desire for long enough. I would not have the whole of Emile's youth spent in killing creatures, and I do not even profess to justify this cruel passion; it is enough for me that it serves to delay a more dangerous passion, so that he may listen to me calmly when I speak of it, and give me time to describe it without stimulating it

There are moments in human life which can never be forgotten.

Such is the time when Emile receives the instruction of which I have spoken; its influence should endure all his life through. Let us try to engrave it on his memory so that it may never fade away. It is one of the faults of our age to rely too much on cold reason, as if men were all mind. By neglecting the language of expression we have lost the most forcible mode of speech. The spoken word is always weak, and we speak to the heart rather through the eyes than the ears. In our attempt to appeal to reason only, we have reduced our precepts to words, we have not embodied them in deed. Mere reason is not active; occasionally she restrains, more rarely she stimulates, but she never does any great thing. Small minds have a mania for reasoning. Strong souls speak a very different language, and it is by this language that men are persuaded and driven to action.

I observe that in modern times men only get a hold over others by force or self-interest, while the ancients did more by persuasion, by the affections of the heart; because they did not neglect the language; of symbolic expression. All agreements were drawn up solemnly, so that they might be more inviolable; before the reign of force, the gods were the judges of mankind; in their presence, individuals made their treaties and alliances, and pledged themselves to perform their promises; the face of the earth was the book in which the archives were preserved. The leaves of this book were rocks, trees, piles of stones, made sacred by these transactions, and regarded with reverence by barbarous men; and these pages were always open before their eyes. The well of the oath, the well of the living and seeing one; the ancient oak of Mamre, the stones of witness, such were the simple but stately monuments of the sanctity of contracts; none dared to lay a sacrilegious hand on these monuments, and man's faith was more secure under the warrant of these dumb witnesses than it is to-day upon all the rigour of the law.

In government the people were over-awed by the pomp and splendour of royal power. The symbols of greatness, a throne, a sceptre, a purple robe, a crown, a fillet, these were sacred in their sight. These symbols, and the respect which they inspired, led them to reverence the venerable man whom they beheld adorned with them; without soldiers and without threats, he spoke and was obeyed. In our own day men profess to do away with these symbols.[1] What are the consequences of this contempt? The kingly majesty makes no impression on all hearts, kings can only gain

[1] The Roman Catholic clergy have very wisely retained these symbols, and certain republics, such as Venice, have followed their example. Thus the Venetian government, despite the fallen condition of the state, still enjoys, under the trappings of its former greatness, all the affection, all the reverence of the people; and next to the pope in his triple crown, there is perhaps no king, no potentate, no person in the world so much respected as the Doge of Venice; he has no power, no authority, but he is rendered sacred by his pomp, and he wears beneath his ducal coronet a woman's flowing locks. That ceremony of the Bucentaurius, which stirs the laughter of fools, stirs the Venetian populace to shed its life-blood for the maintenance of this tyrannical government.

obedience by the help of troops, and the respect of their subjects
is based only on the fear of punishment. Kings are spared the
trouble of wearing their crowns, and our nobles escape from the
outward signs of their station, but they must have a hundred
thousand men at their command if their orders are to be obeyed.
Though this may seem a finer thing, it is easy to see that in the long
run they will gain nothing.

It is amazing what the ancients accomplished with the aid of
eloquence: but this eloquence did not merely consist in fine
speeches carefully prepared; and it was most effective when the
orator said least. The most startling speeches were expressed not
in words but in signs; they were not uttered but shown. A thing
beheld by the eyes kindles the imagination, stirs the curiosity, and
keeps the mind on the alert for what we are about to say, and often
enough the thing tells the whole story. Thrasybulus and Tarquin
cutting off the heads of the poppies, Alexander placing his seal on
the lips of his favourite, Diogenes marching before Zeno, do not these
speak more plainly than if they had uttered long orations? What
flow of words could have expressed the ideas as clearly? Darius,
in the course of the Scythian war, received from the king of the
Scythians a bird, a frog, a mouse, and five arrows. The ambassador
deposited this gift and retired without a word. In our days he
would have been taken for a madman. This terrible speech was
understood, and Darius withdrew to his own country with what
speed he could. Substitute a letter for these symbols and the
more threatening it was the less terror it would inspire; it would
have been merely a piece of bluff, to which Darius would have paid
no attention.

What heed the Romans gave to the language of signs! Different
ages and different ranks had their appropriate garments, toga, tunic,
patrician robes, fringes and borders, seats of honour, lictors, rods
and axes, crowns of gold, crowns of leaves, crowns of flowers, ovations,
triumphs, everything had its pomp, its observances, its ceremonial,
and all these spoke to the heart of the citizens. The state regarded
it as a matter of importance that the populace should assemble in
one place rather than another, that they should or should not behold
the Capitol, that they should or should not turn towards the Senate,
that this day or that should be chosen for their deliberations. The
accused wore a special dress, so did the candidates for election;
warriors did not boast of their exploits, they showed their scars.
I can fancy one of our orators at the death of Cæsar exhausting all
the commonplaces of rhetoric to give a pathetic description of his
wounds, his blood, his dead body; Anthony was an orator, but he
said none of this; he showed the murdered Cæsar. What rhetoric
was this!

But this digression, like many others, is drawing me unawares
away from my subject; and my digressions are too frequent to
be borne with patience. I therefore return to the point.

Do not reason coldly with youth. Clothe your reason with a

body, if you would make it felt. Let the mind speak the language of the heart, that it may be understood. I say again our opinions, not our actions, may be influenced by cold argument; they set us thinking, not doing; they show us what we ought to think, not what we ought to do. If this is true of men, it is all the truer of young people who are still enwrapped in their senses and cannot think otherwise than they imagine.

Even after the preparations of which I have spoken, I shall take good care not to go all of a sudden to Emile's room and preach a long and heavy sermon on the subject in which he is to be instructed. I shall begin by rousing his imagination; I shall choose the time, place, and surroundings most favourable to the impression I wish to make; I shall, so to speak, summon all nature as witness to our conversations; I shall call upon the eternal God, the Creator of nature, to bear witness to the truth of what I say. He shall judge between Emile and myself; I will make the rocks, the woods, the mountains round about us, the monuments of his promises and mine; eyes, voice, and gesture shall show the enthusiasm I desire to inspire. Then I will speak and he will listen, and his emotion will be stirred by my own. The more impressed I am by the sanctity of my duties, the more sacred he will regard his own. I will enforce the voice of reason with images and figures, I will not give him long-winded speeches or cold precepts, but my overflowing feelings will break their bounds; my reason shall be grave and serious, but my heart cannot speak too warmly. Then when I have shown him all that I have done for him, I will show him how he is made for me; he will see in my tender affection the cause of all my care. How greatly shall I surprise and disturb him when I change my tone. Instead of shrivelling up his soul by always talking of his own interests, I shall henceforth speak of my own; he will be more deeply touched by this. I will kindle in his young heart all the sentiments of affection, generosity, and gratitude which I have already called into being, and it will indeed be sweet to watch their growth. I will press him to my bosom, and weep over him in my emotion; I will say to him: " You are my wealth, my child, my handi-work; my happiness is bound up in yours; if you frustrate my hopes you rob me of twenty years of my life, and you bring my grey hairs with sorrow to the grave." This is the way to gain a hearing and to impress what is said upon the heart and memory of the young man.

Hitherto I have tried to give examples of the way in which a tutor should instruct his pupil in cases of difficulty. I have tried to do so in this instance; but after many attempts I have abandoned the task, convinced that the French language is too artificial to permit in print the plainness of speech required for the first lessons in certain subjects.

They say French is more chaste than other languages; for my own part I think it more obscene; for it seems to me that the purity of a language does not consist in avoiding coarse expressions but in having none. Indeed, if we are to avoid them, they must be in our thoughts, and there is no language in which it is so difficult to speak with purity on every subject than French. The reader is always quicker to detect than the author to avoid a gross meaning, and he is shocked and startled by everything. How can what is heard by impure ears avoid coarseness? On the other hand, a nation whose morals are pure has fit terms for everything, and these terms are always right because they are rightly used. One could not imagine more modest language than that of the Bible, just because of its plainness of speech. The same things translated into French would become immodest. What I ought to say to Emile will sound pure and honourable to him; but to make the same impression in print would demand a like purity of heart in the reader.

I should even think that reflections on true purity of speech and the sham delicacy of vice might find a useful place in the conversations as to morality to which this subject brings us; for when he learns the language of plain-spoken goodness, he must also learn the language of decency, and he must know why the two are so different. However this may be, I maintain that instead of the empty precepts which are prematurely dinned into the ears of children, only to be scoffed at when the time comes when they might prove useful, if instead of this we bide our time, if we prepare the way for a hearing, if we then show him the laws of nature in all their truth, if we show him the sanction of these laws in the physical and moral evils which overtake those who neglect them, if while we speak to him of this great mystery of generation, we join to the idea of the pleasure which the Author of nature has given to this act the idea of the exclusive affection which makes it delightful, the idea of the duties of faithfulness and modesty which surround it, and redouble its charm while fulfilling its purpose; if we paint to him marriage, not only as the sweetest form of society, but also as the most sacred and inviolable of contracts, if we tell him plainly all the reasons which lead men to respect this sacred bond, and to pour hatred and curses upon him who dares to dishonour it; if we give him a true and terrible picture of the horrors of debauch, of its stupid brutality, of the downward road by which a first act of misconduct leads from bad to worse, and at last drags the sinner to his ruin; if, I say, we give him proofs that on a desire for chastity depends health, strength, courage, virtue, love itself, and all that is truly good for man—I maintain that this chastity will be so dear and so desirable in his eyes, that his mind will be ready to receive our teaching as to the way to preserve it; for so long as we are chaste we respect chastity; it is only when we have lost this virtue that we scorn it.

It is not true that the inclination to evil is beyond our control, and that we cannot overcome it until we have acquired the habit of yielding to it. Aurelius Victor says that many men were mad enough to purchase a night with Cleopatra at the price of their life, and this is not incredible in the madness of passion. But let us suppose the maddest of men, the man who has his senses least under control; let him see the preparations for his death, let him realise that he will certainly die in torment a quarter of an hour later; not only would that man, from that time forward, become able to resist temptation, he would even find it easy to do so; the terrible picture with which they are associated will soon distract his attention from these temptations, and when they are continually put aside they will cease to recur. The sole cause of our weakness is the feebleness of our will, and we have always strength to perform what we strongly desire. " Volenti nihil difficile! " Oh! if only we hated vice as much as we love life, we should abstain as easily from a pleasant sin as from a deadly poison in a delicious dish.

How is it that you fail to perceive that if all the lessons given to a young man on this subject have no effect, it is because they are not adapted to his age, and that at every age reason must be presented in a shape which will win his affection? Speak seriously to him if required, but let what you say to him always have a charm which will compel him to listen. Do not coldly oppose his wishes; do not stifle his imagination, but direct it lest it should bring forth monsters. Speak to him of love, of women, of pleasure; let him find in your conversation a charm which delights his youthful heart; spare no pains to make yourself his confidant; under this name alone will you really be his master. Then you need not fear he will find your conversation tedious; he will make you talk more than you desire.

If I have managed to take all the requisite precautions in accordance with these maxims, and have said the right things to Emile at the age he has now reached, I am quite convinced that he will come of his own accord to the point to which I would lead him, and will eagerly confide himself to my care. When he sees the dangers by which he is surrounded, he will say to me with all the warmth of youth, " Oh, my friend, my protector, my master! resume the authority you desire to lay aside at the very time when I most need it; hitherto my weakness has given you this power. I now place it in your hands of my own free-will, and it will be all the more sacred in my eyes. Protect me from all the foes which are attacking me, and above all from the traitors within the citadel; watch over your work, that it may still be worthy of you. I mean to obey your laws, I shall ever do so, that is my steadfast purpose; if I ever disobey you, it will be against my will; make me free by guarding me against the passions which do me violence; do not let me become their slave; compel me to be my own master and to obey, not my senses, but my reason."

When you have led your pupil so far (and it will be your own fault if you fail to do so), beware of taking him too readily at his word, lest your rule should seem too strict to him, and lest he should think he has a right to escape from it, by accusing you of taking him by surprise. This is the time for reserve and seriousness; and this attitude will have all the more effect upon him seeing that it is the first time you have adopted it towards him.

You will say to him therefore: "Young man, you readily make promises which are hard to keep; you must understand what they mean before you have a right to make them; you do not know how your fellows are drawn by their passions into the whirlpool of vice masquerading as pleasure. You are honourable, I know; you will never break your word, but how often will you repent of having given it. How often will you curse your friend, when, in order to guard you from the ills which threaten you, he finds himself compelled to do violence to your heart. Like Ulysses who, hearing the song of the Sirens, cried aloud to his rowers to unbind him, you will break your chains at the call of pleasure; you will importune me with your lamentations, you will reproach me as a tyrant when I have your welfare most at heart; when I am trying to make you happy, I shall incur your hatred. Oh, Emile, I can never bear to be hateful in your eyes; this is too heavy a price to pay even for your happiness. My dear young man, do you not see that when you undertake to obey me, you compel me to promise to be your guide, to forget myself in my devotion to you, to refuse to listen to your murmurs and complaints, to wage unceasing war against your wishes and my own. Before we either of us undertake such a task, let us count our resources; take your time, give me time to consider, and be sure that the slower we are to promise, the more faithfully will our promises be kept.

You may be sure that the more difficulty he finds in getting your promise, the easier you will find it to carry it out. The young man must learn that he is promising a great deal, and that you are promising still more. When the time is come, when he has, so to say, signed the contract, then change your tone, and make your rule as gentle as you said it would be severe. Say to him, " My young friend, it is experience that you lack; but I have taken care that you do not lack reason. You are ready to see the motives of my conduct in every respect; to do this you need only wait till you are free from excitement. Always obey me first, and then ask the reasons for my commands; I am always ready to give my reasons so soon as you are ready to listen to them, and I shall never be afraid to make you the judge between us. You promise to follow my teaching, and I promise only to use your obedience to make you the happiest of men. For proof of this I have the life you have lived hitherto. Show me any one of your age who has led as happy a life as yours, and I promise you nothing more."

When my authority is firmly established, my first care will be to avoid the necessity of using it. I shall spare no pains to become more and more firmly established in his confidence, to make myself the confidant of his heart and the arbiter of his pleasures. Far from combating his youthful tastes, I shall consult them that I may be their master; I will look at things from his point of view that I may be his guide; I will not seek a remote distant good at the cost of his present happiness. I would always have him happy always if that may be.

Those who desire to guide young people rightly and to preserve them from the snares of sense give them a disgust for love, and would willingly make the very thought of it a crime, as if love were for the old. All these mistaken lessons have no effect; the heart gives the lie to them. The young man, guided by a surer instinct, laughs to himself over the gloomy maxims which he pretends to accept, and only awaits the chance of disregarding them. All that is contrary to nature. By following the opposite course I reach the same end more safely. I am not afraid to encourage in him the tender feeling for which he is so eager, I shall paint it as the supreme joy of life, as indeed it is; when I picture it to him, I desire that he shall give himself up to it; by making him feel the charm which the union of hearts adds to the delights of sense, I shall inspire him with a disgust for debauchery; I shall make him a lover and a good man.

How narrow-minded to see nothing in the rising desires of a young heart but obstacles to the teaching of reason. In my eyes, these are the right means to make him obedient to that very teaching. Only through passion can we gain the mastery over passions; their tyranny must be controlled by their legitimate power, and nature herself must furnish us with the means to control her.

Emile is not made to live alone, he is a member of society, and must fulfil his duties as such. He is made to live among his fellow-men and he must get to know them. He knows mankind in general; he has still to learn to know individual men. He knows what goes on in the world; he has now to learn how men live in the world. It is time to show him the front of that vast stage, of which he already knows the hidden workings. It will not arouse in him the foolish admiration of a giddy youth, but the discrimination of an exact and upright spirit. He may no doubt be deceived by his passions; who is there who yields to his passions without being led astray by them? At least he will not be deceived by the passions of other people. If he sees them, he will regard them with the eye of the wise, and will neither be led away by their example nor seduced by their prejudices.

As there is a fitting age for the study of the sciences, so there is a fitting age for the study of the ways of the world. Those who learn these too soon, follow them throughout life, without choice or consideration, and although they follow them fairly well they never really know what they are about. But he who studies the ways of the world and sees the reason for them, follows them with more insight, and therefore more exactly and gracefully. Give me a child of twelve who knows nothing at all; at fifteen I will restore him to you knowing as much as those who have been under instruction from infancy; with this difference, that your scholars only know things by heart, while mine knows how to use his knowledge. In the same way plunge a young man of twenty into society; under good guidance, in a year's time, he will be more charming and more truly polite than one brought up in society from childhood. For the former is able to perceive the reasons for all the proceedings relating to age, position, and sex, on which the customs of society depend, and can reduce them to general principles, and apply them to unforeseen emergencies; while the latter, who is guided solely by habit, is at a loss when habit fails him.

Young French ladies are all brought up in convents till they are married. Do they seem to find any difficulty in acquiring the ways which are so new to them, and is it possible to accuse the ladies of Paris of awkward and embarrassed manners or of ignorance of the ways of society, because they have not acquired them in infancy? This is the prejudice of men of the world, who know nothing of more importance than this trifling science, and wrongly imagine that you cannot begin to acquire it too soon.

On the other hand, it is quite true that we must not wait too long. Any one who has spent the whole of his youth far from the great world is all his life long awkward, constrained, out of place; his manners will be heavy and clumsy, no amount of practice will get rid of this, and he will only make himself more ridiculous by trying to do so. There is a time for every kind of teaching and we ought to recognise it, and each has its own dangers to be avoided. At this age there are more dangers than at any other; but I do not expose my pupil to them without safeguards.

When my method succeeds completely in attaining one object, and when in avoiding one difficulty it also provides against another, I then consider that it is a good method, and that I am on the right track. This seems to be the case with regard to the expedient suggested by me in the present case. If I desire to be stern and cold towards my pupil, I shall lose his confidence, and he will soon conceal himself from me. If I wish to be easy and complaisant, to shut my eyes, what good does it do him to be under my care? I only give my authority to his excesses, and relieve his conscience at the expense of my own. If I introduce him into society with no object but to teach him, he will learn more than I want. If I keep him apart from society, what will he have learnt from me? Everything perhaps, except the one art absolutely necessary to a civilised man, the art of living among his fellow-men. If I try to attend to this at a distance, it will be of no avail; he is only concerned with the present. If I am content to supply him with amusement, he will acquire habits of luxury and will learn nothing.

We will have none of this. My plan provides for everything. Your heart, I say to the young man, requires a companion; let us go in search of a fitting one; perhaps we shall not easily find such a one, true worth is always rare, but we will be in no hurry, nor will we be easily discouraged. No doubt there is such a one, and we shall find her at last, or at least we shall find some one like her. With an end so attractive to himself, I introduce him into society. What more need I say? Have I not achieved my purpose?

By describing to him his future mistress, you may imagine whether I shall gain a hearing, whether I shall succeed in making the qualities he ought to love pleasing and dear to him, whether I shall sway his feelings to seek or shun what is good or bad for him. I shall be the stupidest of men if I fail to make him in love with he knows not whom. No matter that the person I describe is imaginary, it is enough to disgust him with those who might have attracted him; it is enough if it is continually suggesting comparisons which make him prefer his fancy to the real people he sees; and is not love itself a fancy, a falsehood, an illusion? We are far more in love with our own fancy than with the object of it. If we saw the object of our affections as it is, there would be no such thing as love. When we cease to love, the person we used to love remains unchanged, but we no longer see with the same eyes; the magic veil is drawn aside, and love disappears. But when I supply the object of imagination, I have control over comparisons, and I am able easily to prevent illusion with regard to realities.

For all that I would not mislead a young man by describing a model of perfection which could never exist; but I would so choose the faults of his mistress that they will suit him, that he will be pleased by them, and they may serve to correct his own. Neither would I lie to him and affirm that there really is such a person; let him delight in the portrait, he will soon desire to find the original. From desire to belief the transition is easy; it is a matter of a little skilful description, which under more perceptible features will give to this imaginary object an air of greater reality. I would go so far as to give her a name; I would say, smiling, Let us call your future mistress Sophy; Sophy is a name of good omen; if it is not the name of the lady of your choice at least she will be worthy of the name; we may honour her with it meanwhile. If after all these details, without affirming or denying, we excuse ourselves from giving an answer, his suspicions will become certainty; he will think that his destined bride is purposely concealed from him, and that he will see her in good time. If once he has arrived at this conclusion and if the characteristics to be shown to him have been well chosen, the rest is easy; there will be little risk in exposing him to the world; protect him from his senses, and his heart is safe.

But whether or no he personifies the model I have contrived to make so attractive to him, this model, if well done, will attach him none the less to everything that resembles itself, and will give him as great a distaste for all that is unlike it as if Sophy really existed. What a means to preserve his heart from the dangers to which his appearance would expose him, to repress his senses by means of his imagination, to rescue him from the hands of those women who profess to educate young men, and make them pay so dear for their teaching, and only teach a young man manners by making him utterly shameless. Sophy is so modest? What would she think of their advances! Sophy is so simple! How would she like their airs? They are too far from his thoughts and his observations to be dangerous.

Every one who deals with the control of children follows the same prejudices and the same maxims, for their observation is at fault, and their reflection still more so. A young man is led astray in the first place neither by temperament nor by the senses, but by popular opinion. If we were concerned with boys brought up in boarding schools or girls in convents, I would show that this applies even to them; for the first lessons they learn from each other, the only lessons that bear fruit, are those of vice; and it is not nature that corrupts them but example. But let us leave the boarders in schools and convents to their bad morals; there is no cure for them. I am dealing only with home training. Take a young man carefully educated in his father's country house, and examine him when he reaches Paris and makes his entrance into society; you will find him thinking clearly about honest matters, and you will find his will as wholesome as his reason. You will find scorn of vice and disgust for debauchery; his face will betray his innocent horror at the very mention of a prostitute. I maintain that no young man could make up his mind to enter the gloomy abodes of these unfortunates by himself, if indeed he were aware of their purpose and felt their necessity.

See the same young man six months later, you will not know him; from his bold conversation, his fashionable maxims, his easy air, you would take him for another man, if his jests over his former simplicity and his shame when any one recalls it did not show that it is he indeed and that he is ashamed of himself. How greatly has he changed in so short a time! What has brought about so sudden and complete a change? His physical development? Would not that have taken place in his father's house, and certainly he would not have acquired these maxims and this tone at home? The first charms of sense? On the contrary; those who are beginning to abandon themselves to these pleasures are timid and anxious, they shun the light and noise. The first pleasures are always mysterious, modesty gives them their savour, and modesty conceals them; the first mistress does not make a man bold but timid. Wholly absorbed in a situation so novel to him, the young man retires into himself to enjoy it, and trembles for fear it should escape him. If he is noisy he knows neither passion nor love; however he may boast, he has not enjoyed.

These changes are merely the result of changed ideas. His heart is the same, but his opinions have altered. His feelings, which change more slowly, will at length yield to his opinions and it is then that he is indeed corrupted. He has scarcely made his entrance into society before he receives a second education quite unlike the first, which teaches him to despise what he esteemed, and esteem what he despised; he learns to consider the teaching of his parents and masters as the jargon of pedants, and the duties they have instilled into him as a childish morality, to be scorned now that he is grown up. He thinks he is bound in honour to change his conduct; he becomes forward without desire, and he talks foolishly from false shame. He rails against morality before he has any taste for vice, and prides himself on debauchery without knowing how to set about it. I shall never forget the confession of a young officer in the Swiss Guards, who was utterly sick of the noisy pleasures of his comrades, but dared not refuse to take part in them lest he should be laughed at. "I am getting used to it," he said, "as I am getting used to taking snuff; the taste will come with practice; it will not do to be a child for ever."

So a young man when he enters society must be preserved from vanity rather than from sensibility; he succumbs rather to the tastes of others than to his own, and self-love is responsible for more libertines than love.

This being granted, I ask you, Is there any one on earth better armed than my pupil against all that may attack his morals, his sentiments, his principles; is there any one more able to resist the flood? What seduction is there against which he is not forearmed? If his desires attract him towards women, he fails to find what he seeks, and his heart, already occupied, holds him back. If he is disturbed and urged onward by his senses, where will he find satisfaction? His horror of adultery and debauch keeps him at a distance from prostitutes and married women, and the disorders of youth may always be traced to one or other of these. A maiden may be a coquette, but she will not be shameless, she will not fling herself at the head of a young man who may marry her if he believes in her virtue; besides she is always under supervision. Emile, too, will not be left entirely to himself; both of them will be under the guardianship of fear and shame, the constant companions of a first passion; they will not proceed at once to misconduct, and they will not have time to come to it gradually without hindrance. If he behaves otherwise, he must have taken lessons from his comrades, he must have learned from them to despise his self-control, and to imitate their boldness. But there is no one in the whole world so little given to imitation as Emile. What man is there who is so little influenced by mockery as one who has no prejudices himself and yields nothing to the prejudices of others. I have laboured twenty years to arm him against mockery; they will not make him their dupe in a day; for in his eyes ridicule is the argument of fools, and nothing makes one less susceptible to raillery than to be beyond the influence of prejudice. Instead of jests he must have arguments, and while he is in this frame of mind, I am not afraid that he will be carried away by young fools; conscience and truth are on my side. If prejudice is to enter into the matter at all, an affection of twenty years' standing counts for something; no one will ever convince him that I have wearied him with vain lessons; and in a heart so upright and so sensitive the voice of a tried and trusted friend will soon efface the shouts of twenty libertines. As it is therefore merely a question of showing him that he is deceived, that while they pretend to treat him as a man they are really treating him as a child, I shall choose to be always simple but serious and plain in my arguments, so that he may feel that I do indeed treat him as a man. I will say to him, You will see that your welfare, in which my own is bound up, compels me to speak; I can do nothing else. But why do these young men want to persuade you? Because they desire to seduce you; they do not care for you, they take no real interest in you; their only motive is a secret spite because they see you are better than they; they want to drag you down to their own level, and they only reproach you with submitting to control that they may themselves control you. Do you think you have anything to gain by this? Are they so much wiser than I, is the affection of a day stronger than mine? To give any weight to their jests they must give weight to their authority; and by what experience do they support their maxims above ours? They have only followed the example of other giddy youths, as they would have you follow theirs. To escape from the so-called prejudices of their fathers, they yield to those of their comrades. I cannot see that they are any the better off; but I see that they lose two things of value—the affection of their parents, whose advice is that of tenderness and truth, and the wisdom of experience which teaches us to judge by what we know; for their fathers have once been young, but the young men have never been fathers.

But you think they are at least sincere in their foolish precepts. Not so, dear Emile; they deceive themselves in order to deceive you; they are not in agreement with themselves; their heart continually revolts, and their very words often contradict themselves. This man who mocks at everything good would be in despair if his wife held the same views. Another extends his indifference to good morals even to his future wife, or he sinks to such depths of infamy as to be indifferent to his wife's conduct; but go a step further; speak to him of his mother; is he willing to be treated as the child of an adulteress and the son of a woman of bad character, is he ready to assume the name of a family, to steal the patrimony of the true heir, in a word will he bear being treated as a bastard? Which of them will permit his daughter to be dishonoured as he dishonours the daughter of another? There is not one of them who would not kill you if you adopted in your conduct towards him all the principles he tries to teach you. Thus they prove their inconsistency, and we know they do not believe what they say. Here are reasons, dear Emile; weigh their arguments if they have any, and compare them with mine. If I wished to have recourse like them to scorn and mockery, you would see that they lend themselves to ridicule as much or more than myself. But I am not afraid of serious inquiry. The triumph of mockers is soon over; truth endures, and their foolish laughter dies away.

You do not think that Emile, at twenty, can possibly be docile. How differently we think! I cannot understand how he could be docile at ten, for what hold have I on him at that age? It took me fifteen years of careful preparation to secure that hold. I was not educating him, but preparing him for education. He is now sufficiently educated to be docile; he recognises the voice of friendship and he knows how to obey reason. It is true I allow him a show of freedom, but he was never more completely under control, because he obeys of his own free will. So long as I could not get the mastery over his will, I retained my control over his person; I never left him for a moment. Now I sometimes leave him to himself because I control him continually. When I leave him I embrace him and I say with confidence: Émile, I trust you to my friend, I leave you to his honour; he will answer for you.

To corrupt healthy affections which have not been previously depraved, to efface principles which are directly derived from our own reasoning, is not the work of a moment. If any change takes place during my absence, that absence will not be long, he will never be able to conceal himself from me, so that I shall perceive the danger before any harm comes of it, and I shall be in time to provide a remedy. As we do not become depraved all at once, neither do we learn to deceive all at once; and if ever there was a man unskilled in the art of deception it is Emile, who has never had any occasion for deceit.

By means of these precautions and others like them, I expect to guard him so completely against strange sights and vulgar precepts that I would rather see him in the worst company in Paris than alone in his room or in a park left to all the restlessness of his age. Whatever we may do, a young man's worst enemy is himself, and this is an enemy we cannot avoid. Yet this is an enemy of our own making, for, as I have said again and again, it is the imagination which stirs the senses. Desire is not a physical need; it is not true that it is a need at all. If no lascivious object had met our eye, if no unclean thought had entered our mind, this so-called need might never have made itself felt, and we should have remained chaste, without temptation, effort, or merit. We do not know how the blood of youth is stirred by certain situations and certain sights, while the youth himself does not understand the cause of his uneasiness—an uneasiness difficult to subdue and certain to recur. For my own part, the more I consider this serious crisis and its causes, immediate and remote, the more convinced I am that a solitary brought up in some desert, apart from books, teaching, and women, would die a virgin, however long he lived.

But we are not concerned with a savage of this sort. When we educate a man among his fellow men and for social life, we cannot, and indeed we ought not to, bring him up in this wholesome ignorance, and half knowledge is worse than none. The memory of things we have observed, the ideas we have acquired, follow us into retirement and people it, against our will, with images more seductive than the things themselves, and these make solitude as fatal to those who bring such ideas with them as it is wholesome for those who have never left it.

Therefore, watch carefully over the young man; he can protect himself from all other foes, but it is for you to protect him against himself. Never leave him night or day, or at least share his room;

never let him go to bed till he is sleepy, and let him rise as soon as he wakes. Distrust instinct as soon as you cease to rely altogether upon it. Instinct was good while he acted under its guidance only; now that he is in the midst of human institutions, instinct is not to be trusted; it must not be destroyed, it must be controlled, which is perhaps a more difficult matter. It would be a dangerous matter if instinct taught your pupil to abuse his senses; if once he acquires this dangerous habit he is ruined. From that time forward, body and soul will be enervated; he will carry to the grave the sad effects of this habit, the most fatal habit which a young man can acquire. If you cannot attain to the mastery of your passions, dear Emile, I pity you; but I shall not hesitate for a moment, I will not permit the purposes of nature to be evaded. If you must be a slave, I prefer to surrender you to a tyrant from whom I may deliver you; whatever happens, I can free you more easily from the slavery of women than from yourself.

Up to the age of twenty, the body is still growing and requires all its strength; till that age continence is the law of nature, and this law is rarely violated without injury to the constitution. After twenty, continence is a moral duty; it is an important duty, for it teaches us to control ourselves, to be masters of our own appetites. But moral duties have their modifications, their exceptions, their rules. When human weakness makes an alternative inevitable, of two evils choose the least; in any case it is better to commit a misdeed than to contract a vicious habit.

Remember, I am not talking of my pupil now, but of yours. His passions, to which you have given way, are your master; yield to them openly and without concealing his victory. If you are able to show him it in its true light, he will be ashamed rather than proud of it, and you will secure the right to guide him in his wanderings, at least so as to avoid precipices. The disciple must do nothing, not even evil, without the knowledge and consent of his master; it is a hundredfold better that the tutor should approve of a misdeed than that he should deceive himself or be deceived by his pupil, and the wrong should be done without his knowledge. He who thinks he must shut his eyes to one thing, must soon shut them altogether; the first abuse which is permitted leads to others, and this chain of consequences only ends in the complete overthrow of all order and contempt for every law.

There is another mistake which I have already dealt with, a mistake continually made by narrow-minded persons; they constantly affect the dignity of a master, and wish to be regarded by their disciples as perfect. This method is just the contrary of what should be done. How is it that they fail to perceive that when they try to strengthen their authority they are really destroying it; that to gain a hearing one must put oneself in the place of our hearers, and that to speak to the human heart, one must be a man. All these perfect people neither touch nor persuade; people always say, " It is easy for them to fight against passions they do not feel." Show your pupil your own weaknesses if you want to cure his; let him see in you struggles like his own; let him learn by your example to master himself and let him not say like other young men, " These old people, who are vexed because they are no longer young, want to treat all young people as if they were old; and they make a crime of our passions because their own passions are dead."

Montaigne tells us that he once asked Seigneur de Langey how often, in his negotiations with Germany, he had got drunk in his king's service. I would willingly ask the tutor of a certain young man how often he has entered a house of ill-fame for his pupil's sake. How often? I am wrong. If the first time has not cured the young libertine of all desire to go there again, if he does not return penitent and ashamed, if he does not shed torrents of tears upon your bosom, leave him on the spot; either he is a monster or you are a fool; you will never do him any good. But let us have done with these last expedients, which are as distressing as they are dangerous; our kind of education has no need of them.

What precautions we must take with a young man of good birth before exposing him to the scandalous manners of our age! These precautions are painful but necessary; negligence in this matter is the ruin of all our young men; degeneracy is the result of youthful excesses, and it is these excesses which make men what they are. Old and base in their vices, their hearts are shrivelled, because their worn-out bodies were corrupted at an early age; they have scarcely strength to stir. The subtlety of their thoughts betrays a mind lacking in substance; they are incapable of any great or noble feeling, they have neither simplicity nor vigour; altogether abject and meanly wicked, they are merely frivolous, deceitful, and false; they have not even courage enough to be distinguished criminals. Such are the despicable men produced by early debauchery; if there were but one among them who knew how to be sober and temperate, to guard his heart, his body, his morals from the contagion of bad example, at the age of thirty he would crush all these insects, and would become their master with far less trouble than it cost him to become master of himself.

However little Emile owes to birth and fortune, he might be this man if he chose; but he despises such people too much to condescend to make them his slaves. Let us now watch him in their midst, as he enters into society, not to claim the first place, but to acquaint himself with it and to seek a helpmeet worthy of himself.

Whatever his rank or birth, whatever the society into which he is introduced, his entrance into that society will be simple and unaffected; God grant he may not be unlucky enough to shine in society; the qualities which make a good impression at the first glance are not his, he neither possesses them, nor desires to possess them. He cares too little for the opinions of other people to value their prejudices, and he is indifferent whether people esteem him or not until they know him. His address is neither shy nor conceited, but natural and sincere, he knows nothing of constraint or concealment, and he is just the same among a group of people as he is when he is alone. Will this make him rude, scornful, and careless of others? On the contrary; if he were not heedless of others when he lived alone, why should he be heedless of them now that he is living among them? He does not prefer them to himself in his manners, because he does not prefer them to himself in his heart, but neither does he show them an indifference which he is far from feeling; if he is unacquainted with the forms of politeness, he is not unacquainted with the attentions dictated by humanity. He cannot bear to see any one suffer; he will not give up his place to another from mere external politeness, but he will willingly yield it to him out of kindness if he sees that he is being neglected and that this neglect hurts him; for it will be less disagreeable to Emile to remain standing of his own accord than to see another compelled to stand.

Although Emile has no very high opinion of people in general, he does not show any scorn of them, because he pities them and is sorry for them. As he cannot give them a taste for what is truly good, he leaves them the imaginary good with which they are satisfied, lest by robbing them of this he should leave them worse off than before. So he neither argues nor contradicts; neither does he flatter nor agree; he states his opinion without arguing with others, because he loves liberty above all things, and freedom is one of the fairest gifts of liberty.

He says little, for he is not anxious to attract attention; for the same reason he only says what is to the point; who could induce him to speak otherwise? Emile is too well informed to be a chatterbox. A great flow of words comes either from a pretentious spirit, of which I shall speak presently, or from the value laid upon trifles which we foolishly think to be as important in the eyes of others as in our own. He who knows enough of things to value them at their true worth never says too much; for he can also judge of the attention bestowed on him and the interest aroused by what he says. People who know little are usually great talkers, while men who know much say little. It is plain that an ignorant person thinks everything he does know important, and he tells it to everybody. But a well educated man is not so ready to display his learning; he would have too much to say, and he sees that there is much more to be said, so he holds his peace.

Far from disregarding the ways of other people, Emile conforms to them readily enough; not that he may appear to know all about them, nor yet to affect the airs of a man of fashion, but on the contrary for fear lest he should attract attention, and in order to pass unnoticed; he is most at his ease when no one pays any attention to him.

Although when he makes his entrance into society he knows nothing of its customs, this does not make him shy or timid; if he keeps in the background, it is not because he is embarrassed, but because, if you want to see, you must not be seen; for he scarcely troubles himself at all about what people think of him, and he is not the least afraid of ridicule. Hence he is always quiet and self-possessed and is not troubled with shyness. All he has to do is done as well as he knows how to do it, whether people are looking at him or not; and as he is always on the alert to observe other people, he acquires their ways with an ease impossible to the slaves of other people's opinions. We might say that he acquires the ways of society just because he cares so little about them.

But do not make any mistake as to his bearing; it is not to be compared with that of your young dandies. It is self-possessed, not conceited; his manners are easy, not haughty; an insolent look is the mark of a slave, there is nothing affected in independence. I never saw a man of lofty soul who showed it in his bearing; this affectation is more suited to vile and frivolous souls, who have no other means of asserting themselves. I read somewhere that a foreigner appeared one day in the presence of the famous Marcel, who asked him what country he came from. "I am an Englishman," replied the stranger. "You are an Englishman!" replied the dancer, "You come from that island where the citizens have a share in the government, and form part of the sovereign power? [1] No, sir, that modest bearing, that timid glance, that hesitating manner, proclaim only a slave adorned with the title of an elector."

I cannot say whether this saying shows much knowledge of the true relation between a man's character and his appearance. I have not the honour of being a dancing master, and I should have thought just the opposite. I should have said, "This Englishman is no courtier; I never heard that courtiers have a timid bearing and a hesitating manner. A man whose appearance is timid in the presence of a dancer might not be timid in the House of Commons." Surely this M. Marcel must take his fellow-countrymen for so many Romans.

He who loves desires to be loved. Emile loves his fellows and desires to please them. Even more does he wish to please the women; his age, his character, the object he has in view, all increase this desire. I say his character, for this has a great effect; men of good character are those who really adore women. They have not the mocking jargon of gallantry like the rest, but their eagerness is more genuinely tender, because it comes from the heart In the presence of a young woman, I could pick out a young man of character and self-control from among a hundred thousand libertines. Consider what Emile must be, with all the eagerness of early youth and so many reasons for resistance! For in the presence of women

---

[1] As if there were citizens who were not part of the city and had not, as such, a share in sovereign power! But the French, who have thought fit to usurp the honourable name of citizen which was formerly the right of the members of the Gallic cities, have degraded the idea till it has no longer any sort of meaning. A man who recently wrote a number of silly criticisms on the "Nouvelle Heloise" added to his signature the title "Citizen of Paimbœuf," and he thought it a capital joke.

I think he will sometimes be shy and timid; but this shyness will certainly not be displeasing, and the least foolish of them will only too often find a way to enjoy it and augment it. Moreover, his eagerness will take a different shape according to those he has to do with. He will be more modest and respectful to married women, more eager and tender towards young girls. He never loses sight of his purpose, and it is always those who most recall it to him who receive the greater share of his attentions.

No one could be more attentive to every consideration based upon the laws of nature, and even on the laws of good society; but the former are always preferred before the latter, and Emile will show more respect to an elderly person in private life than to a young magistrate of his own age. As he is generally one of the youngest in the company, he will always be one of the most modest, not from the vanity which apes humility, but from a natural feeling founded upon reason. He will not have the effrontery of the young fop, who speaks louder than the wise and interrupts the old in order to amuse the company. He will never give any cause for the reply given to Louis XV. by an old gentleman who was asked whether he preferred this century or the last: "Sire, I spent my youth in reverence towards the old; I find myself compelled to spend my old age in reverence towards the young."

His heart is tender and sensitive, but he cares nothing for the weight of popular opinion, though he loves to give pleasure to others; so he will care little to be thought a person of importance. Hence he will be affectionate rather than polite, he will never be pompous or affected, and he will be always more touched by a caress than by much praise. For the same reasons he will never be careless of his manners or his clothes; perhaps he will be rather particular about his dress, not that he may show himself a man of taste, but to make his appearance more pleasing; he will never require a gilt frame, and he will never spoil his style by a display of wealth.

All this demands, as you see, no stock of precepts from me; it is all the result of his early education. People make a great mystery of the ways of society, as if, at the age when these ways are acquired, we did not take to them quite naturally, and as if the first laws of politeness were not to be found in a kindly heart. True politeness consists in showing our goodwill towards men; it shows its presence without any difficulty; those only who lack this goodwill are compelled to reduce the outward signs of it to an art.

"The worst effect of artificial politeness is that it teaches us how to dispense with the virtues it imitates. If our education teaches us kindness and humanity, we shall be polite, or we shall have no need of politeness.

"If we have not those qualities which display themselves gracefully we shall have those which proclaim the honest man and the citizen; we shall have no need for falsehood.

"Instead of seeking to please by artificiality, it will suffice that we are kindly; instead of flattering the weaknesses of others by false-hood, it will suffice to tolerate them.

"Those with whom we have to do will neither be puffed up nor corrupted by such intercourse; they will only be grateful and will be informed by it." [1]

It seems to me that if any education is calculated to produce the sort of politeness required by M. Duclos in this passage, it is the education I have already described.

Yet I admit that with such different teaching Emile will not be just like everybody else, and heaven preserve him from such a fate! But where he is unlike other people, he will neither cause annoyance nor will he be absurd; the difference will be perceptible but not unpleasant. Emile will be, if you like, an agreeable foreigner. At first his peculiarities will be excused with the phrase, " He will learn." After a time people will get used to his ways, and seeing that he does not change they will still make excuses for him and say, " He is made that way."

He will not be fêted as a charming man, but every one will like him without knowing why; no one will praise his intellect, but every one will be ready to make him the judge between men of intellect; his own intelligence will be clear and limited, his mind will be accurate, and his judgment sane. As he never runs after new ideas, he cannot pride himself on his wit. I have convinced him that all wholesome ideas, ideas which are really useful to mankind, were among the earliest known, that in all times they have formed the true bonds of society, and that there is nothing left for ambitious minds but to seek distinction for themselves by means of ideas which are injurious and fatal to mankind. This way of winning admiration scarcely appeals to him; he knows how he ought to seek his own happiness in life, and how he can contribute to the happiness of others. The sphere of his knowledge is restricted to what is profitable. His path is narrow and clearly defined; as he has no temptation to leave it, he is lost in the crowd; he will neither distinguish himself nor will he lose his way. Emile is a man of common sense and he has no desire to be anything more; you may try in vain to insult him by applying this phrase to him; he will always consider it a title of honour.

Although from his wish to please he is no longer wholly indifferent to the opinion of others, he only considers that opinion so far as he himself is directly concerned, without troubling himself about arbitrary values, which are subject to no law but that of fashion or conventionality He will have pride enough to wish to do well in everything that he undertakes, and even to wish to do it better than others; he will want to be the swiftest runner, the strongest wrestler, the cleverest workman, the readiest in games of skill; but he will not seek advantages which are not in themselves clear gain, but need to be supported by the opinion of others, such as to be thought wittier than another, a better speaker, more learned, etc.;

[1] *Considerations sur les mœurs de ce siècle*, par M. Duclos.

still less will he trouble himself with those which have nothing to do with the man himself, such as higher birth, a greater reputation for wealth, credit, or public estimation, or the impression created by a showy exterior.

As he loves his fellows because they are like himself, he will prefer him who is most like himself, because he will feel that he is good; and as he will judge of this resemblance by similarity of taste in morals, in all that belongs to a good character, he will be delighted to win approval. He will not say to himself in so many words, " I am delighted to gain approval," but " I am delighted because they say I have done right; I am delighted because the men who honour me are worthy of honour; while they judge so wisely, it is a fine thing to win their respect."

As he studies men in their conduct in society, just as he formerly studied them through their passions in history, he will often have occasion to consider what it is that pleases or offends the human heart. He is now busy with the philosophy of the principles of taste, and this is the most suitable subject for his present study.

The further we seek our definitions of taste, the further we go astray; taste is merely the power of judging what is pleasing or displeasing to most people. Go beyond this, and you cannot say what taste is. It does not follow that the men of taste are in the majority; for though the majority judges wisely with regard to each individual thing, there are few men who follow the judgment of the majority in everything; and though the most general agreement in taste constitutes good taste, there are few men of good taste just as there are few beautiful people, although beauty consists in the sum of the most usual features.

It must be observed that we are not here concerned with what we like because it is serviceable, or hate because it is harmful to us. Taste deals only with things that are indifferent to us, or which affect at most our amusements, not those which relate to our needs; taste is not required to judge of these, appetite only is sufficient. It is this which makes mere decisions of taste so difficult and as it seems so arbitrary ; for beyond the instinct they follow there appears to be no reason whatever for them. We must also make a distinction between the laws of good taste in morals and its laws in physical matters. In the latter the laws of taste appear to be absolutely inexplicable. But it must be observed that there is a moral element in everything which involves imitation.[1] This is the explanation of beauties which seem to be physical, but are not so in reality. I may add that taste has local rules which make it dependent in many respects on the country we are in, its manners, government, institutions; it has other rules which depend upon age, sex, and character, and it is in this sense that we must not dispute over matters of taste.

Taste is natural to men; but all do not possess it in the same degree,

[1] This is demonstrated in an " Essay on the Origin of Languages " which will be found in my collected works.

it is not developed to the same extent in every one; and in every one it is liable to be modified by a variety of causes. Such taste as we may possess depends on our native sensibility; its cultivation and its form depend upon the society in which we have lived. In the first place we must live in societies of many different kinds, so as to compare much. In the next place, there must be societies for amusement and idleness, for in business relations, interest, not pleasure, is our rule. Lastly, there must be societies in which people are fairly equal, where the tyranny of public opinion may be moderate, where pleasure rather than vanity is queen; where this is not so, fashion stifles taste, and we seek what gives distinction rather than delight.

In the latter case it is no longer true that good taste is the taste of the majority. Why is this? Because the purpose is different. Then the crowd has no longer any opinion of its own, it only follows the judgment of those who are supposed to know more about it; its approval is bestowed not on what is good, but on what they have already ap roved. At any time let every man have his own opinion, and what is most pleasing in itself will always secure most votes.

Every beauty that is to be found in the works of man is imitated. All the true models of taste are to be found in nature. The further we get from the master, the worse are our pictures. Then it is that we find our models in what we ourselves like, and the beauty of fancy, subject to caprice and to authority, is nothing but what is pleasing to our leaders.

Those leaders are the artists, the wealthy, and the great, and they themselves follow the lead of self-interest or pride. Some to display their wealth, others to profit by it, they seek eagerly for new ways of spending it. This is how luxury acquires its power and makes us love what is rare and costly; this so-called beauty consists, not in following nature, but in disobeying her. Hence luxury and bad taste are inseparable. Wherever taste is lavish, it is bad.

Taste, good or bad, takes its shape especially in the intercourse between the two sexés; the cultivation of taste is a necessary consequence of this form of society. But when enjoyment is easily obtained, and the desire to please becomes lukewarm, taste must degenerate; and this is, in my opinion, one of the best reasons why good taste implies good morals.

Consult the women's opinions in bodily matters, in all that concerns the senses; consult the men in matters of morality and all that concerns the understanding. When women are what they ought to be, they will keep to what they can understand, and their judgment will be right; but since they have set themselves up as judges of literature, since they have begun to criticise books and to make chem with might and main, they are altogether astray. Authors who take the advice of blue-stockings will always be ill advised; gal.ants who consult them about their clothes will always be absurdly dressed. I shall presently have an opportunity of speaking of the real talents of the female sex, the way to cultivate these talents, and the matters in regard to which their decisions should receive attention.

These are the elementary considerations which I shall lay down as principles when I discuss with Emile this matter which is by no means indifferent to him in his present inquiries. And to whom should it be a matter of indifference? To know what people may find pleasant or unpleasant is not only necessary to any one who requires their help, it is still more necessary to any one who would help them; you must please them if you would do them service; and the art of writing is no idle pursuit if it is used to make men hear the truth.

If in order to cultivate my pupil's taste, I were compelled to choose between a country where this form of culture has not yet arisen and those in which it has already degenerated, I would progress backwards; I would begin his survey with the latter and end with the former. My reason for this choice is, that tas e becomes corrupted through excessive delicacy, which makes it sensitive to things which most men do not perceive; this delicacy leads to a spirit of discussion, for the more subtle is our discrimination of things the more things there are for us. This subtlety increases the delicacy and decreases the uniformity of our touch. So there are as many tastes as there are people. In disputes as to our preferences, philosophy and knowledge are enlarged, and thus we learn to think. It is only men accustomed to plenty of society who are capable of very delicate observations, for these observations do not occur to us till the last, and people who are unused to all sorts of society exhaust their attention in the consideration of the more conspicuous features. There is perhaps no civilised place upon earth where the common taste is so bad as in Paris. Yet it is in this capital that good taste is cultivated, and it seems that few books make any impression in Europe whose authors have not studied in Paris. Those who think it is enough to read our books are mistaken; there is more to be learnt from the conversation of authors than from their books; and it is not from the authors that we learn most. It is the spirit of social life which develops a thinking mind, and carries the eye as far as it can reach. If you have a spark of genius, go and spend a year in Paris; you will soon be all that you are capable of becoming, or you will never be good for anything at all.

One may learn to think in places where bad taste rules supreme; but we must not think like those whose taste is bad, and it is very difficult to avoid this if we spend much time among them. We must use their efforts to perfect the machinery of judgment, but we must be careful not to make the same use of it. I shall take care not to polish Emile's judgment so far as to transform it, and when he has acquired discernment enough to feel and compare the varied tastes of men, I shall lead him to fix his own taste upon simpler matters.

I will go still further in order to keep his taste pure and whole-some. In the tumult of dissipation I shall find opportunities for useful conversation with him; and while these conversations are always about things in which he takes a delight, I shall take care to make them as amusing as they are instructive. Now is the time to read pleasant books; now is the time to teach him to analyse speech and to appreciate all the beauties of eloquence and diction. It is a small matter to learn languages, they are less useful than people think; but the study of languages leads us on to that of grammar in general. We must learn Latin if we would have a thorough knowledge of French; these two languages must be studied and compared if we would understand the rules of the art of speaking.

There is, moreover, a certain simplicity of taste which goes straight to the heart; and this is only to be found in the classics. In oratory, poetry, and every kind of literature, Emile will find the classical authors as he found them in history, full of matter and sober in their judgment. The authors of our own time, on the contrary, say little and talk much. To take their judgment as our constant law is not the way to form our own judgment. These differences of taste make themselves felt in all that is left of classical times and even on their tombs. Our monuments are covered with praises, theirs recorded facts.

"Sta, viator; heroem calcas."

If I had found this epitaph on an ancient monument, I should at once have guessed it was modern; for there is nothing so common among us as heroes, but among the ancients they were rare.   Instead of saying a man was a hero, they would have said what he had done to gain that name.   With the epitaph of this hero compare that of the effeminate Sardanapalus—

"Tarsus and Anchiales I built in a day, and now I am dead."

Which do you think says most? Our inflated monumental style is only fit to trumpet forth the praises of pygmies. The ancients showed men as they were, and it was plain that they were men indeed. Xenophon did honour to the memory of some warriors who were slain by treason during the retreat of the Ten Thousand. "They died," said he, "without stain in war and in love." That is all, but think how full was the heart of the author of this short and simple elegy. Woe to him who fails to perceive its charm.

The following words were engraved on a tomb at Thermopylæ—

"Go, Traveller, tell Sparta that here we fell in obedience to her laws"

It is pretty clear that this was not the work of the Academy of Inscriptions.

If I am not mistaken, the attention of my pupil, who sets so small a value upon words, will be directed in the first place to these differences, and they will affect his choice in his reading. He will be carried away by the manly eloquence of Demosthenes, and will say, "This is an orator;" but when he reads Cicero, he will say, "This is a lawyer."

Speaking generally Emile will have more taste for the books of the ancients than for our own, just because they were the first, and therefore the ancients are nearer to nature and their genius is more distinct. Whatever La Motte and the Abbé Terrasson may say, there is no real advance in human reason, for what we gain in one direction we lose in another; for all minds start from the same point, and as the time spent in learning what others have thought is so much time lost in learning to think for ourselves, we have more acquired knowledge and less vigour of mind. Our minds like our arms are accustomed to use tools for everything, and to do nothing for themselves. Fontenelle used to say that all these disputes as to the ancients and the moderns came to this—Were the trees in former times taller than they are now. If agriculture had changed, it would be worth our while to ask this question.

After I have led Emile to the sources of pure literature, I will also show him the channels into the reservoirs of modern compilers; journals, translations, dictionaries, he shall cast a glance at them all, and then leave them for ever. To amuse him he shall hear the chatter of the academies; I will draw his attention to the fact that every member of them is worth more by himself than he is as a member of the society; he will then draw his own conclusions as to the utility of these fine institutions.

I take him to the theatre to study taste, not morals; for in the theatre above all taste is revealed to those who can think. Lay aside precepts and morality, I should say; this is not the place to study them. The stage is not made for truth; its object is to flatter and amuse; there is no place where one can learn so completely the art of pleasing and of interesting the human heart. The study of plays leads to the study of poetry; both have the same end in view. If he has the least glimmering of taste for poetry, how eagerly will he study the languages of the poets, Greek, Latin, and Italian! These studies will afford him unlimited amusement and will be none the less valuable; they will be a delight to him at an age and in circumstances when the heart finds so great a charm in every kind of beauty which affects it. Picture to yourself on the one hand Emile, on the other some young rascal from college, reading the fourth book of the *Æneid*, or Tibullus, or the *Banquet* of Plato: what a difference between them! What stirs the heart of Emile to its depths, makes not the least impression on the other! Oh, good youth, stay, make a pause in your reading, you are too deeply moved; I would have you find pleasure in the language of love, but I would not have you carried away by it; be a wise man, but be a good man too. If you are only one of these, you are nothing. After this let him win fame or not in dead languages, in literature, in poetry, I care little. He will be none the worse if he knows nothing of them, and his education is not concerned with these mere words.

My main object in teaching him to feel and love beauty of every kind is to fix his affections and his taste on these, to prevent the corruption of his natural appetites, lest he should have to seek some day in the midst of his wealth for the means of happiness which should be found close at hand. I have said elsewhere that taste is only the art of being a connoisseur in matters of little importance, and this is quite true; but since the charm of life depends on a tissue of these matters of little importance, such efforts are no small thing; through their means we learn how to fill our life with the good things within our reach, with as much truth as they may hold for us. I do not refer to the morally good which depends on a good disposition of the heart, but only to that which depends on the body, on real delight, apart from the prejudices of public opinion.

The better to unfold my idea, allow me for a moment to leave Emile, whose pure and wholesome heart cannot be taken as a rule for others, and to seek in my own memory for an illustration better suited to the reader and more in accordance with his own manners.

There are professions which seem to change a man's nature, to recast, either for better or worse, the men who adopt them. A coward becomes a brave man in the regiment of Navarre. It is not only in the army that *esprit de corps* is acquired, and its effects are not always for good. I have thought again and again with terror that if I had the misfortune to fill a certain post I am thinking of in a certain country, before to-morrow I should certainly be a tyrant, an extortioner, a destroyer of the people, harmful to my king, and a professed enemy of mankind, a foe to justice and every kind of virtue.

In the same way, if I were rich, I should have done all that is required to gain riches; I should therefore be insolent and degraded, sensitive and feeling only on my own behalf, harsh and pitiless to all besides, a scornful spectator of the sufferings of the lower classes; for that is what I should call the poor, to make people forget that I was once poor myself. Lastly I should make my fortune a means to my own pleasures with which I should be wholly occupied; and so far I should be just like other people.

But in one respect I should be very unlike them; I should be sensual and voluptuous rather than proud and vain, and I should give myself up to the luxury of comfort rather than to that of ostentation. I should even be somewhat ashamed to make too great a show of my wealth, and if I overwhelmed the envious with my pomp I should always fancy I heard him saying, " Here is a rascal who is greatly afraid lest we should take him for anything but what he is."

In the vast profusion of good things upon this earth I should seek what I like best, and what I can best appropriate to myself.

To this end, the first use I should make of my wealth would be to purchase leisure and freedom, to which I would add health, if it were to be purchased; but health can only be bought by temperance, and as there is no real pleasure without health, I should be temperate from sensual motives.

I should also keep as close as possible to nature, to gratify the senses given me by nature, being quite convinced that, the greater her share in my pleasures, the more real I shall find them. In the choice of models for imitation I shall always choose nature as my pattern; in my appetites I will give her the preference; in my tastes she shall always be consulted; in my food I will always choose what most owes its charm to her, and what has passed through the fewest possible hands on its way to table. I will be on my guard against fraudulent shams; I will go out to meet pleasure. No cook shall grow rich on my gross and foolish greediness; he shall not poison me with fish which cost its weight in gold, my table shall not be decked with fetid splendour or putrid flesh from far-off lands. I will take any amount of trouble to gratify my sensibility, since this trouble has a pleasure of its own, a pleasure more than we expect. If I wished to taste a food from the ends of the earth, I would go, like Apicius, in search of it, rather than send for it; for the daintiest dishes always lack a charm which cannot be brought along with them, a flavour which no cook can give them—the air of the country where they are produced.

For the same reason I would not follow the example of those who are never well off where they are, but are always setting the seasons at nought, and confusing countries and their seasons; those who seek winter in summer and summer in winter, and go to Italy to be cold and to the north to be warm, do not consider that when they think they are escaping from the severity of the seasons, they are going to meet that severity in places where people are not prepared for it. I shall stay in one place, or I shall adopt just the opposite course; I should like to get all possible enjoyment out of one season to discover what is peculiar to any given country. I would have a variety of pleasures, and habits quite unlike one another, but each according to nature; I would spend the summer at Naples and the winter in St. Petersburg; sometimes I would breathe the soft zephyr lying in the cool grottoes of Tarentum, and again I would enjoy the illuminations of an ice palace, breathless and wearied with the pleasures of the dance.

In the service of my table and the adornment of my dwelling I would imitate in the simplest ornaments the variety of the seasons, and draw from each its charm without anticipating its successor. There is no taste but only difficulty to be found in thus disturbing the order of nature; to snatch from her unwilling gifts, which she yields regretfully, with her curse upon them; gifts which have neither strength nor flavour, which can neither nourish the body nor tickle the palate. Nothing is more insipid than forced fruits. A wealthy man in Paris, with all his stoves and hot-houses, only succeeds in getting all the year round poor fruit and poor vegetables for his table at a very high price. If I had cherries in frost, and golden melons in the depths of winter, what pleasure should I find in them when my palate did not need moisture or refreshment. Would the heavy chestnut be very pleasant in the heat of the dog-days; should I prefer to have it hot from the stove, rather than the gooseberry, the strawberry, the refreshing fruits which the earth takes care to provide for me. A mantelpiece covered in January with forced vegetation, with pale and scentless flowers, is not winter adorned, but spring robbed of its beauty; we deprive ourselves of the pleasure of seeking the first violet in the woods, of noting the earliest buds, and exclaiming in a rapture of delight, "Mortals, you are not forsaken, nature is living still."

To be well served I would have few servants; this has been said before, but it is worth saying again. A tradesman gets more real service from his one man than a duke from the ten gentlemen round about him. It has often struck me when I am sitting at table with my glass beside me that I can drink whenever I please; whereas, if I were dining in state, twenty men would have to call for "Wine" before I could quench my thirst. You may be sure that whatever is done for you by other people is ill done. I would not send to the shops, I would go myself; I would go so that my servants should not make their own terms with the shopkeepers, and to get a better choice and cheaper prices; I would go for the sake of pleasant exercise and to get a glimpse of what was going on out of doors; this is amusing and sometimes instructive; lastly I would go for the sake of the walk; there is always something in that. A sedentary life is the source of tedium; when we walk a good deal we are never dull. A porter and footmen are poor interpreters, I should never wish to have such people between the world and myself, nor would I travel with all the fuss of a coach, as if I were afraid people would speak to me. Shanks' mare is always ready; if she is tired or ill, her owner is the first to know it; he need not be afraid of being kept at home while his coachman is on the spree; on the road he will not have to submit to all sorts of delays, nor will he be consumed with impatience, nor compelled to stay in one place a moment longer than he chooses. Lastly, since no one serves us so well as we serve ourselves, had we the power of Alexander and the wealth of Crœsus we should accept no services from others, except those we cannot perform for ourselves.

I would not live in a palace; for even in a palace I should only occupy one room; every room which is common property belongs to nobody, and the rooms of each of my servants would be as strange to me as my neighbour's. The Orientals, although very voluptuous, are lodged in plain and simply furnished dwellings. They consider life as a journey, and their house as an inn. This reason scarcely appeals to us rich people who propose to live for ever; but I should find another reason which would have the same effect. It would seem to me that if I settled myself in one place in the midst of such splendour, I should banish myself from every other place, and imprison myself, so to speak, in my palace. The world is a palace fair enough for any one; and is not everything at the disposal of the rich man when he seeks enjoyment? "Ubi bene, ibi patria," that is his motto; his home is anywhere where money will carry him, his country is anywhere where there is room for his strong-box, as Philip considered as his own any place where a mule laden with silver could enter.[1] Why then should we shut ourselves up within walls and gates as if we never meant to leave them? If pestilence, war, or rebellion drive me from one place, I go to another, and I find my hotel there before me. Why should I build a mansion for myself when the world is already at my disposal? Why should I be in such a hurry to live, to bring from afar delights which I can find on the spot? It is impossible to make a pleasant life for oneself when one is always at war with oneself. Thus Empedocles reproached the men of Agrigentum with heaping up pleasures as if they had but one day to live, and building as if they would live for ever.

And what use have I for so large a dwelling, as I have so few people to live in it, and still fewer goods to fill it? My furniture would be as simple as my tastes; I would have neither picture-gallery nor library, especially if I was fond of reading and knew something about pictures. I should then know that such collections are never complete, and that the lack of that which is wanting causes more annoyance than if one had nothing at all. In this respect abundance is the cause of want, as every collector knows to his cost. If you are an expert, do not make a collection; if you know how to use your cabinets, you will not have any to show.

Gambling is no sport for the rich, it is the resource of those who have nothing to do; I shall be so busy with my pleasures that I shall have no time to waste. I am poor and lonely and I never play, unless it is a game of chess now and then, and that is more than enough. If I were rich I would play even less, and for very low stakes, so that I should not be disappointed myself, nor see the disappointment of others. The wealthy man has no motive for play, and the love of play will not degenerate into the passion for gambling unless the disposition is evil. The rich man is always more keenly aware of his losses than his gains, and as in games where the stakes are not high the winnings are generally exhausted in the long run, he will usually lose more than he gains, so that if we reason rightly we shall scarcely take a great fancy to games where the odds are against us. He who flatters his vanity so far as to believe that Fortune favours him can seek her favour in more exciting ways; and her favours are just as clearly shown when the stakes are low as when they are high. The taste for play, the result of greed and dullness, only lays hold of empty hearts and heads;

[1] A stranger, splendidly clad, was asked in Athens what country he belonged to. "I am one of the rich," was his answer; and a very good answer in my opinion

and I think I should have enough feeling and knowledge to dispense with its help. Thinkers are seldom gamblers; gambling interrupts the habit of thought and turns it towards barren combinations; thus one good result, perhaps the only good result of the taste for science, is that it deadens to some extent this vulgar passion; people will prefer to try to discover the uses of play rather than to devote themselves to it. I should argue with the gamblers against gambling, and I should find more delight in scoffing at their losses than in winning their money.

I should be the same in private life as in my social intercourse. I should wish my fortune to bring comfort in its train, and never to make people conscious of inequalities of wealth. Showy dress is inconvenient in many ways. To preserve as much freedom as possible among other men, I should like to be dressed in such a way that I should not seem out of place among all classes, and should not attract attention in any; so that without affectation or change I might mingle with the crowd at the inn or with the nobility at the Palais Royal. In this way I should be more than ever my own master, and should be free to enjoy the pleasures of all sorts and conditions of men. There are women, so they say, whose doors are closed to embroidered cuffs, women who will only receive guests who wear lace ruffles; I should spend my days elsewhere; though if these women were young and pretty I might sometimes put on lace ruffles to spend an evening or so in their company.

Mutual affection, similarity of tastes, suitability of character; these are the only bonds between my companions and myself; among them I would be a man, not a person of wealth; the charm of their society should never be embittered by self-seeking. If my wealth had not robbed me of all humanity, I would scatter my benefits and my services broadcast, but I should want companions about me, not courtiers, friends, not protégés; I should wish my friends to regard me as their host, not their patron. Independence and equality would leave to my relations with my friends the sincerity of goodwill; while duty and self-seeking would have no place among us, and we should know no law but that of pleasure and friendship.

Neither a friend nor a mistress can be bought. Women may be got for money, but that road will never lead to love. Love is not only not for sale; money strikes it dead. If a man pays, were he indeed the most lovable of men, the mere fact of payment would prevent any lasting affection. He will soon be paying for some one else, or rather some one else will get his money; and in this double connection based on self-seeking and debauchery, without love, honour, or true pleasure, the woman is grasping, faithless, and unhappy, and she is treated by the wretch to whom she gives her money as she treats the fool who gives his money to her; she has no love for either. It would be sweet to be generous towards one we love, if that did not make a bargain of love. I know only one way of gratifying this desire with the woman one loves without embittering love; it is to bestow our all upon her and to live at her expense. It remains to be seen whether there is any woman with regard to whom such conduct would not be unwise.

He who said, " Lais is mine, but I am not hers," was talking nonsense. Possession which is not mutual is nothing at all; at most it is the possession of the sex not of the individual. But where there is no morality in love, why make such ado about the rest? Nothing is so easy to find. A muleteer is in this respect as near to happiness as a millionaire.

Oh, if we could thus trace out the unreasonableness of vice, how often should we find that, when it has attained its object, it discovers it is not what it seemed! Why is there this cruel haste to corrupt innocence, to make a victim of a young creature whom we ought to protect, one who is dragged by this first false step into a gulf of misery from which only death can release her? Brutality, vanity, folly, error, and nothing more. This pleasure itself is unnatural; it rests on popular opinion, and popular opinion at its worst, since it depends on scorn of self. He who knows he is the basest of men fears comparison with others, and would be the first that he may be less hateful. See if those who are most greedy in pursuit of such fancied pleasures are ever attractive young men—men worthy of pleasing, men who might have some excuse if they were hard to please. Not so; any one with good looks, merit, and feeling has little fear of his mistress' experience; with well-placed confidence he says to her, " You know what pleasure is, what is that to me? my heart assures me that this is not so."

But an aged satyr, worn out with debauchery, with no charm, no consideration, no thought for any but himself, with no shred of honour, incapable and unworthy of finding favour in the eyes of any woman who knows anything of men deserving of love, expects to make up for all this with an innocent girl by trading on her inexperience and stirring her emotions for the first time. His last hope is to find favour as a novelty; no doubt this is the secret motive of this desire; but he is mistaken, the horror he excites is just as natural as the desires he wishes to arouse. He is also mistaken in his foolish attempt: that very nature takes care to assert her rights; every girl who sells herself is no longer a maid; she has given herself to the man of her choice, and she is making the very comparison he dreads. The pleasure purchased is imaginary, but none the less hateful.

For my own part, however riches may change me, there is one matter in which I shall never change. If I have neither morals nor virtue, I shall not be wholly without taste, without sense, without delicacy; and this will prevent me from spending my fortune in the pursuit of empty dreams, from wasting my money and my strength in teaching children to betray me and mock at me. If I were young, I would seek the pleasures of youth; and as I would have them at their best I would not seek them in the guise of a rich man. If I were at my present age, it would be another matter;

I would wisely confine myself to the pleasures of my age; I would form tastes which I could enjoy, and I would stifle those which could only cause suffering. I would not go and offer my grey beard to the scornful jests of young girls; I could never bear to sicken them with my disgusting caresses, to furnish them at my expense with the most absurd stories, to imagine them describing the vile pleasures of the old ape, so as to avenge themselves for what they had endured. But if habits unresisted had changed my former desires into needs, I would perhaps satisfy those needs, but with shame and blushes. I would distinguish between passion and necessity, I would find a suitable mistress and would keep to her. I would not make a business of my weakness, and above all I would only have one person aware of it. Life has other pleasures when these fail us; by hastening in vain after those that fly us, we deprive ourselves of those that remain. Let our tastes change with our years, let us no more meddle with age than with the seasons. We should be ourselves at all times, instead of struggling against nature; such vain attempts exhaust our strength and prevent the right use of life.

The lower classes are seldom dull, their life is full of activity; if there is little variety in their amusements they do not recur frequently; many days of labour teach them to enjoy their rare holidays. Short intervals of leisure between long periods of labour give a spice to the pleasures of their station. The chief curse of the rich is dullness; in the midst of costly amusements, among so many men striving to give them pleasure, they are devoured and slain by dullness; their life is spent in fleeing from it and in being overtaken by it; they are overwhelmed by the intolerable burden; women more especially, who do not know how to work or play, are a prey to tedium under the name of the vapours; with them it takes the shape of a dreadful disease, which robs them of their reason and even of their life. For my own part I know no more terrible fate than that of a pretty woman in Paris, unless it is that of the pretty manikin who devotes himself to her, who becomes idle and effeminate like her, and so deprives himself twice over of his manhood, while he prides himself on his successes and for their sake endures the longest and dullest days which human being ever put up with.

Proprieties, fashions, customs which depend on luxury and breeding, confine the course of life within the limits of the most miserable uniformity. The pleasure we desire to display to others is a pleasure lost; we neither enjoy it ourselves, nor do others enjoy it.[1] Ridicule, which public opinion dreads more than anything, is ever at hand to tyrannise and punish. It is only ceremony that

[1] Two ladies of fashion, who wished to seem to be enjoying themselves greatly, decided never to go to bed before five o'clock in the morning. In the depths of winter their servants spent the night in the street waiting for them, and with great difficulty kept themselves from freezing. One night, or rather one morning, some one entered the room where these merry people spent their hours without knowing how time passed. He found them quite alone; each of them was asleep in her arm-chair.

makes us ridiculous; if we can vary our place and our pleasures, to-day's impressions can efface those of yesterday; in the mind of men they are as if they had never been; but we enjoy ourselves for we throw ourselves into every hour and everything. My only set rule would be this: wherever I was I would pay no heed to anything else. I would take each day as it came, as if there were neither yesterday nor to-morrow. As I should be a man of the people, with the populace, I should be a countryman in the fields; and if I spoke of farming, the peasant should not laugh at my expense. I would not go and build a town in the country nor erect the Tuileries at the door of my lodgings. On some pleasant shady hill-side I would have a little cottage, a white house with green shutters, and though a thatched roof is the best all the year round, I would be grand enough to have, not those gloomy slates, but tiles, because they look brighter and more cheerful than thatch, and the houses in my own country are always roofed with them, and so they would recall to me something of the happy days of my youth. For my courtyard I would have a poultry-yard, and for my stables a cowshed for the sake of the milk which I love. My garden should be a kitchen-garden, and my park an orchard, like the one described further on. The fruit would be free to those who walked in the orchard, my gardener should neither count it nor gather it; I would not, with greedy show, display before your eyes superb espaliers which one scarcely dare touch. But this small extravagance would not be costly, for I would choose my abode in some remote province where silver is scarce and food plentiful, where plenty and poverty have their seat.

There I would gather round me a company, select rather than numerous, a band of friends who know what pleasure is, and how to enjoy it, women who can leave their arm-chairs and betake themselves to outdoor sports, women who can exchange the shuttle or the cards for the fishing line or the bird-trap, the gleaner's rake or grape-gatherer's basket. There all the pretensions of the town will be forgotten, and we shall be villagers in a village; we shall find all sorts of different sports and we shall hardly know how to choose the morrow's occupation. Exercise and an active life will improve our digestion and modify our tastes. Every meal will be a feast, where plenty will be more pleasing than any delicacies. There are no such cooks in the world as mirth, rural pursuits, and merry games; and the finest made dishes are quite ridiculous in the eyes of people who have been on foot since early dawn. Our meals will be served without regard to order or elegance; we shall make our dining-room anywhere, in the garden, on a boat, beneath a tree; sometimes at a distance from the house on the banks of a running stream, on the fresh green grass, among the clumps of willow and hazel; a long procession of guests will carry the material for the feast with laughter and singing; the turf will be our chairs and table, the banks of the stream our side-board, and our dessert is hanging on the trees; the dishes will be served in any order, appetite needs no ceremony; each one of us, openly putting himself first, would gladly see every one else do the same; from this warm-hearted and temperate familiarity there would arise, without coarseness, pretence, or constraint, a laughing conflict a hundredfold more delightful than politeness, and more likely to cement our friendship. No tedious flunkeys to listen to our words, to whisper criticisms on our behaviour, to count every mouthful with greedy eyes, to amuse themselves by keeping us waiting for our wine, to complain of the length of our dinner. We will be our own servants, in order to be our own masters. Time will fly unheeded, our meal will be an interval of rest during the heat of the day. If some peasant comes our way, returning from his work with his tools over his shoulder, I will cheer his heart with kindly words, and a glass or two of good wine, which will help him to bear his poverty more cheerfully; and I too shall have the joy of feeling my heart stirred within me, and I should say to myself—I too am a man.

If the inhabitants of the district assembled for some rustic feast, I and my friends would be there among the first; if there were marriages, more blessed than those of towns, celebrated near my home, every one would know how I love to see people happy, and I should be invited. I would take these good folks some gift as simple as themselves, a gift which would be my share of the feast; and in exchange I should obtain gifts beyond price, gifts so little known among my equals, the gifts of freedom and true pleasure. I should sup gaily at the head of their long table; I should join in the chorus of some rustic song and I should dance in the barn more merrily than at a ball in the Opera House.

"This is all very well so far," you will say, "but what about the shooting? One must have some sport in the country." Just so; I only wanted a farm, but I was wrong. I assume I am rich, I must keep my pleasures to myself, I must be free to kill something; this is quite another matter. I must have estates, woods, keepers, rents, seignorial rights, particularly incense and holy water.

Well and good. But I shall have neighbours about my estate who are jealous of their rights and anxious to encroach on those of others; our keepers will quarrel, and possibly their masters will quarrel too; this means altercations, disputes, ill-will, or law-suits at the least; this in itself is not very pleasant. My tenants will not enjoy finding my hares at work upon their corn, or my wild boars among their beans. As they dare not kill the enemy, every one of them will try to drive him from their fields; when the day has been spent in cultivating the ground, they will be compelled to sit up at night to watch it; they will have watch-dogs, drums, horns, and bells; my sleep will be disturbed by their racket. Do what I will, I cannot help thinking of the misery of these poor people, and I cannot help blaming myself for it. If I had the honour of being a prince, this would make little impression on me; but as I am a self-made man who has only just come into his property, I am still rather vulgar at heart.

That is not all; abundance of game attracts trespassers; I shall soon have poachers to punish; I shall require prisons, gaolers, guards, and galleys; all this strikes me as cruel. The wives of those miserable creatures will besiege my door and disturb me with their crying; they must either be driven away or roughly handled. The poor people who are not poachers, whose harvest has been destroyed by my game, will come next with their complaints. Some people will be put to death for killing the game, the rest will be punished for having spared it; what a choice of evils! On every side I shall find nothing but misery and hear nothing but groans. So far as I can see this must greatly disturb the pleasure of slaying at one's ease heaps of partridges and hares which are tame enough to run about one's feet.

If you would have pleasure without pain let there be no monopoly; the more you leave it free to everybody, the purer will be your own enjoyment. Therefore I should not do what I have just described, but without change of tastes I would follow those which seem likely to cause me least pain. I would fix my rustic abode in a district where game is not preserved, and where I can have my sport without hindrance. Game will be less plentiful, but there will be more skill in finding it, and more pleasure in securing it. I remember the start of delight with which my father watched the rise of his first partridge and the rapture with which he found the hare he had sought all day long. Yes, I declare, that alone with his dog, carrying his own gun, cartridges, and game bag together with his hare, he came home at nightfall, worn out with fatigue and torn to pieces by brambles, but better pleased with his day's sport than all your ordinary sportsmen, who on a good horse, with twenty guns ready for them, merely take one gun after another, and shoot and kill everything that comes their way, without skill, without glory, and almost without exercise. The pleasure is none the less, and the difficulties are removed; there is no estate to be preserved, no poacher to be punished, and no wretches to be tormented; here are solid grounds for preference. Whatever you do, you cannot torment men for ever without experiencing some amount of discomfort; and sooner or later the muttered curses of the people will spoil the flavour of your game.

Again, monopoly destroys pleasure. Real pleasures are those which we share with the crowd; we lose what we try to keep to ourselves alone. If the walls I build round my park transform it into a gloomy prison, I have only deprived myself, at great expense, of the pleasure of a walk; I must now seek that pleasure at a distance. The demon of property spoils everything he lays hands upon. A rich man wants to be master everywhere, and he is never happy where he is; he is continually driven to flee from himself. I shall therefore continue to do in my prosperity what I did in my poverty. Henceforward, richer in the wealth of others than I ever shall be in my own wealth, I will take possession of everything in my neighbourhood that takes my fancy; no conqueror is so deter-

mined as I; I even usurp the rights of princes; I take possession of
every open place that pleases me, I give them names; this is my
park, that is my terrace, and I am their owner; henceforward I
wander among them at will; I often return to maintain my pro-
prietary rights; I make what use I choose of the ground to walk
upon, and you will never convince me that the nominal owner of
the property which I have appropriated gets better value out of
the money it yields him than I do out of his land.   No matter
if I am interrupted by hedges and ditches, I take my park on my
back, and I carry it elsewhere; there will be space enough for it
near at hand, and I may plunder my neighbours long enough before
I outstay my welcome.

This is an attempt to show what is meant by good taste in the
choice of pleasant occupations for our leisure hours; this is the
spirit of enjoyment; all else is illusion, fancy, and foolish pride.
He who disobeys these rules, however rich he may be, will devour
his gold on a dung-hill, and will never know what it is to live.

You will say, no doubt, that such amusements lie within the
reach of all, that we need not be rich to enjoy them.   That is the
very point I was coming to.   Pleasure is ours when we want it;
it is only social prejudice which makes everything hard to obtain,
and drives pleasure before us.   To be happy is a hundredfold easier
than it seems.   If he really desires to enjoy himself the man of taste
has no need of riches; all he wants is to be free and to be his own
master.   With health and daily bread we are rich enough, if we
will but get rid of our prejudices; this is the "Golden Mean" of
Horace.   You folks with your strong-boxes may find some other
use for your wealth, for it cannot buy you pleasure.   Emile knows
this as well as I, but his heart is purer and more healthy, so he will
feel it more strongly, and all that he has beheld in society will only
serve to confirm him in this opinion.

While our time is thus employed, we are ever on the look-out for
Sophy, and we have not yet found her.   It was not desirable that
she should be found too easily, and I have taken care to look for her
where I knew we should not find her.

The time is come; we must now seek her in earnest, lest Emile
should mistake some one else for Sophy, and only discover his error
when it is too late.   Then farewell Paris, far-famed Paris, with all
your noise and smoke and dirt, where the women have ceased to
believe in honour and the men in virtue.   We are in search of
love, happiness, innocence; the further we go from Paris the
better.

BOOK V

WE have reached the last act of youth's drama; we are approaching its closing scene.

It is not good that man should be alone. Emile is now a man, and we must give him his promised helpmeet. That helpmeet is Sophy. Where is her dwelling-place, where shall she be found? We must know beforehand what she is, and then we can decide where to look for her. And when she is found, our task is not ended. "Since our young gentleman," says Locke, "is about to marry, it is time to leave him with his mistress." And with these words he ends his book. As I have not the honour of educating "A young gentleman," I shall take care not to follow his example.

SOPHY, OR WOMAN

Sophy should be as truly a woman as Emile is a man, *i.e.*, she must possess all those characters of her sex which are required to enable her to play her part in the physical and moral order. Let us inquire to begin with in what respects her sex differs from our own.

But for her sex, a woman is a man; she has the same organs, the same needs, the same faculties. The machine is the same in its construction; its parts, its working, and its appearance are similar. Regard it as you will the difference is only in degree.

Yet where sex is concerned man and woman are unlike; each is the complement of the other; the difficulty in comparing them lies in our inability to decide, in either case, what is a matter of sex, and what is not. General differences present themselves to the comparative anatomist and even to the superficial observer; they seem not to be a matter of sex; yet they are really sex differences, though the connection eludes our observation. How far such differences may extend we cannot tell; all we know for certain is that where man and woman are alike we have to do with the characteristics of the species; where they are unlike, we have to do with the characteristics of sex. Considered from these two standpoints, we find so many instances of likeness and unlikeness that it is perhaps one of the greatest of marvels how nature has contrived to make two beings so like and yet so different.

These resemblances and differences must have an influence on the moral nature; this inference is obvious, and it is confirmed by experience; it shows the vanity of the disputes as to the superiority or the equality of the sexes; as if each sex, pursuing the path marked out for it by nature, were not more perfect in that very divergence than if it more closely resembled the other. A perfect man and a perfect woman should no more be alike in mind than in face, and perfection admits of neither less nor more.

In the union of the sexes each alike contributes to the common end, but in different ways. From this diversity springs the first difference which may be observed between man and woman in their moral relations. The man should be strong and active; the woman should be weak and passive; the one must have both the power and the will; it is enough that the other should offer little resistance.

When this principle is admitted, it follows that woman is specially made for man's delight. If man in his turn ought to be pleasing in her eyes, the necessity is less urgent, his virtue is in his strength, he pleases because he is strong. I grant you this is not the law of love, but it is the law of nature, which is older than love itself.

If woman is made to please and to be in subjection to man, she ought to make herself pleasing in his eyes and not provoke him to anger; her strength is in her charms, by their means she should compel him to discover and use his strength. The surest way of arousing this strength is to make it necessary by resistance. Thus pride comes to the help of desire and each exults in the other's victory. This is the origin of attack and defence, of the boldness of one sex and the timidity of the other, and even of the shame and modesty with which nature has armed the weak for the conquest of the strong.

Who can possibly suppose that nature has prescribed the same advances to the one sex as to the other, or that the first to feel desire should be the first to show it? What strange depravity of judgment! The consequences of the act being so different for the two sexes, is it natural that they should enter upon it with equal boldness? How can any one fail to see that when the share of each is so unequal, if the one were not controlled by modesty as the other is controlled by nature, the result would be the destruction of both, and the human race would perish through the very means ordained for its continuance?

Women so easily stir a man's senses and fan the ashes of a dying passion, that if philosophy ever succeeded in introducing this custom into any unlucky country, especially if it were a warm country where more women are born than men, the men, tyrannised over by the women, would at last become their victims, and would be dragged to their death without the least chance of escape.

Female animals are without this sense of shame, but what of that? Are their desires as boundless as those of women, which are curbed by this shame? The desires of the animals are the result of necessity, and when the need is satisfied, the desire ceases; they no longer make a feint of repulsing the male, they do it in earnest. Their seasons of complaisance are short and soon over. Impulse and restraint are alike the work of nature. But what would take the place of this negative instinct in women if you rob them of their modesty?

The Most High has deigned to do honour to mankind; he has endowed man with boundless passions, together with a law to guide them, so that man may be alike free and self-controlled; though swayed by these passions man is endowed with reason by which to control them. Woman is also endowed with boundless passions; God has given her modesty to restrain them. Moreover, he has given to both a present reward for the right use of their powers, in the delight which springs from that right use of them, i.e., the taste for right conduct established as the law of our behaviour. To my mind this is far higher than the instinct of the beasts.

Whether the woman shares the man's passion or not, whether she is willing or unwilling to satisfy it, she always repulses him and defends herself, though not always with the same vigour, and therefore not always with the same success. If the siege is to be successful, the besieged must permit or direct the attack. How skilfully can she stimulate the efforts of the aggressor. The freest and most delightful of activities does not permit of any real violence; reason and nature are alike against it; nature, in that she has given the weaker party strength enough to resist if she chooses; reason, in that actual violence is not only most brutal in itself, but it defeats its own ends, not only because the man thus declares war against his companion and thus gives her a right to defend her person and her liberty even at the cost of the enemy's life, but also because the woman alone is the judge of her condition, and a child would have no father if any man might usurp a father's rights.

Thus the different constitution of the two sexes leads us to a third conclusion, that the stronger party seems to be master, but is as a matter of fact dependent on the weaker, and that, not by any foolish custom of gallantry, nor yet by the magnanimity of the protector, but by an inexorable law of nature. For nature has endowed woman with a power of stimulating man's passions in excess of man's power of satisfying those passions, and has thus made him dependent on her goodwill, and compelled him in his turn to endeavour to please her, so that she may be willing to yield to his superior strength. Is it weakness which yields to force, or is it voluntary self-surrender? This uncertainty constitutes the chief charm of the man's victory, and the woman is usually cunning enough to leave him in doubt. In this respect the woman's mind exactly resembles her body; far from being ashamed of her weakness, she is proud of it; her soft muscles offer no resistance, she professes that she cannot lift the lightest weight; she would be ashamed to be strong. And why? Not only to gain an appearance of refinement; she is too clever for that; she is providing herself beforehand with excuses, with the right to be weak if she chooses.

The experience we have gained through our vices has considerably modified the views held in older times; we rarely hear of violence for which there is so little occasion that it would hardly be credited. Yet such stories are common enough among the Jews and ancient Greeks; for such views belong to the simplicity of nature, and have only been uprooted by our profligacy. If fewer deeds of violence are quoted in our days, it is not that men are more temperate, but because they are less credulous, and a complaint which would have been believed among a simple people would only excite laughter among ourselves; therefore silence is the better course. There is a law in Deuteronomy, under which the outraged maiden was punished, along with her assailant, if the crime were committed in a town; but if in the country or in a lonely place, the latter alone was punished. " For," says the law, " the maiden cried for help, and there was none to hear." From this merciful interpretation of the law, girls learnt not to let themselves be surprised in lonely places.

This change in public opinion has had a perceptible effect on our morals. It has produced our modern gallantry. Men have found that their pleasures depend, more than they expected, on the goodwill of the fair sex, and have secured this goodwill by attentions which have had their reward.

See how we find ourselves led unconsciously from the physical to the moral constitution, how from the grosser union of the sexes spring the sweet laws of love. Woman reigns, not by the will of man, but by the decrees of nature herself; she had the power long before she showed it. That same Hercules who proposed to violate all the fifty daughters of Thespis was compelled to spin at the feet of Omphale, and Samson, the strong man, was less strong than Delilah. This power cannot be taken from woman; it is hers by right; she would have lost it long ago, were it possible.

The consequences of sex are wholly unlike for man and woman. The male is only a male now and again, the female is always a female, or at least all her youth; everything reminds her of her sex; the performance of her functions requires a special constitution. She needs care during pregnancy and freedom from work when her child is born; she must have a quiet, easy life while she nurses her children; their education calls for patience and gentleness, for a zeal and love which nothing can dismay; she forms a bond between father and child, she alone can win the father's love for his children and convince him that they are indeed his own. What loving care is required to preserve a united family! And there should be no question of virtue in all this, it must be a labour of love, without which the human race would be doomed to extinction.

The mutual duties of the two sexes are not, and cannot be, equally binding on both. Women do wrong to complain of the inequality of man-made laws; this inequality is not of man's making, or at any rate it is not the result of mere prejudice, but of reason. She to whom nature has entrusted the care of the children must hold herself responsible for them to their father. No doubt every breach of faith is wrong, and every faithless husband, who robs his wife of the sole reward of the stern duties of her sex, is cruel and unjust; but the faithless wife is worse; she destroys the family and breaks the bonds of nature; when she gives her husband children who are not his own, she is false both to him and them, her crime is not infidelity but treason. To my mind, it is the source of dissension and of crime of every kind. Can any position be more wretched than that of the unhappy father who, when he clasps his child to his breast, is haunted by the suspicion that this is the child of another, the badge of his own dishonour, a thief who is robbing his own children of their inheritance. Under such circumstances the family is little more than a group of secret enemies, armed against each other by a guilty woman, who compels them to pretend to love one another.

Thus it is not enough that a wife should be faithful; her husband, along with his friends and neighbours, must believe in her fidelity; she must be modest, devoted, retiring; she should have the witness not only of a good conscience, but of a good reputation. In a word, if a father must love his children, he must be able to respect their mother. For these reasons it is not enough that the woman should be chaste, she must preserve her reputation and her good name. From these principles there arises not only a moral difference between the sexes, but also a fresh motive for duty and propriety, which prescribes to women in particular the most scrupulous attention to their conduct, their manners, their behaviour. Vague assertions as to the equality of the sexes and the similarity of their duties are only empty words; they are no answer to my argument.

It is a poor sort of logic to quote isolated exceptions against laws so firmly established. Women, you say, are not always bearing children. Granted; yet that is their proper business. Because there are a hundred or so of large towns in the world where women live licentiously and have few children, will you maintain that it is their business to have few children? And what would become of your towns if the remote country districts, with their simpler and purer women, did not make up for the barrenness of your fine ladies? There are plenty of country places where women with only four or five children are reckoned unfruitful. In conclusion, although here and there a woman may have few children,[1] what difference does it make? Is it any the less a woman's business to be a mother? And do not the general laws of nature and morality make provision for this state of things?

Even if there were these long intervals, which you assume, between the periods of pregnancy, can a woman suddenly change her way of life without danger? Can she be a nursing mother to-day and a soldier to-morrow? Will she change her tastes and her feelings as a chameleon changes his colour? Will she pass at once from the privacy of household duties and indoor occupations to the buffeting of the winds, the toils, the labours, the perils of war? Will

---

[1] Without this the race would necessarily diminish; all things considered, for its preservation each woman ought to have about four children, for about half the children born die before they can become parents, and two must survive to replace the father and mother. See whether the towns will supply them?

she be now timid,[1] now brave, now fragile, now robust? If the young men of Paris find a soldier's life too hard for them, how would a woman put up with it, a woman who has hardly ventured out of doors without a parasol and who has scarcely put a foot to the ground? Will she make a good soldier at an age when even men are retiring from this arduous business?

There are countries, I grant you, where women bear and rear children with little or no difficulty, but in those lands the men go half-naked in all weathers, they strike down the wild beasts, they carry a canoe as easily as a knapsack, they pursue the chase for 700 or 800 leagues, they sleep in the open on the bare ground, they bear incredible fatigues and go many days without food. When women become strong, men become still stronger; when men become soft, women become softer; change both the terms and the ratio remains unaltered.

I am quite aware that Plato, in the *Republic*, assigns the same gymnastics to women and men. Having got rid of the family there is no place for women in his system of government, so he is forced to turn them into men. That great genius has worked out his plans in detail and has provided for every contingency; he has even provided against a difficulty which in all likelihood no one would ever have raised; but he has not succeeded in meeting the real difficulty. I am not speaking of the alleged community of wives which has often been laid to his charge; this assertion only shows that his detractors have never read his works. I refer to that political promiscuity under which the same occupations are assigned to both sexes alike, a scheme which could only lead to intolerable evils; I refer to that subversion of all the tenderest of our natural feelings, which he sacrificed to an artificial sentiment which can only exist by their aid. Will the bonds of convention hold firm without some foundation in nature? Can devotion to the state exist apart from the love of those near and dear to us? Can patriotism thrive except in the soil of that miniature fatherland, the home? Is it not the good son, the good husband, the good father, who makes the good citizen?

When once it is proved that men and women are and ought to be unlike in constitution and in temperament, it follows that their education must be different. Nature teaches us that they should work together, but that each has its own share of the work; the end is the same, but the means are different, as are also the feelings which direct them. We have attempted to paint a natural man, let us try to paint a helpmeet for him.

You must follow nature's guidance if you would walk aright. The native characters of sex should be respected as nature's handiwork. You are always saying, "Women have such and such faults, from which we are free." You are misled by your vanity; what would be faults in you are virtues in them; and things would go worse,

[1] Women's timidity is yet another instinct of nature against the double risk she runs during pregnancy.

if they were without these so-called faults. Take care that they do not degenerate into evil, but beware of destroying them.

On the other hand, women are always exclaiming that we educate them for nothing but vanity and coquetry, that we keep them amused with trifles that we may be their masters; we are responsible, so they say, for the faults we attribute to them. How silly! What have men to do with the education of girls? What is there to hinder their mothers educating them as they please? There are no colleges for girls; so much the better for them! Would God there were none for the boys, their education would be more sensible and more wholesome. Who is it that compels a girl to waste her time on foolish trifles? Are they forced, against their will, to spend half their time over their toilet, following the example set them by you? Who prevents you teaching them, or having them taught, whatever seems good in your eyes? Is it our fault that we are charmed by their beauty and delighted by their airs and graces, if we are attracted and flattered by the arts they learn from you, if we love to see them prettily dressed, if we let them display at leisure the weapons by which we are subjugated? Well then, educate them like men. The more women are like men, the less influence they will have over men, and then men will be masters indeed.

All the faculties common to both sexes are not equally shared between them, but taken as a whole they are fairly divided. Woman is worth more as a woman and less as a man; when she makes a good use of her own rights, she has the best of it; when she tries to usurp our rights, she is our inferior. It is impossible to controvert this, except by quoting exceptions after the usual fashion of the partisans of the fair sex.

To cultivate the masculine virtues in women and to neglect their own is evidently to do them an injury. Women are too clear-sighted to be thus deceived; when they try to usurp our privileges they do not abandon their own; with this result: they are unable to make use of two incompatible things, so they fall below their own level as women, instead of rising to the level of men. If you are a sensible mother you will take my advice. Do not try to make your daughter a good man in defiance of nature. Make her a good woman, and be sure it will be better both for her and us.

Does this mean that she must be brought up in ignorance and kept to housework only? Is she to be man's handmaid or his help-meet? Will he dispense with her greatest charm, her companion-ship? To keep her a slave will he prevent her knowing and feeling? Will he make an automaton of her? No, indeed, that is not the teaching of nature, who has given women such a pleasant easy wit. On the contrary, nature means them to think, to will, to love, to cultivate their minds as well as their persons; she puts these weapons in their hands to make up for their lack of strength and to enable them to direct the strength of men. They should learn many things, but only such things as are suitable.

When I consider the special purpose of woman, when I observe her inclinations or reckon up her duties, everything combines to indicate the mode of education she requires. Men and women are made for each other, but their mutual dependence differs in degree; man is dependent on woman through his desires; woman is dependent on man through her desires and also through her needs; he could do without her better than she can do without him. She cannot fulfil her purpose in life without his aid, without his goodwill, without his respect; she is dependent on our feelings, on the price we put upon her virtue, and the opinion we have of her charms and her deserts. Nature herself has decreed that woman, both for herself and her children, should be at the mercy of man's judgment.

Worth alone will not suffice, a woman must be thought worthy; nor beauty, she must be admired; nor virtue, she must be respected. A woman's honour does not depend on her conduct alone, but on her reputation, and no woman who permits herself to be considered vile is really virtuous. A man has no one but himself to consider, and so long as he does right he may defy public opinion; but when a woman does right her task is only half finished, and what people think of her matters as much as what she really is. Hence her education must, in this respect, be different from man's education. " What will people think " is the grave of a man's virtue and the throne of a woman's.

The children's health depends in the first place on the mother's, and the early education of man is also in a woman's hands; his morals, his passions, his tastes, his pleasures, his happiness itself, depend on her. A woman's education must therefore be planned in relation to man. To be pleasing in his sight, to win his respect and love, to train him in childhood, to tend him in manhood, to counsel and console, to make his life pleasant and happy, these are the duties of woman for all time, and this is what she should be taught while she is young. The further we depart from this principle, the further we shall be from our goal, and all our precepts will fail to secure her happiness or our own.

Every woman desires to be pleasing in men's eyes, and this is right; but there is a great difference between wishing to please a man of worth, a really lovable man, and seeking to please those foppish manikins who are a disgrace to their own sex and to the sex which they imitate. Neither nature nor reason can induce a woman to love an effeminate person, nor will she win love by imitating such a person.

If a woman discards the quiet modest bearing of her sex, and adopts the airs of such foolish creatures, she is not following her vocation, she is forsaking it; she is robbing herself of the rights to which she lays claim. " If we were different," she says, " the men would not like us." She is mistaken. Only a fool likes folly; to wish to attract such men only shows her own foolishness. If there were no frivolous men, women would soon make them, and women are more responsible for men's follies than men are for theirs. The woman who loves true manhood and seeks to find favour in its sight will adopt means adapted to her ends. Woman is a coquette by profession, but her coquetry varies with her aims; let these aims be in accordance with those of nature, and a woman will receive a fitting education.

Even the tiniest little girls love finery; they are not content to be pretty, they must be admired; their little airs and graces show that their heads are full of this idea, and as soon as they can understand they are controlled by " What will people think of you? " If you are foolish enough to try this way with little boys, it will not have the same effect; give them their freedom and their sports, and they care very little what people think; it is a work of time to bring them under the control of this law.

However acquired, this early education of little girls is an excellent thing in itself. As the birth of the body must precede the birth of the mind, so the training of the body must precede the cultivation of the mind. This is true of both sexes; but the aim of physical training for boys and girls is not the same; in the one case it is the development of strength, in the other of grace; not that these qualities should be peculiar to either sex, but that their relative values should be different. Women should be strong enough to do anything gracefully; men should be skilful enough to do anything easily.

The exaggeration of femine delicacy leads to effeminacy in men. Women should not be strong like men but for them, so that their sons may be strong. Convents and boarding-schools, with their plain food and ample opportunities for amusements, races, and games in the open air and in the garden, are better in this respect than the home, where the little girl is fed on delicacies, continually encouraged or reproved, where she is kept sitting in a stuffy room, always under her mother's eye, afraid to stand or walk or speak or breathe, without a moment's freedom to play or jump or run or shout, or to be her natural, lively, little self; there is either harmful indulgence or misguided severity, and no trace of reason. In this fashion heart and body are alike destroyed.

In Sparta the girls used to take part in military sports just like the boys, not that they might go to war, but that they might bear sons who could endure hardship. That is not what I desire. To provide the state with soldiers it is not necessary that the mother should carry a musket and master the Prussian drill. Yet, on the whole, I think the Greeks were very wise in this matter of physical training. Young girls frequently appeared in public, not with the boys, but in groups apart. There was scarcely a festival, a sacrifice, or a procession without its bands of maidens, the daughters of the chief citizens. Crowned with flowers, chanting hymns, forming the chorus of the dance, bearing baskets, vases, offerings, they presented a charming spectacle to the depraved senses of the Greeks, a spectacle well fitted to efface the evil effects of their unseemly gymnastics. Whatever this custom may have done for the Greek men, it was well fitted to develop in the Greek women a sound constitution by means of pleasant, moderate, and healthy exercise: while the desire to please would develop a keen and cultivated taste without risk to character.

When the Greek women married, they disappeared from public life; within the four walls of their home they devoted themselves to the care of their household and family. This is the mode of life prescribed for women alike by nature and reason. These women gave birth to the healthiest, strongest, and best proportioned men who ever lived, and except in certain islands of ill repute, no women in the whole world, not even the Roman matrons, were ever at once so wise and so charming, so beautiful and so virtuous, as the women of ancient Greece.

It is admitted that their flowing garments, which did not cramp the figure, preserved in men and women alike the fine proportions which are seen in their statues. These are still the models of art, although nature is so disfigured that they are no longer to be found among us. The Gothic trammels, the innumerable bands which confine our limbs as in a press, were quite unknown. The Greek women were wholly unacquainted with those frames of whalebone in which our women distort rather than display their figures. It seems to me that this abuse, which is carried to an incredible degree of folly in England, must sooner or later lead to the production of a degenerate race. Moreover, I maintain that the charm which these corsets are supposed to produce is in the worst possible taste; it is not a pleasant thing to see a woman cut in two like a wasp— it offends both the eye and the imagination. A slender waist has its limits, like everything else, in proportion and suitability, and beyond these limits it becomes a defect. This defect would be a glaring one in the nude; why should it be beautiful under the costume?

I will not venture upon the reasons which induce women to incase themselves in these coats of mail. A clumsy figure, a large waist, are no doubt very ugly at twenty, but at thirty they cease to offend the eye, and as we are bound to be what nature has made us at any given age, and as there is no deceiving the eye of man, such defects are less offensive at any age than the foolish affectations of a young thing of forty.

Everything which cramps and confines nature is in bad taste; this is as true of the adornments of the person as of the ornaments of the mind. Life, health, common-sense, and comfort must come first; there is no grace in discomfort, languor is not refinement, there is no charm in ill-health; suffering may excite pity, but pleasure and delight demand the freshness of health.

Boys and girls have many games in common, and this is as it should be; do they not play together when they are grown up? They have also special tastes of their own. Boys want movement and noise, drums, tops, toy-carts; girls prefer things which appeal to the eye, and can be used for dressing-up—mirrors, jewellery, finery, and specially dolls. The doll is the girl's special plaything;

this shows her instinctive bent towards her life's work. The art of pleasing finds its physical basis in personal adornment, and this physical side of the art is the only one which the child can cultivate.

Here is a little girl busy all day with her doll; she is always changing its clothes, dressing and undressing it, trying new combinations of trimmings well or ill matched; her fingers are clumsy, her taste is crude, but there is no mistaking her bent; in this endless occupation time flies unheeded, the hours slip away unnoticed, even meals are forgotten. She is more eager for adornment than for food. "But she is dressing her doll, not herself," you will say. Just so; she sees her doll, she cannot see herself; she cannot do anything for herself, she has neither the training, nor the talent, nor the strength; as yet she herself is nothing, she is engrossed in her doll and all her coquetry is devoted to it. This will not always be so; in due time she will be her own doll.

We have here a very early and clearly-marked bent; you have only to follow it and train it. What the little girl most clearly desires is to dress her doll, to make its bows, its tippets, its sashes, and its tuckers; she is dependent on other people's kindness in all this, and it would be much pleasanter to be able to do it herself. Here is a motive for her earliest lessons, they are not tasks prescribed, but favours bestowed. Little girls always dislike learning to read and write, but they are always ready to learn to sew. They think they are grown up, and in imagination they are using their knowledge for their own adornment.

The way is open and it is easy to follow it; cutting out, embroidery, lace-making follow naturally. Tapestry is not popular; furniture is too remote from the child's interests, it has nothing to do with the person, it depends on conventional tastes. Tapestry is a woman's amusement; young girls never care for it.

This voluntary course is easily extended to include drawing, an art which is closely connected with taste in dress; but I would not have them taught landscape and still less figure painting. Leaves, fruit, flowers, draperies, anything that will make an elegant trimming for the accessories of the toilet, and enable the girl to design her own embroidery if she cannot find a pattern to her taste; that will be quite enough. Speaking generally, if it is desirable to restrict a man's studies to what is useful, this is even more necessary for women, whose life, though less laborious, should be even more industrious and more uniformly employed in a variety of duties, so that one talent should not be encouraged at the expense of others.

Whatever may be said by the scornful, good sense belongs to both sexes alike. Girls are usually more docile than boys, and they should be subjected to more authority, as I shall show later on, but that is no reason why they should be required to do things in which they can see neither rhyme nor reason. The mother's art consists in showing the use of everything they are set to do, and this is all the easier as the girl's intelligence is more precocious than the boy's. This principle banishes, both for boys and girls, not only those pursuits which never lead to any appreciable results, not even increasing the charms of those who have pursued them, but also those studies whose utility is beyond the scholar's present age and can only be appreciated in later years. If I object to little boys being made to learn to read, still more do I object to it for little girls until they are able to see the use of reading; we generally think more of our own ideas than theirs in our attempts to convince them of the utility of this art. After all, why should a little girl know how to read and write? Has she a house to manage? Most of them make a bad use of this fatal knowledge, and girls are so full of curiosity that few of them will fail to learn without compulsion. Possibly cyphering should come first; there is nothing so obviously useful, nothing which needs so much practice or gives so much opportunity for error as reckoning. If the little girl does not get the cherries for her lunch without an arithmetical exercise, she will soon learn to count.

I once knew a little girl who learnt to write before she could read, and she began to write with her needle. To begin with, she would write nothing but O's; she was always making O's, large and small, of all kinds and one within another, but always drawn backwards. Unluckily one day she caught a glimpse of herself in the glass while she was at this useful work, and thinking that the cramped attitude was not pretty, like another Minerva she flung away her pen and declined to make any more O's. Her brother was no fonder of writing, but what he disliked was the constraint, not the look of the thing. She was induced to go on with her writing in this way. The child was fastidious and vain; she could not bear her sisters to wear her clothes. Her things had been marked, they declined to mark them any more, she must learn to mark them herself; there is no need to continue the story.

Show the sense of the tasks you set your little girls, but keep them busy. Idleness and insubordination are two very dangerous faults, and very hard to cure when once established. Girls should be attentive and industrious, but this is not enough by itself; they should early be accustomed to restraint. This misfortune, if such it be, is inherent in their sex, and they will never escape from it, unless to endure more cruel sufferings. All their life long, they will have to submit to the strictest and most enduring restraints, those of propriety. They must be trained to bear the yoke from the first, so that they may not feel it, to master their own caprices and to submit themselves to the will of others. If they were always eager to be at work, they should sometimes be compelled to do nothing. Their childish faults, unchecked and unheeded, may easily lead to dissipation, frivolity, and inconstancy. To guard against this, teach them above all things self-control. Under our senseless conditions, the life of a good woman is a perpetual struggle against self; it is only fair that woman should bear her share of the ills she has brought upon man.

Beware lest your girls become weary of their tasks and infatuated with their amusements; this often happens under our ordinary methods of education, where, as Fénelon says, all the tedium is on one side and all the pleasure on the other. If the rules already laid down are followed, the first of these dangers will be avoided, unless the child dislikes those about her. A little girl who is fond of her mother or her friend will work by her side all day without getting tired; the chatter alone will make up for any loss of liberty. But if her companion is distasteful to her, everything done under her direction will be distasteful too. Children who take no delight in their mother's company are not likely to turn out well; but to judge of their real feelings you must watch them and not trust to their words alone, for they are flatterers and deceitful and soon learn to conceal their thoughts. Neither should they be told that they ought to love their mother. Affection is not the result of duty, and in this respect constraint is out of place. Continual intercourse, constant care, habit itself, all these will lead a child to love her mother, if the mother does nothing to deserve the child's ill-will. The very control she exercises over the child, if well directed, will increase rather than diminish the affection, for women being made for dependence, girls feel themselves made to obey.

Just because they have, or ought to have, little freedom, they are apt to indulge themselves too fully with regard to such freedom as they have; they carry everything to extremes, and they devote themselves to their games with an enthusiasm even greater than that of boys. This is the second difficulty to which I referred. This enthusiasm must be kept in check, for it is the source of several vices commonly found among women, caprice and that extravagant admiration which leads a woman to regard a thing with rapture to-day and to be quite indifferent to it to-morrow. This fickleness of taste is as dangerous as exaggeration; and both spring from the same cause. Do not deprive them of mirth, laughter, noise, and romping games, but do not let them tire of one game and go off to another; do not leave them for a moment without restraint. Train them to break off their games and return to their other occupations without a murmur. Habit is all that is needed, as you have nature on your side.

This habitual restraint produces a docility which woman requires all her life long, for she will always be in subjection to a man, or to man's judgment, and she will never be free to set her own opinion above his. What is most wanted in a woman is gentleness; formed to obey a creature so imperfect as man, a creature often vicious and always faulty, she should early learn to submit to injustice and to suffer the wrongs inflicted on her by her husband without complaint; she must be gentle for her own sake, not his. Bitterness and obstinacy only multiply the sufferings of the wife and the misdeeds of the husband; the man feels that these are not the weapons to be used against him. Heaven did not make women attractive and persuasive that they might degenerate into bitterness, or meek that they should desire the mastery; their soft voice was not meant for

hard words, nor their delicate features for the frowns of anger.
When they lose their temper they forget themselves; often enough
they have just cause of complaint; but when they scold they always
put themselves in the wrong. We should each adopt the tone
which befits our sex; a soft-hearted husband may make an over-
bearing wife, but a man, unless he is a perfect monster, will sooner
or later yield to his wife's gentleness, and the victory will be hers.

Daughters must always be obedient, but mothers need not always
be harsh. To make a girl docile you need not make her miserable;
to make her modest you need not terrify her; on the contrary, I
should not be sorry to see her allowed occasionally to exercise a little
ingenuity, not to escape punishment for her disobedience, but to
evade the necessity for obedience. Her dependence need not be
made unpleasant, it is enough that she should realise that she is
dependent. Cunning is a natural gift of woman, and so convinced
am I that all our natural inclinations are right, that I would cultivate
this among others, only guarding against its abuse.

For the truth of this I appeal to every honest observer. I do
not ask you to question women themselves, our cramping institutions
may compel them to sharpen their wits; I would have you examine
girls, little girls, newly-born so to speak; compare them with boys
of the same age, and I am greatly mistaken if you do not find the
little boys heavy, silly, and foolish, in comparison. Let me give
one illustration in all its childish simplicity.

Children are commonly forbidden to ask for anything at table,
for people think they can do nothing better in the way of education
than to burden them with useless precepts; as if a little bit of this
or that were not readily given or refused without leaving a poor
child dying of greediness intensified by hope. Every one knows how
cunningly a little boy brought up in this way asked for salt when
he had been overlooked at table. I do not suppose any one will
blame him for asking directly for salt and indirectly for meat; the
neglect was so cruel that I hardly think he would have been punished
had he broken the rule and said plainly that he was hungry. But
this is what I saw done by a little girl of six; the circumstances were
much more difficult, for not only was she strictly forbidden to ask
for anything directly or indirectly, but disobedience would have been
unpardonable, for she had eaten of every dish; one only had been
overlooked, and on this she had set her heart. This is what she did
to repair the omission without laying herself open to the charge
of disobedience; she pointed to every dish in turn, saying, " I've
had some of this; I've had some of this; " however she omitted the
one dish so markedly that some one noticed it and said, " Have not
you had some of this ? " " Oh, no," replied the greedy little girl
with soft voice and downcast eyes. These instances are typical
of the cunning of the little boy and girl.

What is, is good, and no general law can be bad. This special
skill with which the female sex is endowed is a fair equivalent for
its lack of strength; without it woman would be man's slave, not

Emile

his helpmeet. By her superiority in this respect she maintains her equality with man, and rules in obedience. She has everything against her, our faults and her own weakness and timidity; her beauty and her wiles are all that she has. Should she not cultivate both? Yet beauty is not universal; it may be destroyed by all sorts of accidents, it will disappear with years, and habit will destroy its influence. A woman's real resource is her wit; not that foolish wit which is so greatly admired in society, a wit which does nothing to make life happier; but that wit which is adapted to her condition, the art of taking advantage of our position and controlling us through our own strength. Words cannot tell how beneficial this is to man, what a charm it gives to the society of men and women, how it checks the petulant child and restrains the brutal husband; without it the home would be a scene of strife; with it, it is the abode of happiness. I know that this power is abused by the sly and the spiteful; but what is there that is not liable to abuse? Do not destroy the means of happiness because the wicked use them to our hurt.

The toilet may attract notice, but it is the person that wins our hearts. Our finery is not us; its very artificiality often offends, and that which is least noticeable in itself often wins the most attention. The education of our girls is, in this respect, absolutely topsy-turvy. Ornaments are promised them as rewards, and they are taught to delight in elaborate finery. " How lovely she is!" people say when she is most dressed up. On the contrary, they should be taught that so much finery is only required to hide their defects, and that beauty's real triumph is to shine alone. The love of fashion is contrary to good taste, for faces do not change with the fashion, and while the person remains unchanged, what suits it at one time will suit it always.

If I saw a young girl decked out like a little peacock, I should show myself anxious about her figure so disguised, and anxious what people would think of her; I should say, " She is over-dressed with all those ornaments; what a pity! Do you think she could do with something simpler? Is she pretty enough to do without this or that? " Possibly she herself would be the first to ask that her finery might be taken off and that we should see how she looked without it. In that case her beauty should receive such praise as it deserves. I should never praise her unless simply dressed. If she only regards fine clothes as an aid to personal beauty, and as a tacit confession that she needs their aid, she will not be proud of her finery, she will be humbled by it; and if she hears some one say, " How pretty she is," when she is smarter than usual, she will blush for shame.

Moreover, though there are figures that require adornment there are none that require expensive clothes. Extravagance in dress is the folly of the class rather than the individual, it is merely conventional. Genuine coquetry is sometimes carefully thought out, but never sumptuous, and Juno dressed herself more magnificently than Venus. " As you cannot make her beautiful you are making her fine," said Apelles to an unskilful artist who was painting Helen loaded with jewellery. I have also noticed that the smartest clothes proclaim the plainest women; no folly could be more misguided. If a young girl has good taste and a contempt for fashion, give her a few yards of ribbon, muslin, and gauze, and a handful of flowers, without any diamonds, fringes, or lace, and she will make herself a dress a hundredfold more becoming than all the smart clothes of La Duchapt.

Good is always good, and as you should always look your best, the women who know what they are about select a good style and keep to it, and as they are not always changing their style they think less about dress than those who can never settle to any one style. A genuine desire to dress becomingly does not require an elaborate toilet. Young girls rarely give much time to dress; needlework and lessons are the business of the day; yet, except for the rouge, they are generally as carefully dressed as older women and often in better taste. Contrary to the usual opinion, the real cause of the abuse of the toilet is not vanity but lack of occupation. The woman who devotes six hours to her toilet is well aware that she is no better dressed than the woman who took half an hour, but she has got rid of so many of the tedious hours and it is better to amuse oneself with one's clothes than to be sick of everything. Without the toilet how would she spend the time between dinner and supper. With a crowd of women about her, she can at least cause them annoyance, which is amusement of a kind; better still she avoids a *tête-à-tête* with the husband whom she never sees at any other time; then there are the tradespeople, the dealers in bric-à-brac, the fine gentlemen, the minor poets with their songs, their verses, and their pamphlets; how could you get them together but for the toilet. Its only real advantage is the chance of a little more display than is permitted by full dress, and perhaps this is less than it seems and a woman gains less than she thinks. Do not be afraid to educate your women as women; teach them a woman's business, that they be modest, that they may know how to manage their house and look after their family; the grand toilet will soon disappear, and they will be more tastefully dressed.

Growing girls perceive at once that all this outside adornment is not enough unless they have charms of their own. They cannot make themselves beautiful, they are too young for coquetry, but they are not too young to acquire graceful gestures, a pleasing voice, a self-possessed manner, a light step, a graceful bearing, to choose whatever advantages are within their reach. The voice extends its range, it grows stronger and more resonant, the arms become plumper, the bearing more assured, and they perceive that it is easy to attract attention however dressed. Needlework and industry suffice no longer, fresh gifts are developing and their usefulness is already recognised.

I know that stern teachers would have us refuse to teach little girls to sing or dance, or to acquire any of the pleasing arts. This strikes me as absurd. Who should learn these arts—our boys? Are these to be the favourite accomplishments of men or women? Of neither, say they; profane songs are simply so many crimes, dancing is an invention of the Evil One; her tasks and her prayers are all the amusement a young girl should have. What strange amusements for a child of ten! I fear that these little saints who have been forced to spend their childhood in prayers to God will pass their youth in another fashion; when they are married they will try to make up for lost time. I think we must consider age as well as sex; a young girl should not live like her grandmother; she should be lively, merry, and eager; she should sing and dance to her heart's content, and enjoy all the innocent pleasures of youth; the time will come, all too soon, when she must settle down and adopt a more serious tone.

But is this change in itself really necessary? Is it not merely another result of our own prejudices? By making good women the slaves of dismal duties, we have deprived marriage of its charm for men. Can we wonder that the gloomy silence they find at home drives them elsewhere, or inspires little desire to enter a state which offers so few attractions? Christianity, by exaggerating every duty, has made our duties impracticable and useless; by forbidding singing, dancing, and amusements of every kind, it renders women sulky, fault-finding, and intolerable at home. There is no religion which imposes such strict duties upon married life, and none in which such a sacred engagement is so often profaned. Such pains has been taken to prevent wives being amiable, that their husbands have become indifferent to them. This should not be, I grant you, but it will be, since husbands are but men. I would have an English maiden cultivate the talents which will delight her husband as zealously as the Circassian cultivates the accomplishments of an Eastern harem. Husbands, you say, care little for such accomplishments. So I should suppose, when they are employed, not for the husband, but to attract the young rakes who dishonour the home. But imagine a virtuous and charming wife, adorned with such accomplishments and devoting them to her husband's amusement; will she not add to his happiness? When he leaves his office worn out with the day's work, will she not prevent him seeking recreation elsewhere? Have we not all beheld happy families gathered together, each contributing to the general amusement? Are not the confidence and familiarity thus established, the innocence and the charm of the pleasures thus enjoyed, more than enough to make up for the more riotous pleasures of public entertainments?

Pleasant accomplishments have been made too formal an affair of rules and precepts, so that young people find them very tedious instead of a mere amusement or a merry game as they ought to be. Nothing can be more absurd than an elderly singing or dancing master frowning upon young people, whose one desire is to laugh, and adopting a more pedantic and magisterial manner in teaching his frivolous art than if he were teaching the catechism. Take the case of singing; does this art depend on reading music; cannot the voice be made true and flexible, can we not learn to sing with taste and even to play an accompaniment without knowing a note? Does the same kind of singing suit all voices alike? Is the same method adapted to every mind? You will never persuade me that the same attitudes, the same steps, the same movements, the same gestures, the same dances will suit a lively little brunette and a tall fair maiden with languishing eyes. So when I find a master giving the same lessons to all his pupils I say, " He has his own routine, but he knows nothing of his art! "

Should young girls have masters or mistresses? I cannot say; I wish they could dispense with both; I wish they could learn of their own accord what they are already so willing to learn. I wish there were fewer of these dressed-up old ballet masters promenading our streets. I fear our young people will get more harm from intercourse with such people than profit from their instruction, and that their jargon, their tone, their airs and graces, will instil a precocious taste for the frivolities which the teacher thinks so important, and to which the scholars are only too likely to devote themselves.

Where pleasure is the only end in view, any one may serve as teacher—father, mother, brother, sister, friend, governess, the girl's mirror, and above all her own taste. Do not offer to teach, let her ask; do not make a task of what should be a reward, and in these studies above all remember that the wish to succeed is the first step. If formal instruction is required I leave it to you to choose between a master and a mistress. How can I tell whether a dancing master should take a young pupil by her soft white hand, make her lift her skirt and raise her eyes, open her arms and advance her throbbing bosom? but this I know, nothing on earth would induce me to be that master.

Taste is formed partly by industry and partly by talent, and by its means the mind is unconsciously opened to the idea of beauty of every kind, till at length it attains to those moral ideas which are so closely related to beauty. Perhaps this is one reason why ideas of propriety and modesty are acquired earlier by girls than by boys, for to suppose that this early feeling is due to the teaching of the governesses would show little knowledge of their style of teaching and of the natural development of the human mind. The art of speaking stands first among the pleasing arts; it alone can add fresh charms to those which have been blunted by habit. It is the mind which not only gives life to the body, but renews, so to speak, its youth; the flow of feelings and ideas give life and variety to the countenance, and the conversation to which it gives rise arouses and sustains attention, and fixes it continuously on one object. I suppose this is why little girls so soon learn to prattle prettily, and why men enjoy listening to them even before the child can understand them; they are watching for the first gleam of intelligence and sentiment.

Women have ready tongues; they talk earlier, more easily, and more pleasantly than men. They are also said to talk more; this may be true, but I am prepared to reckon it to their credit; eyes and mouth are equally busy and for the same cause. A man says what he knows, a woman says what will please; the one needs knowledge, the other taste; utility should be the man's object; the woman speaks to give pleasure. There should be nothing in common but truth.

You should not check a girl's prattle like a boy's by the harsh question, " What is the use of that ? " but by another question at least as difficult to answer, " What effect will that have ? " At this early age when they know neither good nor evil, and are incapable of judging others, they should make this their rule and never say anything which is unpleasant to those about them; this rule is all the more difficult to apply because it must always be subordinated to our first rule, " Never tell a lie."

I can see many other difficulties, but they belong to a later stage. For the present it is enough for your little girls to speak the truth without grossness, and as they are naturally averse to what is gross, education easily teaches them to avoid it. In social intercourse I observe that a man's politeness is usually more helpful and a woman's more caressing. This distinction is natural, not artificial. A man seeks to serve, a woman seeks to please. Hence a woman's politeness is less insincere than ours, whatever we may think of her character; for she is only acting upon a fundamental instinct; but when a man professes to put my interests before his own, I detect the falsehood, however disguised. Hence it is easy for women to be polite, and easy to teach little girls politeness. The first lessons come by nature; art only supplements them and determines the conventional form which politeness shall take. The courtesy of woman to woman is another matter; their manner is so constrained, their attentions so chilly, they find each other so wearisome, that they take little pains to conceal the fact, and seem sincere even in their falsehood, since they take so little pains to conceal it. Still young girls do sometimes become sincerely attached to one another. At their age good spirits take the place of a good disposition, and they are so pleased with themselves that they are pleased with every one else. Moreover, it is certain that they kiss each other more affectionately and caress each other more gracefully in the presence of men, for they are proud to be able to arouse their envy without danger to themselves by the sight of favours which they know will arouse that envy.

If young boys must not be allowed to ask unsuitable questions, much more must they be forbidden to little girls; if their curiosity is satisfied or unskilfully evaded it is a much more serious matter, for they are so keen to guess the mysteries concealed from them and so skilful to discover them. But while I would not permit them to ask questions, I would have them questioned frequently, and pains should be taken to make them talk; let them be teased to make them speak freely, to make them answer readily, to loosen mind and tongue while it can be done without danger. Such conversation always leading to merriment, yet skilfully controlled and directed, would form a delightful amusement at this age and might instil into these youthful hearts the first and perhaps the most helpful lessons in morals which they will ever receive, by teaching them in the guise of pleasure and fun what qualities are esteemed by men and what is the true glory and happiness of a good woman.

If boys are incapable of forming any true idea of religion, much more is it beyond the grasp of girls; and for this reason I would speak of it all the sooner to little girls, for if we wait till they are ready for a serious discussion of these deep subjects we should be in danger of never speaking of religion at all. A woman's reason is practical, and therefore she soon arrives at a given conclusion, but she fails to discover it for herself. The social relation of the sexes is a wonderful thing. This relation produces a moral person of which woman is the eye and man the hand, but the two are so dependent on one another that the man teaches the woman what to see, while she teaches him what to do. If women could discover principles and if men had as good heads for detail, they would be mutually independent, they would live in perpetual strife, and there would be an end to all society. But in their mutual harmony each contributes to a common purpose; each follows the other's lead, each commands and each obeys.

As a woman's conduct is controlled by public opinion, so is her religion ruled by authority. The daughter should follow her mother's religion, the wife her husband's. Were that religion false, the docility which leads mother and daughter to submit to nature's laws would blot out the sin of error in the sight of God. Unable to judge for themselves they should accept the judgment of father and husband as that of the church.

While women unaided cannot deduce the rules of their faith, neither can they assign limits to that faith by the evidence of reason; they allow themselves to be driven hither and thither by all sorts of external influences, they are ever above or below the truth. Extreme in everything, they are either altogether reckless or altogether pious; you never find them able to combine virtue and piety. Their natural exaggeration is not wholly to blame; the ill-regulated control exercised over them by men is partly responsible. Loose morals bring religion into contempt; the terrors of remorse make it a tyrant; this is why women have always too much or too little religion.

As a woman's religion is controlled by authority it is more important to show her plainly what to believe than to explain the reasons for belief; for faith attached to ideas half-understood is the main source of fanaticism, and faith demanded on behalf of what is absurd leads to madness or unbelief. Whether our catechisms tend to produce impiety rather than fanaticism I cannot say, but I do know that they lead to one or other.

In the first place, when you teach religion to little girls never make it gloomy or tiresome, never make it a task or a duty, and therefore never give them anything to learn by heart, not even their prayers. Be content to say your own prayers regularly in their presence, but do not compel them to join you. Let their prayers be short, as Christ himself has taught us. Let them always be said with becoming reverence and respect; remember that if we ask the Almighty to give heed to our words, we should at least give heed to what we mean to say.

It does not much matter that a girl should learn her religion young, but it does matter that she should learn it thoroughly, and still more that she should learn to love it. If you make religion a burden to her, if you always speak of God's anger, if in the name of religion you impose all sorts of disagreeable duties, duties which she never sees you perform, what can she suppose but that to learn one's catechism and to say one's prayers is only the duty of a little girl, and she will long to be grown-up to escape, like you, from these duties. Example! Example! Without it you will never succeed in teaching children anything.

When you explain the Articles of Faith let it be by direct teaching, not by question and answer. Children should only answer what they think, not what has been drilled into them. All the answers in the catechism are the wrong way about; it is the scholar who instructs the teacher; in the child's mouth they are a downright lie, since they explain what he does not understand, and affirm what he cannot believe. Find me, if you can, an intelligent man who could honestly say his catechism. The first question I find in our catechism is as follows: "Who created you and brought you into the world?" To which the girl, who thinks it was her mother, replies without hesitation, "It was God." All she knows is that she is asked a question which she only half understands and she gives an answer she does not understand at all.

I wish some one who really understands the development of children's minds would write a catechism for them. It might be the most useful book ever written, and, in my opinion, it would do its author no little honour. This at least is certain—if it were a good book it would be very unlike our catechisms.

Such a catechism will not be satisfactory unless the child can answer the questions of its own accord without having to learn the answers; indeed the child will often ask the questions itself. An example is required to make my meaning plain and I feel how ill equipped I am to furnish such an example. I will try to give some sort of outline of my meaning.

To get to the first question in our catechism I suppose we must begin somewhat after the following fashion.

Nurse. Do you remember when your mother was a little girl?

Child. No, nurse.

M 4

Nurse. Why not, when you have such a good memory?
Child. I was not alive.
Nurse. Then you were not always alive!
Child. No.
Nurse. Will you live for ever?
Child. Yes.
Nurse. Are you young or old?
Child. I am young.
Nurse. Is your grandmamma old or young?
Child. She is old.
Nurse. Was she ever young?
Child. Yes.
Nurse. Why is she not young now?
Child. She has grown old.
Nurse. Will you grow old too?
Child. I don't know.
Nurse. Where are your last year's frocks?
Child. They have been unpicked.
Nurse. Why?
Child. Because they were too small for me.
Nurse. Why were they too small?
Child. I have grown bigger.
Nurse. Will you grow any more?
Child. Oh, yes.
Nurse. And what becomes of big girls?
Child. They grow into women.
Nurse. And what becomes of women?
Child. They are mothers.
Nurse. And what becomes of mothers?
Child. They grow old.
Nurse. Will you grow old?
Child. When I am a mother.
Nurse. And what becomes of old people?
Child. I don't know.
Nurse. What became of your grandfather?
Child. He died.[1]
Nurse. Why did he die?
Child. Because he was so old.
Nurse. What becomes of old people?
Child. They die.
Nurse. And when you are old——?
Child. Oh nurse! I don't want to die!
Nurse. My dear, no one wants to die, and everybody dies.
Child. Why, will mamma die too?

[1] The child will say this because she has heard it said; but you must make sure she knows what death is, for the idea is not so simple and within the child's grasp as people think. In that little peom " Abel " you will find an example of the way to teach them. This charming work breathes a delightful simplicity with which one should feed one's own mind so as to talk with children.

Nurse. Yes, like everybody else. Women grow old as well as men, and old age ends in death.

Child. What must I do to grow old very, very slowly?

Nurse. Be good while you are little.

Child. I will always be good, nurse.

Nurse. So much the better. But do you suppose you will live for ever?

Child. When I am very, very old——

Nurse. Well?

Child. When we are so very old you say we must die?

Nurse. You must die some day.

Child. Oh dear! I suppose I must.

Nurse. Who lived before you?

Child. My father and mother.

Nurse. And before them?

Child. Their father and mother.

Nurse. Who will live after you?

Child. My children.

Nurse. Who will live after them?

Child. Their children.

In this way, by concrete examples, you will find a beginning and end for the human race like everything else—that is to say, a father and mother who never had a father and mother, and children who will never have children of their own.

It is only after a long course of similar questions that we are ready for the first question in the catechism; then alone can we put the question and the child may be able to understand it. But what a gap there is between the first and the second question which is concerned with the definitions of the divine nature. When will this chasm be bridged? " God is a spirit." " And what is a spirit? " Shall I start the child upon this difficult question of metaphysics which grown men find so hard to understand? These are no questions for a little girl to answer; if she asks them, it is as much or more than we can expect. In that case I should tell her quite simply, " You ask me what God is; it is not easy to say; we can neither hear nor see nor handle God; we can only know Him by His works. To learn what He is, you must wait till you know what He has done."

If our dogmas are all equally true, they are not equally important. It makes little difference to the glory of God that we should perceive it everywhere, but it does make a difference to human society, and to every member of that society, that a man should know and do the duties which are laid upon him by the law of God, his duty to his neighbour and to himself. This is what we should always be teaching one another, and it is this which fathers and mothers are specially bound to teach their little ones. Whether a virgin became the mother of her Creator, whether she gave birth to God, or merely to a man into whom God has entered, whether the Father and the Son are of the same substance or of like substance only, whether the

Spirit proceeded from one or both of these who are but one, or from both together, however important these questions may seem, I cannot see that it is any more necessary for the human race to come to a decision with regard to them than to know what day to keep Easter, or whether we should tell our beads, fast, and refuse to eat meat, speak Latin or French in church, adorn the walls with statues, hear or say mass, and have no wife of our own. Let each think as he pleases; I cannot see that it matters to any one but himself; for my own part it is no concern of mine. But what does concern my fellow-creatures and myself alike is to know that there is indeed a judge of human fate, that we are all His children, that He bids us all be just, He bids us love one another, He bids us be kindly and merciful, He bids us keep our word with all men, even with our own enemies and His; we must know that the apparent happiness of this world is naught; that there is another life to come, in which this Supreme Being will be the rewarder of the just and the judge of the unjust. Children need to be taught these doctrines and others like them and all citizens require to be persuaded of their truth. Whoever sets his face against these doctrines is indeed guilty; he is the disturber of the peace, the enemy of society. Whoever goes beyond these doctrines and seeks to make us the slaves of his private opinions, reaches the same goal by another way; to establish his own kind of order he disturbs the peace; in his rash pride he makes himself the interpreter of the Divine, and in His name demands the homage and the reverence of mankind; so far as may be, he sets himself in God's place; he should receive the punishment of sacrilege if he is not punished for his intolerance.

Give no heed, therefore, to all those mysterious doctrines which are words without ideas for us, all those strange teachings, the study of which is too often offered as a substitute for virtue, a study which more often makes men mad rather than good. Keep your children ever within the little circle of dogmas which are related to morality. Convince them that the only useful learning is that which teaches us to act rightly. Do not make your daughters theologians and casuists; only teach them such things of heaven as conduce to human goodness; train them to feel that they are always in the presence of God, who sees their thoughts and deeds, their virtue and their pleasures; teach them to do good without ostentation and because they love it, to suffer evil without a murmur, because God will reward them; in a word to be all their life long what they will be glad to have been when they appear in His presence. This is true religion; this alone is incapable of abuse, impiety, or fanaticism. Let those who will, teach a religion more sublime, but this is the only religion I know.

Moreover, it is as well to observe that, until the age when the reason becomes enlightened, when growing emotion gives a voice to conscience, what is wrong for young people is what those about have decided to be wrong. What they are told to do is good; what they are forbidden to do is bad; that is all they ought to know: this shows how important it is for girls, even more than for boys, that the right people should be chosen to be with them and to have authority over them. At last there comes a time when they begin to judge things for themselves, and that is the time to change your method of education.

Perhaps I have said too much already. To what shall we reduce the education of our women if we give them no law but that of conventional prejudice? Let us not degrade so far the sex which rules over us, and which does us honour when we have not made it vile. For all mankind there is a law anterior to that of public opinion. All other laws should bend before the inflexible control of this law; it is the judge of public opinion, and only in so far as the esteem of men is in accordance with this law has it any claim on our obedience

This law is our individual conscience. I will not repeat what has been said already; it is enough to point out that if these two laws clash, the education of women will always be imperfect. Right feeling without respect for public opinion will not give them that delicacy of soul which lends to right conduct the charm of social approval; while respect for public opinion without right feeling will only make false and wicked women who put appearances in the place of virtue.

It is, therefore, important to cultivate a faculty which serves as judge between the two guides, which does not permit conscience to go astray and corrects the errors of prejudice. That faculty is reason. But what a crowd of questions arise at this word. Are women capable of solid reason; should they cultivate it, can they cultivate it successfully? Is this culture useful in relation to the functions laid upon them? Is it compatible with becoming simplicity?

The different ways of envisaging and answering these questions lead to two extremes; some would have us keep women indoors sewing and spinning with their maids; thus they make them nothing more than the chief servant of their master. Others, not content to secure their rights, lead them to usurp ours; for to make woman our superior in all the qualities proper to her sex, and to make her our equal in all the rest, what is this but to transfer to the woman the superiority which nature has given to her husband?

The reason which teaches a man his duties is not very complex; the reason which teaches a woman hers is even simpler. The obedience and fidelity which she owes to her husband, the tenderness and care due to her children, are such natural and self-evident consequences of her position that she cannot honestly refuse her consent to the inner voice which is her guide, nor fail to discern her duty in her natural inclination.

I would not altogether blame those who would restrict a woman to the labours of her sex and would leave her in profound ignorance of everything else; but that would require a standard of morality at once very simple and very healthy, or a life withdrawn from the world. In great towns, among immoral men, such a woman would be too easily led astray; her virtue would too often be at the mercy of circumstances; in this age of philosophy, virtue must be able to resist temptation; she must know beforehand what she may hear and what she should think of it.

Moreover, in submission to man's judgment she should deserve his esteem; above all she should obtain the esteem of her husband; she should not only make him love her person, she should make him approve her conduct; she should justify his choice before the world, and do honour to her husband through the honour given to the wife. But how can she set about this task if she is ignorant of our institutions, our customs, our notions of propriety, if she knows nothing of the source of man's judgment, nor the passions by which it is swayed? Since she depends both on her own conscience and on public opinion, she must learn to know and reconcile these two laws, and to put her own conscience first only when the two are opposed to each other. She becomes the judge of her own judges, she decides when she should obey and when she should refuse her obedience. She weighs their prejudices before she accepts or rejects them; she learns to trace them to their source, to foresee what they will be, and to turn them in her own favour; she is careful never to give cause for blame if duty allows her to avoid it. This cannot be properly done without cultivating her mind and reason.

I always come back to my first principle and it supplies the solution of all my difficulties. I study what is, I seek its cause, and I discover in the end that what is, is good. I go to houses where the master and mistress do the honours together. They are equally well educated, equally polite, equally well equipped with wit and good taste, both of them are inspired with the same desire to give their guests a good reception and to send every one away satisfied. The husband omits no pains to be attentive to every one; he comes and goes and sees to every one and takes all sorts of trouble; he is attention itself. The wife remains in her place; a little circle gathers round her and apparently conceals the rest of the company from her; yet she sees everything that goes on, no one goes without a word with her; she has omitted nothing which might interest anybody, she has said nothing unpleasant to any one, and without any fuss the least is no more overlooked than the greatest. Dinner is announced, they take their places; the man knowing the assembled guests will place them according to his knowledge; the wife, without previous acquaintance, never makes a mistake; their looks and bearing have already shown her what is wanted and every one will find himself where he wishes to be. I do not assert that the servants forget no one. The master of the house may have omitted no one, but the mistress perceives what you like and sees that you get it; while she is talking to her neighbour she has one eye on the other end of the table; she sees who is not eating because he is not hungry and who is afraid to help himself because he is clumsy and timid. When the guests leave the table every one thinks she has had no thought but for him, everybody thinks she has had no time to eat anything, but she has really eaten more than anybody.

When the guests are gone, husband and wife talk over the events of the evening. He relates what was said to him, what was said and done by those with whom he conversed. If the lady is not always quite exact in this respect, yet on the other hand she perceived what was whispered at the other end of the room; she knows what so-and-so thought, and what was the meaning of this speech or that gesture; there is scarcely a change of expression for which she has not an explanation in readiness, and she is almost always right.

The same turn of mind which makes a woman of the world such an excellent hostess, enables a flirt to excel in the art of amusing a number of suitors. Coquetry, cleverly carried out, demands an even finer discernment than courtesy; provided a polite lady is civil to everybody, she has done fairly well in any case; but the flirt would soon lose her hold by such clumsy uniformity; if she tries to be pleasant to all her lovers alike, she will disgust them all. In ordinary social intercourse the manners adopted towards everybody are good enough for all; no question is asked as to private likes or dislikes provided all are alike well received. But in love, a favour shared with others is an insult. A man of feeling would rather be singled out for ill-treatment than be caressed with the crowd, and the worst that can befall him is to be treated like every one else. So a woman who wants to keep several lovers at her feet must persuade every one of them that she prefers him, and she must contrive to do this in the sight of all the rest, each of whom is equally convinced that he is her favourite.

If you want to see a man in a quandary, place him between two women with each of whom he has a secret understanding, and see what a fool he looks. But put a woman in similar circumstances between two men, and the results will be even more remarkable; you will be astonished at the skill with which she cheats them both, and makes them laugh at each other. Now if that woman were to show the same confidence in both, if she were to be equally familiar with both, how could they be deceived for a moment? If she treated them alike, would she not show that they both had the same claims upon her? Oh, she is far too clever for that; so far from treating them just alike, she makes a marked difference between them, and she does it so skilfully that the man she flatters thinks it is affection, and the man she ill uses think it is spite. So that each of them believes she is thinking of him, when she is thinking of no one but herself.

A general desire to please suggests similar measures; people would be disgusted with a woman's whims if they were not skilfully managed, and when they are artistically distributed her servants are more than ever enslaved.

> " Usa ogn'arte la donna, onde sia colto
> Nella sua rete alcun novello amante;
> Nè con tutti, nè sempre un stesso volto
> Serba; ma cangia a tempo atto e sembiante."
>   TASSO, *Jerus. Del.*, c. iv., v. 87.

What is the secret of this art? Is it not the result of a delicate and continuous observation which shows her what is taking place in a man's heart, so that she is able to encourage or to check every hidden impulse? Can this art be acquired? No; it is born with women; it is common to them all, and men never show it to the same degree. It is one of the distinctive characters of the sex. Self-possession, penetration, delicate observation, this is a woman's science; the skill to make use of it is her chief accomplishment.

This is what is, and we have seen why it is so. It is said that women are false. They become false. They are really endowed with skill not duplicity; in the genuine inclinations of their sex they are not false even when they tell a lie. Why do you consult their words when it is not their mouths that speak? Consult their eyes, their colour, their breathing, their timid manner, their slight resistance, that is the language nature gave them for your answer. The lips always say "No," and rightly so; but the tone is not always the same, and that cannot lie. Has not a woman the same needs as a man, but without the same right to make them known? Her fate would be too cruel if she had no language in which to express her legitimate desires except the words which she dare not utter. Must her modesty condemn her to misery? Does she not require a means of indicating her inclinations without open expression? What skill is needed to hide from her lover what she would fain reveal! Is it not of vital importance that she should learn to touch his heart without showing that she cares for him? It is a pretty story that tale of Galatea with her apple and her clumsy flight. What more is needed? Will she tell the shepherd who pursues her among the willows that she only flees that he may follow? If she did, it would be a lie; for she would no longer attract him. The more modest a woman is, the more art she needs, even with her husband. Yes, I maintain that coquetry, kept within bounds, becomes modest and true, and out of it springs a law of right conduct.

One of my opponents has very truly asserted that virtue is one; you cannot disintegrate it and choose this and reject the other. If you love virtue, you love it in its entirety, and you close your heart when you can, and you always close your lips to the feelings which you ought not to allow. Moral truth is not only what is, but what is good; what is bad ought not to be, and ought not to be confessed, especially when that confession produces results which might have been avoided. If I were tempted to steal, and in confessing it I tempted another to become my accomplice, the very confession of my temptation would amount to a yielding to that temptation. Why do you say that modesty makes women false? Are those who lose their modesty more sincere than the rest? Not so, they are a thousandfold more deceitful. This degree of depravity is due to many vices, none of which is rejected, vices which owe their power to intrigue and falsehood.[1]

[1] I know that women who have openly decided on a certain course of conduct profess that their lack of concealment is a virtue in itself, and

On the other hand, those who are not utterly shameless, who take no pride in their faults, who are able to conceal their desires even from those who inspire them, those who confess their passion most reluctantly, these are the truest and most sincere, these are they on whose fidelity you may generally rely.

The only example I know which might be quoted as a recognised exception to these remarks is Mlle. de L'Enclos; and she was considered a prodigy. In her scorn for the virtues of women, she practised, so they say, the virtues of a man. She is praised for her frankness and uprightness; she was a trustworthy acquaintance and a faithful friend. To complete the picture of her glory it is said that she became a man. That may be, but in spite of her high reputation I should no more desire that man as my friend than as my mistress.

This is not so irrelevant as it seems. I am aware of the tendencies of our modern philosophy which make a jest of female modesty and its so-called insincerity; I also perceive that the most certain result of this philosophy will be to deprive the women of this century of such shreds of honour as they still possess.

On these grounds I think we may decide in general terms what sort of education is suited to the female mind, and the objects to which we should turn its attention in early youth.

As I have already said, the duties of their sex are more easily recognised than performed. They must learn in the first place to love those duties by considering the advantages to be derived from them—that is the only way to make duty easy. Every age and condition has its own duties. We are quick to see our duty if we love it. Honour your position as a woman, and in whatever station of life to which it shall please heaven to call you, you will be well off. The essential thing is to be what nature has made you; women are only too ready to be what men would have them.

The search for abstract and speculative truths, for principles and axioms in science, for all that tends to wide generalisation, is beyond a woman's grasp; their studies should be thoroughly practical. It is their business to apply the principles discovered by men, it is their place to make the observations which lead men to discover those principles. A woman's thoughts, beyond the range of her immediate duties, should be directed to the study of men, or the acquirement of that agreeable learning whose sole end is the formation of taste; for the works of genius are beyond her reach, and she has neither the accuracy nor the attention for success in the exact sciences; as for the physical sciences, to decide the relations between

swear that, with one exception, they are possessed of all the virtues; but I am sure they never persuaded any but fools to believe them. When the natural curb is removed from their sex, what is there left to restrain them? What honour will they prize when they have rejected the honour of their sex? Having once given the rein to passion they have no longer any reason for self-control. " Nec femina, amissa pudicitia, alia abnuerit." No author ever understood more thoroughly the heart of both sexes than Tacitus when he wrote those words.

living creatures and the laws of nature is the task of that sex which is more active and enterprising, which sees more things, that sex which is possessed of greater strength and is more accustomed to the exercise of that strength. Woman, weak as she is and limited in her range of observation, perceives and judges the forces at her disposal to supplement her weakness, and those forces are the passions of man. Her own mechanism is more powerful than ours; she has many levers which may set the human heart in motion. She must find a way to make us desire what she cannot achieve unaided and what she considers necessary or pleasing; therefore she must have a thorough knowledge of man's mind; not an abstract knowledge of the mind of man in general, but the mind of those men who are about her, the mind of those men who have authority over her, either by law or custom. She must learn to divine their feelings from speech and action, look and gesture. By her own speech and action, look and gesture, she must be able to inspire them with the feelings she desires, without seeming to have any such purpose. The men will have a better philosophy of the human heart, but she will read more accurately in the heart of men. Woman should discover, so to speak, an experimental morality, man should reduce it to a system. Woman has more wit, man more genius; woman observes, man reasons; together they provide the clearest light and the profoundest knowledge which is possible to the unaided human mind; in a word, the surest knowledge of self and of others of which the human race is capable. In this way art may constantly tend to the perfection of the instrument which nature has given us.

The world is woman's book; if she reads it ill, it is either her own fault or she is blinded by passion. Yet the genuine mother of a family is no woman of the world, she is almost as much of a recluse as the nun in her convent. Those who have marriageable daughters should do what is or ought to be done for those who are entering the cloisters: they should show them the pleasures they forsake before they are allowed to renounce them, lest the deceitful picture of unknown pleasures should creep in to disturb the happiness of their retreat. In France it is the girls who live in convents and the wives who flaunt in society. Among the ancients it was quite otherwise; girls enjoyed, as I have said already, many games and public festivals; the married women lived in retirement. This was a more reasonable custom and more conducive to morality. A girl may be allowed a certain amount of coquetry, and she may be mainly occupied at amusement. A wife has other responsibilities at home, and she is no longer on the look-out for a husband; but women would not appreciate the change, and unluckily it is they who set the fashion. Mothers, let your daughters be your companions. Give them good sense and an honest heart, and then conceal from them nothing that a pure eye may behold. Balls, assemblies, sports, the theatre itself; everything which viewed amiss delights imprudent youth may be safely displayed to a healthy mind. The more they know of these noisy pleasures, the sooner they will cease to desire them.

I can fancy the outcry with which this will be received. What girl will resist such an example? Their heads are turned by the first glimpse of the world; not one of them is ready to give it up. That may be; but before you showed them this deceitful prospect, did you prepare them to behold it without emotion? Did you tell them plainly what it was they would see? Did you show it in its true light? Did you arm them against the illusions of vanity? Did you inspire their young hearts with a taste for the true pleasures which are not to be met with in this tumult? What precautions, what steps, did you take to preserve them from the false taste which leads them astray? Not only have you done nothing to preserve their minds from the tyranny of prejudice, you have fostered that prejudice; you have taught them to desire every foolish amusement they can get. Your own example is their teacher. Young people on their entrance into society have no guide but their mother, who is often just as silly as they are themselves, and quite unable to show them things except as she sees them herself. Her example is stronger than reason; it justifies them in their own eyes, and the mother's authority is an unanswerable excuse for the daughter. If I ask a mother to bring her daughter into society, I assume that she will show it in its true light.

The evil begins still earlier; the convents are regular schools of coquetry; not that honest coquetry which I have described, but a coquetry the source of every kind of misconduct, a coquetry which turns out girls who are the most ridiculous little madams. When they leave the convent to take their place in smart society, young women find themselves quite at home. They have been educated for such a life; is it strange that they like it? I am afraid what I am going to say may be based on prejudice rather than observation, but so far as I can see, one finds more family affection, more good wives and loving mothers in Protestant than in Catholic countries; if that is so, we cannot fail to suspect that the difference is partly due to the convent schools.

The charms of a peaceful family life must be known to be enjoyed; their delights should be tasted in childhood. It is only in our father's home that we learn to love our own, and a woman whose mother did not educate her herself will not be willing to educate her own children. Unfortunately, there is no such thing as home education in our large towns. Society is so general and so mixed there is no place left for retirement, and even in the home we live in public. We live in company till we have no family, and we scarcely know our own relations we see them as strangers; and the simplicity of home life disappears together with the sweet familiarity which was its charm. In this wise do we draw with our mother's milk a taste for the pleasures of the age and the maxims by which it is controlled.

Girls are compelled to assume an air of propriety so that men may be deceived into marrying them by their appearance. But watch these young people for a moment; under a pretence of coyness they barely conceal the passion which devours them, and already you may read in their eager eyes their desire to imitate their mothers. It is not a husband they want, but the licence of a married woman. What need of a husband when there are so many other resources; but a husband there must be to act as a screen.[1] There is modesty on the brow, but vice in the heart; this sham modesty is one of its outward signs; they affect it that they may be rid of it once for all. Women of Paris and London, forgive me! There may be miracles everywhere, but I am not aware of them; and if there is even one among you who is really pure in heart, I know nothing of our institutions.

All these different methods of education lead alike to a taste for the pleasures of the great world, and to the passions which this taste so soon kindles. In our great towns depravity begins at birth; in the smaller towns it begins with reason. Young women brought up in the country are soon taught to despise the happy simplicity of their lives, and hasten to Paris to share the corruption of ours. Vices, cloaked under the fair name of accomplishments, are the sole object of their journey; ashamed to find themselves so much behind the noble licence of the Parisian ladies, they hasten to become worthy of the name of Parisian. Which is responsible for the evil—the place where it begins, or the place where it is accomplished?

I would not have a sensible mother bring her girl to Paris to show her these sights so harmful to others; but I assert that if she did so, either the girl has been badly brought up, or such sights have little danger for her. With good taste, good sense, and a love of what is right, these things are less attractive than to those who abandon themselves to their charm. In Paris you may see giddy young things hastening to adopt the tone and fashions of the town for some six months, so that they may spend the rest of their life in disgrace; but who gives any heed to those who, disgusted with the rout, return to their distant home and are contented with their lot when they have compared it with that which others desire. How many young wives have I seen whose good-natured husbands have taken them to Paris where they might live if they pleased; but they have shrunk from it and returned home more willingly than they went, saying tenderly, " Ah, let us go back to our cottage, life is happier there than in these palaces." We do not know how many there are who have not bowed the knee to Baal, who scorn his senseless worship. Fools make a stir; good women pass unnoticed.

If so many women preserve a judgment which is proof against temptation, in spite of universal prejudice, in spite of the bad

[1] The way of a man in his youth was one of the four things that the sage could not understand; the fifth was the shamelessness of an adulteress. " Quæ comedit, et tergens os suum dicit; non sum operata malum." Prov. xxx. 20.

education of girls, what would their judgment have been, had it been strengthened by suitable instruction, or rather left unaffected by evil teaching, for to preserve or restore the natural feelings is our main business? You can do this without preaching endless sermons to your daughters, without crediting them with your harsh morality. The only effect of such teaching is to inspire a dislike for the teacher and the lessons. In talking to a young girl you need not make her afraid of her duties, nor need you increase the burden laid upon her by nature. When you explain her duties speak plainly and pleasantly; do not let her suppose that the performance of these duties is a dismal thing—away with every affectation of disgust or pride. Every thought which we desire to arouse should find its expression in our pupils, their catechism of conduct should be as brief and plain as their catechism of religion, but it need not be so serious. Show them that these same duties are the source of their pleasures and the basis of their rights. Is it so hard to win love by love, happiness by an amiable disposition, obedience by worth, and honour by self-respect? How fair are these woman's rights, how worthy of reverence, how dear to the heart of man when a woman is able to show their worth! These rights are no privilege of years; a woman's empire begins with her virtues; her charms are only in the bud, yet she reigns already by the gentleness of her character and the dignity of her modesty. Is there any man so hard-hearted and uncivilised that he does not abate his pride and take heed to his manners with a sweet and virtuous girl of sixteen, who listens but says little; her bearing is modest, her conversation honest, her beauty does not lead her to forget her sex and her youth, her very timidity arouses interest, while she wins for herself the respect which she shows to others?

These external signs are not devoid of meaning; they do not rest entirely upon the charms of sense; they arise from that conviction that we all feel that women are the natural judges of a man's worth. Who would be scorned by women? not even he who has ceased to desire their love. And do you suppose that I, who tell them such harsh truths, am indifferent to their verdict? Reader, I care more for their approval than for yours; you are often more effeminate than they. While I scorn their morals, I will revere their justice; I care not though they hate me, if I can compel their esteem.

What great things might be accomplished by their influence if only we could bring it to bear! Alas for the age whose women lose their ascendancy, and fail to make men respect their judgment! This is the last stage of degradation. Every virtuous nation has shown respect to women. Consider Sparta, Germany, and Rome; Rome the throne of glory and virtue, if ever they were enthroned on earth. The Roman women awarded honour to the deeds of great generals, they mourned in public for the fathers of the country, their awards and their tears were alike held sacred as the most solemn utterance of the Republic. Every great revolution began with the women. Through a woman Rome gained her liberty, through a woman the plebeians won the consulate, through a woman the tyranny of the decemvirs was overthrown; it was the women who saved Rome when besieged by Coriolanus. What would you have said at the sight of this procession, you Frenchmen who pride yourselves on your gallantry, would you not have followed it with shouts of laughter? You and I see things with such different eyes, and perhaps we are both right. Such a procession formed of the fairest beauties of France would be an indecent spectacle; but let it consist of Roman ladies, you will all gaze with the eyes of the Volscians and feel with the heart of Coriolanus.

I will go further and maintain that virtue is no less favourable to love than to other rights of nature, and that it adds as much to the power of the beloved as to that of the wife or mother. There is no real love without enthusiasm, and no enthusiasm without an object of perfection real or supposed, but always present in the imagination. What is there to kindle the hearts of lovers for whom this perfection is nothing, for whom the loved one is merely the means to sensual pleasure? Nay, not thus is the heart kindled, not thus does it abandon itself to those sublime transports which form the rapture of lovers and the charm of love. Love is an illusion, I grant you, but its reality consists in the feelings it awakes, in the love of true beauty which it inspires. That beauty is not to be found in the object of our affections, it is the creation of our illusions. What matter! do we not still sacrifice all those baser feelings to the imaginary model? and we still feed our hearts on the virtues we attribute to the beloved, we still withdraw ourselves from the baseness of human nature. What lover is there who would not give his life for his mistress? What gross and sensual passion is there in a man who is willing to die? We scoff at the knights of old; they knew the meaning of love; we know nothing but debauchery. When the teachings of romance began to seem ridiculous, it was not so much the work of reason as of immorality.

Natural relations remain the same throughout the centuries, their good or evil effects are unchanged; prejudices, masquerading as reason, can but change their outward seeming; self-mastery, even at the behest of fantastic opinions, will not cease to be great and good. And the true motives of honour will not fail to appeal to the heart of every woman who is able to seek happiness in life in her woman's duties. To a high-souled woman chastity above all must be a delightful virtue. She sees all the kingdoms of the world before her and she triumphs over herself and them; she sits enthroned in her own soul and all men do her homage; a few passing struggles are crowned with perpetual glory; she secures the affection, or it may be the envy, she secures in any case the esteem of both sexes and the universal respect of her own. The loss is fleeting, the gain is permanent. What a joy for a noble heart—the pride of virtue combined with beauty. Let her be a heroine of romance; she will taste delights more exquisite than those of Lais and Cleopatra;

and when her beauty is fled, her glory and her joys remain; she alone can enjoy the past.

The harder and more important the duties, the stronger and clearer must be the reasons on which they are based. There is a sort of pious talk about the most serious subjects which is dinned in vain into the ears of young people. This talk, quite unsuited to their ideas and the small importance they attach to it in secret, inclines them to yield readily to their inclinations, for lack of any reasons for resistance drawn from the facts themselves. No doubt a girl brought up to goodness and piety has strong weapons against temptation; but one whose heart, or rather her ears, are merely filled with the jargon of piety, will certainly fall a prey to the first skilful seducer who attacks her. A young and beautiful girl will never despise her body, she will never really deplore sins which her beauty leads men to commit, she will never lament earnestly in the sight of God that she is an object of desire, she will never be convinced that the tenderest feeling is an invention of the Evil One. Give her other and more pertinent reasons for her own sake, for these will have no effect. It will be worse to instil, as is often done, ideas which contradict each other, and after having humbled and degraded her person and her charms as the stain of sin, to bid her reverence that same vile body as the temple of Jesus Christ. Ideas too sublime and too humble are equally ineffective and they cannot both be true. A reason adapted to her age and sex is what is needed. Considerations of duty are of no effect unless they are combined with some motive for the performance of our duty.

> " Quæ quia non liceat non facit, illa facit."
> OVID, *Amor*. I. iii. eleg. iv.

One would not suspect Ovid of such a harsh judgment.

If you would inspire young people with a love of good conduct avoid saying, " Be good; " make it their interest to be good; make them feel the value of goodness and they will love it. It is not enough to show this effect in the distant future, show it now, in the relations of the present, in the character of their lovers. Describe a good man, a man of worth, teach them to recognise him when they see him, to love him for their own sake; convince them that such a man alone can make them happy as friend, wife, or mistress. Let reason lead the way to virtue; make them feel that the empire of their sex and all the advantages derived from it depend not merely on the right conduct, the morality, of women, but also on that of men; that they have little hold over the vile and base, and that the lover is incapable of serving his mistress unless he can do homage to virtue. You may then be sure that when you describe the manners of our age you will inspire them with a genuine disgust; when you show them men of fashion they will despise them; you will give them a distaste for their maxims, an aversion to their sentiments, and a scorn for their empty gallantry; you will arouse a nobler ambition, to reign over great and strong souls, the ambition of the

Spartan women to rule over men. A bold, shameless, intriguing woman, who can only attract her lovers by coquetry and retain them by her favours, wins a servile obedience in common things; in weighty and important matters she has no influence over them. But the woman who is both virtuous, wise, and charming, she who, in a word, combines love and esteem, can send them at her bidding to the end of the world, to war, to glory, and to death at her behest. This is a fine kingdom and worth the winning.

This is the spirit in which Sophy has been educated, she has been trained carefully rather than strictly, and her taste has been followed rather than thwarted. Let us say just a word about her person, according to the description I have given to Emile and the picture he himself has formed of the wife in whom he hopes to find happiness.

I cannot repeat too often that I am not dealing with prodigies. Emile is no prodigy, neither is Sophy. He is a man and she is a woman; this is all they have to boast of. In the present confusion between the sexes it is almost a miracle to belong to one's own sex.

Sophy is well born and she has a good disposition; she is very warm-hearted, and this warmth of heart sometimes makes her imagination run away with her. Her mind is keen rather than accurate, her temper is pleasant but variable, her person pleasing though nothing out of the common, her countenance bespeaks a soul and it speaks true; you may meet her with indifference, but you will not leave her without emotion. Others possess good qualities which she lacks; others possess her good qualities in a higher degree, but in no one are these qualities better blended to form a happy disposition. She knows how to make the best of her very faults, and if she were more perfect she would be less pleasing.

Sophy is not beautiful; but in her presence men forget the fairer women, and the latter are dissatisfied with themselves. At first sight she is hardly pretty; but the more we see her the prettier she is; she wins where so many lose, and what she wins she keeps. Her eyes might be finer, her mouth more beautiful, her stature more imposing; but no one could have a more graceful figure, a finer complexion, a whiter hand, a daintier foot, a sweeter look, and a more expressive countenance. She does not dazzle; she arouses interest; she delights us, we know not why.

Sophy is fond of dress, and she knows how to dress; her mother has no other maid; she has taste enough to dress herself well; but she hates rich clothes; her own are always simple but elegant. She does not like showy but becoming things. She does not know what colours are fashionable, but she makes no mistake about those that suit her. No girl seems more simply dressed, but no one could take more pains over her toilet; no article is selected at random, and yet there is no trace of artificiality. Her dress is very modest in appearance and very coquettish in reality; she does not display her charms, she conceals them, but in such a way as to enhance them. When you see her you say, "That is a good modest girl," but while you are with her, you cannot take your eyes or your thoughts off her, and one might say that this very simple adornment is only put on to be removed bit by bit by the imagination.

Sophy has natural gifts; she is aware of them, and they have not been neglected; but never having had a chance of much training she is content to use her pretty voice to sing tastefully and truly; her little feet step lightly, easily, and gracefully, she can always make an easy graceful courtesy. She has had no singing master but her father, no dancing mistress but her mother; a neighbouring organist has given her a few lessons in playing accompaniments on the spinet, and she has improved herself by practice. At first she only wished to show off her hand on the dark keys; then she discovered that the thin clear tone of the spinet made her voice sound sweeter; little by little she recognised the charms of harmony; as she grew older she at last began to enjoy the charms of expression, to love music for its own sake. But she has taste rather than talent; she cannot read a simple air from notes.

Needlework is what Sophy likes best; and the feminine arts have been taught her most carefully, even those you would not expect, such as cutting out and dressmaking. There is nothing she cannot do with her needle, and nothing that she does not take a delight in doing; but lace-making is her favourite occupation, because there is nothing which requires such a pleasing attitude, nothing which calls for such grace and dexterity of finger. She has also studied all the details of housekeeping; she understands cooking and cleaning; she knows the prices of food, and also how to choose it; she can keep accounts accurately, she is her mother's house-keeper. Some day she will be the mother of a family; by managing her father's house she is preparing to manage her own; she can take the place of any of the servants and she is always ready to do so. You cannot give orders unless you can do the work yourself; that is why her mother sets her to do it. Sophy does not think of that; her first duty is to be a good daughter, and that is all she thinks about for the present. Her one idea is to help her mother and relieve her of some of her anxieties. However, she does not like them all equally well. For instance, she likes dainty food, but she does not like cooking; the details of cookery offend her, and things are never clean enough for her. She is extremely sensitive in this respect and carries her sensitiveness to a fault; she would let the whole dinner boil over into the fire rather than soil her cuffs. She has always disliked inspecting the kitchen-garden for the same reason. The soil is dirty, and as soon as she sees the manure heap she fancies there is a disagreeable smell.

This defect is the result of her mother's teaching. According to her, cleanliness is one of the most necessary of a woman's duties, a special duty, of the highest importance and a duty imposed by nature. Nothing could be more revolting than a dirty woman, and a husband who tires of her is not to blame. She insisted so strongly on this duty when Sophy was little, she required such absolute cleanliness in her person, clothing, room, work, and toilet, that use has become habit, till it absorbs one half of her time and controls the other; so that she thinks less of how to do a thing than of how to do it without getting dirty.

Yet this has not degenerated into mere affectation and softness; there is none of the over refinement of luxury. Nothing but clean water enters her room; she knows no perfumes but the scent of flowers, and her husband will never find anything sweeter than her breath. In conclusion, the attention she pays to the outside does not blind her to the fact that time and strength are meant for greater tasks; either she does not know or she despises that exaggerated cleanliness of body which degrades the soul. Sophy is more than clean, she is pure.

I said that Sophy was fond of good things. She was so by nature; but she became temperate by habit and now she is temperate by virtue. Little girls are not to be controlled, as little boys are, to some extent, through their greediness. This tendency may have ill effects on women and it is too dangerous to be left unchecked. When Sophy was little, she did not always return empty handed if she was sent to her mother's cupboard, and she was not quite to be trusted with sweets and sugar-almonds. Her mother caught her, took them from her, punished her, and made her go without her dinner. At last she managed to persuade her that sweets were bad for the teeth, and that over-eating spoiled the figure. Thus Sophy overcame her faults; and when she grew older other tastes distracted her from this low kind of self-indulgence. With awakening feeling greediness ceases to be the ruling passion, both with men and women. Sophy has preserved her feminine tastes; she likes milk and sweets; she likes pastry and made-dishes, but not much meat. She has never tasted wine or spirits; moreover, she eats sparingly; women, who do not work so hard as men, have less waste to repair. In all things she likes what is good, and knows how to appreciate it; but she can also put up with what is not so good, or can go without it.

Sophy's mind is pleasing but not brilliant, and thorough but not deep; it is the sort of mind which calls for no remark, as she never seems cleverer or stupider than oneself. When people talk to her they always find what she says attractive, though it may not be highly ornamental according to modern ideas of an educated woman; her mind has been formed not only by reading, but by conversation with her father and mother, by her own reflections, and by her own observations in the little world in which she has lived. Sophy is naturally merry; as a child she was even giddy; but her mother cured her of her silly ways, little by little, lest too sudden a change should make her self-conscious. Thus she became modest and retiring while still a child, and now that she is a child no longer, she finds it easier to continue this conduct than it would have been to acquire it without knowing why. It is amusing to see her occasionally return to her old ways and indulge in childish mirth and then suddenly check herself, with silent lips, downcast eyes, and rosy blushes; neither child nor woman, she may well partake of both.

Sophy is too sensitive to be always good humoured, but too gentle to let this be really disagreeable to other people; it is only herself who suffers. If you say anything that hurts her she does not sulk, but her heart swells; she tries to run away and cry. In the midst of her tears, at a word from her father or mother she returns at once laughing and playing, secretly wiping her eyes and trying to stifle her sobs.

Yet she has her whims; if her temper is too much indulged it degenerates into rebellion, and then she forgets herself. But give her time to come round and her way of making you forget her wrong-doing is almost a virtue. If you punish her she is gentle and sub-missive, and you see that she is more ashamed of the fault than the punishment. If you say nothing, she never fails to make amends, and she does it so frankly and so readily that you cannot be angry with her. She would kiss the ground before the lowest servant and would make no fuss about it; and as soon as she is forgiven, you can see by her delight and her caresses that a load is taken off her heart. In a word, she endures patiently the wrong-doing of others, and she is eager to atone for her own. This amiability is natural to her sex when unspoiled. Woman is made to submit to man and to endure even injustice at his hands. You will never bring young lads to this; their feelings rise in revolt against injustice; nature has not fitted them to put up with it.

> " Gravem
> Pelidæ stomachum cedere nescii."
> HORACE, lib. i. ode vi.

Sophy's religion is reasonable and simple, with few doctrines and fewer observances; or rather as she knows no course of conduct but the right her whole life is devoted to the service of God and to doing good. In all her parents' teaching of religion she has been trained to a reverent submission; they have often said, " My little girl, this is too hard for you; your husband will teach you when you are grown up." Instead of long sermons about piety, they have been content to preach by their example, and this example is engraved on her heart.

Sophy loves virtue; this love has come to be her ruling passion; she loves virtue because there is nothing fairer in itself, she loves it because it is a woman's glory and because a virtuous woman is little lower than the angels; she loves virtue as the only road to real happiness, because she sees nothing but poverty, neglect, unhappiness, shame, and disgrace in the life of a bad woman; she loves virtue because it is dear to her revered father and to her tender and worthy mother; they are not content to be happy in their own virtue, they desire hers; and she finds her chief happiness in the hope of making them happy. All these feelings inspire an enthusiasm which stirs her heart and keeps all its budding passions in subjection to this noble enthusiasm. Sophy will be chaste and good till her dying day; she has vowed it in her secret heart, and not before she knew how hard it would be to keep her vow; she made this vow at a time when she would have revoked it had she been the slave of her senses.

Sophy is not so fortunate as to be a charming French woman, cold-hearted and vain, who would rather attract attention than give pleasure, who seeks amusement rather than delight. She suffers from a consuming desire for love; it even disturbs and troubles her heart in the midst of festivities; she has lost her former liveliness, and her taste for merry games; far from being afraid of the tedium of solitude she desires it. Her thoughts go out to him who will make solitude sweet to her. She finds strangers tedious, she wants a lover, not a circle of admirers. She would rather give pleasure to one good man than be a general favourite, or win that applause of society which lasts but a day and to-morrow is turned to scorn.

A woman's judgment develops sooner than a man's; being on the defensive from her childhood up, and intrusted with a treasure so hard to keep, she is earlier acquainted with good and evil. Sophy is precocious by temperament in everything, and her judgment is more formed than that of most girls of her age. There is nothing strange in that, maturity is not always reached at the same age.

Sophy has been taught the duties and rights of her own sex and of ours. She knows men's faults and women's vices; she also knows their corresponding good qualities and virtues, and has them by heart. No one can have a higher ideal of a virtuous woman, but she would rather think of a virtuous man, a man of true worth; she knows that she is made for such a man, that she is worthy of him, that she can make him as happy as he will make her; she is sure she will know him when she sees him; the difficulty is to find him.

Women are by nature judges of a man's worth, as he is of theirs; this right is reciprocal, and it is recognised as such both by men and women. Sophy recognises this right and exercises it, but with the modesty becoming her youth, her inexperience, and her position; she confines her judgment to what she knows, and she only forms an opinion when it may help to illustrate some useful precept. She is extremely careful what she says about those who are absent, particularly if they are women. She thinks that talking about each other makes women spiteful and satirical; so long as they only talk about men they are merely just. So Sophy stops there. As to women she never says anything at all about them, except to tell the good she knows; she thinks this is only fair to her sex; and if she knows no good of any woman, she says nothing, and that is enough.

Sophy has little knowledge of society, but she is observant and obliging, and all that she does is full of grace. A happy disposition does more for her than much art. She has a certain courtesy of her own, which is not dependent on fashion, and does not change with its changes; it is not a matter of custom, but it arises from a feminine desire to please. She is unacquainted with the language of empty compliment, nor does she invent more elaborate compliments of her own; she does not say that she is greatly obliged, that you do her too much honour, that you should not take so much trouble, etc. Still less does she try to make phrases of her own. She responds to an attention or a customary piece of politeness by a courtesy or a mere "Thank you;" but this phrase in her mouth is quite enough. If you do her a real service, she lets her heart speak, and its words are no empty compliment. She has never allowed French manners to make her a slave to appearances; when she goes from one room to another she does not take the arm of an old gentleman, whom she would much rather help. When a scented fop offers her this empty attention, she leaves him on the staircase and rushes into the room saying that she is not lame. Indeed, she will never wear high heels though she is not tall; her feet are small enough to dispense with them.

Not only does she adopt a silent and respectful attitude towards women, but also towards married men, or those who are much older than herself; she will never take her place above them, unless compelled to do so; and she will return to her own lower place as soon as she can; for she knows that the rights of age take precedence of those of sex, as age is presumably wiser than youth, and wisdom should be held in the greatest honour.

With young folks of her own age it is another matter; she requires a different manner to gain their respect, and she knows how to adopt it without dropping the modest ways which become her. If they themselves are shy and modest, she will gladly preserve the friendly familiarity of youth; their innocent conversation will be merry but suitable; if they become serious they must say something useful; if they become silly, she soon puts a stop to it, for she has an utter contempt for the jargon of gallantry, which she considers an insult to her sex. She feels sure that the man she seeks does not speak that jargon, and she will never permit in another what would be displeasing to her in him whose character is engraved on her heart. Her high opinion of the rights of women, her pride in the purity of her feelings, that active virtue which is the basis of her self-respect, make her indignant at the sentimental speeches intended for her amusement. She does not receive them with open anger, but with a disconcerting irony or an unexpected iciness. If a fair Apollo displays his charms, and makes use of his wit in the praise of her wit, her beauty, and her grace; at the risk of offending him she is quite capable of saying politely, "Sir, I am afraid I know that better than you; if we have nothing more interesting to talk about, I think we may put an end to this conversation." To say this with a deep courtesy, and then to withdraw to a considerable distance, is the work of a moment. Ask your lady-killers if it is easy to continue to babble to such an unsympathetic ear.

It is not that she is not fond of praise if it is really sincere, and if she thinks you believe what you say. You must show that you appreciate her merit if you would have her believe you. Her proud spirit may take pleasure in homage which is based upon esteem, but empty compliments are always rejected; Sophy was not meant to practise the small arts of the dancing-girl.

With a judgment so mature, and a mind like that of a woman of twenty, Sophy, at fifteen, is no longer treated as a child by her parents. No sooner do they perceive the first signs of youthful disquiet than they hasten to anticipate its development, their conversations with her are wise and tender. These wise and tender conversations are in keeping with her age and disposition. If her disposition is what I fancy why should not her father speak to her somewhat after this fashion?

" You are a big girl now, Sophy, you will soon be a woman. We want you to be happy, for our own sakes as well as yours, for our happiness depends on yours. A good girl finds her own happiness in the happiness of a good man, so we must consider your marriage; we must think of it in good time, for marriage makes or mars our whole life, and we cannot have too much time to consider it.

" There is nothing so hard to choose as a good husband, unless it is a good wife. You will be that rare creature, Sophy, you will be the crown of our life and the blessing of our declining years; but however worthy you are, there are worthier people upon earth. There is no one who would not do himself honour by marriage with you; there are many who would do you even greater honour than themselves. Among these we must try to find one who suits you, we must get to know him and introduce you to him.

" The greatest possible happiness in marriage depends on so many points of agreement that it is folly to expect to secure them all. We must first consider the more important matters; if others are to be found along with them, so much the better; if not we must do without them. Perfect happiness is not to be found in this world, but we can, at least, avoid the worst form of unhappiness, that for which ourselves are to blame.

" There is a natural suitability, there is a suitability of established usage, and a suitability which is merely conventional. Parents should decide as to the two latters, and the children themselves should decide as to the former. Marriages arranged by parents only depend on a suitability of custom and convention; it is not two people who are united, but two positions and two properties; but these things may change, the people remain, they are always there; and in spite of fortune it is the personal relation that makes a happy or an unhappy marriage.

" Your mother had rank, I had wealth; this was all that our parents considered in arranging our marriage. I lost my money, she lost her position; forgotten by her family, what good did it do her to be a lady born? In the midst of our misfortunes, the union of our hearts has outweighed them all; the similarity of our tastes led us to choose this retreat; we live happily in our poverty, we are all in all to each other. Sophy is a treasure we hold in common, and we thank Heaven which has bestowed this treasure and deprived us of all others. You see, my child, whither we have been led by Providence; the conventional motives which brought about our marriage no longer exist, our happiness consists in that natural suitability which was held of no account.

" Husband and wife should choose each other. A mutual liking should be the first bond between them. They should follow the guidance of their own eyes and hearts; when they are married their first duty will be to love one another, and as love and hatred do not depend on ourselves, this duty brings another with it, and they must begin to love each other before marriage. That is the law of nature, and no power can abrogate it; those who have fettered it by so many legal restrictions have given heed rather to the outward show of order than to the happiness of marriage or the morals of the citizen. You see, my dear Sophy, we do not preach a harsh morality. It tends to make you your own mistress and to make us leave the choice of your husband to yourself.

" When we have told you our reasons for giving you full liberty, it is only fair to speak of your reasons for making a wise use of that liberty. My child, you are good and sensible, upright and pious, you have the accomplishments of a good woman and you are not altogether without charms; but you are poor; you have the gifts most worthy of esteem, but not those which are most esteemed. Do not seek what is beyond your reach, and let your ambition be controlled, not by your ideas or ours, but by the opinion of others. If it were merely a question of equal merits, I know not what limits to impose on your hopes; but do not let your ambitions outrun your fortune, and remember it is very small. Although a man worthy of you would not consider this inequality an obstacle, you must do what he would not do; Sophy must follow her mother's example and only enter a family which counts it an honour to receive her. You never saw our wealth, you were born in our poverty; you make it sweet for us, and you share it without hardship. Believe me, Sophy, do not seek those good things we indeed thank heaven for having taken from us; we did not know what happiness was till we lost our money.

" You are so amiable that you will win affection, and you are not so poor as to be a burden. You will be sought in marriage, it may be by those who are unworthy of you. If they showed themselves in their true colours, you would rate them at their real value; all their outward show would not long deceive you; but though your judgment is good and you know what merit is when you see it, you are inexperienced and you do not know how people can conceal their real selves. A skilful knave might study your tastes in order to seduce you, and make a pretence of those virtues which he does not possess. You would be ruined, Sophy, before you knew what you were doing, and you would only perceive your error when you had cause to lament it.   The most dangerous snare, the only snare which reason cannot avoid, is that of the senses; if ever you have the misfortune to fall into its toils, you will perceive nothing but fancies and illusions; your eyes will be fascinated, your judgment troubled, your will corrupted; your very error will be dear to you, and even if you were able to perceive it you would not be willing to escape from it.   My child, I trust you to Sophy's own reason; I do not trust you to the fancies of your own heart.   Judge for yourself so long as your heart is untouched, but when you love betake yourself to your mother's care.

I propose a treaty between us which shows our esteem for you, and restores the order of nature between us.   Parents choose a husband for their daughter and she is only consulted as a matter of form; that is the custom.   We shall do just the opposite; you will choose, and we shall be consulted.   Use your right, Sophy, use it freely and wisely.   The husband suitable for you should be chosen by you not us.   But it is for us to judge whether he is really suitable, or whether, without knowing it, you are only following your own wishes.   Birth, wealth, position, conventional opinions will count for nothing with us.   Choose a good man whose person and character suit you; whatever he may be in other respects, we will accept him as our son-in-law.   He will be rich enough if he has bodily strength, a good character, and family affection.   His position will be good enough if it is ennobled by virtue.   If everybody blames us, we do not care.   We do not seek the approbation of men, but your happiness."

I cannot tell my readers what effect such words would have upon girls brought up in their fashion.   As for Sophy, she will have no words to reply; shame and emotion will not permit her to express herself easily; but I am sure that what was said will remain engraved upon her heart as long as she lives, and that if any human resolution may be trusted, we may rely on her determination to deserve her parent's esteem.

At worst let us suppose her endowed with an ardent disposition which will make her impatient of long delays; I maintain that her judgment, her knowledge, her taste, her refinement, and, above all, the sentiments in which she has been brought up from childhood, will outweigh the impetuosity of the senses, and enable her to offer a prolonged resistance, if not to overcome them altogether.   She would rather die a virgin martyr than distress her parents by marrying a worthless man and exposing herself to the unhappiness of an ill-assorted marriage.   Ardent as an Italian and sentimental as an Englishwoman, she has a curb upon heart and sense in the pride of a Spaniard, who even when she seeks a lover does not easily discover one worthy of her.

Not every one can realise the motive power to be found in a love of what is right, nor the inner strength which results from a genuine love of virtue.   There are men who think that all greatness is a figment of the brain, men who with their vile and degraded reason will never recognise the power over human passions which is wielded by the very madness of virtue. You can only teach such men by examples; if they persist in denying their existence, so much the worse for them. If I told them that Sophy is no imaginary person, that her name alone is my invention, that her education, her conduct, her character, her very features, really existed, and that her loss is still mourned by a very worthy family, they would, no doubt, refuse to believe me; but indeed why should I not venture to relate word for word the story of a girl so like Sophy that this story might be hers without surprising any one. Believe it or no, it is all the same to me; call my history fiction if you will; in any case I have explained my method and furthered my purpose.

This young girl with the temperament which I have attributed to Sophy was so like her in other respects that she was worthy of the name, and so we will continue to use it. After the conversation related above, her father and mother thought that suitable husbands would not be likely to offer themselves in the hamlet where they lived; so they decided to send her to spend the winter in town, under the care of an aunt who was privately acquainted with the object of the journey; for Sophy's heart throbbed with noble pride at the thought of her self-control; and however much she might want to marry she would rather have died a maid than have brought herself to go in search of a husband.

In response to her parents' wishes her aunt introduced her to her friends, took her into company, both private and public, showed her society, or rather showed her in society, for Sophy paid little heed to its bustle. Yet it was plain that she did not shrink from young men of pleasing appearance and modest seemly behaviour. Her very shyness had a charm of its own, which was very much like coquetry; but after talking to them once or twice she repulsed them. She soon exchanged that air of authority which seems to accept men's homage for a humbler bearing and a still more chilling politeness. Always watchful over her conduct, she gave them no chance of doing her the least service; it was perfectly plain that she was determined not to accept any one of them.

Never did sensitive heart take pleasure in noisy amusements, the empty and barren delights of those who have no feelings, those who think that a merry life is a happy life. Sophy did not find what she sought, and she felt sure she never would, so she got tired of the town. She loved her parents dearly and nothing made up for their absence, nothing could make her forget them; she went home long before the time fixed for the end of her visit.

Scarcely had she resumed her home duties when they perceived that her temper had changed though her conduct was unaltered, she was forgetful, impatient, sad, and dreamy; she wept in secret. At first they thought she was in love and was ashamed to own it; they spoke to her, but she repudiated the idea. She protested she had seen no one who could touch her heart, and Sophy always spoke the truth.

Yet her languor steadily increased, and her health began to give way. Her mother was anxious about her, and determined to know the reason for this change. She took her aside, and with the winning speech and the irresistible caresses which only a mother can employ, she said, " My child, whom I have borne beneath my heart, whom I bear ever in my affection, confide your secret to your mother's bosom. What secrets are these which a mother may not know? Who pities your sufferings, who shares them, who would gladly relieve them, if not your father and myself? Ah, my child! would you have me die of grief for your sorrow without letting me share it? "

Far from hiding her griefs from her mother, the young girl asked nothing better than to have her as friend and comforter; but she could not speak for shame, her modesty could find no words to describe a condition so unworthy of her, as the emotion which disturbed her senses in spite of all her efforts. At length her very shame gave her mother a clue to her difficulty, and she drew from her the humiliating confession. Far from distressing her with reproaches or unjust blame, she consoled her, pitied her, wept over her; she was too wise to make a crime of an evil which virtue alone made so cruel. But why put up with such an evil when there was no necessity to do so, when the remedy was so easy and so legitimate? Why did she not use the freedom they had granted her? Why did she not take a husband? Why did she not make her choice? Did she not know that she was perfectly independent in this matter, that whatever her choice, it would be approved, for it was sure to be good? They had sent her to town, but she would not stay; many suitors had offered themselves, but she would have none of them. What did she expect? What did she want? What an inexplicable contradiction?

The reply was simple. If it were only a question of the partner of her youth, her choice would soon be made; but a master for life is not so easily chosen; and since the two cannot be separated, people must often wait and sacrifice their youth before they find the man with whom they could spend their life. Such was Sophy's case; she wanted a lover, but this lover must be her husband; and to discover a heart such as she required, a lover and husband were equally difficult to find. All these dashing young men were only her equals in age, in everything else they were found lacking; their empty wit, their vanity, their affectations of speech, their ill-regulated conduct, their frivolous imitations alike disgusted her. She sought a man and she found monkeys; she sought a soul and there was none to be found.

" How unhappy I am! " said she to her mother; " I am compelled to love and yet I am dissatisfied with every one. My heart rejects every one who appeals to my senses. Every one of them stirs my passions and all alike revolt them; a liking unaccompanied by respect cannot last. That is not the sort of man for your Sophy; the delightful image of her ideal is too deeply graven in her heart.

She can love no other; she can make no one happy but him, and she cannot be happy without him. She would rather consume herself in ceaseless conflicts, she would rather die free and wretched, than driven desperate by the company of a man she did not love, a man she would make as unhappy as herself; she would rather die than live to suffer."

Amazed at these strange ideas, her mother found them so peculiar that she could not fail to suspect some mystery. Sophy was neither affected nor absurd. How could such exaggerated delicacy exist in one who had been so carefully taught from her childhood to adapt herself to those with whom she must live, and to make a virtue of necessity? This ideal of the delightful man with which she was so enchanted, who appeared so often in her conversation, made her mother suspect that there was some foundation for her caprices which was still unknown to her, and that Sophy had not told her all. The unhappy girl, overwhelmed with her secret grief, was only too eager to confide it to another. Her mother urged her to speak; she hesitated, she yielded, and leaving the room without a word, she presently returned with a book in her hand. " Have pity on your unhappy daughter, there is no remedy for her grief, her tears cannot be dried. You would know the cause: well, here it is," said she, flinging the book on the table. Her mother took the book and opened it; it was *The Adventures of Telemachus*. At first she could make nothing of this riddle; by dint of questions and vague replies, she discovered to her great surprise that her daughter was the rival of Eucharis.

Sophy was in love with Telemachus, and loved him with a passion which nothing could cure. When her father and mother became aware of her infatuation, they laughed at it and tried to cure her by reasoning with her. They were mistaken, reason was not altogether on their side; Sophy had her own reason and knew how to use it. Many a time did she reduce them to silence by turning their own arguments against them, by showing them that it was all their own fault for not having trained her to suit the men of that century; that she would be compelled to adopt her husband's way of thinking or he must adopt hers, that they had made the former course impossible by the way she had been brought up, and that the latter was just what she wanted. " Give me," said she, " a man who holds the same opinions as I do, or one who will be willing to learn them from me, and I will marry him; but until then, why do you scold me? Pity me; I am miserable, but not mad. Is the heart controlled by the will? Did my father not ask that very question? Is it my fault if I love what has no existence? I am no visionary; I desire no prince, I seek no Telemachus, I know he is only an imaginary person; I seek some one like him. And why should there be no such person, since there is such a person as I, I who feel that my heart is like his? No, let us not wrong humanity so greatly, let us not think that an amiable and virtuous man is a figment of the imagination. He exists, he lives, perhaps he is seeking me; he is seeking a soul which is capable of love for him. But who is he, where is he? I know not; he is not among those I have seen; and no doubt I shall never see him. Oh! mother, why did you make virtue too attractive? If I can love nothing less, you are more to blame than I."

Must I continue this sad story to its close? Must I describe the long struggles which preceded it? Must I show an impatient mother exchanging her former caresses for severity? Must I paint an angry father forgetting his former promises, and treating the most virtuous of daughters as a mad woman? Must I portray the unhappy girl, more than ever devoted to her imaginary hero, because of the persecution brought upon her by that devotion, drawing nearer step by step to her death, and descending into the grave when they were about to force her to the altar? No; I will not dwell upon these gloomy scenes; I have no need to go so far to show, by what I consider a sufficiently striking example, that in spite of the prejudices arising from the manners of our age, the enthusiasm for the good and the beautiful is no more foreign to women than to men, and that there is nothing which, under nature's guidance, cannot be obtained from them as well as from us.

You stop me here to inquire whether it is nature which teaches us to take such pains to repress our immoderate desires. No, I reply, but neither is it nature who gives us these immoderate desires. Now, all that is not from nature is contrary to nature, as I have proved again and again.

Let us give Emile his Sophy; let us restore this sweet girl to life and provide her with a less vivid imagination and a happier fate. I desired to paint an ordinary woman, but by endowing her with a great soul, I have disturbed her reason. I have gone astray. Let us retrace our steps. Sophy has only a good disposition and an ordinary heart; her education is responsible for everything in which she excels other women.

In this book I intended to describe all that might be done and to leave every one free to choose what he could out of all the good things I described. I meant to train a helpmeet for Emile, from the very first, and to educate them for each other and with each other. But on consideration I thought all these premature arrangements undesirable, for it was absurd to plan the marriage of two children before I could tell whether this union was in accordance with nature and whether they were really suited to each other. We must not confuse what is suitable in a state of savagery with what is suitable in civilised life. In the former, any woman will suit any man, for both are still in their primitive and undifferentiated condition; in the latter, all their characteristics have been developed by social institutions, and each mind, having taken its own settled form, not from education alone, but by the co-operation, more or less well-regulated, of natural disposition and education, we can only make a match by introducing them to each other to see if they suit each other in every respect, or at least we can let them make that choice which gives the most promise of mutual suitability.

The difficulty is this: while social life develops character it differentiates classes, and these two classifications do not correspond, so that the greater the social distinctions, the greater the difficulty of finding the corresponding character. Hence we have ill-assorted marriages and all their accompanying evils; and we find that it follows logically that the further we get from equality, the greater the change in our natural feelings; the wider the distance between great and small, the looser the marriage tie; the deeper the gulf between rich and poor the fewer husbands and fathers. Neither master nor slave belongs to a family, but only to a class.

If you would guard against these abuses, and secure happy marriages, you must stifle your prejudices, forget human institutions, and consult nature. Do not join together those who are only alike in one given condition, those who will not suit one another if that condition is changed; but those who are adapted to one another in every situation, in every country, and in every rank in which they may be placed. I do not say that conventional considerations are of no importance in marriage, but I do say that the influence of natural relations is so much more important, that our fate in life is decided by them alone, and that there is such an agreement of taste, temper, feeling, and disposition as should induce a wise father, though he were a prince, to marry his son, without a moment's hesitation, to the woman so adapted to him, were she born in a bad home, were she even the hangman's daughter. I maintain indeed that every possible misfortune may overtake husband and wife if they are thus united, yet they will enjoy more real happiness while they mingle their tears, than if they possessed all the riches of the world, poisoned by divided hearts.

Instead of providing a wife for Emile in childhood, I have waited till I knew what would suit him. It is not for me to decide, but for nature; my task is to discover the choice she has made. My business, mine I repeat, not his father's; for when he entrusted his son to my care, he gave up his place to me. He gave me his rights; it is I who am really Emile's father; it is I who have made a man of him. I would have refused to educate him if I were not free to marry him according to his own choice, which is mine. Nothing but the pleasure of bestowing happiness on a man can repay me for the cost of making him capable of happiness.

Do not suppose, however, that I have delayed to find a wife for Emile till I sent him in search of her. This search is only a pretext for acquainting him with women, so that he may perceive the value of a suitable wife. Sophy was discovered long since; Emile may even have seen her already, but he will not recognise her till the time is come.

Although equality of rank is not essential in marriage, yet this equality along with other kinds of suitability increases their value;

it is not to be weighed against any one of them, but, other things being equal, it turns the scale.

A man, unless he is a king, cannot seek a wife in any and every class; if he himself is free from prejudices, he will find them in others; and this girl or that might perhaps suit him and yet she would be beyond his reach. A wise father will therefore restrict his inquiries within the bounds of prudence. He should not wish to marry his pupil into a family above his own, for that is not within his power. If he could do so he ought not desire it; for what difference does rank make to a young man, at least to my pupil? Yet, if he rises he is exposed to all sorts of real evils which he will feel all his life long. I even say that he should not try to adjust the balance between different gifts, such as rank and money; for each of these adds less to the value of the other than the amount deducted from its own value in the process of adjustment; moreover, we can never agree as to a common denominator; and finally the preference, which each feels for his own surroundings, paves the way for discord between the two families and often to difficulties between husband and wife.

It makes a considerable difference as to the suitability of a marriage whether a man marries above or beneath him. The former case is quite contrary to reason, the latter is more in conformity with reason. As the family is only connected with society through its head, it is the rank of that head which decides that of the family as a whole. When he marries into a lower rank, a man does not lower himself, he raises his wife; if, on the other hand, he marries above his position, he lowers his wife and does not raise himself. Thus there is in the first case good unmixed with evil, in the other evil unmixed with good. Moreover, the law of nature bids the woman obey the man. If he takes a wife from a lower class, natural and civil law are in accordance and all goes well. When he marries a woman of higher rank it is just the opposite case; the man must choose between diminished rights or imperfect gratitude; he must be ungrateful or despised. Then the wife, laying claim to authority, makes herself a tyrant over her lawful head; and the master, who has become a slave, is the most ridiculous and miserable of creatures. Such are the unhappy favourites whom the sovereigns of Asia honour and torment with their alliance; people tell us that if they desire to sleep with their wife they must enter by the foot of the bed.

I expect that many of my readers will remember that I think women have a natural gift for managing men, and will accuse me of contradicting myself; yet they are mistaken. There is a vast difference between claiming the right to command, and managing him who commands. Woman's reign is a reign of gentleness, tact, and kindness; her commands are caresses, her threats are tears. She should reign in the home as a minister reigns in the state, by contriving to be ordered to do what she wants. In this sense, I grant you, that the best managed homes are those where the wife has most power. But when she despises the voice of her head, when she desires to usurp his rights and take the command upon herself, this inversion of the proper order of things leads only to misery, scandal, and dishonour.

There remains the choice between our equals and our inferiors; and I think we ought also to make certain restrictions with regard to the latter; for it is hard to find in the lowest stratum of society a woman who is able to make a good man happy; not that the lower classes are more vicious than the higher, but because they have so little idea of what is good and beautiful, and because the injustice of other classes makes its very vices seem right in the eyes of this class.

By nature man thinks but seldom. He learns to think as he acquires the other arts, but with even greater difficulty. In both sexes alike I am only aware of two really distinct classes, those who think and those who do not; and this difference is almost entirely one of education. A man who thinks should not ally himself with a woman who does not think, for he loses the chief delight of social life if he has a wife who cannot share his thoughts. People who spend their whole life in working for a living have no ideas beyond their work and their own interests, and their mind seems to reside in their arms. This ignorance is not necessarily unfavourable either to their honesty or their morals; it is often favourable; we often content ourselves with thinking about our duties, and in the end we substitute words for things. Conscience is the most enlightened philosopher; to be an honest man we need not read Cicero s *De Officiis*, and the most virtuous woman in the world is probably she who knows least about virtue. But it is none the less true that a cultivated mind alone makes intercourse pleasant, and it is a sad thing for a father of a family, who delights in his home, to be forced to shut himself up in himself and to be unable to make himself understood.

Moreover, if a woman is quite unaccustomed to think, how can she bring up her children? How will she know what is good for them? How can she incline them to virtues of which she is ignorant, to merit of which she has no conception? She can only flatter or threaten, she can only make them insolent or timid; she will make them performing monkeys or noisy little rascals; she will never make them intelligent or pleasing children.

There ore it is not fitting that a man of education should choose a wife who has none, or take her from a class where she cannot be expected to have any education. But I would a thousand times rather have a homely girl, simply brought up, than a learned lady and a wit who would make a literary circle of my house and instal herself as its president. A female wit is a scourge to her husband, her chil dren, her friends, her servants, to everybody. From the lofty height of her genius she scorns every womanly duty, and she is always trying to make a man of herself after the fashion of Mlle. de L'Enclos. Outside her home she always makes herself

ridiculous and she is very rightly a butt for criticism, as we always
are when we try to escape from our own position into one for
which we are unfitted. These highly talented women only get a
hold over fools. We can always tell what artist or friend holds the
pen or pencil when they are at work; we know what discreet man
of letters dictates their oracles in private. This trickery is unworthy
of a decent woman. If she really had talents, her pretentiousness
would degrade them. Her honour is to be unknown; her glory is
the respect of her husband; her joys the happiness of her family.
I appeal to my readers to give me an honest answer; when you
enter a woman's room what makes you think more highly of her,
what makes you address her with more respect—to see her busy with
feminine ocupations, with her household duties, with her children's
clothes about her, or to find her writing verses at her toilet table
surrounded with pamphlets of every kind and with notes on tinted
paper? If there were none but wise men upon earth such a woman
would die an old maid.

"Quæris cur nolim te ducere, galla? diserta es."

MARTIAL xi. 20.

Looks must next be considered; they are the first thing that
strikes us and they ought to be the last, still they should not count
for nothing. I think that great beauty is rather to be shunned than
sought after in marriage. Possession soon exhausts our apprecia-
tion of beauty; in six weeks' time we think no more about it, but
its dangers endure as long as life itself. Unless a beautiful woman
is an angel, her husband is the most miserable of men; and even if
she were an angel he would still be the centre of a hostile crowd
and she could not prevent it. If extreme ugliness were not repulsive
I should prefer it to extreme beauty; for before very long the
husband would cease to notice either, but beauty would still have
its disadvantages and ugliness its advantages. But ugliness which
is actually repulsive is the worst misfortune; repulsion increases
rather than diminishes, and it turns to hatred. Such a union is
a hell upon earth; better death than such a marriage.

Desire mediocrity in all things, even in beauty. A pleasant
attractive countenance, which inspires kindly feelings rather than
love, is what we should prefer; the husband runs no risk, and the
advantages are common to husband and wife; charm is less
perishable than beauty; it is a living thing, which constantly
renews itself, and after thirty years of married life, the charms of a
good woman delight her husband even as they did on the wedding-
day.

Such are the considerations which decided my choice of Sophy.
Brought up, like Emile, by Nature, she is better suited to him than
any other; she will be his true mate. She is his equal in birth and
character, his inferior in fortune. She makes no great impression
at first sight, but day by day reveals fresh charms. Her chief
influence only takes effect gradually, it is only discovered in friendly

intercourse; and her husband will feel it more than any one. Her education is neither showy nor neglected; she has taste without deep study, talent without art, judgment without learning. Her mind knows little, but it is trained to learn; it is well-tilled soil ready for the sower. She has read no book but *Barème* and *Telemachus* which happened to fall into her hands; but no girl who can feel so passionately towards Telemachus can have a heart without feeling or a mind without discernment. What charming ignorance! Happy is he who is destined to be her tutor. She will not be her husband's teacher but his scholar; far from seeking to control his tastes, she will share them. She will suit him far better than a blue-stocking and he will have the pleasure of teaching her everything. It is time they made acquaintance; let us try to plan a meeting.

When we left Paris we were sorrowful and wrapped in thought. This Babel is not our home. Emile casts a scornful glance towards the great city, saying angrily, " What a time we have wasted; the bride of my heart is not there. My friend, you knew it, but you think nothing of my time, and you pay no heed to my sufferings." With steady look and firm voice I reply, " Emile, do you mean what you say ? " At once he flings his arms round my neck and clasps me to his breast without speaking. That is his answer when he knows he is in the wrong.

And now we are wandering through the country like true knights-errant; yet we are not seeking adventures when we leave Paris; we are escaping from them; now fast now slow, we wander through the country like knights-errants. By following my usual practice the taste for it has become established; and I do not suppose any of my readers are such slaves of custom as to picture us dozing in a post-chaise with closed windows, travelling, yet seeing nothing, observing nothing, making the time between our start and our arrival a mere blank, and losing in the speed of our journey, the time we meant to save.

Men say life is short, and I see them doing their best to shorten it. As they do not know how to spend their time they lament the swiftness of its flight, and I perceive that for them it goes only too slowly. Intent merely on the object of their pursuit, they behold unwillingly the space between them and it; one desires to-morrow, another looks a month ahead, another ten years beyond that. No one wants to live to-day, no one contents himself with the present hour, all complain that it passes slowly. When they complain that time flies, they lie; they would gladly purchase the power to hasten it; they would gladly spend their fortune to get rid of their whole life; and there is probably not a single one who would not have reduced his life to a few hours if he had been free to get rid of those hours he found tedious, and those which separated him from the desired moment. A man spends his whole life rushing from Paris to Versailles, from Versailles to Paris, from town to country, from country to town, from one district of the town to another; but he would not know what to do with his time if he had not discovered this way of wasting it, by leaving his business on purpose to find something to do in coming back to it; he thinks he is saving the time he spends, which would otherwise be unoccupied; or maybe he rushes for the sake of rushing, and travels post in order to return in the same fashion. When will mankind cease to slander nature? Why do you complain that life is short when it is never short enough for you? If there were but one of you, able to moderate his desires, so that he did not desire the flight of time, he would never find life too short; for him life and the joy of life would be one and the same; should he die young, he would still die full of days.

If this were the only advantage of my way of travelling it would be enough. I have brought Emile up neither to desire nor to wait, but to enjoy; and when his desires are bent upon the future, their ardour is not so great as to make time seem tedious. He will not only enjoy the delights of longing, but the delights of approaching the object of his desires; and his passions are under such restraint that he lives to a great extent in the present.

So we do not travel like couriers but like explorers. We do not merely consider the beginning and the end, but the space between. The journey itself is a delight. We do not travel sitting, dismally imprisoned, so to speak, in a tightly closed cage. We do not travel with the ease and comfort of ladies. We do not deprive ourselves of the fresh air, nor the sight of the things about us, nor the opportunity of examining them at our pleasure. Emile will never enter a post-chaise, nor will he ride post unless in a great hurry. But what cause has Emile for haste? None but the joy of life. Shall I add to this the desire to do good when he can? No, for that is itself one of the joys of life.

I can only think of one way of travelling pleasanter than travelling on horseback, and that is to travel on foot. You start at your own time, you stop when you will, you do as much or as little as you choose. You see the country, you turn off to the right or left; you examine anything which interests you, you stop to admire every view. Do I see a stream, I wander by its banks; a leafy wood, I seek its shade; a cave, I enter it; a quarry, I study its geology. If I like a place, I stop there. As soon as I am weary of it, I go on. I am independent of horses and postillions; I need not stick to regular routes or good roads; I go anywhere where a man can go; I see all that a man can see; and as I am quite independent of everybody, I enjoy all the freedom man can enjoy. If I am stopped by bad weather and I find myself getting bored, then I take horses. If I am tired—but Emile is hardly ever tired; he is strong; why should he get tired? There is no hurry. If he stops, why should he be bored? He always finds some amusement. He works at a trade; he uses his arms to rest his feet.

To travel on foot is to travel in the fashion of Thales, Plato, and Pythagoras. I find it hard to understand how a philosopher can bring himself to travel in any other way; how he can tear himself from the study of the wealth which lies before his eyes and beneath his feet. Is there any one with an interest in agriculture, who does not want to know the special products of the district through which he is passing, and their method of cultivation? Is there any one with a taste for natural history, who can pass a piece of ground without examining it, a rock without breaking off a piece of it, hills without looking for plants, and stones without seeking for fossils?

Your town-bred scientists study natural history in cabinets; they have small specimens; they know their names but nothing of their nature. Emile's museum is richer than that of kings; it is the whole world. Everything is in its right place; the Naturalist who is its curator has taken care to arrange it in the fairest order; Dauberton could do no better.

What varied pleasures we enjoy in this delightful way of travelling, not to speak of increasing health and a cheerful spirit. I notice that those who ride in nice, well-padded carriages are always wrapped in thought, gloomy, fault-finding, or sick; while those who go on foot are always merry, light-hearted, and delighted with everything. How cheerful we are when we get near our lodging for the night! How savoury is the coarse food! How we linger at table enjoying our rest! How soundly we sleep on a hard bed! If you only want to get to a place you may ride in a post-chaise; if you want to travel you must go on foot.

If Sophy is not forgotten before we have gone fifty leagues in the way I propose, either I am a bungler or Emile lacks curiosity; for with an elementary knowledge of so many things, it is hardly to be supposed that he will not be tempted to extend his knowledge. It is knowledge that makes us curious; and Emile knows just enough to want to know more.

One thing leads on to another, and we make our way forward. If I chose a distant object for the end of our first journey, it is not difficult to find an excuse for it; when we leave Paris we must seek a wife at a distance.

A few days later we had wandered further than usual among hills and valleys where no road was to be seen and we lost our way completely. No matter, all roads are alike if they bring you to your journey's end, but if you are hungry they must lead somewhere. Luckily we came across a peasant who took us to his cottage; we enjoyed his poor dinner with a hearty appetite. When he saw how hungry and tired we were he said, "If the Lord had led you to the other side of the hill you would have had a better welcome, you would have found a good resting place, such good, kindly people! They could not wish to do more for you than I, but they are richer, though folks say they used to be much better off. Still they are not reduced to poverty, and the whole country-side is the better for what they have."

When Emile heard of these good people his heart warmed to them. "My friend," said he, looking at me, "let us visit this house, whose owners are a blessing to the district; I shall be very glad to see them; perhaps they will be pleased to see us too; I am sure we shall be welcome; we shall just suit each other."

Our host told us how to find our way to the house and we set off, but lost our way in the woods. We were caught in a heavy rainstorm, which delayed us further. At last we found the right path and in the evening we reached the house, which had been described to us. It was the only house among the cottages of the little hamlet, and though plain it had an air of dignity. We went up to the door and asked for hospitality. We were taken to the owner of the house, who questioned us courteously; without telling him the object of our journey, we told him why we had left our path. His former wealth enabled him to judge a man's position by his manners; those who have lived in society are rarely mistaken; with this passport we were admitted.

The room we were shown into was very small, but clean and comfortable; a fire was lighted, and we found linen, clothes, and everything we needed. "Why," said Emile, in astonishment, "one would think they were expecting us. The peasant was quite right; how kind and attentive, how considerate, and for strangers too! I shall think I am living in the times of Homer." "I am glad you feel this," said I, "but you need not be surprised; where strangers are scarce, they are welcome; nothing makes people more hospitable than the fact that calls upon their hospitality are rare; when guests are frequent there is an end to hospitality. In Homer's time, people rarely travelled, and travellers were everywhere welcome. Very likely we are the only people who have passed this way this year." "Never mind," said he, "to know how to do without guests and yet to give them a kind welcome, is its own praise."

Having dried ourselves and changed our clothes, we rejoined the master of the house, who introduced us to his wife; she received us not merely with courtesy but with kindness. Her glance rested on Emile. A mother, in her position, rarely receives a young man into her house without some anxiety or some curiosity at least.

Supper was hurried forward on our account. When we went into the dining-room there were five places laid; we took our seats and the fifth chair remained empty. Presently a young girl entered, made a deep courtesy, and modestly took her place without a word. Emile was busy with his supper or considering how to reply to what was said to him; he bowed to her and continued talking and eating. The main object of his journey was as far from his thoughts as he believed himself to be from the end of his journey. The conversation turned upon our losing our way. "Sir," said the master of the house to Emile, "you seem to be a pleasant well-behaved young gentleman, and that reminds me that your tutor and you arrived wet and weary like Telemachus and Mentor in the island of Calypso." "Indeed," said Emile, "we have found the hospitality of Calypso." His Mentor added, "And the charms of Eucharis."

But Emile knew the *Odyssey* and he had not read *Telemachus*, so
he knew nothing of Eucharis. As for the young girl, I saw she
blushed up to her eyebrows, fixed her eyes on her plate, and hardly
dared to breathe. Her mother, noticing her confusion, made a
sign to her father to turn the conversation. When he talked of his
lonely life, he unconsciously began to relate the circumstances which
brought him into it; his misfortunes, his wife's fidelity, the con-
solations they found in their marriage, their quiet, peaceful life in
their retirement, and all this without a word of the young girl; it
is a pleasing and a touching story, which cannot fail to interest.
Emile, interested and sympathetic, leaves off eating and listens.
When finally this best of men discourses with delight of the affection
of the best of women, the young traveller, carried away by his
feelings, stretches one hand to the husband, and taking the wife's
hand with the other, he kisses it rapturously and bathes it with his
tears. Everybody is charmed with the simple enthusiasm of the
young man; but the daughter, more deeply touched than the rest
by this evidence of his kindly heart, is reminded of Telemachus
weeping for the woes of Philoctetus. She looks at him shyly, the
better to study his countenance; there is nothing in it to give the
lie to her comparison.

His easy bearing shows freedom without pride; his manners are
lively but not boisterous; sympathy makes his glance softer and his
expression more pleasing; the young girl, seeing him weep, is ready
to mingle her tears with his. With so good an excuse for tears, she
is restrained by a secret shame; she blames herself already for the
tears which tremble on her eyelids, as though it were wrong to weep
for one's family.

Her mother, who has been watching her ever since she sat down
to supper, sees her distress, and to relieve it she sends her on some
errand. The daughter returns directly, but so little recovered
that her distress is apparent to all. Her mother says gently,
"Sophy, control yourself; will you never cease to weep for the
misfortunes of your parents? Why should you, who are their chief
comfort, be more sensitive than they are themselves?"

At the name of Sophy you would have seen Emile give a start.
His attention is arrested by this dear name, and he awakes all at
once and looks eagerly at one who dares to bear it. Sophy!
Are you the Sophy whom my heart is seeking? Is it you that I
love? He looks at her; he watches her with a sort of fear and
self-distrust. The face is not quite what he pictured; he cannot tell
whether he likes it more or less. He studies every feature, he
watches every movement, every gesture; he has a hundred fleeting
interpretations for them all; he would give half his life if she would
but speak. He looks at me anxiously and uneasily; his eyes are
full of questions and reproaches. His every glance seems to say,
"Guide me while there is yet time; if my heart yields itself and is
deceived, I shall never get over it."

There is no one in the world less able to conceal his feelings than

Emile. How should he conceal them, in the midst of the greatest disturbance he has ever experienced, and under the eyes of four spectators who are all watching him, while she who seems to heed him least is really most occupied with him. His uneasiness does not escape the keen eyes of Sophy; his own eyes tell her that she is its cause; she sees that this uneasiness is not yet love; what matter? He is thinking of her, and that is enough; she will be very unlucky if he thinks of her with impunity.

Mothers, like daughters, have eyes; and they have experience too. Sophy's mother smiles at the success of our schemes. She reads the hearts of the young people; she sees that the time has come to secure the heart of this new Telemachus; she makes her daughter speak. Her daughter, with her native sweetness, replies in a timid tone which makes all the more impression. At the first sound of her voice, Emile surrenders; it is Sophy herself; there can be no doubt about it. If it were not so, it would be too late to deny it.

The charms of this maiden enchantress rush like torrents through his heart, and he begins to drain the draughts of poison with which he is intoxicated. He says nothing; questions pass unheeded; he sees only Sophy, he hears only Sophy; if she says a word, he opens his mouth; if her eyes are cast down, so are his; if he sees her sigh, he sighs too; it is Sophy's heart which seems to speak in his. What a change have these few moments wrought in her heart! It is no longer her turn to tremble, it is Emile's. Farewell liberty, simplicity, frankness. Confused, embarrassed, fearful, he dare not look about him for fear he should see that we are watching him. Ashamed that we should read his secret, he would fain become invisible to every one, that he might feed in secret on the sight of Sophy. Sophy, on the other hand, regains her confidence at the sight of Emile's fear; she sees her triumph and rejoices in it.

" No'l mostra già, ben che in suo cor ne rida."
TASSO, *Jerus. Del.*, c. iv. v. 33.

Her expression remains unchanged; but in spite of her modest look and downcast eyes, her tender heart is throbbing with joy, and it tells her that she has found Telemachus.

If I relate the plain and simple tale of their innocent affections you will accuse me of frivolity, but you will be mistaken. Sufficient attention is not given to the effect which the first connection between man and woman is bound to produce on the future life of both. People do not see that a first impression so vivid as that of love, or the liking which takes the place of love, produces lasting effects whose influence continues till death. Works on education are crammed with wordy and unnecessary accounts of the imaginary duties of children; but there is not a word about the most important and most difficult part of their education, the crisis which forms the bridge between the child and the man. If any part of this work is really useful, it will be because I have dwelt at great length on this matter, so essential in itself and so neglected by other authors, and because I have not allowed myself to be discouraged either by false delicacy or by the difficulties of expression. The story of human nature is a fair romance. Am I to blame if it is not found elsewhere? I am trying to write the history of mankind. If my book is a romance, the fault lies with those who deprave mankind.

This is supported by another reason; we are not dealing with a youth given over from childhood to fear, greed, envy, pride, and all those passions which are the common tools of the schoolmaster; we have to do with a youth who is not only in love for the first time, but with one who is also experiencing his first passion of any kind; very likely it will be the only strong passion he will ever know, and upon it depends the final formation of his character. His mode of thought, his feelings, his tastes, determined by a lasting passion, are about to become so fixed that they will be incapable of further change.

You will easily understand that Emile and I do not spend the whole of the night which follows after such an evening in sleep. Why! Do you mean to tell me that a wise man should be so much affected by a mere coincidence of name! Is there only one Sophy in the world? Are they all alike in heart and in name? Is every Sophy he meets his Sophy? Is he mad to fall in love with a person of whom he knows so little, with whom he has scarcely exchanged a couple of words? Wait, young man; examine, observe. You do not even know who our hosts may be, and to hear you talk one would think the house was your own.

This is no time for teaching, and what I say will receive scant attention. It only serves to stimulate Emile to further interest in Sophy, through his desire to find reasons for his fancy. The unexpected coincidence in the name, the meeting which, so far as he knows, was quite accidental, my very caution itself, only serve as fuel to the fire. He is so convinced already of Sophy's excellence, that he feels sure he can make me fond of her.

Next morning I have no doubt Emile will make himself as smart as his old travelling suit permits. I am not mistaken; but I am amused to see how eager he is to wear the clean linen put out for us. I know his thoughts, and I am delighted to see that he is trying to establish a means of intercourse, through the return and exchange of the linen; so that he may have a right to return it and so pay another visit to the house.

I expected to find Sophy rather more carefully dressed too; but I was mistaken. Such common coquetry is all very well for those who merely desire to please. The coquetry of true love is a more delicate matter; it has quite another end in view. Sophy is dressed, if possible, more simply than last night, though as usual her frock is exquisitely clean. The only sign of coquetry is her self-consciousness. She knows that an elaborate toilet is a sign of love, but she does not know that a careless toilet is another of its signs; it shows a desire to be liked not merely for one's clothes but for oneself.

What does a lover care for her clothes if he knows she is thinking of him? Sophy is already sure of her power over Emile, and she is not content to delight his eyes if his heart is not hers also; he must not only perceive her charms, he must divine them; has he not seen enough to guess the rest?

We may take it for granted that while Emile and I were talking last night, Sophy and her mother were not silent; a confession was made and instructions given. The morning's meeting is not unprepared. Twelve hours ago our young people had never met; they have never said a word to each other; but it is clear that there is already an understanding between them. Their greeting is formal, confused, timid; they say nothing, their downcast eyes seem to avoid each other, but that is in itself a sign that they understand, they avoid each other with one consent; they already feel the need of concealment, though not a word has been uttered. When we depart we ask leave to come again to return the borrowed clothes in person, Emile's words are addressed to the father and mother, but his eyes seek Sophy's, and his looks are more eloquent than his words. Sophy says nothing by word or gesture; she seems deaf and blind, but she blushes, and that blush is an answer even plainer than that of her parents.

We receive permission to come again, though we are not invited to stay. This is only fitting; you offer shelter to benighted travellers, but a lover does not sleep in the house of his mistress.

We have hardly left the beloved abode before Emile is thinking of taking rooms in the neighbourhood; the nearest cottage seems too far; he would like to sleep in the next ditch. "You young fool!" I said in a tone of pity, "are you already blinded by passion? Have you no regard for manners or for reason? Wretched youth, you call yourself a lover and you would bring disgrace upon her you love! What would people say of her if they knew that a young man who has been staying at her house was sleeping close by? You say you love her! Would you ruin her reputation? Is that the price you offer for her parents' hospitality? Would you bring disgrace on her who will one day make you the happiest of men?" "Why should we trouble ourselves about the empty words and unjust suspicions of other people?" said he eagerly. "Have you not taught me yourself to make light of them? Who knows better than I how greatly I honour Sophy, what respect I desire to show her? My attachment will not cause her shame, it will be her glory, it shall be worthy of her. If my heart and my actions continually give her the homage she deserves, what harm can I do her?" "Dear Emile," I said, as I clasped him to my heart, "you are thinking of yourself alone; learn to think for her too. Do not compare the honour of one sex with that of the other, they rest on different foundations. These foundations are equally firm and right, because they are both laid by nature, and that same virtue which makes you scorn what men say about yourself, binds you to respect what they say of her you love. Your honour is in your own keeping, her honour depends on others. To neglect it is to wound your own honour, and you fail in what is due to yourself if you do not give her the respect she deserves.

Then while I explain the reasons for this difference, I make him realise how wrong it would be to pay no attention to it. Who can say if he will really be Sophy's husband? He does not know how she feels towards him; her own heart or her parents' will may already have formed other engagements; he knows nothing of her, perhaps there are none of those grounds of suitability which make a happy marriage. Is he not aware that the least breath of scandal with regard to a young girl is an indelible stain, which not even marriage with him who has caused the scandal can efface? What man of feeling would ruin the woman he loves? What man of honour would desire that a miserable woman should for ever lament the misfortune of having found favour in his eyes?

Always prone to extremes, the youth takes alarm at the consequences which I have compelled him to consider, and now he thinks that he cannot be too far from Sophy's home; he hastens his steps to get further from it; he glances round to make sure that no one is listening; he would sacrifice his own happiness a thousand times to the honour of her whom he loves; he would rather never see her again than cause her the least unpleasantness. This is the first result of the pains I have taken ever since he was a child to make him capable of affection.

We must therefore seek a lodging at a distance, but not too far. We look about us, we make inquiries; we find that there is a town at least two leagues away. We try and find lodgings in this town, rather than in the nearer villages, where our presence might give rise to suspicion. It is there that the new lover takes up his abode, full of love, hope, joy, above all full of right feeling. In this way, I guide his rising passion towards all that is honourable and good, so that his inclinations unconsciously follow the same bent.

My course is drawing to a close; the end is in view. All the chief difficulties are vanquished, the chief obstacles overcome; the hardest thing left to do is to refrain from spoiling my work by undue haste to complete it. Amid the uncertainty of human life, let us shun that false prudence which seeks to sacrifice the present to the future; what is, is too often sacrificed to what will never be. Let us make man happy at every age lest in spite of our care he should die without knowing the meaning of happiness. Now if there is a time to enjoy life, it is undoubtedly the close of adolescence, when the powers of mind and body have reached their greatest strength, and when man in the midst of his course is furthest from those two extremes which tell him "Life is short." If the imprudence of youth deceives itself it is not in its desire for enjoyment, but because it seeks enjoyment where it is not to be found, and lays up misery for the future, while unable to enjoy the present.

Consider my Emile over twenty years of age, well formed, well developed in mind and body, strong, healthy, active, skilful, robust,

full of sense, reason, kindness, humanity, possessed of good morals
and good taste, loving what is beautful, doing what is good, free
from the sway of fierce passions, released from the tyranny of
popular prejudices, but subject to the law of wisdom, and easily
guided by the voice of a friend; gifted with so many useful and
pleasant accomplishments, caring little for wealth, able to earn a
living with his own hands, and not afraid of want, whatever may
come. Behold him in the intoxication of a growing passion; his
heart opens to the first beams of love; its pleasant fancies reveal
to him a whole world of new delights and enjoyments; he loves a
sweet woman, whose character is even more delightful than her
person; he hopes, he expects the reward which he deserves.

Their first attachment took its rise in mutual affection, in community of honourable feelings; therefore this affection is lasting.
It abandons itself, with confidence, with reason, to the most delightful madness, without fear, regret, remorse, or any other disturbing
thought, but that which is inseparable from all happiness. What
lacks there yet? Behold, inquire, imagine what still is lacking,
that can be combined with present joys. Every happiness which
can exist in combination is already present; nothing could be added
without taking away from what there is; he is as happy as man can
be. Shall I choose this time to cut short so sweet a period? Shall
I disturb such pure enjoyment? The happiness he enjoys is my
life's reward. What could I give that could outweigh what I
should take away? Even if I set the crown to his happiness I
should destroy its greatest charm. That supreme joy is a hundredfold greater in anticipation than in possession; its savour is greater
while we wait for it than when it is ours. O worthy Emile! love
and be loved! prolong your enjoyment before it is yours; rejoice
in your love and in your innocence, find your paradise upon earth,
while you await your heaven. I shall not cut short this happy
period of life. I will draw out its enchantments, I will prolong them
as far as possible. Alas! it must come to an end and that soon;
but it shall at least linger in your memory, and you will never
repent of its joys.

Emile has not forgotten that we have something to return. As
soon as the things are ready, we take horse and set off at a great
pace, for on this occasion he is anxious to get there. When the
heart opens the door to passion, it becomes conscious of the slow
flight of time. If my time has not been wasted he will not spend his
life like this.

Unluckily the road is intricate and the country difficult. We lose
our way; he is the first to notice it, and without losing his temper,
and without grumbling, he devotes his whole attention to discovering the path; he wanders for a long time before he knows where he
is and always with the same self-control. You think nothing of
that; but I think it a matter of great importance, for I know how
eager he is; I see the results of the care I have taken from his infancy
to harden him to endure the blows of necessity.

We are there at last! Our reception is much simpler and more friendly than on the previous occasion; we are already old acquaintances. Emile and Sophy bow shyly and say nothing; what can they say in our presence? What they wish to say requires no spectators. We walk in the garden; a well-kept kitchen-garden takes the place of flower-beds, the park is an orchard full of fine tall fruit trees of every kind, divided by pretty streams and borders full of flowers. "What a lovely place!" exclaims Emile, still thinking of his Homer, and still full of enthusiasm, "I could fancy myself in the garden of Alcinous." The daughter wishes she knew who Alcinous was; her mother asks. "Alcinous," I tell them, "was a king of Corcyra. Homer describes his garden and the critics think it too simple and unadorned.[1] This Alcinous had a charming daughter who dreamed the night before her father received a stranger at his board that she would soon have a husband." Sophy, taken unawares, blushed, hung her head, and bit her lips; no one could be more confused. Her father, who was enjoying her confusion, added that the young princess bent herself to wash the linen in the river. "Do you think," said he, "she would have scorned to touch the dirty clothes, saying, that they smelt of grease?" Sophy, touched to the quick, forgot her natural timidity and defended herself eagerly. Her papa knew very well all the smaller things would have had no other laundress if she had been allowed to wash them, and she would gladly have done more had she been set to do it.[2] Meanwhile she watched me secretly with such anxiety that I could not suppress a smile, while I read the terrors of her simple heart which urged her to speak. Her father was cruel enough to continue this foolish sport, by asking her, in jest, why she spoke on her own behalf and what had she in common with the daughter of Alcinous. Trembling and ashamed she dared hardly breathe or look at us. Charming girl! This is no time for feigning, you have shown your true feelings in spite of yourself.

[1] "'When you leave the palace you enter a vast garden, four acres in extent, walled in on every side, planted with tall trees in blossom, and yielding pears, pomegranates, and other goodly fruits, fig-trees with their luscious burden and green olives. All the year round these fair trees are heavy with fruit; summer and winter the soft breath of the west wind sways the trees and ripens the fruit. Pears and apples wither on the branches, the fig on the fig-tree, and the clusters of grapes on the vine. The inexhaustible stock bears fresh grapes, some are baked, some are spread out on the threshing floor to dry, others are made into wine, while flowers, sour grapes, and those which are beginning to wither are left upon the tree. At either end is a square garden filled with flowers which bloom throughout the year; these gardens are adorned by two fountains, one of these streams waters the garden, the other passes through the palace and is then taken to a lofty tower in the town to provide drinking water for its citizens.' Such is the description of the royal garden of Alcinous in the 7th book of the *Odyssey*; a garden in which, to the lasting disgrace of that old dreamer Homer and the princes of his day, there were neither trellises, statues, cascades, nor bowling-greens."

[2] I own I feel grateful to Sophy's mother for not letting her spoil such pretty hands with soap, hands which Emile will kiss so often.

To all appearance this little scene is soon forgotten; luckily for Sophy, Emile, at least, is unaware of it. We continue our walk, the young people at first keeping close beside us; but they find it hard to adapt themselves to our slower pace, and presently they are a little in front of us, they are walking side by side, they begin to talk, and before long they are a good way ahead. Sophy seems to be listening quietly, Emile is talking and gesticulating vigorously; they seem to find their conversation interesting. When we turn homewards a full hour later, we call them to us and they return slowly enough now, and we can see they are making good use of their time. Their conversation ceases suddenly before they come within earshot, and they hurry up to us. Emile meets us with a frank affectionate expression; his eyes are sparkling with joy; yet he looks anxiously at Sophy's mother to see how she takes it. Sophy is not nearly so much at her ease; as she approaches us she seems covered with confusion at finding herself *tête-à-tête* with a young man, though she has met so many other young men frankly enough, and without being found fault with for it. She runs up to her mother, somewhat out of breath, and makes some trivial remark, as if to pretend she had been with her for some time.

From the happy expression of these dear children we see that this conversation has taken a load off their hearts. They are no less reticent in their intercourse, but their reticence is less embarrassing, it is only due to Emile's reverence and Sophy's modesty, to the goodness of both. Emile ventures to say a few words to her, she ventures to reply, but she always looks at her mother before she dares to answer. The most remarkable change is in her attitude towards me. She shows me the greatest respect, she watches me with interest, she takes pains to please me; I see that I am honoured with her esteem, and that she is not indifferent to mine. I understand that Emile has been talking to her about me; you might say they have been scheming to win me over to their side; yet it is not so, and Sophy herself is not so easily won. Perhaps Emile will have more need of my influence with her than of hers with me. What a charming pair! When I consider that the tender love of my young friend has brought my name so prominently into his first conversation with his lady-love, I enjoy the reward of all my trouble; his affection is a sufficient recompense.

Our visit is repeated. There are frequent conversations between the young people. Emile is madly in love and thinks that his happiness is within his grasp. Yet he does not succeed in winning any formal avowal from Sophy; she listens to what he says and answers nothing. Emile knows how modest she is, and is not surprised at her reticence; he feels sure that she likes him; he knows that parents decide whom their daughters shall marry; he supposes that Sophy is awaiting her parents' commands; he asks her permission to speak to them, and she makes no objection. He talks to me and I speak on his behalf and in his presence. He is immensely surprised to hear that Sophy is her own mistress, that his happiness depends on her alone. He begins to be puzzled by her conduct. He is less self-confident, he takes alarm, he sees that he has not made so much progress as he expected, and then it is that his love appeals to her in the tenderest and most moving language.

Emile is not the sort of man to guess what is the matter; if no one told him he would never discover it as long as he lived, and Sophy is too proud to tell him. What she considers obstacles, others would call advantages. She has not forgotten her parents' teaching. She is poor; Emile is rich; so much she knows. He must win her esteem; his deserts must be great indeed to remove this inequality. But how should he perceive these obstacles? Is Emile aware that he is rich? Has he ever condescended to inquire? Thank heaven, he has no need of riches, he can do good without their aid. The good he does comes from his heart, not his purse. He gives the wretched his time, his care, his affection, himself; and when he reckons up what he has done, he hardly dares to mention the money spent on the poor.

As he does not know what to make of his disgrace, he thinks it is his own fault; for who would venture to accuse the adored one of caprice. The shame of humiliation adds to the pangs of disappointed love. He no longer approaches Sophy with that pleasant confidence of his own worth; he is shy and timid in her presence. He no longer hopes to win her affections, but to gain her pity. Sometimes he loses patience and is almost angry with her. Sophy seems to guess his angry feelings and she looks at him. Her glance is enough to disarm and terrify him; he is more submissive than he used to be.

Disturbed by this stubborn resistance, this invincible silence, he pours out his heart to his friend. He shares with him the pangs of a heart devoured by sorrow; he implores his help and counsel. "How mysterious it is, how hard to understand! She takes an interest in me, that I am sure; far from avoiding me she is pleased to see me; when I come she shows signs of pleasure, when I go she shows regret; she receives my attentions kindly, my services seem to give her pleasure, she condescends to give me her advice and even her commands. Yet she rejects my requests and my prayers. When I venture to speak of marriage, she bids me be silent; if I say a word, she leaves me at once. Why on earth should she wish me to be hers but refuse to be mine? She respects and loves you, and she will not dare to refuse to listen to you. Speak to her, make her answer. Come to your friend's help, and put the coping stone to all you have done for him; do not let him fall a victim to your care! If you fail to secure his happiness, your own teaching will have been the cause of his misery."

I speak to Sophy, and have no difficulty in getting her to confide her secret to me, a secret which was known to me already. It is not so easy to get permission to tell Emile; but at last she gives me leave and I tell him what is the matter. He cannot get over his surprise at this explanation. He cannot understand this delicacy;

he cannot see how a few pounds more or less can affect his character or his deserts. When I get him to see their effect on people's prejudices he begins to laugh; he is so wild with delight that he wants to be off at once to tear up his title deeds and renounce his money, so as to have the honour of being as poor as Sophy, and to return worthy to be her husband.

"Why," said I, trying to check him, and laughing in my turn at his impetuosity, "will this young head never grow any older? Having dabbled all your life in philosophy, will you never learn to reason? Do not you see that your wild scheme would only make things worse, and Sophy more obstinate? It is a small superiority to be rather richer than she, but to give up all for her would be a very great superiority; if her pride cannot bear to be under the small obligation, how will she make up her mind to the greater? If she cannot bear to think that her husband might taunt her with the fact that he has enriched her, would she permit him to blame her for having brought him to poverty? Wretched boy, beware lest she suspects you of such a plan! On the contrary, be careful and economical for her sake, lest she should accuse you of trying to gain her by cunning, by sacrificing of your own free will what you are really wasting through carelessness.

"Do you really think that she is afraid of wealth, and that she is opposed to great possessions in themselves? No, dear Emile; there are more serious and substantial grounds for her opinion, in the effect produced by wealth on its possessor. She knows that those who are possessed of fortune's gifts are apt to place them first. The rich always put wealth before merit. When services are reckoned against silver, the latter always outweighs the former, and those who have spent their life in their master's service are considered his debtors for the very bread they eat. What must you do, Emile, to calm her fears? Let her get to know you better; that is not done in a day. Show her the treasures of your heart, to counterbalance the wealth which is unfortunately yours. Time and constancy will overcome her resistance; let your great and noble feelings make her forget your wealth. Love her, serve her, serve her worthy parents. Convince her that these attentions are not the result of a foolish fleeting passion, but of settled principles engraved upon your heart. Show them the honour deserved by worth when exposed to the buffets of Fortune; that is the only way to reconcile it with that worth which basks in her smiles."

The transports of joy experienced by the young man at these words may easily be imagined; they restore confidence and hope, his good heart rejoices to do something to please Sophy, which he would have done if there had been no such person, or if he had not been in love with her. However little his character has been understood, anybody can see how he would behave under such circumstances.

Here am I, the confidant of these two young people and the mediator of their affection. What a fine task for a tutor! So fine

that never in all my life have I stood so high in my own eyes, nor
felt so pleased with myself. Moreover, this duty is not without its
charms. I am not unwelcome in the home; it is my business to
see that the lovers behave themselves; Emile, ever afraid of offending me, was never so docile. The little lady herself overwhelms me
with a kindness which does not deceive me, and of which I only take
my proper share. This is her way of making up for her severity
towards Emile. For his sake she bestows on me a hundred tender
caresses, though she would die rather than bestow them on him;
and he, knowing that I would never stand in his way, is delighted
that I should get on so well with her. If she refuses his arm when
we are out walking, he consoles himself with the thought that she
has taken mine. He makes way for me without a murmur, he
clasps my hand, and voice and look alike whisper, " My friend,
plead for me!" and his eyes follow us with interest; he tries to read
our feelings in our faces, and to interpret our conversation by our
gestures; he knows that everything we are saying concerns him.
Dear Sophy, how frank and easy you are when you can talk to
Mentor without being overheard by Telemachus. How freely and
delightfully you permit him to read what is passing in your tender
little heart! How delighted you are to show him how you esteem
his pupil! How cunningly and appealingly you allow him to
divine still tenderer sentiments. With what a pretence of anger
you dismiss Emile when his impatience leads him to interrupt you?
With what pretty vexation you reproach his indiscretion when he
comes and prevents you saying something to his credit, or listening
to what I say about him, or finding in my words some new excuse
to love him!

Having got so far as to be tolerated as an acknowledged lover,
Emile takes full advantage of his position; he speaks, he urges, he
implores, he demands. Hard words or ill treatment make no
difference, provided he gets a hearing. At length Sophy is persuaded, though with some difficulty, to assume the authority of a
betrothed, to decide what he shall do, to command instead of to ask,
to accept instead of to thank, to control the frequency and the
hours of his visits, to forbid him to come till such a day or to stay
beyond such an hour. This is not done in play, but in earnest, and
if it was hard to induce her to accept these rights, she uses them
so sternly that Emile is often ready to regret that he gave them to
her. But whatever her commands, they are obeyed without
question, and often when at her bidding he is about to leave her,
he glances at me his eyes full of delight, as if to say, " You see she
has taken possession of me." Yet unknown to him, Sophy, with
all her pride, is observing him closely, and she is smiling to herself
at the pride of her slave.

Oh that I had the brush of an Alban or a Raphael to paint their
bliss, or the pen of the divine Milton to describe the pleasures of
love and innocence! Not so; let such hollow arts shrink back
before the sacred truth of nature. In tenderness and pureness of

heart let your imagination freely trace the raptures of these young lovers, who under the eyes of parents and tutor, abandon themselves to their blissful illusions; in the intoxication of passion they are advancing step by step to its consummation; with flowers and garlands they are weaving the bonds which are to bind them till death do part. I am carried away by this succession of pictures, I am so happy that I cannot group them in any sort of order or scheme; any one with a heart in his breast can paint the charming picture for himself and realise the different experiences of father, mother, daughter, tutor, and pupil, and the part played by each and all in the union of the most delightful couple whom love and virtue have ever led to happiness.

Now that he is really eager to please, Emile begins to feel the value of the accomplishments he has acquired. Sophy is fond of singing, he sings with her; he does more, he teaches her music. She is lively and light of foot, she loves skipping; he dances with her, he perfects and develops her untrained movements into the steps of the dance. These lessons, enlivened by the gayest mirth, are quite delightful, they melt the timid respect of love; a lover may enjoy teaching his betrothed—he has a right to be her teacher.

There is an old spinet quite out of order. Emile mends and tunes it; he is a maker and mender of musical instruments as well as a carpenter; it has always been his rule to learn to do everything he can for himself. The house is picturesquely situated and he makes several sketches of it, in some of which Sophy does her share, and she hangs them in her father's study. The frames are not gilded, nor do they require gilding. When she sees Emile drawing, she draws too, and improves her own drawing; she cultivates all her talents, and her grace gives a charm to all she does. Her father and mother recall the days of their wealth, when they find themselves surrounded by the works of art which alone gave value to wealth; the whole house is adorned by love; love alone has enthroned among them, without cost or effort, the very same pleasures which were gathered together in former days by dint of toil and money.

As the idolater gives what he loves best to the shrine of the object of his worship, so the lover is not content to see perfection in his mistress, he must be ever trying to add to her adornment. She does not need it for his pleasure, it is he who needs the pleasure of giving, it is a fresh homage to be rendered to her, a fresh pleasure in the joy of beholding her. Everything of beauty seems to find its place only as an accessory to the supreme beauty. It is both touching and amusing to see Emile eager to teach Sophy everything he knows, without asking whether she wants to learn it or whether it is suitable for her. He talks about all sorts of things and explains them to her with boyish eagerness; he thinks he has only to speak and she will understand; he looks forward to arguing, and discussing philosophy with her; everything he cannot display before her is so much useless learning; he is quite ashamed of knowing more than she.

So he gives her lessons in philosophy, physics, mathematics, history, and everything else. Sophy is delighted to share his enthusiasm and to try and profit by it. How pleased Emile is when he can get leave to give these lessons on his knees before her! He thinks the heavens are open. Yet this position, more trying to pupil than to teacher, is hardly favourable to study. It is not easy to know where to look, to avoid meeting the eyes which follow our own, and if they meet so much the worse for the lesson.

Women are no strangers to the art of thinking, but they should only skim the surface of logic and metaphysics. Sophy understands readily, but she soon forgets. She makes most progress in the moral sciences and æsthetics; as to physical science she retains some vague idea of the general laws and order of this world. Sometimes in the course of their walks, the spectacle of the wonders of nature bids them not fear to raise their pure and innocent hearts to nature's God; they are not afraid of His presence, and they pour out their hearts before him.

What! Two young lovers spending their time together talking of religion! Have they nothing better to do than to say their catechism! What profit is there in the attempt to degrade what is noble? Yes, no doubt they are saying their catechism in their delightful land of romance; they are perfect in each other's eyes; they love one another, they talk eagerly of all that makes virtue worth having. Their sacrifices to virtue make her all the dearer to them. Their struggles after self-control draw from them tears purer than the dew of heaven, and these sweet tears are the joy of life; no human heart has ever experienced a sweeter intoxication. Their very renunciation adds to their happiness, and their sacrifices increase their self-respect. Sensual men, bodies without souls, some day they will know your pleasures, and all their life long they will recall with regret the happy days when they refused the cup of pleasure.

In spite of this good understanding, differences and even quarrels occur from time to time; the lady has her whims, the lover has a hot temper; but these passing showers are soon over and only serve to strengthen their union. Emile learns by experience not to attach too much importance to them, he always gains more by the reconciliation than he lost by the quarrel. The results of the first difference made him expect a like result from all; he was mistaken, but even if he does not make any appreciable step forward, he has always the satisfaction of finding Sophy's genuine concern for his affection more firmly established. "What advantage is this to him?" you would ask. I will gladly tell you; all the more gladly because it will give me an opportunity to establish clearly a very important principle, and to combat a very deadly one.

Emile is in love, but he is not presuming; and you will easily understand that the dignified Sophy is not the sort of girl to allow any kind of familiarity. Yet virtue has its bounds like everything else, and she is rather to be blamed for her severity than for indulgence; even her father himself is sometimes afraid lest her lofty pride should degenerate into a haughty spirit. When most alone, Emile dare not ask for the slightest favour, he must not even seem to desire it; and if she is gracious enough to take his arm when they are out walking, a favour which she will never permit him to claim as a right, it is only occasionally that he dare venture with a sigh to press her hand to his heart. However, after a long period of self-restraint, he ventured secretly to kiss the hem of her dress, and several times he was lucky enough to find her willing at least to pretend she was not aware of it. One day he attempts to take the same privilege rather more openly, and Sophy takes it into her head to be greatly offended. He persists, she gets angry and speaks sharply to him; Emile will not put up with this without reply; the rest of the day is given over to sulks, and they part in a very ill temper.

Sophy is ill at ease; her mother is her confidant in all things, how can she keep this from her? It is their first misunderstanding, and the misunderstanding of an hour is such a serious business. She is sorry for what she has done, she has her mother's permission and her father's commands to make reparation.

The next day Emile returns somewhat earlier than usual and in a state of some anxiety. Sophy is in her mother's dressing-room and her father is also present. Emile enters respectfully but gloomily. Scarcely have her parents greeted him than Sophy turns round and holding out her hand asks him in an affectionate tone how he is. That pretty hand is clearly held out to be kissed; he takes it but does not kiss it. Sophy, rather ashamed of herself, withdraws her hand as best she may. Emile, who is not used to a woman's whims, and does not know how far caprice may be carried, does not forget so easily or make friends again all at once. Sophy's father, seeing her confusion, completes her discomfiture by his jokes. The poor girl, confused and ashamed, does not know what to do with herself and would gladly have a good cry. The more she tries to control herself the worse she feels; at last a tear escapes in spite of all she can do to prevent it. Emile, seeing this tear, rushes towards her, falls on his knees, takes her hand and kisses it again and again with the greatest devotion. " My word, you are too kind to her," says her father, laughing; " if I were you, I should deal more severely with these follies, I should punish the mouth that wronged me." Emboldened by these words, Emile turns a suppliant eye towards her mother, and thinking she is not unwilling, he tremblingly approaches Sophy's face; she turns away her head, and to save her mouth she exposes a blushing cheek. The daring young man is not content with this; there is no great resistance. What a kiss, if it were not taken under her mother's eyes. Have a care, Sophy, in your severity; he will be ready enough to try to kiss your dress if only you will sometimes say " No."

After this exemplary punishment, Sophy's father goes about his business, and her mother makes some excuse for sending her out of the room; then she speaks to Emile very seriously. " Sir," she says, " I think a young man so well born and well bred as yourself, a man of feeling and character, would never reward with dishonour the confidence reposed in him by the friendship of this family. I am neither prudish nor over strict; I know how to make excuses for youthful folly, and what I have permitted in my own presence is sufficient proof of this. Consult your friend as to your own duty, he will tell you there is all the difference in the world between the playful kisses sanctioned by the presence of father and mother, and the same freedom taken in their absence and in betrayal of their confidence, a freedom which makes a snare of the very favours which in the parents' presence were wholly innocent. He will tell you, sir, that my daughter is only to blame for not having perceived from the first what she ought never to have permitted; he will tell you that every favour, taken as such, is a favour, and that it is unworthy of a man of honour to take advantage of a young girl's innocence, to usurp in private the same freedom which she may permit in the presence of others. For good manners teach us what is permitted in public; but we do not know what a man will permit to himself in private, if he makes himself the sole judge of his conduct."

After this well-deserved rebuke, addressed rather to me than to my pupil, the good mother leaves us, and I am amazed by her rare prudence, in thinking it a little thing that Emile should kiss her daughter's lips in her presence, while fearing lest he should venture to kiss her dress when they are alone. When I consider the folly of worldly maxims, whereby real purity is continually sacrificed to a show of propriety, I understand why speech becomes more refined while the heart becomes more corrupt, and why etiquette is stricter while those who conform to it are most immoral.

While I am trying to convince Emile's heart with regard to these duties which I ought to have instilled into him sooner, a new idea occurs to me, an idea which perhaps does Sophy all the more credit, though I shall take care not to tell her lover; this so-called pride, for which she has been censured, is clearly only a very wise precaution to protect her from herself. Being aware that, unfortunately, her own temperament is inflammable, she dreads the least spark, and keeps out of reach so far as she can. Her sternness is due not to pride but to humility. She assumes a control over Emile because she doubts her control of herself; she turns the one against the other. If she had more confidence in herself she would be much less haughty With this exception is there anywhere on earth a gentler, sweeter girl? Is there any who endures an affront with greater patience, any who is more afraid of annoying others? Is there any with less pretension, except in the matter of virtue? Moreover, she is not proud of her virtue, she is only proud in order to preserve her virtue, and if she can follow the guidance of her heart without danger, she caresses her lover himself. But her wise mother does not confide all this even to her father; men should not hear everything.

Far from seeming proud of her conquest, Sophy has grown more friendly and less exacting towards everybody, except perhaps the one person who has wrought this change. Her noble heart no longer swells with the feeling of independence. She triumphs modestly over a victory gained at the price of her freedom. Her bearing is more restrained, her speech more timid, since she has begun to blush at the word " lover "; but contentment may be seen beneath her outward confusion and this very shame is not painful. This change is most noticeable in her behaviour towards the young men she meets. Now that she has ceased to be afraid of them, much of her extreme reserve has disappeared. Now that her choice is made, she does not hesitate to be gracious to those to whom she is quite in-different; taking no more interest in them, she is less difficult to please, and she always finds them pleasant enough for people who are of no importance to her.

If true love were capable of coquetry, I should fancy I saw traces of it in the way Sophy behaves towards other young men in her lover's presence. One would say that not content with the ardent passion she inspires by a mixture of shyness and caresses, she is not sorry to rouse this passion by a little anxiety; one would say that when she is purposely amusing her young guests she means to torment Emile by the charms of a freedom she will not allow herself with him; but Sophy is too considerate, too kindly, too wise to really torment him. Love and honour take the place of prudence and control the use of this dangerous weapon. She can alarm and reassure him just as he needs it; and if she sometimes makes him uneasy she never really gives him pain. The anxiety she causes to her beloved may be forgiven because of her fear that he is not sufficiently her own.

But what effect will this little performance have upon Emile? Will he be jealous or not? That is what we must discover; for such digressions form part of the purpose of my book, and they do not lead me far from my main subject.

I have already shown how this passion of jealousy in matters of convention finds its way into the heart of man. In love it is another matter; then jealousy is so near akin to nature, that it is hard to believe that it is not her work; and the example of the very beasts, many of whom are madly jealous, seems to prove this point beyond reply. Is it man's influence that has taught cocks to tear each other to pieces or bulls to fight to the death?

No one can deny that the aversion to everything which may disturb or interfere with our pleasures is a natural impulse. Up to a certain point the desire for the exclusive possession of that which ministers to our pleasure is in the same case. But when this desire has become a passion, when it is transformed into madness, or into a bitter and suspicious fancy known as jealousy, that is quite another matter; such a passion may be natural or it may not; we must distinguish between these different cases.

I have already analysed the example of the animal world in my

Discourse on Inequality, and on further consideration I think I may refer my readers to that analysis as sufficiently thorough. I will only add this further point to those already made in that work, that the jealousy which springs from nature depends greatly on sexual power, and that when sexual power is or appears to be boundless, that jealousy is at its height; for then the male, measuring his rights by his needs, can never see another male except as an unwelcome rival. In such species the females always submit to the first comer, they only belong to the male by right of conquest, and they are the cause of unending strife.

Among the monogamous species, where intercourse seems to give rise to some sort of moral bond, a kind of marriage, the female who belongs by choice to the male on whom she has bestowed herself usually denies herself to all others; and the male, having this preference of affection as a pledge of her fidelity, is less uneasy at the sight of other males and lives more peaceably with them. Among these species the male shares the care of the little ones; and by one of those touching laws of nature it seems as if the female rewards the father for his love for his children.

Now consider the human species in its primitive simplicity; it is easy to see, from the limited powers of the male, and the moderation of his desires, that nature meant him to be content with one female; this is confirmed by the numerical equality of the two sexes, at any rate in our part of the world; an equality which does not exist in anything like the same degree among those species in which several females are collected around one male. Though a man does not brood like a pigeon, and though he has no milk to suckle the young, and must in this respect be classed with the quadrupeds, his children are feeble and helpless for so long a time, that mother and children could ill dispense with the father's affection, and the care which results from it.

All these observations combine to prove that the jealous fury of the males of certain animals proves nothing with regard to man; and the exceptional case of those southern regions were polygamy is the established custom, only confirms the rule, since it is the plurality of wives that gives rise to the tyrannical precautions of the husband, and the consciousness of his own weakness makes the man resort to constraint to evade the laws of nature.

Among ourselves where these same laws are less frequently evaded in this respect, but are more frequently evaded in another and even more detestable manner, jealousy finds its motives in the passions of society rather than in those of primitive instinct. In most irregular connections the hatred of the lover for his rivals far exceeds his love for his mistress; if he fears a rival in her affections it is the effect of that self-love whose origin I have already traced out, and he is moved by vanity rather than affection. Moreover, our clumsy systems of education have made women so deceitful,[1]

---

[1] The kind of deceit referred to here is just the opposite of that deceit becoming in a woman, and taught her by nature; the latter consists in

and have so over-stimulated their appetites, that you cannot rely even on the most clearly proved affection; they can no longer display a preference which secures you against the fear of a rival.

True love is another matter. I have shown, in the work already referred to, that this sentiment is not so natural as men think, and that there is a great difference between the gentle habit which binds a man with cords of love to his helpmeet, and the unbridled passion which is intoxicated by the fancied charms of an object which he no longer sees in its true light. This passion which is full of exclusions and preferences, only differs from vanity in this respect, that vanity demands all and gives nothing, so that it is always harmful, while love, bestowing as much as it demands, is in itself a sentiment full of equi'y. Moreover, the more exacting it is, the more credulous; that very illusion which gave rise to it, makes it easy to persuade. If love is suspicious, esteem is trustful; and love will never exist in an honest heart without esteem, for every one loves in another the qualities which he himself holds in honour.

When once this is clearly understood, we can predict with confidence the kind of jealousy which Emile will be capable of experiencing; as there is only the smallest germ of this passion in the human heart, the form it takes must depend solely upon education: Emile, full of love and jealousy, will not be angry, sullen, suspicious, but delicate, sensitive, and timid; he will be more alarmed than vexed; he will think more of securing his lady-love than of threatening his rival; he will treat him as an obstacle to be removed if possible from his path, rather than as a rival to be hated; if he hates him, it is not because he presumes to compete with him for Sophy's affection, but because Emile feels that there is a real danger of losing that affection; he will not be so unjust and foolish as to take offence at the rivalry itself; he understands that the law of preference rests upon merit only, and that honour depends upon success; he will redouble his efforts to make himself acceptable, and he will probably succeed. His generous Sophy, though she has given alarm to his love, is well able to allay that fear, to atone for it; and the rivals who were only suffered to put him to the proof are speedily dismissed.

But whither am I going? O Emile! what art thou now? Is this my pupil? How art thou fallen! Where is that young man so sternly fashioned, who braved all weathers, who devoted his body to the hardest tasks and his soul to the laws of wisdom; untouched by prejudice or passion, a lover of truth, swayed by reason only, unheeding all that was not hers? Living in softness and idleness he now lets himself be ruled by women; their amusements are the business of his life, their wishes are his laws; a young girl is the arbiter of his fate, he cringes and grovels before her; the earnest Emile is the plaything of a child.

concealing her real feelings, the former in feigning what she does not feel. Every society lady spends her life in boasting of her supposed sensibility, when in reality she cares for no one but herself.

So shift the scenes of life; each age is swayed by its own motives, but the man is the same. At ten his mind was set upon cakes, at twenty it is set upon his mistress; at thirty it will be set upon pleasure; at forty on ambition, at fifty on avarice; when will he seek after wisdom only? Happy is he who is compelled to follow her against his will! What matter who is the guide, if the end is attained Heroes and sages have themselves paid tribute to this human weakness; and those who handled the distaff with clumsy fingers were none the less great men.

If you would prolong the influence of a good education through life itself, the good habits acquired in childhood must be carried forward into adolescence, and when your pupil is what he ought to be you must manage to keep him what he ought to be. This is the coping-stone of your work. This is why it is of the first importance that the tutor should remain with young men; otherwise there is little doubt they will learn to make love without him. The great mistake of tutors and still more of fathers is to think that one way of living makes another impossible, and that as soon as the child is grown up, you must abandon everything you used to do when he was little. If that were so, why should we take such pains in childhood, since the good or bad use we make of it will vanish with childhood itself; if another way of life were necessarily accompanied by other ways of thinking?

The stream of memory is only interrupted by great illnesses, and the stream of conduct, by great passions. Our tastes and inclinations may change, but this change, though it may be sudden enough, is rendered less abrupt by our habits. The skilful artist, in a good colour scheme, contrives so to mingle and blend his tints that the transitions are imperceptible; and certain colour washes are spread over the whole picture so that there may be no sudden breaks. So should it be with our likings. Unbalanced characters are always changing their affections, their tastes, their sentiments; the only constant factor is the habit of change; but the man of settled character always returns to his former habits and preserves to old age the tastes and the pleasures of his childhood.

If you contrive that young people passing from one stage of life to another do not despise what has gone before, that when they form new habits, they do not forsake the old, and that they always love to do what is right, in things new and old; then only are the fruits of your toil secure, and you are sure of your scholars as long as they live; for the revolution most to be dreaded is that of the age over which you are now watching. As men always look back to this period with regret so the tastes carried forward into it from childhood are not easily destroyed; but if once interrupted they are never resumed.

Most of the habits you think you have instilled into children and young people are not really habits at all; they have only been acquired under compulsion, and being followed reluctantly they will be cast off at the first opportunity. However long you remain in prison you never get a taste for prison life; so aversion is increased rather than diminished by habit. Not so with Emile; as a child he only did what he could do willingly and with pleasure, and as a man he will do the same, and the force of habit will only lend its help to the joys of freedom. An active life, bodily labour, exercise, movement, have become so essential to him that he could not relinquish them without suffering. Reduce him all at once to a soft and sedentary life and you condemn him to chains and imprisonment, you keep him in a condition of thraldom and constraint; he would suffer, no doubt, both in health and temper. He can scarcely breathe in a stuffy room, he requires open air, movement, fatigue. Even at Sophy's feet he cannot help casting a glance at the country and longing to explore it in her company. Yet he remains if he must; but he is anxious and ill at ease; he seems to be struggling with himself; he remains because he is a captive. "Yes," you will say, "these are necessities to which you have subjected him, a yoke which you have laid upon him." You speak truly, I have subjected him to the yoke of manhood.

Emile loves Sophy; but what were the charms by which he was first attracted? Sensibility, virtue, and love for things pure and honest. When he loves this love in Sophy, will he cease to feel it himself? And what price did she put upon herself? She required all her lover's natural feelings — esteem of what is really good, frugality, simplicity, generous unselfishness, a scorn of pomp and riches. These virtues were Emile's before love claimed them of him. Is he really changed? He has all the more reason to be himself; that is the only difference. The careful reader will not suppose that all the circumstances in which he is placed are the work of chance. There were many charming girls in the town; is it chance that his choice is discovered in a distant retreat? Is their meeting the work of chance? Is it chance that makes them so suited to each other? Is it chance that they cannot live in the same place, that he is compelled to find a lodging so far from her? Is it chance that he can see her so seldom and must purchase the pleasure of seeing her at the price of such fatigue? You say he is becoming effeminate. Not so, he is growing stronger; he must be fairly robust to stand the fatigue he endures on Sophy's account.

He lives more than two leagues away. That distance serves to temper the shafts of love. If they lived next door to each other, or if he could drive to see her in a comfortable carriage, he would love at his ease in the Paris fashion. Would Leander have braved death for the sake of Hero if the sea had not lain between them? Need I say more; if my reader is able to take my meaning, he will be able to follow out my principles in detail.

The first time we went to see Sophy, we went on horseback, so as to get there more quickly. We continue this convenient plan until our fifth visit. We were expected; and more than half a league from the house we see people on the road. Emile watches them, his pulse quickens as he gets nearer, he recognises Sophy and dismounts quickly; he hastens to join the charming family. Emile is fond of good horses; his horse is fresh, he feels he is free, and gallops off across the fields; I follow and with some difficulty I succeed in catching him and bringing him back. Unluckily Sophy is afraid of horses, and I dare not approach her. Emile has not seen what happened, but Sophy whispers to him that he is giving his friend a great deal of trouble. He hurries up quite ashamed of himself, takes the horses, and follows after the party. It is only fair that each should take his turn and he rides on to get rid of our mounts. He has to leave Sophy behind him, and he no longer thinks riding a convenient mode of travelling. He returns out of breath and meets us half-way.

The next time, Emile will not hear of horses. "Why," say I, "we need only take a servant to look after them." "Shall we put our worthy friends to such expense?" he replies. "You see they would insist on feeding man and horse." "That is true," I reply; "theirs is the generous hospitality of the poor. The rich man in his niggardly pride only welcomes his friends, but the poor find room for their friends' horses." "Let us go on foot," says he; "won't you venture on the walk, when you are always so ready to share the toilsome pleasures of your child?" "I will gladly go with you," I reply at once, "and it seems to me that love does not desire so much show."

As we draw near, we meet the mother and daughter even further from home than on the last occasion. We have come at a great pace. Emile is very warm; his beloved condescends to pass her handkerchief over his cheeks. It would take a good many horses to make us ride there after this.

But it is rather hard never to be able to spend an evening together. Midsummer is long past and the days are growing shorter. Whatever we say, we are not allowed to return home in the dark, and unless we make a very early start, we have to go back almost as soon as we get there. The mother is sorry for us and uneasy on our account, and it occurs to her that, though it would not be proper for us to stay in the house, beds might be found for us in the village, if we liked to stay there occasionally. Emile claps his hands at this idea and trembles with joy; Sophy, unwittingly, kisses her mother rather oftener than usual on the day this idea occurs to her.

Little by little the charm of friendship and the familiarity of innocence take root and grow among us. I generally accompany my young friend on the days appointed by Sophy or her mother, but sometimes I let him go alone. The heart thrives in the sunshine of confidence, and a man must not be treated as a child; and what have I accomplished so far, if my pupil is unworthy of my esteem? Now and then I go without him; he is sorry, but he does not complain; what use would it be? And then he knows I shall not interfere with his interests. However, whether we go together or separately you will understand that we are not stopped by the weather; we are only too proud to arrive in a condition which calls for pity. Unluckily Sophy deprives us of this honour and forbids us to come in bad weather. This is the only occasion on which she rebels against the rules which I laid down for her in private.

One day Emile had gone alone and I did not expect him back till the following day, but he returned the same evening. " My dear Emile," said I, " have you come back to your old friend already ? " But instead of responding to my caresses he replied with some show of temper, " You need not suppose I came back so soon of my own accord; she insisted on it it; is for her sake not yours that I am here." Touched by his frankness I renewed my caresses, saying, " Truthful heart and faithful friend, do not conceal from me anything I ought to know. If you came back for her sake, you told me so for my own; your return is her doing, your frankness is mine. Continue to preserve the noble candour of great souls; strangers may think what they will, but it is a crime to let our friends think us better than we are."

I take care not to let him underrate the cost of his confession by assuming that there is more love than generosity in it, and by telling him that he would rather deprive himself of the honour of this return, than give it to Sophy. But this is how he revealed to me, all unconsciously, what were his real feelings; if he had returned slowly and comfortably, dreaming of his sweetheart, I should know he was merely her lover; when he hurried back, even if he was a little out of temper, he was the friend of his Mentor.

You see that the young man is very far from spending his days with Sophy, and seeing as much of her as he wants. One or two visits a week are all that is permitted, and these visits are often only for the afternoon and are rarely extended to the next day. He spends much more of his time in longing to see her, or in rejoicing that he has seen her, than he actually spends in her presence. Even when he goes to see her, more time is spent in going and returning than by her side. His pleasures, genuine, pure, delicious, but more imaginary than real, serve to kindle his love but not to make him effeminate.

On the days when he does not see Sophy he is not sitting idle at home. He is Emile himself and quite unchanged. He usually scours the country round in pursuit of its natural history; he observes and studies the soil, its products, and their mode of cultivation; he compares the methods he sees with those with which he is already familiar; he tries to find the reasons for any differences; if he thinks other methods better than those of the locality, he introduces them to the farmers' notice; if he suggests a better kind of plough, he has one made from his own drawings; if he finds a lime pit he teaches them how to use the lime on the land, a process new to them; he often lends a hand himself; they are surprised to find him handling all manner of tools more easily than they can themselves; his furrows are deeper and straighter than theirs, he is a more skilful sower, and his beds for early produce are more cleverly planned. They do not scoff at him as a fine talker, they see he knows what he is talking about. In a word, his zeal and attention are bestowed on everything that is really useful to everybody; nor does he stop there. He visits the peasants in their homes; inquires into their circumstances, their families, the number of their children, the extent of their holdings, the nature of their produce, their markets, their rights, their burdens, their debts, etc. He gives away very little money, for he knows it is usually ill spent; but he himself directs the use of his money, and makes it helpful to them without distributing it among them. He supplies them with labourers, and often pays them for work done by themselves, on tasks for their own benefit. For one he has the falling thatch repaired or renewed; for another he clears a piece of land which had gone out of cultivation for lack of means; to another he gives a cow, a horse, or stock of any kind to replace a loss; two neighbours are ready to go to law, he wins them over, and makes them friends again; a peasant falls ill, he has him cared for, he looks after him himself; [1] another is harassed by a rich and powerful neighbour, he protects him and speaks on his behalf; young people are fond of one another, he helps forward their marriage; a good woman has lost her beloved child, he goes to see her, he speaks words of comfort and sits a while with her; he does not despise the poor, he is in no hurry to avoid the unfortunate; he often takes his dinner with some peasant he is helping, and he will even accept a meal from those who have no need of his help; though he is the benefactor of some and the friend of all, he is none the less their equal. In conclusion, he always does as much good by his personal efforts as by his money.

Sometimes his steps are turned in the direction of the happy abode; he may hope to see Sophy without her knowing, to see her out walking without being seen. But Emile is always quite open in everything he does; he neither can nor would deceive. His delicacy is of that pleasing type in which pride rests on the foundation of a good conscience. He keeps strictly within bounds, and never comes near enough to gain from chance what he only desires to win from Sophy herself. On the other hand, he delights to roam about the neighbourhood, looking for the trace of Sophy's steps, feeling what pains she has taken and what a distance she has walked to please him.

The day before his visit, he will go to some neighbouring farm and order a little feast for the morrow. We shall take our walk in that direction without any special object, we shall turn in apparently by chance; fruit, cakes, and cream are waiting for us. Sophy likes sweets, so is not insensible to these attentions, and she is quite ready to do honour to what we have provided; for I always have my share

[1] To look after a sick peasant is not merely to give him a pill, or medicine, or to send a surgeon to him. That is not what these poor folk require in sickness; what they want is more and better food. When you have fever, you will do well to fast, but when your peasants have it, give them meat and wine; illness, in their case, is nearly always due to poverty and exhaustion; your cellar will supply the best draught, your butchers will be the best apothecary.

of the credit even if I have had no part in the trouble; it is a girl's way of returning thanks more easily. Her father and I have cakes and wine; Emile keeps the ladies company and is always on the look-out to secure a dish of cream in which Sophy has dipped her spoon.

The cakes lead me to talk of the races Emile used to run. Every one wants to hear about them; I explain amid much laughter; they ask him if he can run as well as ever. "Better," says he; "I should be sorry to forget how to run." One member of the company is dying to see him run, but she dare not say so; some one else undertakes to suggest it; he agrees and we send for two or three young men of the neighbourhood; a prize is offered, and in imitation of our earlier games a cake is placed on the goal. Every one is ready; Sophy's father gives the signal by clapping his hands. The nimble Emile flies like lightning and reaches the goal almost before the others have started. He receives his prize at Sophy's hands, and no less generous than Æneas, he gives gifts to all the vanquished.

In the midst of his triumph, Sophy dares to challenge the victor, and to assert that she can run as fast as he. He does not refuse to enter the lists with her, and while she is getting ready to start, while she is tucking up her skirt at each side, more eager to show Emile a pretty ankle than to vanquish him in the race, while she is seeing if her petticoats are short enough, he whispers a word to her mother who smiles and nods approval. Then he takes his place by his competitor; no sooner is the signal given than she is off like a bird.

Women were not meant to run; they flee that they may be over-taken. Running is not the only thing they do ill, but it is the only thing they do awkwardly; their elbows glued to their sides and pointed backwards look ridiculous, and the high heels on which they are perched make them look like so many grasshoppers trying to run instead of to jump.

Emile, supposing that Sophy runs no better than other women, does not deign to stir from his place and watches her start with a smile of mockery. But Sophy is light of foot and she wears low heels; she needs no pretence to make her foot look smaller; she runs so quickly that he has only just time to overtake this new Atalanta when he sees her so far ahead. Then he starts like an eagle dashing upon its prey; he pursues her, clutches her, grasps her at last quite out of breath, and gently placing his left arm about her, he lifts her like a feather, and pressing his sweet burden to his heart, he finishes the race, makes her touch the goal first, and then exclaiming, "Sophy wins!" he sinks on one knee before her and owns himself beaten.

Along with such occupations there is also the trade we learnt. One day a week at least, and every day when the weather is too bad for country pursuits, Emile and I go to work under a master-joiner. We do not work for show, like people above our trade; we work in earnest like regular workmen. Once when Sophy's father came to see us, he found us at work, and did not fail to report his wonder to his wife and daughter. "Go and see that young man in the workshop," said he, "and you will soon see if he despises the condition of the poor." You may fancy how pleased Sophy was at this! They talk it over, and they decide to surprise him at his work. They question me, apparently without any special object, and having made sure of the time, mother and daughter take a little carriage and come to town on that very day.

On her arrival, Sophy sees, at the other end of the shop, a young man in his shirt sleeves, with his hair all untidy, so hard at work that he does not see her; she makes a sign to her mother. Emile, a chisel in one hand and a hammer in the other, is just finishing a mortise; then he saws a piece of wood and places it in the vice in order to polish it. The sight of this does not set Sophy laughing; it affects her greatly; it wins her respect. Woman, honour your master; he it is who works for you, he it is who gives you bread to eat; this is he!

While they are busy watching him, I perceive them and pull Emile by the sleeve; he turns round, drops his tools, and hastens to them with an exclamation of delight. After he has given way to his first raptures, he makes them take a seat and he goes back to his work. But Sophy cannot keep quiet; she gets up hastily, runs about the workshop, looks at the tools, feels the polish of the boards, picks up shavings, looks at our hands, and says she likes this trade, it is so clean. The merry girl tries to copy Emile. With her delicate white hand she passes a plane over a bit of wood; the plane slips and makes no impression. It seems to me that Love himself is hovering over us and beating his wings; I think I can hear his joyous cries, "Hercules is avenged."

Yet Sophy's mother questions the master. "Sir, how much do you pay these two men a day?" "I give them each tenpence a day and their food; but if that young fellow wanted he could earn much more, for he is the best workman in the country." "Tenpence a day and their food," said she looking at us tenderly. "That is so, madam," replied the master. At these words she hurries up to Emile, kisses him, and clasps him to her breast with tears; unable to say more she repeats again and again, "My son, my son!"

When they had spent some time chatting with us, but without interrupting our work, "We must be going now," said the mother to her daughter, "it is getting late and we must not keep your father waiting." Then approaching Emile she tapped him playfully on the cheek, saying, "Well, my good workman, won't you come with us?" He replied sadly, "I am at work, ask the master." The master is asked if he can spare us. He replies that he cannot. "I have work on hand," said he, "which is wanted the day after to-morrow, so there is not much time. Counting on these gentlemen I refused other workmen who came; if they fail me I don't know how to replace them and I shall not be able to send the work home at the time promised." The mother said nothing, she was waiting to hear what Emile would say. Emile hung his head in silence.

" Sir," she said, somewhat surprised at this, " have you nothing to say to that ? " Emile looked tenderly at her daughter and merely said, " You see I am bound to stay." Then the ladies left us. Emile went with them to the door, gazed after them as long as they were in sight, and returned to his work without a word.

On the way home, the mother, somewhat vexed at his conduct, spoke to her daughter of the strange way in which he had behaved. " Why," said she, " was it so difficult to arrange matters with the master without being obliged to stay. The young man is generous enough and ready to spend money when there is no need for it, could not he spend a little on such a fitting occasion ? " " Oh, mamma," replied Sophy, " I trust Emile will never rely so much on money as to use it to break an engagement, to fail to keep his own word, and to make another break his ! I know he could easily give the master a trifle to make up for the slight inconvenience caused by his absence; but his soul would become the slave of riches, he would become accustomed to place wealth before duty, and he would think that any duty might be neglected provided he was ready to pay. That is not Emile's way of thinking, and I hope he will never change on my account. Do you think it cost him nothing to stay ? You are quite wrong, mamma; it was for my sake that he stayed; I saw it in his eyes."

It is not that Sophy is indifferent to genuine proofs of love; on the contrary she is imperious and exacting; she would rather not be loved at all than be loved half-heartedly. Hers is the noble pride of worth, conscious of its own value, self-respecting and claiming a like honour from others. She would scorn a heart that did not recognise the full worth of her own; that did not love her for her virtues as much and more than for her charms; a heart which did not put duty first, and prefer it to everything. She did not desire a lover who knew no will but hers. She wished to reign over a man whom she had not spoilt. Thus Circe, having changed into swine the comrades of Ulysses, bestowed herself on him over whom she had no power.

Except for this sacred and inviolable right, Sophy is very jealous of her own rights; she observes how carefully Emile respects them, how zealously he does her will; how cleverly he guesses her wishes, how exactly he arrives at the appointed time; she will have him neither late nor early; he must arrive to the moment. To come early is to think more of himself than of her; to come late is to neglect her. To neglect Sophy, that could not happen twice. An unfounded suspicion on her part nearly ruined everything, but Sophy is really just and knows how to atone for her faults.

They were expecting us one evening; Emile had received his orders. They came to meet us, but we were not there. What has become of us ? What accident have we met with ? No message from us ! The evening is spent in expectation of our arrival. Sophy thinks we are dead; she is miserable and in an agony of distress; she cries all the night through. In the course of the evening a messenger was despatched to inquire after us and bring back news in the morning. The messenger returns together with another messenger sent by us, who makes our excuses verbally and says we are quite well. Then the scene is changed; Sophy dries her tears, or if she still weeps it is for anger. It is small consolation to her proud spirit to know that we are alive; Emile lives and he has kept her waiting.

When we arrive she tries to escape to her own room; her parents desire her to remain, so she is obliged to do so; but deciding at once what course she will take she assumes a calm and contented expression which would deceive most people. Her father comes forward to receive us saying, "You have made your friends very uneasy; there are people here who will not forgive you very readily." "Who are they, papa," said Sophy with the most gracious smile she could assume. "What business is that of yours," said her father, "if it is not you?" Sophy bent over her work without reply. Her mother received us coldly and formally. Emile was so confused he dared not speak to Sophy. She spoke first, inquired how he was, asked him to take a chair, and pretended so cleverly that the poor young fellow, who as yet knew nothing of the language of angry passions, was quite deceived by her apparent indifference, and ready to take offence on his own account.

To undeceive him I was going to take Sophy's hand and raise it to my lips as I sometimes did; she drew it back so hastily, with the word, "Sir," uttered in such a strange manner that Emile's eyes were opened at once by this involuntary movement.

Sophy herself, seeing that she had betrayed herself, exercised less control over herself. Her apparent indifference was succeeded by scornful irony. She replied to everything he said in monosyllables uttered slowly and hesitatingly as if she were afraid her anger should show itself too plainly. Emile half dead with terror stared at her full of sorrow, and tried to get her to look at him so that his eyes might read in hers her real feelings. Sophy, still more angry at his boldness, gave him one look which removed all wish for another. Luckily for himself, Emile, trembling and dumbfounded, dared neither look at her nor speak to her again; for had he not been guilty, had he been able to endure her wrath, she would never have forgiven him.

Seeing that it was my turn now, and that the time was ripe for explanation, I returned to Sophy. I took her hand and this time she did not snatch it away; she was ready to faint. I said gently, "Dear Sophy, we are the victims of misfortune; but you are just and reasonable; you will not judge us unheard; listen to what we have to say." She said nothing and I proceeded—

"We set out yesterday at four o'clock; we were told to be here at seven, and we always allow ourselves rather more time than we need, so as to rest a little before we get here. We were more than half way here when we heard lamentable groans, which came from a little valley in the hillside, some distance off. We hurried towards the place and found an unlucky peasant who had taken rather more wine than was good for him; on his way home he had fallen heavily from his horse and broken his leg. We shouted and called for help; there was no answer; we tried to lift the injured man on his horse, but without success; the least movement caused intense agony. We decided to tie up the horse in a quiet part of the wood; then we made a chair of our crossed arms and carried the man as gently as possible, following his directions till we got him home. The way was long, and we were constantly obliged to stop and rest. At last we got there, but thoroughly exhausted. We were surprised and sorry to find that it was a house we knew already and that the wretched creature we had carried with such difficulty was the very man who received us so kindly when first we came. We had all been so upset that until that moment we had not recognised each other.

"There were only two little children. His wife was about to present him with another, and she was so overwhelmed at the sight of him brought home in such a condition, that she was taken ill and a few hours later gave birth to another little one. What was to be done under such circumstances in a lonely cottage far from any help? Emile decided to fetch the horse we had left in the wood, to ride as fast as he could into the town and fetch a surgeon. He let the surgeon have the horse, and not succeeding in finding a nurse all at once, he returned on foot with a servant, after having sent a messenger to you; meanwhile I hardly knew what to do between a man with a broken leg and a woman in travail, but I got ready as well as I could such things in the house as I thought would be needed for the relief of both.

"I will pass over the rest of the details; they are not to the point. It was two o'clock in the morning before we got a moment's rest. At last we returned before daybreak to our lodging close at hand, where we waited till you were up to let you know what had happened to us."

That was all I said. But before any one could speak Emile, approaching Sophy, raised his voice and said with greater firmness than I expected, "Sophy, my fate is in your hands, as you very well know. You may condemn me to die of grief; but do not hope to make me forget the rights of humanity; they are even more sacred in my eyes than your own rights; I will never renounce them for you."

For all answer, Sophy rose, put her arm round his neck, and kissed him on the cheek; then offering him her hand with inimitable grace she said to him, "Emile, take this hand; it is yours. When you will, you shall be my husband and my master; I will try to be worthy of that honour."

Scarcely had she kissed him, when her delighted father clapped his hands calling, "Encore, encore," and Sophy without further ado, kissed him twice on the other cheek; but afraid of what she had done she took refuge at once in her mother's arms and hid her blushing face on the maternal bosom.

I will not describe our happiness; everybody will feel with us. After dinner Sophy asked if it were too far to go and see the poor invalids. It was her wish and it was a work of mercy. When we got there we found them both in bed—Emile had sent for a second bedstead; there were people there to look after them—Emile had seen to it. But in spite of this everything was so untidy that they suffered almost as much from discomfort as from their condition. Sophy asked for one of the good wife's aprons and set to work to make her more comfortable in her bed; then she did as much for the man; her soft and gentle hand seemed to find out what was hurting them and how to settle them into less painful positions. Her very presence seemed to make them more comfortable; she seemed to guess what was the matter. This fastidious girl was not disgusted by the dirt or smells, and she managed to get rid of both without disturbing the sick people. She who had always appeared so modest and sometimes so disdainful, she who would not for all the world have touched a man's bed with her little finger, lifted the sick man and changed his linen without any fuss, and placed him to rest in a more comfortable position. The zeal of charity is of more value than modesty. What she did was done so skilfully and with such a light touch that he felt better almost without knowing she had touched him. Husband and wife mingled their blessings upon the kindly girl who tended, pitied, and consoled them. She was an angel from heaven come to visit them; she was an angel in face and manner, in gentleness and goodness. Emile was greatly touched by all this and he watched her without speaking. O man, love thy helpmeet. God gave her to relieve thy sufferings, to comfort thee in thy troubles. This is she!

The new-born baby was baptised. The two lovers were its godparents, and as they held it at the font they were longing, at the bottom of their hearts, for the time when they should have a child of their own to be baptised. They longed for their wedding day; they thought it was close at hand; all Sophy's scruples had vanished, but mine remained. They had not got so far as they expected; every one must have his turn.

One morning when they had not seen each other for two whole days, I entered Emile's room with a letter in my hands, and looking fixedly at him I said to him, " What would you do if some one told you Sophy were dead ? " He uttered a loud cry, got up and struck his hands together, and without saying a single word, he looked at me with eyes of desperation. " Answer me," I continued with the same calmness. Vexed at my composure, he then approached me with eyes blazing with anger; and checking himself in an almost threatening attitude, " What would I do ? I know not; but this I do know, I would never set eyes again upon the person who brought me such news." " Comfort yourself," said I, smiling, " she lives, she is well, and they are expecting us this evening. But let us go for a short walk and we can talk things over."

The passion which engrosses him will no longer permit him to devote himself as in former days to discussions of pure reason; this very passion must be called to our aid if his attention is to be given to my teaching. That is why I made use of this terrible preface; I am quite sure he will listen to me now.

"We must be happy, dear Emile; it is the end of every feeling creature; it is the first desire taught us by nature, and the only one which never leaves us. But where is happiness? Who knows? Every one seeks it, and no one finds it. We spend our lives in the search and we die before the end is attained. My young friend, when I took you, a new-born infant, in my arms, and called God himself to witness to the vow I dared to make that I would devote my life to the happiness of your life, did I know myself what I was undertaking? No; I only knew that in making you happy, I was sure of my own happiness. By making this useful inquiry on your account, I made it for us both.

"So long as we do not know what to do, wisdom consists in doing nothing. Of all rules there is none so greatly needed by man, and none which he is less able to obey. In seeking happiness when we know not where it is, we are perhaps getting further and further from it, we are running as many risks as there are roads to choose from. But it is not every one that can keep still. Our passion for our own well-being makes us so uneasy, that we would rather deceive ourselves in the search for happiness than sit still and do nothing; and when once we have left the place where we might have known happiness, we can never return.

"In ignorance like this I tried to avoid a similar fault. When I took charge of you I decided to take no useless steps and to prevent you from doing so too. I kept to the path of nature, until she should show me the path of happiness. And lo! their paths were the same, and without knowing it this was the path I trod.

"Be at once my witness and my judge; I will never refuse to accept your decision. Your early years have not been sacrificed to those that were to follow, you have enjoyed all the good gifts which nature bestowed upon you. Of the ills to which you were by nature subject, and from which I could shelter you, you have only experienced such as would harden you to bear others. You have never suffered any evil, except to escape a greater. You have known neither hatred nor servitude. Free and happy, you have remained just and kindly; for suffering and vice are inseparable, and no man ever became bad until he was unhappy. May the memory of your childhood remain with you to old age! I am not afraid that your kind heart will ever recall the hand that trained it without a blessing upon it.

"When you reached the age of reason, I secured you from the influence of human prejudice; when your heart awoke I preserved you from the sway of passion. Had I been able to prolong this inner tranquillity till your life's end, my work would have been secure, and you would have been as happy as man can be; but, my dear Emile, in vain did I dip you in the waters of Styx, I could not make you everywhere invulnerable; a fresh enemy has appeared, whom you have not yet learnt to conquer, and from whom I cannot save you. That enemy is yourself. Nature and fortune had left you free. You could face poverty, you could bear bodily pain; the sufferings of the heart were unknown to you; you were then dependent on nothing but your position as a human being; now you depend on all the ties you have formed for yourself; you have learnt to desire, and you are now the slave of your desires. Without any change in yourself, without any insult, any injury to yourself, what sorrows may attack your soul, what pains may you suffer without sickness, how many deaths may you die and yet live! A lie, an error, a suspicion, may plunge you in despair.

" At the theatre you used to see heroes, abandoned to depths of woe, making the stage re-echo with their wild cries, lamenting like women, weeping like children, and thus securing the applause of the audience. Do you remember how shocked you were by those lamentations, cries, and groans, in men from whom one would only expect deeds of constancy and heroism. ' Why,' said you, ' are those the patterns we are to follow, the models set for our imitation! Are they afraid man will not be small enough, unhappy enough, weak enough, if his weakness is not enshrined under a false show of virtue.' My young friend, henceforward you must be more merciful to the stage; you have become one of those heroes.

" You know how to suffer and to die; you know how to bear the heavy yoke of necessity in ills of the body, but you have not yet learnt to give a law to the desires of your heart; and the difficulties of life arise rather from our affections than from our needs. Our desires are vast, our strength is little better than nothing. In his wishes man is dependent on many things; in himself he is dependent on nothing, not even on his own life; the more his connections are multiplied, the greater his sufferings. Everything upon earth has an end; sooner or later all that we love escapes from our fingers, and we behave as if it would last for ever. What was your terror at the mere suspicion of Sophy's death? Do you suppose she will live for ever? Do not young people of her age die? She must die, my son, and perhaps before you. Who knows if she is alive at this moment? Nature meant you to die but once; you have prepared a second death for yourself.

" A slave to your unbridled passions, how greatly are you to be pitied! Ever privations, losses, alarms; you will not even enjoy what is left. You will possess nothing because of the fear of losing it; you will never be able to satisfy your passions, because you desired to follow them continually. You will ever be seeking that which will fly before you; you will be miserable and you will become wicked. How can you be otherwise, having no care but your un-bridled passions? If you cannot put up with involuntary privations how will you voluntarily deprive yourself? How can you sacrifice desire to duty, and resist your heart in order to listen to your reason? You would never see that man again who dared to bring you word of the death of your mistress; how would you behold him who would deprive you of her living self, him who would dare to tell you, ' She is dead to you, virtue puts a gulf between you ' ? If you must live with her whatever happens, whether Sophy is married or single, whether you are free or not, whether she loves or hates you, whether she is given or refused to you, no matter, it is your will and you must have her at any price. Tell me then what crime will stop a man who has no law but his heart's desires, who knows not how to resist his own passions.

" My son, there is no happiness without courage, nor virtue without a struggle. The word virtue is derived from a word signifying strength, and strength is the foundation of all virtue. Virtue is the heritage of a creature weak by nature but strong by will; that is the whole merit of the righteous man; and though we call God good we do not call Him virtuous, because He does good without effort. I waited to explain the meaning of this word, so often profaned, until you were ready to understand me. As long as virtue is quite easy to practise, there is little need to know it. This need arises with the awakening of the passions; your time has come.

" When I brought you up in all the simplicity of nature, instead of preaching disagreeable duties, I secured for you immunity from the vices which make such duties disagreeable; I made lying not so much hateful as unnecessary in your sight; I taught you not so much to give others their due, as to care little about your own rights; I made you kindly rather than virtuous. But the kindly man is only kind so long as he finds it pleasant; kindness falls to pieces at the shock of human passions; the kindly man is only kind to himself.

" What is meant by a virtuous man? He who can conquer his affections; for then he follows his reason, his conscience; he does his duty; he is his own master and nothing can turn him from the right way. So far you have had only the semblance of liberty, the precarious liberty of the slave who has not received his orders. Now is the time for real freedom; learn to be your own master; control your heart, my Emile, and you will be virtuous.

" There is another apprenticeship before you, an apprenticeship more difficult than the former; for nature delivers us from the evils she lays upon us, or else she teaches us to submit to them; but she has no message for us with regard to our self-imposed evils; she leaves us to ourselves; she leaves us, victims of our own passions, to succumb to our vain sorrows, to pride ourselves on the tears of which we should be ashamed.

" This is your first passion. Perhaps it is the only passion worthy of you. If you can control it like a man, it will be the last; you will be master of all the rest, and you will obey nothing but the passion for virtue.

" There is nothing criminal in this passion; I know it; it is as pure as the hearts which experience it. It was born of honour and nursed by innocence. Happy lovers! for you the charms of virtue do but add to those of love; and the blessed union to which you are looking forward is less the reward of your goodness than of your affection. But tell me, O truthful man, though this passion is pure, is it any the less your master? Are you the less its slave? And if to-morrow it should cease to be innocent, would you strangle it on the spot? Now is the time to try your strength; there is no time for that in hours of danger. These perilous efforts should be made when danger is still afar. We do not practise the use of our weapons when we are face to face with the enemy, we do that before the war; we come to the battle-field ready prepared.

" It is a mistake to classify the passions as lawful and unlawful, so as to yield to the one and refuse the other. All alike are good if we are their masters; all alike are bad if we abandon ourselves to them. Nature forbids us to extend our relations beyond the limits of our strength; reason forbids us to want what we cannot get, conscience forbids us, not to be tempted, but to yield to temptation. To feel or not to feel a passion is beyond our control, but we can control ourselves. Every sentiment under our own control is lawful; those which control us are criminal. A man is not guilty if he loves his neighbour's wife, provided he keeps this unhappy passion under the control of the law of duty; he is guilty if he loves his own wife so greatly as to sacrifice everything to that love.

" Do not expect me to supply you with lengthy precepts of morality, I have only one rule to give you which sums up all the rest. Be a man; restrain your heart within the limits of your manhood. Study and know these limits; however narrow they may be, we are not unhappy within them; it is only when we wish to go beyond them that we are unhappy, only when, in our mad passions, we try to attain the impossible; we are unhappy when we forget our manhood to make an imaginary world for ourselves, from which we are always slipping back into our own. The only good things, whose loss really affects us, are those which we claim as our rights. If it is clear that we cannot obtain what we want, our mind turns away from it; wishes without hope cease to torture us. A beggar is not tormented by a desire to be a king; a king only wishes to be a god when he thinks himself more than man.

" The illusions of pride are the source of our greatest ills; but the contemplation of human suffering keeps the wise humble. He keeps to his proper place and makes no attempt to depart from it; he does not waste his strength in getting what he cannot keep; and his whole strength being devoted to the right employment of what he has, he is in reality richer and more powerful in proportion as he desires less than we. A man, subject to death and change, shall I forge for myself lasting chains upon this earth, where everything changes and disappears, whence I myself shall shortly vanish! Oh, Emile! my son! if I were to lose you, what would be left of myself? And yet I must learn to lose you, for who knows when you may be taken from me?

"Would you live in wisdom and happiness, fix your heart on the beauty that is eternal; let your desires be limited by your position, let your duties take precedence of your wishes; extend the law of necessity into the region of morals; learn to lose what may be taken from you; learn to forsake all things at the command of virtue, to set yourself above the chances of life, to detach your heart before it is torn in pieces, to be brave in adversity so that you may never be wretched, to be steadfast in duty that you may never be guilty of a crime. Then you will be happy in spite of fortune, and good in spite of your passions. You will find a pleasure that cannot be destroyed, even in the possession of the most fragile things; you will possess them, they will not possess you, and you will realise that the man who loses everything, only enjoys what he knows how to resign. It is true you will not enjoy the illusions of imaginary pleasures, neither will you feel the sufferings which are their result. You will profit greatly by this exchange, for the sufferings are real and frequent, the pleasures are rare and empty. Victor over so many deceitful ideas, you will also vanquish the idea that attaches such an excessive value to life. You will spend your life in peace, and you will leave it without terror; you will detach yourself from life as from other things. Let others, horror-struck, believe that when this life is ended they cease to be; conscious of the nothingness of life, you will think that you are but entering upon the true life. To the wicked, death is the close of life; to the just it is its dawn."

Emile heard me with attention not unmixed with anxiety. After such a startling preface he feared some gloomy conclusion. He foresaw that when I showed him how necessary it is to practise the strength of the soul, I desired to subject him to this stern discipline; he was like a wounded man who shrinks from the surgeon, and fancies he already feels the painful but healing touch which will cure the deadly wound.

Uncertain, anxious, eager to know what I am driving at, he does not answer, he questions me but timidly. "What must I do?" says he almost trembling, not daring to raise his eyes. "What must you do?" I reply firmly. "You must leave Sophy." "What are you saying?" he exclaimed angrily. "Leave Sophy, leave Sophy, deceive her, become a traitor, a villain, a perjurer!" "Why!" I continue, interrupting him; "does Emile suppose I shall teach him to deserve such titles?" "No," he continued with the same vigour. "Neither you nor any one else; I am capable of preserving your work; I shall not deserve such reproaches."

I was prepared for this first outburst; I let it pass unheeded. If I had not the moderation I preach it would not be much use preaching it! Emile knows me too well to believe me capable of demanding any wrong action from him, and he knows that it would be wrong to leave Sophy, in the sense he attaches to the phrase. So he waits for an explanation. Then I resume my speech.

"My dear Emile, do you think any man whatsoever can be happier than you have been for the last three months? If you think so, undeceive yourself. Before tasting the pleasures of life you have plumbed the depths of its happiness. There is nothing more than you have already experienced. The joys of sense are soon over; habit invariably destroys them. You have tasted greater joys through hope than you will ever enjoy in reality. The imagination which adorns what we long for, deserts its possession. With the exception of the one self-existing Being, there is nothing beautiful except that which is not. If that state could have lasted for ever, you would have found perfect happiness. But all that is related to man shares his decline; all is finite, all is fleeting in human life, and even if the conditions which make us happy could be prolonged for ever, habit would deprive us of all taste for that happiness. If external circumstances remain unchanged, the heart changes; either happiness forsakes us, or we forsake her.

"During your infatuation time has passed unheeded. Summer is over, winter is at hand. Even if our expeditions were possible, at such a time of year they would not be permitted. Whether we wish it or no, we shall have to change our way of life; it cannot continue. I read in your eager eyes that this does not disturb you greatly; Sophy's confession and your own wishes suggest a simple plan for avoiding the snow and escaping the journey. The plan has its advantages, no doubt; but when spring returns, the snow will melt and the marriage will remain; you must reckon for all seasons.

" You wish to marry Sophy and you have only known her five months! You wish to marry her, not because she is a fit wife for you, but because she pleases you; as if love were never mistaken as to fitness, as if those, who begin with love, never ended with hatred! I know she is virtuous; but is that enough? Is fitness merely a matter of honour? It is not her virtue I misdoubt, it is her disposition. Does a woman show her real character in a day? Do you know how often you must have seen her and under what varying conditions to really know her temper? Is four months of liking a sufficient pledge for the rest of your life? A couple of months hence you may have forgotten her; as soon as you are gone another may efface your image in her heart; on your return you may find her as indifferent as you have hitherto found her affectionate. Sentiments are not a matter of principle; she may be perfectly virtuous and yet cease to love you. I am inclined to think she will be faithful and true; but who will answer for her, and who will answer for you if you are not put to the proof? Will you postpone this trial till it is too late, will you wait to know your true selves till parting is no longer possible?

" Sophy is not eighteen, and you are barely twenty-two; this is the age for love, but not for marriage. What a father and mother for a family! If you want to know how to bring up children, you should at least wait till you yourselves are children no longer. Do you not know that too early motherhood has weakened the constitution, destroyed the health, and shortened the life of many young women? Do you not know that many children have always been

weak and sickly because their mother was little more than a child
herself? When mother and child are both growing, the strength
required for their growth is divided, and neither gets all that nature
intended; are not both sure to suffer? Either I know very little
of Emile, or he would rather wait and have a healthy wife and
children, than satisfy his impatience at the price of their life and
health.

"Let us speak of yourself. You hope to be a husband and a
father; have you seriously considered your duties? When you become the head of a family you will become a citizen of your country.
And what is a citizen of the state? What do you know about it?
You have studied your duties as a man, but what do you know
of the duties of a citizen? Do you know the meaning of such terms
as government, laws, country? Do you know the price you must
pay for life, and for what you must be prepared to die? You think
you know everything, when you really know nothing at all. Before
you take your place in the civil order, learn to perceive and know
what is your proper place.

"Emile, you must leave Sophy; I do not bid you forsake her; if
you were capable of such conduct, she would be only too happy not
to have married you; you must leave her in order to return worthy
of her. Do not be vain enough to think yourself already worthy.
How much remains to be done! Come and fulfil this splendid task;
come and learn to submit to absence; come and earn the prize of
fidelity, so that when you return you may indeed deserve some
honour, and may ask her hand not as a favour but as a reward."

Unaccustomed to struggle with himself, untrained to desire one
thing and to will another, the young man will not give way; he
resists, he argues. Why should he refuse the happiness which
awaits him? Would he not despise the hand which is offered him
if he hesitated to accept it? Why need he leave her to learn what he
ought to know? And if it were necessary to leave her why not
leave her as his wife with a certain pledge of his return? Let him
be her husband, and he is ready to follow me; let them be married
and he will leave her without fear. "Marry her in order to leave
her, dear Emile! what a contradiction! A lover who can leave his
mistress shows himself capable of great things; a husband should
never leave his wife unless through necessity. To cure your scruples,
I see the delay must be involuntary on your part; you must be able
to tell Sophy you leave her against your will. Very well, be content,
and since you will not follow the commands of reason, you must
submit to another master. You have not forgotten your promise.
Emile, you must leave Sophy; I will have it."

For a moment or two he was downcast, silent, and thoughtful,
then looking me full in the face he said, "When do we start?"
"In a week's time," I replied; "Sophy must be prepared for our
going. Women are weaker than we are, and we must show consideration for them; and this parting is not a duty for her as it
is for you, so she may be allowed to bear it less bravely."

The temptation to continue the daily history of their love up to the time of their separation is very great; but I have already presumed too much upon the good nature of my readers; let us abridge the story so as to bring it to an end. Will Emile face the situation as bravely at his mistress' feet as he has done in conversation with his friend? I think he will; his confidence is rooted in the sincerity of his love. He would be more at a loss with her, if it cost him less to leave her; he would leave her feeling himself to blame, and that is a difficult part for a man of honour to play; but the greater the sacrifice, the more credit he demands for it in the sight of her who makes it so difficult. He has no fear that she will misunderstand his motives. Every look seems to say, " Oh, Sophy, read my heart and be faithful to me; your lover is not without virtue."

Sophy tries to bear the unforeseen blow with her usual pride and dignity. She tries to seem as if she did not care, but as the honours of war are not hers, but Emile's, her strength is less equal to the task. She weeps, she sighs against her will, and the fear of being forgotten embitters the pain of parting. She does not weep in her lover's sight, she does not let him see her terror; she would die rather than utter a sigh in his presence. I am the recipient of her lamentations, I behold her tears, it is I who am supposed to be her confidant. Women are very clever and know how to conceal their cleverness; the more she frets in private, the more pains she takes to please me; she feels that her fate is in my hands.

I console and comfort her; I make myself answerable for her lover, or rather for her husband; let her be as true to him as he to her and I promise they shall be married in two years' time. She respects me enough to believe that I do not want to deceive her. I am guarantor to each for the other. Their hearts, their virtue, my honesty, the confidence of their parents, all combine to reassure them. But what can reason avail against weakness? They part as if they were never to meet again.

Then it is that Sophy recalls the regrets of Eucharis, and fancies herself in her place. Do not let us revive that fantastic affection during his absence " Sophy," say I one day, " exchange looks with Emile; let him have your *Telemachus* that he may learn to be like him, and let him give you his *Spectator* which you enjoy reading. Study the duties of good wives in it, and remember that in two years' time you will undertake those duties." The exchange gave pleasure to both and inspired them with confidence. At last the sad day arrived and they must part.

Sophy's worthy father, with whom I had arranged the whole business, took affectionate leave of me, and taking me aside, he spoke seriously and somewhat emphatically, saying, " I have done everything to please you; I knew I had to do with a man of honour; I have only one word to say. Remembering your pupil has signed his contract of marriage on my daughter's lips."

What a difference in the behaviour of the two lovers! Emile, impetuous, eager, excited, almost beside himself, cries aloud and sheds torrents of tears upon the hands of father, mother, and daughter; with sobs he embraces every one in the house and repeats the same thing over and over again in a way that would be ludicrous at any other time. Sophy, pale, sorrowful, doleful, and heavy-eyed, remains quiet without a word or a tear, she sees no one, not even Emile. In vain he takes her hand, and clasps her in his arms; she remains motionless, unheeding his tears, his caresses, and everything he does; so far as she is concerned, he is gone already. A sight more moving than the prolonged lamentations and noisy regrets of her lover! He sees, he feels, he is heartbroken. I drag him reluctantly away; if I left him another minute, he would never go. I am delighted that he should carry this touching picture with him. If he should ever be tempted to forget what is due to Sophy, his heart must have strayed very far indeed if I cannot bring it back to her by recalling her as he saw her last.

OF TRAVEL

Is it good for young people to travel? The question is often asked and as often hotly disputed. If it were stated otherwise—Are men the better for having travelled?—perhaps there would be less difference of opinion.

The misuse of books is the death of sound learning. People think they know what they have read, and take no pains to learn. Too much reading only produces a pretentious ignoramus. There was never so much reading in any age as the present, and never was there less learning; in no country of Europe are so many histories and books of travel printed as in France, and nowhere is there less knowledge of the mind and manners of other nations. So many books lead us to neglect the book of the world; if we read it at all, we keep each to our own page. If the phrase, "Can one become a Persian," were unknown to me, I should suspect on hearing it that it came from the country where national prejudice is most prevalent and from the sex which does most to increase it.

A Parisian thinks he has a knowledge of men and he knows only Frenchmen; his town is always full of foreigners, but he considers every foreigner as a strange phenomenon which has no equal in the universe. You must have a close acquaintance with the middle classes of that great city, you must have lived among them, before you can believe that people could be at once so witty and so stupid. The strangest thing about it is that probably every one of them has read a dozen times a description of the country whose inhabitants inspire him with such wonder.

To discover the truth amidst our own prejudices and those of the authors is too hard a task. I have been reading books of travels all my life, but I never found two that gave me the same idea of the same nation. On comparing my own scanty observations with what I have read, I have decided to abandon the travellers and I regret the time wasted in trying to learn from their books; for I am quite convinced that for that sort of study, seeing not reading is required. That would be true enough if every traveller were honest, if he only said what he saw and believed, and if truth were not tinged with false colours from his own eyes. What must it be when we have to disentangle the truth from the web of lies and ill-faith?

Let us leave the boasted resources of books to those who are content to use them. Like the art of Raymond Lully they are able to set people chattering about things they do not know. They are able to set fifteen-year-old Platos discussing philosophy in the clubs, and teaching people the customs of Egypt and the Indies on the word of Paul Lucas or Tavernier.

I maintain that it is beyond dispute that any one who has only seen one nation does not know men; he only knows those men among whom he has lived. Hence there is another way of stating the question about travel: "Is it enough for a well-educated man to know his fellow-countrymen, or ought he to know mankind in general?" Then there is no place for argument or uncertainty. See how greatly the solution of a difficult problem may depend on the way in which it is stated.

But is it necessary to travel the whole globe to study mankind? Need we go to Japan to study Europeans? Need we know every individual before we know the species? No, there are men so much alike that it is not worth while to study them individually. When y u have seen a dozen Frenchmen you have seen them all. Though one cannot say as much of the English and other nations, it is, however, certain that every nation has its own specific character, which is derived by induction from the study, not of one, but many of its members. He who has compared a dozen nations knows men, just he who has compared a dozen Frenchmen knows the French.

To acquire knowledge it is not enough to travel hastily through a country. Observation demands eyes, and the power of directing them towards the object we desire to know. There are plenty of people who learn no more from their travels than from their books, because they do not know how to think; because in reading their mind is at least under the guidance of the author, and in their travels they do not know how to see for themselves. Others learn nothing, because they have no desire to learn. Their object is so entirely different, that this never occurs to them; it is very unlikely that you will see clearly what you take no trouble to look for. The French travel more than any other nation, but they are so taken up with their own customs, that everything else is confused together. There are Frenchmen in every corner of the globe. In no country of the world do you find more people who have travelled than in France. And yet of all the nations of Europe, that which has seen most, knows least. The English are also travellers, but they travel in another fashion; these two nations must always be at opposite extremes. The English nobility travels, the French stays at home; the French people travel, the English stay at home. This difference does credit, I think, to the English. The French almost always travel for their own ends; the English do not seek their fortune in other lands, unless in the way of commerce and with their hands full; when they travel it is to spend their money, not to live by their wits; they are too proud to cringe before strangers. This is why they learn more abroad than the French who have other fish to fry. Yet the English have their national prejudices; but these prejudices are not so much the result of ignorance as of feeling. The Englishman's prejudices are the result of pride, the Frenchman's are due to vanity.

Just as the least cultivated nations are usually the best, so those travel best who travel least; they have made less progress than we in our frivolous pursuits, they are less concerned with the objects of our empty curiosity, so that they give their attention to what is really useful. I hardly know any but the Spaniards who travel in this fashion. While the Frenchman is running after all the artists of the country, while the Englishman is getting a copy of some antique, while the German is taking his album to every man of science, the Spaniard is silently studying the government, the manners of the country, its police, and he is the only one of the four who from all that he has seen will carry home any observation useful to his own country.

The ancients travelled little, read little, and wrote few books; yet we see in those books that remain to us, that they observed each other more thoroughly than we observe our contemporaries. Without going back to the days of Homer, the only poet who transports us to the country he describes, we cannot deny to Herodotus the glory of having painted manners in his history, though he does it rather by narrative than by comment; still he does it better than all our historians whose books are overladen with portraits and characters. Tacitus has described the Germans of his time better than any author has described the Germans of to-day. There can be no doubt that those who have devoted themselves to ancient history know more about the Greeks, Carthaginians, Romans, Gauls, and Persians than any nation of to-day knows about its neighbours.

It must also be admitted that the original characteristics of different nations are changing day by day, and are therefore more difficult to grasp. As races blend and nations intermingle, those national differences which formerly struck the observer at first sight gradually disappear. Before our time every nation remained more or less cut off from the rest; the means of communication were fewer; there was less travelling, less of mutual or conflicting interests, less political and civil intercourse between nation and nation; those intricate schemes of royalty, miscalled diplomacy, were less frequent; there were no permanent ambassadors resident at foreign courts; long voyages were rare, there was little foreign trade, and what little there was, was either the work of princes, who employed foreigners, or of people of no account who had no influence on others and did nothing to bring the nations together. The relations between Europe and Asia in the present century are a hundredfold more numerous than those between Gaul and Spain in the past; Europe alone was less accessible than the whole world is now.

Moreover, the peoples of antiquity usually considered themselves as the original inhabitants of their country; they had dwelt there so long that all record was lost of the far-off times when their ancestors settled there; they had been there so long that the place had made a lasting impression on them; but in modern Europe the invasions of the barbarians, following upon the Roman conquests, have caused an extraordinary confusion. The Frenchmen of to-day are no longer the big fair men of old; the Greeks are no longer beautiful enough to serve as a sculptor's model; the very face of the Romans has changed as well as their character; the Persians, originally from Tartary, are daily losing their native ugliness through the intermixture of Circassian blood. Europeans are no longer Gauls, Germans, Iberians, Allobroges; they are all Scythians, more or less degenerate in countenance, and still more so in conduct.

This is why the ancient distinctions of race, the effect of soil and climate, made a greater difference between nation and nation in respect of temperament, looks, manners, and character than can be distinguished in our own time, when the fickleness of Europe leaves no time for natural causes to work, when the forests are cut down and the marshes drained, when the earth is more generally, though less thoroughly, tilled, so that the same differences between country and country can no longer be detected even in purely physical features.

If they considered these facts perhaps people would not be in such a hurry to ridicule Herodotus, Ctesias, Pliny for having described the inhabitants of different countries each with its own peculiarities and with striking differences which we no longer see. To recognise such types of face we should need to see the men themselves; no change must have passed over them, if they are to remain the same. If we could behold all the people who have ever lived, who can doubt that we should find greater variations between one century and another, than are now found between nation and nation.

At the same time, while observation becomes more difficult, it is more carelessly and badly done; this is another reason for the small success of our researches into the natural history of the human race. The information acquired by travel depends upon the object of the journey. If this object is a system of philosophy, the traveller only sees what he desires to see; if it is self-interest, it engrosses the whole attention of those concerned. Commerce and the arts which blend and mingle the nations at the same time prevent them from studying each other. If they know how to make a profit out of their neighbours, what more do they need to know?

It is a good thing to know all the places where we might live, so as to choose those where we can live most comfortably. If every one lived by his own efforts, all he would need to know would be how much land would keep him in food. The savage, who has need of no one, and envies no one, neither knows nor seeks to know any other country but his own. If he requires more land for his subsistence he shuns inhabited places; he makes war upon the wild beasts and feeds on them. But for us, to whom civilised life has become a necessity, for us who must needs devour our fellow-creatures, self-interest prompts each one of us to frequent those districts where there are most people to be devoured. This is why we all flock to Rome, Paris, and London. Human flesh and blood are always cheapest in the capital cities. Thus we only know the great nations, which are just like one another.

They say that men of learning travel to obtain information; not so, they travel like other people from interested motives. Philosophers like Plato and Pythagoras are no longer to be found, or if they are, it must be in far-off lands. Our men of learning only travel at the king's command; they are sent out, their expenses are paid, they receive a salary for seeing such and such things, and the object of that journey is certainly not the study of any question of morals. Their whole time is required for the object of their journey, and they are too honest not to earn their pay. If in any country whatsoever there are people travelling at their own expense, you may be sure it is not to study men but to teach them. It is not knowledge they desire but ostentation. How should their travels teach them to shake off the yoke of prejudice? It is prejudice that sends them on their travels.

To travel to see foreign lands or to see foreign nations are two very different things. The former is the usual aim of the curious, the latter is merely subordinate to it. If you wish to travel as a philosopher you should reverse this order. The child observes things till he is old enough to study men. Man should begin by studying his fellows; he can study things later if time permits.

It is therefore illogical to conclude that travel is useless because we travel ill. But granting the usefulness of travel, does it follow that it is good for all of us? Far from it; there are very few people who are really fit to travel; it is only good for those who are strong enough in themselves to listen to the voice of error without being deceived, strong enough to see the example of vice without being led away by it. Travelling accelerates the progress of nature, and completes the man for good or evil. When a man returns from travelling about the world, he is what he will be all his life; there are more who return bad than good, because there are more who start with an inclination towards evil. In the course of their travels, young people, ill-educated and ill-behaved, pick up all the vices of the nations among whom they have sojourned, and none of the virtues with which those vices are associated; but those who, happily for themselves, are well-born, those whose good disposition has been well cultivated, those who travel with a real desire to learn, all such return better and wiser than they went. Emile will travel in this fashion; in this fashion there travelled another young man, worthy of a nobler age; one whose worth was the admiration of Europe, one who died for his country in the flower of his manhood; he deserved to live, and his tomb, ennobled by his virtues only, received no honour till a stranger's hand adorned it with flowers.

Everything that is done in reason should have its rules. Travel, undertaken as a part of education, should therefore have its rules. To travel for travelling's sake is to wander, to be a vagabond; to travel to learn is still too vague; learning without some definite aim is worthless. I would give a young man a personal interest in learning, and that interest, well-chosen, will also decide the nature of the instruction. This is merely the continuation of the method I have hitherto practised.

Now after he has considered himself in his physical relations to other creatures, in his moral relations with other men, there remains to be considered his civil relations with his fellow-citizens. To do this he must first study the nature of government in general, then the different forms of government, and lastly the particular government under which he was born, to know if it suits him to live under it; for by a right which nothing can abrogate, every man, when he comes of age, becomes his own master, free to renounce the contract by which he forms part of the community, by leaving the country in which that contract holds good. It is only by sojourning in that country, after he has come to years of discretion, that he is supposed to have tacitly confirmed the pledge given by his ancestors. He acquires the right to renounce his country, just as he has the right to renounce all claim to his father's lands; yet his place of birth was a gift of nature, and in renouncing it, he renounces what is his own. Strictly speaking, every man remains in the land of his birth at his own risk unless he voluntarily submits to its laws in order to acquire a right to their protection.

For example, I should say to Emile, " Hitherto you have lived under my guidance, you were unable to rule yourself. But now you are approaching the age when the law, giving you the control over your property, makes you master of your person. You are about to find yourself alone in society, dependent on everything, even on your patrimony. You mean to marry; that is a praiseworthy intention, it is one of the duties of man; but before you marry you must know what sort of man you want to be, how you wish to spend your life, what steps you mean to take to secure a living for your family and for yourself; for although we should not make this our main business, it must be definitely considered. Do you wish to be dependent on men whom you despise? Do you wish to establish your fortune and determine your position by means of civil relations which will make you always dependent on the choice of others, which will compel you, if you would escape from knaves, to become a knave yourself? "

In the next place I would show him every possible way of using his money in trade, in the civil service, in finance, and I shall show him that in every one of these there are risks to be taken, every one of them places him in a precarious and dependent position, and compels him to adapt his morals, his sentiments, his conduct to the example and the prejudices of others.

" There is yet another way of spending your time and money; you may join the army; that is to say, you may hire yourself out at very high wages to go and kill men who never did you any harm. This trade is held in great honour among men, and they cannot think too highly of those who are fit for nothing better. Moreover, this profession, far from making you independent of other resources, makes them all the more necessary; for it is a point of honour in this profession to ruin those who have adopted it. It is true they are not all ruined; it is even becoming fashionable to grow rich in this as in other professions; but if I told you how people manage to do it, I doubt whether you would desire to follow their example.

" Moreover, you must know that, even in this trade, it is no longer a question of courage or valour, unless with regard to the ladies; on the contrary, the more cringing, mean, and degraded you are, the more honour you obtain; if you have decided to take your profession seriously, you will be despised, you will be hated, you will very possibly be driven out of the service; or at least you will fall a victim to favouritism and be supplanted by your comrades, because you have been doing your duty in the trenches, while they have been attending to their toilet."

We can hardly suppose that any of these occupations will be much to Emile's taste. " Why," he will exclaim, " have I forgotten the amusements of my childhood? Have I lost the use of my arms? Is my strength failing me? Do I not know how to work? What do I care about all your fine professions and all the silly prejudices of others? I know no other pride than to be kindly and just; no other happiness than to live in independence with her I love, gaining health and a good appetite by the day's work. All these difficulties you speak of do not concern me. The only property I desire is a little farm in some quiet corner. I will devote all my efforts after wealth to making it pay, and I will live without a care. Give me Sophy and my land, and I shall be rich."

" Yes, my dear friend, that is all a wise man requires, a wife and land of his own; but these treasures are scarcer than you think. The rarest you have found already; let us discuss the other.

" A field of your own, dear Emile! Where will you find it, in what remote corner of the earth can you say, ' Here am I master of myself and of this estate which belongs to me?' We know where a man may grow rich; who knows where he can do without riches? Who knows where to live free and independent, without ill-treating others and without fear of being ill-treated himself? Do you think it is so easy to find a place where you can always live like an honest man? If there is any safe and lawful way of living without intrigues, without lawsuits, without dependence on others, it is, I admit, to live by the labour of our hands, by the cultivation of our own land; but where is the state in which a man can say, 'The earth which I dig is my own?' Before choosing this happy spot, be sure that you will find the peace you desire; beware lest an unjust government, a persecuting religion, and evil habits should disturb you in your home. Secure yourself against the excessive taxes which devour the fruits of your labours, and the endless lawsuits which consume your capital. Take care that you can live rightly without having to pay court to intendents, to their deputies, to judges, to priests, to powerful neighbours, and to knaves of every kind, who are always ready to annoy you if you neglect them. Above all, secure yourself from annoyance on the part of the rich and great; remember that their estates may anywhere adjoin your Naboth's vineyard. If unluckily for you some great man buys or builds a house near your cottage, make sure that he will not find a way, under some pretence or other, to encroach on your lands to round off his estate, or that you do not find him at once absorbing all your resources to make a wide highroad. If you keep sufficient credit to ward off all these disagreeables, you might as well keep your money, for it will cost you no more to keep it. Riches and credit lean upon each other, the one can hardly stand without the other.

"I have more experience than you, dear Emile; I see more clearly the difficulties in the way of your scheme. Yet it is a fine scheme and honourable; it would make you happy indeed. Let us try to carry it out. I have a suggestion to make; let us devote the two years from now till the time of your return to choosing a place in Europe where you could live happily with your family, secure from all the dangers I have just described. If we succeed, you will have discovered that true happiness, so often sought for in vain; and you will not have to regret the time spent in its search. If we fail, you will be cured of a mistaken idea; you will console yourself for an inevitable ill, and you will bow to the law of necessity."

I do not know whether all my readers will see whither this suggested inquiry will lead us; but this I do know, if Emile returns from his travels, begun and continued with this end in view, without a full knowledge of questions of government, public morality, and political philosophy of every kind, we are greatly lacking, he in intelligence and I in judgment.

The science of politics is and probably always will be unknown. Grotius, our leader in this branch of learning, is only a child, and what is worse an untruthful child. When I hear Grotius praised to the skies and Hobbes overwhelmed with abuse, I perceive how little sensible men have read or understood these authors. As a matter of fact, their principles are exactly alike, they only differ in their mode of expression. Their methods are also different:

Hobbes relies on sophism; Grotius relies on the poets; they are agreed in everything else. In modern times the only man who could have created this vast and useless science was the illustrious Montesquieu. But he was not concerned with the principles of political law; he was content to deal with the positive laws of settled governments; and nothing could be more different than these two branches of study.

Yet he who would judge wisely in matters of actual government is forced to combine the two; he must know what ought to be in order to judge what is. The chief difficulty in the way of throwing light upon this important matter is to induce an individual to discuss and to answer these two questions. " How does it concern me; and what can I do ? " Emile is in a position to answer both.

The next difficulty is due to the prejudices of childhood, the principles in which we were brought up; it is due above all to the partiality of authors, who are always talking about truth, though they care very little about it; it is only their own interests that they care for, and of these they say nothing. Now the nation has neither professorships, nor pensions, nor membership of the academies to bestow. How then shall its rights be established by men of that type? The education I have given him has removed this difficulty also from Emile's path. He scarcely knows what is meant by government; his business is to find the best; he does not want to write books; if ever he did so, it would not be to pay court to those in authority, but to establish the rights of humanity.

There is a third difficulty, more specious than real; a difficulty which I neither desire to solve nor even to state; enough that I am not afraid of it; sure I am that in inquiries of this kind, great talents are less necessary than a genuine love of justice and a sincere reverence for truth. If matters of government can ever be fairly discussed, now or never is our chance.

Before beginning our observations we must lay down rules of procedure; we must find a scale with which to compare our measurements. Our principles of political law are our scale. Our actual measurements are the civil law of each country.

Our elementary notions are plain and simple, being taken directly from the nature of things. They will take the form of problems discussed between us, and they will not be formulated into principles, until we have found a satisfactory solution of our problems.

For example, we shall begin with the state of nature, we shall see whether men are born slaves or free, in a community or independent; is their association the result of free will or of force? Can the force which compels them to united action ever form a permanent law, by which this original force becomes binding, even when another has been imposed upon it, so that since the power of King Nimrod, who is said to have been the first conqueror, every other power which has overthrown the original power is unjust and usurping, so that there are no lawful kings but the descendants of Nimrod or their representatives; or if this original power has ceased, has the

power which succeeded it any right over us, and does it destroy
the binding force of the former power, so that we are not bound to
obey except under compulsion, and we are free to rebel as soon as
we are capable of resistance? Such a right is not very different from
might; it is little more than a play upon words.

We shall inquire whether man might not say that all sickness
comes from God, and that it is therefore a crime to send for the
doctor.

Again, we shall inquire whether we are bound by our conscience
to give our purse to a highwayman when we might conceal it from
him, for the pistol in his hand is also a power.

Does this word power in this context mean something different
from a power which is lawful and therefore subject to the laws to
which it owes its being?

Suppose we reject this theory that might is right and admit the
right of nature, or the authority of the father, as the foundation of
society; we shall inquire into the extent of this authority; what
is its foundation in nature? Has it any other grounds but that of its
usefulness to the child, his weakness, and the natural love which
his father feels towards him? When the child is no longer feeble,
when he is grown-up in mind as well as in body, does not he become
the sole judge of what is necessary for his preservation? Is he
not therefore his own master, independent of all men, even of his
father himself? For is it not still more certain that the son loves
himself, than that the father loves the son?

The father being dead, should the children obey the eldest
brother, or some other person who has not the natural affection of
a father? Should there always be, from family to family, one
single head to whom all the family owe obedience? If so, how
has power ever come to be divided, and how is it that there
is more than one head to govern the human race throughout
the world?

Suppose the nations to have been formed each by its own choice;
we shall then distinguish between right and fact; being thus
subjected to their brothers, uncles, or other relations, not because
they were obliged, but because they choose, we shall inquire
whether this kind of society is not a sort of free and voluntary
association?

Taking next the law of slavery, we shall inquire whether a man
can make over to another his right to himself, without restriction,
without reserve, without any kind of conditions; that is to say,
can he renounce his person, his life, his reason, his very self, can he
renounce all morality in his actions; in a word, can he cease to exist
before his death, in spite of nature who places him directly in charge
of his own preservation, in spite of reason and conscience which tell
him what to do and what to leave undone?

If there is any reservation or restriction in the deed of slavery,
we shall discuss whether this deed does not then become a true
contract, in which both the contracting powers, having in this

respect no common master,[1] remain their own judge as to the conditions of the contract, and therefore free to this extent, and able to break the contract so soon as it becomes hurtful,

If then a slave cannot convey himself altogether to his master, how can a nation convey itself altogether to its head? If a slave is to judge whether his master is fulfilling his contract, is not the nation to judge whether its head is fulfilling his contract?

Thus we are compelled to retrace our steps, and when we consider the meaning of this collective nation we shall inquire whether some contract, a tacit contract at the least, is not required to make a nation, a contract anterior to that which we are assuming.

Since the nation was a nation before it chose a king, what made it a nation, except the social contract? Therefore the social contract is the foundation of all civil society, and it is in the nature of this contract that we must seek the nature of the society formed by it.

We will inquire into the meaning of this contract; may it not be fairly well expressed in this formula? As an individual every one of us contributes his goods, his person, his life, to the common stock, under the supreme direction of the general will; while as a body we receive each member as an indivisible part of the whole.

Assuming this, in order to define the terms we require, we shall observe that, instead of the individual person of each contracting party, this deed of association produces a moral and collective body, consisting of as many members as there are votes in the Assembly. This public personality is usually called the *body politic*, which is called by its members the *State* when it is passive, and the *Sovereign* when it is active, and a *Power* when compared with its equals. With regard to the members themselves, collectively they are known as the *nation*, and individually as *citizens* as members of the *city* or partakers in the sovereign power, and *subjects* as obedient to the same authority.

We shall note that this contract of association includes a mutual pledge on the part of the public and the individual; and that each individual, entering, so to speak, into a contract with himself, finds himself in a twofold capacity, *i.e.*, as a member of the sovereign with regard to others, as member of the state with regard to the sovereign.

We shall also note that while no one is bound by any engagement to which he was not himself a party, the general deliberation which may be binding on all the subjects with regard to the sovereign, because of the two different relations under which each of them is envisaged, cannot be binding on the state with regard to itself. Hence we see that there is not, and cannot be, any other fundamental law, properly so called, except the social contract only. This does not mean that the body politic cannot, in certain respects, pledge itself to others; for in regard to the foreigner, it then becomes a simple creature, an individual.

---

[1] If they had such a common master, he would be no other than the sovereign, and then the right of slavery resting on the right of sovereignty would not be its origin.

Emile

425

Thus the two contracting parties, *i.e.*, each individual and the public, have no common superior to decide their differences; so we will inquire if each of them remains free to break the contract at will, that is to repudiate it on his side as soon as he considers it hurtful.

To clear up this difficulty, we shall observe that, according to the social pact, the sovereign power is only able to act through the common, general will; so its decrees can only have a general or common aim; hence it follows that a private individual cannot be directly injured by the sovereign, unless all are injured, which is impossible, for that would be to want to harm oneself. Thus the social contract has no need of any warrant but the general power, for it can only be broken by individuals, and they are not therefore freed from their engagement, but punished for having broken it.

To decide all such questions rightly, we must always bear in mind that the nature of the social pact is private and peculiar to itself, in that the nation only contracts with itself, *i.e.*, the people as a whole as sovereign, with the individuals as subjects; this condition is essential to the construction and working of the political machine, it alone makes pledges lawful, reasonable, and secure, without which it would be absurd, tyrannical, and liable to the grossest abuse.

Individuals having only submitted themselves to the sovereign, and the sovereign power being only the general will, we shall see that every man in obeying the sovereign only obeys himself, and how much freer are we under the social part than in the state of nature.

Having compared natural and civil liberty with regard to persons, we will compare them as to property, the rights of ownership and the rights of sovereignty, the private and the common domain. If the sovereign power rests upon the right of ownership, there is no right more worthy of respect; it is inviolable and sacred for the sovereign power, so long as it remains a private individual right; as soon as it is viewed as common to all the citizens, it is subject to the common will, and this will may destroy it. Thus the sovereign has no right to touch the property of one or many; but he may lawfully take possession of the property of all, as was done in Sparta in the time of Lycurgus; while the abolition of debts by Solon was an unlawful deed.

Since nothing is binding on the subjects except the general will, let us inquire how this will is made manifest, by what signs we may recognise it with certainty, what is a law, and what are the true characters of the law? This is quite a fresh subject; we have still to define the term law.

As soon as the nation considers one or more of its members, the nation is divided. A relation is established between the whole and its part which makes of them two separate entities, of which the part is one, and the whole, minus that part, is the other. But the whole minus the part is not the whole; as long as this relation exists, there is no longer a whole, but two unequal parts.

On the other hand, if the whole nation makes a law for the whole nation, it is only considering itself; and if a relation is set up, it is between the whole community regarded from one point of view, and the whole community regarded from another point of view, without any division of that whole. Then the object of the statute is general, and the will which makes that statute is general too. Let us see if there is any other kind of decree which may bear the name of law.

If the sovereign can only speak through laws, and if the law can never have any but a general purpose, concerning all the members of the state, it follows that the sovereign never has the power to make any law with regard to particular cases; and yet it is necessary for the preservation of the state that particular cases should also be dealt with; let us see how this can be done.

The decrees of the sovereign can only be decrees of the general will, that is laws; there must also be determining decrees, decrees of power or government, for the execution of those laws; and these, on the other hand, can only have particular aims. Thus the decrees by which the sovereign decides that a chief shall be elected is a law; the decree by which that chief is elected, in pursuance of the law, is only a decree of government.

This is a third relation in which the assembled people may be considered, i.e., as magistrates or executors of the law which it has passed in its capacity as sovereign.[1]

We will now inquire whether it is possible for the nation to deprive itself of its right of sovereignty, to bestow it on one or more persons; for the decree of election not being a law, and the people in this decree not being themselves sovereign, we do not see how they can transfer a right which they do not possess.

The essence of sovereignty consisting in the general will, it is equally hard to see how we can be certain that an individual will shall always be in agreement with the general will. We should rather assume that it will often be opposed to it; for individual interest always tends to privileges, while the common interest always tends to equality, and if such an agreement were possible, no sovereign right could exist, unless the agreement were either necessary or indestructible.

We will inquire if, without violating the social pact, the heads of the nation, under whatever name they are chosen, can ever be more than the officers of the people, entrusted by them with the duty of carrying the law into execution. Are not these chiefs themselves accountable for their administration, and are not they themselves subject to the laws which it is their business to see carried out?

If the nation cannot alienate its supreme right, can it entrust it to others for a time? Cannot it give itself a master, cannot it find

---

[1] These problems and theorems are mostly taken from the *Treatise on the Social Contract*, itself a summary of a larger work, undertaken without due consideration of my own powers, and long since abandoned.

representatives? This is an important question and deserves discussion.

If the nation can have neither sovereign nor representatives we will inquire how it can pass its own laws; must there be many laws; must they be often altered; is it easy for a great nation to be its own lawgiver?

Was not the Roman people a great nation?

Is it a good thing that there should be great nations?

It follows from considerations already established that there is an intermediate body in the state between subjects and sovereign; and this intermediate body, consisting of one or more members, is entrusted with the public administration, the carrying out of the laws, and the maintenance of civil and political liberty.

The members of this body are called *magistrates* or *kings*, that is to say, rulers. This body, as a whole, considered in relation to its members, is called the *prince*, and considered in its actions it is called the *government*.

If we consider the action of the whole body upon itself, that is to say, the relation of the whole to the whole, of the sovereign to the state, we can compare this relation to that of the extremes in a proportion of which the government is the middle term. The magistrate receives from the sovereign the commands which he gives to the nation, and when it is reckoned up his product or his power is in the same degree as the product or power of the citizens who are subjects on one side of the proportion and sovereigns on the other. None of the three terms can be varied without at once destroying this proportion. If the sovereign tries to govern, and if the prince wants to make the laws, or if the subject refuses to obey them, disorder takes the place of order, and the state falls to pieces under despotism or anarchy.

Let us suppose that this state consists of ten thousand citizens. The sovereign can only be considered collectively and as a body, but each individual, as a subject, has his private and independent existence. Thus the sovereign is as ten thousand to one; that is to say, every member of the state has, as his own share, only one ten-thousandth part of the sovereign power, although he is subject to the whole. Let the nation be composed of one hundred thousand men, the position of the subjects is unchanged, and each continues to bear the whole weight of the laws, while his vote, reduced to the one hundred-thousandth part, has ten times less influence in the making of the laws. Thus the subject being always one, the sovereign is relatively greater as the number of the citizens is increased. Hence it follows that the larger the state the less liberty.

Now the greater the disproportion between private wishes and the general will, *i.e.*, between manners and laws, the greater must be the power of repression. On the other side, the greatness of the state gives the depositaries of public authority greater temptations and additional means of abusing that authority, so that the more power is required by the government to control the people, the more power should there be in the sovereign to control the government.

From this twofold relation it follows that the continued proportion between the sovereign, the prince, and the people is not an arbitrary idea, but a consequence of the nature of the state. Moreover, it follows that one of the extremes, *i.e.*, the nation, being constant, every time the double ratio increases or decreases, the simple ratio increases or diminishes in its turn; which cannot be unless the middle term is as often changed. From this we may conclude that there is no single absolute form of government, but there must be as many different forms of government as there are states of different size.

If the greater the numbers of the nation the less the ratio between its manners and its laws, by a fairly clear analogy, we may also say, the more numerous the magistrates, the weaker the government.

To make this principle clearer we will distinguish three essentially different wills in the person of each magistrate; first, his own will as an individual, which looks to his own advantage only; secondly, the common will of the magistrates, which is concerned only with the advantage of the prince, a will which may be called corporate, and one which is general in relation to the government and particular in relation to the state of which the government forms part; thirdly, the will of the people, or the sovereign will, which is general, as much in relation to the state viewed as the whole as in relation to the government viewed as a part of the whole. In a perfect legislature the private individual will should be almost nothing; the corporate will belonging to the government should be quite subordinate, and therefore the general and sovereign will is the master of all the others. On the other hand, in the natural order, these different wills become more and more active in proportion as they become centralised; the general will is always weak, the corporate will takes the second place, the individual will is preferred to all; so that every one is himself first, then a magistrate, and then a citizen; a series just the opposite of that required by the social order.

Having laid down this principle, let us assume that the government is in the hands of one man. In this case the individual and the corporate will are absolutely one, and therefore this will has reached the greatest possible degree of intensity. Now the use of power depends on the degree of this intensity, and as the absolute power of the government is always that of the people, and therefore invariable, it follows that the rule of one man is the most active form of government.

If, on the other hand, we unite the government with the supreme power, and make the prince the sovereign and the citizens so many magistrates, then the corporate will is completely lost in the general will, and will have no more activity than the general will, and it will leave the individual will in full vigour. Thus the government, though its absolute force is constant, will have the minimum of activity.

These rules are incontestable in themselves, and other considerations only serve to confirm them. For example, we see the magistrates as a body far more active than the citizens as a body, so that the individual will always counts for more. For each magistrate usually has charge of some particular duty of government; while each citizen, in himself, has no particular duty of sovereignty. Moreover, the greater the state the greater its real power, although its power does not increase because of the increase in territory; but the state remaining unchanged, the magistrates are multiplied in vain, the government acquires no further real strength, because it is the depositary of that of the state, which I have assumed to be constant. Thus, this plurality of magistrates decreases the activity of the government without increasing its power.

Having found that the power of the government is relaxed in proportion as the number of magistrates is multiplied, and that the more numerous the people, the more the controlling power must be increased, we shall infer that the ratio between the magistrates and the government should be inverse to that between subjects and sovereign, that is to say, that the greater the state, the smaller the government, and that in like manner the number of chiefs should be diminished because of the increased numbers of the people.

In order to make this diversity of forms clearer, and to assign them their different names, we shall observe in the first place that the sovereign may entrust the care of the government to the whole nation or to the greater part of the nation, so that there are more citizen magistrates than private citizens. This form of government is called *Democracy*.

Or the sovereign may restrict the government in the hands of a lesser number, so that there are more plain citizens than magistrates; and this form of government is called *Aristocracy*.

Finally, the sovereign may concentrate the whole government in the hands of one man. This is the third and commonest form of government, and is called *Monarchy* or royal government.

We shall observe that all these forms, or the first and second at least, may be less or more, and that within tolerably wide limits. For the democracy may include the whole nation, or may be confined to one half of it. The aristocracy, in its turn, may shrink from the half of the nation to the smallest number. Even royalty may be shared, either between father and son, between two brothers, or in some other fashion. There were always two kings in Sparta, and in the Roman empire there were as many as eight emperors at once, and yet it cannot be said that the empire was divided. There is a point where each form of government blends with the next; and under the three specific forms there may be really as many forms of government as there are citizens in the state.

Nor is this all. In certain respects each of these governments is capable of subdivision into different parts, each administered in one of these three ways. From these forms in combination there may

430 Emile

arise a multitude of mixed forms, since each may be multiplied by all the simple forms.

In all ages there have been great disputes as to which is the best form of government, and people have failed to consider that each is the best in some cases and the worst in others. For ourselves, if the number of magistrates in the various states is to be in inverse ratio to the number of the citizens, we infer that generally a democratic government is adapted to small states, an aristocratic government to those of moderate size, and a monarchy to large states.

These inquiries furnish us with a clue by which we may discover what are the duties and rights of citizens, and whether they can be separated one from the other; what is our country, in what does it really consist, and how can each of us ascertain whether he has a country or no?

Having thus considered every kind of civil society in itself, we shall compare them, so as to note their relations one with another; great and small, strong and weak, attacking one another, insulting one another, destroying one another; and in this perpetual action and reaction causing more misery and loss of life than if men had preserved their original freedom. We shall inquire whether too much or too little has not been accomplished in the matter of social institutions; whether individuals who are subject to law and to men, while societies preserve the independence of nature, are not exposed to the ills of both conditions without the advantages of either, and whether it would not be better to have no civil society in the world rather than to have many such societies. Is it not that mixed condition which partakes of both and secures neither?

"Per quem neutrum licet, nec tanquam in bello paratum esse, nec tanquam in pace securum."—SENECA, *De Trang: Animi*, cap. 1.

Is it not this partial and imperfect association which gives rise to tyranny and war? And are not tyranny and war the worst scourges of humanity?

Finally we will inquire how men seek to get rid of these difficulties by means of leagues and confederations, which leave each state its own master in internal affairs, while they arm it against any unjust aggression. We will inquire how a good federal association may be established, what can make it lasting, and how far the rights of the federation may be stretched without destroying the right of sovereignty.

The Abbé de Saint-Pierre suggested an association of all the states of Europe to maintain perpetual peace among themselves. Is this association practicable, and supposing that it were established, would it be likely to last? These inquiries lead us straight to all the questions of international law which may clear up the remaining difficulties of political law.

1 You will remember that I mean, in this context, the supreme magistrates or heads of the nation, the others being only their deputies in this or that respect.

Finally we shall lay down the real principles of the laws of war, and we shall see why Grotius and others have only stated false principles.

I should not be surprised if my pupil, who is a sensible young man, should interrupt me saying, " One would think we were building our edifice of wood and not of men; we are putting everything so exactly in its place! " That is true; but remember that the law does not bow to the passions of men, and that we have first to establish the true principles of political law. Now that our foundations are laid, come and see what men have built upon them; and you will see some strange sights!

Then I set him to read *Telemachus*, and we pursue our journey; we are seeking that happy Salentum and the good Idomeneus made wise by misfortunes. By the way we find many like Protesilas and no Philocles, neither can Adrastes, King of the Daunians, be found. But let our readers picture our travels for themselves, or take the same journeys with *Telemachus* in their hand; and let us not suggest to them painful applications which the author himself avoids or makes in spite of himself.

Moreover, Emile is not a king, nor am I a god, so that we are not distressed that we cannot imitate Telemachus and Mentor in the good they did; none know better than we how to keep to our own place, none have less desire to leave it. We know that the same task is allotted to all; that whoever loves what is right with all his heart, and does the right so far as it is in his power, has fulfilled that task. We know that Telemachus and Mentor are creatures of the imagination. Emile does not travel in idleness and he does more good than if he were a prince. If we were kings we should be no greater benefactors. If we were kings and benefactors we should cause any number of real evils for every apparent good we supposed we were doing. If we were kings and sages, the first good deed we should desire to perform, for ourselves and for others, would be to abdicate our kingship and return to our present position.

I have said why travel does so little for every one. What makes it still more barren for the young is the way in which they are sent on their travels. Tutors, more concerned to amuse than to instruct, take them from town to town, from palace to palace, where if they are men of learning and letters, they make them spend their time in libraries, or visiting antiquaries, or rummaging among old buildings transcribing ancient inscriptions. In every country they are busy over some other century, as if they were living in another country; so that after they have travelled all over Europe at great expense, a prey to frivolity or tedium, they return, having seen nothing to interest them, and having learnt nothing that could be of any possible use to them.

All capitals are just alike, they are a mixture of all nations and all ways of living; they are not the place in which to study the nations. Paris and London seem to me the same town. Their inhabitants have a few prejudices of their own, but each has as many as the other, and all their rules of conduct are the same. We know the kind of people who will throng the court. We know the way of living which the crowds of people and the unequal distribution of wealth will produce. As soon as any one tells me of a town with two hundred thousand people, I know its life already. What I do not know about it is not worth going there to learn.

To study the genius and character of a nation you should go to the more remote provinces, where there is less stir, less commerce, where strangers seldom travel, where the inhabitants stay in one place, where there are fewer changes of wealth and position. Take a look at the capital on your way, but go and study the country far away from that capital. The French are not in Paris, but in Touraine; the English are more English in Mercia than in London, and the Spaniards more Spanish in Galicia than in Madrid. In these remoter provinces a nation assumes its true character and shows what it really is; there the good or ill effects of the government are best perceived, just as you can measure the arc more exactly at a greater radius.

The necessary relations between character and government have been so clearly pointed out in the book of *L'Esprit des Lois*, that one cannot do better than have recourse to that work for the study of those relations. But speaking generally, there are two plain and simple standards by which to decide whether governments are good or bad. One is the population. Every country in which the population is decreasing is on its way to ruin; and the countries in which the population increases most rapidly, even were they the poorest countries in the world, are certainly the best governed.[1]

But this population must be the natural result of the government and the national character, for if it is caused by colonisation or any other temporary and accidental cause, then the remedy itself is evidence of the disease. When Augustus passed laws against celibacy, those laws showed that the Roman empire was already beginning to decline. Citizens must be induced to marry by the goodness of the government, not compelled to marry by law; you must not examine the effects of force, for the law which strives against the constitution has little or no effect; you should study what is done by the influence of public morals and by the natural inclination of the government, for these alone produce a lasting effect. It was the policy of the worthy Abbé de Saint-Pierre always to look for a little remedy for every individual ill, instead of tracing them to their common source and seeing if they could not all be cured together. You do not need to treat separately every sore on a rich man's body; you should purify the blood which produces them. They say that in England there are prizes for agriculture; that is enough for me; that is proof enough that agriculture will not flourish there much longer.

The second sign of the goodness or badness of the government and the laws is also to be found in the population, but it is to be

[1] I only know one exception to this rule—it is China.

found not in its numbers but in its distribution. Two states equal in size and population may be very unequal in strength; and the more powerful is always that in which the people are more evenly distributed over its territory; the country which has fewer large towns, and makes less show on this account, will always defeat the other. It is the great towns which exhaust the state and are the cause of its weakness; the wealth which they produce is a sham wealth, there is much money and few goods. They say the town of Paris is worth a whole province to the King of France; for my own part I believe it costs him more than several provinces. I believe that Paris is fed by the provinces in more senses than one, and that the greater part of their revenues is poured into that town and stays there, without ever returning to the people or to the king. It is inconceivable that in this age of calculators there is no one to see that France would be much more powerful if Paris were destroyed. Not only is this ill-distributed population not advantageous to the state, it is more ruinous than depopulation itself, because depopulation only gives as produce nought, and the ill-regulated addition of still more people gives a negative result. When I hear an Englishman and a Frenchman so proud of the size of their capitals, and disputing whether London or Paris has more inhabitants, it seems to me that they are quarrelling as to which nation can claim the honour of being the worst governed.

Study the nation outside its towns; thus only will you really get to know it. It is nothing to see the apparent form of a government, overladen with the machinery of administration and the jargon of the administrators, if you have not also studied its nature as seen in the effects it has upon the people, and in every degree of administration. The difference of form is really shared by every degree of the administration, and it is only by including every degree that you really know the difference. In one country you begin to feel the spirit of the minister in the manœuvres of his underlings; in another you must see the election of members of parliament to see if the nation is really free; in each and every country, he who has only seen the towns cannot possibly know what the government is like, as its spirit is never the same in town and country. Now it is the agricultural districts which form the country, and the country people who make the nation.

This study of different nations in their remoter provinces, and in the simplicity of their native genius, gives a general result which is very satisfactory, to my thinking, and very consoling to the human heart; it is this: All the nations, if you observe them in this fashion, seem much better worth observing; the nearer they are to nature, the more does kindness hold sway in their character; it is only when they are cooped up in towns, it is only when they are changed by cultivation, that they become depraved, that certain faults which were rather coarse than injurious are exchanged for pleasant but pernicious vices.

From this observation we see another advantage in the mode of travel I suggest; for young men, sojourning less in the big towns which are horribly corrupt, are less likely to catch the infection of vice; among simpler people and less numerous company, they will preserve a surer judgment, a healthier taste, and better morals. Besides this contagion of vice is hardly to be feared for Emile; he has everything to protect him from it. Among all the precautions I have taken, I reckon much on the love he bears in his heart.

We do not know the power of true love over youthful desires, because we are ourselves as ignorant of it as they are, and those who have control over the young turn them from true love. Yet a young man must either love or fall into bad ways. It is easy to be deceived by appearances. You will quote any number of young men who are said to live very chastely without love; but show me one grown man, a real man, who can truly say that his youth was thus spent? In all our virtues, all our duties, people are content with appearances; for my own part I want the reality, and I am much mistaken if there is any other way of securing it beyond the means I have suggested.

The idea of letting Emile fall in love before taking him on his travels is not my own. It was suggested to me by the following incident.

I was in Venice calling on the tutor of a young Englishman. It was winter and we were sitting round the fire. The tutor's letters were brought from the post office. He glanced at them, and then read them aloud to his pupil. They were in English; I understood not a word, but while he was reading I saw the young man tear some fine point lace ruffles which he was wearing, and throw them in the fire one after another, as quietly as he could, so that no one should see it. Surprised at this whim, I looked at his face and thought I perceived some emotion; but the external signs of passion, though much alike in all men, have national differences which may easily lead one astray. Nations have a different language of facial expression as well as of speech. I waited till the letters were finished and then showing the tutor the bare wrists of his pupil, which he did his best to hide, I said, " May I ask the meaning of this ? "

The tutor seeing what had happened began to laugh; he embraced his pupil with an air of satisfaction and, with his consent, he gave me the desired explanation.

"The ruffles," said he, "which Mr. John has just torn to pieces, were a present from a lady in this town, who made them for him not long ago. Now you must know that Mr. John is engaged to a young lady in his own country, with whom he is greatly in love, and she well deserves it. This letter is from the lady's mother, and I will translate the passage which caused the destruction you beheld.

" ' Lucy is always at work upon Mr. John's ruffles. Yesterday Miss Betty Roldham came to spend the afternoon and insisted on doing some of her work. I knew that Lucy was up very early this morning and I wanted to see what she was doing; I found her busy unpicking what Miss Betty had done. She would not have a single stitch in her present done by any hand but her own.' "

Mr. John went to fetch another pair of ruffles, and I said to his tutor: " Your pupil has a very good disposition; but tell me is not the letter from Miss Lucy's mother a put up job? Is it not an expedient of your designing against the lady of the ruffles?" " No," said he, " it is quite genuine; I am not so artful as that; I have made use of simplicity and zeal, and God has blessed my efforts."

This incident with regard to the young man stuck in my mind; it was sure to set a dreamer like me thinking.

But it is time we finished. Let us take Mr. John back to Miss Lucy, or rather Emile to Sophy. He brings her a heart as tender as ever, and a more enlightened mind, and he returns to his native land all the better for having made acquaintance with foreign governments through their vices and foreign nations through their virtues. I have even taken care that he should associate himself with some man of worth in every nation, by means of a treaty of hospitality after the fashion of the ancients, and I shall not be sorry if this acquaintance is kept up by means of letters. Not only may this be useful, not only is it always pleasant to have a correspondent in foreign lands, it is also an excellent antidote against the sway of patriotic prejudices, to which we are liable all through our life, and to which sooner or later we are more or less enslaved. Nothing is better calculated to lessen the hold of such prejudices than a friendly interchange of opinions with sensible people whom we respect; they are free from our prejudices and we find ourselves face to face with theirs, and so we can set the one set of prejudices against the other and be safe from both. It is not the same thing to have to do with strangers in our own country and in theirs. In the former case there is always a certain amount of politeness which either makes them conceal their real opinions, or makes them think more favourably of our country while they are with us; when they get home again this disappears, and they merely do us justice. I should be very glad if the foreigner I consult has seen my country, but I shall not ask what he thinks of it till he is at home again.

When we have spent nearly two years travelling in a few of the great countries and many of the smaller countries of Europe, when we have learnt two or three of the chief languages, when we have seen what is really interesting in natural history, government, arts, or men, Emile, devoured by impatience, reminds me that our time is almost up. Then I say, " Well, my friend, you remember the main object of our journey; you have seen and observed; what is the final result of your observations? What decision have you come to?" Either my method is wrong, or he will answer me somewhat after this fashion—

" What decision have I come to? I have decided to be what you made me; of my own free will I will add no fetters to those imposed upon me by nature and the laws. The more I study the works of men in their institutions, the more clearly I see that, in their efforts after independence, they become slaves, and that their very freedom is wasted in vain attempts to assure its continuance. That they may not be carried away by the flood of things, they form all sorts of attachments; then as soon as they wish to move forward they are surprised to find that everything drags them back. It seems to me that to set oneself free we need do nothing, we need only continue to desire freedom. My master, you have made me free by teaching me to yield to necessity. Let her come when she will, I follow her without compulsion; I lay hold of nothing to keep me back. In our travels I have sought for some corner of the earth where I might be absolutely my own; but where can one dwell among men without being dependent on their passions? On further consideration I have discovered that my desire contradicted itself; for were I to hold to nothing else, I should at least hold to the spot on which I had settled; my life would be attached to that spot, as the dryads were attached to their trees. I have discovered that the words liberty and empire are incompatible; I can only be master of a cottage by ceasing to be master of myself.

" ' Hoc erat in votis, modus agri non ita magnus.'
HORACE, lib. ii., sat. vi.

"I remember that my property was the origin of our inquiries. You argued very forcibly that I could not keep both my wealth and my liberty; but when you wished me to be free and at the same time without needs, you desired two incompatible things, for I could only be independent of men by returning to dependence on nature. What then shall I do with the fortune bequeathed to me by my parents? To begin with, I will not be dependent on it; I will cut myself loose from all the ties which bind me to it; if it is left in my hands, I shall keep it; if I am deprived of it, I shall not be dragged away with it. I shall not trouble myself to keep it, but I shall keep steadfastly to my own place. Rich or poor, I shall be free. I shall be free not merely in this country or in that; I shall be free in any part of the world. All the chains of prejudice are broken; as far as I am concerned I know only the bonds of necessity. I have been trained to endure them from my childhood, and I shall endure them until death, for I am a man; and why should I not wear those chains as a free man, for I should have to wear them even if I were a slave, together with the additional fetters of slavery?

"What matters my place in the world? What matters it where I am? Wherever there are men, I am among my brethren; wherever there are none, I am in my own home. So long as I may be independent and rich, and have wherewithal to live, and I shall live. If my wealth makes a slave of me, I shall find it easy to renounce it. I have hands to work, and I shall get a living. If my hands fail me, I shall live if others will support me; if they forsake me I shall die; I shall die even if I am not forsaken, for death is not the penalty of poverty, it is a law of nature. Whensoever death comes I defy it; it shall never find me making preparations for life; it shall never prevent me having lived.

" My father, this is my decision. But for my passions, I should be in my manhood independent as God himself, for I only desire what is and I should never fight against fate. At least, there is only one chain, a chain which I shall ever wear, a chain of which I may be justly proud. Come then, give me my Sophy, and I am free."

" Dear Emile, I am glad indeed to hear you speak like a man, and to behold the feelings of your heart. At your age this exaggerated unselfishness is not unpleasing. It will decrease when you have children of your own, and then you will be just what a good father and a wise man ought to be. I knew what the result would be before our travels; I knew that when you saw our institutions you would be far from reposing a confidence in them which they do not deserve. In vain do we seek freedom under the power of the laws. The laws! Where is there any law? Where is there any respect for law? Under the name of law you have everywhere seen the rule of self-interest and human passion. But the eternal laws of nature and of order exist. For the wise man they take the place of positive law; they are written in the depths of his heart by conscience and reason; let him obey these laws and be free; for there is no slave but the evil-doer, for he always does evil against his will. Liberty is not to be found in any form of government, she is in the heart of the free man, he bears her with him everywhere. The vile man bears his slavery in himself; the one would be a slave in Geneva, the other free in Paris.

" If I spoke to you of the duties of a citizen, you would perhaps ask me, ' Which is my country?' And you would think you had put me to confusion. Yet you would be mistaken, dear Emile, for he who has no country has, at least, the land in which he lives. There is always a government and certain so-called laws under which he has lived in peace. What matter though the social contract has not been observed, if he has been protected by private interest against the general will, if he has been secured by public violence against private aggressions, if the evil he has beheld has taught him to love the good, and if our institutions themselves have made him perceive and hate their own iniquities? Oh, Emile, where is the man who owes nothing to the land in which he lives? Whatever that land may be, he owes to it the most precious thing possessed by man, the morality of his actions and the love of virtue. Born in the depths of a forest he would have lived in greater happiness and freedom; but being able to follow his inclinations without a struggle there would have been no merit in his goodness, he would not have been virtuous, as he may be now, in spite of his passions. The mere sight of order teaches him to know and love it. The public good, which to others is a mere pretext, is a real motive for him. He learns to fight against himself and to prevail, to sacrifice his own interest to the common weal. It is not true that he gains nothing from the laws; they give him courage to be just, even in the midst of the wicked. It is not true that they have failed to make him free: they have taught him to rule himself.

"Do not say therefore, 'What matter where I am?' It does matter that you should be where you can best do your duty; and one of these duties is to love your native land. Your fellow-countrymen protected you in childhood; you should love them in your manhood. You should live among them, or at least you should live where you can serve them to the best of your power, and where they know where to find you if ever they are in need of you. There are circumstances in which a man may be of more use to his fellow-countrymen outside his country than within it. Then he should listen only to his own zeal and should bear his exile without a murmur; that exile is one of his duties. But you, dear Emile, you have not undertaken the painful task of telling men the truth, you must live in the midst of your fellow-creatures, cultivating their friendship in pleasant intercourse; you must be their benefactor, their pattern; your example will do more than all our books, and the good they see you do will touch them more deeply than all our empty words.

"Yet I do not exhort you to live in a town; on the contrary, one of the examples which the good should give to others is that of a patriarchal, rural life, the earliest life of man, the most peaceful, the most natural, and the most attractive to the uncorrupted heart. Happy is the land, my young friend, where one need not seek peace in the wilderness! But where is that country? A man of good will finds it hard to satisfy his inclinations in the midst of towns, where he can find few but frauds and rogues to work for. The welcome given by the towns to those idlers who flock to them to seek their fortunes only completes the ruin of the country, when the country ought really to be repopulated at the cost of the towns. All the men who withdraw from high society are useful just because of their withdrawal, since its vices are the result of its numbers. They are also useful when they can bring with them into the desert places life, culture, and the love of their first condition. I like to think what benefits Emile and Sophy, in their simple home, may spread about them, what a stimulus they may give to the country, how they may revive the zeal of the unlucky villagers.

"In fancy I see the population increasing, the land coming under cultivation, the earth clothed with fresh beauty. Many workers and plenteous crops transform the labours of the fields into holidays; I see the young couple in the midst of the rustic sports which they have revived, and I hear the shouts of joy and the blessings of those about them. Men say the golden age is a fable; it always will be for those whose feelings and taste are depraved. People do not really regret the golden age, for they do nothing to restore it. What is needed for its restoration? One thing only, and that is an impossibility; we must love the golden age.

"Already it seems to be reviving around Sophy's home; together you will only complete what her worthy parents have begun. But, dear Emile, you must not let so pleasant a life give you a distaste for sterner duties, if every they are laid upon you; remember that the Romans sometimes left the plough to become consul. If the prince or the state calls you to the service of your country, leave all to fulfil the honourable duties of a citizen in the post assigned to you. If you find that duty onerous, there is a sure and honourable means of escaping from it; do your duty so honestly that it will not long be left in your hands. Moreover, you need not fear the difficulties of such a test; while there are men of our own time, they will not summon you to serve the state."

Why may I not paint the return of Emile to Sophy and the end of their love, or rather the beginning of their wedded love! A love founded on esteem which will last with life itself, on virtues which will not fade with fading beauty, on fitness of character which gives a charm to intercourse, and prolongs to old age the delights of early love. But all such details would be pleasing but not useful, and so far I have not permitted myself to give attractive details unless I thought they would be useful. Shall I abandon this rule when my task is nearly ended? No, I feel that my pen is weary. Too feeble for such prolonged labours, I should abandon this if it were not so nearly completed; if it is not to be left imperfect it is time it were finished.

At last I see the happy day approaching, the happiest day of Emile's life and my own; I see the crown of my labours, I begin to appreciate their results. The noble pair are united till death do part; heart and lips confirm no empty vows; they are man and wife. When they return from the church, they follow where they are led; they know not where they are, whither they are going, or what is happening around them. They heed nothing, they answer at random; their eyes are troubled and they see nothing. Oh, rapture! Oh, human weakness! Man is overwhelmed by the feeling of happiness, he is not strong enough to bear it.

There are few people who know how to talk to the newly-married couple. The gloomy propriety of some and the light conversation of others seem to me equally out of place. I would rather their young hearts were left to themselves, to abandon themselves to an agitation which is not without its charm, rather than that they should be so cruelly distressed by a false modesty, or annoyed by coarse witticisms which, even if they appealed to them at other times, are surely out of place on such a day.

I behold our young people, wrapped in a pleasant languor, giving no heed to what is said. Shall I, who desire that they should enjoy all the days of their life, shall I let them lose this precious day? No, I desire that they shall taste its pleasures and enjoy them. I rescue them from the foolish crowd, and walk with them in some quiet place; I recall them to themselves by speaking of them I wish to speak, not merely to their ears, but to their hearts, and I know that there is only one subject of which they can think to-day.

" My children," say I, taking a hand of each, " it is three years since I beheld the birth of the pure and vigorous passion which is your happiness to-day. It has gone on growing; your eyes tell

me that it has reached its highest point; it must inevitably decline."
My readers can fancy the raptures, the anger, the vows of Emile,
and the scornful air with which Sophy withdraws her hand from
mine; how their eyes protest that they will adore each other till
their latest breath. I let them have their way; then I continue—

" I have often thought that if the happiness of love could continue
in marriage, we should find a Paradise upon earth. So far this has
never been. But if it were not quite impossible, you two are quite
worthy to set an example you have not received, an example which
few married couples could follow. My children, shall I tell you
what I think is the way, and the only way, to do it? "

They look at one another and smile at my simplicity. Emile
thanks me curtly for my prescription, saying that he thinks Sophy
has a better, at any rate it is good enough for him. Sophy agrees
with him and seems just as certain. Yet in spite of her mockery,
I think I see a trace of curiosity. I study Emile; his eager eyes are
fixed upon his wife's beauty; he has no curiosity for anything else;
and he pays little heed to what I say. It is my turn to smile, and
I say to myself, " I will soon get your attention."

The almost imperceptible difference between these two hidden
impulses is characteristic of a real difference between the two sexes;
it is that men are generally less constant than women, and are sooner
weary of success in love. A woman foresees man's future inconstancy,
and is anxious; it is this which makes her more jealous.[1] When his
passion begins to cool she is compelled to pay him the attentions he
used to bestow on her for her pleasure; she weeps, it is her turn to
humiliate herself, and she is rarely successful. Affection and kind
deeds rarely win hearts, and they hardly ever win them back. I
return to my prescription against the cooling of love in marriage.

" It is plain and simple," I continue. " It consists in remaining
lovers when you are husband and wife."

" Indeed," said Emile, laughing at my secret, " we shall not find
that hard."

" Perhaps you will find it harder than you think. Pray give me
time to explain.

" Cords too tightly stretched are soon broken. This is what
happens when the marriage bond is subjected to too great a strain.
The fidelity imposed by it upon husband and wife is the most sacred
of all rights; but it gives to each too great a power over the other.
Constraint and love do not agree together, and pleasure is not to
be had for the asking. Do not blush, Sophy, and do not try to
run away. God forbid that I should offend your modesty! But
your fate for life is at stake. For so great a cause, permit a con-

[1] In France it is the wives who first emancipate themselves; and necessarily so, for having very little heart, and only desiring attention, when
a husband ceases to pay them attention they care very little for himself.
In other countries it is not so; it is the husband who first emancipates
himself; and necessarily so, for women, faithful, but foolish, importune
men with their desires and only disgust them. There may be plenty of
exceptions to these general truths; but I still think they are truths.

versation between your husband and your father which you would not permit elsewhere.

"It is not so much possession as mastery of which people tire, and affection is often more prolonged with regard to a mistress than a wife. How can people make a duty of the tenderest caresses, and a right of the sweetest pledges of love? It is mutual desire which gives the right, and nature knows no other. The law may restrict this right, it cannot extend it. The pleasure is so sweet in itself! Should it owe to sad constraint the power which it cannot gain from its own charms? No, my children, in marriage the hearts are bound, but the bodies are not enslaved. You owe one another fidelity, but not complaisance. Neither of you may give yourself to another, but neither of you belongs to the other except at your own will.

"If it is true, dear Emile, that you would always be your wife's lover, that she should always be your mistress and her own, be a happy but respectful lover; obtain all from love and nothing from duty, and let the slightest favours never be of right but of grace. I know that modesty shuns formal confessions and requires to be overcome; but with delicacy and true love, will the lover ever be mistaken as to the real will? Will not he know when heart and eyes grant what the lips refuse? Let both for ever be master of their person and their caresses, let them have the right to bestow them only at their own will. Remember that even in marriage this pleasure is only lawful when the desire is mutual. Do not be afraid, my children, that this law will keep you apart; on the contrary, it will make both more eager to please, and will prevent satiety. True to one another, nature and love will draw you to each other."

Emile is angry and cries out against these and similar suggestions. Sophy is ashamed, she hides her face behind her fan and says nothing. Perhaps while she is saying nothing, she is the most annoyed. Yet I insist, without mercy; I make Emile blush for his lack of delicacy; I undertake to be surety for Sophy that she will undertake her share of the treaty. I incite her to speak, you may guess she will not dare to say I am mistaken. Emile anxiously consults the eyes of his young wife; he beholds them, through all her confusion, filled with a voluptuous anxiety which reassures him against the dangers of trusting her. He flings himself at her feet, kisses with rapture the hand extended to him, and swears that beyond the fidelity he has already promised, he will renounce all other rights over her. "My dear wife," said he, "be the arbiter of my pleasures as you are already the arbiter of my life and fate. Should your cruelty cost me life itself I would yield to you my most cherished rights. I will owe nothing to your complaisance, but all to your heart."

Dear Emile, be comforted; Sophy herself is too generous to let you fall a victim to your generosity.

In the evening, when I am about to leave them, I say in the most solemn tone, "Remember both of you, that you are free, that there is no question of marital rights; believe me, no false deference.

Emile will you come home with me? Sophy permits it." Emile is ready to strike me in his anger. " And you, Sophy, what do you say? Shall I take him away?" The little liar, blushing, answers, " Yes." A tender and delightful falsehood, better than truth itself!

The next day. . . . Men no longer delight in the picture of bliss; their taste is as much depraved by the corruption of vice as their hearts. They can no longer feel what is touching or perceive what is truly delightful. You who, as a picture of voluptuous joys, see only the happy lovers immersed in pleasure, your picture is very imperfect; you have only its grosser part, the sweetest charms of pleasure are not there. Which of you has seen a young couple, happily married, on the morrow of their marriage? their chaste yet languid looks betray the intoxication of the bliss they have enjoyed, the blessed security of innocence, and the delightful certainty that they will spend the rest of their life together. The heart of man can behold no more rapturous sight; this is the real picture of happiness; you have beheld it a hundred times without heeding it; your hearts are so hard that you cannot love it. Sophy, peaceful and happy, spends the day in the arms of her tender mother; a pleasant resting place, after a night spent in the arms of her husband.

The day after I am aware of a slight change. Emile tries to look somewhat vexed; but through this pretence I notice such a tender eagerness, and indeed so much submission, that I do not think there is much amiss. As for Sophy she is merrier than she was yesterday; her eyes are sparkling and she looks very well pleased with herself; she is charming to Emile; she ventures to tease him a little and vexes him still more.

These changes are almost imperceptible, but they do not escape me; I am anxious and I question Emile in private, and I learn that, to his great regret, and in spite of all entreaties, he was not permitted last night to share Sophy's bed. That haughty lady had made haste to assert her right. An explanation takes place. Emile complains bitterly, Sophy laughs; but at last, seeing that Emile is really getting angry, she looks at him with eyes full of tenderness and love, and pressing my hand, she only says these two words, but in a tone that goes to his heart, " Ungrateful man! " Emile is too stupid to understand. But I understand, and I send Emile away and speak to Sophy privately in her turn.

" I see," said I, " the reason for this whim. No one could be more delicate, and no one could use that delicacy so ill. Dear Sophy, do not be anxious, I have given you a man; do not be afraid to treat him as such. You have had the first fruits of his youth; he has not squandered his manhood and it will endure for you.

" My dear child, I must explain to you why I said what I did in our conversation of the day before yesterday. Perhaps you only understood it as a way of restraining your pleasures to secure their continuance. Oh, Sophy, there was another object, more worthy of my care. When Emile became your husband, he became your head, it is yours to obey; this is the will of nature. When the wife is like Sophy, it is, however, good for the man to be led by her; that is another of nature's laws, and it is to give you as much authority over his heart, as his sex gives him over your person, that I have made you the arbiter of his pleasures. It will be hard for you, but you will control him if you can control yourself, and what has already happened shows me that this difficult art is not beyond your courage. You will long rule him by love if you make your favours scarce and precious, if you know how to use them aright. If you want to have your husband always in your power, keep him at a distance. But let your sternness be the result of modesty not caprice; let him find you modest not capricious; beware lest in controlling his love you make him doubt your own. Be all the dearer for your favours and all the more respected when you refuse them; let him honour his wife's chastity, without having to complain of her coldness.

"Thus, my child, he will give you his confidence, he will listen to your opinion, will consult you in his business, and will decide nothing without you. Thus you may recall him to wisdom, if he strays, and bring him back by a gentle persuasion, you may make yourself lovable in order to be useful, you may employ coquetry on behalf of virtue, and love on behalf of reason.

"Do not think that with all this, your art will always serve your purpose. In spite of every precaution pleasures are destroyed by possession, and love above all others. But when love has lasted long enough, a gentle habit takes its place and the charm of confidence succeeds the raptures of passion. Children form a bond between their parents, a bond no less tender and a bond which is sometimes stronger than love itself. When you cease to be Emile's mistress you will be his friend and wife; you will be the mother of his children. Then instead of your first reticence let there be the fullest intimacy between you; no more separate beds, no more refusals, no more caprices. Become so truly his better half that he can no longer do without you, and if he must leave you, let him feel that he is far from himself. You have made the charms of home life so powerful in your father's home, let them prevail in your own. Every man who is happy at home loves his wife. Remember that if your husband is happy in his home, you will be a happy wife.

"For the present, do not be too hard on your lover; he deserves more consideration; he will be offended by your fears; do not care for his health at the cost of his happiness, and enjoy your own happiness. You must neither wait for disgust nor repulse desire; you must not refuse for the sake of refusing, but only to add to the value of your favours."

Then, taking her back to Emile, I say to her young husband, "One must bear the yoke voluntarily imposed upon oneself. Let your deserts be such that the yoke may be lightened. Above all, sacrifice to the graces, and do not think that sulkiness will make you more amiable." Peace is soon made, and everybody can guess its terms. The treaty is signed with a kiss, after which I say to my pupil, " Dear Emile, all his life through a man needs a guide and counsellor. So far I have done my best to fulfil that duty; my lengthy task is now ended, and another will undertake this duty. To-day I abdicate the authority which you gave me; henceforward Sophy is your guardian."

Little by little the first raptures subside and they can peacefully enjoy the delights of their new condition. Happy lovers, worthy husband and wife! To do honour to their virtues, to paint their felicity, would require the history of their lives. How often does my heart throb with rapture when I behold in them the crown of my life's work! How often do I take their hands in mine blessing God with all my heart! How often do I kiss their clasped hands! How often do their tears of joy fall upon mine! They are touched by my joy and they share my raptures. Their worthy parents see their own youth renewed in that of their children; they begin to live, as it were, afresh in them; or rather they perceive, for the first time, the true value of life; they curse their former wealth, which prevented them from enjoying so delightful a lot when they were young. If there is such a thing as happiness upon earth, you must seek it in our abode.

One morning a few months later Emile enters my room and embraces me, saying, " My master, congratulate your son; he hopes soon to have the honour of being a father. What a responsibility will be ours, how much we shall need you! Yet God forbid that I should let you educate the son as you educated the father. God forbid that so sweet and holy a task should be fulfilled by any but myself, even though I should make as good a choice for my child as was made for me! But continue to be the teacher of the young teachers. Advise and control us; we shall be easily led; as long as I live I shall need you. I need you more than ever now that I am taking up the duties of manhood. You have done your own duty; teach me to follow your example, while you enjoy your well-earned leisure.

Everyman
A selection of titles

* indicates volumes available in paperback

Complete lists of Everyman's Library and Everyman Paperbacks are available from the Sales Department, J.M. Dent and Sons Ltd, Aldine House, 33 Welbeck Street, London W1M 8LX.

BIOGRAPHY

Bligh, William. *A Book of the 'Bounty'*
Boswell, James. *The Life of Samuel Johnson*
Byron, Lord. *Letters*
* Chesterfield, Lord. *Letters to His Son and Others*
Cibber, Colley. *An Apology for the Life of Colly Cibber*
Dana. *Two Years Before the Mast*
* De Quincey, Thomas. *Confessions of an English Opium-Eater*
Forster, John. *Life of Charles Dickens* (2 vols)
* Gaskell, Elizabeth. *The Life of Charlotte Brontë*
* Gilchrist, Alexander. *The Life of William Blake*
* Hudson, W.H. *Far Away and Long Ago*
* Johnson, Samuel. *Lives of the English Poets: a selection*
Pepys, Samuel. *Diary* (3 vols)
Thomas, Dylan
    * *Adventures in the Skin Trade*
    * *Portrait of the Artist as a Young Dog*
Tolstoy. *Childhood, Boyhood and Youth*
Vasari, Giorgio. *Lives of the Painters, Sculptors, and Architects* (4 vols)

ESSAYS AND CRITICISM

Arnold, Matthew. *On the Study of Celtic Literature*
* Bacon, Francis. *Essays*
* Coleridge, Samuel Taylor. *Biographia Literaria*
* Jerome. *Idle Thoughts of an Idle Fellow*
* Emerson, Ralph. *Essays*

*Milton, John. *Prose Writings*
Montaigne, Michael Eyquem de. *Essays* (3 vols)
Spencer, Herbert. *Essays on Education and Kindred Subjects*
*Swift, Jonathan. *Tale of a Tub and other satires*

FICTION

*American Short Stories of the Nineteenth Century
Austen, Jane
    Emma
    Mansfield Park
    Northanger Abbey
    Persuasion
    Pride and Prejudice
    Sense and Sensibility
*Australian Short Stories
Bennett, Arnold
    The Old Wives' Tale
    The Card
Boccaccio, Giovanni. *The Decameron*
Brontë, Anne
    Agnes Grey
    The Tenant of Wildfell Hall
Brontë, Charlotte
    Jane Eyre
    The Professor and *Emma* (a fragment)
    Shirley
    Villette
*Brontë, Emily. *Wuthering Heights* and *Poems*
*Bunyan, John. *Pilgrim's Progress*
*Carroll. *Alice in Wonderland*
Collins, Wilkie
    The Moonstone
    The Woman in White
Conrad, Joseph
    *The Nigger of the 'Narcissus', Typhoon, Falk and other
       stories*
    Nostromo
    Youth, Heart of Darkness and *The End of the Tether*

Hardy, Thomas
  *Far from the Madding Crowd
  *Jude the Obscure
  *The Mayor of Casterbridge
  *Stories and Poems
  *Tess of the d'Urbervilles
*Hartley, L.P. The Travelling Grave
James, Henry
  *Selected Tales
  *The Golden Bowl
  *The Turn of the Screw
*Jefferies, Richard. Bevis: The Story of a Boy
*Lawrence, D.H. Short Stories
*Mansfield, K. Short Stories
*Maupassant, Guy de. Short Stories
*Modern Short Stories to 1940
*Modern Short Stories 2 (1940–1980)
*Oliphant, Margaret. Kirsteen
Peacock, Thomas Love. Headlong Hall and Nightmare Abbey
*Poe, Edgar Allan. Tales of Mystery and Imagination
*Pushkin, Alexander. The Captain's Daughter and other stories
Richardson, Samuel
    Clarissa (4 vols)
    *Pamela (2 vols)
*Russian Short Stories
*Saki. Short Stories 1 and 2
Scott, Walter
    The Abbott
    *The Bride of Lammermoor
    *Heart of Midlothian
    *Ivanhoe
    *Redgauntlet
    *Rob Roy
    *The Talisman
    *Waverley
*Shelley, Mary Wollstonecraft. Frankenstein
*Smollett, Tobias. Roderick Random
*Somerville, E. and Ross, M. Some Experiences of an Irish R.M.
      and Further Experiences of an Irish R.M.

*Sterne, Lawrence. *Tristram Shandy*
Stevenson, R.L.
   **Dr Jekyll and Mr Hyde, The Merry Men* and other tales
   *Kidnapped
   **The Master of Ballantrae* and *Weir of Hermiston*
*Stowe, Harriet Beecher. *Uncle Tom's Cabin*
*Swift, Jonathan. *Gulliver's Travels*
*Thackeray, W.M. *Vanity Fair*
Thirteen Famous Ghost Stories
Thomas, Dylan
   *Miscellany 1
   *Miscellany 2
   *Miscellany 3
*Tolstoy, Leo. *Master and Man and other parables and tales*
Trollope, Anthony
   Barchester Towers
   *The Warden
   Dr Thorne
   **Framley Parsonage*
   Small House at Allington
   Last Chronicle of Barset
*Twain. *Tom Sawyer* and *Huckleberry Finn*
*Voltaire, *Candide and other tales*
Wells, H.G.
   *The Time Machine
   **The Wheels of Chance*
*Wilde, Oscar. *The Picture of Dorian Gray*
*Wood, Mrs Henry. *East Lynne*
Woolf, Virgina. *To the Lighthouse*

HISTORY

---

*The Anglo-Saxon Chronicle
*Burnet, Gilbert. *History of His Own Time*
*Crèvecoeur. *Letters from an American Farmer*
Gibbon, Edward. *The Decline and Fall of the Roman Empire*
   (6 vols)
Green, John. *A Short History of the English People* (2 vols)
Prescott, W.H. *History of the Conquest of Mexico*

LEGENDS AND SAGAS

*Beowulf and Its Analogues
*Chrétien de Troyes. *Arthurian Romances*
*Egils saga
  Holinshed, Raphael. *Chronicle*
*Layamon and Wace. *Arthurian Chronicles*
*The Mabinogion
*The Saga of Gisli
*The Saga of Grettir the Strong
  Snorri Sturluson. *Heimskringla* (3 vols)
*The Story of Burnt Njal

POETRY AND DRAMA

*Anglo-Saxon Poetry
*American Verse of the Nineteenth Century
*Arnold, Matthew. *Selected Poems and Prose*
*Blake, William. *Selected Poems*
*Brontës, The. *Selected Poems*
*Browning, Robert. *Men and Women and other poems*
*Burns, Robert. *The Kilmarnock Poems*
*Chaucer, Geoffrey. *Canterbury Tales*
*Clare, John. *Selected Poems*
*Coleridge, Samuel Taylor. *Poems*
*Donne, John. *The Complete English Poems*
*Elizabethan Sonnets
*English Moral Interludes
*Everyman and Medieval Miracle Plays
*Everyman's Book of Evergreen Verse
*Gay, John. *The Beggar's Opera and other eighteenth-century
      plays*
*The Golden Treasury of Longer Poems
*Hardy, Thomas. *Selected Poems*
*Herbert, George. *The English Poems*
*Hopkins, Gerard Manley. *The Major Poems*
  Ibsen, Henrik
      A Doll's House; The Wild Duck; The Lady from the Sea
      Hedda Gabler; The Master Builder; John Gabriel Borkman

*Keats, John. *Poems*
*Langland, William. *The Vision of Piers Plowman*
*Marlowe, Christopher. *Complete Plays and Poems*
*Marvell, Andrew. *Complete Poetry*
*Milton, John. *Complete Poems*
*Middleton, Thomas. *Three Plays*
*Palgrave's Golden Treasury
*Pearl, Patience, Cleanness, and Sir Gawain and the Green Knight
*Poems of the Second World War
*Pope, Alexander. *Collected Poems*
*Restoration Plays
*The Rubáiyát of Omar Khayyám and other Persian poems
*Shelley, Percy Bysshe. *Selected Poems*
*Spenser, Edmund. *The Faerie Queene: a selection*
*The Stuffed Owl
*Synge, J.M. *Plays, Poems and Prose*
*Tennyson, Alfred. *In Memoriam, Maud and other poems*
  Thomas, Dylan
    *Collected Poems, 1934–1952
    *The Poems
    *Under Milk Wood
*Wilde, Oscar. *Plays, Prose Writings and Poems*
*Wordsworth, William. *Selected Poems*

RELIGION AND PHILOSOPHY

---

*Bacon, Francis. *The Advancement of Learning*
*Berkeley, George. *Philosophical Works including the works on
    vision*
*The Buddha's Philosophy of Man
*Chinese Philosophy in Classical Times
*Descartes, René. *A Discourse on Method*
*Hindu Scriptures
*Kant, Immanuel. *A Critique of Pure Reason*
*The Koran
*Leibniz, Gottfried Wilhelm. *Philosophical Writings*
*Locke, John. *An Essay Concerning Human Understanding
    (abridgment)*
*More, Thomas. *Utopia*

Pascal, Blaise. *Pensées*
Plato. *The Trial and Death of Socrates*
*Spinoza. *Ethics* and *On the Correction of the Understanding*
*The Ramayana and Mahábhárata

SCIENCES: POLITICAL AND GENERAL

Aristotle. *Ethics*
*Coleridge, Samuel Taylor. *On the Constitution of the Church
    and State*
*Darwin, Charles. *The Origin of Species*
Derry, John. *English Politics & the American Revolution*
Harvey, William. *The Circulation of the Blood and other
    writings*
*Hobbes, Thomas. *Leviathan*
*Locke, John. *Two Treatises of Government*
*Machiavelli, Niccolò. *The Prince and other political writings*
*Malthus, Thomas. *An Essay on the Principle of Population*
*Mill, J.S. *Utilitarianism; On Liberty; Representative
    Government*
*Plato. *The Republic*
*Ricardo, David. *The Principles of Political Economy and
    Taxation*
Rousseau, J.-J.
    ✓*Emile*
    The Social Contract and *Discourses*
*Wollstonecraft, Mary. *A Vindication of the Rights of Woman*

TRAVEL AND TOPOGRAPHY

Boswell, James. *The Journal of a Tour to the Hebrides*
*Darwin, Charles. *The Voyage of the 'Beagle'*
*Hudson, W.H. *Idle Days in Patagonia*
*Stevenson, R.L. *An Inland Voyage; Travels with a Donkey; The
    Silverado Squatters*
*Thomas, Edward. *The South Country*
Travels of Marco Polo
*White, Gilbert. *The Natural History of Selborne*